THE CHURCH'S BIBLE

General Editor

Robert Louis Wilken

•　　•

The Song of Songs
Richard A. Norris Jr.

1 Corinthians
Judith L. Kovacs

1 CORINTHIANS

Interpreted by
Early Christian Commentators

Translated and Edited by

Judith L. Kovacs

WILLIAM B. EERDMANS PUBLISHING COMPANY

GRAND RAPIDS, MICHIGAN / CAMBRIDGE, U.K.

© 2005 Wm. B. Eerdmans Publishing Co.
All rights reserved

Wm. B. Eerdmans Publishing Co.
255 Jefferson Ave. S.E., Grand Rapids, Michigan 49503 /
P.O. Box 163, Cambridge CB3 9PU U.K.
www.eerdmans.com

Printed in the United States of America

10 09 08 07 06 05   7 6 5 4 3 2 1

ISBN-10: 0-8028-2577-X
ISBN-13: 978-0-8028-2577-3

Contents

Series Preface	vii
Acknowledgments	ix
Interpreting the New Testament	x
An Introduction to 1 Corinthians	xx
On the Author: Saint Paul	1
General Comments on the Letter	8
1 Corinthians 1	12
1 Corinthians 2	36
1 Corinthians 3	47
1 Corinthians 4	69
1 Corinthians 5	83
1 Corinthians 6	92
1 Corinthians 7	104
1 Corinthians 8	131
1 Corinthians 9	144
1 Corinthians 10	159
1 Corinthians 11	177
1 Corinthians 12	195
1 Corinthians 13	214
1 Corinthians 14	229
1 Corinthians 15	242

CONTENTS

1 Corinthians 16   282

APPENDIX 1: *Authors of Works Excerpted*   293

APPENDIX 2: *Sources of Texts Translated*   299

APPENDIX 3: *Glossary of Proper Names*   314

Bibliography: Editions of Patristic Works   317

Index of Names   320

Index of Subjects   322

Index of Scripture References   330

Series Preface

The volumes in The Church's Bible are designed to present the Holy Scriptures as understood and interpreted during the first millennium of Christian history. The Christian Church has a long tradition of commentary on the Bible. In the early Church all discussion of theological topics, of moral issues, and of Christian practice took the biblical text as the starting point. The recitation of the psalms and meditation on books of the Bible, particularly in the context of the liturgy or of private prayer, nurtured the spiritual life. For most of the Church's history theology and scriptural interpretation were one. Theology was called *sacra pagina* (the sacred page), and the task of interpreting the Bible was a spiritual enterprise.

During the first two centuries interpretation of the Bible took the form of exposition of select passages on particular issues. For example, Irenaeus, bishop of Lyons, discussed many passages from the Old and New Testaments in his defense of the apostolic faith against the Gnostics. By the beginning of the third century Christian bishops and scholars had begun to preach regular series of sermons that followed the biblical books verse by verse. Some wrote more scholarly commentaries that examined in greater detail grammatical, literary, and historical questions as well as theological ideas and spiritual teachings found in the texts. From Origen of Alexandria, the first great biblical commentator in the Church's history, we have, among others, a large verse-by-verse commentary on the Gospel of John, a series of homilies on Genesis and Exodus, and a large part of his *Commentary on the Epistle to the Romans.* In the course of the first eight hundred years of Christian history Christian teachers produced a library of biblical commentaries and homilies on the Bible.

Today this ancient tradition of biblical interpretation is known only in bits and pieces, and even where it still shapes our understanding of the Bible, for example, in the selection of readings for Christian worship (e.g., Isaiah 7 and Isaiah 9 read at Christmas), or the interpretation of the Psalms in daily prayer, the spiritual world that gave it birth remains shadowy and indistinct. It is the purpose of this series to make available the richness of the Church's classical tradition of interpretation for clergy, Sunday school and Bible class teachers, men and women living in religious communities, and all serious readers of the Bible.

Anyone who reads the ancient commentaries realizes at once that they are deeply spiritual, insightful, edifying, and, shall we say, "biblical." Early Christian thinkers moved in the world of the Bible, understood its idiom, loved its teaching, and were filled with awe before its mysteries. They believed in the maxim, "Scripture interprets Scripture." They knew something that has largely been forgotten by biblical scholars, and their commentaries are an untapped resource for understanding the Bible as a book about Christ.

The distinctive mark of The Church's Bible is that it draws extensively on the ancient commentaries, not only on random comments drawn from theological treatises, sermons, or devotional works. Its volumes will, in the main, offer fairly lengthy excerpts from the ancient commentaries and from series of sermons on specific books. For example, in the first volume on the Song of Songs, there are long passages from Origen of Alexandria's *Commentary on the Song of Songs,* from Gregory of Nyssa's *Homilies on the Song,* and from Bernard of Clairvaux's sermons on the Song. Some passages will be as brief as a paragraph, but many will be several pages in length, and some longer. We believe that only through a deeper immersion in the ancient sources can contemporary readers enter into the inexhaustible spiritual and theological world of the early Church and hence of the Bible.

It is also hoped that longer passages will be suitable for private devotional reading and for spiritual reading in religious communities, in Bible study groups, and in prayer circles.

ROBERT LOUIS WILKEN
General Editor

Acknowledgments

From the time this series was proposed to Bill Eerdmans he has been an enthusiastic and unfailing supporter. We thank him for his interest, encouragement, and backing. We also wish to thank the Homeland Foundation and the Community of Christ in the City for their help in making this project possible. This book is a publication of the Center for Catholic and Evangelical Theology.

ROBERT LOUIS WILKEN

I am grateful to David Kovacs, who translated the excerpts from the Latin fathers, and to Charles Schulz, who contributed an initial draft of many of the excerpts from John Chrysostom. Clare Hall, Cambridge University, fostered my work on this book by electing me to a visiting fellowship for the academic year 2000-2001 and providing a stimulating and congenial setting for my research. I am also indebted to the University of Virginia for a semester of research leave in 2003. Finally, to J. Louis Martyn, under whose wise guidance I first read 1 Corinthians in Greek, I offer heartfelt thanks for teaching me to listen attentively to Paul's words, and to love them.

JUDITH L. KOVACS

Interpreting the New Testament

The traditional greeting on Easter morning is "Christ is risen!" To which the response is: "He is risen indeed. Alleluia!" This ancient phrase echoes the greeting of the angel to Mary Magdalene and Mary the mother of James and Joseph as they arrived at the sepulchre to anoint the body of Jesus: "He is not here; for he has risen, as he said" (Matt 28:6). After the two disciples recognized Christ in the breaking of bread on the road to Emmaus, they immediately rose and returned to the others gathered in Jerusalem, announcing: "The Lord has risen indeed, and has appeared to Simon!" (Luke 24:34).

The resurrection of Christ is the ground of Christian belief and the wellspring from which the books of the New Testament flow. The Gospels culminate in the resurrection, at the beginning of the Epistle to the Romans Paul invokes the resurrection as warrant for his apostleship, and he brings 1 Corinthians to a close with a magnificent peroration on the resurrected body. In places 1 Peter reads like an Easter baptismal sermon ("we have been born anew to a living hope through the resurrection of Jesus Christ from the dead" [1 Pet 1:3]), and in the Acts of the Apostles the disciples of Christ are portrayed again and again as "witnesses" to the resurrection (1:22; 2:32; 3:15, et al.).

The New Testament is a collection of books whose authors bore witness in their lives (and some in their deaths) to the living Christ. "It is no longer I who live," writes St. Paul in Galatians, "but Christ who lives in me" (Gal 2:20). Before there was a book, there were persons who handed on Christ's sayings and told of the marvelous things God had worked in him. First came Christ, then the witnesses, then the books. This ordering of things is at the heart of the early interpretation of the New Testament. The goal was to delve more deeply into the mystery of God revealed in Christ, to whom the writings bear witness. In introducing the volumes on the New Testament in this series it may be helpful to say a few things about how the early Christians approached this task.

We are inclined to begin with the book, with historical context and social setting, words and idioms, grammar and literary forms, religious and theological vocabulary, and the many other topics that command our attention. But the early Christians began with the risen Christ, and long before there was a book the faith was handed on orally. Although St. Paul said that he had received his commission "through a revelation of Jesus Christ" (Gal 1:12), not from a human intermediary, he associated himself with traditions that he had received from others. "For I *delivered* to you as of first importance what I also *received,* that Christ died for our sins in accordance with the scriptures, that he was buried, that he was raised on the third day in accordance with the scriptures, and that he appeared to Cephas, then to the twelve. Then he appeared to more than five hundred brethren at one time, most of whom are still alive, though some have fallen asleep. Then he appeared to James, then to all the apostles. Last of all, as to one untimely born, he appeared to me" (1 Cor 15:3-8).

The memory of Christ centered on his death and resurrection, and the brief narrative of his birth, suffering, death, burial, and resurrection formed the core of early Christian tradition. It was complemented by "sayings" of Jesus, but the sayings were understood in light of the events, as the structure of the Gospels makes plain. The setting of the early confessions of faith was almost certainly Christian worship, and they reflect local catechetical instruction. The details varied from place to place, but the central narrative remained constant. Here, for example, is a somewhat freer (and idiosyncratic) form that appears in 1 Peter: "For Christ also *died for sins once for all,* the righteous for the unrighteous, that he might bring us to God, *being put to death in the flesh but made alive in the spirit;* in which he went and preached to the spirits in prison, who formerly did not obey when God's patience waited in the days of Noah, during the building of the ark, in which few, that is, eight persons, were saved through water. Baptism, which corresponds to this, now saves you, not as a removal of dirt from the body but as an appeal to God for a clear conscience, through the *resurrection of Jesus Christ, who has gone into heaven and is at the right hand of God,* with angels, authorities, and powers subject to him" (1 Pet 3:18-22).

The mention of Baptism indicates that the early tradition also included how one was to understand Christian practices. In 1 Corinthians Paul's language about the Lord's Supper is similar to what he had used about the resurrection: "For I *received* from the Lord what I also *delivered* to you, that the Lord Jesus on the night when he was betrayed took bread, and when he had given thanks, he broke it, and said, 'This is my body which is for you. Do this in remembrance of me.' In the same way also the cup, after supper, saying, 'This cup is the new covenant in my blood. Do this, as often as you drink it, in remembrance of me.' For as often as you eat this bread and drink this cup, you proclaim the Lord's death until he comes" (1 Cor 11:23-26). Though Paul says that he had received the account about the Last Supper directly from the Lord, the terms "received" and "delivered" are the customary words for handing on tradition. Paul is repeating word for word what he has received from others.

Early in the Church's history, then, the living Christ was identified by verbal formulas and practices, notably Baptism and the Eucharist. The purpose of the creedlike summaries of faith was primarily catechetical, but they served as guarantors of the truth of what had taken place during Christ's lifetime and unlocked the Jewish scriptures, what Christians would later call the Old Testament. This is evident in an illuminating testimony from Ignatius, bishop of Antioch, at the end of the first century. The Christians in Philadelphia in western Asia Minor were divided over some aspects of Christian teaching, and Ignatius exhorted them to abandon their contentiousness. Apparently some had argued that the only way the matter could be settled was by appeal to what they called "the archives," that is, the Old Testament. "If I do not find it in the archives, I do not believe it to be in the gospel," they said. Ignatius, however, demurred. "For me," he writes,

"the archives are Jesus Christ, the inviolable archives are his cross and death and his resurrection and faith through him. . . ."[1] Although most, if not all, of the books of the New
Testament had been written by the time he became bishop, Ignatius makes no mention of
Christian writings to settle the dispute. He appeals only to the person of Christ and the
brief narrative of his saving deeds, not to written documents.

The time was fast approaching, however, when oral tradition would be complemented by written documents. But not replaced! Even after the writings of the apostles
formed the "canon" of writings we call the New Testament, the oral witness of the apostles remained alive. Irenaeus, bishop of Lyons, at the end of the second century still conceived of apostolic tradition in terms of persons first, books second. "The Lord of all gave
to his apostles the power of the gospel, and through them we have learned the truth, that
is, the teaching of the Son of God. . . . We have not learned the plan of our salvation from
any others than those through whom the gospel came to us. They first proclaimed it, and
then later by the will of God handed it down to us in writings. . . ."[2] For St. Irenaeus the
most authentic tradition was oral, what "the elders, the disciples of the apostles, have
handed on to us."[3]

At the same time Irenaeus is the first writer to draw on the apostolic writings as
part of an authoritative collection. He does not use the term "New Testament" but its
basic structure of Gospels, the Acts of the Apostles, and epistles is clearly visible in his
works. In fact, a large part of his work against the Gnostics is given over to the exegesis of
specific passages from the New Testament that were in dispute. But the books did not
stand on their own. They needed to be explained and individual passages fitted into the
pattern of God's saving work in Christ. For this task the oral tradition confessed in the
rule of faith and explained by teachers whose lineage could be traced back to the apostles
was indispensable. Without a grasp of the plot that holds the books together, said
Irenaeus, the Bible is as vacuous as a mosaic in which the tiny colored stones have been
arbitrarily rearranged without reference to the original design. Even the apostolic writings, the Christian scriptures, required a framework of interpretation, a canopy of beliefs
and practices to envelop the texts.

The oral tradition took form in a tripartite, that is, trinitarian, rule of faith that
identified God by narrating key events recorded in the Scriptures, the creation of the
world, the inspiration of the prophets, the coming of Christ in the flesh, his death and
resurrection, the outpouring of the Holy Spirit. Though drawn from the New Testament,
the rule was distinct from the apostolic writings; it was a brief confession handed on at
Baptism that provided a key to the Scriptures. In other words, the Scriptures were read
and interpreted in light of the Church's tradition. Or, to put it more precisely, the tradition embodied in the apostolic writings, that is, the New Testament, was complemented
by the tradition, equally apostolic, that had been handed on orally (primarily in Christian worship) from one generation to another. The New Testament was the book of the
Church, and interpretation took place within a context of shared beliefs and practices.

1. *Philadelphians* 8.
2. *Against Heresies* 3, preface.
3. *Demonstration of the Apostolic Preaching* 3.

For example, during the great debate over the relation of the Son to the Father in the fourth century, Athanasius, bishop of Alexandria, used Irenaeus's principle of interpretation to marshall scriptural support for the decrees of the Council of Nicea. Arius, whose teaching had been condemned at the council, had called attention to the word "therefore" in Phil 2:9, "*Therefore* God has highly exalted him [Christ] and bestowed on him the name which is above every name." In his view the "therefore" implied that the Son had "become" God and was not God from eternity. Athanasius showed that this was an idiosyncratic and "private" interpretation contrary to the "Church's sense of the Scripture" handed on orally and expressed in other texts in the New Testament, for example, John 1:1, "and the Word was God," or Heb 1:6, "Let all God's angels worship him." For good measure he points out that three verses earlier St. Paul had said that Christ, who was "in the form of God, did not count equality with God a thing to be grasped" (Phil 2:6).[4]

By the third century the canon of the New Testament was universally recognized, though certain books remained in dispute, for example, the Apocalypse. Writers such as Tertullian in North Africa and Clement and Origen in Alexandria had at their disposal a Christian Bible composed of two parts, Old Testament and New Testament. But the written Scripture never replaced the living tradition, and its interpretation was guided by the rule of faith and Christian practice. The engine that drove interpretation was the Church's faith in the triune God confessed in the baptismal creed, made present through Christ in the consecrated bread and wine of the Eucharist, whose power and love were confirmed in the lives of the faithful by the searing flame of the Holy Spirit. Once there was a written Scripture, interpretation inevitably entered a new phase. The church fathers did not doubt that the apostolic writings bore witness to the one God, creator of all things, to the Son Jesus Christ the Lord, and to the outpouring of the Holy Spirit to call into one fellowship a new people. But interpretation not only has to do with the big picture but is most decidedly an exercise in particularity, how specific words and passages are to be understood and related to the faith delivered to the apostles. This was a demanding assigment that could be accomplished only through study, prayer, and, let it not be forgotten, argument and debate. Even in the early centuries the New Testament required interpretation, and its readers no less than we had to train their minds and tutor their affections to discern its meaning. All this took time and hard labor, and the number and variety of commentaries and homilies on books and passages of the New Testament during the early centuries of the Church's history is astonishing. Yet the purpose of commentary was always kept in sight. Interpretation was a spiritual voyage of discovery, a way of exploring the luminous world revealed in the coming of Christ.

A good illustration is Gregory of Nyssa's interpretation of the word "righteousness" or "justice" (either a possible translation of a single Greek word), which occurs twice in the Beatitudes: "Blessed are those who hunger and thirst for righteousness (or justice), for they shall be satisfied." And: "Blessed are those who are persecuted for the sake of justice (or righteousness), for theirs is the kingdom of heaven" (Matt 5:6, 10). The same term occurs in the writings of St. Paul, and Gregory of Nyssa, a fourth-century Greek com-

---

4. *Against the Arians* 1.37-44.

mentator, noted in particular its use in 1 Corinthians: "[God] is the source of your life in Christ Jesus, whom God made our wisdom, our *righteousness* (or justice) and sanctification and redemption" (1 Cor 1:30).

In a homily on the fourth beatitude Gregory asks: "What is justice?", to which he gives a traditional philosophical answer: justice is to give to each according to his worth. But then he observes that there is a higher form of justice, not based on merit. This is the justice we are to desire; hence the beatitude speaks of those who "hunger and thirst for justice." Here the homily takes a surprising turn as Gregory offers what he calls a "bolder interpretation": in the beatitude the Lord proposes to his followers that he himself is what they desire, "for he became for us wisdom from God, justice, sanctification, and redemption" (1 Cor 1:30).

By appealing to 1 Corinthians Gregory opens the beatitude to a christological interpretation. In his view it is speaking about hungering and thirsting for the living God, as David said in the psalm, "My soul thirsts for the living God" (Ps 42:2). By interpreting the words of Jesus with the help of St. Paul, a procedure, one might observe, that would be shunned by a modern interpreter, Gregory is able to transform the beatitude into an invitation to seek not only "justice" but the living God, or, better, to find justice by knowing Christ. The one who tastes the Lord "has received God into himself and is filled with him for whom he has thirsted and hungered. He acknowledges that he has been filled with the one he desires when he says, 'Christ lives in me' (Gal 2:20)."[5]

Some texts posed perplexing theological problems, as, for example, the passage at the beginning of the Gospel of John: "No one has ever seen God" (John 1:18). The text is straightforward enough: God has never been seen. 1 Tim 6:16 went further: "no one has ever seen or can see [God]."[6] Yet the prophet Isaiah said explicitly that he had seen God: "In the year that King Uzziah died I *saw* the Lord sitting upon a throne, high and lifted up" (Isa 6:1). How was one to reconcile these passages and relate the words of John to other texts, for example, the report in the book of Genesis that Jacob saw God "face to face" (Gen 32:30)?

For many modern interpreters theological questions, for example, what it means to see God, are quite secondary to the task of interpretation and the unity of the Bible; that is, how one book in the Scriptures is to be understood in relation to other parts of the Bible is peripheral to their exegesis. Isaiah is Isaiah, and John is John. But early Christian commentators believed that the Bible spoke with a single (though nuanced) voice, and they took apparent inconsistencies between biblical authors as an invitation to probe beneath the surface of the inspired words, that is, to penetrate the spiritual reality about which the text spoke, in this case to grasp what it means to see God. "Seeing," they explained, was a form of knowledge, and they claimed that when all the relevant passages are considered, the Scriptures teach that God can be known, although the fullness of his divinity, his ineffable nature or essence, is beyond our comprehension. "It is one thing to see," writes Augustine, "it is another to grasp the whole by seeing."[7] One writer said that

---

5. *Homily 4 on the Beatitudes* (Gregorii Nysseni Opera VII/II.122-23).

6. 1 John 4:12, "No man has ever seen God," was also cited.

7. *Letter* 147.8.21. This letter, a little treatise "on seeing God," discusses the relevant biblical texts.

in the Scriptures "see" means the same as "possess," citing the words of the psalmist: "May you see the good things of Jerusalem" (Ps 128:5), where "see" means "to find." Hence he concludes that one who sees God "possesses all that is good."[8] By drawing on the many uses of the word "see" in the Scriptures (including the beatitude, "Blessed are the pure in heart, for they shall see God" [Matt 5:8]) Christian thinkers were able to explore the place of the vision of God in Christian life and hope.[9]

At times a single biblical word could inspire a preacher to lyrical heights. In a memorable sermon on the phrase "that God may be all in all" (1 Cor 15:28), Augustine asked, "What is the meaning of 'all'? [God] will be for you whatever you desired here on earth, whatever you valued. What did you want here, what did you love? To eat and drink? He himself will be food for you, he himself will be drink. What did you want here? A fragile and transient bodily health? He himself will be immortality for you. What did you look for here? Wealth? Greedy man, what is it that will satisfy you if God himself does not? Well, what did you love? Glory, honors? God will be your glory."[10]

When they listened to the Scriptures read in divine worship or pondered its words in prayer, the early Christians heard the Word of God spoken to their communities and to their lives. In his *Commentary on the Gospel of John* Origen of Alexandria, the first and greatest biblical scholar in the early Church, explained that "a gospel" is a "discourse containing an account of things that have happened which, because of the good they bring, are a source of joy to the hearer." The gospel is a "word that makes present something good for the believer or a word that the promised good is present." Its subject, continues Origen, is the "presence of Jesus Christ, the firstborn of all creation (Col 1:15), among men for their salvation." Accordingly, the Gospels are the "firstfruits" of the Scriptures, and the "firstfruits" of the Gospels is the Gospel according to John, "whose meaning cannot be understood unless one reclines on Jesus' breast (John 13:23) and accepts Mary from Jesus as his own mother."[11]

Anyone who wrote a commentary on the Gospels in this spirit would discover much in the biblical text that a strictly historical approach would miss. And the reader of Origen's *Commentary on John* will not be disappointed. Not only was Origen engaged with the spiritual and theological meaning of the text, but he also assumed that to understand the Gospel one must know Christ, in his words "recline on Jesus' breast." But his commentary is also a work of great scholarship and learning. In the first book he devotes many pages to a single word, "beginning," in the opening sentence, "In the beginning was the Word." Because "beginning" is the first significant term to appear in the Gospel, it sends him off on a discussion of the many uses of "beginning" in the Scriptures. And this in turn allows him to explain why Christ is identified with "beginning." Christ, writes Origen, is the beginning of those "made in the image of God" because he is the "firstborn of all creation" (Col 1:15); he is the beginning of knowledge because he is called "Wisdom" (1 Cor 1:24); he is the beginning of life because he is the "firstborn from the dead"

8. Gregory of Nyssa, *Homily on the Beatitudes* (Gregorii Nysseni Opera VII/II.138).

9. Jerome, *Commentary on Isaiah* 6:1 (Corpus Christianorum 73:84-85); Gregory the Great, *Moralia*, 18.88.

10. *Sermon* 158.9.

11. *Commentary on John* 1.27.

(Col 1:18); the beginning of creation, that is, the agent of creation, because he is "the beginning of [God's] ways for his work" (Prov 8:22).[12]

Origen is interpreting Scripture by Scripture, an axiom accepted by all early Christian writers. "The entire Scripture is one book and was spoken by the one Holy Spirit," wrote Cyril of Alexandria, another prolific biblical commentator.[13] Accordingly, it was presumed that the interpreter would draw on passages from the entire Bible to illuminate and explain the text under discussion. The technique most often used was word association, seeking words or images that are the same or similar to what is found in the text, as Origen did when he explained "beginning" in his *Commentary on John*. The term could be "life," or "water," or "rock," or "rain," or "man," or "mountain," or a myriad of other words or images. As the expositors sought appropriate texts, they were led to yet more passages, and the commentaries and homilies often read like a pastiche of biblical verses. Yet there was method in their exegetical artistry. As words and phrases were invested with meanings drawn from elsewhere in the Scriptures, they acquired a theological clarity and sonority that only the Bible could give. In effect the words of the Gospel of John become "biblical" rather than simply Johannine; that is, the context of understanding was formed by the Bible as a whole, not just the Gospel of John.

We are so accustomed to think of context as literary or historical that we forget that the words of the Bible have a life that transcends their original setting. Think how a verse from the New Testament can sound when read in Christian worship. It is traditional to read from the book of Titus on Christmas Eve: "For the grace of God has appeared for the salvation of all men, training us to renounce irreligion and worldly passions, and to live sober, upright, and godly lives in this world . . ." [Tit 2:11-13]). When this passage is read in the Liturgy for the Nativity of Christ, the word "appear" rings out clearly like the peal of a single bell announcing the birth of Christ, the Incarnation of the divine Word. While this understanding of the verse is certainly implicit within the text, the liturgical setting gives the word "appear" a concreteness and directness that it does not have in the context of the epistle, and the Liturgy, in turn, acquires a word so fitting and right that Tit 2:11 seems composed primarily for the occasion.

Under the tutelage of the church fathers, one learns to read the Bible very closely and to pay particular attention to the subtlety and resonance of its words. As Augustine once remarked: "My heart is exercised by the pounding of the *words* of your Holy Scripture."[14] One also learns to see things whole, to interpret individual texts in light of the central biblical narrative and the Christ confessed in the creeds and celebrated in the Church's worship.

But there is something else to keep in mind while reading the volumes in this series. For the church fathers biblical interpretation had to do with the bearing of the text on the present. The interpreter is not a disinterested observer, a voyeur; rather, he is a participant in the mystery about which he speaks. This can be illustrated by a story told about St. Antony, the monk of the Egyptian desert.

12. *Commentary on John* 1.90-108.
13. *Commentary on Isaiah 29:11-12* (Patrologia Graeca 70:655a).
14. *Confessions* 12.1.

Once some visitors came to Antony and asked him for a good word. He told them that they should heed the Scriptures. When they pressed him for specifics, he said they should follow the word of Jesus in Matthew: "If anyone strikes you on one cheek, turn to him the other also" (Matt 5:39). But they objected, "We can't do that!" So Antony tempered the exhortation: "If you can't do that, at least allow one cheek to be struck." Again they replied, "We cannot do that." So Antony revised the saying another time: "If you are not able to do that, at least do not return evil for evil." But again they protested. Realizing that it was futile to try to teach such folk how to understand the Bible, he instructed his disciples to "Take a little porridge" to them because "they are ill." And to the visitors he said, "If you cannot do this, or that, what can I do for you? What you need is prayers."[15]

The Bible is a book about how to live in the knowledge of God and of oneself. God's Word is not something to be looked at but something to be acted on. St. Bernard said it well: the interpreter must see himself in that which is said. It is not enough, observes Origen, to say, "'Christ was crucified'; one must say with St. Paul, 'I am crucified with Christ' (Gal 2:20). Likewise it is not enough to say, 'Christ is raised'; one who knows Christ says, 'We shall also live with him'(Rom 6:8)."[16] This is why St. Augustine said that anyone who "thinks he has understood the divine scriptures . . . but does not build up the double love of God and neighbor, has not succeeded in understanding them."[17]

The first major commentaries on the New Testament were written by Origen of Alexandria in the early third century. Like many of the biblical commentaries from the early Church, they have come down to us in fragmentary condition. Fortunately, we still possess large sections of his massive *Commentary on the Gospel of John*. It is not certain whether he completed it, but it took him six books just to reach John 1:29. In addition, he authored a *Commentary on the Gospel of Matthew* and delivered series of homilies on the Gospel of Luke. Others followed his example — some writing commentaries, others delivering homilies that went through a book chapter by chapter. For the Fourth Gospel we have homilies by John Chrysostom and Augustine as well as commentaries by Theodore of Mopsuestia and Cyril of Alexandria. On Matthew there are commentaries by Jerome and Cyril and homilies by Ambrose and John Chrysostom, to mention some of the more important. The Gospel of Mark did not receive a commentary until the Venerable Bede in the eighth century.

Origen also expounded the Pauline epistles. From his commentary on Romans we have only fragments in Greek, but a Latin translation of it was made in the early Church. Homilies on the letters to the Corinthians and commentaries on Paul's minor epistles exist only in fragments. The Latin commentator Ambrosiaster wrote a complete commentary on the Pauline epistles, and Jerome also commented on a number of the letters, including Galatians and Ephesians. Theodore of Mopsuestia wrote a commentary on the minor Pauline epistles, John Chrysostom preached homilies on all of Paul's letters (in-

15. Patrologia Graeca 65:84c.
16. *Against Celsus* 2.69.
17. *On Christian Doctrine* 1.86.

cluding Hebrews), and Theodoret of Cyrus also commented on the entire corpus. Only fragments of Cyril of Alexandria's commentaries on St. Paul remain. John Chrysostom is one of the few who have preached an entire series of homilies on the Acts of Apostles. Augustine delivered a series of sermons on 1 John, and Victorinus and Jerome wrote on the Apocalypse.

Even this partial survey gives some idea of the extent to which the church fathers devoted their energies to expounding the New Testament. Commentaries and homilies, however, are only a small part of the exegetical harvest of the early Church. There are sermons and lengthy letters on particular texts, for example, Gregory of Nyssa on 1 Cor 15:28 and Augustine on Jas 2:10, and homilies on sections of books, for example, the Beatitudes or the Lord's Prayer.[18] In the new English translation of Augustine's sermons, three volumes are devoted to sermons on passages from the New Testament,[19] and Gregory the Great has a series of forty homilies dealing with select texts from the New Testament.[20] There are also works dealing specifically with the infancy narratives of the Gospels and essays that attempt to harmonize the Gospels. Finally, there are wide-ranging discussions of many texts from the New Testament in theological essays, spiritual tracts, and the like.

Given this vast, diffuse, and often formless body of material, it is often difficult to learn how early Christian thinkers interpreted specific passages in the New Testament. In recent years some of the commentaries from the early Church on the New Testament have been translated into English for the first time. For example, Origen's commentaries on the Gospel of John and Romans and his homilies on Luke are now available,[21] as are Ambrose's homilies on Luke,[22] Theodoret of Cyrus on the Pauline epistles,[23] and Origen and Jerome on Ephesians.[24] Nevertheless, the great body of commentaries and homilies remain untranslated in English, and may never be translated.

The Church's Bible will provide commentaries on select books of the New Testament drawn from the writings of the church fathers, and in some cases from medieval authors. We have made a selection of passages from the ancient commentaries and homilies that treat books chapter by chapter. In addition, we have included occasional com-

---

18. *St. Gregory of Nyssa: The Lord's Prayer; The Beatitudes,* trans. Hilda C. Graef (New York: Newman Press, 1954).

19. *The Works of Saint Augustine: A Translation for the 21st Century,* III.3-5, trans. Edmund Hill, O.P. (Brooklyn and New Rochelle, N.Y.: New City Press, 1990-92), 3:3-5.

20. *Gregory the Great: Forty Gospel Homilies,* trans. Dom David Hurst (Kalamazoo: Cistercian Publications, 1990).

21. *Origen: Commentary on the Gospel according to John,* trans. Ronald E. Heine, 2 vols. (Washington, D.C.: Catholic University of America Press, 1989, 1993); *Origen: Homilies on Luke; Fragments on Luke,* trans. Joseph T. Lienhard, S.J. (Washington, D.C.: Catholic University of America Press, 1996); *Origen. Commentary on the Epistle to the Romans,* trans. Thomas P. Schreck, 2 vols. (Washington, D.C.: Catholic University of America Press, 2001, 2002).

22. *Exposition of the Holy Gospel according to Saint Luke: Saint Ambrose of Milan,* trans. Theodosia Tomkinson (Etna, Calif.: Center for Traditionalist Studies, 2003).

23. *Commentary on the Letters of St. Paul by Theodoret of Cyrus,* trans. Robert C. Hill (Brookline, Mass.: Holy Cross Orthodox Press, 2002).

24. Robert E. Heine, *The Commentaries of Origen and Jerome on St. Paul's Epistle to the Ephesians* (New York: Oxford University Press, 2002).

ments on particular verses drawn from theological writings, sermons, and other early Christian writings. Our aim is not a comprehensive survey of early Christian exegesis of the books of the New Testament, but commentaries that we hope will be interesting, theologically significant, and spiritually uplifting to readers of the New Testament today.

In the excerpts the specific text under discussion is printed in bold. When a passage is cited from elsewhere in the Scriptures, it is printed in italics.

The authors and works from which the selections are taken are given in the appendixes.

ROBERT LOUIS WILKEN

An Introduction to 1 Corinthians

"We would not miss the mark," John Chrysostom says, "if we were to call Paul's soul a field of virtues and a spiritual paradise: so richly does it blossom with grace and so worthy of that grace is the discipline it exhibits."[1] One cannot overestimate the importance of Paul and his letters for the early Church. The church fathers quote, paraphrase, and interpret his words so frequently that it is difficult to find any theological or moral treatise, sermon, or commentary in which he is not cited as an authority. For them he is "the divine apostle" or simply "*the* apostle."

The letters of Paul, written in the 50s A.D., are the earliest Christian documents we possess. Most of them were originally addressed to individual churches, but they were soon gathered together and circulated as a collection. The ancient Church credited Paul with fourteen letters: Romans, 1 and 2 Corinthians, Galatians, Ephesians, Philippians, Colossians, 1 and 2 Thessalonians, 1 and 2 Timothy, Titus, Philemon, and Hebrews.[2] By the second century Paul's letters are called Scriptures,[3] and detailed comment on them makes its appearance in the mid-third century, beginning with Origen of Alexandria, who wrote commentaries or series of homilies (sermons) on at least ten of them.[4] The fourth and fifth centuries saw the flowering of this exegetical tradition in the works of men such as John Chrysostom, Theodoret of Cyrus, Cyril of Alexandria, and the anonymous author called Ambrosiaster.

This volume makes available in English translation, for one of Paul's letters, selections from this rich tradition of Greek and Latin commentary. The introductory essay

---

1. *In Praise of Paul* 1.1.1-11, Sources chrétiennes 300:112.

2. Stylistic differences between Hebrews and the other letters occasioned debate about its authorship. Tertullian, for example, thought it was written by Paul's associate, Barnabas. Modern scholars attribute some of the other letters to followers of Paul.

3. See 2 Pet 3:15-16.

4. Origen seems to have written commentaries on Romans, Galatians, Ephesians, Philippians, Colossians, 1-2 Thessalonians, Titus, Philemon, and Hebrews and series of homilies on 1 Corinthians, 2 Corinthians, Galatians, 1 Thessalonians, Titus, and Hebrews; see Pierre Nautin, *Origène, Sa Vie et Son Oeuvre* (Paris: Beauchesne, 1977), 243-54 and 385-6. Of Origen's works on Paul, only the commentary on Romans survives, and only in an abridged Latin translation. Of the commentaries on Ephesians and Galatians and the homilies on 1 Corinthians we have only fragments; of the others nothing.

will discuss: (1) the contents and particular character of 1 Corinthians; (2) the extent of the church fathers' commentary on the letter; (3) the nature of the patristic commentary; and (4) the organization of this book.

1 Corinthians: Its Contents and Particular Character

Among Paul's letters to early Christian communities, 1 Corinthians is the most rooted in the concrete here and now of a particular historical situation,[5] and it gives us a fascinating glimpse of the life of one group of early Christians and Paul's interactions with them. Written to a church Paul knows especially well,[6] in response to a letter from the Corinthians asking him for guidance (see 7:1), it gives advice on such matters as how to heal factions in the community, how to conduct common worship, and how to live out the Christian life in the everyday world. The letter begins with a powerful presentation of the cross of Christ as the paradoxical revelation of God's wisdom and power (1:17-25) and concludes with an extended discussion of the general resurrection of the dead and God's final triumph over evil (15:1-58). It includes a long discussion of marriage and sexual relations (7:1-40), the earliest version we have of the words of institution of the Eucharist (11:23-25), and a hymn in praise of self-giving love (13:1-13).

The letter reveals much about Paul's understanding of the good news of Christ's death and resurrection and how that good news is to be lived out in daily life. The confession of faith in the crucified and resurrected Jesus and the hope for his triumphant return have concrete consequences in the here and now. When, for example, Paul writes, "Christ, our Passover, has been sacrificed for us. Therefore let us keep the feast" (1 Cor 5:7-8), "keeping the feast" means renouncing those things that threaten the health of the church — among them sexual license and lack of community discipline.

Apart from its opening and closing salutations (1:1-9 and 16:1-12) the letter can be divided into five parts:

(1) In 1:10–4:21 Paul responds to reports that the new church in Corinth is riven by faction. To counter this he asks the Corinthians to reflect on the meaning of the cross of Christ. Challenging their arrogant claims to individual superiority, he presents the cross as a demonstration of God's wisdom and power, which appears paradoxically as folly and weakness (1:17–2:16). Wisdom based on anything else, he says, is false wisdom. He uses himself as an example of humble and faithful service to God; in imitation of Christ he does not seek his own glory and is content to seem foolish and weak (3:1–4:13).

(2) The next three chapters (5:1–7:40) are devoted largely to issues of sexual morality that troubled the Corinthian community. One man was sleeping with his father's second wife, while other Corinthians interpreted Paul's message of freedom in Christ as li-

---

5. This is also true of the brief personal letter to Philemon.

6. According to Acts 18:1-17, which relates the story of Paul's founding of the church at Corinth, Paul spent a year and a half there. In addition to 1 and 2 Corinthians, Paul wrote at least one other letter to this community, alluded to in 1 Cor 5:9.

cense to consort with prostitutes. Paul addresses these problems and also discusses marriage and divorce and the role of sex within marriage. Another issue addressed is whether Christians may make use of secular courts to settle their disputes (6:1-11).

(3) In 8:11–10:33 Paul takes up further questions about how to live in a non-Christian world, in particular whether Christians were allowed to eat meat that had been sacrificed to Greek gods and sold in the marketplace and whether it was permissible to attend dinners held in the precincts of these gods' temples (8:10; 10:27). Paul has a distinctive approach to such issues. Instead of laying down a firm law, he advises the Corinthians to act in such a way as to "build up" the whole community (8:1; 10:23). Eating meat offered to idols is intrinsically harmless, he says, but only if it does not threaten the faith of weaker Christians. In the middle of this discussion about not causing needless offense, Paul pictures himself as one who has "become all things to all men" in service of Christ (9:1-26).

(4) Chapters 11–14 consider a variety of questions that relate to worship: the dress of women who prophesy (11:2-16), the manner of celebrating the Lord's Supper (11:17-34), the form of worship services, including the exercise of "spiritual gifts" such as prophecy and speaking in tongues (12:11–4:40), and whether women are allowed to speak in the assemblies (14:33-36). Here again Paul appeals to the principle of "building up": the Corinthians are to use special gifts such as ecstatic speech to build up, rather than divide, the community. He drives the point home through the striking image of the Church as the "body of Christ": like the parts of a body, the members of the Church have different gifts and functions, but all are necessary for the health of the whole "body" (12:12-30). Rising to unusual poetic and rhetorical heights, Paul reinforces his point by an extended praise of *agapē*, self-giving love (13:1-13).

(5) Paul devotes chapter 15 to the general resurrection of the dead, a central point of his preaching about which the Corinthians were confused. Repeating an early summary of the Christian faith that centers on the death and resurrection of Christ (15:1-7), Paul goes on to argue that Christ's resurrection necessarily implies that *all* the dead will be raised. This will take place at Christ's second coming, when he will complete his victory over evil and death and usher in God's kingdom, so that God may be "all in all" (15:28). The resurrection will involve the present body, which God will transform into a "spiritual body" (15:44).

The Extent of Patristic Commentary on 1 Corinthians

This volume, like others in the The Church's Bible series, focuses especially on interpretations found in the patristic commentaries and series of homilies (or sermons), some of which survive complete and others only in fragments. But to form an accurate picture of how 1 Corinthians figured in early Christian thought and practice it is necessary to pay attention also to comments made in other kinds of works — in theological treatises, works of practical instruction, letters, liturgies, and sermons on other parts of Scripture. The earliest comments we possess on the letter are not in the form of a running commentary. Accordingly, I will discuss these "occasional" sources before turning to the commentaries and homilies on 1 Corinthians and introducing the authors whose words will be heard most often in this book.

Certain chapters of 1 Corinthians received sustained attention already in the second and third centuries. In the debates with Gnostic Christians Paul was bound to figure — for his claim to superior *gnōsis* (knowledge) made him an important figure for Gnostics — and the fathers used 1 Corinthians 15 to counter those who denied the physical resurrection of believers. In formulating a Christian view of marriage, authors such as Clement of Alexandria and Tertullian naturally turned to 1 Corinthians 7. In the fourth and fifth centuries, as the ascetic ideal became increasingly popular, fathers such as Athanasius, John Chrysostom, Gregory of Nyssa, Ambrose, and Augustine wrote separate treatises on virginity or on marriage in which this chapter plays a prominent role. Verses from the letter, notably 8:6 and 15:28, also figured in christological and trinitarian debates. Gregory of Nyssa, for example, devoted a whole treatise to 15:28 ("When all things are subjected to him, then the Son himself will also be subjected to the one who put all things in subjection under him, that God may be all in all") to counter an interpretation that made the Son inferior to the Father. Several sections that speak of the Spirit, including 1 Cor 2:10-16 and 12:4-13, were cited in treatises on the Holy Spirit (e.g., those of Athanasius and Basil of Caesarea) to demonstrate the biblical basis for the Trinity and for the full divinity of the Spirit. Passages from the letter also informed discussions of purgatory (1 Cor 3:13-15), the prophetic activity of women (11:2-16), and the beatific vision of God (13:12-13).

The letter was fundamental for the way the Old Testament was read. In 10:1-11 Paul gives an allegorical interpretation of texts from Exodus and Numbers that describe the ancient Israelites' exodus from Egypt and their journey to the Promised Land. Claiming that these events happened "as examples for us" (10:6) that were "written down for our edification" (10:11), Paul interprets them as referring to Christ and the experience of Christians in the present time. This exegesis was much cited by the fathers, along with the allegory of Sarah and Hagar in Gal 4:21-31, as basis for the view that Scripture has other senses beyond the literal meaning. "No Christian," Augustine claims, "would dare to maintain that [scriptural] narrative is not to be taken in a figurative sense since the apostle Paul says, 'Now these things happened to them as figures' (1 Cor 10:6)."[7] Two other passages from the letter, 2:10-16 and 9:9-10, reinforce this view, as is evident in the writings of Origen, who is particularly known for his allegorical exegesis.

Verse-by-verse comment on the letter, in commentaries and sermons, begins in the third century. The earliest series of homilies, by Origen of Alexandria, are extant only in fragments. We owe these, as well as fragments from many other authors such as Severian of Gabala, Didymus the Blind, Theodore of Mopsuestia, and Cyril of Alexandria, to medieval works called *catenae* (from Lat. *catena*, "chain"), which consisted of extracts from earlier writers linked together.[8] These works attest the admiration of later Christian gen-

---

7. Augustine, *The Literal Meaning of Genesis* 1.1.1 (Patrologia Latina 34:247).

8. Fragments of commentary preserved in the *catenae* can be found in K. Staab, ed., *Pauluskommentar aus der griechischen Kirche aus Katenhandschriften gesammelt* (Münster: Aschendorff, 1933). For editions of the fragments of Origen and Cyril of Alexandria, see below, "Bibliography of Editions."

erations for the exegesis of the church fathers and their determination to preserve them as precious resources. The forty-four homilies on 1 Corinthians by the fourth-century preacher John Chrysostom are preserved in their entirety. They were taken down stenographically while he preached and have reached us intact. We also have complete versions of the commentaries by Theodoret of Cyrus, Pelagius, Ambrosiaster, Cassiodorus, and John of Damascus.

The authors whose comments are translated in this book include both well-known and obscure figures. Those cited most frequently are Origen, John Chrysostom, Cyril of Alexandria, Theodoret, Gregory of Nyssa, and Augustine. Origen, of Alexandria and later of Caesarea in Palestine (ca. 185–ca. 254), was the most brilliant theologian and exegete of the early Greek church. Some of his views were later condemned as heretical, with the result that many of his works survive only in fragments or in Latin translation. Nonetheless, his interpretation of Scripture had wide influence in the ancient Church, on Greek fathers such as Basil of Caesarea and Gregory of Nyssa and on theologians such as Ambrose and Jerome in the Latin West. Origen wrote a series of homilies on 1 Corinthians, as he did on several other Pauline epistles. The importance of this letter for his theology is apparent in his sermons on other biblical books and in his major works *On First Principles* and *Against Celsus*. Although known especially for his allegorical or spiritual exegesis, Origen also concerns himself with historical and philological questions; for example, he pays careful attention to the definitions of words, to shades of meaning expressed by similar phrases, and to textual variants A central theme in his homilies on 1 Corinthians is that Scripture entails a complex divine pedagogy, as the divine Word addresses individual souls in the present time, in the way most appropriate to each, and gradually leads them all up to perfection. Origen understands different parts of 1 Corinthians to be addressed to two groups in Corinth who are at different stages on the road to perfection, in regard both to morality and to knowledge. The task of the interpreter is to encourage his audience to imitate those Corinthians who have progressed further along this path.

John Chrysostom (ca. 347-407), whose forty-four homilies on 1 Corinthians were beloved in medieval times, studied rhetoric under the pagan orator Libanius and theology under Diodorus of Tarsus, head of the Christian school of Antioch. He became a priest at Antioch and later bishop in Constantinople. He was known especially for his moral exhortation, his courage in the face of trying political circumstances, and his eloquence, reflected in his honorific title "Chrysostom," which means "golden-tongued." His sermons on 1 Corinthians resemble a commmentary in that they go through the book verse by verse and deal with both historical and theological questions. But his hearers are always kept in view, especially in the moral exhortation that takes up the last half of most sermons. He particularly emphasizes the dangers of wealth and the importance of caring for the poor.

Of those fathers who wrote commentaries on 1 Corinthians, the ones cited most frequently in this book are Cyril of Alexandria and Theodoret from the Greek East, and Ambrosiaster from the Latin West. Cyril (d. 444) was the patriarch of Alexandria and an influential theologian who played an important role in the formulation of the classic doctrine of the person of Christ. His writings include theological treatises, letters, and commentaries. A noteworthy feature of his commentary on 1 Corinthians, of which fragments were preserved in the medieval *catenae,* is his exploration of how Paul's words relate to the books of the Old Testament. Theodoret (ca. 393–ca. 460), bishop of Cyrus in Syria (near Antioch), was educated in Antioch, and he defended Antiochene views on Christology against the criticisms of Cyril. His works include an apology that compares Christian and pagan teaching, a church history, biographies of monks, and a refutation of heresies, as well as commentaries on many Old Testament books and on all the letters of Paul. Ambrosiaster is a name given by scholars to an anonymous early Christian who wrote commentaries on thirteen letters of Paul, perhaps in Rome at the time of Pope Damasus (366-84). The name reflects early manuscripts in which these commentaries were wrongly attributed to St. Ambrose. His commentary on 1 Corinthians contains succinct comments that focus on the historical sense of the text and on theological and moral themes, and he exhibits a particular interest in the Jews and Jewish institutions.

The most significant of those who made "occasional" comments on 1 Corinthians are Gregory of Nyssa and Augustine. Gregory (ca. 330–ca. 395) was bishop of Nyssa in Cappadocia (in modern Turkey) and an important theologian and mystical writer. He championed the creed of Nicea (325) against Neo-Arians[9] who denied the full divinity of Christ, as is illustrated by the extracts included here from his treatise on 1 Cor 15:28 and from his polemical work *Against Eunomius.* Among his many writings are the *Great Catechism,* an introduction to the Christian faith and sacraments; *On Virginity,* which recommends the ascetic life; *The Life of Moses;* and homilies on the Beatitudes, the Lord's Prayer, and the Song of Songs, which he understands as an allegory of the love between God and the human soul. Gregory's exegesis, which was influenced by that of Origen, emphasizes the spiritual meaning of Scripture.

Augustine, bishop of Hippo in North Africa (354-430), is the most influential and important Latin theologian of the patristic period. The immense corpus of his writings includes the autobiographical *Confessions, On the Trinity,* and *The City of God,* in which he answers pagan critics of Christianity through a synthesis of philosophical, theological, and political ideas that was to become foundational for Western civilization. Among his many commentaries on Scripture are those on Genesis, the Psalms, the Gospel of John, Galatians, and part of a commentary on Romans. Although Augustine did not compose a commentary or a series of homilies on 1 Corinthians, his works are full of comments on the letter. Included in this volume are selections from the major works just mentioned as well as from such minor works as *On the Usefulness of Fasting, On the Good of Marriage, On the Predestination of the Saints, On Rebuke and Grace,* and *On the Work of Monks.* The largest number of excerpts included here are from his sermons, of which more than five hundred have been preserved, which contain comments on every chapter of 1 Corinthians.

---

9. See Appendix 3 for an explanation of Arians and Neo-Arians.

The Nature of Patristic Commentary on 1 Corinthians

For the church fathers, all discussions of theology, morals, and Christian practice begin with the Bible. In their commentaries and homilies on 1 Corinthians, interpreters bring Paul's words to bear on new situations and explore their implications for the theological issues of their own day. For example, the rise of the prophetic movement called Montanism, in which women had prominent roles, prompted the anonymous author of *The Dialogue of a Montanist with an Orthodox Christian* to take a close look at what Paul says about women prophets in 1 Corinthians 11. Gregory of Nyssa, writing amid fourth-century debates about the relation of Jesus Christ to God the Father, pays particular attention to 1 Cor 8:6 — "For us there is one God, the Father, from whom are all things and for whom we exist, and one Lord, Jesus Christ, through whom are all things and through whom we exist" — in which he finds clear evidence against the claim of Arius and his followers that Christ the Son has a nature different from that of God the Father. Athanasius, Cyril of Alexandria, and Theodoret explore Paul's discussion of spiritual gifts in 1 Corinthians 12 in the context of contemporary debates about the Trinity. "The blessed Paul," Athanasius writes, "does not divide the Trinity," since he presents the Father as the source of spiritual gifts, which are distributed by the Spirit through the Son. Patristic commentary on 1 Corinthians refers frequently to figures such as Marcion, Arius, Eunomius, Mani, and Donatus,[10] whose views, though deemed inadequate by the fathers of the Church, provoked much reflection and inspired much of the creative theology of Origen, Gregory of Nyssa, Augustine, and others.

Like modern exegetes, patristic commentators ask historical questions and try to imagine the situation of Paul and his original addressees. So John Chrysostom prefaces his series of homilies with a summary of the letter's argument, in which he uses hints in the letter and other sources to reconstruct what was happening in the Corinthian church. The fathers also pose philological questions and consider textual variants. For example, Origen compares two different Greek translations of the quotation from Isaiah in 1 Cor 14:21, that of Aquila and that of the Septuagint (LXX), the version of the Old Testament in common use in the church. Augustine, in a comment on 1 Cor 13:10-12, cites 2 Kings 5:26 in two different versions, the Septuagint and Jerome's Latin translation, which was based on the Hebrew text. Patristic commentary also anticipates modern interest in the rhetorical analysis of Paul's letters. This is especially evident in the homilies of John Chrysostom, which give close attention to Paul's rhetorical strategy in every section of the letter.[11]

The primary concern of patristic commentaries and homilies, however, is not to reconstruct past history or praise Paul's rhetorical skill. For the fathers Paul's letters are above all a witness to the activity of the Lord Jesus Christ, who was also at work in their own day. The God of whom Paul speaks is not only a subject for theological reflection and debate but a living reality toward which one's whole life is to be oriented. To under-

---

10. For brief biographies of these figures see Appendix 3.

11. On this point see Margaret M. Mitchell, *The Heavenly Trumpet: John Chrysostom and the Art of Pauline Interpretation* (Tübingen: Mohr Siebeck, 2000).

stand Paul's letters, the fathers believed, the interpreter needs the guidance of the Holy Spirit,[12] as Paul says in 1 Cor 2:11: "So also no one comprehends the thoughts of God except the Spirit of God." The final goal of exegesis, as of the Christian life in general, is perfect knowledge of God and communion with him. So Augustine identifies the reward that Paul describes in 1 Cor 2:9 — "What eye has not seen, nor ear heard, and has not come up into the heart of man, what God has prepared for those who love him" — to be this: "God has promised himself to us as our reward. See if you can find something better. . . . Do not seek anything from God except God. Love him for nothing, ask him only for himself."[13] The implications of the biblical text for how one is to live and think about one's own life are never far from the fathers' thoughts.

This theological and existential orientation is reflected in several other characteristics of patristic interpretation. First, as the title of our series, The Church's Bible, suggests, the setting of patristic exegesis is the life and worship of the Church. This is obvious in the case of sermons, as well as in liturgies such as *The Liturgy of Saint James*. But it is also true of the material taken from commentaries, theological treatises, and letters. The fathers are speaking in and for a community of faith, and they read Paul's words in a spirit of worship and awe. So, for example, Origen says that one is to read the words of the prophets with "care," "attention," and "reverence" (*On First Principles* 4.1.6).

Second, the fathers read Paul's letters in the context of the whole Bible. They see the Old and New Testaments as one divine revelation, with Christ as the center. They know much of the Bible by heart. Interpreting Scripture by means of Scripture, they bring together different parts of the biblical revelation, not forcibly harmonizing them but thoughtfully considering how texts illuminate each other. So, for example, Gregory of Nyssa relates Paul's claim that Christ is "our righteousness" (1 Cor 1:24) to Matt 5:6, in which Jesus pronounces happy "those who hunger and thirst for righteousness." Words from the Gospel of John and the Psalms complete his picture of Christ as the ultimate end of the soul's longing. The fragments of Cyril of Alexandria's commentary on 1 Corinthians are particularly rich in such intrabiblical interpretation.

Third, the fathers encourage their readers and hearers to savor the words of Scripture and meditate on them, to pause and let them sink in. Augustine, in a comment on 1 Cor 2:2 — "I decided to know nothing among you except Jesus Christ and him crucified." — urges his hears to stop and unwrap this treasure:

> "Christ crucified," Paul says. What great things does that treasure contain? . . . Stay, do not pass on, do not despise, do not insult. Wait, examine. There may be something within that will give you much delight. You may find "what no eye has seen, nor ear heard, nor the heart of man conceived." (1 Cor 2:9)[14]

Images from different parts of Scripture are brought together in a creative way and allowed to work together on the mind and heart of the reader. When Paul says rather enig-

---

12. See Origen, *On First Principles* 4.1.4, and John Chrysostom, *Homilies on Genesis* 21.1.

13. *Sermon* 362.29 (Patrologia Latina 39:1632-33).

14. *Sermon* 160.1-5 (Patrologia Latina 38:874-875).

matically in 1 Cor 12:13: "we were all made to drink of one Spirit," Cyril of Alexandria brings to mind the "water of eternal life" and the "rivers of living water" promised by Jesus in John 4:13-14 and 7:38-39, as well as the "river of God" in Ps 65:9. This river, Cyril says, is "full of waters, the richly flowing winter torrent, which God the Father is said to give those who love him to drink. Why, then, should his Spirit not be thought of as a life-giving cup of water?"

Finally, for all their erudition and acumen, the fathers' emphasis is not on the interpreter making judgments about the text but rather on the transformation the text occasions in the interpreter. This idea of spiritual growth through engagement with the words of Scripture is a central thread running through Origen's homilies on 1 Corinthians, and it explains why he emphasizes that the original recipients of this letter were a mixed group, some of whom were "mature" and "spiritual" but most of whom were "babes" and "fleshly ones." Paul writes the letter, Origen says, to encourage both groups to make progress in their spiritual journey; he adapts his teaching so that it will challenge Christians at different stages, giving "milk" to beginners in the faith and "solid food" to those who are more mature (1 Cor 3:1-3). There are different levels of teaching in both moral matters — for example Paul's allowing marriage but recommending celibacy in chapter 7 — and theology, as Paul hints when he speaks of the "wisdom" he reserves for the "mature" in 1 Cor 2:6-11. According to Origen, Paul's letter serves a similar function for all those in later ages who encounter his words. So, in the first extant fragment of his homilies, Origen expresses his own eagerness to imitate the more mature of the Corinthians and urges his hearers to join him in leaving behind the immature Corinthians and following those who are more spiritual and ready to receive God's "mysteries."

A similar sense of deep personal engagement with the words of Scripture is also evident in the sermons and treatises of Augustine. Behind his brilliant rhetoric one always hears the beating heart of the author of the *Confessions,* for whom the most important question is always how his hearers and readers — and he himself — may be brought nearer to communion with God, the only source of their blessing.

The Organization of This Book

The substance of this book is the words of the church fathers, in translations from Greek or Latin made for this volume. The book begins with two general chapters of patristic comment, one on the life and character of the apostle Paul and the other summarizing the main themes of 1 Corinthians. Patristic comment on each of the sixteen chapters of Paul's letter follows, with commentary from one or more sources on each section of the text. At the beginning of each chapter I have summarized the principal themes in Paul's text and the main lines of patristic comment on them. Paul's words are then quoted, paragraph by paragraph, followed by the fathers' commentary. I cite 1 Corinthians from the Revised Standard Version except where the fathers construe the words differently or cite a variant text. The same holds for biblical quotations within the fathers' commentary. One cause of minor variants is that fathers cite the Old Testament from the Greek Septuagint (LXX) or a Latin translation, not the Hebrew, whereas the RSV and other modern translations are based on the Hebrew text.

In the fathers' commentary, bold type is used to signal verses, words, or phrases from the paragraph of 1 Corinthians under discussion. All other biblical citations are printed in italics. From the huge number of quoted words and phrases readers can see the extent to which the *words* of the Bible — not only its ideas — have formed the language and thought of the fathers.[15] When a father's comment is drawn from two or more of his works or different parts of the same work, I separate the selections by means of a blank line.

Appendix 1 contains brief biographies of all the ancient authors whose words are quoted in this book. Appendix 2 gives the sources from which the excerpts are taken. Appendix 3 explains proper names (e.g., Arius, Donatus, Montanists, Manicheans) mentioned by the fathers. The Bibliography cites the editions from which the translations were made.

JUDITH L. KOVACS

---

15. On this point, see Robert L. Wilken, *The Spirit of Early Christian Thought: Seeking the Face of God* (New Haven: Yale University Press, 2003), 76-77.

On the Author: Saint Paul

In his On Illustrious Men *Jerome draws on the book of Acts, Paul's letters, and church tradition to describe Paul's life. He presents Paul as the author of fourteen letters, a view commonly held in the early Church, though he admits that there is some doubt about the authorship of Hebrews and gives several possible explanations of its composition. The selections from Augustine focus on Paul's persecution of Christians and his conversion, and show how Paul's life illustrates the radical dependence of human beings on God's grace — a point to which Augustine returns many times in his comments on 1 Corinthians. Augustine, Origen, and John Chrysostom all comment on Paul's adaptability (see 1 Cor 9:19-23): Chrysostom notes Paul's success in dealing with widely differing situations, while Augustine and Origen applaud his versatility in accommodating his teaching to the capabilities of different audiences, some of whom were more advanced in the faith than others.*

The excerpts from John Chrysostom come from his seven "panegyrics," speeches in praise of Paul, which may have been composed for the feast day of St. Paul (28 December). One of the conventions of the panegyric genre in classical antiquity was the use of comparisons. Thus Chrysostom praises his hero by comparing him with various biblical figures to show that he possesses all the virtues for which the others were famous.

(1) Jerome

The apostle Paul, previously called Saul — not one of the twelve apostles — was of the tribe of Benjamin and the town of Giscala in Judaea. When the town was captured by the Romans, he moved with his parents to Tarsus. Sent by them to Jerusalem to study the law, he was taught by the learned Gamaliel, mentioned by Luke (Acts 22:3). But after he took part in the slaying of the martyr Stephen and had set out for Damascus with written authority from the high priest of the temple to persecute believers in Christ, he was conscripted into the faith by the revelation described in the Acts of the Apostles and became a *chosen instrument* (Acts 9:15) instead of a persecutor. When the proconsul of Syria, Sergius Paulus, had become a believer through his preaching, Saul took Paulus's name since he had conquered him and made him obedient to the Christian faith.[1] Then he took Barnabas with him and made a journey to many cities. Returning to Jerusalem, he was ordained Apostle of the Gentiles by Peter, James, and John.

Since the course of Paul's life is fully described in the Acts of the Apostles, I will say only this, that in the twenty-fifth year after the Lord's passion, that is, the second year of Nero's reign, at the time when Festus succeeded Felix as procurator of Judea, Paul was sent to Rome in chains. He remained there for two years, under guard but free to move about, and engaged in daily discussions with the Jews about the coming of Christ. We should note that at his first trial, when Nero's reign was not yet firmly established and he had not yet committed the monstrous crimes the historians relate, Paul was acquitted by Nero and thus was able to preach the gospel of Christ in the West also, as he says in his Second Letter to Timothy, written at the time of his martyrdom and dictated from prison: *At my first defense no one took my part; all deserted me. May it not be charged against them! But the Lord stood by me and gave me strength to proclaim the message fully, that all the Gentiles might hear it. So I was rescued from the lion's mouth* (2 Tim 4:16-17). Clearly the reference here is to the cruelty of Nero. Immediately thereafter Paul says, *The Lord will rescue me from every evil and will save me for his heavenly kingdom* (2 Tim 4:18). This means, of course, that he was aware that his martyrdom was imminent. He had already said in the same epistle, *I am already on the point of being sacrificed; the time of my departure has come* (2 Tim 4:6). Accordingly, in the fourteenth year of Nero, on the same day that Peter died, Paul was beheaded at Rome for Christ's sake, and was buried on the road to Ostia in the thirty-seventh year after the Lord's passion.

Paul wrote nine letters to seven churches: one to the Romans, two to the Corinthians, one to the Galatians, one to the Ephesians, one to the Philippians, one to the Colossians, and two to the Thessalonians. He also wrote letters to his disciples: two to Timothy, one to Titus, and one to Philemon. The Epistle to the Hebrews is not thought to be his because it differs in style and language. Tertullian thought it was by Barnabas, and others by Luke the Evangelist or Clement, afterward bishop of Rome. It is said that Clement ordered and embellished Paul's ideas with his own style; another possibility is that Paul was writing to Hebrews, and because of their animosity toward him he omitted his name from the opening salutation. Being a Hebrew, he wrote in his own language most eloquently: what was eloquently written in Hebrew, was translated into more eloquent Greek, and this, it is claimed, is the reason why this letter seems different from his others. There is also a letter to the Laodiceans under Paul's name, but its authenticity is rejected by everyone.

(2) Origen

[*The following description of Paul is part of an exegesis of Lev 6:8-13, which concerns the ritual of the burnt offering. Origen gives a symbolic interpretation of the two different garments*

---

1. Jerome is thinking of the custom whereby a Roman general took an additional name from a people he had subdued; for example, Scipio was called Africanus for his defeat of Carthage.

the priest is to wear, one when he performs the sacrifice and the other put on when he leaves the altar.]

We should notice that the priest wears one garment when he is making sacrifices and another when he goes out to the people. This is what Paul, the most learned of pontiffs and the most expert of priests, did as well. When he was in the assembly of the perfect, standing as it were inside the *holy of holies* (see Exod 30:29) and clothed in the garment of perfection, he said, *Yet among the mature we do impart wisdom, although it is not a wisdom of this age or of the rulers of this age, who are doomed to pass away. But we impart a secret and hidden wisdom of God, which God decreed before the ages for our glorification. None of the rulers of this age understood this; for if they had, they would not have crucified the Lord of glory* (1 Cor 2:6-8). But after saying this, as if he were going out to the people (see Num 11:24), he changed his garment and put on a much inferior one. And what does he say? *I decided to know nothing among you except Jesus Christ and him crucified* (1 Cor 2:2). You see how this most learned priest, when he is inside, in the midst of the perfect, as in the *holy of holies,* wears one doctrinal *garment.* But when he goes out to those who are not able to understand, he changes his verbal *garment* and teaches things less elevated. To some, as *babes,* he gives *milk* to drink (1 Cor 3:2); others he nourishes with *vegetables* since they are *weak* (Rom 14:2). For others who *have their faculties trained by practice to distinguish good from evil* (Heb 5:14) he prepares *solid food.*

(3) Augustine

Let us listen to the apostle Paul, as the festival of his martyrdom approaches, talking confidently about the crown prepared for him: *I have fought the good fight, I have finished the race, I have kept the faith. Henceforth there is laid up for me the crown of righteousness, which the Lord, the righteous judge, will award to me on that Day, and not only to me but also to all who have loved his appearing* (2 Tim 4:7-8). . . .

When Paul the apostle, previously Saul, was the cruelest and most monstrous persecutor, he deserved nothing good and merited severe punishment: he deserved to be damned, not chosen. But note that when he was doing evil and deserved evil, he was thrown to the ground by a heavenly voice. He was cast down as a persecutor and raised up as a preacher. Listen to him confessing this very thing: *I formerly blasphemed and persecuted and insulted him; but I received mercy* (1 Tim 1:13). Did he say, "The just judge will award it to me"? No, he said, *I received mercy:* I deserved evil and received good. *He did not deal with us according to our sins* (Ps 103:10). *I received mercy:* what was owed to me was not paid. If what was owed had been paid, Paul would have been punished. . . .

As far as the east is from the west, so far does he remove our transgressions from us (Ps 103:12). Turn away from the west and turn toward the east. Here is one man, Saul also called Paul. Saul is in the west, Paul is in the east; the persecutor is in the west, the preacher in the east. On the one side his sins are setting, on the other his righteousness is rising; in the west is the old man, in the east the new, in the west is Saul, in the east Paul. How did this happen to Saul, the cruel man, the persecutor, the one who was no shepherd? He was *a ravenous wolf* (Gen 49:27), *a member of the tribe of Benjamin* (Rom 11:1), as he himself says.[2] It was said in the prophecy, *Benjamin is a ravenous wolf, in the morning devouring the prey, and at even dividing the food* (Gen 49:27). Previously he devoured, later he was a shepherd. He was a predator, indeed very much the predator. Read about it, read the Acts of the Apostles. Paul had received letters from the priests authorizing him to bring back in chains for punishment whomever he found following the way of Christ. He went, he raged, he breathed *threats and murder* (Acts 9:1). Here he is a predator. But it is still morning, and there is *vanity under the sun* (Eccl 1:14). It becomes evening for him when he is struck with blindness. His eyes are closed to the vanity of this world, and his inner eyes are filled with light. Previously a vessel of destruction (cf. Rom 9:22), he became a *chosen instrument* (Acts 9:15). And here the phrase *he will divide the food* (Gen 49:27) is fulfilled. The account of Paul's dividing up the food is recited everywhere. Notice how he divides the food. He knows what is suitable for whom. He divides and does not distribute to all or at random. He divides, that is, he chooses to whom he will give. He does not dispense to all or haphazardly. He speaks *wisdom among the perfect* (1 Cor 2:6). But to others, those who are not strong enough to take solid food, he divides and says, *I gave you milk to drink* (1 Cor 3:2).

That is what he does who previously did — what? I do not want to remember: no, let me remember the man's wickedness so that I may demonstrate God's mercy. The one at whose hands Christ suffered suffered on behalf of Christ. He became Paul instead of Saul, a true witness instead of a false one. He who scattered gathers together. How did all these things come to Saul? Let us listen to him. He asks, "Do you ask how this came to me? This is not from me": *I received mercy* (1 Tim 1:13).

Again the apostle says, *I received mercy* (1 Tim 1:13). What a confession! He does not say, "I received mercy because I was faithful" but *I received mercy so that I might be faithful* (1 Cor 7:25).

Let us look at Paul's early life, let us see Saul raging and in a fury, let us watch him breathing out hatred and thirsting for blood. Let us watch him, my brothers, for he is a great spectacle. Here is the situation: after the murder of Stephen, after stones had caused the blood of God's witness to be spilled, and Saul had kept the cloaks of the stoners so that he might stone with their hands as well as his own, the brethren who had gathered at Jerusalem were scattered (Acts 7:54–8:2). And that madman, not satisfied with seeing Stephen's blood being poured out, received letters from the chief priests to go to Damascus and bring back in chains whatever Christians he found there (Acts 9:1-3). And he was on his way. This was the way of Paul, for Christ was not yet the way for him: this was Saul's road, not yet Paul's. He was on his way. What was in his heart? What except evil? Tell me what he deserves. If you ask for his deserts, they are damnation, not liberation. He was on his way to commit acts of rage against the members of Christ's body, he went to shed blood, he, the shepherd-to-be, went as a wolf. That is the way he went. He could go in no other way toward that goal for which he was heading. And when he was walking in this way, his thoughts were of murder and he breathed out slaughter. Wrath moved his foot-

2. Augustine here understands the prophecy about Benjamin in Gen 49:27 as applying to Paul since he was of the tribe of Benjamin.

4

steps, hatred set his limbs in motion. As he went on his way, it was as a slave who serves cruelty. But lo, a voice came from heaven, *Saul, Saul, why do you persecute me?* (Acts 9:4). That is why he said, *I received mercy that I might be faithful* (1 Cor 7:25). He was faithless; indeed, he was cruel in his faithlessness. But he received mercy that he might be faithful.

(4) John Chrysostom

We would not miss the mark if we were to call Paul's soul a field of virtues and a spiritual paradise: so richly does it blossom with grace and so worthy of that grace is the discipline it exhibits. Since Paul became a *chosen instrument* (Acts 9:15) and purified himself thoroughly, the gift of the Spirit was poured out upon him in abundance. From this Spirit he brought forth for our benefit those amazing *rivers* (John 7:38), not four in number like the springs of paradise (Gen 2:10-14), but many more, which keep flowing each day. These rivers do not water the earth but raise up human souls for a harvest of virtue. . . .

What is the proper starting point for our accolades? It is none other than to demonstrate that Paul possessed all the good things anyone ever possessed. For whatever noble qualities prophets or patriarchs or righteous ones or apostles or martyrs manifested, Paul has joined them all together and possessed them to a greater degree than any of the others possessed even a single virtue. . . .

Consider the following. Abel made a sacrifice (Gen 4:4), and for that reason his name is remembered. But Paul's sacrifice is as superior to Abel's as heaven is superior to earth. Do you want me to tell you what kind of sacrifice Paul made? It was not just one. For he sacrificed himself completely every day, and in doing this he made a double offering. On one hand, he died *every day* (1 Cor 15:31); on the other hand, he *carried in* his *body the death of Jesus* (2 Cor 4:10). . . .

But Paul was not satisfied with these sacrifices. When he had completely consecrated himself, he made an offering of the whole world, both land and sea, both Greek and non-Greek, and to every land where the sun shines he went, as if on wings. And not only did he travel; he also pulled up the weeds of sin and sowed the word of godliness, driving out deceit, restoring the truth, making men into angels, or rather turning men from demons into angels. Thus, when he was about to die, after much labor and numerous victories, he encouraged his disciples by saying, *Even if I am to be poured as a libation upon the sacrificial offering of your faith, I am glad and rejoice with you all. Likewise you also should be glad and rejoice with me* (Phil 2:17-18). . . .

Everyone admires Abraham because when he heard, *Go from your country and your kindred* (Gen 12:1), he left his fatherland and home, his friends and relatives. God's command was everything to him, and this we admire. But how could anyone equal Paul? For the sake of Jesus he left not fatherland and home and relatives, but the world itself. Or, rather, he made little of heaven or the heaven of heavens and sought one thing only, to love Jesus. Listen to him as he makes this clear, *Not things present, nor things to come . . . nor height, nor depth, will be able to separate us from the love of God* (Rom 8:38-39). . . .

[*Chrysostom then shows how Paul is superior to both Isaac and Jacob.*] Does the Scripture admire Isaac's son Jacob for his patient endurance? Yet what steely soul could exhibit the patience of Paul? He did not serve [as Jacob did] for twice seven years (Gen 29:15-30), but served his whole life for the sake of the *bride* of Christ (Rev 21:9; 2 Cor 11:2; Eph 5:23).[3] And not only did he suffer the heat of the day and the frost of the night; he also endured a thousand stormy trials, at one time being scourged (Acts 22:24), at another having his body beaten with stones (Acts 14:19; 2 Cor 11:25), at one time fighting wild beasts (2 Cor 15:32), at another contending with the open sea (2 Cor 11:25-26), being in constant hunger day and night, suffering icy cold (2 Cor 11:27), and constantly leaping over the pits and snatching his sheep away from the jaws of the devil. . . .

[*In a section omitted here Chrysostom compares Paul to Joseph and Job.*] Who else could astonish us? Moses of course! But Paul surpasses even him, and to a considerable degree. Moses did many great things, but the chief and crowning accomplishment of that saintly soul was that he chose to be blotted out of God's book for the sake of the salvation of the Jews (Exod 32:31-32). But while Moses chose to perish together with the others, Paul did not choose to perish with them but to have himself cut off from unending glory while others were saved (Rom 9:3-4). Moses contended with the pharaoh, but Paul contended every day against the devil. . . .

Consider how great were the things God found Paul worthy to receive even before the resurrection that is to come. He snatched him up to paradise; he led him up to the third heaven; he made him privy to things so secret that it is not permitted to utter them to anyone who shares human nature (2 Cor 12:2-4). And this was absolutely fitting since even when he walked on the earth, Paul did everything as if consorting with angels. Even while he was bound to his mortal body, his purity was angelic. And although he was subjected to great trials, he was eager not to fall short of the heavenly powers. For he traversed the known world as if he had wings; like an incorporeal being, he was contemptuous of hardships and perils. As if already enjoying his place in heaven, he disdained earthly things; and he kept constant vigil as though in the very presence of incorporeal powers. . . .

Tell me, then, how was it that this frequenter of the marketplace (Acts 17:17), who stood in his workshop wielding his knife (see Acts 18:3), exhibited such a disciplined way of life and also won over others — nations and cities and country regions? He did this despite displaying no power of eloquence; quite to the contrary, he lacked the most rudimentary education. Listen to what he says with no trace of embarrassment, *Even if I am unskilled in speaking, I am not in knowledge* (2 Cor 11:6). He had no money — he says so himself: *To the present hour we hunger and thirst, we are . . . buffeted* (1 Cor 4:11). But why am I talking about money when often he did not have even the bare minimum of food or a cloak to cast about himself? And his disciple[4] shows that Paul was not distinguished in his occupation, when he says, *Because he was of the same trade he stayed with them [Priscilla and Aquila], for by trade they were tentmakers* (Acts 18:3). Nor was Paul remarkable on account of his ancestors. How could he be, in view of his trade? He was not notable because of his native land or race. Nonetheless, when he appeared in public, his ap-

---

3. Chrysostom is comparing Paul's labor for the sake of the church, the bride of Christ, to Jacob's serving Laban in order to earn Leah and Rachel as brides.

4. That is. Luke, the author of Acts.

pearance alone confounded and upset all opposition. Like fire lighting on straw or grass, he burned up the realm of demons and transformed everything according to his will. . . .

As I have said repeatedly about Paul and will not quit saying, no one facing such wholly adverse conditions was so perfectly equal to each of them. At any rate, no one had such a desire for the present life, not even those who are cowardly in the face of death. Yet no one so despised this present life, not even those who practice excessive self-mortification. Paul was purified of every desire and cared nothing for this present world; he would always temper his own desire by the will of God. At one point he says that living in this world is more necessary than to be found with Christ and communing with him (Phil 1:24), at another he says that this life is so wearying and burdensome that he groans and longs to be released (2 Cor 5:4; Phil 1:23). He desires only what will benefit him before God, even if that means the opposite of what he previously desired. Paul was a complex and many-sided person: he was no hypocrite (God forbid!), but he became whatever the proclamation of the gospel and the salvation of human beings required (see 1 Cor 9:22). In this, too, he imitates his master. . . .

Whenever the royal standard bearers enter a city, with trumpets blaring before them and many soldiers leading the way, everyone comes running to hear the sound, see the insignia lifted on high, and behold the valor of the standard bearer. Therefore, since today Paul is entering not a city but the entire world, let us all come running. For he does not bear the standard of an earthly king but the cross of Christ who reigns above, and it is not men who lead the way but angels, whose role it is to honor that which is borne and secure the safety of the bearer. . . .

Since God has honored our human race by deeming one man worthy to accomplish so much, let us be zealous to imitate Paul, let us be eager to become like him, and let us not think that this is beyond our reach. What I have often said before I will say again: Paul had the same body we have, he ate the same food, and he had the same soul. Yet his will was great and his zeal magnificent. And it was this that made him what he was. Therefore, let none of you despair; let no one give up. . . .

General Comments on the Letter

Ancient commentaries on Scripture often begin with a summary of a book's content and its argument. Ambrosiaster's brief introduction enumerates the many issues discussed in the first seven chapters of the letter. John Chrysostom begins his introductory summary with a description of the city of Corinth and then paraphrases the account in Acts 18 of Paul's experiences in Corinth. Turning to the letter itself, he identifies its central problem as discord in the community. Two causes of dissension that Chrysostom particularly emphasizes are the influence of Greek philosophy and the Corinthians' arrogance about spiritual gifts. His introduction concludes with a discussion of Paul's sources of information about the situation at Corinth and his rhetorical strategy. Theodoret, like the other two commentators, interprets the letter in light of the statement in Acts 18:11 that Paul spent a long time in Corinth. In his view this explains why the letter contains more concrete advice than discussion of doctrinal matters. Paul had had sufficient time with the Corinthians to give them full instruction.

(1) Ambrosiaster

In obedience to the Lord's command, the apostle lived with the Corinthians for a year and a half, and taught the word of God in their midst (see Acts 18:11). This is why he shows great confidence and affection in his dealings with them, sometimes advising, sometimes admonishing, sometimes coaxing them as if they were his children. There are many reasons why he writes to them. First, like heretics they were at variance with one another. They attached themselves to individuals and chose to be called Paulinists, Petrians, and Apollonians, not Christians, a practice the apostle sharply criticizes. But there were some who set themselves against all these leaders and were devoted to Christ alone (1 Cor 1:10-12). Second, the Corinthians had begun to take pleasure in eloquence and earthly philosophy (1:17), and in the name of Christ they adopted teachings contrary to the faith. Third, they grew bold because they were sure that the apostle was not coming to see them (4:18). The fourth reason is that they allowed a brother who was a fornicator to remain in their midst (5:1). Fifth, Paul reminds them of a previous epistle (5:9), which he had written before this letter which is called the first [to the Corinthians]. Sixth, they were unjust and deceitful to one another and wanted their disputes to be tried by unbelievers (6:1). Seventh, he claims that he has the right to accept money for his expenses but disdains to do so in order not to provide a pretext for false apostles to defraud them (9:4-12). Eighth, he replies to their letter because heretics had sown confusion on the subject of marriage (7:1). Ninth, he declares that each individual should remain in the state in which he first came to faith (7:17). His tenth reason regards virgins, about whom he had received no instructions (7:25). The other reasons will be brought to light in the body of the commentary.

(2) John Chrysostom

Today Corinth is the most prominent city in Greece, and in ancient times the citizens took pride in the city's many advantages, above all, in its abundant wealth. This is why one of the pagan authors called the place "rich."[1] The city is located on the Isthmus of the Peloponnesus in a setting well-suited for trade. It was full of rhetoricians and philosophers. One of the so-called Seven Sages is from this city.[2] I say these things not to show off or to display the breadth of my education — for what is the significance of knowing these things? — but because they help us understand the subject matter of the letter.

Paul had many experiences in this city. In addition to everything else, Christ appeared to him there and said, *Do not be silent, but speak; for I have many people in this city* (Acts 18:10). Paul stayed there for two years. It was here, too, that the demon was cast out, at whose hands the Jews suffered terribly when they tried to exorcise it (Acts 19:13-17).[3] Here too those who were converted gathered the books of the magicians and burned them, fifty thousand in all, as it turned out (Acts 19:19). In this city, while Gallio was proconsul, Paul was beaten before the judgment seat (Acts 18:17).[4]

Now the devil realized that this great and populous city had embraced the truth, and he knew that it was a city noted for its wealth. At that time it was the chief city of Greece — for the Athenians and the Spartans were in a sorry state, having long ago lost their preeminence. What did he do when he saw that the Corinthians had accepted the word of God with great enthusiasm? He sowed division. For he knew that even the strongest kingdom in the world will not stand if it is divided within itself (Matt 12:25). And he used the wealth and wisdom of the inhabitants as the occasion of his attack. The wealthy and the wise had formed groups among themselves and appointed themselves leaders of the masses, and people were attached to one or another of these leaders, to some because of their wealth, and to others because of their wisdom and their ability to provide advanced instruction. As they welcomed adherents, these teachers actually boasted that their speech surpassed what the apostle had said. Paul refers to this obliquely when he says, *I could not address you as spiritual men* (1 Cor 3:1). Clearly it was the Corinthians' weakness, not Paul's inability, that kept them from hearing much of what he had to teach,

1. Homer, *Iliad* 2.570.

2. That is, Periander of Corinth, who figures prominently in Plutarch's *Banquet of the Seven Sages.*

3. Actually this story and the following one take place in Ephesus; Chrysostom seems to be quoting from memory.

4. In Acts it is only Sosthenes who is described as having been beaten before the tribunal.

as Paul makes clear when he says, *Without us you have become rich* (4:8). It is an extremely destructive thing for the church to be torn apart by divisions.

Furthermore there was another sin that they committed brazenly: a man slept with his stepmother, and instead of being rebuked, he even attracted followers who boasted about him. For this reason Paul exclaims, *And you are arrogant! Ought you not rather to mourn?* (5:2). Next, some of the so-called "more perfect ones," who in their gluttony ate food sacrificed to idols and dined in temples, were wrecking everything (8:1-2). And others brought their conflicts and quarrels about money to pagan courts to be arbitrated (6:1). Furthermore there were many long-haired men among them, whom Paul orders to cut their hair (11:14). There was also another sin — and no small one: they ate by themselves in their assemblies and did not share with the needy (11:17-20). They also acted improperly in yet another way: they were arrogant about spiritual gifts (12:1), and this made them jealous of each other. This was the main cause of the divisions in the church.

In addition, the teaching about the resurrection was not firmly established among them. For some of them did not really believe that there was a resurrection of bodies (15:12), because they were still afflicted with Greek folly. In fact, all of their problems sprang from the foolishness of pagan philosophy, the mother of all evils. That is why they were divided into sects, something else they learned from the philosophers, who are constantly competing. They opposed each other's teachings because they were arrogant and desired to be first and were keen to go beyond their predecessors in making discoveries (see Acts 17:21). These things were the result of their absolute commitment to rational arguments.

The Corinthians had sent a letter to Paul through Fortunatus and Stephanas and Achaicus, and through them Paul also sends his letters. He makes this clear at the end of the letter (16:17), although not everything discussed in Paul's letter responds to their letter but only what he says about marriage and virginity. That is why he says, *Concerning the things about which you wrote to me* (7:1). Paul's own letter treats subjects about which the Corinthians had written him as well as topics they had not mentioned, since he was well informed about all their deficiencies. In addition to the letter, he also sends Timothy (16:10). He knew that, despite the powerful nature of his letter, the presence of his disciple would add considerably to its effectiveness.

Those who caused divisions in the church were ashamed to be seen as acting out of ambition, so they devised a cloak for what they were doing: they claimed to teach a more perfect doctrine and to be wiser than others. To pluck out the root of the trouble and the spirit of division that sprang from it, Paul first takes a stand against the real disease. And he speaks very boldly, because the Corinthians were his closest disciples. This why he says, *If to others I am not an apostle, at least I am to you; for you are the seal of my apostleship* (9:2). Further, they were in a weaker state than others, so Paul says, *I did not speak to you as to spiritual men, for you were not ready for it, and even yet you are not ready* (3:1-2). He says this so that they would not think that he was speaking only about the past, which is why he added: *and even yet you are not ready.* It is likely, however, that not all were corrupted. Some were very holy. Paul makes this clear in the middle of the letter when he says, *But with me it is a very small thing that I should be judged by you* (4:3), and adds, *I have applied all this to myself and to Apollos* (4:6).[5] Since, then, all the Corinthians' troubles were born of folly and of the claim to know something special, Paul begins by dealing with this problem.

(3) Theodoret

The holy Paul was the first to bring the message of salvation to the Corinthians, and he spent a long time with them, as the Master had explicitly commanded. *Speak,* the Lord said to Paul, *and do not be silent, for I have many people in this place* (Acts 18:9-10). When a year and a half had passed, Paul traveled to other cities to preach the gospel, but the Corinthians reveled in idle disputes and rivalries. They were divided into many factions, and chose eloquent men as their leaders and teachers. Each group was constantly praising its own teacher and competing with the other groups. One of those who took pride in their eloquence went so far as to commit a most serious sin, sleeping with his stepmother (5:1). Overlooking this sin, his partisans only praised his smooth words.

This is why the divine apostle begins the letter by condemning what was thought to be wisdom. He shows that preaching the gospel, even though unadorned by such wisdom, has more power than anything else. He also censures those who disagreed about other things and who turned to civil leaders for adjudication. In addition, he forbids eating meat sacrificed to idols and suggests that some dared to do even this. In the course of the letter he gives appropriate advice concerning virgins and widows. Further, he includes an extended discussion of spiritual gifts (12:1–14:33), which explains the differences among the various gifts, and he enjoins the Corinthians to use the gift of speaking in tongues to serve the community, not to win praise.

He also teaches them about the resurrection since some, it seems, had spoken out against the doctrine of the resurrection of the body (15:12). Paul put many other things in his letter to them — for brevity's sake I will not list them all — which were useful to the addressees and beneficial for everyone else as well. And yet he said little about doctrinal matters because he had spent considerable time among them and had taught them carefully and thoroughly what was to be believed. In addition, the distinguished Apollos, who arrived after Paul, had confirmed the apostolic teaching. So Paul, like a good doctor, offered remedies corresponding to the malady.

---

5. Chrysostom's point is not entirely clear here, but he seems to take 1 Cor 4:3-6 as an indication that some of the Corinthians were more righteous than others and that they had been subjected to unjust criticism. He thinks Paul is indirectly defending these people when he uses himself as an example.

1 Corinthians 1

Paul's greetings and thanksgivings (vv. 1-9) anticipate some of the main themes of the letter: divine grace, wisdom, fellowship in Christ, spiritual gifts, and the judgment that awaits at the last day. In vv. 10-17 he addresses the problem of the division of the Christian community in Corinth into rival groups. This is followed by a powerful presentation of the gospel as hidden divine wisdom, which appears to be foolishness to the wise of this world (vv. 18-31).

In their comments on the introductory greetings the fathers pay careful attention to individual words. Thus Severian (on vv. 1-3) notes how often Paul mentions "the Lord Jesus Christ" and sees here an anticipation of the theme of unity that is so important in this letter. Theodoret's interpretation of the preposition "by" in v. 9 ("God, by whom you were called") reflects the christological controversies of the early Church, as do many other comments included in this volume (compare Ambrosiaster on v. 2). Origen's comments on these verses introduce some of the main emphases of his Homilies on 1 Corinthians. *In the phrases "church of God" and "all those who call on the name" (v. 2) he sees a clue to understanding the whole letter. He takes the phrases to refer to two distinct groups, the perfect "church" and those who invoke the name of Christ but have not yet achieved perfection. Reading this letter as a call to pursue perfection, Origen admonishes his hearers to imitate the perfect among the Corinthians. Another theme that runs through Origen's homilies is how one is to interpret the Bible. Origen repeatedly looks to Paul's words for guidance in this matter (see his discussion of "all knowledge" in vv. 6-7). Other frequently occurring motifs are Origen's strictness on moral matters and his humility before God (both exemplified in the comments on the "day of our Lord" in vv. 7-8). Also characteristic of Origen is that he often suggests more than one interpretation (see, e.g., his comments on "testimony" at v. 7).*

A prominent feature of John Chrysostom's Homilies on 1 Corinthians *is his careful attention to Paul's style and rhetoric (see the comments on vv. 10-17). He presents Paul as a psychologically astute writer who uses classical rhetoric to tailor his argument to the situation and the condition of his hearers — very much like John himself, who was called Chrysostom, or "golden mouth," because of his great rhetorical skill. Nonetheless, he emphasizes the difference between Paul's preaching and human wisdom (v. 17) and argues that the grace of the gospel is all the more miraculous because it was preached by a man like Paul who did not have a Greek education. Ambrosiaster's primary interest in these verses is to identify the teachers Paul opposes in the letter.*

Paul's depiction of the paradoxical power and wisdom of the cross (vv. 18-25) occasioned much reflection. Origen, who interprets the crucifixion as a victory over Satan, elucidates verse 18 by comparing other Pauline texts and also the pagan practice of making human sacrifices to avert a plague. To explain why Paul calls Christ the "power of God" (v. 24) he points to the spread of the gospel to the ends of the earth and adds that, according to Scripture, Christ has also taken possession of the heavens and the infernal regions. Ambrosiaster understands the "wisdom of the world," which the cross shows to be foolish (v. 20), to refer to teaching that denies God's providence and his future judgment. Cyril makes a similar point in his comments on verses 22-25: the divine plan to save the world through the incarnation, death, and resurrection of Christ seems foolish to Greeks, even though it manifests God's inexpressible power. He quotes several gospel texts as examples of how the "Jews demand signs" (v. 22). Such intrabiblical exegesis — illuminating one biblical text by adducing others that contain similar terms or themes — is a common practice of the fathers and is particularly frequent in Cyril's commentary. John Chrysostom, in his comments on verses 18-21, describes a debate he had with a pagan who argued that the cross showed Christ's weakness. Chrysostom interprets the "wisdom of God" that should have led the world to recognize God (v. 21) as a reference to the miraculous works of creation. To explain how the wisdom of the gospel can seem to be folly (v. 23) Theodoret compares how the sun appears to be dark to those who are blind.

The chapter concludes with an appeal to the experience of Paul's hearers (vv. 26-31): they too were foolish, weak, and insignificant, as the gospel appears to be, but through Christ, who is the wisdom and power of God, they have been redeemed, sanctified, and justified. Both Origen and John of Damascus call attention to the words "not many" in v. 26 ("not many were wise"), from which they conclude that there were some educated people among the Corinthian Christians. Ambrosiaster explains the four epithets given to Christ in v. 30 — wisdom, righteousness, sanctification, and redemption — as different ways of expressing his salvific work. Gregory of Nazianzus considers these words together with titles from John 1, Colossians 1, and other New Testament texts. These four terms also stimulated Gregory of Nyssa's reflections on the spiritual life. Like Gregory of Nazianzus, he relates the terms to christological titles from other parts of the Bible. For example, by linking Christ as "righteousness" with the blessing of those who "hunger and thirst after righteousness" in Matt 5:5 he portrays Christ as the ultimate end of the soul's longing. Basil of Caesarea quotes verse 31 in a homily and sets it in the context of passages from many other scriptural books. Augustine, for whom the primary sin is pride, emphasizes the prohibition of boasting in verse 31, which he relates to Paul's preaching of the humility of the cross (1 Cor 2:1-2). "He who boasts in himself," Augustine says, "boasts in a fool."

1 Corinthians 1:1-3

₁**Paul, called by the will of God to be an apostle of Christ Jesus, and our brother Sosthenes, ₂To the church of God which is at Corinth, to those sanctified in Christ Jesus, called to be saints together with all those who in every place call on the name of our Lord Jesus Christ, both their [Lord] and ours:[1] ₃Grace to you and peace from God our Father and the Lord Jesus Christ.**

1. Or "with all who call on the name of the Lord Jesus Christ in every place of theirs and ours." For this alternative construal of the Greek text, see the commentary of Ambrosiaster.

(1) Severian of Gabala

[**By the will of God**] Paul does not add this phrase without reason, but to show that it is God's will that all should be called after Christ and that there be apostles. With one stroke he enlists on his side this will, as something known to the Corinthians, and at the same time he cuts off the arrogance of those who are elated by their own talk. When he calls them one **church** and **of God**, he combats the unfortunate division that had arisen. He adds **in Christ Jesus** — not in so-and-so and what's-his-name. One should note how often, within a few words, Paul mentions **Christ Jesus.** He teaches them, from the very beginning of the letter, that it is wrong to be named after anyone else than the Lord Jesus Christ. By constantly mentioning Jesus Christ, he heals the wound created by their dividing into groups named for different people.

 To those sanctified in Christ Jesus: It is not a man who has sanctified you, Paul says, but God acting in Christ. If you call upon a man, he says, take your name from him. But if you call upon Jesus Christ, take your name from him on whom you call. Wisely he says, **together with all those who call on the name.** Not only you, but all those everywhere who are believers call upon Christ and take their name from him, not from men. Do not, then, be the only ones to act strangely and introduce an impious innovation. Paul did not say "with all those who name the name" but **together with those who call on** it, showing thereby that the Son of God is God. For it is God upon whom one calls in prayer. **In every place, their [Lord] and ours.** Since every place calls upon Jesus Christ, imitate the majority and do not do something at variance with the others. The phrase **theirs and ours** is to be taken with **the Lord.** It means: "both we who write and you who benefit from what we write have one Christ Jesus."

(2) Ambrosiaster

Paul began his letter to the Romans differently since the case he argued there was different; to these Corinthians, however, he writes that he is an **apostle of Christ Jesus by the will of God** because everything he did was by the will of the Son of God, who said to him, *Depart, for I will send you far away to the Gentiles* (Acts 22:21). Hence he is called **apostle,** that is, someone who is sent **by the will of God,** to the Gentiles. By this Paul also criticizes those whom Christ had not sent and whose teaching was not true. He names God and Christ frequently in order to show that Christ, who is God, is not the Father, yet that Christ the Son exists just as God the Father exists; they are not a single entity since he is clearly called *Son.* For many sects had emerged that proclaimed the gospel of Christ in accordance with their own personal judgment — dry branches of these sects are still in evidence now — and their partisans were subverting the churches. That is why the apostle sets down everything contrary to these heresies and claims that he is the true preacher who was sent by Christ **by the will of God.**

 And our brother Sosthenes. Paul commends Sosthenes, too, as his associate. **To the church of God which is at Corinth, to those sanctified in Christ Jesus.** He writes to the church because at that time individual churches did not have overseers. And even though he reproves them in many respects, still he says, **to those sanctified in Christ Jesus.** This is because they are sanctified by being reborn in Christ, though afterward they had begun to behave badly. Paul wanted to show that the whole church was sanctified in Christ but that certain of them had turned aside from the tradition of the truth because of the evil teachings of the false apostles.

Called to be saints. That is, your calling is to be saints. Sanctification is the rule laid down for you, and you must not step aside from it. **With all who in every place call on the name of the Lord Jesus Christ, theirs and ours.** That is, he joins the Gentiles to the true Jews since *salvation is from the Jews* (John 4:22), so that in every place where there are Gentiles who call upon the name of our Lord Jesus Christ and where there are also the Jews already mentioned, they may all be one in like fashion. For the false apostles, who preached the name of Christ by means of the *wisdom of the world* (1 Cor 1:20), that is, with an admixture of philosophy, rejected the ancient Law and the Prophets. They denied that Christ was actually crucified and maintained that he only appeared to be crucified, as Marcion and Manicheus[2] did. Hence the apostle says, *we preach Christ crucified* (1 Cor 1:23). They also did not admit the resurrection of the flesh, something Isaiah the prophet proclaims when he says, *Those who are in the tombs shall rise again* (Isa 26:19).

(3) Origen on verse 2

If all the Corinthians were meant by the term **church,** why would there be any need for Paul to add, **together with all those who call on the name?** If all were calling upon the name in the same way, why did Paul need to write not only **together with those who call upon the name** but, in addition to these, also **to the church of God?** We have shown that only the praiseworthy ought to be called **church.** Those who deserve blame, although they are not deserters who have become entrenched in sin but are still **calling on the name,** have not yet become **the church.** Let us, then, move quickly beyond **calling on the name** and ascend to the spotless and blameless **church.**

1 Corinthians 1:4-9

4I give thanks to my God always for you because of the grace of God which was given you in Christ Jesus, 5that in every way you were enriched in him with all speech and all knowledge — 6even as the testimony to Christ was confirmed among you — 7so that you are not lacking in any spiritual gift, as you wait for the revealing of our Lord Jesus Christ; 8who will sustain you to the end, guiltless in the day of our Lord Jesus Christ. 9God is faithful, by whom you were called into the fellowship of his Son, Jesus Christ our Lord.

---

2. On Marcion and Manicheus, see "Glossary of Proper Names" in Appendix 3.

(1) Ambrosiaster on verses 4 and 7

I give thanks to my God always for you. Although he writes to everyone in the church, he writes in such a way — at times criticizing and at times praising — that each person who reads his words may understand what is being said in praise of him and what in condemnation. For within a single audience Paul addresses two populations in such a way that when he criticizes, those who behave badly should know that it is written to them, and likewise when he praises, those who stick steadfastly to the rule should know that this is said to them. And this is why Paul declares, **I give thanks to my God always for you for the grace of God which was given to you in Christ Jesus**. He says that grace was given by God in Christ Jesus. This grace is given in Christ Jesus because it is God's plan that whoever believes in Christ is saved without works. By faith alone he receives as a gift the forgiveness of sins. . . .

    So that you are not lacking in any spiritual gift, as you wait for the revealing of our Lord Jesus Christ. It is clear that whoever is cautious and careful awaits the day of judgment, that is, the future judgment of God in which our Lord will be revealed both to the faithful and to unbelievers. On that day unbelievers will know that what they refused to believe is true and will perish, but the faithful will rejoice in finding more blessings than they anticipated.

(2) Origen

These remarks of Paul are not appropriate for sinners, nor are the later remarks appropriate for the righteous, I mean this verse: *I appeal to you, brethren, through the name of our Lord Jesus Christ, that you all agree and that there be no divisions* (1:10) and similar remarks. The church, then, was mixed, if we may call *church* (1:2) this whole mixture of righteous and unrighteous people. Let us say instead that those who were gathered together were a mixture. For this reason, when the apostle was about to censure the sins of those who were gathered together in wickedness, he first has to praise those who *meet together* for good (1 Cor 11:17, 20). **I give thanks to God always.** It is right to give thanks for those whom he calls praiseworthy, not to give thanks at some times and at other times not, but **always** to give thanks. If I see a person who sometimes acts well and sometimes sins, I do not give thanks for him **always,** but when he acts well. I do the same in my own case. For whom will Paul give thanks, when he gives thanks? For his own disciples, whose father he has become by God's will. Just as, then, a father gives thanks for his sons whenever they are healthy and are faring well, in the same way, whenever the teacher sees his students *boiling in the Spirit* (Rom 12:11) or being rich in the *word of wisdom* (1 Cor 2:1) and worthy of praise, he **gives thanks always** for them.

    Let us consider the grace possessed by those Corinthians Christians who were deserving of praise, so that we might imitate it. **That in every way you were enriched in him.** Blessed are those who are **enriched in every way** and who **are lacking** none of the gifts of God, but practice every virtue and enjoy his rich and abundant gifts **in all speech and all knowledge**. Therefore, they are not at a loss to interpret any Scripture but always *seek and find* (Matt 7:7), and when they must interpret Scripture, they use **all [kinds of] speech** — both that called discursive and the method of question and answer. They are also prepared to speak against every heresy and to come to the defense of true doctrine, and to fulfill the saying of the apostle: *Always be ready to give a defense to everyone who asks you for an account of the faith that is in you* (1 Pet 3:15). Similarly, **in all knowledge,** not only knowledge of the Scriptures but also the knowledge that allows a person to say, *For he gave me true knowledge of the things that are* (Wis 7:17) and the words that follow. Note that **knowledge** indicates only the act of knowing, while **speech** means interpreting what is known.

Even as the witness of Christ was confirmed among you. Christ, we might say, is the chief witness, and while there are many who witness to Christ through their death, he is the first of the witnesses.[3] This **witness of Christ** is firm among some, but among others it is not firm but wavers. For if a person's faith in what is attested is such that he can say, out of a true inner conviction, *I am convinced that neither death nor life,* nor the other things, *will be able to separate us from the love of God that is in Christ Jesus our Lord* (Rom 8:38-39), then **the witness** is firm in such a person. But if we are not like this, but waver according to the circumstances, **the witness of Christ** is not yet **confirmed** in us. And, again, we can understand this verse in another sense: every Scripture that bears witness concerning Christ is a **testimony to Christ.** It is a good thing, then to be **confirmed** in the **testimony to Christ** that comes from the Scriptures. Another interpretation: behold the **testimony to Christ,** *when [God] added his testimony to him by signs and wonders and various miracles, and by gifts of the Holy Spirit, distributed according to his will* (Heb 2:4). And **the testimony to Christ is confirmed** among *the saints* (1:2).

So that you are not lacking in any spiritual gift. There are many spiritual gifts, a point to which Paul returns later in this letter (1 Corinthians 12–14). Paul explains that there are many spiritual gifts **as you wait for the revealing of our Lord Jesus Christ**: the righteous person does not put his hope in this age, but when he suffers or is in danger, he awaits *the revealing of our Lord Jesus Christ,* that is, the revelation Christ Jesus makes.

Who will sustain you to the end. Who sustains? Christ Jesus, *the Word* (John 1:1) and *Wisdom* (1 Cor 1:24). And **the testimony** that is **confirmed** is not for a few days, but **to the end. [So that you may be] guiltless on the day of our Lord Jesus Christ.** Until we arrive there, we are not yet beyond reproach. For we do not know *what the morrow will bring* (Prov 27:1), and though someone may think he is beyond reproach at present, [he will know it only] **on the day of our Lord Jesus Christ.**

God is faithful, by whom you were called into the fellowship of his Son, Jesus Christ our Lord. Believe in him always. Paul says that **you were called** in order that we might be totally under the power of Jesus. It is a great thing that God grants to the saints. We were called **into the fellowship of his Son.** Therefore, *we are heirs of God and fellow heirs with Christ* (Rom 8:17).

---

3. The Greek word *martyr* can mean both "witness" (or "testimony") and "martyr."

(3) Theodoret

I give thanks to my God always for you because of the grace of God that has been given you in Christ Jesus. Since he is about to criticize them, the apostle first soothes the ears of his audience so that they will accept his medicine. And what he says is true, for he gives thanks to God for the gifts given to them. He says this more clearly in what follows: **That in every way you were enriched in him with all speech and all knowledge — even as the testimony to Christ was confirmed among you.** These are forms of the gifts of the Spirit. *To one,* Paul says, *is given through the Spirit the utterance of wisdom, and to another the utterance of knowledge according to the same Spirit* (1 Cor 12:8). He continually repeats the name of the Lord, in order to teach that one must not be named after any other name, except the One who has given us salvation.

The preaching of Christ he calls a **testimony.** For those who preach bear a sort of witness. So when he writes to Timothy, Paul says: *I bear witness in the presence of God who gives life* to the dead (1 Tim 6:13). So also the Lord says in the holy Gospels: *And this gospel of the kingdom will be preached . . . to all nations as a testimony* to them (Matt 24:14). Paul calls the miraculous working of signs a confirmation of the gospel. For by them the truth of the preaching is demonstrated.

So that you are not lacking in any spiritual gift. For the Corinthians also shared in the gift of prophecy and were speaking in various tongues, as Paul shows more clearly in what follows (1 Corinthians 12–14). **As you wait for the revealing of our Lord Jesus Christ.** You have had the benefit of this gift so that you might wait for the second coming of the Savior. **Who will sustain you to the end, guiltless in the day of our Lord Jesus Christ.** Paul prayed that they might be made firm and **guiltless.** With the word **guiltless** he indicates that formerly they were guilty.

God is faithful, by whom you were called into the fellowship of his Son, Jesus Christ our Lord. The One who has granted us the gift of adoption will do this. For Paul designates adoption as **the fellowship of his Son.** The word **faithful** means without falsity and true. Here also Paul uses the phrase **by whom** to describe the Father, thereby shutting the impudent mouths of the heretics and teaching that this phrase does not indicate inferiority.[4] When he has thus conciliated his hearers with pleasant words and blessings, Paul begins his accusations, not introducing them baldly but beginning with an exhortation.

1 Corinthians 1:10-17

10**I appeal to you, brethren, by the name of our Lord Jesus Christ, that all of you agree and that there be no dissensions among you, but that you be united in the same mind and the same judgment.** 11**For it has been reported to me by Chloe's people that there is quarreling among you, my brethren.** 12**What I mean is that each one of you says, "I be-**

---

4. The Arians, followers of the third-century Alexandrian theologian Arius (d. 336), had interpreted the preposition "by" in John 1:3 ("by whom all things were made") as a sign that the Son was inferior to the Father.

long to Paul," or "I belong to Apollos," or "I belong to Cephas," or "I belong to Christ." ₁₃Is Christ divided? Was Paul crucified for you? Or were you baptized in the name of Paul? ₁₄I am thankful that I baptized none of you except Crispus and Gaius; ₁₅lest any one should say that you were baptized in my name. ₁₆(I did baptize also the household of Stephanas. Beyond that, I do not know whether I baptized any one else.) ₁₇For Christ did not send me to baptize but to preach the gospel, and not with eloquent wisdom, lest the cross of Christ be emptied of its power.

(1) John Chrysostom

I appeal to you, brethren, by the name of our Lord Jesus Christ. I have always maintained that one should deliver criticism gently and little by little. Here Paul does just this. When he is about to embark on a subject full of perils, which could tear up the church from her foundations, he uses gentle language. He says that he **appeals** to them, and he appeals **by Christ**, as if he were not capable of making this supplication by himself and winning their assent. . . .

That each one of you says, "I belong to Paul," or "I belong to Apollos," or "I belong to Cephas." I'm not talking, Paul says, about **quarreling** in private matters but something more serious: **that each one of you says.** The corruption ranged not over a part but over the whole church. Yet the Corinthians were not actually calling on the name of Paul himself or Peter or Apollos. Paul shows that, if it is wrong to take these men as your foundation, much more is it wrong to rely on others. He indicates in what follows that the Corinthians were not speaking about the apostles: *I have applied all this to myself and Apollos for your benefit, that you may learn by us not to pride yourself beyond what is written* (1 Cor 4:6). For if it was not right for them to call themselves by the names of Paul and Apollos and Cephas, still less should they call themselves so by the names of others. If it was not right to enroll themselves under the teacher who was the first of the apostles and who had instructed so many people, should they not avoid this even more in the case of those who are of no account? Paul writes these names, therefore, using hyperbole, because he is eager to draw his hearers out of their sickness. In addition, he makes his word less offensive by not naming those who were dividing the church but concealing them, as if by masks, under the names of the apostles.

"I belong to Paul," or "I belong to Apollos," or "I belong to Cephas." It is not in order to give himself greater honor that Paul places Peter last, but to give Peter much greater honor than himself. He makes his argument using the rhetorical figure called "climax";[5] we should not think that he is acting out of ill will or depriving the others of honor because of envy. This is why he put himself first in the list. He who disqualifies himself first does not do so out of love for honor but because he thoroughly despises such glory. . . .

But why does he add, **"I belong to Christ"**? For if those who devoted themselves to

---

5. In this stylistic device the last important word of a clause is repeated as the first significant word of the next clause, and each clause is more important than the preceding one.

men sinned, surely those who devoted themselves to Christ did not. But it is not their calling themselves by the name of Christ that Paul criticizes but only that not all did so. I think Paul has added this phrase to what they said because he wants to intensify the reproach and to show that — even if the Corinthians did not make this claim explicitly — by their behavior they were handing Christ over to one faction. He makes clear in what follows that this is what he means, saying: **Is Christ divided?** What he means is, "You have dismembered Christ and divided up his body." Do you see his anger? Do you see the rebuke? Do you see how his speech is filled with indignation? For Paul does not mount an argument but only raises questions, whenever the point at issue is admittedly absurd. . . .

[*In a section omitted here, Chrysostom discusses how the Corinthians had prided themselves on the stature of the person who baptized them.*] **Not with eloquent wisdom, lest the cross of Christ be emptied of its power.** After criticizing the conceit of those who think highly of themselves because of their baptism, Paul then turns to those who boast in pagan wisdom, and against them he produces stronger weapons.[6] . . . If this pagan wisdom wars against the cross and fights with the Gospels, one should not boast of it but be overcome with shame. This is the reason the apostles were not wise, not because God's gift to them was weak but so that the gospel would not suffer harm. Those, then, who boasted of their wisdom, instead of advancing the teaching of the cross, were actually ravaging it.[7] But it is the uneducated who *confirm* (1:7) this teaching. This fact has the power to punish arrogance, to restrain excess, and to persuade people to be moderate. . . .

If I were to ask you to give me a demonstration that Peter and Paul were eloquent, you could not do it. For they were *uneducated* and *common* (Acts 4:13). . . . Thus when the Greeks accuse the disciples of being uneducated, let us outdo them in this charge. Let no one say that Paul was wise. While we praise the great men of the Greeks for their wisdom and admire them for their eloquence, let us say that all our great ones were uneducated. For on this point we have no small victory over them — so splendid will be our triumph.

I have said these things because I once heard a Christian debating with a Greek in a ridiculous way, and as they contended against each other, each was destroying his own case. For the Greek was saying what the Christian should have said. And the Christian made the case the Greek ought to have made. In a dispute about Paul and Plato, the Greek attempted to show that Paul was ignorant and uneducated, while the Christian, out of naïveté, was eager to establish that Paul was more learned than Plato. And so the Greek gained the victory, since his argument was stronger. For if Paul were more eloquent than Plato, many would be likely to object that it was not by grace but by eloquence that he prevailed. Thus what the Christian said was an argument for the Greek's position, and what the Greek said argued for the Christian's view. For if Paul was uneducated and defeated Plato, the victory (as I have said) was glorious. For he who was ig-

---

6. That is, here Paul does not merely hint at his criticisms, as he did in the previous section, but states them directly.

7. The verb Chrysostom employs here is used in Acts 8:3 to describe the activity of the pre-Christian Saul.

norant took all of the other man's disciples and won them over and brought them to his side. From this it is clear that his preaching has prevailed not by human wisdom but by the grace of God.

Therefore, to avoid having the same thing happen to us and to keep from being ridiculed for arguing like this with Greeks, in every debate we have with them we should accuse the apostles of lack of learning. For this accusation is actually a commendation. And whenever they say that the apostles were bumpkins, let us add to this that they were also ignorant and without learning and poor and lowly and unintelligent and insignificant. This is not to slander the apostles; on the contrary, it is a marvelous thing that such people proved to be more glorious than all the world. These uneducated and uncultured and ignorant men so completely defeated the wise and powerful, the absolute rulers, and those famous for wealth, splendor, and all external things, as to make them seem less than human. From this it is clear that the power of the cross is great and that these things did not happen by human might.

(2) Ambrosiaster

What I mean is that each one of you says, "I belong to Paul," "I belong to Apollos," "I belong to Cephas," "I belong to Christ." Paul reveals their error but does not reveal the names of those who caused it. These men did not stay in one place but traveled around upsetting the simple. Those whom he does name were doubtless good teachers, but Paul uses their names to criticize the false apostles: if Paul forbids boasting in the good teachers, how much more would he forbid boasting in evil teachers, to whose false teaching he alludes in what follows? Nevertheless, he names certain people among them who said that they belonged to Christ, and not to a man, and these he had praised earlier.

Christ is divided.[8] He says that Christ is divided because men divided his glory among themselves. Just like the heretics, who do not shrink from being called Photinians or Arians or Cataphrygians or Novatianists or Donatists or Manicheans, so too the Corinthians had begun to enroll themselves under the names of different heretics with the result that they seemed to be venerating men in place of Christ. Since these heretics accept different doctrines about Christ, they divide Christ. For one of them accepts Christ as only a man, another confesses him as pure God without man, one says that Christ was predicted by the prophets, but another denies that the prophets spoke of Christ. Since, therefore, the one Christ is God and man, these men, in making different claims, divide Christ.

And because by using these names they form many churches, he adds: **Was Paul crucified for you?** He begins with himself, not wishing it to be thought that he rejects other persons in order to commend himself. For, he asks, if Christ died for you, how is it that you ascribe his grace and benefit to men, thereby wronging Christ? **Or were you baptized in the name of Paul?** Moreover, he says, if we were baptized into Christ when

---

8. Ambrosiaster understands this as a statement, while Chrysostom and many modern translations take it as a question. The earliest Greek manuscripts of the New Testament contained no punctuation.

we became believers, why should we treat men as the authors of this faith and forget the faith with which we began? . . .

Not with eloquent wisdom, lest the cross of Christ be emptied of its power. Because Christian preaching does not need pomp or carefully cultivated speech, uneducated fishermen were chosen to preach the gospel so that the truth of the teaching should commend itself by the power of its testimony; otherwise it would seem to have won acceptance because of the cleverness and astuteness of human wisdom rather than because of its truth. In the case of teachings invented by men, people do not look for reason or for power but for verbal facility. Whoever seeks to adorn the faith of Christ by words seeks his own glory. In fact, he obscures the faith by the splendor of his speech, with the result that it is he himself and not the faith that wins praise.

1 Corinthians 1:18-25

18For the word of the cross is folly to those who are perishing, but to us who are being saved it is the power of God. 19For it is written, "I will destroy the wisdom of the wise, and the cleverness of the clever I will thwart" [Isa 29:14]. 20Where is the wise man? Where is the scribe? Where is the debater of this age? Has not God made foolish the wisdom of the world? 21For since, in the wisdom of God, the world did not know God through wisdom, it pleased God through the folly of what we preach to save those who believe. 22For Jews demand signs and Greeks seek wisdom, 23but we preach Christ crucified, a stumbling block to Jews and folly to Gentiles, 24but to those who are called, both Jews and Greeks, Christ the power of God and the wisdom of God. 25For the foolishness of God is wiser than men, and the weakness of God is stronger than men.

(1) Origen on verses 18 and 24

The name of the cross is thought to be a stumbling block. But if someone opens his ears to the word of God and to grace, he will see that *this* too is *a great mystery* (Eph 5:32). Even the Gentiles hand on traditions that severe plagues or heavy rains or droughts often ceased when a person sacrificed himself for the sake of the community. Why, then, does it cause amazement that, when the whole world was suffering a plague of error, it was necessary for *one man to die* (John 18:14) in order to end this plague of ignorance, darkness, and destruction? But who could undergo this sacrifice? Not a prophet, not an apostle, not any other righteous person. It was necessary for a divine power to descend from heaven, a power capable of taking upon itself *to die on behalf of all* (2 Cor 5:15) in a way that involved public shame, so that through that death a victory over the devil might be won. And in fact worldly victors who lead their enemies in triumphal procession (see Col 2:14-18) are accustomed to set up trophies of victory over the defeated in the form of a cross. The cross, then, is a sign of victory over Satan.

For this reason Paul says: *May I never boast of anything except the cross* (Gal 6:14), since he recognizes what the **power** of the cross is — that I was set free from evil because he died in order to rescue me from death. *Except the cross of our Lord Jesus Christ, by which the world has been crucified to me, and I to the world* (Gal 6:14). It is a great good that *the world has been crucified to me.* Through what has this good come to me? *Through the cross of Christ.* It is a great good for me that *I have been crucified to the world.* For if I have died to the world, I have been crucified with Christ *to the world.* But if I live in sin, I have not yet been deemed worthy of the good that follows upon the cross. At the same time let us also prepare ourselves against temptations and be ready for martyrdom, knowing that *whoever denies* (Matt 10:33) does not possess salvation. . . .

Behold the greatness of the Lord:[9] *in every land the sound of his teaching has gone forth, and his words to the ends of the earth* (Ps 19:4). Our Lord Jesus, because he is the **power of God**, is spread through all the earth, and he is at this moment with us, just as the apostle says: *when you are assembled, and my spirit is present, with the power of our Lord Jesus* (1 Cor 5:4). The **power** of the Lord our Savior is also with those in Britain, who are separated from our part of the world, and with those who are in Mauritania, and with all people under the sun who have believed in his name. See, then, how the greatness of the Savior is spread throughout the whole world.

But in fact I have not yet set forth the Savior's true greatness. Ascend into heaven and see how he has filled the heavenly places, if indeed *he appeared to angels* (1 Tim 3:16). Descend, in your imagination, into the abyss, and you will see that he has descended there as well. For *he who descended is the same one who also ascended . . . that he might fill all things* (Eph 4:10), *that at the name of Jesus every knee should bow, in heaven and on earth and under the earth* (Phil 2:10). Consider how the **power** of the Lord has filled the world — that is, the sky, the earth, and what is under the earth — and how it has pierced the heaven itself and climbed to the very summit. For we read that the Son of God *passed through the heavens* (Heb 4:14). If you have seen these things, you will understand as well that Scripture's saying *he will be great* is not just an offhand comment (Luke 1:32); the word has been fulfilled by the deed. Whether he is present or absent, our Lord Jesus is "great," and he gives a share of his power also to this our assembly and community. Let us pray to the Lord Jesus that each of us might be worthy to receive this; *to him belong glory and dominion for ever and ever. Amen* (1 Pet 4:11).

(2) Ambrosiaster on verse 20

Has not God made foolish the wisdom of the world? The **wisdom of this world** has been **made foolish**; thinking itself to be wise, it has been found to be foolish. What the world judged to be impossible — that God should be concerned for men — has been declared possible. Is there anything more foolish than to assert that God made the world and yet has no care for it? Why did he make it if what he has made does not concern him? But because the wise of the world see that certain people prosper while others are op-

---

9. In this second excerpt Origen cites 1 Cor 1:24 in the context of a comment on Luke 1:32: "he [Jesus] will be great."

pressed and that those who do good are looked down upon while men of ill will exult, they have come to believe that God has no concern for men. Anyone who says God lacks concern must admit that he is malevolent and unjust: either he is going to judge the world or he unjustly ignores good people and allows evil to happen. If, therefore, such men would lay aside their hatred of the divine law and pay attention, they could see that we have argued this case to its conclusion. We look for the judgment of God in which those oppressed by violence will be exalted and those who practice violence will be brought low. *God shows no partiality* (Rom 2:11).

(3) John Chrysostom on verses 18-21

No speech can explain the great things of God. Consider this: when I say, "[Christ] was crucified," a Greek asks, "What kind of sense can this make? When he was being crucified and tested, he did not help himself. So, after this, how did he rise again and help others? If he had the power, he should have helped himself before his death." This is what the Jews were saying (see Matt 27:41-42). "How can the one who did not help himself help others? It does not make sense," they say. This is quite right, for the cross is beyond reason, my friend, and it has an indescribable **power**. It demonstrates Christ's infinite **power** that when he was in great danger he proved superior to it, and grappled with it, and conquered. This resembles the case of the three youths (Dan 3:19-26): it was more amazing that they entered the furnace and trampled the flames than if they had not entered it at all. And in the case of Jonah, it was a much greater thing that he entered the belly of the sea monster and suffered no harm from the beast than if he had not entered it at all. So also in the case of Christ. The most amazing thing is that by dying he destroyed death, more amazing than his escaping death would have been, for then he would not have destroyed death. Therefore do not say, "Why did he not help himself on the cross?" He was eager to wrestle with death itself. He did not descend from the cross because he was unable to do so but because he did not wish to. How could the nails of the cross restrain one whom the tyranny of death could not restrain? . . .

For since, in the wisdom of God, Paul says, **the world did not know God through wisdom**, the cross appeared. What is the meaning of **in the wisdom of God**? It is the wisdom apparent in his works, through which he wished to be made known. He made the things that can be seen so that by reasoning from them we might worship their maker (Rom 1:20). The heaven is great, and earth boundless. Stand in awe, therefore, before the Creator. In fact, not only did he make this great heaven — he did so with ease, and the boundless earth he also brought forth effortlessly. This is why Scripture says concerning God, *The heavens are the work of your fingers* (Ps 102:25), and concerning the earth, *He who made the earth as if it were nothing* (Isa 40:23). Since the world did not wish to know God **through** this **wisdom**, he persuaded men through the apparent foolishness of the gospel, not through a process of reasoning but through faith.

Now where the **wisdom of God** is, there is no more need of human wisdom. To assert that the One who created so great a world must by logical inference be a god of inconceivable and inexpressible power, and on this basis to apprehend him, would be reasoning on the basis of human wisdom. Now, however, rational deduction is no longer required, but faith alone. To believe in the One who was crucified and buried, and to be fully convinced that this very One rose again and is seated above, requires not wisdom or reasoning, but faith. And in fact the apostles went forth not in wisdom but in faith, and they proved wiser and loftier than the pagan wise men, inasmuch as receiving the things of God in faith is greater than mounting arguments. This gift transcends human understanding.

(4) Cyril of Alexandria on verses 22-25

For Jews demand signs and Greeks seek wisdom. On both points Paul's statement is true. For once, when Christ was driving the sellers of sheep, cattle, pigeons, and doves out of the sacred precincts and said, *Stop making my Father's house a marketplace* (John 2:16), [the Jews] opposed him, asking *What sign can you show us for doing this?* (John 2:18) and *Who gave you this authority?* (Matt 21:23). And after a demonstration of signs of the most impressive kind, some of the scribes also approached him and said with malice, *Teacher, we wish to see a sign from you* (Matt 12:38). So, because they utterly disregarded the words of the holy prophets, from which they could have learned that he was the Christ, they sought signs from heaven. Hence the Savior said to those who were sent by John: *Return and report to John what you hear and see: the blind recover their sight, the lame walk*, and what follows (Matt 11:4).

As for the **Greeks,** who seek glory in speech and eloquence, they consider the divine plan of the incarnation to be foolishness. They ask, "Why did the Word who comes from God, who was God by nature and able by an act of will — by a mere nod — to accomplish what was pleasing to him, why did this Word have any need to become man and to endure death? And how could it happen that a virgin gave birth? And how will what is destroyed by death rise again?" Well, it is quite natural that they say such things, *For the natural man does not receive the things of the Spirit, for they are foolishness to him* (1 Cor 2:14).

But to us the incarnate Word is **the power and wisdom of God.** Through him God the Father has saved everything under the heavens, as through a **power** that is naturally present in him and through an ineffable **wisdom** that is clearly his own. For the Son is **the wisdom and power of God** the Father, through which all things have been brought to birth and, once created, are now maintained. If someone, Paul says, should choose to compare the **power** that is in **God** with human powers, he will see quite clearly that the divine works that seem to have been accomplished in weakness, and without God's using his power to the fullest, are far superior to anything that comes from human power. And the case is the same as regards **wisdom**: that what seems to be **foolish** in God is wiser than men. It is as if a person should wish to compare the smallest and most insignificant of creatures to the grandeur and beauty of the elements — I mean heaven and the sun and the rest of the stars, and fire and water and the other elements. The power and wisdom of the former will prove to be exceedingly paltry. . . .

It is true, therefore, that **the weakness of God is stronger than men, and the wis-**

dom of God is wiser than men. Thus the divine plan of salvation possesses perfect wisdom. For in wisdom Christ has become the wise ruler over all the world.

(5) Theodoret on verses 22-25

For Jews demand signs and Greeks seek wisdom. Jews demanded the working of wonders from the Lord, as the Evangelists teach us. And, furthermore, to judge from what the divine apostle says, they must also have urged the apostles to exhibit signs. But the Greeks ridiculed the apostles' lack of education. For instance, they asked in Athens, *What would this babbler [i.e., Paul] say?* (Acts 17:18). But Paul says: we despise the foolishness of both groups and proclaim the suffering of the Master, although we know full well that both groups speak openly against us.

And what is the benefit of the preaching? **But to those who are called, both Jews and Greeks, Christ the power of God and the wisdom of God.** The same thing is both **wisdom** and **folly**, both **power** and **weakness**. While it is **folly** and **weakness** to unbelievers, to those who believe it is **wisdom** and **power**. The sun is light to those who see but darkness to those who are blind. Yet it does not itself produce the darkness, but it is the condition of blindness that blocks the radiance of the sun's rays. Thus unbelief, like a disease of the eye, keeps the light of divine knowledge from illuminating the soul.

Of course, we must understand that it is not the deity of the Only Son that the divine apostle indicates by the words **wisdom** and **power** but rather preaching about the cross. And Paul refutes the followers of Arius and Eunomius, who wickedly attempt to show from this text that by **wisdom** is meant God, the Word. From this text and the utterance [of Wisdom] in Proverbs[10] they devise their blasphemous view.[11]

For the foolishness of God is wiser than men, and the weakness of God is stronger than men. Paul calls the mystery of the cross the **weakness** and **folly of God** — this is how it appears to the foolish. But he shows that it has prevailed over both the wise and the powerful.

1 Corinthians 1:26-31

26For consider your call, brethren; not many of you were wise according to the flesh, not many were powerful, not many were of noble birth; 27but God chose what is foolish in the world to shame the wise, God chose what is weak in the world to shame the strong, 28God chose what is low and despised in the world, even things that are not, to bring to nothing things that are, 29so that no human being might boast in the presence of God. 30You are from him in Christ Jesus, whom God made our wisdom, our righteousness and sanctification and redemption; 31therefore, as it is written, "Let him who boasts, boast of the Lord" (Jer 9:24).

---

10. See Prov 8:22: "The Lord created me [Wisdom] at the beginning of his work." Early Christians identified the personified "Wisdom" in this text with Christ, the divine Word.

11. The view that the Son is a creature, subordinate to the Father.

(1) Origen on verses 26-27

To the words **not many of you were wise** Paul adds **according to the flesh,** since he knows that there are different sorts of wise people, and some are wise **according to the flesh** and some are wise according to the Spirit (see Rom 8:8-17; Gal 5:16-23). The **wise according to the flesh** are those who are concerned with mere niceties of style and who can embellish anything at all to make it seem true, even though it is not. Nevertheless, even these words of Paul do not exclude the **wise according to the flesh** from the faith. For he did not say that "no" person who is wise **according to the flesh** comes to the Word, but "very few." The **powerful according to the flesh** are those who have authority. But you will understand the meaning of *powerful according to the Spirit* if you observe how the Savior was not **powerful according to the flesh.** For he was handed over and *crucified in weakness* (2 Cor 13:4). But he was **powerful** according to the Spirit, *healing every disease and every infirmity among the people* (Matt 4:23). In the same way consider the lives of the apostles, and see how they were **powerful** according to the Spirit. Anyone who lives by the Spirit and who *by the Spirit* puts to death *the deeds of the body* (Rom 8:13) is also powerful according to the Spirit.

The same interpretation applies to those of noble birth. **Those of noble birth, according to the flesh**, are those who come of wealthy and famous fathers. But those **of noble birth** according to the Spirit are *sons of God* (Rom 8:13), concerning whom it is written: *all who received him . . . he gave power to become children of God* (John 1:12).

What things, then, did **God choose** (v. 27)? Not **what is foolish** without qualification but **what is foolish in the world.** We who believe are foolish in the sight of the world. They ridicule us as fools, saying: "The Christians say that there is a resurrection of the dead and that we live after death and that Jesus whom the Jews crucified was born from a virgin," and other such things. Let them ridicule us and call us fools. For *the unspiritual man does not receive the gifts of the Spirit of God, for they are folly to him* (1 Cor 2:14).

(2) John of Damascus

For consider your call, brethren; not many of you were wise according to the flesh, that is, according to appearance, and according to the present life and according to pagan education. But to avoid contradicting himself — for there were also wise and noble people among them — he adds, **not many.** Even if he granted the presence of the latter group, the others were much more numerous. Why are few Christians **wise according to the flesh?** Because those who are wise by worldly standards are burdened with a high degree of folly. Such a person is a fool when he refuses to reject corrupt teaching. **Not many were powerful, not many were of noble birth.** For such people are filled with pride. There is no greater impediment to accurate knowledge of God than being rich and foolish.

But God chose what is foolish in the world to shame the wise. This is the greatest part of God's victory, how he conquers by means of the uneducated. For the Greeks feel less shame when they are defeated by wise men. **God chose what is weak in the world to shame the strong; God chose what is low and despised in the world.** He called not only uneducated people, but the poor, those easily despised, and the undistinguished, in order that he might humble those who had power. **Even things that are not, to bring to nothing things that are.** And what does Paul mean by **the things that are not?** Those who are considered to be nothing because they are ordinary. Thus God showed his great power by bringing down the great through those who seem to be nothing.

So that no human being might boast in the presence of God. God does everything in order to put pride and arrogance in their place and destroy boasting. For it is from boasting that sin comes. People claimed to be wiser than the divine laws because they did not wish to receive them as he established them. Therefore they did not learn them at all.

You are from him in Christ Jesus, whom God made our wisdom, our righteousness and sanctification and redemption. You are children of God, Paul says, having become so through Christ. For when he says, **God chose what is foolish in the world and what is low,** he shows that they are the noblest of all, since they have God as their Father. And the cause of this nobility, he says, is not this or that person, but Christ himself, who made us wise and righteous and holy. For this is the meaning of **whom God made our wisdom, our righteousness and sanctification and redemption.**

(3) Severian of Gabalda on verses 29-30

So that no flesh might boast in the presence of God. That is, so that people may not ascribe the success of preaching to their own excellence. Paul said **flesh** and not soul, to make light of human boasting. Why does he say **in the presence of God** and not in the presence of men? Because he sets boasting in our own accomplishments over against boasting in God. The things we ought to ascribe to God, the Corinthians ascribed to human beings. For this reason he says, **in the presence of God.** The boasting that takes place in the presence of the One who sees everything is impious. . . .

You are from him in Christ Jesus. All interpreters alike say that these words refer to salvation, not to creation, as it says elsewhere: *Who were born, not of blood nor of the will of the flesh . . . but of God* (John 1:13). If, therefore, **You are from him,** how should we boast in our own accomplishments? **In Christ Jesus, whom God made our wisdom, our righteousness and sanctification and redemption.** It is not human wisdom that has brought salvation — for it was led astray — but he became **wisdom** for us in order to bring knowledge of God. It was not human understanding, but Jesus the crucified, who grasped this. Human beings did not redeem us. Therefore, the one who brought salvation is entitled to boast, not the ones who are saved.

(4) Ambrosiaster on verses 30-31

You are from him in Christ Jesus. Paul says that we are from him, that is, from God, in the faith of Christ. For it is the purpose of God that we should learn his truth and his mercy through Christ. His truth is the mystery of the Trinity; his mercy is that when we were captives he redeemed us.

He has been made wisdom for us by God, and righteousness and sanctification and redemption. In order to strengthen believers Paul says that Christ did what he did by the will of God, so that we may know that we have truly been taught wisdom, sanctified, justified, and redeemed by God through Christ. No one redeems something unless it is his own. Whether, therefore, because we have been redeemed or because we have been sanctified (i.e. cleansed from the works of the flesh and the impurity of idols) or because we have been made just — for it is just to worship the Creator and scorn other things — or because we have become wise by learning that worldly men are ignorant, all these benefits given by God come through Christ. **Our redemption,** however, consists in this: Christ offered himself to the devil, when the devil demanded, in order that he might take upon himself the cancelling of sin and thus rescue those held captive by the devil.

Therefore, as it is written, "Let him who boasts, boast of the Lord." This is written in the prophet Jeremiah (9:23-24). What the prophet says is right, that we should boast in the Lord, since he who boasts in the Lord cannot be put to shame. His works and his magnificence appear in what he has done. Therefore it says, *Let them be put to shame in their idols, which do not cause it to rain and have not made heaven and earth* (Ps 97:7). The same is true of those who boast in men, who they know have no power. That is why Scripture says, *Hope in man is vain* (Jer 17:5).

(5) Gregory of Nazianzus on verse 30

Perhaps it would be worthwhile to add to what I have said an explication of the meaning and mystical significance of each of the titles Scripture gives to the Son. These terms are many, reflecting many aspects of our understanding of him, and should not be passed over.

[*In a section omitted here Gregory considers various descriptions of God in the Old Testament before turning to scriptural titles for the Son.*] . . . Let us now return to our original concern: the names of the Son. It seems to me that he is called "Son" because he is identical to the Father in essence. And not for this reason only but also because he derives from the Father. And the reason he is called *the Only Son* (John 1:18) is not that he is the only Son from the only Father and only a Son, but that his relationship as Son to the Father is special, not like the relation of bodies to one another. And he is *Logos* or *Word* (John 1:1) since he is related to the Father as word relates to mind. This is not only due to his generation apart from passion but also because he is closely joined to the Father and makes him known (John 1:18; Matt 11:27). Perhaps we could also say that the *Logos* [Word] relates to the Father as a definition relates to the thing it defines, for *logos* also means "definition." For Scripture states that he who has known the Son (for this is what the text means when it says, *He who has seen [the Son]*) *has* known *the Father* (John 14:9). And in the Son we have a concise and easily grasped demonstration of the nature of the Father, because everything that is begotten is a silent "word" that expresses what has begotten it. And if someone should say that the Son is called *Logos* because he is present in all things that exist, he would not be wrong. For what is there that is not *held together* (Col 1:17) by the Word?

The Son is also called **Wisdom,** as being the knowledge of things divine and human. For how could he who has made all things (Col 1:16; John 1:4) be ignorant of the meaning of what he has made? He is called *Power* (1 Cor 1:24) as being the One who sustains all things created and enables them to hold together (Col 1:17). And *Truth* (John 14:6) since he is by nature one and not many (for truth is single, but falsehood has many forms), and also because he is the pure *Seal* (John 6:27) and unerring *Stamp* (Heb 1:3) of the Father. He is called *Image* (Col 1:15) since he shares the Father's nature and is of the Father (and not the Father of him). For it is the nature of an image to be a copy of the archetype for which it is named. But in this case there is more involved: ordinarily an image is an unchanging representation of an object that has motion, but in this case the image is a living representation of the Living One. And this image resembles the archetype even more exactly than Seth did Adam (Gen 4:25), or any child its father. For beings whose nature is simple are such that they are not alike in one particular and unlike in another, but rather the image as a whole represents the whole archetype, and the two are the same rather than merely alike.

The Son is also called *Light* (John 1:4-5; 8:12) since he is the illumination of souls that are being purified in both word and deed. For if ignorance and sin are *darkness* (John 12:35, 46), *Light* will mean knowledge and life in God. The Son is called *Life* (John 1:4; 14:6) because he is *Light* and because he creates and holds together (Col 1:17) every rational being. *For in him we live and move and have our being* (Acts 17:28), by the power breathed into us through a double inspiration. For we have all received breath from him (Gen 2:7), and in addition all who are able have received the Holy Spirit, insofar as we have *opened the mouth* of our understanding (Ps 119:130-31).

The Son is also called **righteousness** because he distributes according to merit (Rom 2:6), and because he judges equitably those *under the law* and those *under grace* (Rom 6:14), and also soul and body — so that soul should rule and the body be ruled and thus the superior part have power over the inferior lest it rise against its better. And he is **sanctification**, as being purity, so that what is pure may be contained by purity. And **redemption**, since he liberates us, who were dominated by sin, and gives himself for us as a ransom that purifies the whole world. And he is called *resurrection* (John 11:25) because he raises us up — since we were dead because we tasted [the forbidden fruit] (Gen 2:17) — and leads us to life.

(6) Gregory of Nyssa on verse 30

The bride [i.e., the soul] *washed her feet* (Cant 5:3) and put off, along with her sandals, all earthly soil.[12] Therefore, she keeps her feet undefiled on the marble-paved way, as did David, who, when he had washed off the slime of the clay, set his feet upon the rock and uttered these words: *He drew me up from the desolate pit, out of the miry bog, and set my feet upon a rock, making my steps secure* (Ps 40:2).

12. This passage is a comment on Cant 5:3, in which a bride speaks and asks, "I had put off my garment, how could I put it on? I had bathed my feet, how could I soil them?" Gregory understands the bride as an image of the soul, who longs for Christ, her bridegroom.

We understand this *rock* to be the Lord (1 Cor 10:4), who is *light* (John 1:4), *truth* (John 14:6), *incorruptibility* (1 Cor 15:53-57), and **righteousness**, and these things are the paving stones of the spiritual road. If we avoid stepping off the path to either side, we keep our footsteps unstained by the mire of pleasure. These are the means, it seems to me, by which the bride opens the door to the Word (Cant 5:5). Her vow not to take up again the mud she has put off and not to accept any earthly defilement on her life's journey becomes the way that **sanctification** enters the soul that has been prepared by these means. And the Lord is **sanctification**.

Blessed, Christ says, *are those who hunger and thirst for righteousness, for they shall be satisfied* (Matt 5:6). . . . If I may attempt a bold interpretation, it seems to me that in this teaching about virtue and righteousness what the Lord offers to his hearers as the object of their desire is himself, he **whom God made our wisdom, our righteousness and sanctification and redemption.** He is also *bread coming down from heaven* (John 6:50) and *living water* (John 4:10), for which David *thirsts,* according to one of the Psalms in which he offers up to God this most blessed passion of the soul, when he says, *My soul thirsts for the living God, my strength. When shall I come and appear before the face of God?* (Ps 42:2). David, it seems to me, was given a preview of the lofty teachings of the Lord by the power of the Holy Spirit, and thus he goes on to describe the satisfaction of his desire. For he says, *As for me, I will appear before thy face in righteousness; I shall be satisfied with beholding thy form* (Ps 17:15; cf. Matt 5:6). This, it seems to me, is the true virtue, the good that is unmixed with evil, the concern of every thought about what is good, namely, God the Word himself, the virtue that *covered the heavens,* as Habakkuk says (Hab 3:3). And those *who hunger* for this *righteousness* are properly counted *blessed* (Matt 5:6). For in truth, the one who has tasted the LORD (Ps 34:8), as the Psalm says — that is, who has received God into himself — will be full of that for which he hungered and thirsted. This was promised by the One who said: the Father and I *will come to him and make our home with him* (John 14:23) — since, of course, the Holy Spirit had already taken up his dwelling there.

(7) Maximus the Confessor on verse 30

Now it is clear that the Word of God is the substance of the virtue that each person possesses. For our Lord Jesus Christ is himself the substance of all the virtues, as it is written: **whom God made our wisdom, our righteousness and sanctification and redemption.** Of course these words apply to him in an absolute sense since he is **wisdom** itself and likewise **righteousness** and **sanctification**. These things are not merely attributed to him, as they are in our case, as, for example, when one speaks of a "wise person" or a "just person." Such statements clearly mean that everyone who partakes of virtue as a steadfast habit partakes of God, who is the substance of the virtues. When someone cultivates, by free choice, the true seeds of goodness that are sown into our nature, he demonstrates that the end is the same as the beginning, and the beginning the same as the end, or rather that the beginning and the end are the identical thing (Rev 21:6), for he is in genuine harmony with God. For we believe that the goal ordained for everything consists in its beginning and its end. It is from God that a person receives this, that is, both his existence and the good that is in his nature through his participation in God. And God is the end, when a person zealously pursues to the end, by his own will and choice, the meritorious course that leads straight back to the beginning. And by this a person becomes God, being made God by God himself. For to the natural good of the *image* is added the divine *likeness* (Gen 1:26), acquired by one's own choice through the practice of virtue. For it belongs to our nature to ascend and appropriate for ourselves the beginning from which we come. In such a person, furthermore, the word of the apostle is fulfilled: *In him we live and move and have our being* (Acts 17:28).

(8) Basil of Caesarea on verses 30-31

[*From a sermon on humility*]

What is thought to be the greatest and most enduring of human possessions is knowledge or wisdom. Yet even this involves vain pride and false exaltation. If we lack the wisdom that comes from God, all our wisdom comes to nothing. . . . Therefore, no one who is sensible will feel pride either in his own wisdom or in the other things I mentioned earlier. Instead he will be moved by the wise exhortations of the blessed Hannah[13] and those of Jeremiah the prophet: *Let not the wise man glory in his wisdom, let not the mighty man glory in his might, let not the rich man glory in his riches* (Jer 9:23). But what is the true basis for boasting, and what makes a person really great? Jeremiah replies: *Let him who glories glory in this: that he understands and knows that I am the Lord* (Jer 9:24). This is our true exaltation, glory, and greatness: to have true understanding of what is great and cling to it, and to seek glory from the *Lord of glory* (1 Cor 2:8).

For the apostle says: **Let him who boasts, boast of the Lord**. He says that Christ has become **our wisdom, our righteousness and sanctification and redemption; therefore, as it is written, "Let him who boasts, boast of the Lord"** (Jer 9:24; 1 Cor 1:30-31). For our true and perfect boasting in God is this: when we take no pride in our own righteousness and realize that we lack true righteousness but are made righteous solely through faith in Christ. So Paul boasts that he despises his own righteousness and seeks *the righteousness from God that depends on faith, that I may know him and the power of his resurrection, and may share his sufferings, becoming like him in his death, that if possible I may attain the resurrection from the dead* (Phil 3:9-11). Here all proud exaltation has fallen away. No grounds for boasting remain for you, my friend, when your boast and your hope rests in putting to death your boasting and all your own accomplishments and seeking the life promised in Christ.

And we have the *firstfruits* (2 Cor 1:22) of this life and already live with these blessings, if we live entirely by the grace and free gift of God: *for God is at work in you, both to will and to work for his good pleasure* (Phil 2:13). Through his own Spirit God reveals his

---

13. The song of Hannah, the mother of the prophet Samuel, in 1 Sam 2:1-10 includes these words: "Talk no more so very proudly, let not arrogance come from your mouth; for the Lord is a God of knowledge, and by him actions are weighed" (v. 3).

wisdom decreed before the ages for our glorification (1 Cor 2:7). God also gives us strength in the midst of our toils, as Paul writes: *I worked harder than any of them, though it was not I, but the grace of God which is with me* (1 Cor 15:10). When all human hope is gone, God rescues us from dangers. *We felt,* Paul says, *that we had received the sentence of death; but that was to make us rely not on ourselves but on God who raises the dead; he delivered us from so deadly a peril, and he will deliver us; on him we have set our hope that he will deliver us again* (2 Cor 1:9-10).

Tell me, then, why do you pride yourself on your own accomplishments instead of giving thanks to the giver for his gifts? *What have you that you did not receive? If then you received it, why do you boast as if it were not a gift?* (1 Cor 4:7). It is not you who have come to know God through your own righteousness, but God, in his kindness, has known you, as it says: *now that you have come to know God, or rather to be known by God* (Gal 4:9). You did not gain Christ through your virtue, but Christ gained you through his coming. *But I press on,* Paul says, *to make [God's righteousness] my own, because Christ has made me his own* (Phil 3:12). *You did not choose me,* says the Lord, *but I chose you* (John 15:16).

(9) Augustine on verse 31

Therefore, "let him who boasts, boast in the Lord." What is less worrisome than boasting in One who will never put you to shame? If you boast in a man, something — no, many things — may be discovered in him to shame the boaster. Now if it is true that you should not boast in man, you should certainly not boast in yourself — a human being. If, therefore, you boast in yourself, you boast in man, and this is foolish and reprehensible. If you boast in a just and wise man, the one in whom you boast will not be boasting in himself. But if you boast in yourself, you are neither wise nor just. So if you should not boast in a wise man, much less ought you to boast in a fool. But whoever boasts in himself boasts in a fool; for only a fool boasts in himself. . . .

Recognize the **righteousness of God** and do not attempt to claim any righteousness you may have as your own. If you live a good life, if you do what God commands, do not regard this as your own; for that springs from a desire to claim righteousness as your own. If you recognize from whom you have received it, you see that what you possess is what you have received. For you have nothing that was not given you. *If you have received it, why do you boast as if it were not a gift?* (1 Cor 4:7). When you boast as if you had not received it, you boast in yourself. And then what becomes of **Let him who boasts, boast of the Lord**? Hold fast to what is given, but recognize the giver. When the Lord promised that he would give his Holy Spirit, he declared, *If anyone is thirsty, let him come to me and drink. He who believes in me, out of his heart shall flow rivers of living water* (John 7:37-38). Whence came this river in you? Recall your original dryness. For if you had not been dry, you would not have thirsted. If you had not thirsted, you would not have drunk. What does it mean that if you had not thirsted, you would not have drunk? If you had not found yourself to be empty, you would not have believed in Christ. Before he said, *out of his heart shall flow rivers of water,* he said, *If anyone thirst, let him come to me and drink.* Therefore, you will have a *river of water* because you drink. You do not drink if you are not thirsty. But if you were thirsty, why did you wish to boast as if it were your own river? **Therefore, "Let him who boasts, boast in the Lord."**

And when I came to you, brethren, Paul says, *I did not come proclaiming to you the testimony of God in lofty words or wisdom* (1 Cor 2:1). He also says, *I decided to know nothing among you except Jesus Christ and him crucified* (1 Cor 2:2). If he knew that, he knew everything. It is a great thing to *know Christ crucified.* But Paul has placed it before the eyes of the babes (1 Cor 3:1-2) as a treasure wrapped up in a cloth. *Christ crucified,* he says. What great things does that treasure contain? Then in another place, when he was afraid that certain people might be led astray from Christ by *philosophy and vain deceit,* he promised a treasure of the knowledge and wisdom of God in Christ. *See to it that no one makes a prey of you by philosophy and empty deceit, according to human tradition, according to the elemental spirits of the universe, and not according to Christ, in whom are hid all the treasures of wisdom and knowledge* (Col 2:8, 3). *Christ crucified, hidden treasures of wisdom and knowledge.* Do not be deceived, therefore, Paul says, by the name of wisdom. Bring yourselves to this wrapped treasure; ask that it be unwrapped for you. O foolish philosopher of this world, what you are looking for is nothing. But he whom you do not look for [is everything].[14] What good does it do you that you are thirsty and yet spurn the spring and pass by it? You despise humility because you do not understand majesty. . . .

Why do they mock unless it is because they see the lowly garment draped around the outside and do not see the treasure lying hidden within? Someone sees flesh, sees a man, sees a cross, sees death. He despises these things. Stay, do not pass on, do not despise, do not insult. Wait, examine. There may be something within that will give you much delight. You may find *what no eye has seen, nor ear heard, nor the heart of man conceived* (1 Cor 2:9). . . .

Far be it from me, Paul says, *to glory except in the cross of our Lord Jesus Christ* (Gal 6:14). He could have said "in the wisdom of our Lord Jesus Christ," and he would have been saying the truth; he could have said, "in the majesty of our Lord Jesus Christ," and he would have been saying the truth; he could have said, "in the power of our Lord Jesus Christ," and he would have been saying the truth. But he said, *in the cross.* Where the philosopher of the world felt shame, there the apostle finds a treasure. He did not despise the lowly covering and arrived at the precious thing that was wrapped in it. . . .

You have heard in the Gospel about the sons of Zebedee. They sought a lofty station, asking that one of them sit at the right hand of their great father and the other at his left (Mark 10:37). They sought an exalted station, truly great. But because they had given no thought how they should get there, Christ reminds them of the path they must travel. How does he answer their request for such a lofty position? *Are you able to drink the cup that I shall drink?* (Mark 10:38). What cup is that if not the cup of humility, of suffering? When he was about to drink it, making our weakness strong in himself, he said to the Father, *My Father, if it be possible, let this cup pass from me* (Matt 26:39). In his own person he transforms into strength the weakness of those who refused to drink such a cup and who were seeking an exalted station while neglecting the way of humility, and asks, *Are you able to drink the cup that I shall drink?* You seek Christ raised above: return to the cru-

14. There is a gap in the text here; words in brackets are supplied by the translator.

34

cified one. You wish to reign and to boast of a seat next to Christ: first learn to say, *Far be it from me to glory except in the cross of our Lord Jesus Christ* (Gal 6:14). This is Christian doctrine: the teaching of humility, recommending humility and boasting only in the cross of our Lord Jesus Christ.

1 Corinthians 2

In chapter 2 Paul continues his discussion of the preaching of the cross as apparent folly. Admitting that he came to them in fear and weakness, he reminds the Corinthians that his preaching among them was marked by the "demonstration of the Spirit," not human eloquence (vv. 1-5). John Chrysostom, who often advocates the imitation of biblical characters, encourages his hearers to emulate Paul's courage in the face of fear. He takes "weakness" in v. 3 to refer to the persecutions Paul endured. Interpreting the "demonstration of the Spirit" (v. 5) to mean miracles, he discusses why such miracles are less evident in his own time.

In verses 6-8 Paul's argument takes a surprising turn, as he now claims that he does impart a secret wisdom to those who are "mature" (or "perfect"), a wisdom unknown to the "rulers of this world." Origen thinks that Paul is speaking of pedagogical reserve: the deep wisdom of the gospel must be introduced gradually. In a discussion of the principles of biblical exegesis in On First Principles *he cites this passage (together with vv. 12-16) as justification for the practice of spiritual exegesis, seeing here a reference to the third and most elevated of three senses of Scripture. Cyril of Alexandria interprets the "rulers" who crucify the Lord because they do not understand God's secret wisdom (v. 8) to refer to Satan and the powers of evil, while Oecumenius considers the possibility that "rulers" refers to the human authorities responsible for Christ's death.*

In verses 9-12 Paul explains that the secret meaning of the cross is revealed to believers by the Holy Spirit. Patristic authors found these verses very rich. Verse 9 is often used to describe the unimaginable blessings that await the faithful at the end time. Both Augustine and Leo the Great say that the verse refers to sharing in God himself — for what reward could be greater? Verses 10-12, along with several verses later in the letter, figured in debates about the divinity of the Holy Spirit.[1] Athanasius, disputing a claim that the Holy Spirit is a created being, inferior to God the Father, says that the Spirit, if "from God" as Paul states in v. 12, cannot have been created from nothing. Basil of Caesarea cites the Spirit's intimate knowledge of the Father (vv. 10-11) as proof of the unity of the Trinity.

Paul says that his own teaching comes from the Spirit and that it can be understood only by those who are "spiritual," who have the "mind of Christ" (vv. 13-16). Origen highlights the phrase "taught by the Spirit" in verse 13, pointing out that ultimately one must not rely on any human

---

1. See also the comments on 3:16-17 (Athanasius), 8:6 (John Chrysostom), 12:3 (Basil), 12:4-7, 11, 13 (Athanasius), and 14:24-25 (Basil) translated below.

teacher, even one as great as Paul. John of Damascus takes "interpreting spiritual things by spiritual things" (v. 13) to refer to using Old Testament texts to explain the events of the gospel. He thinks that the "unspiritual person" of verse 14 is a person who relies on rational arguments alone and does not recognize the need for divine instruction.

1 Corinthians 2:1-5

1When I came to you, brethren, I did not come proclaiming to you the testimony of God in lofty words or wisdom. 2For I decided to know nothing among you except Jesus Christ and him crucified. 3And I was with you in weakness and in much fear and trembling; 4and my speech and my message were not in plausible words of wisdom, but in demonstration of the Spirit and power, 5that your faith might not rest in the wisdom of men but in the power of God.

(1) John Chrysostom

And I was with you in weakness and in much fear and trembling. Here we find another very important point. Not only are the believers uncultured and the speaker utterly unskillful and the message itself enough to cause an uproar — for the message proclaimed was the cross and death. In addition to all these things, there were other obstacles: perils and plots and constant fear and the experience of persecution. For Paul often calls persecutions **weakness**, as he does in another text: *you did not despise* my *weakness* in *the flesh* (Gal 4:4, 13). And again: *If I must boast, I will boast of the things that show my weakness* (2 Cor 11:30). What sort of weakness? *The governor under King Aretas guarded the city of Damascus in order to seize me* (2 Cor 11:32). Again he observes, therefore, *I am content with weaknesses* (2 Cor 12:10). Then he adds to explain what kind of weaknesses: *with insults, hardships, calamities.* In the present text Paul says the same thing. For after saying, **I came in weakness**, he does not stop; rather, in order to make clear that he refers to perils as **weakness**, he adds, **and in much fear and trembling I came to you.**

What do you say to this? Was even Paul afraid of perils? Yes, he was afraid, and he suffered extreme anxiety. Even though he was Paul, he was still a man. This is not meant as a criticism. Rather, even as we call his nature weak, we praise his deliberate moral choice: even though he feared death and beatings, this fear made him do nothing unworthy. Those who deny that he feared being beaten fail to do him honor and take away much of the praise he deserves. For if he was afraid, what great perseverance and discipline did he show when he endured danger? Paul has my admiration because although he was afraid of perils — and not only afraid but even **trembling** — yet through all this he *ran* as one crowned victor (1 Cor 9:24-25), and in none of the perils did he give way, as he purified the whole world and sowed the gospel everywhere on earth and on sea. . . .

That your faith might not rest in the wisdom of men but in the power of God. . . . Demonstration through actions and signs is much clearer than demonstration through words. But perhaps an opponent might ask: "If the gospel must prevail and if it does not require words — *lest the cross be emptied* (1 Cor 1:17) — why are miracles withheld now? . . . How is it, then, that miracles were useful in earlier times but not now?" . . . When Christ comes and all his angels with him, when he is shown to be God, and all things are subjected to him (1 Cor 15:25-28), will not even the Greek believe? Clearly, even if he is exceedingly stubborn, the Greek will then worship Christ and call him God. For who, seeing the heavens opened and Christ coming on the clouds and the whole assembly of the heavenly powers in throngs around him and rivers of fire flowing forth and everyone standing by and trembling — who will not worship him and consider him to be God? Tell me, then, will such worship and knowledge be reckoned to the Greek as faith? Certainly not. Why not? Because it is not faith but something brought about by compulsion and the clear appearance of visible things (see Heb 11:1). It does not depend on free choice, but the mind is compelled by the magnitude of what it sees. It follows that the more obvious and compelling the events, the less room there is for faith. This is why miracles do not happen now. And as proof that this is the case, hear what Jesus says to Thomas, *Blessed are those who have not seen and yet believe* (John 20:29). So the clearer the demonstration of a miracle, the smaller the reward for faith. Thus if miracles occurred now, the result would be the same as at the second coming. Paul makes clear that at that time we will no longer know Christ by faith, when he declares: Now *we walk by faith, not by sight* (2 Cor 5:7). Therefore, just as in that future time believing what is evident will bring you no credit, the same would hold true today if miracles like those of the former time were still happening. When we accept things that we cannot discover through reasoning, this is faith.

1 Corinthians 2:6-8

6Yet among the mature[2] we do impart wisdom, although it is not a wisdom of this age or of the rulers of this age, who are doomed to pass away. 7But we impart the hidden wisdom of God, in a mystery which God decreed before the ages for our glorification. 8None of the rulers of this age understood this; for if they had, they would not have crucified the Lord of glory.

(1) Origen

Paul adds these words to prevent someone saying, "Well then, since he gave demonstrations of the faith in power and in the Spirit (v. 5), this means he had no wisdom; the *mystery of our religion* (1 Tim 3:16) is only belief, and there is no promise of wisdom in it." **Yet among the mature we do impart wisdom, although it is not a wisdom of this age or of the rulers of this age, who are doomed to pass away.** It is one thing to lead people to faith and another to reveal the **wisdom of God.** Therefore, we disclose the **wisdom of God** not to novices or beginners or those who have not yet demonstrated soundness in their conduct. But when a person *has trained his faculties by practice* in the appropriate

2. Or "perfect."

way *to distinguish good from evil* (Heb 5:14) and becomes capable of hearing wisdom, then **we speak wisdom among the mature.** . . . Therefore, we must seek **wisdom** also in teaching, but only after coming to faith and leading a disciplined life, just as Scripture puts it: *If you desire wisdom, keep the commandments* (Sir 1:26).

Now that we have indicated briefly that the divine Scriptures are inspired by God, we must explain how they are to be read and understood: many mistakes have been made because most interpreters have not discovered how one must progress through the Scriptures. . . . Now it seems that the interpreters I mentioned earlier[3] held false opinions and impious or uninformed views about God because they failed to understand Scripture in a spiritual sense and interpreted it according to the bare letter. Therefore, we must explain to the faithful that the Scriptures are not human compositions but were written and delivered to us by the mind of the Holy Spirit, by the will of the Father of all, through Jesus Christ. And we must show what ways of interpretation seem correct to us, as we hold fast to the rule of the heavenly church that belongs to Jesus Christ by apostolic succession. . . .

What must we say about the prophecies, which we all know are full of riddles and dark sayings (Prov 1:6)? Even when we come to the Gospels, to understand their exact sense, which is the *mind of Christ* (1 Cor 2:16), we need the grace that was given to the one who said, *But we have the mind of Christ* (2:16), *that we might understand the gifts bestowed on us by God. And we impart this in words not taught by human wisdom but taught by the Spirit* (2:12-13). And who could read the revelations to John without being amazed at the ineffable mysteries concealed there, whose presence is evident even to those who do not understand what is written? And what person trained in literary interpretation could think that the letters of the apostles are clear and easy to understand, when even here there are so many passages that give a tiny glimpse, as if through a peephole, of a great number of profound thoughts?

Since these things are so and since so many have gone astray, it is a dangerous thing, when we read the Scriptures, to make the rash claim that we understand things that require the *key of knowledge* (Luke 11:52). . . . *And write these things three times in your counsel and in your knowledge, so as to respond with words of truth to those who question you* (Prov 22:20-21 LXX) Therefore, a person must inscribe the thoughts of the holy Scriptures three times in his own soul. The simpler believer will be edified as it were by the "flesh" of the Scripture (by this we mean the obvious interpretation), and the one who is somewhat advanced will be edified as it were by its "soul." But the **mature one** will be edified by the *spiritual law* (Rom 7:14), which contains *a shadow of the good things to come* (Heb 10:1). He is like those of whom the apostle speaks: **Yet among the mature we do impart wisdom, although it is not a wisdom of this age or of the rulers of this age, who are doomed to pass away. But we impart the hidden wisdom of God, in a mystery which God decreed before the ages for our glorification.** For just as a person consists of body and soul and spirit (see 1 Thess 5:23), the same is true of Scripture, which is given by divine providence for human salvation.

3. In a section omitted here Origen discusses misinterpretation of Scripture by Jews, Christian heretics, and simple believers.

(2) Cyril of Alexandria

For if they had [known God's wisdom], they would not have crucified the Lord of glory. The verse makes an excellent point. Through his own cross Christ has *triumphed* over the evil and opposing powers, *nailing to the cross the bond which stood against us* (Col 2:14). He has thrown off Satan's tyrannical rule over us; he has nullified the sin of the world. By opening the gates of Hades to the spirits below, he destroyed the power of death. Is not Christ's passion on the cross hateful to the foul demons? **They would not have crucified** him if they had understood clearly that he was the Redeemer and **the Lord of glory.** For the divinely inspired John demonstrates that the crucifixion of Christ by the Jews was a savage act inspired by demons when he says concerning Judas, *After the morsel, Satan entered into him* (John 13:27). Satan did not know that Jesus was God. For if he had known and been persuaded of it, how would he have tested him in the wilderness, saying, *If you are the Son of God, command these stones to become loaves of bread* (Matt 4:3)? And it is consistent with this that the Savior was eager to escape the notice of the **rulers of this world,** so that he might suffer without their notice and by his own blood lay claim to the earthly realms for himself and for his Father.

(3) Oecumenius

If you take **the rulers of this world** to refer to Herod and Pilate, you will understand what follows in a simpler way.[4] **For if they had known,** Paul says, **they would not have crucified the Lord of glory.** They would not have behaved with such insanity unless jealousy was behind it. If you understand **rulers** to refer to the high priests and scribes, who knew that he was the Christ — as is clear from what the farmers of the vineyard said: *This is the heir; come, let us kill him and* the vineyard will be ours (Matt 21:38) — they at any rate were blinded by jealousy. In that case you will understand the next words as follows: **if they had known** that so great a salvation would come to the Gentiles through the cross, they would not have proceeded to crucify him. They would have preferred to waste away with jealousy rather than have the Gentiles be saved, with God casting out the Jews and putting the Gentiles in their place.

1 Corinthians 2:9-12

9But, as it is written, "What no eye has seen, nor ear heard, nor the heart of man conceived, what God has prepared for those who love him,"[5] 10God has revealed to us through the Spirit.[6] For the Spirit searches everything, even the depths of God. 11For

---

4. The context of this comment has not been preserved. Perhaps Oecumenius had first explained the "rulers" as referring to demonic powers, as Cyril does.

5. This text is not found in Scripture. There are partial parallels in Isa 52:15; 64:4; Jer 3:16, and Sir 1:10.

6. The Greek term here and in the following verses can denote either the divine Spirit or the human spirit.

what person knows a man's thoughts except the spirit of the man which is in him? So also no one comprehends the thoughts of God except the Spirit of God. 12Now we have received not the spirit of the world, but the Spirit which is from God, that we might understand the gifts bestowed on us by God.

(1) Leo the Great on verse 9

Happy are the pure in heart, for they shall see God (Matt 5:8). Beloved, great is the happiness of the man for whom such a great reward is prepared. What then is it to have a pure heart if not to be full of zeal for the virtues? But what mind can conceive or what tongue can set forth what great happiness there is in seeing God? Yet when our human nature is transformed, we will behold the Godhead itself, no longer *in a mirror dimly* but *face to face* (1 Cor 13:12); we will behold it as it is, see *what no man has ever seen or can see* (1 Tim 6:16), and attain by the unutterable joy of eternal contemplation **what no eye has seen, nor ear heard, nor the heart of man conceived**. It is right that this happiness is promised to the pure in heart. Eyesight that is blurred will not be able to see the splendor of the true light, and what gives pleasure to minds that are pure brings pain to those that are impure. Therefore, let the mists of earthly vanities be put aside, and let our inner eyes be cleansed from all stain of iniquity so that our unclouded vision may be fed by such a great vision of God.

(2) Augustine on verse 9

God has given us our nature, our existence. He has given us a soul to make us alive, a mind so that we might understand, and nourishment to sustain our mortal life. He gave us light from the sky, springs of water from the earth. But all these gifts are common, belonging both to the good and the wicked. If he gave these to the wicked, does he not keep something especially for the good? He does indeed. And what is it that he keeps for the good? **What no eye has seen, nor ear heard, and what has not come up[7] into the heart of man**. What has **come up into the heart of man** was below the heart of man. That is why it **comes up** into the heart, because the heart, to which it is coming up, is above it. As for what he is keeping for the good, the heart comes up to that. God is keeping for you not **what has come up into** your heart but that to which your heart goes up. Do not turn a deaf ear to the words, "Lift up your heart."[8]

So God has prepared **what no eye has seen, nor ear heard, and what has not come up into the heart of man. Eye has not seen** it, for it is not a color. **Ear has not heard** it, for it is not a sound. It **has not come up into the heart**, for it is no earthly thought. . . .

At this point you will perhaps ask me what it is. Ask him who has begun to dwell in you. I myself can only say what I hear from that source. You ask what God keeps espe-

---

7. RSV, "entered"; Augustine's Latin text differs from the Greek on which the RSV is based.

8. Latin: *sursum corda*. Augustine is quoting a phrase from the eucharistic liturgy.

cially for the good if he gives so much both to the good and to the wicked. And when I reply, **What eye has not seen, nor ear heard, and has not come up into the heart of man**, there are people who will ask, "What do you think this is?" The reward that God is saving for the good alone, for those he himself has made good, is briefly set forth by the prophet: *I will be your God, and you shall be my people* (Lev 26:12; 2 Cor 6:16). *I will be your God:* God has promised himself to us as our reward. See if you can find something better. If I said, "He promised gold," you would be glad. If I say, "He promised himself," will you be sad? If a rich man does not have God, what does he have? Do not seek anything from God except God. Love him for nothing, ask him only for himself. Do not fear poverty: he gives himself to us, and for us he is enough. Let him give himself to us, and let him be enough for us! Listen to Philip the apostle in the Gospel: *Lord, show us the Father, and we shall be satisfied* (John 14:8). Why, therefore, be surprised that lovers of God have endured martyrdom in order to win God?

(3) Athanasius on verses 11-12

Created things came from nothing and have a beginning to their existence.[9] For *in the beginning God created the heavens and the earth* and all that is in them (Gen 1:1). But the Spirit is said to be **of God. For what person knows a man's thoughts except the spirit of the man which is in him? So also no one comprehends the thoughts of God except the Spirit of God. Now we have received not the spirit of the world, but the Spirit which is from God.** Given what has been said, what kinship can the Spirit have with creatures? For creatures once did not exist, but God exists fully, and from him comes the Spirit. That which is **of God** could not be from what is not, nor could it be a creature. By their logic the one from whom the Spirit comes would also be a creature. Who, then, could put up with such fools, who say *in their heart, "There is no God"* (Ps 14:1)? For as no one **knows a man's thoughts except the spirit of the man which is in him, so also no one knows the thoughts of God except the Spirit** which is in **God.** Then how would it not be shocking to say that **the Spirit** that is in **God,** which **searches even the depths of God**, is a creature?

(4) Basil of Caesarea on verses 10-12

They say:[10] "Let the Spirit be glorified, but not with the Father and the Son." But what sense does it make to give up the place the Lord assigned to the Spirit and invent another place for him? And why deprive of a share in glory the One who is joined with the Godhead in all these things: in our confession of the faith [in the creed], in baptism for redemption, in the working of miracles, in his abiding in the saints, in the gifts given to

9. Athanasius is arguing against a group called the Tropici, who denied the divinity of the Holy Spirit, whom they called a "creature."

10. This discussion is taken from Basil's treatise *On the Holy Spirit,* in which he is concerned to demonstrate the full divinity of the Holy Spirit against the so-called Pneumatomachians (or "fighters against the Spirit"), who denied it. On the divinity of the Holy Spirit, see also Basil's comments on 14:24-25, cited below.

those who are obedient? For without the Holy Spirit no gift whatever reaches creation. Indeed, it is not possible to speak a single word in defense of Christ unless helped by the Spirit, as we have learned from what our Lord and Savior says in the Gospels (see Matt 10:19-20). But I do not see how anyone who partakes of the Spirit could approve of people who discount all these things, forget that the Spirit participates in all God's works, and separate him from the Father and the Son.

Where, then, shall we rank the Spirit? With the creatures? But every creature is enslaved (Rom 8:20-21), while the Spirit is free. *Where the Spirit of the Lord is, there is freedom* (2 Cor 3:17). . . . The Spirit is good by nature, as the Father is good and the Son is good. But the creature participates in goodness by choosing the good. The Spirit knows **the depths of God** (v. 10), while a creature receives the revelation of mysteries **through the Spirit** (vv. 9-10). The Spirit makes alive, together with the Father who engenders all things and the Son who gives life. *He who raised Christ Jesus from the dead,* it says, *will give life to your mortal bodies also through his Spirit which dwells in you* (Rom 8:11). And again, *My sheep hear my voice [the Son says], and I give them eternal life* (John 10:27-28), but it also states that *the Spirit gives life* (John 6:63), and likewise, *The Spirit is life because of righteousness* (Rom 8:10). The Lord also bears witness that *the Spirit gives life, the flesh is of no avail* (John 6:63). How, then, can we separate the Spirit from his life-giving power and assimilate him to what by its nature is in need of life? Who is so contentious, who so far from the heavenly gift and with so little experience of the good words of God? Who is so lacking in the eternal hope as to separate the Spirit from the Godhead and classify him with the creatures?

"The Spirit," they say, "is in us as a gift from God. But surely the gift is not to be given the same honors as the giver." The Spirit is indeed a gift of God, but this gift gives life. For Scripture says, *The law of the Spirit of life has set me free* (Rom 8:2). And the Spirit is a gift of power. *You shall receive power when the Holy Spirit has come upon you* (Acts 1:8). Is this a reason to despise the Spirit? Was not the Son also given as a gift to men? *He who did not spare his own Son but gave him up for us all, will he not also give us all things with him* (Rom 8:32)? And elsewhere it says, [**Now we have received . . . the Spirit**], **that we might understand the gifts bestowed on us by God** (v. 12) — meaning by "gifts" the mystery of the incarnation.

But the greatest proof that the Spirit is united with the Father and the Son is that the Spirit is said to have the same relationship to God as the spirit within each of us has with us: **For what person knows a man's thoughts except the spirit of the man which is in him? So also no one comprehends the thoughts of God except the Spirit of God.**

(5) Augustine on verses 11-12

You saw, O God, everything that you made, and, behold, it was very good (Gen 1:31). We too see it, and, behold, it is very good. . . . [*In a section omitted here Augustine describes how he prayed to God for help in understanding the creation story.*] I heard your answer, my Lord God, I sucked out a drop of sweetness from your truthfulness, and I understood that there are some who are displeased by your works. They claim that you made many of them under compulsion, such as the structure of the heavens and their constellations.[11] These, they say, you did not make of your own accord, but they were created elsewhere and by another power. They say that you assembled them and fitted and wove them into a whole, when after conquering your enemies you were constructing the walls of the universe. This construction was to hem them in and keep them from rebelling against you. Other things you neither created nor formed, such as all kinds of flesh and all tiny creatures and everything with its roots in the earth: it was some hostile mind, some nature you did not create, a nature contrary to yours, that begets and forms these things in the lower regions of the earth. Those who say these things are insane: they do not see your works by means of your Spirit and do not recognize you in them.

But as for those who see these things by means of your Spirit, your vision is at work in them. Therefore, when they see that your creation is good, you see it in them. Whatever is pleasing to us because of you is pleasing to you in us. **For what person knows a man's thoughts except the spirit of the man which is in him? So also no one comprehends the thoughts of God except the Spirit of God. Now we have received not the spirit of the world, but the Spirit which is from God, that we might understand the gifts bestowed on us by God.** I am prompted to ask, "Certainly no one knows what is of God except the Spirit of God. How, therefore, can we know the gifts God has given us?" My answer is that the things that we know by the Spirit of God are nevertheless known only by God. Just as it is truly said to those who speak in the Spirit, "It is not you who are speaking," so it is truly said to those who know in the Spirit, "It is not you who know." And so it is equally proper to say to those who see in the Spirit, "It is not you who see." So whatever it is whose goodness they see in the Spirit, it is not they themselves but God who sees that it is good. It is one thing for someone to suppose that what is good is bad, like the people described above. It is another for someone to see that what is good is good, like those who take pleasure in your creation, but do not, in enjoying this creation, enjoy you in it, preferring to have the benefit of it rather than of you. It is a third thing if when someone sees the goodness of a thing, it should be God who sees that it is good, so that God is loved in the things he has made. He could not, however, be loved except by the Spirit he has given, since *love for God has been poured into our hearts through the Holy Spirit which has been given to us* (Rom 5:5). It is through the Spirit that we see the goodness of everything that exists in any degree because it comes from the One who does not have being to a certain degree but is simply *He who is* (cf. Exod 3:14).

1 Corinthians 2:13-16

13And we impart this in words not taught by human wisdom but taught by the Spirit, interpreting spiritual things by spiritual things. 14The unspiritual[12] man does not re-

---

11. Augustine is referring to the Manicheans (see Appendix 3).

12. Or "natural" or "animal." The adjective *psychikos* is derived from the word "soul" and describes the natural human being, consisting of body animated by soul, in contrast to the person who is animated by the divine Spirit.

ceive the gifts of the Spirit of God, for they are folly to him, and he is not able to understand them because they are spiritually discerned. 15The spiritual man judges all things, but is himself to be judged by no one. 16"For who has known the mind of the Lord so as to instruct him?" [Isa 40:13 LXX]. But we have the mind of Christ.

(1) John of Damascus

When something is spiritual and beyond our power to express, we draw testimonies to it from **spiritual things**.[13] For example, when I say that Christ is risen or that he was born from a virgin, I adduce testimonies and figures and demonstrations: the sojourn of Jonah in the big fish and his subsequent release, the birth of children from the barren women, Sarah and Rebekah and the rest. Again, when I say that Christ was born of a virgin, I cite the sprouting of trees in paradise even though no seeds had been planted or rains sent down or furrows plowed (see Gen 1:11-12). The things to come were modeled and described in earlier events, as in a shadow, so that when they happened they might be believed.

Again, I will point out how people are brought forth from the earth and how a woman is brought forth from a man alone without any sexual intercourse (Gen 2:9-23), and how the earth produces without a consort, since the Creator's power is sufficient for everything. In this way I **interpret spiritual things by spiritual things**, and I have no need of pagan wisdom, or arguments, or rhetorical preparation.

The unspiritual man does not receive the gifts of the Spirit of God. Unspiritual is the one who attributes everything to the soul's rational arguments and thinks there is no need of any help from above — which is folly! God has given us our ability to reason, so that we might understand and ask for his help, not so that we should consider ourselves self-sufficient.

(2) Cyril of Alexandria on verse 14

The unspiritual man is one who lives *according to the flesh* (1 Cor 3:1) and whose mind has not yet been illumined by the Spirit but who has only the natural human understanding, which the Creator puts into the souls of all.

(3) Origen

And we impart this, Paul says, **in words not taught by human wisdom but taught by the Spirit** (and what follows). All the wisdoms of this world (v. 6) are **words taught** by men, the teachings of various rational systems.[14] But Paul does not teach the things **taught by**

13. That is, the Scriptures.
14. Probably a reference to philosophical schools.

the Spirit. One cannot say that the teacher teaches them, because he has been **taught** the substance of what he teaches **by the Spirit**. The **Spirit** that is in him shines upon him as he seeks and finds the truth, and thus *by the renewal of his mind* (Rom 12:2) he always discovers what he has not learned from human beings. For this reason the Savior says: Do not seek a teacher *on earth; for you have one teacher, your Father who is in heaven,* or again, *you have one master, Christ* (Matt 23:8-10). A human teacher suggests a few things, for example, when Paul teaches Timothy. And Timothy, taking this as his starting point, comes himself to the spring to which his teacher Paul had come [the Scriptures], and he draws from it and becomes equal to Paul.

1 Corinthians 3

In chapter 3 Paul returns to the problem of cliques that had formed around different teachers (vv. 1-5, compare 1:10-12). Using himself and Apollos as examples, he argues that teachers do not in themselves deserve reverence since they are only servants who carry out the work of God (vv. 6-9). He compares the Corinthian church with a building whose foundation is Christ, and warns other teachers that they will be judged on the last day for the quality of what they build on this foundation (vv. 10-15). The church is the temple of God, in which God's Spirit dwells (vv. 16-17). At the end of the chapter, Paul returns to the theme of God's wisdom, which is folly in the sight of men (vv. 18-23; compare 1:18-25).

Paul claims that the division into cliques shows that the Corinthians are still "of the flesh," and not yet spiritual. As "babes" they cannot receive "solid food" but only the simpler "milk" (vv. 1-3). Some interpreters think that Paul practiced secrecy, or at least pedagogical reserve (Origen), but Augustine argues that "milk" and "solid food" indicate different levels of understanding, not differences in the teaching given. The fathers give various interpretations of the symbols "milk" and "solid food." For Severian they mean respectively a faith based on miracles and an understanding of the divine plan revealed in Christ's passion. Origen takes "milk" to refer to less rigorous moral commandments and to simpler interpretations of biblical texts. According to Augustine, both images refer to Paul's proclamation of "Christ crucified" (1 Cor 2:2), which is "milk" when it is merely accepted in faith and taken as a moral example but "solid food" when it is understood as the locus of divine grace. Commenting on verse 3, John Chrysostom warns his hearers that, even if they do not practice sexual immorality, they are still "of the flesh" if they give way to jealousy. He notes Paul's diplomacy in presenting himself and Apollos as "servants of God" (vv. 6-9). Ambrosiaster elucidates the word "servant" by citing several biblical examples of people who were reluctant servants of God's purposes.

Origen relates Paul's images of planting and watering (vv. 6-9) to biblical texts that portray God as a planter who expects his vines to produce good fruit. Theodoret focuses on the word "labor" in verse 8 ("each shall receive his wages according to his labor") and draws from this a more general point: those who serve God, for example, by their chastity, will be rewarded according to the effort required, not according to the magnitude of what they produce.

John Chrysostom expands on the image of Christ as "foundation" (vv. 9-11) by comparing other biblical images that express the intimate connection between Christ and the believer, while Cyril of Alexandria adduces several passages that emphasize the centrality of Christ. The images of metals, precious stones, wood, and hay laid upon this foundation (vv. 12-15) suggested various lessons. Origen takes them as a warning that he should be very careful about what he "lays down" in his teaching. Then, in a second interpretation, he applies the images to the spiritual life of every believer. John Chrysostom says that the different materials symbolize the actions of those who receive instruction, not those of their teachers. These two interpreters disagree about the meaning of being "saved as if through fire" (v. 15), a phrase that played a role in the development of the idea of purgatory. While Chrysostom emphasizes the threat of eternal hellfire, Origen sees the fire as temporary and understands the purpose of divine punishment as purification, not retribution (so also Ambrosiaster).

Ambrosiaster relates the "temple of God" in vv. 16-17 to similar imagery in 1 Corinthians 6. Origen offers two interpretations of the image: the temple is the church, in which all the stones must be harmonious (for this he compares 1 Cor 1:10-12). It also symbolizes the individual Christian in whom the Spirit dwells.

As examples of gospel teachings that are "folly" to the wise of this world (v. 18) the fathers mention divine providence (Origen), the incarnation, the resurrection of the flesh (Ambrosiaster), and Christ's command to turn the other cheek (Pelagius). Origen mentions Epicurean teachers met by Paul in Athens to illustrate how the "wise" of this world are shown to be foolish (vv. 19-20). He explains "all things are yours" (vv. 21-22) by comparing a saying about the wise man common among Stoic teachers.

1 Corinthians 3:1-3

₁But I, brethren, could not address you as spiritual men, but as men of the flesh, as babes in Christ. ₂I fed you with milk, not solid food; for you were not ready for it; and even yet you are not ready, ₃for you are still of the flesh. For while there is jealousy and strife among you, are you not of the flesh, and behaving like ordinary men?

(1) Ambrosiaster

But I, brethren, could not address you as spiritual men, but as men of the flesh. Now Paul speaks to those who, because they were still slaves to the pleasures of the world, were **of the flesh.** Although they had already been baptized and had received the Holy Spirit, nevertheless because, after baptism, they immediately returned to the *old man* (Eph 4:22; Col 3:9) whom they had renounced, they are said to be **of the flesh.** For the Holy Spirit remains in a person into whom he has poured himself only if the person remains fixed in his resolve of new birth. If not, the Spirit departs, with the understanding, however, that if the person reforms, he will return to him. For the Spirit is always ready for good and loves penitence.

As babes in Christ, I fed you with milk, not solid food. Although they were reborn in Christ, nevertheless it was not fitting to entrust them with spiritual things. Having received faith, which is a kind of spiritual seed, they produced no fruit worthy of God and thus were not worthy to learn the words of perfection: like babes they were eager for the sensations that belong to the imperfect state. The apostle, a man of God and a spiritual doctor, entrusted as much truth to each as each could handle, so that no one should stumble in spiritual things because of imperfection and ignorance.

For you were not yet ready for it. Paul shows clearly that it is wrong for them to hear what is for the ears of those who are firmly grounded. **And even yet you are not ready, for you are still of the flesh.** Here Paul completely refutes the brashness of those who had long complained that they had not heard spiritual things, though in fact they were unworthy to hear them. The false apostles taught everyone without distinction in the same manner, without discerning anyone's character. They sought to win acceptance, commended by their hypocrisy. Yet it is clear that our Lord and Master Christ spoke in one way to the people and in another to his disciples (see Mark 4:10-12). He even made a distinction among the disciples. To three disciples he showed his glory on the mountain, telling them to say nothing of what they had seen until he rose from the dead (Matt 17:1-9).

(2) Origen

Among Paul's addressees some are *mature* (1 Cor 2:6), the **spiritual men** we spoke about earlier. The others, whom the apostle describes as believers in Christ but not **spiritual**, are **babes in Christ** and **men of the flesh in Christ**. (For I take **in Christ** to modify both descriptions.) Those, then, who are less *mature* and have not yet been *trained* (see Heb 5:14) in the holy Scriptures require elementary lessons. Paul calls these lessons **milk**. For he says, **I fed you with milk, not solid food; for you were not ready for it; and even yet you are not ready.** Now among spiritual foods, I think there is an ascending progression: **milk, solid food,** *true food* (John 6:55), *substantial food* (Heb 5:12, 14), *flesh* of the Word (John 6:55) — and also spiritual *vegetables* (Rom 14:2). Now I dare to say this because I trust the Scriptures. For our Lord has not said that every spiritual food is *true food* (John 6:55), since he says, *My flesh is true food* (John 6:55).

As regards that which is *not substantial food* (Heb 5:12), Paul has in mind ethical matters and especially moral teachings that are less stringent, spoken *by way of concession* and not *as a command* (1 Cor 7:6), in accommodation to the weakness of the hearers. But as for the more perfect teaching about morality, given to those who are eager to learn and ready to work, I would say that in the realm of ethics the following are *substantial food:* the teaching about perfect purity, about virginity or chastity, and about martyrdom.

Among the mystical teachings, *substantial food* (Heb 5:12) is the teaching about the Father and the Son. Thus the Law [the Old Testament] sometimes imparts *substantial food* and sometimes elementary food. For example, take the teaching about the snakes that were killing the sons of Israel because of their grumbling (Num 21:4-9). If we read this on the simpler level, we say, *Do not grumble, as some of them grumbled, and they were destroyed by snakes* (1 Cor 10:9-10). But if the student is able to receive mystical teaching, we say what the snakes are and who is the snake who was hung on the tree (see John 3:14; Gal 3:13), and how a person is saved when he looks on that snake — and in similar fashion for each spiritual Scripture.

Now Peter, in his epistle, makes it clear who is given **milk** to drink when he says, *Like newborn babes, long for the pure spiritual milk* (1 Pet 2:2). And in the Letter to the Hebrews it says: *You need milk and not substantial food; for everyone who lives on milk is unskilled in the word of righteousness, for he is a child. But substantial food is for the mature, for those who have their faculties trained by practice to distinguish good from evil* (Heb 5:12-14).

(3) Severian of Gabala

Unbelievers are more inclined than believers to follow after miracles. For this reason "I gave you a teaching," Paul says, "that was not in truth the perfect 'hidden wisdom' (compare 1 Cor 2:6-7) — the divine plan shown in the passion." This only the *mature* (1 Cor 2:1) among the believers receive. Furthermore, he refers figuratively to teaching about ethics and to a faith based on miracles as **milk**, and calls **solid food** the conveying of divine doctrines. The easier commandments, such as *Honor your father and your mother* (Exod 20:12; Matt 15:4) and *You shall not commit adultery* (Exod 20:14; Matt 5:27), and *Come, follow me* (Matt 19:21), could also be **milk**. When Paul says, **you are of the flesh** and **behaving like ordinary men,** he means, "You esteem human things and do not seek the things of God."

(4) Augustine

I remember that a difficult question arose concerning the Lord's words, *I have yet many things to say to you, but you cannot bear them now* (John 16:12), and that I put off answering it so that I could treat it at leisure: my last discourse had reached its proper length, and I had to stop. So now, since the time has come to fulfill what was promised, let the question be treated as the Lord, who put it into my heart to raise it, shall grant. The question is this: Do spiritual men have anything in their teaching which they reveal to the spiritual and conceal from the carnal? If we say No, someone will reply, "What was it that Paul was talking about to the Corinthians, **I could not address you as spiritual men, but as men of the flesh, as babes in Christ. I fed you with milk, not solid food; for you were not ready for it; and even yet you are not ready, for you are still of the flesh?**" But if we say Yes, we must be fearful and on our guard, for under this pretext unlawful things could be taught as secret doctrine, and it might be thought that, under the claim that they are spiritual things that the fleshly cannot understand, they deserve not only to be excused but also to be praised from the pulpit.

In the first place, you should know that it was *Christ* himself *crucified* (1 Cor 2:2) on whom the apostle says that he fed the babes as if on milk. But his very flesh, where his death took place and where piercing and striking produced true wounds and blood, is not perceived in the same way by the fleshly as by the spiritual: for the former it is **milk**, for the latter **solid food**. The latter, even if they do not hear more, understand more. What is received equally by both in faith is not equally grasped by the minds of both.

That is why, when the apostles preached *Christ crucified*, it was *a stumbling block to Jews and folly to Gentiles, but to those who are called, both Jews and Greeks, Christ the power of God and the wisdom of God* (1 Cor 1:23-24). **Fleshly** babes accept this only as a matter of belief, but **spiritual** people, who have greater capacities, perceive it with their understanding. So to the former it is like **milk**, to the latter like **solid food**. It is not that the one group understands in one way in public and the other another way in their private chambers. Rather, what both hear in the same way when it is spoken openly each understands differently and in his own way. . . .

All who were **spiritual** among them understood by their spiritual understanding the same thing that the others heard as **men of the flesh**. So we must understand the words **I could not address you as spiritual men, but as men of the flesh** in the sense "You could not grasp what I said as spiritual men, but as men of the flesh." *The unspiritual man,*[1] that is, the man of ordinary human understanding, called "soulful" from soul and **of the flesh** from flesh since the whole man consists of flesh and soul, *does not perceive what belongs to the Spirit of God* (1 Cor 2:14).[2] That is, he does not perceive the grace the cross of Christ confers on believers and thinks that the cross merely provides an example for us to follow as we fight to death on behalf of truth. For if ordinary men, who want only to be men, knew how Christ crucified was made *our wisdom, our righteousness and sanctification and redemption; therefore, as it is written, "Let him who boasts, boast of the Lord"* (1 Cor 1:30-31; Jer 9:23-24), then they would certainly not boast of man or say in their fleshly way, *"I am of Paul," "I am of Apollos," or "I of Cephas,"* but they would say spiritually, *"I am of Christ"* (1 Cor 1:12). . . .

Even in the food we eat, **solid food** is not contrary to **milk**; solid food can even become milk in order to be suitable for babies, reaching them through the flesh of their mother or nurse. That is how Mother Wisdom acted: although she is the **solid food** of angels on high, she deigned to become **milk** for babes when *the Word became flesh and dwelt among us* (John 1:14). But the man Christ, who in his true flesh, true cross, true death, and true resurrection is called the **milk** of **babes**, is found, when understood by **the spiritual**, to be the Lord of angels. Accordingly, babes are not to be fed with milk in such a way that they fail to understand that Christ is God, or so weaned from it that they leave behind Christ as man. Or, to put it another way, babes are not to be fed with milk in such a way that they fail to understand that Christ is creator, or so weaned that they leave behind Christ as mediator. Indeed, the simile of mother's **milk** and **solid food** does not fit this situation as well as the simile of a *foundation* (1 Cor 3:10). For the child, once weaned from the food of his infancy, eats his solid food and never again looks for the breasts he had sucked. But "Christ crucified" is **milk** to the nurslings and **solid food** to those who are progressing. The simile of a "foundation" is more appropriate since to complete the building we do not remove the foundation but add on top of it.

Since this is so, then all of you, doubtless including many **babes in Christ**, should advance to the **solid food** of the mind, not of the belly. Advance to the separation of good

---

1. The Latin is *animalis*, which, like the Greek *psychikos,* is derived from "soul."

2. Augustine here equates the "unspiritual man" of 1 Cor 2:14 with the "man of the flesh" of 1 Cor 3:1.

from evil and cleave more and more to the Mediator, through whom you are freed from evil. Evil is not to be physically removed from you but cured in your hearts. But suppose someone says to you, "Don't believe that Christ was truly man or that the bodies of men or other creatures were created by the true God or that the Old Testament was given by God," or other things of this nature.[3] "These things," he might continue, "were not said to you at first because your food was milk and you did not have a heart fit to receive the truth." It is not food but poison that such a one is preparing for you. . . .

But any **spiritual** person can teach another person what he knows if the Holy Spirit enables the hearer to make progress. In this the teacher may also learn something more, so that both are taught by God.

That those who are separated from the church do not have the Spirit is made very plain by the apostle Jude when he says, *Those who separate themselves, worldly people, devoid of the Spirit* (Jude 19). That is why, in the church itself, the apostle Paul reproved those who were creating divisions in the name of men (1 Cor 1:10-12), though these men lived within the unity of the church. Among other things he says, *The unspiritual man does not perceive the things belonging to the Spirit of God, for they are folly to him, and he is not able to understand them because they are spiritually discerned* (1 Cor 2:14). Paul shows that by *does not perceive* he means, "does not grasp the word of knowledge." Those persons, living in the unity of the church, he calls **babes**, not yet spiritual but still carnal and needing to be fed milk, not solid food. **Like babes in Christ**, he says, **I fed you with milk, not solid food; for you were not yet ready for it; and even yet you are not ready.** Where **not yet** and **even yet** are used, we do not give up hope, provided that progress is being made toward realizing what does not yet exist. **For you are still of the flesh**, he says. And to show how they are of the flesh, he says, **For while there is jealousy and strife among you, are you not men of the flesh, and behaving like ordinary men?** Then he makes it plainer: *For when one says, "I belong to Paul," and another, "I belong to Apollos," are you not merely men? What then is Apollos? What is Paul? Servants through whom you believed* (1 Cor 3:4-5). These men, then, Paul and Apollos, are of one mind in the bond of peace. And yet since the Corinthians began to divide up these men among themselves and *puff themselves up on behalf of one of them against the other* (1 Cor 4:6), they are called **ordinary men**, and **of the flesh**, and *unspiritual* since they do not *perceive what belongs to the Spirit of God* (1 Cor 2:14). But since the offenders are not separated from the church, they are called **babes in Christ**. Paul wants them to be angels or gods and so accuses them of being **ordinary men**. In other words, in these quarrels they *are not on the side of God but of men* (Matt 16:23; Mark 8:33). But about those who have separated themselves from the church it is not said, *not perceiving the things that belong to the Spirit* (that would make it a matter of perceiving the Spirit) but *not having the Spirit* (Jude 19). It does not, however, follow that everyone who has the Spirit knows that he has it.

Babes in Christ, living within the church though still *unspiritual* (1 Cor 2:14) and **fleshly**, have this Spirit though they cannot *perceive*, that is, know and understand, what

---

3. Such things were taught by the Manicheans, to whom Augustine once belonged, and by earlier Gnostic sects.

they have. How could they be **babes in Christ** unless they were born again by the Holy Spirit? It should cause no surprise that someone should have a thing and not know what he has. Leaving aside the divine power of the Almighty and the unity of the unchangeable Trinity, who really knows what a soul is? Yet who does not have a soul? We can be sure that **babes in Christ** who do not perceive what is of the Spirit of God nevertheless have the Spirit of God, because a little later on the apostle makes this criticism: *Do you not know that you are God's temple and that God's Spirit dwells in you?* (1 Cor 3:16). He would, of course, never have said this to those separated from the church, who are described as not having the Spirit.

(5) John Chrysostom on verse 3

For while there is jealousy and strife among you, are you not of the flesh, and behaving like ordinary men? Although Paul could have mentioned their fornication and licentiousness, he mentions instead this sin, which he has long been eager to correct. Now if **jealousy** produces people who are **of the flesh**, it is time for us all to make loud lamentations, put on sackcloth, and smear ourselves with ashes. For who is unstained by this passion? — unless I am merely making assumptions about others based on myself. If **jealousy** makes them **of the flesh** and does not permit them to be **spiritual**, even though they were prophesying and displaying other astonishing powers (1 Cor 14:26-33), how will we who do not have such great gifts evaluate ourselves when we have been convicted not only of this sin but of even greater ones?

From this we learn the truth of Christ's statement: *no one who does evil comes to the light* (John 3:20). And we see that an unclean life is an impediment to receiving transcendent teaching since it keeps the perceptive faculty of the mind from showing itself. If a person is in error but lives an upright life, he cannot remain in error. In the same way, then, it is not easy for a person who is raised in wickedness to look up all at once to the height of our doctrines. Rather, one who intends to track down the truth must be purified from all the passions. Being freed from these, he will also be freed from error and attain truth.

1 Corinthians 3:4-8

4For when one says, "I belong to Paul," and another, "I belong to Apollos," are you not merely men? 5What then is Apollos? What is Paul? Servants through whom you believed as the Lord assigned to each. 6I planted, Apollos watered, but God gave the growth. 7So neither he who plants nor he who waters is anything, but only God who gives the growth. 8He who plants and he who waters are equal, and each shall receive his wages according to his labor.

(1) John Chrysostom on verse 5

What then is Paul, and **what is Apollos?** After setting forth and demonstrating his facts, Paul accuses them more plainly. He uses his own case to avoid any harshness and to prevent their being angry at what he says. For if Paul is not bothered by being of no account, much less should they be annoyed. Thus he has two ways of making things easier for them, first by referring to himself, then by not taking everything away from them, as if they were contributing nothing. For though the credit he grants them is small, he grants it nonetheless. For having asked, **What is Paul?** and **What is Apollos?** he adds, **servants through whom you believed.** Now in itself this is a great thing and deserving of great reward, but in comparison with the archetype and the source of good things it is nothing: it is not the servant who mediates God's blessings to us but the One who provides and grants them who is our benefactor. And Paul did not say "preachers," but **servants,** which is more. They had not only preached the gospel, but had also served us; this is not only a matter of speech but involves deeds as well.

(2) Ambrosiaster

What then is Apollos? What is Paul? The servants of the One whom you believed.[4] And because they are **servants,** our hope does not lie in them but in the Lord, of whom they are ministers. We must thank the One who made the gift. But these are servants, who must give even if they don't wish to. Was not Moses compelled to go to the pharaoh (Exod 3:10-12)? Was not Jonah sent against his will to preach to the people of Nineveh (Jonah 1:1–3:3)? Was not Ananias sent, under protest, to lay hands on Saul (Acts 9:10-16)?

As the Lord assigned to each. That is, just as he wished and decided, the Lord divided among individuals the offices of ministry.

I planted, Apollos watered, but God gave the growth. To plant is to evangelize and draw people to faith; to water is to baptize with the proper words; but to forgive sins and give the Spirit belongs to God alone. If, therefore, God's gift produces salvation, man has no glory from this. We know that it has happened that the Holy Spirit was given by God even without the laying on of hands and that someone not baptized has obtained the forgiveness of his sins.

(3) Origen on verse 6

If Paul **planted,** he planted together with God who is the chief planter. If **Apollos watered,** he watered together with Christ who is the chief provider of water. For it is God who plants; that is why it is written: *Every plant which my heavenly Father has not planted will be rooted up* (Matt 15:13). And again: *My Father is the vinedresser* (John 15:1). Let us, then, *produce fruit,* lest we be *cut down* like the unfruitful *fig tree* (Luke 13:6-7). For *every*

---

4. Ambrosiaster's text of v. 5 differs from that translated by the RSV.

tree that does not bear good fruit is cut down and thrown into the fire (Matt 7:19). Let us take care that the following Scripture not be applied to us: *I looked for it to yield grapes, but it produced thorns* (Isa 5:4). For if God says these things about us, he will also apply to us the following: *I will remove its hedge, and it shall be devoured; I will break down its wall, and it shall be trampled down* (Isa 5:5).

(4) Augustine on verse 6

[*From a sermon preached on the anniversary of Augustine's ordination to the priesthood*] Ever since there was placed on my shoulders that burden for which I must render a strict accounting, I have always been stricken with anxiety about the honor I have received. But today I am all the more troubled by such thoughts, when the anniversary of that day makes me remember it, setting it before my eyes so that I feel as if today I were about to take up a burden I took up long ago. . . . Let me therefore have the assistance of your prayers that God may deign to bear with me the burden he has imposed. When you pray, you are praying for yourselves. For what is this burden of mine I speak of if not yourselves? Pray for me then, just as I pray that the burden of you may not be too heavy.

Therefore, my brethren, *commanding, we entreat you not to accept the grace of God in vain* (2 Cor 6:1). Make my ministry fruitful. *You are God's field* (1 Cor 3:9). From outside yourselves receive the one who **plants** and **waters** you; but from within receive the one who **gives the growth** (1 Cor 3:6). The fractious have to be corrected, the fainthearted consoled, the weak taken up, the scoffers refuted, the plotters guarded against, the ignorant instructed, the indolent stirred up, the contentious checked, the proud put down, the litigious made peaceable, the poor helped, the oppressed set free, the good approved, the wicked endured, and all loved. In such a great, multiple, and varied responsibility help me, both by praying and by obeying, so that I may have the joy of being not so much your ruler as your benefactor.

(5) Theodoret on verse 8

He who plants and he who waters are equal in their service. Both serve the divine will. They are not, however, the same in what they do or in their zeal. In these matters there is a great difference among those who serve. Paul himself says, **Each shall receive his wages according to his labor** — that is, not simply according to what he does but according to the **labor** expended on it. It often happens that one person brings two hundred people to the Savior with great ease, while another frees only one or two from error at the cost of great effort. We can see this also in the case of fasting and chastity. One person, aided by his nature, achieves chastity without toil, but another, whose nature opposes him, achieves his goal only with the greatest effort. It is very painful for a person who has a more intense disposition to fast until evening, while another can get through two or three days eating nothing yet endure no great distress. This is why the righteous judge considers not what is done but the **labor**.

1 Corinthians 3:9-11

9For we are God's fellow workers; you are God's field, God's building. 10According to the grace of God given to me, like a skilled master builder I laid a foundation, and another man is building upon it. Let each man take care how he builds upon it. 11For no other foundation can any one lay than that which is laid, which is Jesus Christ.

(1) Origen

If you wish to see proof that Paul is **a skilled master builder,** listen to him as he says: *From Jerusalem and as far round as Illyricum I have fully preached the gospel of God, thus making it my ambition to preach the gospel, not where Christ has already been named, lest I build on another man's foundation* (Rom 15:19-20). And not only did he lay a **foundation, like a skilled master builder;** he also wrote books that were like building plans, which teach how **the master builder** must *build a house* (Luke 6:48), and what kind of person *the bishop must be* (1 Tim 3:2), and also the presbyters and the deacons and all who make up the church. These are all, as it were, the directives of the **master builder. Another man,** he says, **is building upon it. Let each man take care how he builds.**

(2) John Chrysostom on verse 11

For no other foundation can any one lay than that which is laid, which is Jesus Christ.... See how Paul constructs the whole argument on the basis of commonly held beliefs. What he means is this: I proclaimed Christ, I handed the **foundation** over to you. Be careful how you build on it, see whether you are building with vainglory, whether you are *drawing the disciples* after men (Acts 20:30). Let us therefore pay no attention to heresies. **For no other foundation can any one lay than that which is laid.** Let us build on this one **foundation** and let us hold fast to it as a branch clings to the vine (John 15:5), and let nothing come between us and Christ.

If anything comes between, we are immediately lost. The branch draws nourishment through its connection to the vine, and a building stands on account of its being fastened together. If it separates from its foundation, it is destroyed since it has nothing to rest on. So let us not only cling to Christ; let us be joined to him. For if we are separated, we perish. As Scripture says, *For lo, those who are far from thee shall perish* (Ps 73:27). Let us then be joined to him, let us be joined by our works. *For he who keeps my commandments,* says Christ, *remains* in me (John 14:21; 15:10).

And in fact Paul speaks of this union using several images. Christ himself is the *head,* we the *body* (1 Cor 12:12-20; Eph 5:23). Can there be any empty space between the head and the body? He is the **foundation,** we the **building.** He is the *vine,* we the *branches* (John 15:5). He is the *bridegroom,* we the *bride* (Matt 25:1-7; Eph 5:23; Rev 21:2, 9). He is the *shepherd,* we the *sheep* (John 10:11). He is the *way,* we the travelers (John 14:6; Jer 6:16). Again, we are the *temple,* he the occupant (Rom 8:11; 1 Cor 3:16; 6:19; 2 Cor 6:16). He is the *firstborn,* we his *brothers* (Rom 8:29; Col 1:18; Heb 2:11, 17; 12:23). He is the *heir* (Matt 21:38), we the *fellow heirs* (Rom 8:17; Gal 3:29; 4:7; Heb 1:2, 14). He is the *life,* we the living (John 14:6, 19). He is the *resurrection,* we the ones who are raised (John 11:25; Rom 6:4). He is the *light* (John 1:9; 9:5; 8:12), we the ones being *enlightened* (Eph 1:18, Heb 10:32). All these things demonstrate unity. They do not allow any gap, not even the smallest one. Whoever distances himself a little will keep on moving further away. In fact, a little gash made by a sword is enough to destroy the body. And if a building develops cracks, even small ones, it falls apart. A branch, if it is partly severed from the root, becomes useless. So these small separations are not really small, but involve the whole. Therefore, whenever we commit a small offense or are a little neglectful, we must pay attention to these small matters because what is ignored quickly becomes more serious. Similarly, a small tear in a garment, if neglected, ruins the whole. And if a few tiles fall off a roof and we do nothing, the whole house will soon be destroyed.

(3) Cyril of Alexandria

Concerning this **foundation** God the Father promised through the prophet, *Behold, I am laying in Zion for a foundation a stone, a precious cornerstone: "he who believes in it will not be put to shame"* (Isa 28:16). Therefore, Paul says that he himself has laid the **foundation** well, and while others can carry on his work and build upon it, they cannot lay **another foundation than that which is laid, which is Jesus Christ.** *For there is no other name under heaven given among men by which we must be saved* (Acts 4:12). *There is one God, the Father, from whom are all things and for whom we exist, and one Lord, Jesus Christ, through whom are all things and through whom we exist* (1 Cor 8:6). *And he is the head of the body, the church* (Col 1:18). If, then, someone denies **the foundation** and rejects the *rock* (1 Cor 10:4), he does not build on the rock but *upon the sand* (Matt 7:24-27). Therefore, the building will be very easily demolished. For that which Christ does not support is unstable and easily moved.

(4) Augustine

[From a sermon preached at the dedication of a church.]
Only faith, which has the eye of piety in its heart, can see when the good works the faithful accomplish with their temporal and earthly means are laid up in heavenly treasure houses. And that is why when the eye of the flesh looks at this building made for gatherings of religious people, the inmost heart rejoices at what the external eye beholds, and seeing this by means of visible light, it has reason to rejoice in a truth that is unseen. Faith does not spend its time noticing how beautiful the parts of this dwelling are; it cares rather to know what beauty of the inward person has produced these works of love. God, therefore, will repay the faithful for acting so piously, joyfully, and devotedly by putting the faithful themselves into the fabric of his building, into which they hasten to fit as *living stones* (1 Pet 2:5), formed by faith, made solid by hope, and fitted together by love

(1 Cor 13:13). In this building that wise **master builder**, the apostle, put Jesus Christ as both his **foundation** and the supreme *cornerstone* (Isa 28:16), which, as Peter reminds us in a quotation from prophecy, was *rejected by men but in God's sight chosen and precious* (1 Pet 2:4; Ps 118:22). By adhering to this stone we are made peaceable, and by resting on it we are made strong. He is at once a stone of **foundation** because he guides us, and a *cornerstone*, since he joins us together. He is the very *rock* on which the wise man builds his house, which keeps him safe against all the temptations of this age; he does not slip when the rain rushes upon him, nor is he overturned when the river floods, or shaken when the wind blows (Matt 7:24-25; 1 Cor 10:4). . . .

Therefore, just as this visible building has been made for us to gather in physically, so that building, which is ourselves, is being constructed as a spiritual dwelling place for God. *For God's temple is holy, and that temple you are* (1 Cor 3:17). Just as we are constructing this temple with earthly materials, so let us erect that one with the building blocks of virtuous lives. This one is now being dedicated during my visit, but that one will be dedicated at the end of the age with the coming of the Lord, when *this perishable nature must put on the imperishable, and the mortal put on immortality* (1 Cor 15:53) because *he will change our lowly body to be like his glorious body* (Phil 3:21). . . .

But when the day comes to dedicate the eternal house, when we will be told, *Come, O blessed of my Father, inherit the kingdom prepared for you from the foundation of the world* (Matt 25:34), how we will exult, how free we will be from care! Those who have achieved glory will sing aloud, and yet those who are weak will not feel pain. When he shows himself to us, the one who has loved us and given himself for us and appeared before us as one born of his mother, he will appear as the creator God, which he was by virtue of his Father (John 1:3). When he, who has dwelt in it for all time, enters his home, now perfected and adorned, made firm in unity, and clothed in immortality, he will fill all things, shed his radiance on all things, and *God* will be *all in all* (1 Cor 15:28).

1 Corinthians 3:12-15

12Now if any one builds on the foundation with gold, silver, precious stones, wood, hay, straw — 13each man's work will become manifest; for the Day will disclose it, because it will be revealed with fire, and the fire will test what sort of work each one has done. 14If the work which any man has built on the foundation survives, he will receive a reward. 15If any man's work is burned up, he will suffer loss, though he himself will be saved, but only as through fire.

(1) Cassiodorus

There are three types of honor in the church: good, better, and best, and three types of dishonor: bad, worse, and worst. These are compared to **wood, hay, and straw**. Others have the following interpretation of this passage: the man who **builds gold, silver, and precious stones** upon the **foundation** is one who has given away his property and goes into a monastery, or one who lives removed from the world's activities, or one who lives on his property in such a way as if he did not possess it (see 1 Cor 7:29-31). It is as if he possessed another's property on loan and was prepared to lose his goods for Christ, so that if persecution came he might be found unencumbered and ready. On the other hand, those who **build with wood, hay, and straw** are those who, although faithful Christians, are entangled by too great a love of their possessions. When persecution comes or they are required to either give up their property or deny Christ, they do not value their possessions more highly than Christ and so they give them up. Yet since they love them more than they ought, their loss causes them pain and tribulation. So they **will be saved, but only as through fire**, that is, by tribulation. **And the fire will test what sort of work each one has done. If the work which any man has built on the foundation survives, he will receive a reward.** That is, his work will be tested by a trial or a present tribulation, which is often compared to fire. **Gold and silver** are made brighter in the **fire; wood, hay, and straw** will burn up. **If any man's work is burned up, he will suffer loss.** If anyone teaches carelessly, either by example or by word, he labors in vain because the product is paltry. **Though he himself will be saved.** He will be saved in virtue of his own righteousness. **But only as through fire.** The word **as** refers to something true,[5] for example, in the passage *as of the only begotten of the Father* (John 1:14). If the man who is just is **saved as through fire**, why was he not concerned that his building be strong and lasting? What of those who build up by word but tear down by example?

(2) John Chrysostom

The subject of our present discussion is no trivial matter, but one of great moment and of interest to everyone: whether there is an end to the fire of hell. That it has no end Christ has declared plainly, saying, *where the worm does not die, and the fire is not be quenched* (Mark 9:48).

I know that you grow numb from listening to these things. But what can I do? For in truth God commands us to din them constantly into your ears, saying, *Admonish this people* (Exod 19:10, 21; Ezek 3:18-19). We have been appointed to the ministry of the word and so must be tiresome to our hearers, not because we want to be but because we have to be. But if you like, we will stop being tiresome: Paul says that if you do good, you should not fear (Rom 13:3). Thus you can listen to what we say without feeling resentment, but with pleasure.[6]

Now Christ himself declares plainly that hellfire has no end. Paul also shows that punishment is unending when he writes that sinners *shall suffer the punishment of eternal destruction* (2 Thess 1:9). Again he says, *Do not be deceived; neither the immoral, nor idolaters, nor adulterers, nor sexual perverts . . . will inherit the kingdom of God* (1 Cor 6:9-10). He also commands the Hebrews, *Strive for peace with all men, and for the holiness without*

---

5. That is, it is not just metaphorical. In light of the earlier interpretation of "fire," this apparently means that the teacher will experience real tribulation.

6. That is, if you "do good" you have no need to find our admonitions tiresome.

which no one will see the Lord (Heb 12:14). And to those who had said, *Did we not . . . do many mighty works in your name?* Christ says, *Depart from me, you evildoers. I do not know you* (Matt 7:22-23). Also, the virgins who had been shut out could no longer enter (Matt 25:1-13). As for those who did not feed him, Christ says, *They will go away into eternal punishment* (Matt 25:46). . . .

Whenever anyone mistreats someone who has done him no wrong, justice requires that he be punished. How much forgiveness, then, does someone deserve who acts insolently toward a benefactor who has done countless good things for him while receiving no benefits in turn, a benefactor who is the sole cause of his existence, that is, his God, who breathed his soul into being, bestowed countless gifts of grace, and willed to lead him up to heaven? What if a person, after such benefactions, not only insults the benefactor but does so daily by his actions? What forgiveness does he deserve? Do you not see that God punished Adam on account of a single sin? . . .

This topic is vexatious and causes the hearer pain. I know this from my own experience. Indeed, my own heart trembles and quivers. The more I see the teaching about hell laid out, the more I quake and shrink back in fear. But it is necessary to say these things so that we may not be cast into hell. It is not the Garden of Eden, or trees and plants, that you have received, but heaven itself and all the blessings it contains. If Adam, who received less, was condemned and could make no case for his acquittal, all the more will we, who sin more and have been called to greater things, suffer harm that cannot be healed. . . .

The image of the *building* (1 Cor 3:9) seems to me to indicate our actions, although some maintain that the subject here is teachers and disciples and corrupt heresies. But this second interpretation does not make sense of Paul's argument. For if this is his meaning, why does Paul say that **the work** will be destroyed, while the one who "builds" this work **will be saved** even if **through fire?** It is the guilty party who ought to perish; but Paul says that the builder who "lays down" the work will pay more dearly. For if the teacher is the cause of the wickedness, he deserves to pay a greater penalty. How, then, shall he **be saved**? If, however, he is not the cause and his disciples become corrupt because of their own perversity, the teacher deserves no punishment whatsoever, and he should not suffer any loss since he built well. What, then, does Paul mean by saying that **he will suffer loss**? From this it is clear that Paul's subject in this text is the disciples' actions [not different kinds of teachers]. . . .

If Paul were speaking of disciples and teachers, the teacher ought not to **suffer loss** for his disciples' refusal to hear. That is why he says, *Each shall receive his wages according to his labor* (1 Cor 3:8), not according to the result but according to the **labor. . . .** What he means is this: if someone has correct beliefs but leads a wicked life, his faith will not protect him from being punished since his **work** will be burned up. The expression **burned up** means that it will not withstand the intensity of the fire. . . . Therefore, Paul also says that **he will suffer loss**. This is one punishment. **Though he himself will be saved, but only as through fire**. See, a second punishment. What Paul means is this. The person himself will not be lost in the same way as his works, that is, by suffering annihilation. He will remain in the fire. However, someone will object that Paul calls this state "salvation." But not without qualification. This is why he adds, **as through fire**. For, in fact, we too are in the habit of saying "it is preserved in the fire" with reference to logs that are not burned up but are simply covered with ashes. But do not think, when you hear **fire**, that those being burnt cease to exist. And do not be surprised if Paul even calls punishment like this "salvation." He tends to use euphemisms for unpleasant things and to describe good things by their opposites. For example, the word "captivity" seems to refer to some grievous situation, but Paul uses it for something good when he says, *take every thought captive to obey Christ* (2 Cor 10:5). Again, he uses a euphemism for something evil when he says, *sin reigned* (Rom 5:21), even though the word "reign" has rather a nice sound. So when Paul now says, **he himself will be saved**, he implies nothing other than the prolongation of punishment, as if he were saying, "He himself will keep being punished continuously." . . .

Nothing is so irrational as sin, nothing is so senseless and foolish and violent. Wherever it bursts it overturns and confounds and destroys everything.

(3) Origen

Let each man take care how he build upon it (v. 10). Now Paul says this also to me, in order that I not build in a careless way, since I know that on that **day the fire will test what sort of work** I build. I *take care* in building not to add on **wood, hay, or straw.** For if I carelessly add wicked souls to the church, I have attached to the good **foundation**, Christ Jesus, **wood,** and others who are **hay,** and others who are **straw.** On the other hand, it will be clear that I have built **precious stones** upon the foundation if some who belong to the building shine brilliantly — and so brilliantly that they are like those stones in the description of Jerusalem and the temple: *chosen stones and stones of crystal* and stones *of saphire* and all the other stones named there (Isa 54:11-12; Rev 21:19-21). The *temple of God* (1 Cor 3:16) and the *building of God* (1 Cor 3:9) are to have **gold** like the temple that Solomon built as the archetype of a temple that has much gold and silver (1 Kings 6:20-22). Thus if someone else comes and builds, the gold he adds to the building will prove to be more precious than the silver. I myself must take care: I do not wish that through me **wood** and **hay** and **straw** should be introduced. Even if I am considered worthy of salvation on other grounds (since Paul writes, **he himself will be saved, but only as through fire**), it is not my wish — *wretched man that I am* (Rom 7:24) — that I be saved in such a way as to fill the building with **wood, hay,** and **straw,** through not being receptive to grace and not building well. This is not what God's word intends. For **the fire will test what sort of work each one has done.** . . .

Let us now examine the plain sense of the text — this interpretation is relevant for each of us. Each of us, when we received the word of the gospel, received **Jesus Christ** as **the foundation**, so that in everything we do and say and think we may build on this **foundation**. If, then, we have good thoughts and intentions, we build with **gold**. If we speak in a pure way, uttering every word in a holy fashion, then we build as if with **silver**. If every action we do is good, then we build as if with **precious stones**, and God judges both the value and the quality of the stones. If, however, after the **foundation** is laid, I act sinfully, my serious sins will be **wood**, the lesser sins will be **hay**, and even smaller ones will be **straw**. And perhaps [in a different interpretation] the roots are thoughts, and whenever thoughts are errant, they are **wood**, for thoughts are the source of evils. And **hay** could indicate words, and **straw** deeds. For action has less importance than thinking.

If we depart from this life with both sins and good deeds, will we be saved because of the good deeds and absolved for the sins we have committed knowingly? Or will we be punished because of the sins but receive no reward for any of the good deeds? Neither the first alternative — I mean receiving what is worse and failing to receive what is better — nor the other, that is, receiving what is better and failing to receive what is worse, is consistent with the justice of God. For the just God wants to destroy and expel evil. Imagine that after the laying of **the foundation, Jesus Christ,** whom you have been taught, you have built not only with **gold** and much **silver** and **precious stones**. Suppose you have **gold**, whether much or little, and that you have **silver** and **precious stones**. And not only this, but suppose that you also have **wood** and **hay** and **straw**. What do you wish to happen to you after your death? Do you want to enter into the holy places with your **wood** and your **hay** and your **straw** so as to defile the kingdom of God? Or are you willing to remain in the **fire** because of your **hay**, your **wood**, and your **straw**, and to receive nothing for your **gold** and **silver** and **precious stones**? This is not reasonable either. What is the answer then? It follows that because of your **wood**, at "first"[7] you receive the **fire** that consumes the **wood**, and hay, and straw.

(4) Ambrosiaster on verse 15

Though he himself will be saved, but only as through fire. Paul says that a person will be saved because the substance of which he consists will not perish the way false doctrine perishes: the latter does not belong to the person's essence. He says **but only as through fire** to show that this salvation does not come without any penalty. He does not say "he will be saved through fire," which would mean that by his own merit he is not burned up by the fire and is saved, being tested by the fire. When he says **but only as through fire,** he shows that though he will be saved, he will nevertheless suffer the penalty of fire, so that, being cleansed by fire, he might be saved and not be tortured by eternal fire forever, as the faithless are. This is so that there may be some benefit from having believed in Christ.

1 Corinthians 3:16-17

16Do you not know that you are God's temple and that God's Spirit dwells in you? 17If any one destroys God's temple, God will destroy him. For God's temple is holy, and that temple you are.

---

7. With this word Origen is referring to Jer 16:18, which is the primary text in this discussion: "And first I will doubly recompense their iniquity and their sin." From the word "first" Origen deduces that divine punishment cannot be eternal.

(1) Origen

If you wish to come to know **God's** true **temple**, seek *living stones* (1 Pet 2:5) hewn out pure and laid down by the Word and standing *foursquare* (Rev 21:16), in no way unstable or rolling about. For even if holy stones roll about on the ground, the stone cutters do not allow them to roll about forever. You, then, *like living stones,* are *built into a spiritual house, to be a holy priesthood, to offer spiritual sacrifices acceptable to God through Jesus Christ* (1 Pet 2:5). And in Paul's letter it is said: *We are the temple of God* (2 Cor 6:16), all of us one temple since each one of us is a stone of the temple. And he writes the following in the Letter to the Ephesians: *So then you are no longer strangers and sojourners, but you are fellow citizens with the saints and members of the household of God, built upon the foundation of the apostles and prophets, Christ Jesus himself being the chief cornerstone, in whom the whole structure is joined together and grows into a holy temple in the Lord; in whom you also are built into it for a dwelling place of God in the Spirit* (Eph 2:19-22).

No stone, then, must be out of harmony with the building. Christ says, *If two of you agree on earth about anything they ask, it will be done for them by my Father in heaven* (Matt 18:19). How much more effective and powerful will their prayer be if all the stones agree in a single harmony and *the heart and soul* of all *is one* (Acts 4:32)? It is, then, a good thing that we *all agree* so that we might be *united in the same mind and in the same judgment* (1 Cor 1:10). In this way you are a *structure joined together into a holy temple in the Lord* (Eph 2:21).

But in another way each one by himself can be a **temple**. For if a temple is that which *has the glory of the Lord* (Rev 21:11; 1 Kings 8:11), everyone who has the glory of God in himself is by that fact a **temple** of God. And the person who acts *in order to glorify the name of the Father in heaven* (Matt 5:16) has more or less glory on account of his acts. Therefore, it is written, *I will glorify those who glorify me* (1 Sam 2:30). Thus we will be most especially a **temple of God** when we prepare ourselves to receive the Spirit of God. A person who has a spirit of any sin cannot, however, be a temple of God, since *the Spirit of God dwells* (1 Cor 6:19) only where he decides to dwell.

If any one destroys the temple of God, God will destroy him. Each person, as far as in him lies — even if he is only a stone — **destroys the temple of God** if he sins, and a person who provides the church with any grounds for stumbling **destroys the temple of God.** In a more specific sense, the one who commits sexual sin **destroys the temple of God** since *your bodies are a temple of the Holy Spirit within you, which you have from God. . . .*

(2) Athanasius on verses 16-17

We are all said to partake of God through the Spirit. **Do you not know that you are God's temple and that God's Spirit dwells in you? If any one destroys God's temple, God will destroy him. For God's temple is holy, and that temple you are.** If the Holy Spirit were a creature,[8] we would not have any fellowship with God through him. If we were joined to

---

8. Athanasius here argues against people who denied the divinity of the Spirit; compare his comments on 12:4-7, 11, 13, translated below.

a creature, we would be alienated from the divine nature since we would have no share in it. But in fact, when we are called participants in Christ and participants in God, it is made clear that our anointing and sealing have the nature not of created things but of the Son, through the Spirit that is in him and that joins us to the Father. For, as we said earlier, John taught this when he wrote, *By this we know that we abide in [God] and he in us, because he has given us of his own Spirit* (1 John 4:13). If by participation in the Spirit we become *partakers of the divine nature,* it would be insane to say that the Spirit is by nature a creature and not God. This is the reason why those in whom the Spirit comes to dwell are made divine. And if the Spirit makes us divine, there is no doubt that his nature is of God.

An even clearer argument against this heresy is found in the words sung in the hundred-and-third Psalm,[9] as we said earlier, *When thou takest away their breath, they die and return to their dust. When thou sendest forth thy Spirit, they are created; and thou renewest the face of the ground* (Ps 103:29-30 LXX). And Paul writes to Titus, *by the washing of regeneration and renewal in the Holy Spirit, which he poured out upon us richly through Jesus Christ our Savior* (Tit 3:5-6). If the Father creates and renews all things through the Word in the Holy Spirit, what likeness or kinship is there between the Creator and the creatures? How could the One in whom all things are created be a creature?

(3) Augustine on verses 16-17

Let no one say in his heart, "God doesn't care about sins of the flesh." **Do you not know**, asks the apostle, **that you are the temple of God, and the Spirit of God dwells in you? Whoever violates God's temple, God will destroy him**. *Let no one deceive himself* (v. 18). But perhaps someone will say, "God's temple is my mind, not my body," adding as proof, *All flesh is grass, and all the splendor of the flesh as the flower of grass* (Isa 40:6). What a miserable interpretation! What a culpable way to think! *Flesh* is called *grass* because it dies, but you must take care that what dies for a time doesn't rise stained by sin. Here is the plain truth about this. *Do you not know,* asks the same apostle, *that your body is a temple of the Holy Spirit in you, which you have from God* (1 Cor 6:19)? Were you making light of bodily sin? Do you think it a small matter to profane a temple? Your very body is the temple of God's Spirit in you. Don't you see what you are doing to God's temple?

If you deliberately choose to commit adultery in the church, within these four walls, could any act be more criminal than yours? But now you yourself are **God's temple**. You come in as a temple, as a temple you go out; as a temple you stay at home, as a temple you get up. Take care what you do, take care that you don't offend the God who dwells in the temple, for fear he will abandon you and you will fall into ruin. *Do you not know,* he asks, *that your body* (he is talking about fornication, to keep the Corinthians from making light of bodily sins) *is a temple of the Holy Spirit in you, which you have from*

---

9. According to the numbering in the Septuagint. This is Psalm 104 in the Hebrew text, followed in modern translations.

God, and *you are not your own? For you have been bought with a great price* (6:19-20). If you feel contempt for your body, consider what you cost.

(4) Theodore of Mopsuestia on verse 16

The person who believes in Christ *by the washing of regeneration* (Tit 3:5) has the Holy Spirit dwelling in him, and he is *spiritual* (1 Cor 3:1). But those who are enslaved to worldly passions are *men of the flesh* (1 Cor 3:1). Paul says that although you have become *spiritual* by your confession, you live in a fleshly way and insult the Holy **Spirit** who dwells **in you.** Thus, since his audience has obtained the Holy **Spirit** they are a **temple of God,** and because they are entangled in fleshly things they are called *men of the flesh.* The apostle does not contradict himself when he calls the same people both **of God** and *men of the flesh* (1 Cor 3:1).

(5) Ambrosiaster on verse 17

If any one destroys God's temple, God will destroy him. For God's temple is holy, and that temple you are. He makes these remarks in order to sting with remorse those who by shameful living corrupt and violate their bodies, especially the man who had his father's wife (1 Cor 5:1). Paul wants him to stand accused even before his case comes into the discussion. In due course Paul speaks in similar — no, the same — fashion when he judges this man's case: *Do you not know that your body is a temple of the Holy Spirit . . . which you have from God?* (1 Cor 6:19). In the earlier passage he says **temple of God,** but in the latter *temple of the Holy Spirit.* Hence who can doubt that by "Holy Spirit" he means God?

1 Corinthians 3:18-23

18**Let no one deceive himself. If any one among you thinks that he is wise in this world, let him become a fool that he may become wise.** 19**For the wisdom of this world is folly with God. For it is written, "He catches the wise in their craftiness"** [Job 5:13], 20**and again, "The Lord knows that the thoughts of the wise are futile"** [Ps 94:11]. 21**So let no one boast of men. For all things are yours,** 22**whether Paul or Apollos or Cephas or the world or life or death or the present or the future, all are yours;** 23**and you are Christ's; and Christ is God's.**

(1) Ambrosiaster on verse 18

Let no one deceive himself. That is, let no one imagine that by his own, or human, thinking, he does himself any good. Paul returns to his earlier train of thought: **If any one**

among you thinks that he is wise in this age, let him become a fool that he may become wise. His meaning is that if anyone understands the promised salvation and the mystery of our Lord Jesus Christ's incarnation, he must become a fool, that is, flee from the wisdom of the world in order to be judged a fool in its eyes, and then he will be wise. The fool to the world is wise before God in that he believes that God has done those things which the world's reason does not comprehend. . . . But the false apostles wished to seem wise in the world, and they did not preach that God had a son or that there was a true incarnation or that flesh could be resurrected.

(2) Pelagius on verse 18

Let no one deceive himself. Deceived either by his own or by another's flattery. **If anyone among you seems to be wise in this world, let him become a fool so that he may be wise.** Here Paul explicitly criticizes the wise of the world, those whose human wisdom keeps them from perceiving divine things. Another explanation: If anyone thinks that he is wise in repaying injury by giving the same in return, let him become a fool. In this world he who wishes to fulfill the gospel teaching is a fool: he who turns the other cheek to the smiter (Matt 5:39) is a fool by choice, not by nature.

(3) Origen

Since the Corinthians prided themselves on their worldly wisdom, Paul says to them: **If anyone among you thinks that he is wise** — not "if someone *is* wise" — but if someone **thinks that he is wise among you, let him become a fool in this world.**[10] He does not say simply "a fool" but **a fool in this world**, since they call us fools in regard to this world. **Let** a person, then, **become a fool in this world**, in order that by becoming a fool in this world he might become truly wise. **For the wisdom of this world is folly with God.** For how is a person who denies that there is providence not a fool? Or one who says that all things have come into existence out of atoms and out of a void, or that pleasure is the supreme good,[11] or who utters all the other things that silly and idle people take from the apparent wisdom of the pagans? Such a person and such doctrines are truly foolish. To speak generally, if you examine every Greek and barbarian philosophy, you can say that wherever it is at odds with the teaching of Christ, it is folly.

    For it is written, "He catches the wise in their own craftiness" (Job 5:13). It seems to me that it is not surprising if God, acting as God, **catches the wise in their craftiness**. But what is extraordinary is if he does this through Paul, who declares, *Although we live in the flesh, we are not carrying on a worldly war, for the weapons of our warfare are not worldly but have divine power to destroy strongholds. We destroy arguments and every*

---

    10. Or: "in this age"; the Greek word *aiōn* can have either sense. Origen takes the phrase with what follows, the RSV and other modern translations with what precedes.

    11. Origen refers here to teachings of the Epicureans.

proud obstacle to the knowledge of God (2 Cor 10:3-5). In order to understand this more clearly, consider Paul dwelling in Athens and asking questions of *those who happened to be there* with the result that *some of the Epicurean and Stoic philosophers met him* (Acts 17:17-18). On that occasion, by the grace of Christ, he "caught" them and pointed out their sophisms. I think that in the present text (1 Cor 3:19) **the wise** designates the sophists, who utter complicated sophisms but do not teach the truth. **And again, "The Lord knows that the thoughts of the wise are futile."** It is no surprise if the Lord **knows** in himself **that the thoughts of the wise are futile.** But I am eager that the Lord who has come to be in me should know **that the thoughts of the wise are futile.** If *Christ* has come to be *in me* (Gal 2:20), he can show me how **the thoughts of the wise** of the world **are futile,** and how only the *wisdom of God* (1 Cor 1:24) shines brightly, conquering and trampling down all apparent wisdom.

Let no one boast of men. The person who is able to *bid farewell* (Luke 9:61) to all human things and become completely worthy to boast in Christ does not **boast of men.**

But how is **death** mine (v. 22)? That I might *die to sin* (Rom 6:2), that I might say: *If we have died, we shall also live with him* (2 Tim 2:11). For the other death is not mine, the one by which *the soul that sins shall die* (Ezek 18:4). **The present** is ours because we gather together in the present world, because we hear the holy Scriptures, because we pray. And **the future** is ours, for *when that which is perfect comes, then that which is imperfect will pass away* (1 Cor 13:10). It is not possible to come to **the future** if I do not first have **the present.**

All things are yours. There is a Greek saying that is much admired: "All things belong to the wise man, and nothing belongs to the base one." But the word of God was the first to teach this, because it says that everything belongs to the one who is holy. To the believer, Scripture teaches, belongs all the money in the world; to the unbeliever not even a penny. The unbeliever owns things as a thief does because he neither knows the right use of his wealth nor the God who created it. Because he fails to hear God when he says, *The silver is mine, and the gold is mine [says the* LORD*]* (Hag 2:8), he does not possess those things as from God. But we see that **all things** are ours. All the money in the world belongs to the believer, but not even a penny to the unbeliever.

(4) Theodore of Mopsuestia on verse 21

All things are yours, that is, they exist for your sake. Alternatively, Paul says **all things are yours** because we have authority to choose what we wish, either what is better or what is worse.

(5) Severian of Gabala on verse 21

After exhorting them not to accept pagan wisdom, Paul teaches them further not to **boast of** wise **men.** Such boasting is worthless since **all things are yours:** the apostles, who were sent for the sake of their beneficiaries, and **the world** is **yours** (for it came to be for your enjoyment), and **life** is **yours,** since you are saved, and likewise **death** — for if death did not cause fear, we would not set so high a value on the life that is to come. For the same reason he mentions **the present** and **the future**. Those who despise **the present,** on the grounds that it is temporary, gain **the future. All** the aforementioned **things are yours** because **you** have come to be **Christ's,** and those who are united with Christ are pleasing to God.

1 Corinthians 4

Paul begins chapter 4 by reminding his readers that it is only the final judgment of God that matters, not the judgments of men (vv. 1-5). Then, in a highly ironic passage, he contrasts his humble service of God, which has brought him many sufferings, with the arrogance of some in the Corinthian community (vv. 6-13). He appeals to the Corinthians, as his "beloved children," to imitate him and to order their community in preparation for his imminent visit (vv. 14-21).

In verse 1 Paul calls himself both "servant of Christ" and "steward of the mysteries of God." Origen understands these phrases to refer to two different types of teaching, Paul's basic teaching and a second, more advanced teaching that needs to be meted out with care. To illustrate how a steward can be "trustworthy" (v. 2) John Chrysostom cites from Scripture several descriptions of Peter and Paul. He attempts to reconstruct the situation in Corinth that had occasioned Paul's warning against premature judgment (vv. 3-5). Origen ponders the apparent contradiction between this warning and Paul's later statement that Christians should be judged by their fellows, not by outsiders (1 Cor 5:12). Augustine argues that we should not anticipate the judgment of God upon sinners and heretics because repentance is possible throughout earthly life.

John Chrysostom and Photius examine why Paul uses himself as an example (see especially the comments on v. 6). Chrysostom gives a moral interpretation to Paul's words "already you are filled" (v. 8): being able to be easily filled is the mark of a weak soul. Both he and Ambrosiaster point out that Paul is using irony.

In verses 9-13 Paul describes the sufferings he endured for the sake of his faithful service to God. These include being "sentenced to death" (v. 9), an expression for which Origen proposes several interpretations. Augustine contrasts Paul's having become a "spectacle" (v. 9) to the godless spectacle of the games celebrated in his own city. He compares Paul's humiliations with the mockery endured by Jesus and the sufferings of martyrs whose stories are recounted in his church. From Paul's descriptions of his deprivations (v. 11) John Chrysostom draws a more general moral: Christians should not fear things commonly regarded as shameful, such as living in poverty or having a low position in society, but should fear only what is shameful in the eyes of God.

To elucidate Paul's command to follow his example (v. 16) Augustine cites several texts that show what qualities of Paul are to be imitated, noting, for example, his willingness to suffer and his ardor for Christ. John Chrysostom compares Paul's imitation of Christ to the work of painters and sculptors; he cites scriptural texts to illustrate the beauty of Paul's various features. Theodoret thinks that Paul's concluding warnings (vv. 17-21) apply especially to the man who committed im-

morality (1 Cor 5:1). Severian notes that when Paul in verse 21 gives the Corinthians the alterna-
tive of his coming "with the rod" or "with love," he is leaving things up to their free choice. John
Chrysostom applies this verse to himself and his hearers and urges them to exert themselves so as
to gain the kingdom of God.

1 Corinthians 4:1-2

₁This is how one should regard us, as servants of Christ and stewards of the mysteries
of God. ₂Moreover, it is required of stewards that they be found trustworthy.

(1) Origen

**This is how one should regard us, as servants of Christ and stewards of the mysteries
of God.** Someone who is not advanced enough in the teaching to understand the mysteries hidden in Scripture can be a **servant of Christ** but not a **steward of the mysteries of
God**. A **steward** has control of the things entrusted to him and knows the **mysteries of
God**. Perhaps the **servant of Christ** means the person who presides over the more ordinary service, while the **steward of the mysteries of God** is in charge of the dispensation
of mysteries known to him: he must not broadcast these in a haphazard way or hand
them on without due consideration. Instead, he imparts transcendent teaching only after
he has purified his future pupil, prepared him, and distanced him from this world. **We,**
Paul says, **are servants of Christ**. The apostle devoted more time to the service of Christ
than to stewardship of the mysteries of God. He distributed the **mysteries of God,** for example, to Luke, so that he could write his Gospel, and to Timothy, so that he could over-
see those in Ephesus who had received more extensive teaching (1 Tim 1:3) and administer the mysteries of God. And I make bold to say that in Corinth Paul was a **servant of
Christ,** but in Ephesus he was a **steward of the mysteries of God.**

Paul has learned from the words of the Savior: *Who then is the faithful and wise
steward, whom the Lord will set over his household, to give at the proper time the share of
food* to his fellow servants (Luke 12:42)? Thus he says, **Moreover, it is required of stewards that they be found trustworthy.** Having knowledge is not enough, nor should the
one who has knowledge speak at random. Rather, he must understand how *to give* to his
fellow servants *at the proper time the share of food,* and he must consider which of his fellow servants ought to receive a greater *share* **of the mysteries of God**, and which a lesser
share, and when. If he carries out his stewardship well and without fault, what is promised to him? *The master,* he says, *will set him over all his possessions* (Luke 12:44).

But if Paul is anxious when he speaks about himself and Cephas and Apollos, how
much more should stewards like us feel anxious that they be found faithful?

(2) John Chrysostom

Moreover, it is required of stewards that they be found trustworthy. That is, it is required that a steward not usurp what belongs to his master by claiming it for himself as if he were master, but that he administer it like a manager. . . . Would you like to see faithful managers? Listen to what Peter says: *Why do you stare at us, as though by our own power or piety we had made him walk* (Acts 3:12)? And he said to Cornelius, *We also are men, of like nature with you.*[1] And to Christ Peter said, *Lo, we have left everything and followed you* (Matt 19:27). And when Paul says, *I worked harder than any of them,* he adds, *though it was not I, but the grace of God which is with me* (1 Cor 15:10). And elsewhere, referring to the same people [i.e., the Corinthians] he asks, *What have you that you did not receive?* (1 Cor 4:7). For nothing you have is your own, not your property or your learning or your soul itself. Yes, even this belongs to the Master. . . .

Everything we have is from Christ. It is through him that we have our very existence and our life and breath, and also light and air and earth. If he cuts off any of these, we are dead, utterly destroyed. For we are *aliens and exiles* (1 Pet 2:11). "Mine" and "yours" are only empty words. They have no application to reality. If you say your house is your own, this is a word devoid of substance. The air, the land, and the building materials all belong to the Creator, as do you yourself who built the house, and everything else as well. Whether you will have the use of it — even this is uncertain, not only on account of the threat of death but also because even short of death the world is in constant flux.

1 Corinthians 4:3-5

3But with me it is a very small thing that I should be judged by you or by any human court. I do not even judge myself. 4I am not aware of anything against myself, but I am not thereby acquitted. It is the Lord who judges me. 5Therefore do not pronounce judgment before the time, before the Lord comes, who will bring to light the things now hidden in darkness and will disclose the purposes of the heart. Then every man will receive his commendation from God.

(1) John Chrysostom

Somehow or other, along with all the other sins, the disease of nosiness and inappropriate meddling was introduced to human nature. Christ himself criticized this when he said, *Judge not, that you be not judged* (Matt 7:1). This sin, unlike other transgressions, brings no pleasure at all but only punishment and retribution. We ourselves, who are brim full of sins and carrying *logs* in our eyes, become exacting inquisitors of our neighbor's transgressions, though they are no bigger than *specks* (Matt 7:3). This is what was

---

1. The words quoted here were actually spoken by Paul to the inhabitants of Lystra in Acts 14:15, but in Acts 10:26 Peter says something similar to Cornelius: "Stand up; I too am a man."

happening in Corinth. They were ridiculing and rejecting devout men who were friends of God on the grounds that they lacked learning, but were commending those guilty of countless sins merely because of their smooth speech. Then, as self-appointed judges, they recklessly cast their votes, saying, "This man is worthy," "That man is better than the other," "This man is inferior to that one, and that one is superior to this one." And because they ceased to *mourn* (1 Cor 5:2) for their own sins, they became judges of others, and thus they caused bitter disputes. . . .

It was not in order to exalt himself but to humble other people and to restrain those who were exalting themselves and persuade them to show moderation that Paul said, **with me it is a very small thing that I should be judged by you or by any human court.** Notice how gently he treats them: someone hearing that Paul disdains all alike and does not consent to be judged by anyone will no longer be hurt, as if he were the only one whose judgment is rejected. If Paul had merely said, **by you,** and nothing more, this might have been enough to make them feel hurt that he held them in contempt. But in fact when he adds, **or by any human court,** he softens the blow by showing that he holds others in contempt as well. Once again, he treats them with the same gentleness when he says: **I do not even judge myself.** Notice that this is not said out of arrogance: Paul admits that even he himself is incapable of such exactness in judgment. . . .

We cannot be free from blame even if we are **not aware of anything against** ourselves, and we are also liable to punishment if we do something good without the proper intention. Consider, therefore, how badly people err in their judgments. Nothing of our interior life is accessible to human beings, but only to the unsleeping eye of God. Even if we deceive men, we will never deceive him. Therefore do not say, "Darkness and walls surround me. Who sees me?" He who by himself formed our hearts knows everything, because *darkness* will not be *dark* to him (Ps 139:12). But the sinner who says, "Darkness and walls surround me," is quite right, for if darkness were not in his heart he would not have cast out the fear of God and acted so boldly. If reason is not first darkened, sin cannot boldly enter in. Therefore, do not ask, "Who sees me?" For there is one who *pierces to the soul and spirit, the joints and marrow* (Heb 4:12). But you do not see yourself and cannot cut through the cloud: you are as incapable of looking up to heaven as if you had a wall surrounding you on all sides.

(2) Origen

Before the Lord comes (v. 5). We are under judgment, and the only true judgment is the one that belongs to the Lord, who knows how to judge our thoughts, weigh our words in the balance, search out all our deeds, and render to each his due. Therefore, even if we find someone to be at fault, let us not condemn him. For we do not know how seriously he has sinned or in what state of mind, or if he has good deeds to compensate for his sin. If we are cautious, we will not judge **before the time,** but we will refer everything to the judgment of God, acting through our savior, Jesus Christ.

In this text Paul says, **do not pronounce judgment before the time** and what follows. But elsewhere in the letter he adds, *Is it not those inside the church whom you are to* *judge? God judges those outside* (1 Cor 5:12). Do these Scriptures contradict each other? Must we both judge and not judge, with the word meaning the same thing in both texts? If you who have been entrusted with judging *those inside* do not do so, the church will be *a company of evildoers* (Ps 22:16). But if *those inside* are to be judged, how is it written, *Judge not, that you be not judged* (Matt 7:1)? Here is my explanation: those entrusted with judging *those inside* are not so foolish as to say, as they judge, "We are pronouncing the judgment of God." Rather, they exercise judgment for the sake of the good of the church. If it benefits the church for this person to be excommunicated (1 Cor 5:5), they pronounce this judgment and carry it out. Likewise it is for the good of the church that they commend people; they do not pronounce the judgment of God but only exercise the judgment delegated to them. For we do not "search hearts," nor do we know the reasons behind each person's deeds. Those who judge according to the gospel leave *the secret things to the LORD God,* but *the things that are revealed,* as Scripture says, *are for you and your children* (Deut 29:29). They judge whatever comes to their attention and what is known to them. Let us never, then, anticipate the judgment of God and say, "This man is lost," or call someone blessed and say, "That man is saved." We do not know how to measure or compare one action — or one reason or thought — with another. **Do not pronounce judgment**, then, **before the time, before the Lord comes, who will bring to light the things hidden in darkness and will disclose the purposes of the heart.**

(3) Augustine

As long as a person lives in the body, it is impossible to judge the impenitence of his heart. We should not give up hope for anyone as long as God's patience is calling him to repentance and he has not been snatched from this life in a state of unbelief: God does not *desire the death of the wicked, but rather that he should turn from his way and live* (Ezek 18:23). "He is a pagan today," you say. But how do you know he won't be a Christian tomorrow? "He's an unbelieving Jew today." But what if he should believe in Christ tomorrow? "He's a heretic today." But what if tomorrow he should become a follower of catholic truth? "He's a schismatic today." But what if tomorrow he embraces catholic peace? Those whom you find to be involved in any sort of error, whom you condemn as beyond hope — what if before leaving this life they were to repent and find the true life in the world to come?

Therefore, brethren, on this matter as well you should be guided by the apostle: **judge nothing before the appropriate time.** As long as they are still in this life, it is impossible to identify in anyone that blasphemy against the Spirit for which there is no forgiveness (Matt 12:31).

1 Corinthians 4:6-8

6I have applied all this to myself and Apollos for your benefit, brethren, that you may learn by us not to go beyond what is written, that none of you may be puffed up in fa-

vor of one against another. 7For who sees anything different in you? What have you that you did not receive? If then you received it, why do you boast as if it were not a gift? 8Already you are filled! Already you have become rich! Without us you have become kings! And would that you did reign, so that we might share the rule with you!

(1) John Chrysostom

As long as he needed to speak harshly, Paul disguised his words and spoke as if he were himself the one being discussed. He wanted to preserve the dignity of those being censured so that his charges might not cause them to explode in violent anger. But when the time came for gentler words, he removed the mask and showed who was concealed under the names "Paul" and "Apollos." That is why he says, **I have applied all this to myself and Apollos for your benefit, brethren.** When a sick child rejects the food offered by his doctors, those taking care of him call his father or his tutor and ask them to take the doctors' food and offer it to the child. This is so that the child, out of respect for them, might eat it and be well. Similarly, when Paul wants to censure his hearers in relation to certain ones he thought were being wronged and others who were given too much honor, he does not identify these persons. Instead, he exhorts them by speaking about himself and Apollos, so that the Corinthians, out of respect for them, would accept the cure he was offering. . . .

For who sees anything different in you? What have you that you did not receive? At this point Paul dismisses the followers and turns to the leaders. This is what he says: "How is it evident that you deserve praise? Has any judgment taken place? Has any inquiry, any trial or exact test, gone forward? You can't maintain that it has. And even if people do cast their votes, their judgment is often incorrect. But let us suppose that you really are worthy of praise, that you have a heavenly gift and that the judgment of men has not been corrupt. Not even so would it be appropriate for you to be proud. You have nothing of your own, but only what you have received from God. Why then do you pretend to have something you do not have?" . . .

If then you received it, why do you boast as if it were not a gift? Since Paul has now made his case by means of rhetorical concession, he indicates that they are in fact lacking a great deal. . . . In the beginning he only hinted at this, saying, *I could not address you as spiritual men* (1 Cor 3:1) and *I decided to know nothing among you except Jesus Christ and him crucified* (2:2).

But here he speaks in a way designed to shame them when he says: **Already you are filled! Already you have become rich!** That is, you need nothing further, you have become perfect, you have gained the very summit. You think you need no one, neither apostles nor teachers. **Already you are filled!** The word **already** is well chosen; Paul makes use of time words to show how ridiculous their statements are and how unreasonable their notion of themselves. He is being sarcastic and ironic when he says to them: "So quickly have you reached the end" — which they could not in fact have done by that time, because we will receive what is perfect only in the future (see 1 Cor 13:9-10). But a soul that is "full" with a little is a weak soul, while to imagine that one is **rich** on the basis of a little is the mark of a sick and miserable soul. True piety is not easily exhausted, and it is the mark of a childish mind to equate learning the elementary lessons with mastery of the whole subject. Likewise it is childish when you are not even at the beginning to boast as if you have reached the end.

(2) Photius

Why does Paul say: **I have applied all this to myself and Apollos for your benefit? For your benefit** means "in order that I not distress you if I criticize you by name." He was eager to correct them but wary of distressing them. In this way, he says, you can have it both ways, if you like: you can be corrected but feel less pain as you hear the words of correction. He did this to avoid giving the impression that it was merely out of human sympathy or antipathy that he reproached certain people, criticizing some while leaving others unscathed. Another reason is that he did not wish, by making such a distinction, to throw those he criticized into despair or make them angrier or more contentious — or, on the other hand, to make those he did not mention more arrogant and vain. That is why he did not criticize them by name but applied his reproach to himself and to Apollos, thus making his general admonition less offensive and easier to accept.

(3) Ambrosiaster on verse 8

Already you are filled! Already you have become rich! Without us you have become kings! This is what we call "irony." These are the words of one who is angry, not one who approves of them. He says that those he has rebuked for such great faults **have become kings**. For that is what they thought, since they gloried in what the false apostles had taught them.

And would that you did reign, so that we might share the rule with you! Like a kind father, he wishes even his ungrateful children well. How could it happen that they should be **kings** without the apostles? Whatever is not taught by the apostles is brimful of wrongdoing.

The normal expression would be "so that you might share rule with us." But because he starts his sentence, **And would that you did reign**, he can only say, **so that we might share rule with you**. To **reign** is to have confidence in the hope and promises of Christ and to rejoice in any adversities undergone in the name of Christ since they bring profit, not loss. That is why Paul says in another place, *When I am weak, then I am strong* (2 Cor 12:10).

(4) Augustine

Let no arguments uproot this faith and this true piety from your hearts, I mean the faith that prevents us from taking pride in our free will and our good works. If someone has received the capacity for good works, he should receive it in such a way that he recognizes the giver. One who ignores the giver is like a sick man, or a man healed by another, who treats his doctor with scorn. Preserve what you have received. **For what have you that you did not receive?** To acknowledge God truly is to say what the apostle said, *We have not received the spirit of this world* (1 Cor 2:12). The spirit of this world makes people proud and arrogant; it causes them to think they are something when they are nothing. But what does Paul say against the spirit of the world? Against the spirit of this world, which is proud, puffed up, swollen with haughtiness, conceit, and lacking in solidity, what does he say? *We have received not the spirit of this world, but the Spirit which is from God, that we might understand the gifts bestowed on us by God* (1 Cor 2:12).

So let us listen to our Lord's words, *Apart from me you can do nothing* (John 15:5), and *No one can receive anything except what is given him from heaven* (John 3:27). And again, *I am the vine, you are the branches. As the branch cannot bear fruit by itself, unless it abides in the vine, neither can you, unless you abide in me* (John 15:4-5). And consider the solemn attestation of James, *Every good endowment and every perfect gift is from above, coming down from the Father of lights* (Jas 1:17). Hear too what the apostle Paul shouts aloud in order to put down the presumption of those who are proud of their free will, **What have you that you did not receive? If then you received it, why do you boast as if it were not a gift?** And again, *For by grace you have been saved through faith; and this is not your own doing, it is the gift of God — not because of works, lest any man should boast* (Eph 2:8-9). And again, *For it has been granted to you that for the sake of Christ you should not only believe in him but also suffer for his sake* (Phil 1:29). And again, *God, who began a good work in you, will bring it to completion at the day of Jesus Christ* (Phil 1:6).

1 Corinthians 4:9-13

9**For I think that God has exhibited us apostles as last of all, like men sentenced to death; because we have become a spectacle to the world, to angels and to men.** 10**We are fools for Christ's sake, but you are wise in Christ. We are weak, but you are strong. You are held in honor, but we in disrepute.** 11**To the present hour we hunger and thirst, we are ill-clad and buffeted and homeless,** 12**and we labor, working with our own hands. When reviled, we bless; when persecuted, we endure;** 13**when slandered, we try to conciliate; we have become, and are now, as the refuse of the world, the offscouring of all things.**

(1) Origen

The more a person lays claim to the true heavenly prizes, the more he becomes, out of humility, the **last one** of all. I think that Paul had something like this in mind when he said: *To me, as to the least of all the saints, was this grace given* (Eph 3:8). . . . It is fitting for those **exhibited** by God **as last** to be first in the sight of God; truly *the last* are *first* (Matt 20:16).

It is also fitting for them to be **sentenced to death.** Insofar as a person lives a more perfect Christian life, he is **sentenced to death.** Such a person is always in danger since he reproaches the sinner, who often has more worldly power and can mete out punishment, and he lives in places *where Christ has not been named* (Rom 15:20), and *lays a foundation* (1 Cor 3:10) that shocks and upsets his audience. Paul spoke truly when he exclaimed, *I protest, brethren, by my pride in you, which I have in Christ Jesus our Lord, I die every day!* (1 Cor 15:31). But it seems to me as I study this text that **sentenced to death** can be taken in two ways. The first is that it is necessary *always to bear the death of Jesus in the body* (2 Cor 4:10). In the other sense the one **sentenced to death** is the righteous one, who is conformed to the death of Christ (Phil 3:10) and who dies constantly to the world. Thus is it fitting that **God exhibited the apostles,** who belong to Christ, as being both **sentenced to death** and **last.**

(2) Augustine on verse 9

What more remarkable gift could come from the Lord Jesus Christ, the Son of God who was even willing to become Son of Man — what more remarkable gift could he bestow on us than to add to his flock not only those who watch these worthless shows, but also some of those who used to be part of the spectacle? The Lord hunted down for salvation not only those who loved to watch hunting but even the hunters themselves. He himself was made **a spectacle.** Before he was made a spectacle, he himself said what was going to happen. Indeed, he predicted it, described it as if it had already happened, announced it in advance by prophetic utterance when he said in the psalm, *They have pierced my hands and feet, they have counted all my bones* (Ps 22:16-17). . . . He became a spectacle to mock at, oggled at by people who had not come to cheer him on in that show but to mistreat him cruelly.

In the same way he made his martyrs **a spectacle** from the beginning: the apostle writes, **We have become a spectacle to the world, to angels and to men.** But there are two kinds of people who watch such spectacles, those who are *fleshly* and those who are *spiritual* (1 Cor 3:1). The fleshly look on and regard the martyrs as pitiable because they are exposed to wild beasts, beheaded, and set on fire; they are filled with loathing and horror. Others, however, look on like the holy angels, not fixing their attention on the laceration of their bodies but instead marveling that the martyrs' faith remains whole. What a great show is offered to the eyes of the mind when the spirit is intact and unbroken even as the body is torn to pieces! When accounts of this are read in the church, the **spectacle** is one on which the eyes of our hearts gaze with pleasure.

(3) John Chrysostom

To the present hour we hunger and thirst, we are ill-clad and buffeted and homeless, and we labor, working with our own hands. This means: I am not telling you ancient history but speaking of the present time. We take no notice of human things or of external distinctions. We look to God alone. Indeed, we must always do this. Not only are we being observed by **angels**, but also ahead of them stands the one who presides over the contest. Let us not expect anyone else to praise us. It is an insult to God, when we pass him over as if his admiration were not sufficient and run to our fellow servants. . . . Those others will stand with us before the judgment seat, and they will do us no good. But God, whom we are now despising, shall himself pass judgment on us. Even though we know these things, we still are overawed at human beings, which is the first sin. . . .

Many consider it a great disgrace to live in poverty. So we flee poverty, not because it really is a disgrace or because we have been persuaded that it is, but because our masters think it a disgrace and we stand in awe of them. Again, many regard being dishonored and despised and deprived of any sort of power to be shameful and contemptible. We shun these things, not because we ourselves condemn them but because of the opinion of our masters. On the other hand, we suffer the same sort of indignity in the other extreme. To be rich is considered good, and so is haughtiness and a high reputation and being in the public eye. Again we pursue all this, not because we have come to regard these things as inherently good but because we have been persuaded by the opinion of our masters. Public opinion is our master. The vast mob is a cruel overlord and a harsh tyrant. There is no need for it to issue commands in order to be obeyed; it is enough that we know its wishes, and we submit without hearing a command — such is the goodwill we feel toward it. The God who threatens and promises day after day finds no hearing, while the great mob, undisciplined and disorderly, has no need to command. It needs only to show what it finds pleasing, and immediately we obey.

How, Paul asks, could anyone escape such masters? Be wiser than they are, consider the nature of things, condemn the judgment of the crowd; consider the things that are truly disgraceful instead of those other things, and train yourself to fear not men but rather the eye that never sleeps. And as you pursue good things, seek your laurels from him. . . . And how, Paul asks, can this happen? Think what a man is and what God is; think which one you are abandoning and to which you are fleeing for refuge, and at once everything becomes clear. Man is subject to the same sin as you, the same judgment and chastisement. Man has been likened to futility (see Eccl 1:2); he does not judge rightly, he needs restoration from above. Man is dust and ashes, and if he offers approval, he will often do so thoughtlessly, or as a favor, or out of spite. If he rejects or condemns, he will act from the same motives. God is different: his verdict is faultless and his judgment pure (see Ps 12:6). This is why we must always take refuge in him. And not only for this reason, but also because he created you, and he spares you more than all the others do, and he loves you more than you love yourself.

(4) Ambrosiaster on verses 11-12

Since the apostles proclaimed Christ freely according to the true faith and without any flattery and criticized evil lives, they did not enjoy favor among men but were **buffeted**, that is, persecuted wrongfully. They were **homeless** because people chased them off to prevent their staying in one place and teaching more people. The reason they were **working with** their **own hands** was not only that they did not enjoy favor with men but also that they thought it unworthy to accept anything from followers of error, as it says in the Psalm: *the oil of the wicked will never anoint my head* (Ps 141:5). A man errs and loses his freedom to criticize when he receives gifts from someone who gives to escape criticism.

1 Corinthians 4:14-16

14I do not write this to make you ashamed, but to admonish you as my beloved children. 15For though you have countless guides in Christ, you do not have many fathers. For I became your father in Christ Jesus through the gospel. 16I urge you, then, be imitators of me, [as I am of Christ].[2]

(1) Augustine

Imitate Christ the redeemer: **Be imitators of me, as I am of Christ.** How did Paul imitate Christ? Notice what he says beginning with *In hunger and thirst . . . in cold and nakedness,* and so on, up to *Who is scandalized, and I am not on fire?* (2 Cor 11:27-29). *I have become all things to all men, that I may gain all* (1 Cor 9:22). *I will bridle my mouth, so long as the wicked are in my presence* (Ps. 39:1). What are Paul's words, brothers? *Who will separate me from the love of Christ?* Notice the end: *Who will separate me from the love of Christ? Shall trouble, or distress, or persecution, or nakedness, or danger* (Rom 8:35)? Oh what a loving man, how ardent, how he runs, how he attains the goal! How much this soul suffered! How passionate he was, what a teacher he was! *Who will separate me from the love of Christ? Shall distress?* and so on, as far as *or the sword?* How much this man suffered! And so that no one should think that he was proud as a result of it all, he said, *Brothers, I consider I have not achieved anything yet* (Phil 3:13).

(2) John Chrysostom

I beg you, then: be imitators of me as I am of Christ. How great is the boldness of Paul the teacher! How exact must his image be, given that he exhorts others to follow it! But he does this not to exalt himself but to show that virtue is attainable. Do not say to me, "I cannot imitate you. You are a teacher and a great man." For the distance between me and you is smaller than that between Christ and me, and nonetheless I have imitated him. . . .

Let us see, then, how Paul imitated Christ. This imitation does not require time and skill but only a decision to do it. Now if we go into the studio of an artist, we will not be able to imitate his painting, even if we look at it again and again. But in the case of Paul, we can imitate him merely by listening to his words. Do you want us, then, to take out the

---

2. The phrase "as I am of Christ" is added in the Latin version and in some Greek manuscripts; apparently it has been added from a similar statement in 1 Cor 11:1. It is quoted in the commentaries of Augustine and John Chrysostom.

portrait and describe to you Paul's way of living? If so, we will set forth a portrait much more dazzling than the images of emperors. The raw material is not boards joined together or cloth that has been stretched, but the work of God. For this portrait is made of soul and body, and the soul is the work of God not men, and the same is true of the body. . . .

Then let the portrait, the soul of Paul, be set forth before us. At one time this portrait was covered with dirt and full of spider webs, for there is nothing worse than blasphemy. But when the One who transforms everything came, he saw that it was not due to laziness or lassitude that the portrait was drawn as it was, but because Paul in his inexperience lacked the bright colors of piety. He had zeal, but the colors were not ready to hand, and he *did not have zeal in accordance with knowledge* (Rom 10:2). Then God gave him the bright color of truth, that is, grace, and made his image wholly regal. When Paul had acquired the colors and learned the things of which he had been ignorant, in no time he presented himself as the consummate artist. And first he showed the *head* to be royal (see Eph 1:22-23) when he proclaimed Christ, and then the rest of the *body,* with its strict way of life.

Painters shut themselves away and do all their work with strict discipline and in deep silence, opening their doors to no one. But Paul, setting his canvas in front of the whole world, with everyone opposing him and shouting and causing trouble, nevertheless created his imperial image effortlesly. That is why he said: *We have become a spectacle to the world* (1 Cor 4:9), since he painted his image in the midst of land and sea, heaven and earth, the physical and the spiritual universe.

Do you want to see the other parts of this image as well, moving downward from the head? Or would you like us to begin our description from the bottom? Consider a golden statue, or rather something even more precious than this, worthy to stand in heaven, not anchored with lead or fixed in one place, but racing *from Jerusalem as far round as Illyricum* (Rom 15:19) and going off to Spain (Rom 15:24) and being carried as if on wings throughout the inhabited world. What could be more beautiful than those feet, which visited every land that lies under the sun? It is a beauty proclaimed of old by the prophet when he said: *How beautiful are the feet of the one who brings good tidings . . . of peace* (Isa 52:7).

Have you seen how beautiful the feet are? Do you wish to see his chest as well? I will show you this too, and you will see that it is far more splendid than those beautiful feet, and also more impressive than the chest of the ancient lawgiver. Moses carried stone tablets, but Paul had Christ himself within him. He bore the kingly image of the atoning sacrifice. For this reason he was more to be revered than the cherubim. . . .

Do you wish also to behold the beauty of his belly? Hear what he says about it: *If food causes my brother to stumble, I will never eat meat* (1 Cor 8:13). It is a good thing not to eat meat, or drink wine, or to do anything that causes a brother to take offense or stumble or to be weak: *Foods are for the belly and the belly for food* (1 Cor 6:13). What could be more beautiful than this belly, trained to be still and instructed in all moderation, knowing how to endure hunger, famine, and thirst? For like a well-trained horse that has received a golden bridle, Paul's belly marched on gracefully, having triumphed over the compulsion of nature. For Christ was marching in it. . . .

If someone had gave me power over the whole world, I would consider Paul's fingernail more powerful than that entire kingdom, his poverty more powerful than all splendor, his nakedness than all riches, the buffeting of that precious head more powerful than all security, and the stoning he received than any crown (2 Cor 11:23-24).

1 Corinthians 4:17-21

17Therefore I sent to you Timothy, my beloved and faithful child in the Lord, to remind you of my ways in Christ, as I teach them everywhere in every church. 18Some are arrogant, as though I were not coming to you. 19But I will come to you soon, if the Lord wills, and I will find out not the talk of these arrogant people but their power. 20For the kingdom of God does not consist in talk but in power. 21What do you wish? Shall I come to you with a rod, or with love in a spirit of gentleness?

(1) Theodoret

Paul revealed his attitude toward them by sending Timothy, and he revealed his tender love for Timothy by calling him **beloved child**. He revealed Timothy's other virtues when he called him **faithful in the Lord**. Timothy, Paul says, will recount my deeds. For he calls deeds **ways**. He does not say that Timothy will teach them these deeds, but that he will **remind** them. The text accuses them of forgetfulness. For the Corinthians had seen the apostle's virtue with their own eyes. He adds further that it was his custom to give this same teaching in all the churches. After making these accusations against the whole community, he then issues a judgment against the one who committed sexual sin (see 1 Cor 5:1).

Some are arrogant, as though I were not coming to you. The holy apostle, foreseeing the man's repentance, does not give his name, not wishing to reveal it to all. Instead he uses the indefinite expression **some**.

But I will come to you soon, if the Lord wills, and I will find out not the talk of these arrogant people but their power. For I do not seek eloquence but actions. Then he puts this more strongly: **For the kingdom of God does not consist in talk but in power.** It is not sufficent for salvation to proclaim the kingdom; one must also perform actions worthy of the kingdom.

(2) Severian of Gabala on verse 21

What do you wish? Shall I come to you with a rod, or with love in a spirit of gentleness? There are two sorts of correction: admonishing for those who are open to persuasion, and force and compulsion for the stiff-necked. Paul kindly leaves the choice up to them so that they might repent and correct themselves. He calls the compelling power of the Spirit a **rod**, which Paul used against Elymas (Acts 13:8-11) and which God uses against Paul himself (Acts 9:3-6).

(3) John Chrysostom on verse 21

See the wisdom of Paul. Although he himself has authority, he entrusts the outcome to others, saying, **What do you wish?** The matter lies in your hands. The same is true of us. We too have the power to produce one result or the other, either being cast into hell or obtaining the kingdom. This is God's will. Look, he says, *fire and water: stretch out your hand for whichever you wish* (Sir 15:16). And *If you are willing and obedient, you shall eat the good of the land* (Isa 1:19).

But perhaps someone will say, "I desire it — and no one is so senseless as not to — but it is not enough for me to desire." But it is enough if you desire as you ought to and act accordingly. If you like, let us consider an analogy. Tell me, is a man who wants to marry content with wishing? By no means; he finds women to speak on his behalf, he asks friends to stay up at night with him, he gets money together. Again, the merchant is not content to sit at home and wish: he hires a ship, hires sailors and rowers, borrows money, makes inquiries about the market and the price of merchandise. Is it not strange that men should show such zeal for earthly things, but when they intend to set off for heaven, they are content with wishing?

1 Corinthians 5

In verses 1-5 Paul denounces the Corinthians for tolerating a case of incest and orders them to exclude the offender from their fellowship: "you are to deliver this man to Satan for the destruction of the flesh" (v. 5). Origen, who often emphasizes the pedagogical purpose of God's punishments, argues that the "flesh" Paul wants to be destroyed is not the body, but instead, as in Rom 8:6-7, an attitude of the mind. Paul's aim is to bring about the man's repentance. Cyril compares the situation in Corinth to stories in the Old Testament and in Greek literature.

In verses 6-8 Paul uses images from the story of the exodus from Egypt to describe Christ's sacrifice and the Christian life. From ancient times verses 7-8 have been used in the eucharistic liturgy: "Christ our Passover has been sacrificed for us. Therefore let us keep the feast." John Chrysostom picks up the image of "feast," portraying the Christian life as one big festival that celebrates Christ's taking on flesh and bringing deliverance from death. Expanding on Paul's imagery, he interprets the crossing of the Red Sea as a type of baptism and the exodus from Egypt as a symbol of deliverance from demons. As in his comments on earlier chapters, so here, too, Origen understands different parts of the chapter to refer to two distinct groups in Corinth. Here this serves to explain why Paul first tells his hearers to cleanse out the old leaven and then says they are already unleavened (v. 7).

In verses 9-11 Paul explains a directive he gave in an earlier letter not to associate with immoral people. Origen's comments illustrate two sides of his exegesis. The comment on verse 9 reflects his interest in historical analysis. He notes two possible interpretations: either Paul is referring to an earlier letter to Corinth, now lost,[1] or the reference is to something said in the present letter (this second explanation of "I wrote to you" is taken up later by Photius). Origen's comment on verse 11 illustrates the way he often interprets Paul's words as directly addressing the reader in the present time. Noting that Paul's catalogue of sins that justify exclusion from the church includes not only such major offenses as incest and idolatry but also that of "reviling," or abusive speech, Origen says: "I fear for myself, lest somehow I might be found guilty." Augustine's interpretation of this verse focuses on Paul's condemnation of drunkards. In a letter to another bishop, he tells the story of how he used this verse to address a specific problem in his church, the overly raucous celebration of a saint's day. He cites the verse, along

---

1. As modern exegetes generally assume; see, for example, Gordon D. Fee, *The First Epistle to the Corinthians* (Grand Rapids: Eerdmans, 1987), 221-22.

with Exod 32, Matt 7:6, and 1 Cor 6:9-11, to rouse the Christians of Hippo to celebrate in a more spiritual way.

Paul concludes the chapter with an exhortation to practice discipline (vv. 12-13), reinforced by a quotation from Deuteronomy 17. Origen asserts that this exhortation refers not only to church discipline, exercised by the bishop, but also to each person's banishing evil from his own life. The citation from Deuteronomy prompts John Chrysostom to explore various divine punishments in the Old Testament and compare them with those described in the New Testament.

1 Corinthians 5:1-5

₁**It is actually reported that there is immorality among you, and of a kind that is not found even among pagans; for a man is living with his father's wife. ₂And you are arrogant! Ought you not rather to mourn? Let him who has done this be removed from among you. ₃For though absent in body I am present in spirit, and as if present, I have already pronounced judgment ₄in the name of the Lord Jesus on the man who has done such a thing. When you are assembled, and my spirit is present, with the power of our Lord Jesus, ₅you are to deliver this man to Satan for the destruction of the flesh, that his spirit may be saved in the day of the Lord Jesus.**

(1) Cyril of Alexandria

It is actually reported that there is immorality among you, and of a kind that is not found even among pagans; for a man is living with his father's wife. Holy Scripture, speaking through the voice of Joel,[2] treats such immortality in Israel: *A man and his father go in to the same maiden, so that my holy name is profaned* (Amos 2:7). This **immorality**, Paul says, **is not even** heard of **among the pagans.** He had probably heard somewhere that Theseus, angry at his own son, cursed and in fact killed him, since he had been slandered by his stepmother.[3]

(2) Origen

For the destruction of the flesh. He is handed over not for the destruction of the soul or of the spirit, but **for the destruction of the flesh.** He is handed over so **that his spirit may be saved in the day of the Lord.** Paul expelled such a person without knowing if he would *turn and repent* (Joel 2:14) but wishing to discipline him. It is one thing to cut off someone on the grounds that he is incapable of repentance and correction, another to reject him for the present and expel him from the flock, as a shepherd casts out a sheep that has a skin disease to prevent its spreading to the whole flock.

2. The text is actually found in Amos.

3. See Euripides' *Hippolytus,* which portrays the love of Phaedra, wife of Theseus, for her stepson Hippolytus. When he rejected her, she falsely accused him of raping her, which led to the young man's death.

Therefore, let those with evil lives be treated by being put outside of the flock, let them confess and lament their own sins and show evidence of repentance by fasting, mourning, weeping, and the like. They are handed over [to Satan] in order to be disciplined, so that **the flesh** might be **destroyed,** that is, *the way of thinking characteristic of the flesh* (Rom 8:6-7). . . .

By naming the man's superior part, Paul refers to his entire salvation; he does not say, "so that his spirit and soul and body might be saved on the day of the Lord," but **that his spirit might be saved,** referring to the salvation of the whole person by that of his most important faculty. In his Second Letter Paul gives orders that this man be taken back into the church in order that he may be saved (2 Cor 2:7).

It is characteristic of Paul and those like him to be **absent in body though present in spirit.** He says elsewhere, *For though I am absent in body, yet I am with you in spirit, rejoicing to see your good order and the firmness of your faith in Christ* (2 Cor 2:7). But none of us can say [if we are physically absent]: "I am present, and I see the excellent qualities of the church, or *your good order and the firmness of your faith in Christ.*" Elisha was like Paul in this. Even though he was not present in body, he went along with his servant Gehazi and asked him: *Did I not go with you in spirit* when you took the two talents of silver and the festal garments from Naaman the Syrian? (see 2 Kings 5:23-26).[4] Now if Elisha possessed this gift, did Paul the apostle of Christ, who *earnestly desired the higher gifts, especially that he might prophesy* (1 Cor 12:31; 14:1) not have the same gift? Indeed, he did; I declare with confidence that Paul was not only an apostle but also a prophet.

1 Corinthians 5:6-8

₆**Your boasting is not good. Do you not know that a little leaven leavens the whole lump?** ₇**Cleanse out the old leaven that you may be a new lump, as you really are unleavened. For Christ, our paschal lamb, has been sacrificed.** ₈**Let us, therefore, celebrate the festival, not with the old leaven, the leaven of malice and evil, but with the unleavened bread of sincerity and truth.**

(1) John Chrysostom

Your boasting is not good. Paul shows that up to the present time they did not allow the offender to repent because of their boasting in him. Then he makes clear that the purpose of expelling this person is not only to spare him but the others as well. That is why he adds: **Do you not know that a little leaven leavens the whole lump?** For, Paul says, even though the sin belongs to that man, if it is overlooked it can destroy the rest of the body of the church: when the one who first sinned is not punished, others will quickly commit the same sins. Paul says these things to show that the struggle affects the whole

---

4. Origen alludes to the aftermath of the story of the prophet Elisha's healing of the Syrian commander Naaman in 2 Kings 5.

church, not just one person. That is why he needed the image of the leaven. For, he says, just as leaven, though small, transforms the whole lump into its own nature, so also if that man and his sin go unpunished, it will bring ruin to the others as well.

Cleanse out the old leaven. That is, that wicked person. Or rather, Paul speaks not only about him but is referring indirectly to the others as well. The **old leaven** is not only sexual immorality but all wickedness. And he did not say "cleanse" but **cleanse out**[5] — cleanse with thoroughness, so that there will be no remnant or shadow of such evil. By saying **cleanse out,** he shows that there is still wickedness among them. And by saying **that you may be a new lump, as you really are unleavened,** he gives a clear indication that the evil did not have power over very many of them. . . .

For Christ, our paschal lamb, has been sacrificed. Let us, therefore, celebrate the festival, not with the old leaven, the leaven of malice and evil, but with the unleavened bread of sincerity and truth. Christ also called teaching *leaven* (Matt 16:6). Paul expands on the metaphor, reminding them of ancient stories, of Passover and the unleavened bread (see Exodus 12) and the blessings received both in those days and now, and also of punishments and retributions.

The present, then, is a time of festival. When Paul said, **let us celebrate the festival,** he did not say this because Passover was at hand, or the feast of Pentecost, but to show that all time is a festal time for Christians, because of the abundance of blessings bestowed on them. What blessing has not come to pass? The Son of God has become man for your sake. He has delivered you from death and called you to the kingdom. Since you have received and are receiving such things, how should you not **celebrate the festival** throughout your whole life? Therefore, let no one be downcast because of poverty or illness or plots against him. For all of our time is festal time. That is why Paul commands, *Rejoice in the Lord always, again I will say, Rejoice* (Phil 4:4).

On feast days no one puts on filthy garments. Therefore, we should not do so either. For a marriage feast has taken place, a spiritual one. *The kingdom of heaven may be compared to a king* who wished to *give a marriage feast for his son* (Matt 22:2). When a king gives a marriage feast, a feast for his son, what could be greater than this? Let no one, then, come clad in rags (see Matt 22:11-14). But I am not talking about clothing, but about impure actions. . . .

This is not the only reason Paul reminds them of the unleavened bread, but also to show the kinship of the Old and New Testaments, and further to show that after eating the unleavened bread, it is not possible to return to Egypt; if anyone wishes to return, he will suffer the same things the Israelites did.[6] For those earlier events were a shadow of these Christian ones. . . .

Let us consider why the leaven is expelled from all the Israelites' borders. What is the hidden meaning? The believer must be freed from all evil. For just as that person perished in whose house **old leaven** was found, so in our case this happens where evil is found. Surely if there was such great punishment in the case of what is a foreshadowing,

5. Chrysostom here calls attention to a prefix on the Greek verb used by Paul that intensifies its meaning.
6. Chrysostom alludes to the forty years of trials the Israelites experienced in the wilderness after their departure from Egypt.

the punishment will be much greater in our case. If the Jews thoroughly cleansed the leaven from their houses, down even to the mouse holes, how much more must we examine our souls, so as to expel every impure thought?

(2) Origen

The one who *puts off the old man with his practices* (Col 3:9) and who has in himself nothing of the **old leaven**, having made the **new lump** in accordance with Christ Jesus — this one has performed the festival of the unleavened bread (see Exod 12:21). Then, after the festival of the unleavened bread, the **new** leaven appears: Jesus Christ is the new leaven. Let us, then, first eat unleavened bread by refraining from any evil or wickedness. Paul teaches about these things when he says: **Cleanse out the old leaven that you may be a new lump, as you really are unleavened.** Just as is done among the Jews, who clean out all the **old leaven** when the day of unleavened bread dawns, and inspect every place in the house in case any leaven should be there, so should you consider the things stored up in you to prevent there being any leaven there, **that you may be a new lump.**

As you really are unleavened. Since there were in Corinth some who were holy and some who were not holy but were sinners — as we said already in commenting on the preface to the letter — Paul says, **as you really are unleavened**, on account of the ones who are worthy of praise.

For Christ, our paschal lamb, has been sacrificed. Because he sees that, according to the law of Moses, first the Passover occurs and the sheep is sacrificed, then after the sheep they eat unleavened bread, Paul says, **Christ, our paschal lamb, has** already **been sacrificed.**

Let us, therefore, celebrate the festival, not with the old leaven, the leaven of malice and evil, but with the unleavened bread of sincerity and truth. Of sincerity: this refers to conduct. **Of truth**: this refers to knowledge. The true unleavened bread is characterized by both of these.

1 Corinthians 5:9-11

₉I wrote to you in my letter not to associate with immoral men; ₁₀not at all meaning the immoral of this world, or the greedy and robbers, or idolaters, since then you would need to go out of the world. ₁₁But rather I wrote to you not to associate with anyone who bears the name of brother if he is guilty of immorality or greed, or is an idolater, reviler, drunkard, or robber — not even to eat with such a one.

(1) Origen

Some suppose, based on this passage, that before this first letter the apostle had written another letter to the Corinthians, which no longer survives, and that in that letter, to judge from the present text, he told them **not to associate with immoral men**. Paul then heard of the confusion of the Corinthians, who thought that they were being told **not to associate with immoral men,** that is, with men of this world — which is impossible since in this life we must associate with non-Christian co-workers, tradesmen, and other such people. So Paul, on this interpretation, clarifies his earlier command and says, "I am not talking about **the immoral of this world** but about those who are called **brothers** even though they are not holy." But others claim there was no other letter before the present one and say that this verse refers to something said in the present letter. They think Paul means: **I wrote to you in** this **letter not to associate with immoral men,** and by **immoral men** I meant another group, not the one you think.

It appears that the apostle compares various kinds of immoral men and finds those in our midst far worse than others. The immoral man who is not a Christian does not *destroy God's temple* (1 Cor 3:17), does not *take the members of Christ and make them members of a prostitute* (1 Cor 6:15), does not *leaven the whole lump* (1 Cor 5:6). The non-Christian, if he wishes, repents and receives remission of his sins, but he who commits fornication after becoming a believer does not receive remission of his sins even though he later repents but can only *cover* them. For Scripture says (Ps 32:1), *Blessed are they whose transgression is forgiven,* that is, those who are converted from paganism, *and those whose sins are covered,* that is, those who sin after receiving faith but who cover their sins with good works, for example, covering their licentiousness by their great chastity. . . .

But rather I wrote to you not to associate with any one who bears the name of brother if he is guilty of immorality. Paul aptly says that such a one is no longer a **brother** except in name. Now as regards such sins, most of us can feel that our consciences are clear. But in the case of the words that follow, I am afraid that somehow I might be found guilty of these other sins. For Paul adds: **or a reviler, drunkard, or robber** — **not even to eat with such a one.** Notice with what serious sinners Paul associates the **reviler**: the **immoral, the greedy, the idolater.** Therefore, the **reviler** is also an enemy of the church. That is why we hear the Lord saying, *Bless those who curse you* (Matt 5:44), and the apostle saying, *When reviled, we bless* (1 Cor 4:12). For a **reviler** *does not inherit the kingdom of God* (1 Cor 6:10). It is essential then, to keep our mouths pure.

(2) Photius

I wrote to you. Where did he write? Where he says: *Ought you not rather to mourn? Let him who has done this be removed from among you* (1 Cor 5:2). He does not specify this one or that one but refers to whatever person is like this. And again he orders, *Cleanse out the old leaven* (1 Cor 5:7), not this leaven or that one but all the *old leaven.* Taking his starting point from the man who had committed sexual sin, Paul moves the discussion to a general level by talking about everyone who is sexually immoral. And then he suggests an even more general point, applying the same commandment to those who commit similar sins, such as those who are **guilty of greed, or idolaters,** or the like.

(3) Augustine

I must not fail to tell you, my brother[7] in Christian love, what has taken place: you prayed with me for this mercy before we received it, and now you may thank God with me that it has been received. I was told after your departure, as I had been told earlier, that some were engaging in riotous feasting and, in spite of the prohibition against it, insisted on celebrating the festival they call Laetitia[8] in a vain attempt to give a fair name to drunkenness. Most opportunely, by the hidden providence of almighty God, it happened that on the fourth day of the feast the Gospel text to be expounded was: *Do not give dogs what is holy; and do not throw your pearls before swine* (Matt 7:6). I talked about dogs and swine in such a way as to force those who obstinately bark against God's ordinances and who give themselves up to the filth of carnal pleasures to blush for shame; I ended by showing them how offensive it was, within the walls of the church, under the name of religion, to engage in behavior which, if regularly practiced by them in their own houses, would necessarily debar them from *that which is holy* and from the *pearls* of the church. . . .

[*Augustine then describes how in a second sermon he cited the story of Jesus' cleansing of the temple and the conduct of the Israelites, who never feasted in their temple.*] Then I handed back the book of Exodus and, in the time I had, enlarged on the crime of drunkenness, taking up the writings of the apostle Paul to show with what sins he classes it. I read this passage: **But rather I wrote to you not to associate with any one who bears the name of brother if he is guilty of immorality or greed, or is an idolater, reviler, drunkard, or robber — not even to eat with such a one.** I reminded them with tears how great a risk we were running if we ate even with those who get drunk in their own houses. I also read a passage that comes a little later in the epistle: *Do not be deceived; neither the immoral, nor idolaters, nor adulterers, nor sexual perverts, nor thieves, nor the greedy, nor drunkards, nor revilers, nor robbers will inherit the kingdom of God. And such were some of you. But you were washed, you were sanctified, you were justified in the name of the Lord Jesus Christ and in the Spirit of our God* (6:9-11). After reading these passages, I told them to consider how believers could listen to the words *But you were washed* if they still allowed their own hearts — that is, God's inner temple — to be defiled by the kind of lusts excluded from the kingdom of heaven. Then I turned to this passage: *When you meet together, it is not the Lord's supper that you eat. For in eating, each one goes ahead with his own meal, and one is hungry and another is drunk. What! Do you not have houses to eat and drink in? Or do you despise the church of God?* (1 Cor 11:20-22). After reading this, I laid stress on the point that not even decorous and sober feasts should be held in the church, since the apostle asks, not "Do you not have houses to get drunk in?" (as if it was only drunkenness that was not allowed in the church), but *Do you not have houses to eat and to drink in?* Eating and drinking are blameless in themselves, but not allowed in the church when people have houses for taking their necessary nourishment. Yet we have been reduced to such corruption and laxity that we no longer insist on moderation in feasting but merely try to confine excess to the home. . . .

7. Augustine's old friend Alypius, who was bishop of Thagaste, not far from Hippo.
8. That is, "Joy." Augustine is talking about a feast the African churches held in honor of Leontius, a bishop of Hippo in the second century.

[*In a section omitted here, Augustine describes how the next morning, the feast day of Bishop Leontius, he responded to the continued feasting by inviting his congregation to assemble at noon to celebrate the feast in an appropriate way, with the singing of psalms.*] In the afternoon a greater crowd gathered than in the morning, and reading alternated with singing up to the hour at which I was to appear with the bishop [Valerius]; after our arrival, two psalms were read. Then, although I did not want to and would gladly have seen such a critical day come to an end, the old bishop ordered me to say something to the people. I delivered a short discourse giving thanks to God. And since we heard the noise of the heretics' usual feasting issuing from their church, heretics who lingered in their cups while we were listening to the psalms, I said that just as the beauty of day is heightened by contrast with night and the pleasingness of white increases when black is next to it, so our spiritual feast would have been less sweet to us if it had not been contrasted with sensual gluttony. I told them that they should eagerly desire feasts like theirs, seeing that they had tasted how sweet the Lord is (see Ps 34:8). But, I added, those who seek as their chief good something that will one day be destroyed should be afraid. . . . I said everything on this subject that the Lord gave me to say, and the regular daily evening worship was held. As the bishop and I were leaving the church, the brethren remained and sang a hymn, and a considerable multitude of both sexes stayed in the church and sang psalms until sunset.

1 Corinthians 5:12-13

12**For what have I to do with judging outsiders? Is it not those inside the church whom you are to judge?** 13**God judges those outside. "Drive out the wicked person from among you"** (Deut 17:7).

(1) Origen

Paul assigned to all of us the task of judging sinners inside the church. We bring the sin to the bishop, so that such a person might be lawfully expelled from the church.

Drive out the wicked person from among you. On the one hand, this means **drive out the wicked person** from their midst. But make sure that in your willingness to **drive out the wicked person**, you recognize that you have a wicked person within yourself. Therefore, spare no effort to **drive out the wicked person** from yourself. For when he departs, Christ Jesus will dwell within you.

(2) John Chrysostom

Drive out the wicked person from among you. Paul mentions a verse from the Old Testament to show two things: first, that the Corinthians will reap substantial benefit from this, as if they were delivered from a terrible plague; and second, that this is not an innovation, but that from the beginning the giver of the law thought it good that such people should be cut off. In the Old Testament this was done with greater severity; here, however, there is a milder way. . . . There the adulterer and the murderer are immediately put to death,[9] whereas here, if they are cleansed through repentance, they escape punishment. In the New Testament, nonetheless, one can see examples of more severe punishments and in the Old of milder ones, which shows that throughout the two covenants are closely related to each other and come from the same lawgiver. And in both testaments one sometimes sees punishments that are immediate, but at other times the punishments come long afterward. And often they do not occur at all, even long afterward, if God is satisfied with repentance alone. And in fact in the Old Testament David, after committing adultery and murder, was saved through repentance (see 2 Samuel 12), but in the New Testament Ananias perished with his wife because he kept back a small portion of the price of the field (Acts 5:1-11).

9. See, for example, Lev 20:10-16.

1 Corinthians 6

In chapter 6 Paul takes up other problems in the church in Corinth. He criticizes the Corinthians for bringing their disputes into pagan lawcourts instead of adjudicating them themselves (vv. 1-6) and then goes on to say that bringing lawsuits in any court is a serious moral failing (vv. 7-8). John Chrysostom, paying close attention to Paul's choice of words, points out that Paul calls the pagan judges "the unrighteous," not simply "unbelievers" (v. 1). Construing the preposition in verse 2 to mean "in," not "by" as most interpreters do, he says that "the world is to be judged in you" means that the Christians' righteous lives provide the standard according to which others are judged. Severian understands the "angels" whom the saints are to judge (v. 3) as false teachers, citing as evidence a text from Malachi that calls wicked priests "angels." Theodoret seeks to explain how Paul's advice to avoid pagan courts squares with his command to obey the ruling powers in Romans 13: in verses 7-8 Paul gives what Theodoret calls "the more perfect commandment" — to avoid lawsuits entirely and choose to suffer injustice instead. To show how suffering injustice willingly can be a victory, Chrysostom cites the examples of Job, Paul, and Christ himself.

In verses 9-11 Paul adduces a list of unrighteous actions that will bring exclusion from the kingdom of God and reminds the Corinthians that, although they may have been guilty of such things in the past, in baptism they have been "washed, sanctified, and made righteous." Origen relates this discussion of "the unrighteous" to Paul's assertion in 1 Cor 1:30 that Christ is "righteousness"; he equates being in the "kingdom of God" with being "in Christ."

The chapter concludes with a discussion of another specific problem, the claim of certain Corinthians that they are free to do whatever they want, including sleeping with prostitutes (vv. 12-20). Paul begins his response with these words: "All things are lawful for me" (v. 12). Theodoret reads this as a question. Augustine and Oecumenius puzzle over why Paul singles out sexual immorality as a sin against one's own body (v. 18). To encourage holy conduct, Paul reminds the Corinthians that they are "the body of Christ" and the "temple of the Holy Spirit" (v. 19). Augustine relates Paul's high regard for Christians' bodies to the high valuation of the human body expressed in the incarnation of Christ. Chrysostom explains Paul's concluding exhortation to "glorify God in your body" (v. 20) by noting the many ways in which the virtuous servant of God can inspire others to praise God.

1 Corinthians 6:1-6

₁When one of you has a grievance against a brother, does he dare go to law before the unrighteous instead of the saints? ₂Do you not know that the saints will judge the world? And if the world is to be judged by you,[1] are you incompetent to try trivial cases? ₃Do you not know that we are to judge angels? How much more, matters pertaining to this life! ₄If then you have such cases, why do you lay them before those who are least esteemed by the church? ₅I say this to your shame. Can it be that there is no man among you wise enough to decide between members of the brotherhood, ₆but brother goes to law against brother, and that before unbelievers?

(1) John Chrysostom

Observe how Paul speaks. He does not say "before the unbelievers" but **before the unrighteous,** using an expression appropriate for the point he is discussing, in order to draw them away from pagan courts. Since his subject was judgment and since those who go to court desire above all that the judges have a genuine concern for what is just, he uses this phrase to dissuade them, saying in effect, "Where are you hurrying off to and what are you doing, my friend? Your desire leads to the reverse of what you are seeking, and you are entrusting yourself to unjust men in order to obtain justice." Because it would offend them to be told at the outset not to go to court, he does not put this idea forward at once but merely suggests a change in the judges, leading litigants away from pagan judges to those within the church.

At that time, more than was the case later on, it was considered disgraceful to make use of Christian judges — perhaps because they were not competent to resolve cases, not being trained in law and in rhetoric as pagan judges were. For most of them had little education. Notice, therefore, how Paul presents them as trustworthy: he begins by calling them **saints.**

But since this term attests to the purity of their lives, not to their skill in hearing cases, notice how carefully he handles this point as well, when he asks, **Do you not know that the saints will judge the world?** You then, who are going to judge the unrighteous at that time, how can you now put up with being judged by them? The saints will not judge by sitting as judges and demanding an account; rather, they will be the source of condemnation. Paul makes this clear when he asks, **And if the world is to judged in you, are you incompetent to try trivial cases?** He did not say, "by you," but **in you**, as when Jesus said, *The queen of the South will arise and condemn this generation* (Matt 12:42), and *The men of Nineveh will arise and condemn this generation* (Matt 12:41). For when it is made plain that all behold the same sun and share in the same things but that we were believers while others lacked faith, they will not be able to take refuge in a claim of ignorance. For we will condemn them by the very deeds we have done.

1. Or "in you"; see the commentary of John Chrysostom.

(2) Severian of Gabala

Whereas earlier Paul had said, *Is it not those inside the church whom you are to judge? God judges those outside* (1 Cor 5:12-13), here he makes the entire **world** subject to the judgment of the saints. In the former passage they judge the lives of believers in order to correct them. Here they are entrusted with judgment of the world, not in order to correct sinful ways but to expose and condemn them. The twelve apostles will judge the twelve tribes (Matt 19:28) since they are Jews descended from those Jews who believed in the prophets. The tribes, however, did not believe in the prophets, and for this reason they rejected the Christ. The other saints, that is, the Gentile Christians, will pass judgment on those who did not turn from idols and believe in the true God. Thus there is no disagreement between the Evangelist and the apostle — for Christ was speaking in both. It is written, *The queen of the South will arise at the judgment with this generation and condemn it,* and *The men of Nineveh will rise up and condemn* you (Matt 12:42, 41). . . .

Now by **angels** Paul means not actual angels, but subordinate priests, teachers of the people. It is reasonable for these to be judged by **the saints** for teaching false things about the Christ. When Paul exclaims, **How much more, matters pertaining to this life!** he shows that he was not speaking of actual angels, but about those who have the rank of angels and have spiritual occupations. But if he does mean **angels** in the proper sense, clearly he is referring to the apostate angels, who had fallen away from God.[2] But the priests are called **angels** by Malachi, who says: *For the lips of a priest will guard knowledge, and men will seek instruction from his mouth, for he is the messenger of the LORD of hosts* (Mal 2:7). We are the judges of those priests who lead the people astray, as we are of the fathers of heresies and those who have perverted the teaching of Christ.

(3) Theodoret

Paul points out that the most insignificant member of the church is better than those whom outsiders consider expert. But he is not ordering that the most insignificant in the church should serves as judges, as the following verses make this clear: **I say this to your shame. Can it be that there is no man among you wise enough to decide between members of the brotherhood, but brother goes to law against brother, and that before unbelievers?**

He points out many absurdities. First, that a believer should go to court. (For by **brother** Paul means a believer). Then, that he brings a case against a fellow believer. But the most serious offense is that Christians go before a judge who is an unbeliever. We must realize, however, that these things do not contradict what Paul wrote to the Romans. There Paul orders us not to resist our rulers (Rom 13:1-2), but here he commands victims of injustice not to go before these rulers. They could decide whether to suffer injustice or be tried by fellow believers. After this (v. 7) he introduces the more perfect commandment: to refrain from all lawsuits.

---

2. For stories of fallen angels, see 1 Enoch 6–16, which is an interpretation of Gen 6:1-4.

1 Corinthians 6:7-8

7To have lawsuits at all with one another is defeat for you. Why not rather suffer wrong? Why not rather be defrauded? 8But you yourselves wrong and defraud, and that even your own brethren.

(1) John Chrysostom

If you commit an injustice, it is clear that you cannot be righteous. But if you suffer wrong and endure it (for this is characteristic of a righteous person), you have no need of pagan laws. Someone will ask, "How can I put up with being wronged?" Yet Christ enjoined something greater than this. He ordered us not only to put up with being wronged but also to give lavishly to the one who wrongs us and, in our eagerness to suffer, to outdo his desire to treat us badly. Christ did not simply say, "If any one would sue you and take your coat, let him have your coat," but *Give your cloak as well* (Matt 5:40). *Overcome him,* Jesus commands, *by suffering evil, not by doing it.* This is the clear and splendid victory.

This is why Paul goes on to say, **To have lawsuits at all with one another is defeat for you. Why not rather suffer wrong? Why not rather be defrauded? . . .** If you endure the injustice, you are victorious; you are deprived of money but not of the victory won by a disciplined life. Your opponent cannot compel you to do what you do not wish to do. Here is the proof: tell me, who was victorious, the envious one [i.e., Satan] or the one on the dunghill (Job 1–2; 42)? Who was defeated, Job who was robbed of everything, or the devil who robbed him? Clearly the devil who robbed him. Whose victory do we admire, that of the devil who afflicted Job, or that of Job who was afflicted? Clearly Job, even though he could not hold onto his perishable wealth or save his children. And why do I speak of wealth and children? Job could not even protect his own body. But nonetheless Job, who lost all his possessions, is the victorious one. He could not hold onto his money, but he held onto his piety with the utmost strictness. . . .

If it were an evil thing to suffer injustice, God would not have told us to do it, for God does not enjoin what is evil. Do you not know that he is the God of glory? He does not wish to cover us with shame and ridicule and loss but to give us the opposite of these. For this reason he orders us to suffer injustice, and he does everything he can to separate us from worldly things and to make us see what is glory and what is shame, what is loss and what is gain (Phil 3:7).

But someone will say, "It is a terrible thing to suffer wrong and be maltreated." No, my friend, it is not terrible, not at all. How long will you be distressed about present things? God would not have commanded this if it were terrible. Consider this: the one who has committed injustice leaves the court with money but with a bad conscience, but the one who has suffered injustice, even if he is deprived of his money, has confidence before God, a possession more precious than countless treasures. . . .

But someone will object, "What are you saying? I have been deprived of all my possessions; do you order me to keep silent? I was maltreated; do you exhort me to bear it meekly? How can I?" You are quite mistaken; it is easy, if you look up to heaven, if you behold its beauty and see where God has promised to receive you if you suffer injustice nobly. Look up to heaven, therefore, and, as you do so, consider that you have become like the One who sits there above the cherubim (see Heb 9:5, 25). He too was insulted and bore it, he too was reproached and did not seek revenge, he was struck and did not strike (Matt 26:67-68). He repaid his enemies, who had done such things, with innumerable acts of kindness, and he ordered us to be imitators of him. Consider that you came naked from your mother's womb, and you will return naked — both you and the one who has done you wrong. In fact, your oppressor will depart with countless wounds, which produce worms. Consider that present things are temporary; take note of the tombs of your ancestors. Observe clearly what has happened, and you will see that the one who wronged you has made you stronger. He has made his own passion fiercer — I mean his love of money — but he has weakened your passion by taking away what nourishes that wild beast. Further, he has set you free from anxious thoughts, struggles, the envy of slanderers, trouble, upset, and constant worry. And this mass of evils he has heaped upon his own head.

"What, then, if I am gripped by hunger?" someone will ask. You suffer this in company with Paul, who says: *Up to the present hour we hunger and thirst and are poorly clad* (1 Cor 4:11). "But Paul did it because of God," you will object. You too should do it because of God. For when you do not go on the attack, you do this for the sake of God. "But the one who treated me unjustly lives in luxury with the wealthy." No, rather, with the devil. But you win your crown along with Paul.

1 Corinthians 6:9-11

9Do you not know that the unrighteous will not inherit the kingdom of God? Do not be deceived; neither the immoral, nor idolaters, nor adulterers, nor effeminate men nor those men who sleep with men,³ 10nor thieves, nor the greedy, nor drunkards, nor revilers, nor robbers will inherit the kingdom of God. 11And such were some of you. But you were washed, you were sanctified, you were justified in the name of the Lord Jesus Christ and in the Spirit of our God.

(1) Origen

If the **kingdom of God** is in Christ and Christ is *righteousness* (1 Cor 1:30), then the righteous person inherits the **kingdom of God** in Christ, who is righteousness. It follows that the person who is in the opposite state [i.e., unrighteousness] does not **inherit the kingdom of God**.

Do not be deceived. Neither the immoral, and what follows. *Let no one deceive you with* persuasive *words* (Eph 5:6; 1 John 3:7), saying: "God is merciful, kind, and benevolent. He forgives sins." *We all must appear before the judgment seat of Christ, so that each*

---

3. The RSV combines two terms in v. 9 and translates them together as "sexual perverts." Here they are rendered separately.

one may receive good or evil, according to what he has done in the body (2 Cor 5:10). Let no one make excuses: "I was young, I was unmarried, I committed sexual sin before I married." But why did you not marry? Do you not believe that *if someone destroys the temple of God, God will destroy him* (1 Cor 3:17)? Do you *take the members of Christ and make them members of a prostitute* (1 Cor 6:15)? A person who commits sexual sin commits impiety against the Lord of the universe.

Neither the immoral, nor idolaters, nor adulterers: The person who commits sexual sin *destroys God's temple* (1 Cor 3:17). Additionally, the man who commits adultery sins against the woman's husband. This is why Paul says, **nor adulterers**. But **effeminate men** will not inherit either. Therefore, I exhort you, too, O children, to keep your youth pure and not to *be defiled* with such a womanish defilement (Rev 14:4). **Nor those men who sleep with men . . . will inherit the kingdom of God.** But far be it from us that even one such person be found in the church. Next Paul goes on to what seem to be lesser sins when he says, **Nor thieves.**

1 Corinthians 6:12-14

12All things are lawful for me,[4] but not all things are helpful. All things are lawful for me, but I will not be enslaved by anything. 13Food is meant for the stomach and the stomach for food — and God will destroy both one and the other. The body is not meant for immorality, but for the Lord, and the Lord for the body. 14And God raised the Lord and will also raise us up by his power.

(1) Theodoret

Are all things lawful for me? We must understand this as a question. Then Paul says in reply, **But not all things are helpful.** So too the next words: **Are all things lawful for me? But I will not be enslaved by anything.** You may say "all things are lawful" because you do not live under the law and have free will and your judgment is independent. But it is not beneficial to use your liberty in every case. When you do something wicked, you renounce your authority and become a slave of sin.

Food is meant for the stomach and the stomach for food — and God will destroy both one and the other. If you wish to use your liberty in these matters, do so. For food was created for the sake of the belly. Yet you should be aware that these things will have an end. After death food is superfluous, and the life to come has no need of it. Just as, in our Lord's words, *they do not marry, nor are they given in marriage* (Matt 22:30), so they do not eat or drink. Paul has used the word **will destroy** in a prophetic sense.

---

4. The RSV places the phrase "all things are lawful for me" in vv. 12 and 13 and "food is meant for the stomach and the stomach for food" in v. 13 in quotation marks because the translators regard them as quotations of something said by the Christians in Corinth. Here the quotation marks are omitted because the patristic commentary does not understand the phrases in this way. Theodoret takes the first phrase as a question.

The body is not for immorality but for the Lord, and the Lord is for the body. Paul often calls the Lord our *head* (see Eph 1:22; 4:15). Now the body is joined to him as the head. Although the stomach was made as a receptacle for food, the body has not been created for the sake of sexual immorality.

And God raised the Lord and will also raise us up by his power. Do not be contemptuous of the Master as if he were a dead man. For he has been raised. And the God who raised him will also raise us by the power of the One who was raised up. He shows clearly that he was raised in human fashion, but it is like God that he will raise us up.

(2) Severian of Gabala

The words **by anything** do not refer to people but to wicked deeds and passions. Paul speaks in the first person to encourage others to practice self-control. Since he knows that the belly is the cause of their greed — for most people will do anything for the sake of the pleasures of the stomach — he teaches that it is misguided to serve the belly. We know that **food is** appointed **for the stomach** and the stomach for food. Nonetheless these things are temporary, and God will bring them to an end; after the resurrection, when we are granted immortality, food will be superfluous. Why, then, are you eager for transient things, which lead to sexual immorality and wicked pleasures? It is clear that food and eating are transient. But **the body is not** appointed **for immorality, but for the Lord, and the Lord for the body.** And the body is not transient but will be raised to eternity following the model of Christ.

1 Corinthians 6:15-18

15Do you not know that your bodies are members of Christ? Shall I therefore take the members of Christ and make them members of a prostitute? Never! 16Do you not know that he who joins himself to a prostitute becomes one body with her? For, as it is written, "The two shall become one flesh" [Gen 2:24]. 17But he who is united to the Lord becomes one spirit with him. 18Shun immorality. Every other sin which a man commits is outside the body; but the immoral man sins against his own body.

(1) Augustine

We have heard the words of the apostle rebuking and checking human lusts and asserting, **Do you not know that your bodies are members of Christ? Shall I therefore take the members of Christ and make them members of a prostitute? Never!** He says that our bodies are members of Christ, for Christ is our *head* since he became man for our sake, the head of which it is said: *He himself is the savior of our body* (Eph 5:23). But his body is the Church (Col 1:18). If, therefore, our Lord Jesus Christ had taken on only a human soul, only our souls would be members of him. But he has taken a body, by which he became our *head* since we consist of soul and body; therefore, our bodies are also members of him.

So if anyone, from a desire to commit fornication, had little value in his own eyes and was despising himself, let him not despise Christ in himself. Let him not say, I will do it, I am of no account, for *all flesh is grass* (Isa 40:6). Your body is a member of Christ. Where were you headed? Come back! From what precipice were you eager to hurl yourself? Have mercy on Christ in yourself, recognize Christ in yourself! **Shall I therefore take the members of Christ and make them members of a prostitute?** The prostitute is the one who agrees to commit adultery with you. Perhaps she is a Christian and takes the members of Christ and makes them members of an adulterer. You are despising Christ in each other, failing to recognize your Lord or to consider the *price* with which you were bought (1 Cor 6:20). What sort of Lord is one who makes his slaves into his brothers? Yet "brothers" was too little for him — he made us into his **members.** Is being so highly valued of so little account? It was conferred on us so graciously: shall it not be treated respectfully? If this gift were not given to us, we would wish it given; shall we, because it is given, treat it with contempt?

But these bodies of ours, which the apostle calls **members of Christ** — since he took a body of the same nature as ours — these bodies are described by the same apostle as the *temple* within us *of the Holy Spirit,* whom we have received from God (1 Cor 6:19). Because of Christ's body, our bodies are members of Christ; because of the indwelling spirit of Christ, our bodies are a temple of the Holy Spirit. Which of these two things within you will you treat with contempt? Christ, whose member you are, or the Holy Spirit, whose temple you are? . . .

Perhaps a wicked man, unjust, adulterous, shameless, and a fornicator, rejoices in what he does, grows old (though his lust does not), and asks himself, "Is it really true that *the face of the Lord is against evildoers, to cut off the remembrance of them from the earth*" (Ps 34:16)? Here I am, an old man, one who from my earliest youth up to the present has done so many wicked deeds, and I have buried many chaste men before me — even leading the funeral procession of many chaste young men. I have outlived, rogue that I am, many virtuous men. What do the words *the face of the Lord is against evildoers, to cut off the remembrance of them from the earth* really amount to?" But there is another land where no fornicator dwells, there is another land in the kingdom of God. *Do not be deceived; neither the immoral, nor idolaters, nor adulterers, nor effeminate men, nor those who sleep with men, nor thieves, nor the greedy, nor drunkards, nor revilers, nor robbers will inherit the kingdom of God* (1 Cor 6:9-10). This means that he will *cut off the remembrance of them from the earth.* Many who commit such sins feel hopeful. It is because of those who live immoral lives and yet hope for the kingdom of God, a place they will never reach, that Scripture says, *he will cut off the remembrance of them from the earth.* There will be a new heaven and a new earth (Rev 21:1), which the righteous will inhabit. The godless, the wicked, the impure will not be allowed to live there. Anyone who is like this should choose now where he wants to live, for there are two dwelling places, one in eternal fire, the other in the eternal kingdom. . . .

Nevertheless, if you avoid adultery because you are afraid of burning in eternal fire, you do not yet deserve praise. To be sure, we need not grieve for you, as we did before, but you do not yet deserve praise. . . . I ask you, if God did not see you commit fornication and no one could convict you of it in his courtroom, would you still do it? Each of you should see to himself. You cannot reply to all my words but must consider yourself. Would you do it? If you would, you are afraid of punishment but do not yet have love. You are afraid the way a slave is afraid. What motivates you is fear of the bad, not love of the good. Nevertheless, go on fearing so that this fear may be your guardian and bring you to love. The fear of hell that keeps you from sinning acts as a restraint. Though your inner self wants to sin, fear does not allow it to. Just as the law once served as a pedagogue or tutor, fear is a kind of guardian (Gal 3:24). Fear is the threatening letter of the law, not the grace that aids us. But let this fear keep watch over you as you refrain from wrongdoing, and in time love will arrive. Insofar as it enters your heart, fear departs. It was fear that kept you from doing wrong; but love wills no wrong even if it could be done with impunity.

I have said what you should fear and what you should desire. Follow after love; let love enter. At first receive her into yourself by being afraid to sin, receive a love that does not sin, a love that lives a virtuous life. . . . When she has fully entered, there will be no more fear, for *perfect love casts out fear* (1 John 4:18).

The topic before us is the passage in 1 Corinthians where Paul says, **Every other sin which a man commits is outside the body; but the fornicator sins against his own body.** I do not know if the difficulties in this text can be completely cleared up, though with the Lord's help a possible solution may be given; the water is deep here. . . .

The difficulty is this: isn't it impossible to commit the other vices and crimes [mentioned in 6:9-11 and 15] apart from the body? What reasonable person would deny that this is so? The body has been bought with the precious blood of Christ and made a temple of the Holy Spirit (1 Cor 6:19-20). The apostle in this whole passage has been defending it from being polluted with such vices, to keep it as God's inviolate habitation. So why does he add these words, the source of our difficulty: **Every other sin which a man commits is outside the body; but the immoral man sins against his own body?** For the other sins of this kind, which are similar in impurity to fornication, are also performed through the body. . . .

It seems that the blessed apostle, through whom Christ was speaking, wished to make the evil of fornication greater than other sins. These others, although they are committed through the body, do not bind and subjugate the human soul to fleshly lust as the overpowering force of sexual desire does. Only the sexual act makes the soul mingle with the body, fastening the one to the other with a kind of glue. The result is that the person engaged in such vice has a mind submerged and drowned in carnal lust and can think of or intend nothing else. . . .

So much, then, about fornication in the specific and bodily sense. But since fornication is used in Scripture not only in this specific sense but also with a more general meaning, let us try, with God's help, to say something plausible on this subject as well. Fornication in a more general sense is clearly indicated by the psalm, where it is said, *For lo, those who are far from thee shall perish; thou dost put an end to those who fornicate against you* (Ps 73:27). Then the psalmist goes on to show how such fornication can be avoided and shunned when he says, *But for me it is good to cleave to God* (Ps 73:28). From this we can easily see that fornication of the human soul, in an extended sense, means not cleaving to God but cleaving to the world. . . . Whenever someone does not cleave to God but cleaves to the world, loving and lusting after temporal things, it is proper to say that he **sins against his own body**; that is, he is devoted and given over to universal fleshly lust. He is completely the slave of the creature and alienated from the Creator because of that pride which is the origin of all sin, the pride whose beginning, as Scripture says, is *to depart from the Lord* (Sir 10:12).

(2) Oecumenius

[**Every other sin which a man commits is outside the body; but the immoral man sins against his own body.**] One explanation of why Paul says this is that the other sins have an additional cause in the passion of the soul, for example, in anger that leads to murder or vanity that leads to a desire for wealth. But for sexual immorality the body is the source of the desire. Paul wants to emphasize the seriousness of sexual immorality since this is the subject of his present exhortation. But it is not the case that sexual immorality is the worst of all sins.

The holy Severian[5] . . . gives several interpretations of this verse, one that he says is identical with that of the sainted John Chrysostom, and another one. His first interpretation is that the person who commits sexual immorality sins against his own human frame and against the formation of the body and insults the womb in which his body is formed. Alternatively, the human being is **the body of Christ** and his parts are **members of Christ** (1 Cor 6:15; 12:12). So he who sins against his own body sins against Christ, our *head* (Eph 1:22; Col 1:18), whose *temple* the body is (1 Cor 6:19).

Along with all these interpretations, consider the following, if you will. Paul, who wishes to emphasize the seriousness of sexual immorality, wants to say something like this: that the fornicator deserves limitless punishment — for how can one who does not keep from defiling his own body keep from defiling another's? If a person does evil to himself, how can he be good to another?

Another interpretation: it is written about man and woman: **The two shall become one flesh** (Gen 2:24). If a man does not rely on lawful and godly marriage but commits fornication — despite the commandment to hold marriage *in honor* and the marriage bed *undefiled* (Heb 13:4) — by his fornication and the resultant impurity he insults both marriage and his wife. The person who does this sins against his own body since he sins against his wife, who is **one body** with her husband, just as she is his rib and as she was taken from him (Gen 2:21-23). . . .

There is another interpretation by the holy Athanasius in his treatise "Concerning Holy Marriage."[6] And, in addition to all these interpretations, someone else proposes the following: Paul, who is writing to people who live luxurious lives and love the flesh,

5. Severian of Gabala (fl. ca. 400) was an exegete of the Antiochene school. See Appendix 1.
6. Now lost. Staab, *Pauluskommentar,* 435, suggests that the work in question was a homily.

makes use of their love of the flesh to dissuade them from fornication. He says that while other sins harm the soul alone, the person who commits immorality wrongs his body along with his soul, corrupting and weakening it and destroying its natural and lively vigor, as if to say, "Spare your bodies: honor and cherish them and look out for them."

One might ask: Doesn't envy cause the body to waste away? Why, then, does Paul say that only fornication does this? The apostle expresses himself very carefully. For he says, **Every other sin which a person commits is outside the body.** Envy is not something we "do," but it works on us. We are subject to envy, then, but we do not *commit* envy. It is an emotion, not an action. But in this text Paul is talking about actions — for he says, **Every other sin which a person commits** — not emotions.

1 Corinthians 6:19-20

19**Do you not know that your body is a temple of the Holy Spirit within you, which you have from God? You are not your own;** 20**you were bought with a price. So glorify God in your body.**

(1) Theodoret

You were bought with a price. The Lord's blood has been shed for your sake. We belong to another. Paul adds these words to *All things are lawful for me* (1 Cor 6:12) to teach that we belong to a master, and we must live according to his laws. He adds, **glorify God in your body and in your spirit, which are from God.**[7] God is the creator of both our souls and our bodies. And he has not only made them but also freed them from the power of the devil. We must therefore glorify him both through the body and through the soul, doing and saying what will lead all to praise him.

By this time the apostle has established his first point. But let us remember his exhortation, and let us both *present* our *bodies as a living sacrifice, holy and pleasing to God* (Rom 12:1) and also sanctify our souls by the memory of his many and various benefactions. Then we may be truly called temples of God in the present life and enjoy his promised blessings, by the grace and benevolence of our Lord Jesus Christ, to whom with the Father and the Holy Spirit belong glory and magnificence, now and always, forever and ever. Amen.

(2) John Chrysostom

So glorify God in your body. This is the reason that in the Lord's Prayer we are bidden to say, *Hallowed be thy name* (Matt 6:9). And Christ also says, *Let your light so shine before men, that they may see your good works and give glory to your Father who is in heaven* (Matt

---

7. Theodoret, along with several Greek manuscripts, has a longer version of v. 20.

5:16). In the same way the heavens also **glorify** God, not because they speak but because the sight of them inspires wonder and they render glory to the Creator (see Ps 19:1-4).

In the same way let us also glorify him, or, rather, let us do so even more than the heavens do. We can do this, if we are willing. A holy soul glorifies God far more than heaven, day, or night does. Just as someone who looks at the beauty of heaven says, "Glory be to you, O God, for great is the work you have created," so when he sees the virtue of a man, he will glorify God even more. Not everyone glorifies God on account of seeing his creation. Many say that the world arose by chance, while others commit a great and unpardonable sin by attributing the creation and care of the world to demons. But a virtuous person cannot be ignored: when someone sees a servant of God living virtuously, he will always glorify God.

Who will not be amazed when a human being who shares our common nature and lives in our midst is as unyielding as steel in the face of the passions that beset him? Or who, when surrounded by fire and sword and wild beasts, proves stronger than iron and conquers all because of his godliness? Or when treated shamefully, blesses (Luke 6:28; 1 Cor 4:12)? Or when slandered, responds with praises? Or when mistreated, prays for those who treat him unjustly (Luke 6:28)? Or when plotted against, does good to the enemies who contrive against him? These things and others like them will glorify God much more than the heavens do.

When the Greeks behold the heavens, they are not humbled. But when they see a holy man living a conscientious and disciplined life, they retreat and condemn themselves. For when one who shares their nature is far better than they — further even than the heavens are above the earth — the Greek must admit, against his will, that a divine power produces these results. For this reason Jesus says, *And that they might give glory to your Father who is in heaven* (Matt 5:16).

Would you like to learn from another source how God is glorified by the life of his servants as well as by miracles? Nebuchadnezzar once put the three youths into the furnace. When he saw that the fire did not prevail over them, he said, *Blessed be God, who has sent his angel and delivered his servants from the furnace, because they put their trust in him and set at nought the king's command* (Dan 3:28 LXX). What will you say, O Nebuchadnezzar? When you are treated with contempt — do you show honor to those who spit upon you? "Yes," he says, "I do, for this very reason, that they did not honor me." This provoked his admiration. Thus it was not only because of the miracle that God received glory on that occasion, but also because of the righteous acts of those who were thrown into the furnace.

1 Corinthians 7

Patristic commentary on this chapter reflects the wide influence of the ascetic ideal in the early centuries of the Church, evident, for example, in the many treatises on virginity composed by fathers such as Athanasius, Ambrose, John Chrysostom, and Gregory of Nyssa (see especially the commentary on vv. 32-35). Most commentators, taking their clue from verse 38 where Paul says that marriage is "good" but remaining single is "better," agree that the celibate life is superior to married life. Nonetheless, there is strong opposition to groups such as the Marcionites and the Manicheans, who totally rejected marriage on the grounds that it was an institution of the inferior creator god (see Origen and Augustine on vv. 1-7 and Theodoret on vv. 36-40). The fathers insist that celibacy is motivated not by hatred of the created world but rather by a desire to serve the loving Creator with undivided attention.

Within this widespread consensus, some fathers give a more positive assessment of marriage than others. Clement of Alexandria devotes a whole book of his Miscellanies *to a discussion of marriage and sex, in which he takes strong exception to Gnostic groups who depreciate marriage. He points out that the apostles Peter and Philip were married and even suggests, on the basis of Paul's reference to his "consort" (or "yokefellow") in Phil 4:3, that Paul himself was married. Like other fathers, however, Clement sees sexual desire as a threat to the spiritual life. He advocates continence within marriage and, like many other fathers, says that sexual relations are allowable only for the purpose of procreation (see his comments on vv. 1-7). Origen views marriage as a "concession" (v. 6) to those who are too weak to observe sexual purity but admits that marriage is a "special gift" (v. 7) that can foster the virtue of "harmony."*

The Roman monk Jovinian (quoted in Jerome's comments on vv. 1-7) aroused Jerome's ire by arguing that married and celibate Christians have equal merit, a position he supports by quoting verse 39 ("A wife is bound to her husband as long as he lives. If the husband dies, she is free to be married to whom she wishes, only in the Lord"), along with Heb 13:4 and several passages from 1 Timothy. In response, Jerome gives an interpretation of 1 Corinthians 7 that emphasizes verse 1: "It is well for a man not to touch a woman." From this Jerome concludes: "If it is good not to touch a woman, it is bad to touch one." Augustine agrees with Jerome about the merit of celibacy but argues that, according to verse 38, marriage is still a "good," not just the lesser of two evils. He presents marriage as an indissoluble bond and gives a positive picture of the social and spiritual companionship offered by marriage (see the comments on vv. 1-7 and 10-11).

Paul says in verse 5 that married people are to refrain from sexual relations only for limited periods, so as to devote themselves to prayer. From this verse Origen concludes that the prayers of the celibate are purer than those of people who have conjugal relations. John Chrysostom, on the other hand, argues that the point of this verse is that Christians should have time for zealous devotion to prayer; Paul is not talking about different degrees of purity. Both these fathers emphasize that in the matter of sexual relations, Paul treats wives and husbands equally (v. 4). Augustine calls attention to Paul's statement that the wife has authority over her husband's body, which was a surprising thing to say in a time when husbands were clearly "masters" of their wives.

This chapter from 1 Corinthians also figured in patristic discussions of second marriage, which many fathers discouraged (see Clement of Alexandria on vv. 12-14 and Theodoret on vv. 36-40). Tertullian cites the chapter in a letter to his wife in which he advises her not to remarry in the case of his death; he argues against certain interpreters who claim that Paul even allows a second marriage to an unbeliever (on vv. 12-14).

The lessons the fathers found in this chapter were not limited to the areas of marriage and sexual relations. Clement of Alexandria uses verses 1-5 and 9 to argue that continence is not only a matter of sexual practice but should be reflected in the whole of life. John Chrysostom elaborates on Paul's words about slavery and freedom in verses 21-23 by considering the story of Joseph and Potiphar's wife: although Joseph was a slave in the pharaoh's house, he was truly free, while the woman who desired him was the real slave. Basil was particularly fond of verse 24, "So, brethren, in whatever state each was called, there let him remain with God," which he quotes in five of his Shorter Rules (100, 125, 136, 141, 147). For Basil this verse encapsulates the virtue of a well-ordered and obedient life, which is at the heart of his monastic ideal. Augustine finds Paul's words about not clinging to possessions (vv. 29-32) a powerful reminder that we must cling to God alone: "We cannot love what is eternal unless we cease to love what is temporal."

Verses 32-35, which contrast the distractions of married life to a celibate life devoted to pleasing the Lord, occasioned much comment. Clement of Alexandria argues that the married can be just as holy and undistracted in their love for the Lord as the unmarried. John Chrysostom reminds the celibate that Paul's main concern is not sexual practice but freedom from worldly anxiety. The fathers read these words in the context of other Scriptures. Basil associates them with Phil 3:20 ("our citizenship is in heaven"), Jesus' call to renounce everything in order to be his disciple (Luke 14:33), and his telling the disciples: "You are not of this world" (John 15:19). Other fathers elucidate these verses by citing Scriptures in which marriage imagery is used to express the intimate, undistracted relationship between the believer and the Lord. So Augustine cites the royal wedding psalm, Psalm 45, and the instructions to wives in 1 Pet 3:3-4, while Athanasius compares Gen 3:24 and the description of Christ as "bridegroom" in Eph 5:24, 32. Quoting the "greatest commandment" from Luke 10:27 (Deut 6:5), Gregory of Nyssa says that it is impossible for the person who is devoted to pleasing men to "Love God with your whole heart" and all your might.

1 Corinthians 7:1-7

1Now concerning the matters about which you wrote. It is well for a man not to touch a woman. 2But because of the temptation to immorality, each man should have his own wife and each woman her own husband. 3The husband should give to his wife her conjugal rights,[1] and likewise the wife to her husband. 4For the wife does not rule over her own body, but the husband does; likewise the husband does not rule over his own body, but the wife does. 5Do not refuse one another except perhaps by agreement for a season, that you may devote yourselves to prayer; but then come together again, lest Satan tempt you through lack of self-control. 6I say this by way of concession, not of command. 7I wish that all were as I myself am. But each has his own special gift from God, one of one kind and one of another.

(1) Clement of Alexandria

Abstaining from sex is not a virtue unless it is done out of love for God. Now the blessed Paul has this to say about those who despise marriage: *In later times some will depart from the faith by giving heed to deceitful spirits and doctrines of demons . . . who forbid marriage and enjoin abstinence from foods* (1 Tim 4:1, 3). Again Paul says, *Let no one disqualify you, insisting on* voluntary *self-abasement and severity to the body* (Col 2:18, 23). He also writes this: *Are you bound to a wife? Do not seek to be free. Are you free from a wife? Do not seek marriage* (1 Cor 7:27), and this: **Each man should have his own wife, lest Satan tempt you.** What are we to think? Did not the righteous of ancient times partake thankfully of what God created? Some of them lived chastely in marriage and had children. Ravens brought food to Elijah, both bread and meat (1 Kings 17:6), and Samuel the prophet brought the remainder of the thighbone, from which he had eaten, and gave it to Saul to eat (1 Sam 9:24). . . .

Do those who revile marriage reject the apostles as well? For Peter and Philip had children, and Philip gave his daughters in marriage (Acts 21:8-9). And even Paul does not hesitate in one of his letters to address his consort (Phil 4:3),[2] whom he did not take on his journeys so as not to complicate his ministry. So he writes in a letter, *Do we not have the right to be accompanied by a wife, as the other apostles?* (1 Cor 9:5). But the other apostles, as was appropriate to their ministry, gave undivided attention (1 Cor 7:35) to their preaching and took their wives along not as spouses but as sisters who could assist with the ministry to women who stayed at home. Through them the Lord's teaching reached the women's quarters without causing any scandal. For we know the instructions about female deacons given by the noble Paul in one of his letters to Timothy (1 Tim 5:9-10). In addition, he himself asserts that *the kingdom of God is not food and drink,* nor indeed is it abstaining from wine and meat, *but righteousness and peace and joy in the Holy Spirit* (Rom 14:17). . . .

Now continence, seen in purely human terms (I refer to the views of Greek philosophers), demands that we fight against desire and not serve it through our actions. But we understand continence to mean having no desire at all; the point is not to be steadfast under the assaults of desires but to control the act of desiring itself. This continence can be attained only by the grace of God. . . .

1. Literally: "debt."
2. Clement is referring to Phil 4.3: "And I ask you also, true companion, help these women." The word translated "companion" can refer to either a man or a woman.

To state in a general way our teaching about marriage and food and other such things: we should do nothing out of desire, but our will should be directed only toward those things that are necessary. For we are children not of desire but of will (John 1:13). And the man who marries to have children must be continent, feeling no sexual desire for his wife. He ought to love her and beget children with a will that is holy and chaste. For we have learned to *make no provision for the flesh. Let us conduct ourselves becomingly as in the day,* that is, in Christ, and in enlightened conduct that is worthy of the Lord, *not in reveling and drunkenness, not in debauchery and licentiousness, not in quarreling and jealousy* (Rom 13:14, 13). But we must pay attention to continence not only in regard to sexual pleasures but also in regard to the other things the self-indulgent soul desires when it is not content with what it needs but busies itself in the pursuit of luxury. Continence means having contempt for money, luxury, and property, disdaining pleasant sights, controlling the tongue, and mastering evil thoughts.

(2) Origen

There are two basic types of sin: people either fall short of the commandments or exceed them. For we miss the mark when we act without knowledge, not knowing the appropriate measure of what righteousness requires. Sometimes when we go beyond the standard, believing that we are doing something greater, we actually fall short of what is required. The *standard,* therefore, which is neither excessive not deficient but in due measure (Prov 20:10), is to know how we should live. *Are you bound to a wife?* (1 Cor 7:27). If so, then you are acting according to an excessive standard if you do not consider your wife but say, "I can practice continence and live in a purer way." Be aware that your wife will *perish* if she cannot endure your purity, she *for whom Christ died* (Rom 14:15).

Something like this happened in Corinth, and there was dissension in the households of the brethren: in some the men and in others the women were seeking to be continent, and they were at odds with each other. And so the Corinthians wrote a letter about this to the apostle, and in response to their letter Paul writes the words recorded here. And, since he is a *wise steward* (1 Pet 4:10; 1 Cor 4:1) he does not speak so vehemently about purity as to nullify the teaching about marriage. Nor does he nullify the teaching about virginity by expressing a preference for marriage. Instead, throughout the discussion, in one way or another, he aims at one goal, encouraging them to be pure. After allowing himself to come down to their level, he once again urges them to practice purity. And when he has urged them to practice purity, he says again that they must accommodate the weakness of those who are less strong.

Paul does not begin with the course that is less than ideal, for that would not be right. Instead he begins with the more perfect course, saying: **Now concerning the matters about which you wrote. It is well for a man not to touch a woman.** This means: I praise the desire for purity in those of you who abstain from intercourse with a woman, but you should consider not only *your own interests* (Phil 2:4) but also those of your wives. For *love does not insist on its own way* (1 Cor 13:5). So **because of the temptation to immorality, each man should have his own wife and each woman her own husband.**

Let one who is stronger **have his own wife**, not because of his own **immorality**, but because his wife might commit immorality because of her husband's continence or the husband might commit immorality because of his wife's continence. For it is preferable for the two of them to be saved while engaging in marital relations than that one of them fall away from the hope that is in Christ because of the resolve of the other. For how will the husband be saved if he is responsible for the death of his wife? The chastity of the man, then, is not holy unless the wife agrees that both should abstain in order to **devote** themselves to **prayer** (v. 5).

The husband should give to his wife her conjugal rights, and likewise the wife to her husband. In this passsage Paul is concerned to heal human weakness and to give the most appropriate advice he can for the situation he addresses. This is why he says that the husband ought to give his wife **conjugal rights** and also that the wife owes them to her husband. Then, so as not to make the married feel ashamed, as if they were slaves to each other, he says that they should undertake the discipline of purity only by mutual agreement: **For the wife does not rule over her own body, but the husband does; likewise the husband does not rule over his own body, but the wife does.** The husband, then, has authority over the body of his wife, and, if he wishes, he also has the authority not to make use of this authority. *Nevertheless, we have not made use of this authority* (1 Cor 9:12), the apostle says. I think that he is teaching about this when he asks, *Do we not have the right to be accompanied by a wife, as the other apostles and the brothers of the Lord and Cephas?* (1 Cor 9:5). Therefore, does not the wife also have authority over her husband's body, and can she not forbear to exercise this authority? The word **likewise**, which Paul uses twice in this passage, indicates that the man must not consider himself superior to his wife in matters pertaining to marriage. For there is similarity and equality between the two parties to a marriage.

Do not refuse one another except perhaps by agreement for a season, that you may devote yourselves to prayer; but then come together again. For you both ought to know that prayer offered when husband and wife are pure is not the same as prayer offered when they are having marital relations. For if there are times when the Greeks purify themselves for the sake of their idols, how much more should you who pray to the God of All do so? While it is a good thing, then, to make an accommodation to weakness, it is also good to endure abstinence for the sake of prayer. Moses, too, purifies the people and says, *Do not go near a woman for three days* (Exod 19:15),[3] so that their purified state might enable them to become hearers of God. And in the book of Kings, Abiathar, or Abimelech the priest,[4] wants to offer the *holy bread* to David, who was fleeing the plots of Saul; and when he wants to give David the *holy bread*, what does he say but *if the young men have kept themselves from women* (1 Sam 21:4)? This does not refer to keeping away from other women but from their wives. So, if a man must abstain from relations with a woman in order to receive the *bread of the Presence* (1 Sam 21:6), does he not need a far

---

3. This is said in preparation for Moses' ascent to Sinai to receive the Ten Commandments.

4. In 1 Sam 21:1-6 the priest Ahimelech gives David and his companions the holy "bread of the Presence" to eat. Origen's mention of Abiathar as well suggests that he knows a variant text. In other Old Testament passages, there is confusion about the relationship between Ahimelech and Abiathar: 1 Sam 22:20-23 calls Abiathar the son of Ahimelech, while 2 Sam 8:17 calls Ahimelech the son of Abiathar.

greater degree of purity in order to receive the greater *bread of the Presence,* over which the names of God and Christ and the Holy Spirit have been pronounced?[5] Otherwise we will in fact receive the bread *for judgment* (1 Cor 11:34) and not for salvation. . . .

I say this by way of concession, not of command. In order to correct his hearers, Paul's practice is to moderate his teaching on account of their weakness and then make it demanding again. **I wish that all were as I myself am. But each has his own special gift from God, one of one kind and one of another.** When the spouses behave with moderation, marriage partakes of a **special gift,** namely, harmony (v. 4). We can say truly that in some cases marriage is a **special gift,** when there is no *dissension* and there is absolute *peace* (1 Cor 14:33), when there is total agreement. . . . But the followers of Marcion also cite this text, and they forbid marriage for foolish reasons, claiming that it is another God, invented by them, and not the creator God, who requires purity. But we can show them from the present verse that they are wrong to forbid marriage and to divide the godhead. For if one has a **special gift** of **one kind** and another of **another kind,** then marriage is a **special gift.** And if marriage is a special gift, it is wrong to forbid the special gift of marriage. If **one of one kind and one of another** is **from God,** it is clear that it is one God who has given both purity and marriage, and that there is one God of both the law and the gospel, who was proclaimed first by the prophets and later by Christ Jesus.

(3) John Chrysostom

Once Paul has set them right on the three most difficult problems — first, the division in the church (1 Cor 1:10-16), second, the immoral brother (1 Cor 5:1-8), and third, the matter of the covetous man (5:9–6:11) — in the rest of the letter he uses a gentler tone. He interposes counsel and advice about marriage and virginity and gives his audience relief from more unpleasant topics. . . . **It is well for a man not to touch a woman.** "If you are seeking the most excellent good," Paul says, "it is better if you refrain entirely from intimacy with a woman. But if you are looking for a safe way to alleviate your weakness, be joined in marriage." It was likely that the same thing was happening in Corinth as happens now: the man wants to have sexual relations but the woman does not, or the other way around. Notice how Paul addresses each possibility. Some people claim that this passage is addressed to priests, but judging from what follows, I would not agree. For in that case Paul would not have given such a general admonition. . . . Elsewhere, both in the Old Testament and in the New, the man takes precedence: *Your desire shall be for your husband, and he shall rule over you* (Gen 3:16). And Paul makes a similar distinction when he writes, *Husbands, love your wives* (Eph 5:25), but *let the wife see that she respects her husband* (Eph 5:33). In the passage before us, however, there is no superiority or inferiority, but the spouses' authority is the same. Why is this so? Because Paul's subject is self-control. *At other times,* he says, *the husband can have his advantage, but not here,* where he is talking about self-control. **The husband does not rule over his own body**, nor does **the wife** rule over hers. Their privileges are entirely equal; neither one has any advantage at all. . . .

5. That is, the bread of the Eucharist.

Do not refuse one another except perhaps by agreement for a season, that you may devote yourselves to fasting and prayer. . . . Here Paul is referring to especially zealous prayer. For if he forbids those who have sexual relations with each other from praying, how would it be possible to *pray constantly* (1 Thess 5:17)? Therefore, it must be possible to be intimate with a woman and devote oneself to prayer. But chastity makes prayer more genuine. Paul did not simply say "that you may pray" but that **you may devote yourselves to prayer**, because sexual relations take time, not because they make impure.

(4) Jerome and Jovinian

A few days ago my holy brothers in Rome sent me the treatises of a certain Jovinian, asking me to reply to the foolish ideas they contain and crush this Christian Epicurus with the force of the gospel and of the apostles. . . . Jovinian says that virgins, widows, and married women, once they have been cleansed by Christ, have equal merit as long as their other actions are similar. He also argues that those who have perfect faith and have been born again in baptism cannot be subverted by the devil. His third point is that there is no difference between abstaining from food and receiving it with thanksgiving. The fourth and last is that all who have kept their baptismal vows will have the same reward in heaven. . . .

[*In a section omitted here Jerome summarizes how Jovinian uses Old Testament texts to argue that marriage and virginity have equal merit; he then turns to the New Testament.*] Suddenly Jovinian passes over to the Gospel and adduces Zechariah and Elizabeth, Peter and his mother-in-law, and the rest of the apostles. His attack on our position remains consistent: "If [those who claim that virginity is superior to marriage] offer the weak argument that the world needed to be populated in its earliest days,[6] let them listen to Paul, who says: *I would have younger widows marry, bear children, and manage their households* (1 Tim 5:14); and *Let marriage be held in honor by all, and let the marriage bed be kept undefiled* (Heb 13:4); and *A wife is bound to her husband as long as he lives. If the husband dies, she is free to be married to whom she wishes, only in the Lord* (1 Cor 7:39); and *Adam was not deceived, but the woman was deceived and became a transgressor. Yet she will be saved through childbearing, provided they continue in faith and love and holiness, with modesty* (1 Tim 2:14-15). . . . From this it is clear that you [who discourage marriage] are following the doctrine of the Manichaeans, who forbid marriage and eating food that God created for use, and who have *consciences seared as with a hot iron* (1 Tim 4:2)." . . .

[*Jerome responds to Jovinian's assertions.*] We must fight the enemy with all our might and marshall our battle lines to repulse the disorderly forces of the enemy, who fight like brigands, not soldiers. In the front rank I will set the apostle Paul, and since he is a very brave general, I will equip him with his own weapons, that is, his own words. For when the Corinthians asked repeatedly about this matter, the instructor of the Gentiles and teacher of the Church gave a full reply. We should regard what he set down as the law of Christ who speaks in him (see 1 Cor 2:16). . . .

---

6. With the implication that marriage was necessary at that time but is no longer.

Let us return to the chief point of Paul's witness: **It is well**, he says, **for a man not to touch a woman**. If it is good not to touch a woman, it is bad to touch one; for nothing is the opposite of good except bad. But if it is bad and what is bad is pardoned, then Paul is making a **concession** (v. 6) in order to prevent something worse than that which is bad. But a thing that is conceded only to prevent something worse cannot be not good to any great degree. . . .

That you may devote yourselves to prayer; but then come together again. . . . The apostle's wish is one thing; his concession is another. If we carry out his wish, we are acting meritoriously; if we act on his concession, we are making improper use of a thing. Do you want to know the apostle's wish? Read what follows: **I wish that all were as I myself am.** Blessed is the one who is like Paul! Happy is the one who listens to the apostle's commands, not his concessions. "This," he says, "I wish, this I desire, that you *be imitators of me as I also am of Christ* (1 Cor 11:1), who was a virgin born of a virgin, uncorrupted son of a mother who was uncorrupted." Because we are human, we cannot imitate our Savior's birth, but let us at least imitate his life. . . . For he who believes in Christ *ought to walk just as he walked* (1 John 2:6).

(5) Augustine

Every person is a part of the human race, which is naturally social, and accordingly each possesses as a great natural blessing the capacity for friendship. God wished to create the whole race from one person (see Acts 17:26) so that in their relations with one another people might be bound together not only by their being of the same species but also by the bond of kinship. Accordingly, the first connection in human society is that between husband and wife. These God did not create individually, with separate origins, and afterward join together; instead he made the woman from the man, signifying the strength of their union by her being taken and shaped from the side of the man (Gen 2:18-23). For it is at the side that those who walk together and look in the same direction are joined. The next bond of community between them is children. These are the sole honorable result, not of the marriage of male and female, but of their sexual relations; for even without sexual intercourse there could be between them a true union of friendship, with one of them ruling and the other obeying. . . .

The point I am arguing is this: since we are born into an existence limited by birth and death, marriage between male and female is a good. Holy Scripture commends this compact so strongly that a woman divorced by her husband is not allowed to marry as long as her husband is alive, and likewise a man divorced by his wife may not take another during the lifetime of the woman who has left him (Rom 7:2-3). And in the Gospels the Lord confirmed that marriage is a good not only by forbidding divorce except in cases of adultery (Matt 5:32; 19:9) but also by accepting an invitation to a wedding (John 2:1-11).

Now it is reasonable to ask why marriage is a good. In my opinion it is not merely for the sake of the procreation of children but also because there is a natural affinity between the sexes. If this were not the case, we could not call it a marriage when the spouses are old or have lost their children or never had any at all. But in actuality in a good marriage, no matter how old the partners, even if the youthful ardor between the husband and the wife has withered away, the ordered love between them continues. The better the partners are, the sooner they refrain from intercourse **by agreement** (v. 5), so that their abstinence not be merely a matter of necessity because of inability in their later years to act on their desire. Instead it is to their credit if they decline to do what they are able to do. Accordingly, if both sexes are faithful and render to each other honor and the **debt** (vv. 3-4) they owe each other, though their bodies are failing and nearly corpse-like, still the chastity of souls that have been joined together remains all the purer for being more tested and all the safer for being more serene. Marriage produces a further good: it uses carnal and youthful incontinence, which is a fault, for the honorable task of begetting children, so that intercourse within marriage creates something good out of the evil of lust. Furthermore, the desire of the flesh is subdued and its blazing passion becomes more moderate since parental love tempers it. A certain seriousness is imposed upon the heat of their pleasure, since in the act of cleaving together they are intending to become father and mother.

A further point is that in the very act by which married people pay the **debt** they owe each other, even if they seek it with too little temperance and self-control, they owe fidelity to each other. The apostle sets such a high value on this fidelity that he calls it **authority**, when he says that **the wife does not have authority over her own body, but her husband does, and likewise the husband does not have authority over his own body, but his wife does.**

My brothers, my sons, be chaste, love chastity, embrace chastity, esteem purity: God is the promoter of purity in his temple, which is what you are (1 Cor 3:16); he asks for it. He expels the unclean from his temple. Be contented with your wives since you want your wives to be contented with you. You do not want her to engage in anything without you: neither do so without her. You are the master, and she is the servant. God created both of you. Scripture says, *Sarah obeyed Abraham, calling him lord* (1 Pet 3:6). It is true: the bishop has put his signature on the marriage contract, and your wives are your servants and you their masters. But when it comes to the matter in which the sexes differ and each is joined to the other, **The wife does not have authority over her own body, but her husband does.** You were glad to hear that, you felt exalted, lifted up, and you said: "Bravo, bravissimo, hurray for the apostle, this *chosen instrument* (Acts 9:15), for asserting that **the wife does not have authority over her own body, but her husband does!** For I am the master." You praised Paul. Now listen to what follows, listen to something you do not want but which I am asking you to want. "What is that?" Listen: **the husband,** that lord and master, **does not have authority over his own body, but his wife does.** Hear this with gladness. What is being taken from you is not authority but vice. What is happening is that you are being forbidden to commit adultery, not that women are being raised to your level. You are a man: show it. "Vir" (man) is derived from "virtus" (manliness or virtue), or "virtus" from "vir." Do you possess "virtus"? Then conquer lust. *The head of a woman is her husband,* Scripture says (1 Cor 11:3). If you are the head, lead, and let her follow. But look where you are leading her. Be the head, and let her follow. But do not lead her where you do not wish her to follow. To avoid tumbling down a precipice, make sure that you follow the straight path.

1 Corinthians 7:8-11

8To the unmarried and the widows I say that it is well for them to remain single as I do. 9But if they cannot exercise self-control, they should marry. For it is better to marry than to be aflame with passion.[7] **10To the married I give charge, not I but the Lord, that the wife should not separate from her husband 11(but if she does, let her remain single or else be reconciled to her husband) — and that the husband should not divorce his wife.**

(1) Cyril of Alexandria

Interpreters of the Gospel sayings who have a superior understanding of the good and who have Christ himself speaking in them (see 1 Cor 2:16; 2 Cor 2:17; 12:19) are right to teach boldly and with authority, even in cases where the Holy Scriptures had said nothing about what was to be done. And such an interpreter was the divine apostle Paul, who says: **To the unmarried and the widows I say that it is well for them to remain single as I do** and what follows. For in a case where there is no divine law Paul has to add, **I say.** But where it is Christ who gives the commandment Paul says, **I give charge,** and immediately adds, **not I but the Lord.** Now which of the necessary things were overlooked by Christ when he gave the law? What did the Christian teachers devise that was better than what he had said? And is it not incredibly foolish to think that Christ's teachings were not perfect? What shall we say to this? That the divine message of the gospel does not forbid marriage, and I think this is because God was adapting his commandment to human nature. For when the Pharisees test Christ and ask, *Is it lawful to divorce one's wife* for a cause other than adultery? (Matt 19:3), he replies, *he who divorces his wife, except for unchastity, makes her an adulteress* (Matt 19:9). And his disciples respond to this: *If such is the case of a man with his wife, it is not expedient to marry* (Matt 19:10). And the Lord replies, *There are eunuchs who have been so from birth, and there are eunuchs who have been made eunuchs by men, and there are eunuchs who have made themselves eunuchs for the sake of the kingdom of heaven. He who is able to receive this, let him receive it* (Matt 19:12). Christ proposes this for those who wish to be perfect; he does not, however, include it as a law, because he knew that not all could control the inclinations of the flesh.

And all this is foreshadowed in the Old Testament law. For it prescribes different sacrifices to be offered for the glory of God: some for deliberate sins and unintentional sins, others for purification and the removal of defilement, and others for the sabbath and new moon and festivals. Moreover, in addition to these, the law also permits certain freewill offerings to be brought to God. These sacrifices were voluntary. Springing from a

---

7. Or: "For it is better to marry than to burn."

commendable and reverent zeal, they went beyond what was required by the law. Now while it was not allowed to neglect the sacrifices required by the law, those who supplemented these with sacrifices performed on their own initiative were commended by God. And I think that divine providence intends something similar in the present text. For if we choose to marry as allowed by the law, Christ does not forbid this, but nothing prevents us from doing what is better than this if we are eager to achieve the greatest possible glory. Paul then gives excellent advice when he says: **To the unmarried and the widows I say that it is well for them to remain single as I do. To the married I give charge, not I but the Lord, that the wife should not separate from her husband.** And he offers his own situation as an example of choosing a life without distractions and greatly prefers the celibate life to the married state. Therefore, Paul says that if a person has in fact put off the yoke of the law (Rom 7:1-4), he should remain celibate. *For thus says the LORD: "To the eunuchs who keep my sabbaths, who choose the things that please me and hold fast my covenant, I will give in my house and within my walls a monument and a name better than sons and daughters; I will give them an everlasting name which shall not be cut off"* (Isa 56:4-5). Thus the reward of celibacy is precious. Paul does not, however, allow a man who is already bound in marriage to leave his lawfully wedded wife because he does not want his preaching of salvation to fill the world with confusion. And Jesus Christ, the Savior of all of us, does not praise divorce even if the law allowed it as an accommodation for the men of old, because of what he calls *the hardness of their hearts* (Matt 19:8).

(2) Clement of Alexandria

Continence, then, means having contempt for the body as a result of our confession of faith in God. It refers not only to sexual matters but also to all the other things the soul wickedly desires when it is not content with what is necessary for life. For there is also continence in speaking, and in having and using possessions, and in desiring. And this continence is not merely a teaching about self-control; it is also the bestowing of self-control on us, since it is a divine power and grace. Here is what we Christians think on this point: we consider abstinence from sex and those to whom this capacity has been granted by God (Matt 19:10-12) to be blessed. We approve of monogamy and the holiness of marriage to one spouse and claim that we ought to *suffer together* (Rom 8:17) and *bear one another's burdens* (Gal 6:2), lest someone, *thinking that he stands*, should *fall* (1 Cor 10:12). But when the apostle says, "If he is **aflame with passion** (v. 9), let him marry," he is speaking of second marriage.

*　　*　　*

To the married I give charge, not I but the Lord, that the wife should not separate from her husband (but if she does, let her remain single or else be reconciled to her husband) — and that the husband should not divorce his wife. *To the rest I say, not the Lord, that if any brother* (1 Cor 7:12) — along with the rest of this passage through the words: *but as it is they are holy* (7:14) — how is this explained by those who criticize both the law [i.e., the Old Testament] and marriage and claim that marriage was only a *concession* (7:6) allowed by the law but not by the New Testament? What do those who abhor begetting and birth have to say about Paul's injunctions? For Paul also ordains that a bishop who is to rule over the church must be a man who *manages his household well* (1 Tim 3:4), and marriage to one wife constitutes a household of the Lord (1 Tim 3:2; Tit 1:6).

(3) John Chrysostom on verse 9

Do you see how wise Paul is, how he shows that continence is better, and yet he does not compel anyone who is incapable of it because he is concerned that some might fall into sin? **For it is better to marry than to be aflame with passion**. Paul reveals what a great tyrant desire is. His meaning is something like this: if you suffer from a strong compulsion and passion, end your distress and strenuous effort lest you stagger and fall.

(4) Augustine

He who is able to receive this [the teaching about refraining from marriage], let him receive it (Matt 19:12). "But I can't," says someone. Can't you? "No, I can't," you say. Here you can appeal for help to the authority of the apostle, who gives you *milk,* not *solid food,* to eat (1 Cor 3:2) and says, **If they cannot exercise self-control, they should marry**. There has to be some way we may be pardoned: only pardon can prevent our being sent to eternal punishment. We must do what is allowable so that what is otherwise prohibited may be forgiven. This is indicated by what follows: **it is better to marry than to burn**. That is, Paul makes a *concession* (v. 6) to his hearers' lack of self-control because he fears something worse. He fears eternal punishment, he fears what awaits adulterers. Even if married persons, overcome by lust, consort with one another more than is necessary for begetting children, I see this as one of those things for which we pray every day: *Forgive us our debts, as we also have forgiven our debtors* (Matt 6:12).

Every one who divorces his wife, except on the ground of unchastity, makes her an adulteress (Matt 5:32). The compact of marriage is a matter of such sacredness that it is not nullified even by separation. For if a wife marries while her husband is still alive, even if he has left her, she commits adultery, and he who left her is the cause of this evil.

I wonder, however, whether, just as one can renounce an adulterous wife, it is also possible to marry another when one has renounced her. Holy Scripture makes this a difficult problem since the apostle says, on the authority of the Lord, that a woman should not leave her husband; but that if she does so, she must **remain unmarried or be reconciled to her husband**. Yet she should not in any case leave her husband and remain unmarried unless he is an adulterer; for by leaving him she might cause one who was not an adulterer before to commit adultery (Matt 5:32). Still, if she cannot exercise continence, she may properly be reconciled to her husband if she puts up with him or if he changes his ways. But I do not see how a man could be allowed to marry another when he has left an adulterous wife since a woman is not allowed to marry another man if she leaves an adulterous husband.

Since this is so, the bond of fellowship between the spouses is so strong that although they are joined together for the sake of begetting children, this bond is not to be broken in order to beget them. A man might divorce a barren woman and marry a woman who would bear him children, but this is not allowed. And in our time Roman custom forbids having more than one living wife by taking an additional wife. To be sure, if a man or a woman were to abandon an adulterous spouse and marry another, more children would be produced. But since the divine rule seems to forbid this, it makes very clear the strength of the marriage bond. I do not think that it could ever have such great force unless there were attached to it the sacral power[8] of something greater than this weak mortality of ours, a bond which, although people abandon it and desire to nullify it, still remains unshaken and able to bring them punishment.

1 Corinthians 7:12-16

12To the rest I say, not the Lord, that if any brother has a wife who is an unbeliever, and she consents to live with him, he should not divorce her. 13If any woman has a husband who is an unbeliever, and he consents to live with her, she should not divorce him. 14For the unbelieving husband is consecrated through his wife, and the unbelieving wife is consecrated through her husband. Otherwise, your children would be unclean, but as it is they are holy. 15But if the unbelieving partner desires to separate, let it be so; in such a case the brother or sister is not bound. For God has called us to peace. 16Wife, how do you know whether you will save your husband? Husband, how do you know whether you will save your wife?

(1) Tertullian

Just recently, my fellow servant whom I love in the Lord,[9] I have discussed to the best of my ability what should be the conduct of a Christian woman when her marriage has come to an end for any reason. Now I turn to a second set of recommendations, bearing in mind human weakness and warned by the example of certain women. These women, when divorce or the death of their husbands gave them the opportunity to practice celibacy, threw away the possibility of realizing such a great good. What is more, in marrying they were unwilling even to heed the teaching that they should marry *only in the Lord* (1 Cor 7:39). . . .

In recent days a woman was married outside the church and united to an unbeliever, as others, I remember, did previously. I wondered at the audacity of the women themselves or else the duplicity of those who advised them, since there is no scripture that gives permission for this. Can it be, I asked, that they flatter themselves with that passage in the First Letter to the Corinthians? There it is written, **If a brother has a wife**

8. The Latin word used here is "sacramentum."
9. Tertullian is addressing his wife.

116

who is not a believer, and she agrees to live with him, let him not divorce her. And if a woman has a husband who is not a believer, and he agrees to live with her, let her not divorce her husband. For the unbelieving husband is made holy through the wife, and the unbelieving wife is made holy through the brother, since otherwise your children are impure. Perhaps by understanding this admonition concerning married believers in an unrestricted sense they think it is permissible to marry unbelievers. God forbid! Anyone who interprets this way knowingly ensnares himself! It is plain that this scripture names those who were found by the grace of God when already married to a non-believer.

(2) John Chrysostom

Tell me, what harm would there be if those already married [i.e., a Christian married to an unbeliever] stay together and not cause needless enmity — provided that religious duties are observed and that there are good reasons to hope for the unbeliever? Paul is not addressing those who had never married, but those already married. He does not say, "If someone wants to marry an unbeliever," but If any has a spouse who is an unbeliever. This means: if someone received the Christian faith after marrying, and the partner remains an unbeliever but is content to continue living together, the Christian should not seek a divorce. For the unbelieving husband is consecrated through his wife. So abundant is your purity! What, then? Does this mean that the unbeliever is holy? Not at all. Paul does not say, "he is holy," but he is consecrated through his wife. He says this not to show that the husband is holy but to dispel the woman's fear [of being defiled] and to lead the husband to a desire for the truth. Impurity does not come from the bodies that come together, but from what one chooses and thinks. Next comes Paul's proof: if the husband is impure, and you the wife, remain with him and conceive a child,[10] the child would not come from you alone, and thus it might be considered impure or half-pure. But in fact, it is not impure. That is why Paul added, Otherwise, your children would be unclean, but as it is they are holy, that is, they are not impure. He calls them holy, using a strong word to remove any fear they might have.

(3) Augustine on verse 14

"Holy parents," my opponent[11] objects, "ought to produce holy children. For, the apostle says, Otherwise your children would be impure, but in fact they are holy." How do you understand this? In what sense do you take it? That the child of believing parents is so holy that he does not need to be baptized? You may understand holiness in a variety of ways, for there are many kinds of holiness and many kinds of sanctification. Not every-

---

10. I have emended a corrupt text here.

11. Augustine is arguing against the Pelagians, who denied original sin and hence could not explain why the Church permits the baptism of infants.

thing that is sanctified is on its way to the kingdom of heaven. About our food the apostle says, *It is consecrated by the word of God and prayer* (1 Tim 4:5). Yet we all know, do we not, where our food is destined to go, for all that it is consecrated? Know, therefore, that there is a type of sanctification, a sort of foreshadowing [of the true sanctification], that is not sufficient to gain salvation. There is a difference between these types: how large it is, is known to God. Though we do not know, let us quickly take the child of believers to be baptized. The parents should not make the mistake of thinking that by his birth he has already become a believer. They can say that he is born, not that he is born again. Here is the way to understand what it means that the children of believers are **holy** (I shall avoid a discussion here of how this happens since it would be lengthy): take an unbelieving husband married to a believing wife. **The unbelieving husband is made holy through the wife, and the unbelieving wife is made holy through the brother.** Now because there is a kind of sanctification by which an **unbelieving husband is made holy** in **the believing wife**, should he feel assurance that he will enter the kingdom of God even if he is not baptized, regenerated, or redeemed by the blood of Christ? Clearly not. So just as the unbelieving husband is sanctified in the wife and yet perishes unless he is baptized, so the children of believers, though sanctified in some sense, perish if they are not baptized.

1 Corinthians 7:17-24

17Only, let every one lead the life which the Lord has assigned to him, and in which God has called him. This is my rule in all the churches. 18Was any one at the time of his call already circumcised? Let him not take back the foreskin.[12] Was any one at the time of his call uncircumcised? Let him not seek circumcision. 19For neither circumcision counts for anything nor uncircumcision, but keeping the commandments of God. 20Every one should remain in the state in which he was called. 21Were you a slave when called? Never mind. But if you can gain your freedom, avail yourself of the opportunity. 22For he who was called in the Lord as a slave is a freedman of the Lord. Likewise he who was free when called is a slave of Christ. 23You were bought with a price; do not become slaves of men. 24So, brethren, in whatever state each was called, there let him remain with God.

(1) John Chrysostom

Just as circumcision does no good and not being circumcised does no harm, so slavery and freedom bring neither profit nor harm. And to show this in the clearest possible way, Paul says, **But if you can gain your freedom, avail yourself of the opportunity.** He means, avail yourself of the opportunity given by slavery. But why does he tell someone who can be set free to remain a slave? He wants to show that slavery causes no harm, but on the contrary it even brings benefit.

12. RSV: "Let him not seek to remove the marks of circumcision."

I know that some assert that **avail yourself of the opportunity** is said with reference to freedom.[13] They claim that if someone can win his freedom, he should do so. If this is what Paul intends to say, it is quite contrary to his usual approach. It would offer no encouragement to the slave, nor show him that slavery does not harm him, if Paul had told him to be free. For then a slave could ask, "What does this mean? If I cannot go free, am I not suffering harm and being diminished?" This is why Paul did not say this, but by what he does say he seeks to make clear that those who are free have no advantage in their freedom. Even if you can control whether you are set free or not, continue rather to serve. . . . **You were bought with a price; do not become slaves of men.** This word is directed not only to household slaves but also to those who are free. It is possible to be a slave and yet free, and to be a free man and yet a slave. When is the one who is a slave not a slave? When he does everything for the sake of God, when he acts without pretense and not with *eye-service* of men (Eph 6:6; Col 3:22). This is to be free, even while serving human masters. On the other hand, when is a free person a slave? Whenever he does something base in service to men, either because of gluttony or the love of money or power. Indeed, such a person is the most servile of all even if he is "free."

Consider both these cases: Joseph was a slave, but not a **slave of men.** Thus, in his slavery he was freer than all those who were free. He did not give in to his master's wife, to the desires of the woman who owned him (Genesis 39). Again, she was free but more a slave than anyone when she flattered and entreated her attendant. But she did not persuade that free man to do what he did not want to do. This, then, was not slavery but the greatest freedom. How did slavery hinder Joseph from being virtuous? Let slaves and free alike pay attention: Who was the slave? The man who was prized or the woman who prized him? The woman who entreated him or the man who disdained her entreaty? . . .

Every one should remain in the state in which he was called. . . . From this it is clear that Paul does not abolish slavery in the literal sense, but the slavery found even among free people, due to sin. This slavery is much worse, even if the person enslaved to sin is a free man. What benefit did Joseph's brothers enjoy in their freedom? Were not they more servile than any slave when they lied to their father, and told the traders and their brother things that were not true? A free man never acts like this, but he is truthful in all places and all situations. Nothing could enslave Joseph, not chains, not the condition of servitude, not the lust of his master's wife, not living in a foreign land. He remained absolutely free. This is the greatest freedom, when it shines forth even in slavery.

(2) Basil of Caesarea on verse 24

[*In his* Shorter Rules *Basil responds to a series of questions about life in the monastery.*]
Question: If all must all gather together at dinnertime, how should we deal with a person
  who is missing and comes after the meal?
Rule: If he is absent because of the nature or location or his work and he is obeying the

13. Paul's text says literally "avail yourself more" or "use all the more," without any explicit direct object. The object could be slavery, or freedom, or perhaps the "call" of v. 18.

commandment of the one who said: **brethren, in whatever state each was called, there let him remain,** then the monk in charge of community discipline will investigate and pardon him. But if he could have been on time but failed to make an effort, even though he knew that carelessness incurs blame, let him go without food until the appointed time on the next day. . . .

Question: Should guests be received in the workshops, or should some of those working there leave their appointed place to receive them?

Rule: Except for those entrusted with overseeing the workers or distributing what they produce, whoever leaves his work to receive guests and destroys the harmonious order of the parts (1 Cor 12:12-20) is not to be permitted even the usual breaks from the workplace. Let him sit in a place suitable for discipline and perform his work without distraction and with special diligence, until he learns to observe what the apostle said: **in whatever state each was called, there let him remain.** . . .

Question: If a person is busy working in the cellar or the kitchen or with another such work and fails to come at the hour appointed for psalms and prayer, does his soul suffer any harm?

Rule: Each person observes his own rule in his own work, like a part of the body (1 Cor 12:12-20). He suffers harm if he neglects the task entrusted to him, and he is in even more serious danger if he does something that hurts the common good. Therefore, let him fulfill in his thoughts what is written: *Singing and making melody to the Lord with your hearts* (Eph 5:19). Even if he does not appear physically to assemble with the others, let him suffer no condemnation, since he is doing what was commanded: **in whatever state each was called, there let him remain.** But care must be taken that a person who is able to finish his work in good time and be an example to others not use the demands of his work as an excuse and cause others to stumble, thereby incurring the judgment due those who are careless.

1 Corinthians 7:25-31

25Now concerning virgins,[14] I have no command of the Lord, but I give my opinion as one who by the Lord's mercy is trustworthy. 26I think that in view of the present distress it is well for a person to remain as he is. 27Are you bound to a wife? Do not seek to be free. Are you free from a wife? Do not seek marriage. 28But if you marry, you do not sin, and if a girl marries she does not sin. Yet those who marry will have worldly troubles, and I would spare you that. 29I mean, brethren, the appointed time has grown very short; from now on, let those who have wives live as though they had none, 30and those who mourn as though they were not mourning, and those who rejoice as though they were not rejoicing, and those who buy as though they had no goods, 31and those who deal with the world as though they had no dealings with it. For the form of this world is passing away.

---

14. RSV: "the unmarried."

(1) Jerome and Jovinian on verses 25-26

[In this passage Jerome first presents Jovinian's interpretation of verses 25-26.] Having discussed the married and the celibate, Paul comes at last to the virgins and says: **Now concerning virgins, I have no command of the Lord, but I give my opinion as one who by the Lord's mercy is trustworthy. I think that in view of the present distress it is well for a person to remain as he is.** Here our opponent goes mad with exultation. With this as his strongest battering ram to shake the fortress of virginity, he says, "See, the apostle admits that as regards virgins he has no commandment of the Lord, and even Paul, who gave authoritative orders regarding husbands and wives, does not dare to command what the Lord has not taught. He acted properly. For what is taught is an order, anything that is an order must be carried out, and failure to carry out what must be done is punished: it is pointless to issue an order if the decision to carry it out is left to the judgment of the recipient. If the Lord had commanded virginity, he would have seemed to condemn and destroy marriage, the source of human procreation, from which virginity itself is born. If he had cut off the root, how could he expect the fruit?" . . .

[In response to this interpretation Jerome emphasizes the superior merit of virginity.] The apostle will reply on my behalf, "Do you want me to give orders where the Lord has offered something rather than commanding it? The Creator and Fashioner, knowing the weakness of the vessel he made, left virginity open to his hearers; and shall I, the teacher of the Gentiles, who have *become all things to all men that I might gain all* (1 Cor 9:22) begin by imposing the burden of perpetual chastity upon weak believers? Let them learn to take a holiday from the marriage bond and give themselves time for prayer (1 Cor 7:5) so that when they have had a taste of chastity they may desire to have perpetually that which brought them delight for a short time." The Lord was tested by the Pharisees, and when he was asked whether according to the law of Moses it was allowable to put away one's wife, he forbade it. The disciples thought about this and said to him: *If such is the case of a man with his wife, it is not expedient to marry.* But he said to them, *Not all men can accept this saying, but only those to whom it is given. For there are eunuchs who have been so from birth, and there are eunuchs who have been made eunuchs by men, and there are eunuchs who have made themselves eunuchs for the sake of the kingdom of heaven. He who is able to receive this, let him receive it* (Matt 19:10-12). It is plain why the apostle says, **Now concerning virgins I have no command of the Lord.** For the Lord had already said, *Not all men can accept this saying, but only those to whom it is given* and *He who is able to receive this, let him receive it.* The Lord offers the reward and invites us to enter the race; he holds in his hand the prize of virginity, points to the most pure source of water, and cries aloud, *If any one thirst, let him come to me and drink* (John 7:37).

(2) Augustine

Therefore, let there be no fornication. *You are God's temple and God's Spirit dwells in you. If anyone destroys God's temple, God will destroy him* (1 Cor 3:16-17). Marriage is permissible: do not ask for anything beyond it. No great burden has been imposed on you. Upon virgins their greater love has imposed a greater burden. Virgins have declined to take what they could have taken in order to be more pleasing to him to whom they have devoted themselves. They have sought a greater beauty of the heart. It is as if they were saying, "What is your command to us? Do you ask that we should not be adulterers? Out of love for you we are doing more than you command." **Now concerning virgins,** says the apostle, **I have no commandment of the Lord.** So why are they doing this? **But I give my advice.** Now these loving women, in whose eyes earthly marriage is of no value and who do not desire earthly embraces, have accepted the **commandment** in such a way that they do not refuse the **advice,** and in order to be more pleasing they have adorned themselves the more. The more one seeks the adornment of the body, the physical and outer person, the greater the harm to the inner person, while the less one seeks the adornment of the outer person, the more the inner person is adorned with good character.

The glory of marriage, therefore, is chastity in procreation and fidelity in paying the *debt* (1 Cor 7:3) owed to the flesh. This is the task of marriage, and the apostle defends it from all accusation when he says, **And if you marry, you have not sinned; and if a virgin marries, she has not sinned** and *let him do as he wishes; he does not sin; let him marry* (7:36). Moreover, an immoderate demand by either partner for the marriage *debt* is permitted as a *concession* (7:6) to the married for the reasons Paul gave earlier. So the words *the unmarried woman or virgin is concerned about the things of the Lord, that she may be holy both in body and in spirit* (7:34) are not to be understood to mean that the chaste wife is not holy in body. Paul asks all the faithful, *Do you not know that your body is a temple of the Holy Spirit within you, which you have from God?* (1 Cor 6:19). Holy, therefore, are the bodies also of married people who are faithful to each other and to the Lord.

We cannot love what is eternal unless we cease to love what is temporal. Think of human love as the hand of the soul. If it is holding something, it cannot hold anything else. In order to be able to hold a gift it has been given, it must let go of what it is holding. This is what I am saying, and note that I am putting it plainly: he who loves the world cannot love God; his hand is occupied. God says to him, "Take in your hand what I am giving you," but he does not wish to let go of what he holds and so cannot receive what is being offered. Have I said, "Let no one whatsoever possess anything"? No: if someone is able, if his perfection requires this of him, let him cease to possess. But if he is not able to do this and is held back by ties and obligations, let him possess, but without being possessed. Let him be the master, not the slave, of his property. As the apostle says, **This is what I mean, brothers: the time is short. For the time that remains, let those who have wives be as if they did not have them. And let those who mourn be as if they were not mourning, and those who rejoice as if they were not rejoicing. And let those who buy be as if they had no possessions, and those who use the things of the world as if they are not using them. For the present shape of this world is passing away. I want you to be free from care.** What does it mean not to love what you possess in this world? Let it not hold your hand, the hand by which you are to hold onto God. Let not your love be occupied, the love by which you can move toward God and cling to the one who created you.

You reply, "God knows that it is without guilt that I hold what I possess." But tribulation will test this if you are cut off from your possessions and you blaspheme. (It was not long ago that we had to endure such tribulation.) You are cut off from your possessions, and it turns out that you are now not the man you were: clearly your words now are one thing and your words of yesterday quite another. . . .

Hearing this, direct your hearts toward God. Do not deceive yourselves. When things are going well for you in the world, that is the time to question yourselves. That is the time to ask whether you love or do not love this world. Learn to dismiss it before you are dismissed by it. What does it mean to dismiss it? Not to love it in your heart. While that which you must lose is still with you — and either during your life or when you die you will lose it, it cannot be always with you — while it is still with you, loosen your love for it, be prepared, by the will of God, to fasten your love upon God. Hold fast to him whom you cannot lose against your will so that if it should happen that you lose these temporal things you may say, *The Lord gave, and the Lord has taken away; as it has pleased the Lord, so has it come to pass. Blessed be the name of the Lord* (Job 1:21). But if it should happen — and if it is God's will — that your possessions are with you up to the end, you will receive, when you are freed from this life, an immense reward, and perfect blessedness will be yours when you sing "Alleluia." . . .

And so, my brethren, love of the world and friendship with the world make us enemies of God. The world does not keep its promises but is a liar and a deceiver. That is why in this world men never cease to hope, yet few achieve everything they hope for. Whatever you achieve becomes straightway a mere trifle in your eyes. You form new desires, new hopes. And while you wait for these to be achieved, you set no value on your earlier achievements. So, hold onto God: he never loses his value, and nothing is more beautiful than he is. Those other things lose their value because they cannot last and are not what he is. O soul, only he who created you is sufficient for you. Whatever else you grasp is poor stuff: only he can satisfy you who has made you in his own image. The words, *Lord, show us the Father, and we shall be satisfied* (John 14:8) are God's own saying. Only in him is there complete security. And where there is security, there there is a kind of insatiable satisfaction: you will not be sated and wish to depart, yet you will lack nothing and experience no want.

I exhort you, my brethren, in the words of the apostle: **The time is short. For the time that remains, let those who have wives be as if they did not have them. And let those who mourn be as if they were not mourning, and those who rejoice as if they were not rejoicing. And let those who buy be as if they had no possessions, and those who use the things of the world as if they are not using them.** The apostles let go of what they had, and that is why Peter said *Lo, we have left everything* (Matt 19:25). What did you leave, Peter? One little boat, one net. He might reply to me, "I have left the whole world since I have kept nothing for myself." It is always true that poverty, that is, the poor man, has small resources but large desires. God does not pay attention to what he has but to what he desires. It is his will that is being judged and observed by One who is unseen. And so the apostles left all and left the world entirely because they cut away all that they hoped for in this world, followed the one who made the world, and believed his promises. And afterward many others did the same. Is it not surprising to learn who did this? The very men who killed the Lord! There in Jerusalem, when the Lord had ascended into heaven and after ten days kept his promise by sending the Holy Spirit, the disciples, filled with the Holy Spirit, spoke in the languages of all the nations (Acts 2). Then many Jews who were in Jerusalem heard it and felt awe before the gracious gift of the Savior. And while in their astonishment they discussed among themselves why it had taken place, the apostles told them that it was a gift from the Spirit of the one whom they had killed. They asked how they might be saved. For they dared not hope that their crime would be forgiven since they had killed the Lord of all creation. They received consolation from the apostles, and when they had been promised pardon and remission of their punishment, they believed. And selling all that they had, they laid the price of their property at the feet of the apostles, being made all the better because they were so afraid (Acts 2:43-45). Their great fear drove out their love of luxury. Now this was done by those who killed the Lord, it was done later by many others, and it is being done today by many. We know, we see the instances, we receive consolation and joy from many examples, for the word of God is not without effect in those who hear it with faith. . . . And when persecution came, they were approved because they **used the world as if they were not using it**. Not only common folk, the ordinary, the poor and resourceless, but also many men of great wealth, senators, and women of high station renounced all when persecution came in order to bring the tower to completion (see Luke 14:28). By sincere courage and piety they overcame the lying and deceitful devil.

1 Corinthians 7:32-35

32I want you to be free from anxieties. The unmarried man is anxious about the affairs of the Lord, how to please the Lord; 33but the married man is anxious about worldly affairs, how to please his wife, 34and his interests are divided. And the unmarried woman or girl is anxious about the affairs of the Lord, how to be holy in body and spirit; but the married woman is anxious about worldly affairs, how to please her husband. 35I say this for your own benefit, not to lay any restraint upon you, but to promote good order and to secure your undivided devotion to the Lord.

(1) Clement of Alexandria

Yes, Paul does say, **the unmarried man is anxious about the affairs of the Lord, but the married man how to please his wife**. What does this mean? Cannot those who please their wives in a godly way give thanks to God? Is the married man not allowed to **be anxious about the affairs of the Lord** together with his wife? But just as **the unmarried woman is anxious about the affairs of the Lord, how to be holy in body and spirit**, so also the **married woman is anxious about** the affairs of her husband and about the affairs of the Lord, **how to be holy in body and spirit**. For both are holy in the Lord, the one as a wife, the other as a virgin.

(2) John Chrysostom on verses 34-35

I say this for your own benefit, not to lay any restraint upon you, but to promote good order and to secure your undivided devotion. Let the virgins hear that virginity is not defined by one point alone [i.e., sexual abstinence]. For a woman who is anxious about the things of the world cannot be a virgin or be worthy of respect. For when Paul said, **The wife is divided from the virgin,**[15] Paul then adds that the point on which the two differ is anxiety; it is this that divides the two. In defining the virgin and the one who is not a virgin, he mentions not marriage or chastity but freedom from worries and engagement with worries. For it is not sexual relations that are wrong but being kept from a contemplative life.

(3) Basil of Caesarea

Question 5: On having an undistracted mind

We must recognize that we cannot fulfill the commandment to love God or our neighbor, or any other commandment, when our thoughts are wandering in this direction and that. For a person who is constantly embarking on something new cannot excel in any skill or area of knowledge. Nor can he master any subject if he is not acquainted with the things that relate to his goal. Our actions must be consistent with our goals since no rational end is accomplished by inappropriate means. You cannot achieve the metal-worker's task by being a potter, nor are athletic honors achieved by learning to play the pipe. Instead, every goal requires specific efforts appropriate to it. Thus we achieve the discipline that is pleasing to God, and in accordance with the gospel of Christ, by withdrawing from the **anxieties** of the world and becoming completely estranged from its **distractions.** For this reason the apostle, even though he allows marriage and gives it his blessing, contrasts the busyness marriage requires with **anxiety** for God, the two being mutually exclusive. He says, **The unmarried man is anxious about the affairs of the Lord, how to please the Lord; but the married man is anxious about worldly affairs, how to please his wife.** So too the Lord attests to the pure and single-minded attitude of his disciples when he says, *You are not of this world* (John 15:19). On the other hand, he declares that the world cannot receive the knowledge of God or accept the Holy Spirit. For he says, *O righteous Father, the world has not known thee* (John 17:25) and also, *the Spirit of Truth, whom the world cannot receive* (John 14:17).

Therefore, one who truly follows God must dissolve the bonds that bind him to this life. This is accomplished by complete withdrawal and by forgetting old habits. We must become totally alienated from the ties that bind us to the fleshly life as if removed to another world through our participation in it, as Paul says: *Our citizenship is in heaven* (Phil 3:20). Otherwise we cannot achieve the goal of **pleasing** God, since the Lord has decreed:

---

15. In Greek the subject of the first verb in v. 34 ("is divided") is not expressed. Most modern translations take the subject to be "the married man" mentioned in v. 33. John Chrysostom understands it to be the "wife" who is "divided from," that is, contrasted with, the virgin.

So therefore, whoever of you does not renounce all that he has cannot be my disciple (Luke 14:33). And once we have done this, we must watch our hearts closely so that our awareness of God is never lost and the memory of his marvelous deeds is never sullied by thoughts of vain things. A holy awareness of God, imprinted on our souls like an indelible seal through a pure and continuous recollection of him, must be our constant companion. In this way the love of God will prevail in us and rouse us to fulfill the Lord's commandments, which in turn make our love for God abiding and unchanging. The Lord also speaks of this when he says on one occasion, *If you love me, you will keep my comandments* (John 14:15). And at another time he says, *If you keep my commandments, you will abide in my love,* and, expressing himself even more persuasively, *Just as I have kept my Father's commandments and abide in his love* (John 15:10).

(4) Athanasius

[*In his work* On Virginity *Athanasius addresses a woman who has dedicated herself to a life of celibacy.*] Pay attention, handmaid of Christ, and all who wish to be saved, and give ear to my words. May your ears receive words inspired by God. For *this mystery is a profound one* (Eph 5:32), as the blessed Paul said, that whenever a man *joins himself* to a wife, they are both *one body* (1 Cor 6:16). And so again he says that every man or women *who is united to the Lord becomes one spirit with him* (1 Cor 6:17). If those who marry in this world leave father and mother to be united with mortal spouses (Gen 3:24), how much more should a virgin who practices continence leave all earthly things and be joined to the Lord alone. And the apostle himself confirms this point when he says, **And the unmarried woman is anxious about the affairs of the Lord, how to be holy in body and spirit; but the married woman is anxious about worldly affairs, how to please her husband, and her interests are divided.** This is what I mean: if a virgin or a widow who lives a celibate life is concerned about something in this world, this concern is her "husband." And if she has possessions or goods, her anxiety about them defiles her mind. For just as the body is defiled by the husband, so also worldly possessions defile the soul and the body of the continent woman, and she is not **holy in body and spirit**. But she whose concern is the work of God has Christ as her bridegroom (Eph 5:23-24). For the woman who is married to a mortal husband does the will of her husband, for so it is written, *For the wife does not rule over her own body, but the husband does* (1 Cor 7:4), and again, *As the church is subject to Christ, so let wives also be subject in everything to their husbands* (Eph 5:24). We can, if we wish, use such worldly matters to understand the higher things: the one who is joined to the heavenly bridegroom also does the will of her husband.

And this is the will of Christ: that those who are joined to him not be troubled by anything in this world or anxious about any earthly thing, but only bear the cross of the one who was crucified for them (Luke 14:27) and care about praising him night and day with ceaseless hymns and doxologies. He wills that the eye of the mind be enlightened so that we know his will and do it, with sincere hearts and pure minds, and that we be merciful so that, just as Christ himself is compassionate and merciful, we too should follow him (Luke 6:36). We are to be humble and gentle, long-suffering, and not render evil for evil.

(5) Augustine

[*Augustine comments on verse 34 in the context of a discussion of 1 Pet 3:3-4, "Let not yours be the outward adorning . . . but let it be the hidden person of the heart."*] God's young women, the holy virgins, eager for these adornments, have neither desired what they were within their rights to have [i.e., marriage] nor given their consent if they were forced into it. Many of them overcame the opposition of their parents with the fire of heavenly love. The father was angry, the mother in tears, but the virgin herself did not care since she had before her eyes *one lovely in beauty above the sons of men* (Ps 45:2). It was for him that she wished to adorn herself so that she might care for him alone. For **the married woman is anxious about worldly affairs, how to please her husband**, whereas the unmarried woman **is anxious about the affairs of the Lord, how to please the Lord**. Notice what is involved in love. Paul does not say, "She is anxious that she may not be condemned by God." For that is still a matter of slavish fear. Such fear, to be sure, stands guard over wicked persons so that they will refrain from wicked behavior and by refraining become worthy to receive the gift of love. But these virgins are not thinking how to avoid being punished by God but rather how they may please God by their inner beauty, the loveliness of "the hidden person," the loveliness of the heart, where they are naked before God's eyes. They are naked inwardly, not outwardly, but their goodness is both inward and outward.

(6) Gregory of Nyssa

[*This excerpt is from the introduction to a treatise on virginity.*]
The purpose of this treatise is to arouse in its readers a desire for the virtuous life. In ordinary life there are many distractions, as the apostle says. So we are compelled to propose the life of virginity as a door to the holier life. Those who are entangled in ordinary life find it difficult to meditate in peace on the godly life, but for those who have renounced entirely this troublesome life it is easy to give themselves without interruption and with **undivided devotion** to the higher things. Now advice by itself is unpersuasive, and it is hard to get a person to do what is beneficial merely by exhorting, without first demonstrating the importance of the goal toward which you are urging him. Thus I will begin my discussion with praise of virginity and end it with advice. And because excellence of any sort is easier to comprehend when it is contrasted with its opposite, we must also mention the unpleasant aspects of ordinary life. Then in due course we will describe the contemplative life and show that it cannot be attained by a person who has worldly cares. And since bodily desire becomes weaker in those who renounce such cares, we will next consider what is the true object of desire, that for the sake of which the one who created our nature gave us the capacity to desire. And when we have explained this to the best of our ability, the next step will be to show how we may attain this good: it will be shown that true virginity, undefiled by any sin, is the proper means to this end. . . .

We think it is beneficial for weaker Christians to take refuge in virginity, as in a secure fortress, and not to descend into the ordinary course of life. Otherwise they bring temptations upon themselves and become entwined, through the passions of the flesh (Gal 5:24), with the things that are *at war with the law of our mind* (Rom 7:23). They should consider what is at stake in this life: not lands or wealth or some other earthly goal but our preeminent hope. For no one who has turned toward this world, taken on its cares, and devoted himself to pleasing men (1 Cor 7:33-34; Gal 1:10) can fulfill the first and great commandment of the Lord, which is *to love God with your whole heart* and all your might (Luke 10:27). For how will someone love God with his whole heart when his heart is **divided** between God and the world, and when he steals the love he owes to God alone and uses it up in human affections? **The unmarried man is anxious about the affairs of the Lord, but the married man is anxious about worldly affairs.**

1 Corinthians 7:36-40

36**If any one thinks that he is not behaving properly toward his virgin daughter,**[16] **if she is of marriageable age,**[17] **and it has to be, let him do as he wishes: let them marry — it is no sin.** 37**But whoever is firmly established in his heart, being under no necessity but having his desire under control, and has determined this in his heart, to keep her as a virgin, he will do well.** 38**So that he who gives his virgin in marriage does well; and he who refrains from marriage will do better.** 39**A wife is bound to her husband as long as he lives. If the husband dies, she is free to be married to whom she wishes, only in the Lord.** 40**But in my judgment she is more blessed**[18] **if she remains as she is. And I think that I have the Spirit of God.**

(1) Theodoret

If any one thinks that he is not behaving properly toward his virgin daughter, if she is of marriageable age, and it has to be, let him do as he wishes: let them marry — it is no sin. If a father thinks that his daughter's remaining unmarried is a disgrace and so wishes to unite her with a husband, let him do as he sees fit. For there is no sin in marriage. Here once again Paul's directives are aimed at women who have not yet chosen a life of virginity. . . . **So that he who marries his virgin does well; and he who refrains from marriage will do better.** Paul makes clear that the first choice is good and the other is best of all, and thus he silences the heretics who condemn marriage. And he also finds it neccessary to give widows advice suitable to their situation: **A wife is bound to her husband as long as he lives. If the husband dies, she is free to be married to whom she wishes, only in the Lord.** That is, she is free to marry a fellow Christian who is pious, temperate, and law-

---

16. Here and in vv. 37-38 the Greek reads simply "virgin." In both cases the RSV translates "his betrothed." Theodoret takes this as a reference to a father's "virgin daughter"; see the following note.

17. RSV: "if his passions are strong." The Greek of this verse can be understood to refer either to a father's giving his daughter in marriage (so Theodoret) or to a man marrying a virgin to whom he is engaged (so the RSV).

18. RSV: "happier."

abiding. **But in my judgment she is more blessed if she remains as she is.** Once again Paul does not lay down the law but instead gives advice. And to inspire his hearers' trust he adds: **And I think that I have the Spirit of God.** These words, he says, do not come from me but from the Holy Spirit, whose instrument I am. We should notice, however, that the woman who remains unmarried is not called simply "blessed"; instead Paul describes her as **more blessed.** This is to teach that a woman who enters into a second marriage is not miserable, but blessed, if she marries in acccordance with the apostle's intructions. For by using the comparative, he declares that the one who remarries is also blessed. And this is sufficient refutation of the Novatianists, who denounce second marriage as fornication — which is clearly contrary to the apostle's instructions.

(2) Augustine on verse 38

So *let marriage be held in honor among all, and let the marriage bed be undefiled* (Heb 13:4). We do not call marriage good only by comparison with fornication. For in that case there would be two evils, of which the second was worse. On that showing fornication would also be good because adultery is worse (since it is worse to violate another's marriage than to consort with a prostitute), and adultery would be good because incest is worse (since it is worse to lie with your mother than with another's wife), and so forth until we come to those things which, as the apostle says, *it is a shame even to speak of* (Eph 5:12). Everything would be good in comparison with what is worse.

But who can doubt that such reasoning is false? It is therefore not true that marriage and fornication are two evils, with the latter being worse; rather, there are two goods, marriage and celibacy, of which the latter is better.

So there are humble celibates and proud ones. The proud should not promise themselves the kingdom of God. Yes, the place to which celibacy leads is a higher one, but *every one who exalts himself will be humbled* (Luke 14:11). Why do you seek a loftier place out of a desire for loftiness when you can reach it by holding onto your humility? If you raise yourself up, God casts you down, but if you cast yourself down, God raises you up (Luke 1:51-52). This is the word of the Lord: nothing can be added or subtracted. But celibates are commonly so proud that they are ungrateful not only to people in general but also to their parents and consider themselves superior to them. Why? Because the parents had children, while they themselves spurned marriage. But where would the ungrateful people who spurn marriage come from if their parents had not begotten them? The son is **better** than his married father because he has not taken a wife, and the daughter is **better** than her married mother because she has not sought a husband. Yet if they are prouder, they are in no way better, and if they are better, then assuredly they are more humble. If you wish to be better, question your soul to see whether it is *puffed up* (1 Cor 8:1). If it is puffed up, it is also vain and empty. When the devil finds emptiness, it is there that he contrives to build a nest.

Finally, my brethren, I make bold to say that it is a beneficial thing for proud celibates to fall so that they may be humbled in the very thing in which they exalt themselves.

What good does chastity do a person if he is mastered by pride? He has despised that by which human beings are born and desired that by which the devil fell [i.e., pride]. You have spurned marriage, you have done well. You have chosen something **better** — but do not grow proud. It is from marriage that man is born, but it is by pride that the angels fell. If I consider your blessings separately, the celibate man is better than his father for spurning marriage and the celibate woman than her mother. For virgin holiness is better than conjugal chastity. If these two things are compared, the one gift is greater than the other, as no one will doubt. But if we take pride and humility into consideration and I ask you which is better, pride or humility, you reply "Humility." So, join this to virgin holiness. But pride has no business being joined to your virgin holiness — or residing in your mother. If you hold onto pride and your mother to humility, the mother will be better than the daughter. I will make one more comparison. When I was looking only at virginity and marriage, I found you **better**. But now when I look at two qualities, I do not hesitate to prefer the humble wife to the proud virgin. Notice how it is that I made my preference when I was first comparing. Conjugal chastity is a good thing, virgin holiness a **better** one. I was comparing two goods, distinguishing not bad from good but good from **better**. But when it comes to the second pair, pride and humility, can we say that pride is good but humility is better? Surely not. What do we say? Pride is bad, humility good. If, therefore, one of the two is good and the other bad, and we join the bad to your greater good, the whole becomes bad. If it is joined to your mother's lesser good, the result is a great good. The mother, who is married, will have a lesser place in the kingdom of heaven than the daughter, who is a virgin . . . but both will be there. Just as with a bright star and a star of lesser magnitude, both will be in the heavens. But if your mother is humble and you are proud, she will have some sort of place there and you will have none.

1 Corinthians 8

In chapter 8 Paul turns to questions of how the Corinthian converts are to handle interactions with non-Christians. Here, and again in chapter 10, he considers whether Christians may eat meat that has been dedicated to a pagan god (some of which would end up in the butcher shops), and also whether it is permissible to attend dinner parties held in rooms that belong to a pagan temple. Arguing against those who claim freedom to eat such meat because of their superior knowledge, Paul begins the chapter by considering the relation of knowledge and love (vv. 1-3). John Chrysostom points out the wisdom of Paul's rhetorical strategy, in particular how he appeals to the "stronger" members of the community. To illustrate the perils knowledge can bring, Ambrosiaster compares it with wine, while Augustine explores how knowledge relates to pride, the cardinal sin. Gregory of Nyssa applies Paul's words about the limits of human knowledge to the knowledge of God: since God is infinite, the quest to know him will never end.

In verses 4-5 Paul considers the nature of the Greek gods and the cult statues ("idols") worshiped by non-Christians. He contrasts the so-called gods with the "one God" and "one Lord, Jesus Christ" Christians worship (v. 6). This last phrase proved very useful in the christological debates of the fourth century. Gregory of Nyssa, for example, cites verse 6 to disprove the Neo-Arian claim that the Son was a "servant" who was not equal to God (see also John Chrysostom, Theodoret, and Ambrosiaster on v. 6). John Chrysostom, noting that Paul does not mention the Holy Spirit here, adduces other texts where Paul ranks the Spirit together with the Father and the Son in order to demonstrate that the Spirit is also divine.

Paul next turns to the specific situation of those he calls the "weaker brothers," whose faith is shaken when they see their fellow Christians ("the strong") eating meat offered to idols (vv. 7-9). Ambrosiaster explains that such people have not yet given up the notion that idols contain something divine. John Chrysostom's comments indicate how much the Church's situation had changed between Paul's day and the fourth century: he has to admonish his audience to imagine a time when pagan religion was in full swing and the Christians a small minority. Nonetheless, Christians of the late fourth century were much closer than we are to the circumstances of Paul's time. Augustine's comments on verses 10-13 indicate that the question Paul addresses here — whether Christians could share table fellowship with pagans — was still an issue in his own time. Gregory of Nyssa applies Paul's statement "I will never eat meat" (v. 13) and, by implication, all of this chapter to a very different issue, using it to explain and defend certain theological statements made by his brother Basil.

1 Corinthians 8:1-3

1Now concerning food offered to idols: we know that all of us possess knowledge. Knowledge puffs up, but love builds up. 2If any one imagines that he knows something, he does not yet know as he ought to know. 3But if one loves God, one is known by him.

(1) Ambrosiaster

Now concerning food offered to idols: we know that all of us possess knowledge. Now Paul is about to speak of knowledge, and he does not say at first what knowledge is but reveals this as he addresses the matter at hand by asserting *that an idol has no real existence* (1 Cor 8:4).

Knowledge puffs up. It is obvious that one who has knowledge glories in that very fact: even if prudence keeps him from doing so outwardly, he glories in his heart. It is in the nature of knowledge that one glories in oneself; hence it **puffs up**.

But love builds up. And so knowledge is great and useful in itself if it is humbled by love so that it grows the more. It is tempered by love with the result that it is not so undiluted that it inebriates the knower, causing him to exalt himself. Just as wine unmixed with water clouds the mind, so too knowledge causes pride unless it is tempered. All foods and drinks, taken alone, are unpleasant and harmful: bread by itself is not good to eat, nor are other foods pleasant unless they are mixed with something, but they are noxious. And so **love builds up**. Love itself, though called by a single name, consists in many things. For it cannot build up without patience or humility or simplicity of heart.

(2) John Chrysostom

What, then, was the charge that Paul lodged against the Corinthians at that time? It was a serious one and the cause of much trouble. What was it? Many of them had learned that what *goes into* a person does not *defile* him, but only *what comes out* (Matt 15:17-18), and that idols, which are wood and stones and mere demons, can cause neither harm nor benefit (1 Cor 8:4; 12:2). They had used this perfect knowledge of theirs in an inconsiderate way, injuring others as well as themselves. They went to the idols and took part in their feasts and in this way caused serious harm. For those who still feared the idols and did not yet know enough to make light of them also participated in those meals, because they saw the more advanced Christians doing so. Consequently, they were particularly injured by this. For they did not handle what was set before them in the same spirit as the others, but regarded it as **food offered to idols**, and so the practice was conducive to idolatry. . . . But the blessed apostle, intending to set things straight, does not resort at once to impassioned speech. For in fact this was more a matter of ignorance than of malice. So at first exhortation was required, rather than anger and stern rebuke. . . .

Now concerning food offered to idols: we know that all of us possess knowledge.

As he usually does, Paul leaves the *weak* alone and addresses himself first to the *strong*.[1] He does this also in the Epistle to the Romans, where he asks, *Why do you pass judgment on your brother?* (Rom 14:10). A strong person can take even a sharp rebuke easily. And so here Paul first deprives them of their pride by showing that the "perfect knowledge" they had considered their own special possession was actually common knowledge. **We know**, he says, **that all of us possess knowledge. . . .** By showing right off that this knowledge is common, he checks their pride. For people who possess something great and admirable become especially proud when it is theirs alone. But if it is clear that they share it with others, they no longer feel the same way. . . .

With this first blow Paul strikes down their pride; with the second he does so even more forcefully. . . . For he says, **all of us possess knowledge**, and then adds: **Knowledge puffs up, but love builds up.** Thus when knowledge is without love, it leads to folly. . . .

Boasting tends to cause divisions; love, however, both unites and leads to knowledge. Paul expresses this clearly in the words, **if one loves God, one is known by him. . . .** Do you see how he is already playing the prelude to his discourse on love (1 Corinthians 13)? All those terrible things came from this one source — not from perfect knowledge but rather from failure to love warmly and to be considerate of the neighbor. This was the reason they were torn asunder and filled with pride, and were guilty of all the other faults he identifies in them. And before this passage as well as later in the Letter Paul constantly speaks of love and strives to restore this fount of blessings. . . . If you know more than your neighbor, because of your love for him you will not be proud but will instead lead him to the same knowledge. This is why Paul says: **Knowledge puffs up, but love builds up. . . .**

But if one loves God, one is known by him. See how many ways Paul employs to bring down their pride. First, by saying **all of us possess knowledge**, he shows that they were not the only ones who knew what they knew. Then he asserts that what they are doing is harmful since it lacks love: **Knowledge puffs up.** Next he says that even when it is accompanied by love, knowledge is not complete or perfect: **If anyone imagines that he knows something, he does not yet know,** Paul says, **as he ought to know.** In addition, he points out that they do not have this knowledge from themselves, but by the free gift of God. He does not say, "he knows God," but **he is known by God.** Then he says that this knowledge itself comes from love, which they did not have as they ought to have: **if one loves God, one is known by him.**

(3) Augustine

Knowledge, says the apostle, **puffs up**. What are we to conclude? That you ought to avoid knowledge and choose to know nothing rather than be puffed up? Why would I address you if ignorance is better than knowledge? Why would I argue with you? . . . Why remind you of what you know, why instruct you in what you don't know, if we should avoid knowledge so that it won't **puff us up**? So then, love knowledge, but put love ahead of it.

1. On the "weak" and the "strong," see 1 Cor 8:7-8; Rom 14:1-2, 21; 15:1.

If knowledge is by itself, it **puffs up**. But because **love builds up**, it does not permit knowledge to be puffed up. Knowledge puffs up when love does not build up. But when it builds up, knowledge is set firm. There is no puffing up where a *rock* is the foundation (1 Cor 10:4; Matt 16:18).

How great a temptation it is to be puffed up, that is, proud! Even the great apostle said that because of this vice he was given *a thorn in the flesh, a messenger of Satan, to buffet me* (2 Cor 12:7). Now he who is buffeted receives blows to the head, so that he cannot raise it up. And it is in the head that knowledge creates the danger of pride. So in a situation where great things were being revealed, pride was a danger: *And to keep me from being too elated by the abundance of revelations, a thorn was given me in the flesh, a messenger of Satan, to buffet me, to keep me from being too elated. Three times I besought the Lord about this, that it should leave me; but he said to me, "My grace is sufficient for you, for my power is made perfect in weakness"* (2 Cor 12:7-9).

(4) Gregory of Nyssa on verse 2

[*The following is from a commentary on the Song of Songs, in which Gregory interprets the love of the bridegroom and the bride as a description of the relationship between the human soul and God.*]

Now when . . . the soul that gazes toward God has been raised to such a great height, it **does not yet know,** Paul says, **as** it **ought to know**. Nor does it *consider that it has comprehended,* but it continues to run toward what is beyond, *straining forward to what lies ahead* (Phil 3:13). The words that follow suggest that we understand the soul as speaker: *Upon the handles of the bolt, I opened to my beloved,* and the text continues, *My beloved had gone; my soul failed me when he spoke* (Cant 5:5-6). Through these words we are taught that there is only one way of comprehending the power that transcends all understanding (1 Cor 2:9): not to be content with what we have understood but always to seek greater understanding, never standing still.

1 Corinthians 8:4-6

4Hence, as to the eating of food offered to idols, we know that an idol has no real existence, and that there is no God but one. 5For although there may be so-called gods in heaven or on earth — as indeed there are many "gods" and many "lords" — 6yet for us there is one God, the Father, from whom are all things and for whom we exist,[2] and one Lord, Jesus Christ, through whom are all things and through whom we exist.

---

2. The Latin text used by Ambrosiaster reads, "in whom we exist."

(1) John Chrysostom

See what a tight spot Paul has fallen into! He wants to argue two different points: that it is necessary to refrain from such a meal but also that it cannot harm those who partake of it. These things do not fit together easily. For if the Corinthians learned that the meal was harmless, they would be prone to treat it lightly, as if it were a matter of indifference. On the other hand, if they were prohibited from touching such food, they would suspect that they were being forbidden something that could do them harm. . . .

[We know] that an idol has no real existence, and that there is no God but one. Is it true that there are no idols, no carved statues? There are, but they do not have any power, and they are not gods but only stones and demons. . . . **For although there may be so-called gods — as indeed there are,** not simply gods but only **so-called gods,** since they are gods in word only, not in reality. **In heaven or on earth.** The phrase **in heaven** refers to the sun, the moon, and the stars, which complete the heavenly choir. And in fact the Greeks worshiped these things. By things **on earth,** Paul means the demons and all those men who were made into gods.[3] **Yet for us there is one God, the Father.** First Paul speaks of **God** without adding "the Father," and says that **there is no other God.** Now that he has excluded the pagan gods entirely, he adds the word "Father." And then he also adds, as the greatest evidence of divinity, **from whom are all things,** for this shows that the pagan gods are not gods. "Away with gods who did not make the heaven and the earth," Paul says.

Next he adds something no less significant: **and for whom we exist.** When he says, **from whom all things are,** he means the creation, the passage from nonexistence to existence. But when he adds, **and for whom we exist,** he is speaking of faith and being made God's own. This repeats what he said earlier: *He is the source of your life in Christ Jesus* (1 Cor 1:30). We are in a double sense from him, first in coming from nonexistence into existence, and second in coming to be believers. For this, too, is creation, as Paul says elsewhere, *that he might create in himself one new man in place of the two* (Eph 2:15).

And one Lord, Jesus Christ, through whom are all things and through whom we exist. . . . But if you should claim that the title "God" is not appropriate for the Son because Paul says **there is one God,** notice that the same issue arises from what he says about the Son. The Son is called the **one Lord,** but this does not lead us to say that the title "Lord" suits him alone. Thus the word "one" has the same force in the case of the Father and of the Son. Paul does not exclude the Father from being Lord, as the Son is Lord, just because he calls the Son the **one Lord.** Likewise, he does not exclude the Son from being God, as the Father is God, just because the Father is called the **one God.**

But if someone should ask why Paul makes no mention of the Spirit, we would answer that he was talking to idolaters and arguing about **many gods** and **many lords.** . . . Up to now, Paul's argument has been directed against idolaters, to show that for Christians there is no multiplicity of gods. For this reason, he constantly uses the word **one,** as when he says, **there is no God but one,** and **yet for us there is one God** and **one Lord.**

---

3. Chrysostom may be thinking of Euhemerus (d. 315 B.C.), who argued that all the gods of the Greek pantheon were actually good men who came to be regarded as gods.

From this it is clear that Paul speaks in this way as a concession to the weakness of his audience, and this is why he makes no mention of the Spirit. . . . At any rate, when he feels no such necessity, notice how he adds the Spirit to the others: *The grace of our Lord Jesus Christ and the love of the Father and the fellowship of the Holy Spirit be with you all* (2 Cor 13:14). And again: *Now there are varieties of gifts, but the same Spirit; and there are varieties of service, but the same Lord; and there are varieties of working, but it is the same God* (1 Cor 12:4).

(2) Theodore of Mopsuestia

For although there may be so-called gods in heaven or on earth. The addition of **so-called** is highly appropriate. For by this Paul makes clear that they are falsely so called and are not truly gods. Therefore, just as **there are many so-called gods** among those who go astray, but among us, who *possess knowledge* (8:1), there is **one God,** so there is also **one Lord.**

(3) Gregory of Nyssa on verse 6

Eunomius[4] claims that it is the nature of the Son to be ruled by the Father. Here are his exact words: "He who has his existence and life because of the Father does not claim the Father's dignity for himself, since the being that rules even the Son draws to itself the whole notion of being."[5] Now if these were the views of some pagan philosopher, he would not have to bother with the Gospels and the rest of the teaching of the divinely inspired Scriptures. For *what fellowship* is there (2 Cor 6:14) between Christian teaching and the *wisdom* that has been *made foolish* (1 Cor 1:20)? But if Eunomius seeks support from Scripture, let him only adduce such a statement from holy Scripture, and we will be silent.

I hear Paul crying aloud: **There is one Lord, Jesus Christ.** But Eunomius responds that Christ is a servant. For we acknowledge no other sign of servitude than being subject and being ruled. A servant is a servant in all respects, but by his nature a servant cannot be a lord, even if he be called "lord" in an extended sense of the word. But why do I adduce the words of Paul as testimony to the lordship of the Lord? Paul's Master himself tells his disciples that he is truly Lord. Accepting the confession of those who call him **Lord** and "teacher," he says, *You call me Teacher and Lord; and you are right, for so I am* (John 13:13). He also commanded them to address the Father by this same name, saying: Do not call anyone on earth teacher, *for you have one teacher,* Christ. *And call no man your father on earth, for you have one Father, who is in heaven* (Matt 23:8-9).

Caught between these voices, to whom shall we listen? On the one hand, the Lord

---

4. Eunomius, bishop of Cyzicus (d. 394), claimed that the Son was unlike the Father in essence and, as a creature, was subordinate to him (see Appendix 3).

5. In other words, being in the full sense belongs only to God.

himself and likewise Paul, who has Christ speaking in him (see 1 Cor 2:16), tell us not to consider Christ a servant, but to honor him in the same way as the Father is honored. Eunomius, on the other hand, charges that the Lord is a servant, claiming that the One on whom the rule of the universe rests is subject to rule. Is there any doubt which we should choose? Is it hard to determine which is better? Shall I disdain the counsel of Paul, O Eunomius? Shall I consider the voice of the Truth (John 14:6) less reliable than your deceit? But Christ says, *If I had not come and spoken to them, they would not have sin* (John 15:22). He has spoken to them [i.e., to Eunomius and his followers] himself, saying that he truly is Lord, not that he is falsely so called, for he says, *for so I am* (John 13:13). Therefore, how must we treat someone whose punishment is inevitable because it was promised beforehand?

(4) Theodoret

Yet for us there is one God, the Father, from whom are all things and for whom we exist, and one Lord, Jesus Christ, through whom are all things and through whom we exist. Those who are surrounded by the dark gloom of ignorance go astray after many gods, gods that have no real existence (1 Cor 8:4). But we know that there is **one God, the Father**, and **one Lord, Jesus Christ**. Here again we can admire the apostle's wisdom. For he has already shown that the title **Lord** is equivalent to the title **God** [in 8:5], and now he distinguishes the two, using **God** for the Father and **Lord** for the Son, which he does to remedy his hearers' weakness. For anyone who wants to can easily learn from the Scriptures that Paul often calls the Son "God." For he says, *awaiting the appearing of our great God and Savior Jesus Christ* (Tit 2:13). And also, *Of their race [i.e., the Jews], according to the flesh, is the Christ, who is God over all* (Rom 9:5). And *in the kingdom of Christ, [who is] God* (Eph 5:5). And there are countless other texts like these.

But in our passage Paul calls the one **God** and the other **Lord** because he does not want to provide those who had just escaped from pagan error and learned the truth with an excuse for returning to the error of polytheism. Now if the followers of Arius and Eunomius[6] should say that the phrase [**there is**] **one God** excludes the Son from the divinity of the Father, let them hear what follows: **and one Lord.** Now if it were true that, because the Father is **one God**, the Son is not God, then neither would the Father be Lord, since [**there is**] **one Lord, Jesus Christ.** But let this blasphemous idea be turned back on their own heads. For the divine apostle shows the equality of Father and Son by using the word **one** for Father and Son alike, and also by showing that "Lord" is the equivalent of "God." In a similar way the Old Testament shows that these two titles belong together. For it says, *I am the LORD your God, who brought you out of the land of Egypt* (Exod 20:2), *Hear, O Israel: The LORD our God is one LORD* (Deut 6:4), and *O LORD my God, thou art very great!* (Ps 104:1).

6. On Eunomius see Gregory of Nyssa's comments on 1 Cor 8:6, quoted above, and the note *ad loc.;* on Arius see Appendix 3.

(5) Ambrosiaster

Yet for us there is one God, the Father, from whom are all things, and in whom we exist. All things, whatever and wherever they are, are **from** him, but in saying that we are **in** him he separates us from all other things: although other things are **from** him, they are nevertheless not **in** him since they are not believers.

And one Lord, Jesus Christ, through whom are all things and through whom we exist. All things are from the Father but were created through the Son. But when he says **through whom we exist,** he means that we have been remade by the one who created us: having been created through him along with others, and having fallen into mental stupor and ignorance, through him we have come to know the mystery of one God. And so Paul speaks of **one God, the Father,** and **one Lord, Jesus** his Son so that, since **God** must necessarily be **Lord,** in like manner **Lord** shall also be understood to be **God.** Thus he shows that there is **one God** and **Lord** by twice naming a single first cause.

1 Corinthians 8:7-9

₇**However, not all possess this knowledge. But some, through being hitherto accustomed to idols, eat food as really offered to an idol; and their conscience, being weak, is defiled. ₈Food will not commend us to God. We are no worse off if we do not eat, and no better off if we do. ₉Only take care lest this liberty of yours somehow become a stumbling block to the weak.**

(1) Ambrosiaster

However, not all possess this knowledge. That is, not all believers know the mystery of *one God* (1 Cor 8:6). Some believers think that idols are in some sense divine. Moreover, some who believe in the reality of idols **eat food as really offered to an idol.** Some of the common folk, still honoring the idol, ate food sacrificed to it in the belief that it was a god.

And their conscience, being weak, is defiled. The conscience receives a stain if its faith in the one God is weakened. **Food will not commend us to God.** It is true that we will not please God because we eat everything or offend him if we reject some things. **We are no worse off if we do not eat, and no better off if we do.** If we reject the food of idols, we will not necessarily go hungry, and if we take it, there will not be such great plenty that we lack nothing. Such food must be rejected since we can live without it and it is a stumbling block for our brothers.

(2) John Chrysostom

But some, through being hitherto accustomed to idols, eat food as really offered to an idol; and their conscience, being weak, is defiled. They still tremble before idols, Paul says. Don't think of the present situation, where several generations of your forebears were Christians. Carry your mind back to those earlier times. Imagine a time when the Christian gospel was just beginning to be proclaimed, when pagan impiety still held sway, fires burned on the altars, sacrifices and libations were being performed, and the pagans were in the majority. Imagine people who had inherited paganism from their ancestors and were descendants of pagan fathers, grandfathers, and great-grandfathers, people on whom these demons had inflicted much suffering. Consider what their situation would be when all at once they converted, how they would tremble in fear at the demons' designs. . . .

Suppose someone who follows Jewish custom considers himself unclean if he touches a corpse. If he should see others touching a corpse with a clear conscience and then do the same without sharing their understanding, he would be defiled. This is what these people [the "weak" in Corinth] were experiencing at that time. . . .

Food will not commend us to God. See how Paul disparages a practice the Corinthians thought arose from perfect knowledge! . . . Paul says, **take care lest this liberty of yours somehow become a stumbling block to** the brothers who are **weak**. He does not say that your liberty *is* a stumbling block, nor does he denounce them, which might make them even more impudent. But what does he say? **Take care.** He makes them feel fear and shame and leads them to stop what they are doing. And he does not say, "this knowledge of yours," which would have been somewhat laudatory. Nor does he say, "this perfection of yours," but rather **this liberty**, which is akin to heedlessness, stubbornness, and boastful pride.

1 Corinthians 8:10-13

10**For if any one sees you, a man of knowledge, at table in an idol's temple, might he not be encouraged, if his conscience is weak, to eat food offered to idols?** 11**And so by your knowledge this weak man is destroyed, the brother for whom Christ died.** 12**Thus, sinning against your brethren and wounding their conscience when it is weak, you sin against Christ.** 13**Therefore, if food is a cause of my brother's falling, I will never eat meat, lest I cause my brother to fall.**

(1) John Chrysostom

So the brother who is **weak** will be **destroyed by your** eating — **the brother for whom Christ died**. When you commit such an injury, there are two things that make it difficult to pardon: first, that the injured one is **weak**, and, second, that he is a **brother**. In addition, there is a third, even weightier than the others. What is this? That while Christ was willing even to die for him, you don't have the patience even to make allowance for his condition. By these words Paul reminds the mature Christian what he himself used to be and that **Christ died** for him. . . . But after your weak brother has been saved in this way, will you allow him to perish, and — what is even worse — for the sake of food? . . . In the end, there are four accusations, and very weighty ones at that: that the man is a brother, and a brother who is weak, and one whom Christ valued so highly that he died for him, and, on top of all this, that he is destroyed for the sake of food. . . .

And how do they **sin against Christ**? First, because Christ treats as his own what affects his servants. Second, because those who are **wounded** belong to his body and are his members (1 Cor 12:12-20). Third, these men, for the sake of their own ambition, are destroying Christ's work, which he established by his self-sacrifice. . . .

In fact, it is the height of folly for us if we regard those who were so precious to Christ that he chose to die for them as so insignificant that we cannot even abstain from food for their sake. And this accusation could be addressed not only to the Corinthians but also to us, who care nothing about the salvation of our neighbors and utter words worthy of Satan. For to say, "What does it matter to me if this man **falls** or that one is destroyed?" is to partake of the cruelty and inhumanity of the devil. . . .

Therefore,[7] whenever you see someone chopping wood, or using a hammer, or covered with soot, do not despise him but instead admire him for this. For Peter, too, girded himself and handled the nets and went fishing after the resurrection of the Lord (John 21:3, 7). And why do I speak of Peter? Paul himself, after he had made countless journeys and performed such great miracles, stood in a tentmaker's shop and sewed hides together, and angels stood in awe of him, and demons trembled. And he was not ashamed to say, *These hands ministered to my necessities* (Acts 20:34).

(2) Cyril of Alexandria

Thus, sinning against your brethren and wounding their conscience when it is weak, you sin against Christ. If we **cause** our brothers **to fall**, we will sin against **Christ,** who **died** for the sake of the salvation of all of us. What sin could equal this? **And so by your knowledge this weak man is destroyed,** and *that which is good* becomes our sin (Rom 7:13), and the firmness of our faith becomes a **cause** of our **brother's falling**, and our knowledge becomes a pitfall.

It is a very serious matter when we trample on the weaknesses of our brothers instead of taking pains to strengthen their weak consciences. For you must *not put a stumbling block or hindrance in the way of a brother* (Rom 14:13), and you should remember what Scripture says, *Do not despise one of these little ones; for their angels always behold the face of my Father who is in heaven* (Matt 18:10). How, then, is it not a very serious matter to be accused before the holy angels?

---

7. In a section omitted here Chrysostom focuses on Paul's repeated use of the word "brother," on which he bases an exhortation to treat all Christians — especially the poor and the humble — with respect and concern.

(3) Augustine

[*In this sermon Augustine uses Paul's words to upbraid his parishioners for participating in pagan dinner parties, where there were altars on which were displayed statues of the "genius," or guiding spirit, of the city of Carthage. He understands "the weak" of verses 9-11 to refer both to immature Christians and to pagans whom Paul wants to convert.*]

If any one sees you, a person who has knowledge, eating in the temple of an idol, will not his conscience, if he is weak, be encouraged to eat food as sacrificed to idols? So the one who is weak is destroyed by your knowledge — the brother for whom Christ died. Can you not imagine how people are led astray by images if they think the images are being honored by Christians? "God knows my mind," someone demurs. But your brother doesn't know your heart. If you are weak yourself, watch out for a worse illness; if you are strong, care for your brother's weakness. Those who see you do these things are encouraged to do other things: they want not only to eat in the temple but also to sacrifice. Look at the result: **the one who is weak is destroyed by your knowledge.** Listen, brother. Even if you pay no attention to a weak man, will you also pay no heed to a brother? Wake up. What if you are sinning against Christ himself? . . .

"But I'm afraid," you will say, "that I will offend someone more important." Yes, do be afraid of offending someone more important — and then you will not offend God. You there, who are afraid of offending someone more important, see if there isn't perhaps someone who is more important than the one you are afraid of offending. . . . Is it not clear that you should least offend the one who is greatest of all? . . .

Let me be brief. As Christians you have heard that **by sinning against your brothers and wounding their conscience when it is weak, you sin against Christ.** Don't make light of this if you don't want to be blotted out of *the book of life* (Rev 3:5, Exod 32:33). . . . We want the rest of the pagans to be converted, but you are rocks in their path; though they want to come, they stumble over these rocks and turn back. They say in their hearts, "Why should we abandon the gods when Christians themselves worship them as much as we do?" "Far be it from me," the Christian says, "to worship the gods of the nations. I know, I understand, I believe." But what are you doing about the conscience of the weak man, which you are wounding? . . .

And to refute the idea that you are sinning only against a weak man, and that this is a trivial and unimportant sin, Paul says: **you sin against Christ.** . . . Do you not see the results of these harmful meals? Do you not see how *Bad company corrupts good morals* (1 Cor 15:33)? You can't speak about the gospel there, and you have to listen to talk about idols. You lose sight of the fact that Christ is God, and what you drink at these meals you vomit up in the Church.

"It isn't a god," [the Christian who attends a pagan party] says; "it's the guiding spirit of Carthage." As though it would only be a god if it were Mars or Mercury! But you must look to see how the others regard it, not what it is. We both know that it is only a stone. If a "guiding spirit" is merely some kind of adornment, then, provided the citizens of Carthage live well, they will be the "guiding spirit" of Carthage. But in fact the "guiding spirit" is a demon, as you have also heard in the same letter: *What the Gentiles sacrifice, they sacrifice to demons and not to God. I do not want you to become the companions of demons* (1 Cor 10:20). We know it isn't a god; would that the others also had this knowledge! But because they are **weak** and do not know this, we ought not to **wound** their **conscience**. That is how the apostle bids us act. As for the pagans, the altar makes it obvious that they consider the guiding spirit a god and its statue a god. What is the altar doing there if the image is not regarded as a god? . . . It shows clearly the mind of all who worship there; does it not also show clearly the mind of those who eat there? . . .

We speak to pagans differently, as to those who are **weak**. We must speak coaxingly to them so that they will listen to the truth. In your case we must apply the knife to the rotting flesh. If you want to know how the pagans are to be won over, how they are to be enlightened, how they are to be called to salvation, you must abandon their celebrations and their nonsense. If they don't agree with our truth, let them blush because their own numbers are so few.

(4) Gregory of Nyssa on verse 13

[*In this excerpt from his* Against Eunomius, *Gregory defends his brother Basil against criticisms made by the Neo-Arian Eunomius.*]
This people honors me with their lips, but their heart is far from me (Matt 15:8; Isa 29:13). What does Scripture mean by this? That the condition of the soul in relation to truth is of more importance in the sight of the divine Judge, who hears *sighs too deep for words* (Rom 8:26), than the impressiveness of the words we speak. The same words can be used in opposite senses since the speaker enjoys free use of them and the tongue is a ready servant of his will. But the One who sees hidden things (Matt 6:18) sees the disposition of the soul in its true light.

[Basil] affirms and accepts the word "ungenerated" as a description of God the Father when it is understood in a sense consistent with piety, but he urges that it not be used when it gives those who commit crimes against correct teaching the means to act impiously. Why, then, is he accused of being "inconsistent" and "hasty" — or even "wicked"?[8] Now if Basil had said that we should not think of God as "ungenerated," perhaps there would be reason to make such reproaches against him, and stronger ones as well. But in fact he does affirm this word as it is commonly understood by the faithful, and merely makes the following recommendation, which befits his role as a teacher: "Avoid this word, for it leads to disaster." What is more, he uses different words to express the point that God [the Father] is ungenerated. In all this Basil deserves none of these reproaches.

Doesn't the Truth teach us to cast off things of value if they are contributing to evil? What else is Christ telling us to do when he orders us to *cut off the right eye or hand or foot* if one of these *causes sin* (Matt 5:29-30)? Is he not telling us that even things that seem to

8. Both Gregory and his brother Basil wrote works against Eunomius, a Neo-Arian who denied the divinity of Christ. One of Eunomius's arguments was that by general agreement "ungenerated" *(agennētos)* was a title of God; thus the Son, who is "generated" (see John 1:18), could not be God. To this Basil had replied that, when faced with this argument, one should not call the Father "unbegotten." This led Eunomius to accuse Basil of being "inconsistent," "hasty," and "wicked," a charge Gregory quotes shortly before the present excerpt.

be good are useless and unprofitable if, because of the way foolish people use them, they lead men astray into some evil? Is it not better for a person to be saved by having these extremities that lead to sin lopped off than that he cling to them and perish on their account?

And what does Paul, the *imitator of Christ* (1 Cor 11:1), say? He, too, speaking from the depth of his wisdom, teaches the same doctrine. For although he pronounces all things *good* and says that *nothing is to be rejected if it is received with thanksgiving* (1 Tim 4:4), sometimes, on account of a conscience that is weak (8:10), he takes back something that he had approved and orders us to avoid it. For he says, if **my brother** comes to grief on account of **food, I will never eat meat**. This, then, is what Basil, the imitator of Paul, does as well. He saw that in the wicked usage of the heretics the word "ungenerated" made more persuasive the deceitful teaching of those who maintain that the Son is dissimilar to the Father. Therefore, while counseling us to keep the pious understanding of the "ungenerated" Father in our hearts, he bids us not to be overzealous about using this word since *for those who are perishing* (1 Cor 1:18) it had provided support to sin.

1 Corinthians 9

In this chapter, which comes between two chapters that discuss whether Christians can eat meat dedicated to pagan gods, Paul offers his life as an example of the self-restraint he wants the Corinthians to practice. He also responds to criticisms of his ministry (see v. 3), defending his right to receive compensation for his work of evangelism even though he has not taken advantage of this right. Patristic authors, like modern scholars, ponder how this chapter fits into the context (John Chrysostom on vv. 1-3; Origen on v. 7). In addition to the central point about self-restraint, the fathers identify several other general lessons here. Running through Origen's comments (see on vv. 16-17, 23-24) is the idea that Paul teaches a higher way that transcends elementary faith and leads to perfection. For example, in verses 16-17 Paul speaks of doing things of his "own will." Origen sees this as a reference to voluntary practices such as fasting and sexual asceticism, which merit a greater reward than fulfilling the basic commandments. In verses 12-18 Paul discusses the right of priests and apostles to receive food from the people they serve but says that he would rather "endure anything" than cause offense (v. 12). This leads John Chrystostom to a general exhortation to feed the poor: if Paul was willing to forego pay and go hungry, he says, we should certainly be willing to share our surplus. Augustine's interpretation of these verses, as well as his comments on verses 3-7 and 19-23, come from his On the Work of Monks. *In this treatise he quotes most of 1 Corinthians 9 and uses it to correct a group of monks who claimed that their devotion to higher things exempted them from performing manual work.*

The fathers identify several specific points that need clarification. In verse 5 ("Do we not have the right to be accompanied by a wife/woman?") Augustine explains a word that can be translated either as "wife" or "woman" as a reference to holy women who provided for Paul's material needs, while Severian leaves open the possibility that the word means "wife." The images Paul uses in verse 7 (soldier, farmer, and shepherd) proved intriguing. Origen explicates them by comparing other Scriptures, while John Chrysostom reflects on the force of the comparisons and how they fit Paul's situation. Paul's comment that God does not care about oxen (v. 9) was more disturbing. Both Augustine and John Chrysostom are concerned to show that God really does care for all his creatures. Chrysostom uses this verse as support for a general exegetical principle: Old Testament laws on subjects such as animals and plants are really intended as prescriptions for human life. Origen makes a similar point in his symbolic interpretation of the plowman (vv. 9-11). Severian and Origen are both concerned that verse 24 — "only one receives the prize" — not be misunderstood. Origen's explanation of the verse reflects

144

his vision of the Christian life as involving different levels of perfection, each with a corresponding reward.

In verses 19-23 Paul moves beyond the special question of material support to make a more general point: that he accommodates himself to all sorts of people in order to win as many as possible for the gospel. Origen's comments reveal his philological interests, as he carefully defines Paul's terms (e.g., the difference between "the Jews" and "those under the law"), and show his high valuation of ascetic practices. The chapter concludes with several images taken from athletics that reinforce Paul's call to self-control (vv. 24-27). Augustine uses these last verses in a treatise on fasting to describe the Christian's struggle to control the flesh with its "earthy appetites."

1 Corinthians 9:1-2

1Am I not free? Am I not an apostle? Have I not seen Jesus our Lord? Are not you my work[1] in the Lord? 2If to others I am not an apostle, at least I am to you; for you are the seal of my apostleship in the Lord.

(1) John Chrysostom

Paul said, *If food causes offense to my brother, I will never eat meat* (1 Cor 8:13). He had not actually abstained from meat, but he promised to do so, if need be. He did not want anyone to be able to say: "Paul, you boast in vain; you practice discipline in word only; you make empty promises, which I or anyone else could do just as easily. But if you speak these things from the heart, show by your actions what you have renounced for the sake of not *causing offense to the brother.*" This is why Paul was forced to give a proof in what follows and to show how he abstained from things that were permitted in order to avoid "causing offense," even though no law required this. Such restraint is not admirable in itself. It becomes admirable, however, when Paul abstains from things permitted to avoid *causing offense* and does so amid great hardship and danger to himself. "Why, indeed," he asks, "must I speak about *meats offered to idols?*" For although the Lord enjoined that those preaching the gospel should get their living from the people they teach (1 Cor 9:14), I did not do this. Instead I chose to waste away my life in hunger, if it should come to that, and to die the most painful death, rather than take anything from those I teach." Paul says this, not because his hearers would be *offended* if he did not take anything, but because this would cause them to be *built up* (1 Cor 8:1) in their faith, which was a much more important matter.

And if Paul himself did more than the law required to avoid *causing offense,* and if in order to *build up* others he refrained from things permitted him, what punishment did those who ate *meat offered to idols* deserve, especially when this caused many to be lost? But quite apart from any concern about giving offense, this practice should be shunned because it involves *the table of demons* (1 Cor 10:21).

1. RSV: "workmanship."

So much by way of summary of the argument Paul develops in many verses. Let us now follow the argument more closely from the beginning. . . . Paul is leading up to saying that he did not accept anything from the Corinthians, but he does not state this right off. First he mentions his standing. **Am I not an apostle? Am I not free?** To prevent them from saying, "Even if you took nothing, this was because you had no right to receive anything," Paul first enumerates the reasons why he had the right to receive support from them, if he so desired. . . .

Paul sees that it was necessary to praise himself (for this is way the Corinthians were to be set straight), but he does not want to make great claims for himself. Notice how he balances these things and speaks what the situation requires, praising himself to a certain extent, not as much as he could have but as much as the present situation demands. For he could have said, "It was fitting for me, more than for anyone else, to receive aid, and I had more right than the others, because *I worked harder*" (1 Cor 15:10). But he does not say this since he thought it excessive. Instead he mentions only those things in which the other apostles were also great and on account of which they rightly accepted support. . . .

Are you not my work in the Lord? This **work** is what really counts. The other things bring no benefit at all without this. Even Judas was **an apostle** and was **free** and saw **the Lord**, but these things availed him nothing since he did not do the **work** of an apostle. Therefore, Paul also adds this point, for which he calls the Corinthians themselves as witnesses. And notice how, once he has uttered such a great claim, he takes care to keep it within bounds by adding, **in the Lord**. That is, the **work** is God's, not mine.

1 Corinthians 9:3-7

₃**This is my defense to those who would examine me. ₄Do we not have the right to our food and drink? ₅Do we not have the right to be accompanied by a woman, a sister,[2] as the other apostles and the brothers of the Lord and Cephas? ₆Or is it only Barnabas and I who have no right to refrain from working for a living? ₇Who serves as a soldier at his own expense? Who plants a vineyard without eating any of its fruit? Who tends a flock without getting some of the milk?**

(1) Augustine

Notice how he first shows what is permitted him, permitted because he is an apostle. He begins with this point: *Am I not free? Am I not an apostle?* And he proves that he is an apostle by asking, *Have I not seen Jesus our Lord? Are not you my work in the Lord?* (1 Cor 9:1). After he has demonstrated this, he shows that he has the same rights as the other

---

2. That is, a fellow Christian; the RSV does not translate this word and renders the previous word as "wife." On the ambiguity of this Greek word, which can be translated either "woman" or "wife," see the comments of Severian and Augustine, excerpted below.

apostles, that is, the right to be exempt from manual labor and to earn his living from preaching the gospel, according to the Lord's commandment, as he clearly shows in what follows. Faithful women who had earthly possessions used to go with the apostles and minister to them from what they possessed so that they would lack none of the goods necessary for this life. Paul shows that he has the same right as the other apostles, but reveals later that he declined to make use of it.

Some who fail to understand the question, **Do we not have the right to be accompanied by a woman, a sister?** have taken the word **woman** as "wife," misled by the ambiguity of the Greek, where the same word means both "woman" and "wife." The apostle, however, composed the sentence in a way that its meaning should have been clear since he does not merely say "a woman" but **a woman, a sister,** and does not say "marry" but **be accompanied by.** Other interpreters were not misled by this ambiguity but rendered the word as "woman," not "wife."

If anyone considers it impossible that women of holy life accompanied the apostles wherever they preached the gospel and used their goods to minister to their needs, he should hear the gospel and realize that they did this by precedent of our Lord himself (see Luke 8:1-3). . . .

The apostle Paul, therefore, did more than was required since he served, as he says, **at his own expense.** *Soon afterward Jesus went on through cities and villages, preaching and bringing the good news of the kingdom of God. And the twelve were with him, and also some women who had been healed of evil spirits and infirmities: Mary called Magdalene, from whom seven demons had gone out, and Joanna the wife of Chuza, Herod's steward, and Susanna, and many others, who provided for them out of their means* (Luke 8:1-3). The apostles imitated this precedent of the Lord in order to receive the food they needed.

(2) Severian of Gabala on verse 5

By saying **wife** and then adding the word **sister,** Paul indicates clearly that the traveling companion was fittingly chaste and pure, whether she was a wife or not. He means that, along with Peter and the other apostles, there traveled women who desired instruction from them. Paul does not say this to slander the other apostles — God forbid! — but he exhibits the superlative discipline of his own life and entreats the Corinthians not to live carelessly and thereby cause offense to others.

(3) Origen on verse 7

The apostle, speaking as a God-fearing soldier, asks, **Who serves as a soldier at his own expense?** And as a person entrusted with *God's field* (1 Cor 3:9), who farms the church, he asks, **Who plants a vineyard without eating any of its fruit?** And as a disciple of the *Good Shepherd,* who laid down *his life for his sheep* (John 10:11), Paul asks, **Who tends a flock without getting some of the milk?** As a **soldier** Paul teaches us to fight when he says, *No soldier on service gets entangled in civilian pursuits, since his aim is to satisfy the* *one who enlisted him* (2 Tim 2:4). And as farmer he teaches that we, too, should farm: *I planted, Apollos watered, but God gave the growth* (1 Cor 3:6). The prophets also teach us about **flocks** when they describe the wages of the good shepherds and report the punishments of the bad.[3]

Now if someone is not paying close attention to Scripture, it may seem that in this section the apostle is forgetting the subject under discussion. But this is not true; Paul is sticking closely to his argument. His concern is to teach about *food offered to idols* (1 Cor 8:1), so that if someone claiming to have knowledge says he is not hurt by consuming *food offered to idols* but becomes the cause of harm for others, he will be obliged to care about his neighbor and not become the reason other people come to ruin. So he offers examples, saying, "Because we have a *right* to something, we should not in all cases *make full use of the right* (1 Cor 9:18). For if someone is a **soldier**, he does not **serve as a soldier** so as to have nothing left over from his wages for himself. Or if he is a **farmer**, he is not content with his wages, but he also **eats** from the grapes. If he is a **shepherd**, in addition to his wages he gets a share of the **milk**. So too I ought to receive in this world, in addition to the promises made to me if I **serve** well **as a soldier** or farmer or shepherd, a share in the things I need from the soldiers who serve under me or from the fields I farm or the flocks I tend."

But nonetheless, even if I [Paul] have a *right* to the things I need, in consideration of what *builds up* (1 Cor 8:1), I do not *make full use of this right* (1 Cor 9:18). I am careful not to *put an obstacle in the way of the gospel of Christ* (1 Cor 9:12) or to give an excuse to those who are *living in idleness* and *not doing any work* but are also *mere busybodies* (2 Thess 3:11). Therefore, just as I do not make use of the right my teaching gives me, so also you who claim to be wise should not make use of your *right* but should take thought for the *building up* of your neighbors. And if some of you should think this teaching has no support and is merely human reasoning, let them hear the law which says: *You shall not muzzle an ox when it is treading out the grain* (Deut 25:4; 1 Cor 9:8).

(4) John Chrysostom on verse 7

When Paul had cited the example of the apostles as strong proof that he was allowed to receive his living, he proceeds to produce further examples from common experience, as he often does. He says, **Who serves as a soldier at his own expense?** Please notice how his illustrations are quite appropriate for the present subject, and how he first mentions dangerous things — armies and weapons and battles. For this is what the apostolate is like, and even more so than the things Paul mentions. For the apostles fought not only against human enemies but also against demons, and they marshalled themselves against the prince of demons. What Paul means is this: even civil rulers, who are cruel and unjust, do not demand that their soldiers fight and risk danger and at the same time support themselves from their own resources. How then would Christ ever have demanded this? And Paul is not content with this one example. . . .

3. See Isa 55:1; Jer 23:4; 25:34; 33:12; Ezek 34:2; Zeph 2:6; Zech 10:3.

Therefore, he goes on to yet another illustration and asks, **Who plants a vineyard without eating any of the fruit?** With the previous example he had displayed the perils of the apostolate, and with this second one he illustrates their labor, toil, and watchful care. Then he adds a third example, asking, Or **who tends a flock without getting some of the milk?** This shows the great concern a teacher properly has toward those over whom he rules. And in fact the apostles were **soldiers** and **farmers** and **shepherds**, not shepherds of irrational beasts or farmers of the earth or solders in physical battles, but shepherds of rational souls, and soldiers in the battle against demons.

1 Corinthians 9:8-12a

8Do I say this on human authority? Does not the law say the same? 9For it is written in the law of Moses, "You shall not muzzle an ox when it is treading out the grain" [Deut 25:4]. **Is it for oxen that God is concerned?[4] 10Does he not speak entirely for our sake? It was written for our sake, because the plowman should plow in hope and the thresher thresh in hope of a share in the crop. 11If we have sown spiritual good among you, is it too much if we reap your material benefits? 12If others share this rightful claim upon you, do not we still more?**

(1) Augustine

[*The context of this discussion is a sermon on divine providence.*] You, my dearest brothers and sisters, who have already come to believe in Christ, must not be influenced by unbelievers so as to think that God does not care how human beings live: he sees to it that not only human beings but also cattle, fish, and birds have the means to live. I mean, we mustn't let the apostle's words about **God** not caring **about oxen** lead us to assume that the birth and feeding of animals doesn't come under God's providence. For the Lord Jesus uses the clearest examples of this sort in order to provoke and stir up our faith, telling us to consider how God feeds the birds in the sky and clothes the grass of the field and, therefore, to trust him not to neglect the feeding and clothing of man, his own servant (Matt 6:25-32).

But the reason the apostle says, **For God does not care about oxen** was to keep us from thinking that the text, *You shall not muzzle the mouth of the ox that is threshing* (Deut 25:4), refers only to oxen, and not in fact to people. God's concern in holy Scripture is not to prescribe how we should treat our animals, but this does not mean that he has no concern for nature; for he provides for the birth and proper nourishment of all kinds of animals.

---

4. Some of the fathers (see Augustine's comments) seem to have taken this as a statement: "God does not care about oxen."

(2) John Chrysostom

For it is written in the law of Moses, "You shall not muzzle an ox when it is treading out the grain" (Deut 25:4). . . . Then, so that no one might say, "And why is he talking to us about oxen?" Paul carefully explains this by asking, **Is God concerned about oxen?** Tell me this: Is it true that God has no concern for oxen? No, he does care about them. But not in such a way that he makes a law on this subject. If he were not intimating something important, if he were not training the Jews through irrational animals to be compassionate and using the example of animals to address the Jews about teachers, God would not have taken the trouble to write a law about not muzzling oxen. From this Paul also shows something else: that the labor of teachers both is, and ought to be, great.[5]

Paul makes a further point as well. What is it? That whatever is said in the Old Testament about the care of irrational animals is intended primarily to teach about human beings. The same is true of all the other commandments, for example, about mixed garments, vineyards, seeds, not mixing different crops, leprosy, and virtually everything else. Since men are slow-witted, God addresses them on this basis and educates them little by little. . . .

If we have sown spiritual good among you, is it too much if we reap your material benefits? . . . To prevent those who supported their teachers from becoming too proud Paul shows that they were receiving greater things than they were giving. For even farmers receive back whatever they sow. But we sow spiritual things in your souls and harvest only earthly things — for the food they provided to the teachers was earthly. And then he adds something designed to abash them even more: **If others share this rightful claim upon you, do not we still more?** Notice here yet another argument, also based on examples, but not like the others. Here Paul refers neither to Peter nor to the apostles but to certain impostors with whom he will contend later, and about whom he says, *if a man . . . preys upon you, or takes advantage of you, or puts on airs, or strikes you in the face* (2 Cor 11:20). And in this passage Paul's dispute with them is already anticipated.

(3) Origen

Therefore, these things are said for us (1 Cor 10:11) who have received the new covenant, and they are written about men since the apostle understands Scripture in a spiritual sense. What is this sense? **Because the plowman should plow in hope and the thresher thresh in hope of a share in the crop.** Paul, the farmer, **plows** the soul he is instructing, making furrows in the student's soul, as the divine Jeremiah instructs them: *Break up your fallow ground* (Jer 4:3). Clearly this is for the reception of seeds, about which it is written, *A sower went out to sow* (Matt 13:3). And Paul, when he is sowing the furrows, says: "I keep watch over the seeds, lest *the birds* of heaven come and take what was sown (Matt 13:4). And when the seeds *bear fruit* (Matt 13:23; Rom 7:4) and produce the *fruit of righteousness* (Phil 1:11) — when they are *already ripe for harvest* (John 4:35), then I may at

---

5. The analogy is that oxen are large beasts who can pull heavy loads.

last receive the fruit. For someone will not take offense when he remembers how much effort I have taken to plow his soul and sow it, and how I waited until it was full grown and gathered it into the barn. And for this reason I am permitted to receive food from him. But I have made no use of this *right* (1 Cor 9:12), and instead do this work **in hope**, in order to present the produce to the master of the house (since I am a tiller of the soil). I do not do this in order to put into my own barns what ought to be given to God." Then the apostle gives further teaching on this same subject, when he says, **If we have sown spiritual good among you, is it too much** and what follows.

1 Corinthians 9:12b-18

12bNevertheless, we have not made use of this right, but we endure anything rather than put an obstacle in the way of the gospel of Christ. 13Do you not know that those who are employed in the temple service get their food from the temple, and those who serve at the altar share in the sacrificial offerings? 14In the same way, the Lord commanded that those who proclaim the gospel should get their living by the gospel. 15But I have made no use of any of these rights, nor am I writing this to secure any such provision. For I would rather die than have any one deprive me of my ground for boasting. 16For if I preach the gospel, that gives me no ground for boasting. For necessity is laid upon me. Woe to me if I do not preach the gospel! 17For if I do this of my own will, I have a reward; but if not of my own will, I am entrusted with a commission. 18What then is my reward? Just this: that in my preaching I may make the gospel free of charge, not making full use of my right in the gospel.

(1) John Chrysostom on verse 12

We have not made use of this right. And, indeed, it is an even greater thing that no one could say it was because we were well provided for that we did not exercise our right. Even with necessity weighing down upon us, we did not yield to it. Paul repeats this in his second letter, *I robbed other churches by accepting support from them in order to serve you, and when I was with you and was in want, I did not burden any one* (2 Cor 11:8-9). And also in this verse: *we hunger and thirst, we are ill-clad and buffeted and homeless* (1 Cor 4:11). And in our passage he intimates the same thing when he says, rather, **we endure anything**. In saying **we endure anything**, he hints at hunger and dire hardship and everything else. "But not even in this situation," Paul points out, "were we constrained to break the rule which we established for ourselves." Why was this? **Rather than put an obstacle in the way of the gospel of Christ.** Since the Corinthians were weak, he says: "So that we would not harm you by taking food, we chose to do more than what was commanded **rather than put an obstacle in the way of the gospel,** that is, your instruction. But if we refrained, even though we were suffering greatly and had the apostles as a precedent, **rather than put an obstacle** . . . how much more ought you . . . to abstain?" He makes this whole argument because of those who were offending the weaker brethren through [eating] *food offered to idols.*

Let us listen to these things, my beloved brethren, so as not to disdain those who take offense, or **put an obstacle in the way of the gospel of Christ**. For if we do this, we will betray our own salvation. When a brother takes offense, don't tell me that there are no restrictions against whatever caused the offense; don't tell me that it is permitted. I tell you something greater: even if Christ himself has allowed something, if you see someone being hurt by it, stop and forego your liberty. Paul himself did this. Although Christ granted that he could receive support, he did not take it. The Master, being compassionate, tempered his commandments with great gentleness, so that in many cases we should not only follow the commandments but also exercise our own judgment.

If Christ had not intended this, he could have extended the commandments and said, "Whoever does not fast strictly is to be punished. Whoever does not remain a virgin is to be castigated. Whoever does not rid himself of all his possessions is to be given the ultimate sentence." But he did not do this. Instead he granted you an honor to strive for, if you choose. Thus when he discussed virginity, his practice was to say, *He who is able to receive this, let him receive it* (Matt 19:12). And on the subject of wealth he gave some commandments but left other things up to our own judgment. For he did not say, "Sell your possessions," but *If you would be perfect . . . sell* (Matt 19:21).

We, on the other hand, not only fail to strive for honor and surpass the commandments, but we even fall far short of what has been commanded. Paul suffered hunger **rather than put an obstacle in the way of the gospel**. But we do not even dare to touch food we have stored away for ourselves, though we pass by thousands of disheartened souls. "Let the moth nibble away," someone says, "but not the poor man! Let the worm devour, but let not the naked be clothed! Let time consume everything, but do not feed Christ, though he is hungry."

(2) Oecumenius on verse 13

By **those employed in the temple service** Paul means the levites, who received the tithe. And by **those who serve at the altar** he means the priests, who received the choice parts of the sacrifices. And Paul uses the word **share** advisedly. For whole burnt offerings were made, and these belonged entirely to the altar, and in the case of ordinary sacrifices the blood was poured out upon the altar and the fat was burned, but the priest received a choice part of the meat, for example, the right foreleg, the breast, and the stomach (Deut 18:3).

(3) Augustine

Paul returns once more to this theme of the apostolic right to support and repeatedly tells the Corinthians what he is allowed to do and yet does not do. **Do you not know that those who are employed in the temple service get their food from the temple, and those who serve at the altar share in the sacrificial offerings? In the same way, the Lord commanded that those who proclaim the gospel should get their living by the gospel.**

But I have made no use of any of these rights. What is plainer than this? My only worry is that when I try to expound it, the clarity and force of his words may be obscured. Those who do not understand Paul's words or pretend they don't will understand my words still less — or if they understand them, they will not admit it.[6] Though perhaps they will understand my words more quickly because they know they can mock them, whereas they know they can't mock the apostle's words. Hence, when such folks can't interpret Paul to suit their own views, they claim that clear and obvious words are obscure and uncertain: they can't call his words wicked and wrong.

The minister of God says emphatically: **the Lord commanded that those who proclaim the gospel should get their living by the gospel. But I have made no use of any of these rights.** Here his human critics attempt to twist what is straightforward, to close an open book, and to becloud a clear sky. They say, "Paul was doing a spiritual work, and that was the source of his life. That being so, **he got his living by the gospel.**" Why then does Paul say, **the Lord commanded that those who proclaim the gospel should get their living by the gospel. But I have made no use of any of these rights?** Or if they wish to interpret the **living** Paul speaks of as spiritual life, this would imply that the apostle would then have no hope in God since he said, **I made no use of any of these rights.** But because Paul says, **I made no use of any of these rights**, he puts it beyond doubt that it is in regard to our life in the flesh that the Lord **commanded that those who proclaim the gospel should get their living**, that is to say, they should get from the gospel that life which needs food and clothing, as he said earlier of his fellow apostles (v. 4).

Hence the Lord himself said, *The laborer deserves his food* (Matt 10:10) and *the laborer deserves his wages* (Luke 10:7). The apostle does not lay claim to the food and wage for sustaining life, owed to the preacher by those to whom he preaches, when he says, **I made no use of any of these rights.**

(4) Origen on verses 16-17

For if I preach the gospel, that gives me no ground for boasting. For necessity is laid upon me. Woe to me if I do not preach the gospel! For if I do this of my own will, I have a reward; but if not of my own will, I am entrusted with a commission. We are taught that whatever we do out of **necessity** provides no **ground for boasting.** But whatever we do by free choice, without having **necessity laid** upon us, provides **ground for boasting.** For example, while a person who does not commit adultery or murder has no **ground for boasting**, one who lives a life of virginity does. For he does not come to the life of virginity out of **necessity** but by free choice. Where there is **woe if I do not** do something, I have **no ground for boasting.** This is why Paul says, **For if I do this of my own will, I have a reward; but if not of my own will, I am entrusted with a commission.** Furthermore, we are given a general teaching: some things we do **of** our own **will** with our whole

6. In this treatise Augustine is addressing the issue of monks who refuse to perform manual work. They had interpreted Paul's statement about his own labor in 1 Corinthians 9 (and also the command to work in 2 Thess 3:6-12) as referring to spiritual, not manual work.

heart, and some we do but not **of** our **own will** or with our whole heart, but under duress or out of **necessity**. There is a reward for the things we do willingly. But for the things we do under duress there is neither reward nor punishment. For example, I give alms. If I do it **of my own will**, I have a reward. **But if not of my own will,** at least I am not accused with those who are told, *You gave me no food* and what follows (Matt 25:41-46).

1 Corinthians 9:19-23

19**For though I am free from all things,**[7] **I have made myself a slave to all, that I might win the more.** 20**To the Jews I became as a Jew, in order to win Jews; to those under the law I became as one under the law — though not being myself under the law — that I might win those under the law.** 21**To those outside the law I became as one outside the law — not being without law toward God but under the law of Christ — that I might win those outside the law.** 22**To the weak I became weak, that I might win the weak. I have become all things to all men, that I might by all means save some.** 23**I do it all for the sake of the gospel, that I may share in its blessings.**

(1) Origen

To be **free from all things**[8] is characteristic of the perfected[9] apostle. Someone can be free from sexual sin but a slave to anger, free from avarice but a slave to vanity. He can be free from one sin but a slave to another. But to say **I am free from all things** belongs to the perfected apostle. Such a one was Paul. In the present context this is what he means. **To the Jews I became as a Jew, in order to win Jews.** Although he was **free** from Judaism, he **made** himself **a slave** to Jews **in order to win Jews**. Although I am **free** from being **under the law**, I made myself **as one under the law, that I might win those under the law**. For Paul practiced accommodation in the synagogues of the Jews: he went to the Jews and acted according to their customs without doing anything harmful, and not out of hypocrisy but in order to capture some of them.

Some have raised the question: What is the difference between those **under the law** and **the Jews**? Our view is that those **under the law** means something different from the Jews, for example, the Samaritans.

To those outside the law I became as one outside the law. Paul came to Athens and found philosophers there. And when he spoke to the Athenians he did not use the teachings of the prophets or the law, but he mentioned to them whatever Greek learning he had from his basic schooling. For he says, *As even some of your poets have said, "For we are*

7. RSV: "all men"; the Greek word can be either masculine or neuter (so Origen).
8. As Origen goes on to explain, he takes this to mean being free from all sin and from all unruly emotions.
9. Or "perfect" (or, in other contexts: "mature"). The word "perfect" is for Origen a relative term. Running through his *Homilies on 1 Corinthians* is the notion that Paul is teaching about the path to perfection, that is, moral, spiritual, and intellectual maturity in the faith.

indeed his offspring" (Acts 17:28). In Athens he **became as one outside the law to those outside the law** so that he **might win those outside the law**. And he proceeded to say, *For as I passed along, and observed the objects of your worship, I found also an altar with this inscription, "To an unknown god." What therefore you worship as unknown, this I proclaim to you* (Acts 17:23). And by this means he begins to instruct them about the true religion.

To those outside the law, then, **I became as one outside the law — not being without law toward God but under the law of Christ**. "In accommodating myself to them I did not behave in a lawless way, but regarded myself as **under the law of Christ — that I might win those outside the law**." In all this Paul expresses himself carefully: **To the Jews I became as a Jew**: in this case Paul does not say, "not being a Jew." For he was a *Jew in secret*, not *outwardly* (Rom 2:28-29). Again he says, **To those under the law [I became] as one under the law — though not being myself under the law.** Here he has to add, **though not being under the law.** For *Christ redeemed us from the curse of the law, having become a curse for us* (Gal 3:13). It is as if he had said, "not being a Samaritan."

To those outside the law I became as one outside the law — not being without law toward God. But someone might suppose that I[10] became an apostate from the law and **without law toward God**. I declare that even if I do not keep the law according to the letter I am not **without law toward God but under the law of Christ**, since I observe the way of life of the gospel, **that I might win those outside the law.**

To the weak I became weak. Here Paul did not say, "not being weak myself," for that would be boastful and arrogant. To say "not being weak myself" would not be like the apostle, who heard the Lord say, *My power is made perfect in weakness,* and who for this reason boasts *in* his *weakness* (2 Cor 12:9). And how is Paul **weak to the weak**? When he allows those who were burning with desire to marry, when he shows sympathy for those who have lost their husbands (1 Cor 7:9), when he says, *But because of the temptation to immorality, each man should have his own wife and each woman her own husband* (1 Cor 7:2), and so forth. In giving these counsels Paul became **weak to the weak that** he **might win the weak.**

Then, after these things, Paul says, **I have become all things to all men, that I might by all means save some.** If you consider any person, he belongs to one of these five categories: either he is a **Jew**, or **under the law**, or **outside the law**, or **weak**, or **all things**. A person who is perfected is **all things**. For this reason Paul says, "Among those who are **all things**, that is, among those who are perfected, **I have become** perfected in order to win all. For he says, *among the perfected we do impart wisdom* (1 Cor 2:6), and what follows. The one who is perfected can say, *I am under obligation both to Greeks and to barbarians, both to the wise and to the foolish* (Rom 1:14). Only the one who is perfected can say these words of the apostle who is perfected in the Lord, **I do it all for the sake of the gospel.** For the person who sins cannot say this.

10. In this paragraph "I" seems to designate Origen as well as Paul. Origen was criticized for his practice of nonliteral exegesis, and he might be appealing to the example of Paul as a justification for his practice. In *On First Principles* 4.2-6 Origen uses several texts from Paul as warrants for spiritual exegesis.

(2) Augustine

It is one thing to be **under the law**, another to be "in the law," another to be **without the law. Under the law** were the carnal Jews, "in the law" were spiritual persons, Jews and Christians. The spiritual Jews kept their ancestral customs while not imposing unusual burdens on believing Gentiles.[11] For this reason this group too were circumcised. **Without the law** are the Gentiles who have not yet believed. The apostle made himself like them out of mercy and compassion, not from craftiness or deceit. He wanted to give the carnal Jew or pagan the same kind of help he would have wished to receive had he been one of them. He bore their weakness by compassionately becoming like them; he did not deceive them by lying pretense, as his next words make clear, **I became weak to the weak, that I might win the weak**. Paul here expresses himself in such a way as to include his former statements; his becoming **weak to the weak** was no lie, and the same applies to his earlier statements. For what does he mean by "weakness" toward the weak except his suffering with them? Paul did this so that he might not seem to be putting the gospel up for sale or impede the course of the word of God among those who did not know it by incurring their suspicions. He did this to such a degree that he refused to accept what was owed him as a right the Lord had given him. If he had not refused, even then he would not be telling a lie since this was truly his due. And since he refused it, he did not tell a lie since he did not deny it was his due but only claimed that he had made no use of his right and did not wish to. He was **weak** by the very fact that he refused to use his power. This is how merciful Paul's attitude was: he considered how he himself would wish to be treated if he, like his hearers, were so weak that if he saw preachers of the gospel receiving support, he would suppose they were putting the gospel up for sale.

1 Corinthians 9:24-27

24**Do you not know that those who run in the stadium all compete,[12] but only one receives the prize? So run that you may obtain it.** 25**Every athlete exercises self-control in all things. They do it to receive a perishable wreath, but we an imperishable.** 26**Well, I do not run aimlessly, I do not box as one beating the air;** 27**but I pommel my body and subdue it, lest after preaching to others I myself should be disqualified.**

(1) Severian of Gabala on verse 24

This does not mean that out of all Christians **one** is preferred — for in that case people would have given up on themselves and refused to run the race in view of its difficulties. But Paul has clearly taken up this image of the race for the sake of the Gentiles to whom he is speaking. **All**, he says, compete in this life as **in the stadium**, Jews according to the

---

11. See Rom 2:29 for "the spiritual Jew" and Acts 15:19-29 on not imposing burdens on Gentiles.
12. RSV: "Do you not know that in a race all the runners compete?"

law and Greeks in error, but the true teaching is **one**, which conquers and **receives the prize. Run,** therefore, lest you be left behind with the others. . . .

"Why is it a great thing," Paul asks, "if for the sake of your Christian brother you exercise self-control with regard to the flesh?" **The one who is competing** must **exercise self-control in all things,** abstaining from anger, concern for glory, and all the rest. **They do it to receive a perishable wreath, but we an imperishable.**

(2) Origen

Is it the case, then, that we **all compete** and **only one receives the prize**, while the rest of us perish? For Paul says that **one receives the prize,** although many **compete. All** those who are being saved are *one* and *one body* (Gal 3:28; 1 Cor 12:12). For *we* are all *one bread* and *we partake of the* same *bread* (1 Cor 10:17). And *you are* all *the body of Christ* (1 Cor 12:27). **All,** then, applies to those who are being saved, but there is **one** who **receives the prize. In the stadium,** then, **all compete,** all, that is, who live by a certain doctrine, both those of the sectarians who live by doctrine,[13] and next the Jews, and also those who live by the doctrines of the Greeks as philosophers. And these are the **all who run in a race.** The church also **runs.** But **one receives the prize,** the one man about whom the apostle says, *until we attain to the perfect man, the measure of the stature of the fullness of Christ* (Eph 4:13). Now the perfect judgment of God about **all who compete in the stadium** will need to take place, so that one takes the first prize, and after him each one according to his merits.

(3) Augustine

[*From a treatise on fasting*] We have seen that there is a certain marriage of spirit and flesh. So how is it that *the flesh lusts against the spirit, and the spirit against the flesh* (Gal 5:17)? . . . Why is it said, *In Adam all die* (1 Cor 15:22)? And how is it that the apostle says, *We too were once by nature children of wrath, like the others* (Eph 2:3)? It is because the father from whom we are all born [Adam] received the penalty of death, and we inherit from him something to be overcome. We lust against the flesh in order to tame and subject it to ourselves and draw it into obedience.

Do we therefore hate the thing we want to obey us? . . . Suppose you win a victory over your son so that he obeys you: Do you hate him, consider him an enemy? You love and chastise your servant [the flesh], and in chastising him you make him obedient. On this point you have the plain and full judgment of the apostle himself: **I do not run aimlessly,** he says; **I do not box as one beating the air; but I pommel my body and subdue it, lest after preaching to others I myself should be disqualified.** So the flesh, as a result of its mortal condition, has, as it were, its own earthly appetites. Against these you may apply the bit and bridle. Let your Master be your ruler so that your subject may be ruled by

---

13. These would include Christians who belong to Gnostic groups.

you. Below you is your flesh; above you is your God. When you demand that your flesh serve you, you are reminded how you ought to serve your God. You pay heed to what is below you; pay heed also to what is above you. You have no laws related to your inferior except those given by your superior. You are a servant, and you have a servant. But the Lord has two servants. Your servant is more in the power of your Lord than in your power. So you wish to be obeyed by the flesh. Can you be obeyed in all things? In all things the flesh obeys your Lord, but in all things it does not obey you. "How is that?" you ask. You walk, you move your feet, it follows: but will it go with you as far as you desire? It is animated by you; but is it animated as much as you desire? Do you feel pain when you wish? Are you well when you wish? No, for your Lord often trains you by means of your servant. Since you were a despiser of the Lord, you deserve to be corrected by a servant.

1 Corinthians 10

Paul returns to the question raised in chapter 8 of whether Christians were allowed to eat food that had been dedicated to pagan gods. The chapter begins (vv. 1-11) with an extended exegesis of the stories of the exodus from Egypt (Exodus 1–15) and the wandering of the Israelites in the wilderness (Exodus 16 through Numbers 21), which Paul understands as "types"[1] or "figures" that foreshadow Christian realities. For example, he understands the crossing of the sea (Exodus 14–15) as a type of baptism, and the eating of manna (Exodus 16) as a figure of the Eucharist. Paul uses these stories to warn the Corinthians against immorality and "idolatry" (vv. 6-14), that is, involvement with pagan religion, and he reminds them that baptism and the Eucharist do not give magical protection from the consequences of sin (vv. 15-22).

Paul's spiritual exegesis had considerable influence on patristic interpretation of the Old Testament. Origen says that Paul "has taught the church . . . how she ought to interpret the books of the law." Origen sees in this chapter a model of how to interpret the rest of the Jewish Scriptures in that it points to a spiritual meaning that goes beyond the merely literal or historical meaning. Augustine makes a similar point when he argues that the apostle "by explaining one passage gives the key to the others." "No Christian," Augustine claims, "would dare to maintain that [an Old Testament] narrative is not to be taken in a figurative sense since the apostle Paul says, 'Now these things happened to them as figures' [v. 6]." Both fathers connect Paul's words about the Israelites' eating "spiritual food" (v. 2) with Jesus' claim in John 6:42-49 to be the true manna, the "bread from heaven."

Augustine shows how the model of exegesis given in 1 Corinthians 10 can be applied to other texts by comparing additional features of the exodus and wilderness narratives, not mentioned by Paul, to the different stages of the Christian's battle against sin. John Chrysostom points out that a special feature of Paul's interpretation of Scripture is the way he inserts Christ into his retelling of the Old Testament events. Cyril's comments on verses 6-10 focus especially on the story of the Israelites' idolatrous association with foreign women at Baal-Peor in Num 25:1-3.

In verses 11-12 Paul sums up with a warning to "stand" and not to "fall" into temptation. John Chrysostom plays on the words "stand" and "fall" when he portrays his own congregation as needing even more correction than the Corinthians did. Origen found the next verse — "No temptation has overtaken you that is not human" (v. 13) — very suggestive. He takes "human

---

1. In v. 6 Paul uses the Greek word *typos*, which means "form," "figure," "pattern," and "model."

temptation" to mean a lesser temptation occasioned by life in the body, in contrast to the more serious spiritual temptation posed by evil spirits. That "God will not let you be tempted beyond your strength" (v. 13) means for Origen that God trains each individual by assigning struggles with the flesh and with demons that are specifically suited to his degree of maturity in the faith and his spiritual strength.

Paul next focuses on the Eucharist (vv. 14-22), arguing that participation in the table of Christ excludes any sharing in the "table of demons." Commenting on the phrase "cup of blessing" in verse 16, John Chrysostom reminds his hearers of the awesome nature of the holy sacrament, while Clement of Alexandria (on vv. 18-22) contrasts the food of the glutton with the "true food" of divine contemplation.

From Paul's instruction about food offered to idols in verses 23-26, which includes the statement that "all things are lawful, but not all things are helpful," Clement draws a more general lesson about food: Christians should be moderate in eating, practice self-restraint, and direct their attention to God. "The table of the Truth," he says, "is far removed from the food that excites lust." John Chrysostom compares the advice given in these verses to what Paul says in his other letters. In verses 27-33 Paul offers himself as a model of being thankful to God in all things and putting the good of one's neighbor before one's own advantage. Theodoret ponders whether Paul's claim that he tries "to please all men" (v. 33) makes him a flatterer. John Chrysostom adduces several Old Testament examples of the selfless conduct Paul advocates and then concludes that Paul is the most selfless of all.

1 Corinthians 10:1-5

1I want you to know, brethren, that our fathers were all under the cloud [Exod 13:21], **and all passed through the sea** [Exod 14:22], **2and all were baptized into Moses in the cloud and in the sea, 3and all ate the same spiritual² food** [Exod 16:4-35], **4and all drank the same spiritual drink. For they drank from the spiritual Rock which followed them,³ and the Rock was Christ** [Exod 17:1-7; Num 20:2-13]. **5Nevertheless with most of them God was not pleased; for they were overthrown in the wilderness** [Num 14:29-30].

(1) Origen

The apostle Paul, *teacher of the Gentiles in faith and truth* (1 Tim 2:7), has taught the Church which he gathered from the Gentiles how she ought to interpret the books of the law. She received these books from others, and they were previously unknown and very

---

2. RSV: "supernatural"; the same word also appears twice in v. 4, where the RSV again renders "supernatural." The reference is to the manna that appeared miraculously to feed the Israelites during their sojourn in the wilderness; see Exod 16:4-35; 17:6; Num 20:7-11.

3. Paul is here drawing on Jewish tradition. Because there are two accounts of the miraculous provision of water from a rock (Exod 17:1-7 and Num 20:2-13), some rabbis said that the rock must have followed the Israelites as they traveled through the wilderness.

strange to her. Paul was afraid that the Church, receiving teachings foreign to her and not knowing the principle behind them, would be in doubt what to do with this strange document. So he himself in several places gives examples of how to interpret them. His aim is for us to do likewise in other passages. We are not to suppose that, because our text looks like a document of the Jews, we have become their disciples. Paul wants to distinguish the disciples of Christ from those of the synagogue in this, that the latter by misunderstanding the law rejected Christ, whereas we by understanding it in a spiritual sense show that it was proper to give it to the Church for her instruction.

The Jews, accordingly, understand only that *the children of Israel journeyed* from Egypt, that their first departure was *from Rameses,* that they departed from there and came *to Succoth* (Exod 12:37), and that *they moved on from Succoth* and came *to Etham* (Exod 13:20) at Epauleus next to the sea; then that in that place a cloud went before them (Exod 13:21), that they were followed by a rock, from which they drank water, and that they passed through the Red Sea and came into the desert of Sin (Exod 14:22; 16:1). Let us see, however, what rule of interpretation Paul gives us. Writing to the Corinthians, he says in one place, **I want you to know, brethren, that our fathers were all under the cloud, and all passed through the sea, and all were baptized into Moses in the cloud and in the sea, and all ate the same spiritual food, and all drank the same spiritual drink. For they drank from the spiritual Rock which followed them, and the Rock was Christ.**

Do you see how much Paul's teaching differs from the literal or historical reading? What the Jews thought was the crossing of a sea Paul calls a baptism. What they regarded as a cloud is in reality, Paul claims, the Holy Spirit. The meaning he finds here is like what our Lord taught in the Gospels, *Unless one is born of water and the Spirit, he cannot enter the kingdom of God* (John 3:5). Again manna, which the Jews regarded as food to satisfy their bellies, Paul calls **spiritual food.** And this is not peculiar to Paul, for our Lord in the Gospel says about the same food: *Your fathers ate the manna in the wilderness, and they died. But anyone who eats the bread which I give him will never die.* And after that he says, *I am the living bread which came down from heaven* (John 6:49-51). About the **Rock which followed them** Paul speaks explicitly: **and the Rock was Christ.**

What then shall we do, having received such training in interpretation from Paul, the Church's teacher? Does it not seem right to apply the principle we have been given to other cases? Or shall we take the advice of some and turn again to *Jewish myths* (Tit 1:14), leaving the teaching of the great Paul aside? In my judgment, I would be surrendering to the enemies of Christ if I were to interpret these matters differently from the apostle.

(2) John Chrysostom on verse 2

What does **they were baptized into Moses** mean? Just as we, once we have confessed Christ and his resurrection, are baptized so that we may partake of these mysteries [of the Eucharist], . . . in the same way the Israelites, because they had confidence in Moses — that is, because they had seen him cross over first — also braved the waters of the sea. But since Paul wants to relate the *figure* (1 Cor 10:6) closely to the truth [of its Christian fulfillment], he does not explain this as I have done but instead uses the terms that characterize the fulfillment for the *figure* itself. The crossing of the sea is a symbol of the washing [i.e., baptism], and the event that follows is a symbol of the holy table. Just as you eat the body of the Lord, so they ate the manna; just as you drink the blood, so they drank water from the rock. Although the events were physical, Paul presents them in a spiritual way, not as events that followed in the natural order but as gifts of grace, as events that nurtured the soul along with the body and moved it toward faith.

(3) Augustine

Now about the departure of Israel from Egypt let the apostle speak instead of me. **I want you to know, brethren, that our fathers were all under the cloud, and all passed through the sea, and all were baptized into Moses in the cloud and in the sea, and all ate the same spiritual food, and all drank the same spiritual drink. For they drank from the spiritual Rock which followed them, and the Rock was Christ**. By explaining one passage he gives the key to the others. For if the **rock** was Christ because of its firmness, is not the manna also Christ since it is the living bread *which came down from heaven* (John 6:42)? Those who truly eat of it are spiritually alive. For those who received this figure only in the carnal sense are dead. But when the apostle says that **all ate the same spiritual food**, he shows that the manna is to be understood spiritually as Christ. Similarly, he explains why he calls their drink **spiritual** when he says that **the Rock was Christ**, an explanation that clarifies the whole. Then is not the cloud Christ? And the pillar also because it is straight and firm and supports our infirmity? The sea is red, and likewise our baptism is consecrated by the blood of Christ. The enemies chasing us perish, as do our past sins.

The Old Testament is the promise made in symbols. The New Testament is the promise spiritually understood. . . . According to the Old Testament, the people are liberated from Egypt. According to the New Testament, the people are freed from the devil. The Egyptian persecutors and the pharaoh pursued the Jews as they left Egypt. The people of Christ are pursued by their own sins and the devil, prince of all sins. But just as the Egyptians pursued the Jews up to the sea, so Christians are pursued by their sins up to baptism. . . . After the Red Sea the Jews went out and journeyed through the wilderness. In like manner Christians after their baptism are not yet in the land of promise but live in hope.

Now this age is a wilderness. For the Christian after baptism it is a wilderness indeed if he understands what he has received. If he has experienced not only the bodily sign of baptism but also its spiritual effect, he realizes that this world is a wilderness, that he journeys far from his home, that he misses his country. . . . And just as temptations occur in the wilderness, so they occur after baptism. For the Egyptians who pursued the Israelites from Egypt were not their only enemies — they were their past enemies, just as everyone is pursued by his past life and his past sins, which are accompanied by their leader, the devil — but there were also enemies in the wilderness who wanted to hinder their journey, whom they fought and conquered.[4] So after baptism, when the Christian has begun to make the journey his heart must make to obtain God's promises, let him not turn aside. Temptations occur, which hold out some other object — the delights of this world, another kind of life — in order to deflect us from the path and turn us from our purpose. But if you overcome these desires, these suggestions, the enemy along the way is overcome, and the people are led to their own land.

Hear what the apostle says, telling us that these are figures for us: **I want you to know, brethren, that our fathers were all under the cloud.** If they were under a cloud, they were under a mist. What does it mean to be under a mist? That they did not have a spiritual understanding of what was happening to them physically.[5] **And all passed through the sea, and all were baptized into Moses, and all ate the same spiritual food.** They were given manna in the wilderness, just as we are given the sweetness of the Scriptures, to give us endurance in the wilderness of human life. Christians know what kind of manna they receive, for the psalm tells them: *O taste and see that the* LORD *is good!* (Ps 34:8). **All**, Paul says, **ate the same spiritual food**. What is meant by **the same**? With the same meaning. **And all drank the same spiritual drink.** Observe how he expounds one item and says nothing about the others: **For they drank from the spiritual rock that followed them, and that Rock was Christ.** *Now these things are figures for us* (1 Cor 10:6). These figures were exhibited to them, but they are figures for us: they were shown physically to them but were given spiritual meaning for us.

1 Corinthians 10:6-11

6Now these things are figures[6] for us, so that we do not desire evil as they did. 7Do not be idolaters as some of them were; as it is written, "The people sat down to eat and drink and rose up to dance" [Exod 32:4, 6]. 8We must not indulge in immorality as some of them did, and twenty-three thousand fell in a single day [Num 25:1-18]. 9We must not put the Lord to the test, as some of them did and were destroyed by serpents [Num 21:5-6]; 10nor grumble, as some of them did and were destroyed by the Destroyer [Num 16:14, 49]. 11Now these things happened to them as figures,[7] but they were written down for our instruction, upon whom the end of the ages has come.

---

4. Augustine extends Paul's spiritual exegesis by referring to additional episodes such as Exod 17:8-13 and Num 31:1-54.

5. Perhaps Augustine is thinking of 2 Cor 3:12-18, where Paul says that the Jews, who do not have a spiritual understanding of Scripture, read it as through a veil. For a different understanding of the "cloud" of Exod 13:21, see Cyril of Alexandria's comments on 1 Cor 10:6-11, translated below.

6. Or "types"; the RSV translates "warnings": "Now these things are warnings for us, not to desire evil as they did." On the fathers' interpretation of this word, see editor's introduction to this chapter.

7. Or "as types"; RSV: "as a warning."

(1) Cyril of Alexandria

Paul has already ordered those who made false claims to perfect knowledge not to eat *meat sacrificed to idols* (1 Cor 8:1-13). Now he uses what happened to the ancients to try to persuade them that this practice is not beneficial but dangerous and that they cannot associate with people who are accustomed to sinning without themselves suffering harm. For such association entices them to do what is not permitted, given how easily the human mind is stirred up, little by little, to do what is not proper. Therefore, Paul cites as an analogy what happened to the Israelites in the wilderness — and this not a poorly chosen example, but one that resembles the situation in Corinth very closely. He shows very forcefully that the wish to associate with unbelievers is harmful to those who entertain it.

What Paul says is this: those who were redeemed from slavery were initiated at the sea by the cloud, when the cloud was hanging over them and Moses was acting as mediator. They ate the bread from heaven; they drank the life-giving drink. For Christ, who was himself the *Rock* (1 Cor 10:4), gave them to drink. He is the *Rock* because, as God, he is indestructible, even though he willingly suffered death's assault. We call such things "prefigurations" of spiritual things.

And what happened to the ancients after these things? How did they give offense? They committed sacrilege at Shittim; they served idols, they became initiates of Baal-Peor (Num 25:1-3). Notice how those who were baptized *in the cloud and in the sea* (1 Cor 10:2) became caught up in the worship of idols, even though they had eaten the bread from heaven and drunk the *spiritual drink* (1 Cor 10:4). Since they lived with idolaters and frequented the idolatrous table, they were open to seduction from the start, and they slipped into apostasy and joined the women in their dances. And *the people deliberately became entangled with a harlot* (Hos 4:14), as the prophet says. For this is what **and they rose up to play** means. Thus it is dangerous to associate with the wicked and with unbelievers. Indeed, Solomon says somewhere: *He who walks with wise men becomes wise, but the companion of fools will be known* (Prov 13:20 LXX).

We, too, before we had faith in Christ, were subjected to demons and oppressed by them, and we served a spiritual pharaoh, that is, Satan, the author of evil. In vain we toiled for him, as the ancient Israelites did in mud and the making of bricks, and we engaged in the works of the flesh. And *the mediator between God and men, the man Christ Jesus, who gave himself as a ransom for all* (1 Tim 2:6), delivered us, too. He carried us too across the surging waters of the present life, as across a sea, and he initiated us through holy baptism.

For he is the spiritual cloud from above, who supplies *living water* (John 4:10) to those who love him. *Living water* means the Spirit. And Christ said, *He who believes in me, as the Scripture has said: "Out of his heart shall flow rivers of living water"* (John 7:38; Prov 18:4). And the divinely inspired Evangelist, in a clear explanation of this saying, immediately adds to what was already said: *Now this he said about the Spirit, which those who believed in him were to receive* (John 7:39). We also ate bread that is truly life-giving; we drank *the spiritual drink,* just as they too clearly drank the water from the rock. *Now the Rock was Christ* (1 Cor 10:4), and it was for our sake that he made his own blood, mixed with water, gush out from his side (John 19:34) when the soldiers of Pilate pierced him with the spear.

Paul adduces the whole of the account in Numbers to teach that, although they had been baptized *in the cloud and in the sea* (1 Cor 10:2) and considered worthy of *spiritual food* (1 Cor 10:3), they fell because they ate with the worshipers of idols. And when he says, **and they rose up to play,** this means that they committed fornication with the Midianite women.[8]

(2) Augustine

All sacred Scripture is divided into two parts — as our Lord hints when he says, *Every scribe who has been trained for the kingdom of heaven is like a householder who brings out of his treasure what is new and what is old* (Matt 13:52) — which are called respectively the two testaments. Now in all sacred Scripture we must consider the eternal truths that are intimated, the past events that are narrated, the future events that are foretold, and the precepts and warnings that are given. In the case of a narrative the question arises whether it is all to be taken exclusively in the figurative sense or whether we must proclaim and defend it as a record of events that happened. For no Christian would dare to maintain that the narrative is not to be taken in a figurative sense since the apostle Paul says, **Now these things happened to them as figures.**

1 Corinthians 10:12-13

12Therefore let any one who thinks that he stands take heed lest he fall. 13No temptation has overtaken you that is not human.[9] God is faithful, and he will not let you be tempted beyond your strength, but with the temptation will also provide the way of escape, that you may be able to endure it.

(1) John Chrysostom

It is a good thing that Paul says, **any one who thinks that he stands.** For placing confidence in oneself is not the way one ought to **stand.** A person who does this will quickly fall. For even those Corinthians would not have experienced problems if they had been modest, instead of proud and overconfident. From this it is clear that it is vain boasting, above all, that is the fountainhead of such problems, along with laziness and gluttony. Therefore, even if you stand, be on guard against falling. For to stand in this present life is

---

8. Exod 32:6 refers to the Israelites' construction and worship of the golden calf. Cyril understands this verse in the context of stories such as Num 25:6-9 (to which Paul alludes in the next verse), which speaks of an Israelite's association with a Midianite woman.

9. RSV: "not common to man."

not to stand safely until we are freed from the tempests of this present life (Job 11:16) and sail into our sheltered haven. Do not, therefore, be proud of standing, but guard against falling. For if Paul, the strongest of all, was wary, we should be much more so.

The apostle said, **Therefore, let any one who thinks that he stands take heed lest he fall**. But we cannot even say that we stand since practically all of us have fallen and been laid low and cast to the ground. To whom could I utter Paul's words? To the one who plunders day after day? But he has already had a great fall. To the fornicator then? But he has been thrown to the ground. To the drunkard then? He, too, lies fallen, and he does not even know it. Therefore, it is not the time for this word of Paul, but rather for the prophetic word that was spoken to the Jews as well as to us, *When a man falls, does he not rise again?* (Jer 8:4). For all are lying fallen and do not want to get up. So the exhortation appropriate for us is not about not falling, but about being able to rise after a fall.

Therefore, beloved ones, let us rise; even though it is late, let us rise at last and stand nobly. How long will we lie fallen? How long will we be drunk, stupefied by our great desire for earthly life? Now is a fitting time to ask, *To whom shall I speak and bear witness?* (Jer 6:10 LXX). Everyone has become so deaf to the teaching of virtue and, as a result, filled with a multitude of sins! If it were possible to see our souls laid bare, the Church would be like a military camp after the battle, where one sees some dead and others wounded. So I beg and exhort you: let us reach out to one another and stand up. And in fact I, too, am among the wounded who need someone to give me medicine.

(2) Origen on verse 13

We must now examine how, according to the Scriptures, hostile powers and the devil himself fight against the human race by provoking and inciting sin. First, we are told in the book of Genesis that a serpent led Eve astray (Gen 3:1-7). . . .

[*In a section omitted here Origen then goes on to cite other Old Testament references to evil spirits, before turning to the New Testament.*] We should note also in the New Testament the passage where Satan comes to our Savior to tempt him (Matt 4:1-11). Moreover, evil spirits and unclean demons, which had besieged certain folk, were put to flight from the bodies of their victims, who, we are told, were liberated by the Savior.[10] Judas as well, when the devil had put it in his heart to betray Christ (John 13:2), later received Satan whole into himself: as the scripture says, *after the morsel Satan entered into him* (John 13:27). The apostle Paul teaches us not to give way to the devil (Eph 4:27) but says, *Put on the whole armor of God, that you may be able to stand against the wiles of the devil* (Eph 6:11); by this he indicates that the saints had to fight *not against flesh and blood, but against principalities, against powers, against the world rulers of this present darkness, against the spiritual hosts of wickedness in the heavenly places* (Eph 6:12). He also says that the Savior was crucified by *the rulers of this age* (1 Cor 2:8), who will be destroyed, whose *wisdom*, Paul says, he does not speak (1 Cor 2:6). By these words, then, holy Scripture teaches us that there exist certain invisible foes who fight against us, and it instructs us to arm ourselves against them. As a result, some

---

10. See, for example, Matt 8:28-34.

of the simpler among the believers in Christ think that all sins arise from these hostile powers' influence on the minds of those who commit them, and that in that unseen contest these powers are superior. They think, for example, that if the devil did not exist, no one would sin at all. We, however, who consider the matter more carefully, do not believe this in view of what happens in us by physical necessity. . . .

Just as in good things the human will all by itself is inadequate to perfecting the good (and any perfection it achieves is the result of divine help), so also in bad things we receive the initial impulses and, as it were, the seeds of sin from desires given us by nature, but when we indulge these immoderately and fail to resist the first promptings toward intemperance, the power of the enemy, finding an opening in this first sin, goads us and presses us in every way, desiring to increase our sins. Though it is we who have provided the opportunity and first beginnings of sin, it is the hostile powers who multiply them far and wide and, if possible, endlessly. That is the way we slip into greed: we first desire a little money, and then this fault increases and the power of greed grows stronger. Afterward, when mental blindness caused by this passion comes over us as the result of the temptings and promptings of hostile powers, we no longer simply long for money but seize it by force and even commit murder to obtain it. . . .

That, however, there are certain sins that do not come from the hostile powers but arise from the natural motions of the body is clearly declared by the apostle Paul when he says, *The desires of the flesh are against the Spirit, and the desires of the Spirit are against the flesh; for these are opposed to each other, to prevent you from doing what you would* (Gal 5:17). If, therefore, the flesh lusts against the spirit and the spirit against the flesh, we must at times *contend against flesh and blood* (Eph 6:12), that is, when we are human and walk according to the flesh and are not allowed to be tempted by any temptation greater than human, when it is said of us: **No temptation has overtaken you that is not common to man. God is faithful, and he will not let you be tempted beyond your strength.**

Those who are in charge of athletic contests do not allow entrants to compete indiscriminately or by chance, but after careful examination of their physique and age they join them up in proper pairings, for example, boys with boys and men with men, pairs who are alike in age and strength. So we must understand that divine providence arranges with most righteous care all who enter the contests of this life, taking account of each one's virtue: this is known only to providence, which knows the hearts of men. Thus one person fights against this kind of flesh, another against that kind; one for this length of time, another for that; one is goaded by the flesh into this act, another into a different act; one resists this hostile power, another that, a third two or three together. . . . **But God is faithful, and he will not let you be tempted beyond your strength,** that is to say, individuals are tempted in proportion to the degree and strength of their virtue.

And just because we have said that the righteous judgment of God causes each to be tempted in proportion to his strength, we should not suppose that he who is tempted must in all ways be victorious. For neither is an athlete, justly paired though he may be with his competitor, bound to be victorious at all times. But if the contestants' strength were not equal, there would be no justice in the victor's palm nor would it be right to blame the vanquished. Therefore, God allows us to be tempted, but not **beyond our strength**: we are tempted in proportion to our strength. But Scripture does not say that "he will provide a way to escape from enduring it" but that he **will also provide the way of escape, that you may be able to endure it**, that is, he grants us the ability to endure. But it lies with us how we make use of this power given to us, whether vigorously or feebly. There is no doubt that in every temptation we have the power of enduring, provided that we make proper use of the power thus granted. To have the power to overcome is not the same thing as to overcome, as the careful language of the apostle makes clear: **God will also provide the way of escape, that you may be able to endure it**, not "so that you will endure it." Many do not endure but are vanquished in temptation. But God grants not that we will endure (otherwise there would seem to be no contest) but the power to endure.

1 Corinthians 10:14-17

14Therefore, my beloved, shun the worship of idols. 15I speak as to sensible men; judge for yourselves what I say. 16The cup of blessing which we bless, is it not a participation in the blood of Christ? The bread which we break, is it not a participation in the body of Christ? 17Because there is one bread, we who are many are one body, for we all partake of the one bread.

(1) John Chrysostom

The cup of blessing which we bless, is it not a participation in the blood of Christ? Blessed Paul, what are you saying? When you want to shame your audience and call to mind awesome mysteries, do you refer to the cup that inspires fear and awe as a **cup of blessing**? "Yes," he says, "and this was not spoken lightly. For when I speak of **blessing**, I open up the whole treasury of God's beneficence and call to mind those magnificent gifts." And in fact by invoking over the cup God's inexpressible beneficence and all the benefits we enjoy, we make it our own and share in it. We give thanks that he delivered the human race from sin; that he *brought near* those who were *far off* (Eph 2:13); that he made those *having no hope and without God in the world* (Eph 2:12) into his own brothers and co-heirs (Rom 8:17; Eph 3:6; Heb 2:11). We approach the cup as a **cup of blessing** when we give thanks for these and all other such things.

"How, then," Paul asks the Corinthians, "is it not a contradiction when you thank God for delivering you from idols but then run back to their tables?" **The cup of blessing which we bless, is it not a participation in the blood of Christ?** Paul expresses both strong faith and awe. What he means is this: what is in the cup is the very thing that flowed from Christ's side (John 19:34-35), and of this we partake. He calls it a **cup of blessing** because, as we hold it in our hands, we chant our praise to him. We marvel and are amazed at his indescribable gift (2 Cor 9:15), and we bless God for pouring out this very thing so that we might not remain in error. And he not only poured it out but also gave all of us a share in it. "Therefore," Christ says, "if you desire blood, do not stain the idols' altar with the blood of brute beasts, but stain my altar with my own blood." Tell me, what is more awe-inspiring than this? What could be more loving?

This is how lovers behave. When a man sees that his beloved desires another man's goods and feels contempt for what she has, he persuades her to keep away from the other man by bestowing his own possessions on her. Now lovers compete with money and clothes and possessions, and no one ever did so with blood. But this is how Christ demonstrated his care and his fervent love toward us. In the Old Testament, because the Jews were immature, God condescended to accept blood, which they were used to offering to idols, in order to draw them away from the idols. This was itself an act of inexpressible love. But here [in the New Testament] he exchanged such sacrifice for something much more awesome and grand by changing the offering itself and by bidding us to offer his very self instead of slaughtering brute beasts. . . .

The bread which we break, is it not a participation in the body of Christ? Why did he say **participation in,** not "partaking of"? Because he wants to indicate something greater and to reveal the closeness of the connection. For we "participate" not only in partaking of and sharing the bread but also in becoming one. . . . **Because there is one bread, we who are many are one body.** "Why do I speak of participating in?" Paul asks. "We are that very body." What is the bread? The *body of Christ* (12:27). What do those who partake of it become? The *body of Christ* — not many bodies but **one body.** For a loaf of bread is a unity made up of many grains and such that the grains are nowhere visible. Although the grains still exist, when they are joined together their distinction can no longer be seen. In the same way we are united to one another and to Christ. For you are not nourished by one body and your neighbor by a different one, but all by **one body.**

Consequently, Paul adds, **For we all partake of the same bread.** But if all are of the same body and all become the same body, why do we not show the same love and become one in this as well? And in fact this was true for our Christian ancestors in the early days. *Now the company of those who believed,* it says (Acts 4:32), *were of one heart and soul.* But this is not the case now — quite the opposite. We all constantly battle with one another. Although we are *members* of one another (1 Cor 12:25), we rage against each other like wild beasts. Christ has made you one with himself, even though you had set yourself apart, but you cannot even bring yourself to be united closely with your brother, as you should. Instead, you cut yourself off, even though you have enjoyed so much love and life from the Master. For he did more than merely give up his own body. When the original fleshly nature, formed from the earth, came to die because of sin and to be bereft of life, then Christ introduced his own flesh, as a sort of second, leavened loaf, which had the same nature yet was free from sin and filled with life. He gave it to us all to partake of together, so that when we feed on it and put aside the former dead flesh (Eph 2:1; Col 2:13), we might be united and brought into immortal life by means of this table.

1 Corinthians 10:18-22

18Consider the people of Israel; are not those who eat the sacrifices partners in the altar? 19What do I imply then? That food offered to idols is anything, or that an idol is anything? 20No, I imply that what pagans sacrifice they offer to demons and not to God. I do not want you to be partners with demons. 21You cannot drink the cup of the

Lord and the cup of demons. You cannot partake of the table of the Lord and the table of demons. 22Shall we provoke the Lord to jealousy? Are we stronger than he?

(1) John Chrysostom

Shall we provoke the Lord to jealousy? Are we stronger than he? That is, are we testing him to see if he can punish us and goading him by defecting to his opponents and siding with his enemies? Paul says this to remind the Corinthians of the ancient story about the transgression of our fathers. This is why he uses the same language Moses once used to rebuke the Jews for their idolatry, when he spoke in the person of God. *They have stirred me to jealousy,* Moses says, *with what is no god; they have provoked me with their idols* (Deut 32:21). **Are we stronger than he?** Do you see how Paul strikes his hearers with fear and awe, how he jolts their nerves and attacks them through this *reductio ad absurdum* and destroys their pride?

Someone might ask, "Why did Paul not establish these points at the outset, since they would have been especially effective in bringing them around?" Paul's practice is to employ several different arguments to achieve his purpose, and to put the strongest points last and produce more arguments than he needs to win the day. This is why he started off with lesser points and then progressed to the most serious of their troubles. For this made it easier for them to accept what he says, since their minds had been prepared by his previous arguments.

(2) Clement of Alexandria

At this point we must discuss that which is called **food offered to idols** and how we are commanded to abstain from it. . . . **I do not want you to be partners with demons**, the apostle says, because those who are being saved and those who are perishing have separate foods. We must abstain from this food, then, not because we are afraid of it (for the food has no power in itself), but for the sake of our consciences, which are holy (1 Cor 10:28-29), and out of revulsion, since we abhor the demons to whom the food is dedicated. A further reason for abstaining is the instability of those who have a shaky grasp of many things. *Their conscience, being weak, is defiled. Food will not commend us to God* (1 Cor 8:7-8). *Not what goes into the mouth defiles a man* [Christ says], *but what comes out of the mouth, this defiles a man* (Matt 15:11). There is neither moral benefit nor blame in the normal consumption of food.

We are no worse off if we do not eat, and no better off if we do (1 Cor 8:8). But for those considered worthy to share divine and spiritual food, it is not a good idea to partake of the **table of demons**. *Do we not have the right to our food and drink?* says the apostle. *Do we not have the right to be accompanied by a wife* (1 Cor 9:4)? But clearly if we control our pleasures, this keeps lusts in check. *Only take care lest this liberty of yours somehow become a stumbling block to the weak* (1 Cor 8:9).

Therefore, it is not right for us to use up the Father's gifts in riotous living, like the wealthy son described in the Gospel (Luke 15:11-13). Instead we should be masters over them, making use of them without becoming attached to them. And in fact we were appointed to rule and have dominion (Gen 1:28), not to be slaves to food. How wonderful it is, then, to lift our eyes up to the truth and cling to the divine food that comes from above (John 6:32-35, 48-51), to be filled with the endless contemplation of what is truly real and taste of the pleasure that is secure, stable, and pure! For this is what it means to feed on Christ — that we must share in this feast of love. But it is totally irrational, futile, and subhuman to feed like pigs being fattened up for death, as earthly creatures whose gaze is always toward the ground, who bend over tables and pursue the life of gluttony. . . . We must, then, shun gluttony and partake of only a few foods, those that are necessary to life.

1 Corinthians 10:23-26

23**All things are lawful,**[11] **but not all things are helpful. All things are lawful, but not all things build up.** 24**Let no one seek his own good, but the good of his neighbor.** 25**Eat whatever is sold in the meat market without raising any question on the ground of conscience.** 26**For "the earth is the Lord's, and everything in it"** (Ps 24:1).

(1) Clement of Alexandria

If it is **lawful** for me to partake of **all things**, still **not all things are helpful**. For those who do everything the law allows quickly fall into doing what is not lawful. And just as greediness does not produce justice nor licentiousness temperance, so a Christian life is not achieved through luxury. For the *table* (1 Cor 10:21) of the Truth is far removed from the food that excites lust. And even if *all things were made* (John 1:3) for the sake of human beings, it is not good to make use of everything or to do so on all occasions. And in fact what is beneficial for the one who is being trained depends largely on the occasion, the length of time, the manner, and the intention of an action. And eating appropriately can undo the life of gluttony caused by wealth, which does not see clearly[12] — or rather which is caused by superfluity, which makes a person blind to gluttony. No one is poor in respect of what is necessary for life, and no one is ever overlooked [by God]. For he who feeds the birds and the fish and, in a word, all irrational animals is one — that is, God. And the animals lack nothing whatsoever even if they are not *anxious* about food (Matt 6:25-26). But we are superior to the animals in that we are lords (Gen 1:28; Ps 8:6-8), and dearer to God in that we have greater self-control. But we were not made to eat and drink but so that we might come to know God.

11. The RSV encloses the phrase "all things are lawful" in quotation marks, here and in the next sentence, to reflect the translators' view that Paul is quoting a saying that was current in the church in Corinth. The fathers do not understand the text in this way.

12. Clement may be alluding to Aristophanes' *Wealth,* in which the god of wealth, Plutus, is depicted as blind.

(2) John Chrysostom

Paul adds, **Let no one seek his own good.** Paul says this repeatedly, both throughout the present epistle and in the one to the Romans, as when he says, *For Christ did not please himself* (Rom 15:3). And again, *just as I try to please all men in everything I do, not seeking my own advantage* (1 Cor 10:33), and also in the present passage, although Paul does not elaborate here. This is because earlier in the Letter he had made a full argument and demonstrated that he never sought his own good but *to the Jews* he became *as a Jew* (1 Cor 9:20), and *to those outside the law . . . as one outside the law* (1 Cor 9:21), and that he did not make careless use of his own *freedom* and *authority* but was a servant to all for the benefit of all (1 Cor 9:1, 12, 18-19). In the present text, content with a few words, he moves on, having used this brief reference to remind his hearers of all he had told them.

1 Corinthians 10:27-33

27If one of the unbelievers invites you to dinner and you are disposed to go, eat whatever is set before you without raising any question on the ground of conscience. 28(But if some one says to you, "This has been offered in sacrifice," then out of consideration for the man who informed you, and for conscience' sake — 29I mean his conscience, not yours — do not eat it.) For why should my liberty be determined by another man's scruples? 30If I partake with thankfulness, why am I denounced because of that for which I give thanks? 31So, whether you eat or drink, or whatever you do, do all to the glory of God. 32Give no offense to Jews or to Greeks or to the church of God, 33just as I try to please all men in everything I do, not seeking my own advantage, but that of many, that they may be saved.

(1) Clement of Alexandria

And **if one of the unbelievers invites** us **to dinner and** we decide **to go** (for it is a good idea not to associate with those who are disorderly), Paul bids us **eat whatever is set before** us **without raising any question on the ground of conscience**. And similarly he bids us buy what comes from **the meat market** (1 Cor 10:25) without posing unnecessary questions. It is not required that we avoid all variety in what we eat, but we should not value it too highly. We must partake of what is **set before** us, as is fitting for a Christian, showing respect for our host by our innocent and moderate participation in the social gathering, but being indifferent toward the luxuriousness of what is provided and disdaining the delicacies that will soon perish. *Let not him who eats despise him who abstains, and let not him who abstains pass judgment on him who eats* (Rom 14:3). A little further on Paul will explain the reason for this commandment, when he says: *He who eats, eats in honor of the Lord and gives thanks to God. And he who abstains, abstains in honor of the Lord and gives thanks to God* (Rom 14:6). Thus eating judiciously is to give thanks. And a person who is always giving thanks has no leisure for pleasures. And if we want to influence some of our fellow diners to embrace virtue, then we have all the more reason to avoid these rich foods and to offer ourselves as clear models of virtue, just as we ourselves have Christ as our model. . . . And **whether you eat or drink . . . do all to the glory of God**, aiming for true simplicity. It seems to me that the Lord indicated this symbolically when he blessed the loaves of bread and the cooked fish he gave his disciples to eat (Matt 14:19; John 21:9) and provided a good example of simple food.

(2) Theodoret

So, whether you eat or drink, or whatever you do, do all to the glory of God. Paul was right to include everything — sitting, walking, discussing, showing mercy, and giving instruction — since he regards the goal of all of these actions to be **the glory of God.** So too the Lord commanded: *Let your light so shine before men, that they may see your good works and give glory to your Father who is in heaven* (Matt 5:16). The same point is made in the present text: **Give no offense to Jews or to Greeks or to the church of God.** Let no cause for scandal come from you, whether among the unbelievers or among those who have already believed.

Just as I try to please all men in everything I do. But this is characteristic of flatterers. What Paul goes on to say, however, does not describe a flatterer: **not seeking my own advantage, but that of many, that they may be saved.** Flatterers do not seek the **advantage** of the other person, but their **own advantage.** Or, rather, they do not actually seek their own **advantage**, for they mistreat themselves even more than they do other people. But the divine apostle did not seek his **own advantage**; instead he labored for the salvation of others, and by saving them he stored up for himself imperishable wealth.

(3) John Chrysostom on verses 32-33

Give no offense to Jews or to Greeks or to the church of God. This means: do not give anyone any reason to be offended. For in fact the brother may take offense, and the Jew, even more, will hate and condemn you, and the Greek likewise will deride you as a glutton and a hypocrite. You must not only avoid shocking your brothers in the faith, but as far as possible even those outside. For if we are *light* (Matt 5:14) and *leaven* (Matt 13:33) and *lights* (Phil 2:15) and *salt* (Matt 5:13), we ought to shine and not be dark, to bind together and not break apart, to win the unbelievers over to ourselves, not drive them away. Why, then, are you chasing away those you should be drawing to yourself? For the Greeks are stunned when they see us reverting to such things.[13] They do not understand that the soul is above all physical defilement. The Jews and the weaker among the brothers will also believe the same thing.

Do you notice how many reasons Paul gives for us to abstain from meat sacrificed to idols? It is unprofitable; it is unnecessary; it causes injury to the brother, blasphemy

---

13. That is, partaking of meat dedicated to idols.

among the Jews, and slander among the Greeks. One must not have fellowship with demons (1 Cor 10:20). And the activity itself is a form of idolatry. Then, after he has said, **Give no offense**, and has accused them of injuring Greeks and Jews, and when his words weigh heavily upon his hearers, see how he lightens his point and makes it easy to accept by focusing on himself and saying: **Just as I try to please all men in everything I do, not seeking my own advantage, but that of many, that they may be saved.** *Be imitators of me, as I am of Christ* (1 Cor 11:1). . . .

No achievement can be very great if it does not benefit others. This is shown by the servant who returned the talent safe and sound and then was severely punished because he had not increased it (Matt 25:24-30). Accordingly, you too, my brother — even if you fast continuously, sleep on the ground, eat ashes, constantly lament your sins — if you help no one else, you will not accomplish very much.

In fact, helping others was what those great and noble men of old most desired to do. Examine their lives carefully, and you will see clearly that not a single one of them was ever preoccupied with his own affairs, but each looked after the good of his neighbor. And this made them all the more glorious. In particular, consider Moses: although many great signs and wonders were done through him, nothing made him so great as did his blessed utterance to God, *If thou wilt forgive their sin, forgive — and if not, blot me . . . out* (Exod 32:32). David was the same sort of man. Thus he too said, *I, the shepherd, have sinned, and I have done wickedly; but these sheep, what have they done? Let thy hand . . . be against me and against my father's house* (2 Sam 24:17). In the same way, Abraham also was **not seeking** his **own advantage, but that of the many**. This is why he exposed himself to perils and entreated God on behalf of those who were not related to him (Gen 18:22-33).

Now in this way those men won glory. But consider how others, who were preoccupied with their own affairs, suffered harm. For example, when Abraham's nephew was told, *If you take the right hand, then I will go to the left* (Gen 13:9), in making his choice, he sought his own benefit but did not achieve it. The land he chose was scorched by fire, while the other part remained unscathed (Gen 19:24-29). Again, consider Jonah, who when he did not seek **the advantage of the many**, but only his own, was in danger of losing his life. The city of Nineveh stood firm, but he was tossed and rolled around and thrown into the sea. Yet, when he sought **the advantage of the many**, then he also reaped benefit for himself.

In the same way, although Jacob did not seek his own gain from the flocks, he enjoyed tremendous wealth (Gen 30:29-30). And when Joseph sought the advantage of his brothers, he found his own. Indeed, when he was sent by his father to his brothers (Gen 37:13), he did not say, "What is this? Did you not hear that they wanted to tear me to pieces on account of my vision? And that they accused me because of my dreams and punished me because you love me? What will they do once they catch me among them?" Joseph said none of this, nor did he think it; instead, he put service to his brothers before everything else. This is why he enjoyed all the blessings that followed, which brought him great fame and glory.

Moses was also like this — there is no reason not to mention him a second time to point out how he neglected his own affairs and sought the advantage of others. He lived in a palace, but since *he considered the suffering of abuse . . . greater wealth than the treasures of Egypt* (Heb 11:26), he threw it all away and shared with the Hebrews in their sufferings (Exod 2:11-15). And not only did he escape becoming enslaved himself, but he also delivered them from slavery. These great deeds are worthy of angels.

But the case of Paul is much greater. While all those others gave up their own advantage and chose to share in the troubles of their neighbors, Paul did something much greater. Instead of wishing to share the misfortunes of others, he chose to be in dire straits himself so that others could have the benefits. . . . This is not all, but Paul surpasses all the aforementioned examples in another, more important way. For Abraham and all the others embraced the perils of this present life, and every one of them longed for a death met in this way.[14] But Paul prayed that he might be deprived of the coming glory for the sake of the salvation of others (Rom 9:3). . . .

You see the greatness of Paul's soul and the grandeur of his mind, which surpasses heaven itself. Imitate this. But if you cannot manage this, imitate those who achieved glory in the Old Testament. For you will find your **own advantage** if you seek that of your neighbor. Therefore, when you hesitate to care for your brother, be aware that without this caring you cannot be saved, and, for your own sake if for no other reason, champion him and his concerns.

Enough has been said to prove that there is no other way to gain advantage for ourselves. But if you would like additional examples, taken from everyday life, to help you understand this, consider the following: suppose a house catches on fire, and some of the neighbors are preoccupied with their own concerns and unwilling to fight against the danger. So they shut themselves in and remain at home because they fear that someone might sneak in to steal something they have inside. How great a penalty will they pay? In fact, the approaching fire will burn up everything they have. And since they do not look to the advantage of their neighbors, they destroy their own property as well. Indeed, because God desired to bind all people together, he built into things this necessary consequence: that a person's advantage is bound up with that of his neighbor.

The whole world is arranged in this way. Thus on a ship, if a storm arises and the captain abandons **the advantage of the many** and seeks only his own advantage, he will quickly sink both himself and the others. And if each profession were to seek only its own advantage, life could never be secure, nor could the profession seeking its own advantage be secure. For this reason the farmer does not sow just enough grain to satisfy himself; otherwise he would have destroyed both himself and others long ago. Instead, he seeks **the advantage of the many**. The soldier, too, doesn't face perils just to preserve himself, but to secure safety for entire cities. The trader, as well, does not transport only enough for himself, but for many others as well. . . .

[*Chrysostom goes on to describe higher motivations for seeking the advantage of one's neighbor, namely, the desire to please God and the love of which Paul speaks in 1 Cor 13:3.*] Let us then not seek our own advantage, so that we might find it. We must realize that neither voluntary poverty nor martyrdom nor any other such thing can commend us if we do not have perfect love (1 Cor 13:3). So let us practice this love before everything else,

---

14. That is, with confident expectation of a reward in heaven. See Heb 11:1-40, especially v. 10.

in order that through it we might obtain the other blessings as well, both those available now and those promised for the future. And may we all attain these by the grace and benevolence of our Lord Jesus Christ, to whom, along with the Father and the Holy Spirit, be glory, power, and honor, now and always, world without end. Amen.

1 Corinthians 11

In chapters 11–14 Paul addresses several concerns the relate to the worship of the Corinthian community: the activity and dress of prophets (11:1-16), the celebration of the Lord's Supper (11:17-34), and the exercise of spiritual gifts such as speaking in tongues (chaps. 12–14). In 11:1-16 Paul's main concern is to tell women to cover their heads when they prophesy, but subsequent commentary has focused less on this and more on the justification he gives for this directive: that the head of a woman is her husband, and the head of the man is Christ (v. 3). Patristic commentaries on this text assume with most ancient thinkers that the subordination of women to men is a fact of nature, necessitated by their physical and moral weakness and their smaller intelligence (a view that was reinforced by interpretation of the stories of creation and the fall in Genesis 2–3). There is some difference of opinion, however (see Severian and John Chrysostom), on what constitutes the image of God (1 Cor 11:7, citing Gen 1:26-27) and whether women possess the image as well as men. That some early Christians recognized women prophets is illustrated by the Dialogue of a Montanist and an Orthodox Christian.

Other comments on this passage focus on Christology. Arius and his followers used the hierarchy of "heads" in verse 3 to argue that the Son is subordinate to the Father, a view that is countered in different ways by John Chrysostom and Cyril. Theodore of Mopsuestia gives a soteriological interpretation of this verse by relating it to the Adam/Christ typology of 1 Cor 15:45-46.

Particularly important for Christian theology and practice is 11:23-26, the earliest version we possess of the words of institution of the Eucharist. The selection from The Liturgy of St. James illustrates how the prayers of the early Church elaborate on this text. The excerpts from Gregory of Nyssa and Ambrose are examples of early Christian reflection on the meaning of the Eucharist. Gregory explains how the eating and drinking of bread and wine bring about the sanctification of the Christian's body (a view also reflected in the Liturgy of Saint James). Ambrose relates the Eucharist to Old Testament precedents and argues that it is the words of our Lord spoken over the elements that make them become his body and blood.

Paul frames the words of institution with a description of the situation in Corinth, on the one hand (vv. 17-22; see John Chrysostom's reconstruction of the specific situation Paul addresses), and his own theological interpretation, on the other (vv. 27-34). In these closing verses Paul warns of the serious consequences of misusing the Eucharist. Theodore of Mopsuestia's comments on this last section show that some Christians had responded to Paul's warning by avoiding the Eucharist as much as possible — a view Theodore is at pains to refute. Paul's observation that *"there must be factions" (v. 19) provided encouragement to later Christians as they faced serious theological disputes within the church (see the comments of Augustine and Clement of Alexandria).*

1 Corinthians 11:1-2

₁**Be imitators of me, as I am of Christ.** ₂**I commend you because you remember me in everything and maintain the traditions even as I have delivered them to you.**

(1) Ambrosiaster

Be imitators of me, as I am of Christ. Paul's statement that we should be imitators of the teacher given us by God is an accommodation to human limitation. If the apostle, a human being, is the imitator of God, should we not imitate this man? God the Father sent Christ as teacher and author of life; but because we were not able to be imitators of Christ, he sent apostles to us so that we could imitate them. For that is what our Lord said to the Father: *As thou didst send me into the world, so I send them into the world* (John 17:18). And since they were going to be worthy of their mission and be his imitators, he adds, *And for their sake I consecrate myself* (John 17:19).

(2) John Chrysostom

It is clear from the way Paul begins this passage that he had already exhorted them about these matters while he was with them. Otherwise why, when he has said nothing about this earlier in the letter but dealt with other problems, does he suddenly say, **I commend you because you remember me in everything and maintain the traditions even as I have delivered them to you?** Clearly some, whom Paul praises, were obedient, but others were disobedient. These he corrects in what follows, saying, *If any one is disposed to be contentious, we recognize no such practice* (1 Cor 11:16). For some were acting rightly and others were disobedient, and if Paul had accused them all equally, he would have made the latter more insolent and the former more careless. But, in fact, by praising some and rebuking others, he encourages the obedient and humbles the others. For the rebuke was strong in its own right, but when juxtaposed with the praise of those who act rightly, the sting was more bitter.

In the present passage Paul starts not with accusations but with generous compliments, saying, **I commend you because you remember me in everything.** It was Paul's custom to give strong compliments for little things. Yet this is not flattery — God forbid! How could that be when Paul had no desire for money or glory or anything else of the sort? Rather, he does everything for the sake of their salvation. So he praises them, saying, **I commend you because you remember me in everything.**

1 Corinthians 11:3-9

₃But I want you to understand that the head of every man is Christ, the head of a woman is her husband, and the head of Christ is God. ₄Any man who prays or prophesies with his head covered dishonors his head, ₅but any woman who prays or prophesies with her head unveiled dishonors her head — it is the same as if her head were shaven. ₆For if a woman will not veil herself, then she should cut off her hair; but if it is disgraceful for a woman to be shorn or shaven, let her wear a veil. ₇For a man ought not to cover his head, since he is the image and glory of God [Gen 1:27]; but woman is the glory of man. ₈(For man was not made from woman, but woman from man. ₉Neither was man created for woman, but woman for man [Gen 2:18-24].)

(1) Theodore of Mopsuestia on verse 3

But I want you to understand that the head of every man is Christ, the head of a woman is her husband, and the head of Christ is God. Paul means that we advance from Christ to the God from whom he comes, and we advance from the man to Christ. For it is from Christ that we will derive our second life, and in that resurrection we shall all be immortal like him when we participate in the grace of the Spirit that is in him. Now, because we are subject to passions, we regard Adam, from whom we received our existence, as **our head**. But when we become impassible we consider our **head** to be **Christ**, from whom we receive our impassible life. And in a similar way there is a progression from the **woman** to the **man**, since she has her being from him. . . .

Not only men but also women prophesied. At that time the baptized received spiritual gifts in a more obvious way, and various forms of prophecy were prominent, according to the needs of the church. In particular, prophets exposed the false pretenses of those who entered the church in order to test it (1 Cor 14:24-25).

(2) John Chrysostom on verses 3-5

The head of a woman is her husband, and the head of Christ is God. At this point, the heretics pounce on us and twist these words to mean that the Son is inferior.[1] But they fall into their own trap. For if **the head of a woman is her husband**, and the head [the man] has the same substance as the body, and **the head of Christ is God**, then the Son has the same substance as the Father. "But," objects the heretic, "with these words we are not trying to demonstrate a difference in substance, but rather that the Son is subordinate." What can we say to this? Chiefly that when something is said about the humility of the Son when he was in the flesh (Phil 2:6-8), this does take away from his divine nature, since what is said about his incarnation is part of the divine plan (see Phil 2:9-11).

But tell me, how will you argue from the present passage that just as a husband

---

1. Chrysostom seems to be arguing against the Neo-Arians. See Appendix 3 on Arius and Eunomius.

rules over a wife, so the Father rules over Christ? Would it not follow that the Father rules over the Son just as Christ rules over the man? **The head of every man**, he says, **is Christ**. Who would ever accept this? For if the Father is as much exalted over the Son as the Son is over us, see how lowly you make the Son. . . .

Perhaps someone might see another difficulty here and ask what offense there is in women's baring their heads or for men to cover theirs. What is the offense? Consider this: men and women are marked by different characteristics — the man to rule, the woman to be subject. She covers her head while he keeps his bare. If, then, such things are distinctive marks, they both sin if they violate the proper order and the command of God and transgress their proper boundaries, with the man descending to her inferior status, and the woman, through her outward appearance, rising up over him. For if it is not permitted for them to exchange garments and for her to wear a woolen cloak while he wears a mantle or a veil — *A woman shall not wear anything that pertains to a man, nor shall a man put on a woman's garment* (Deut 22:5) — then it is even more important that there be no confusion about whether to cover one's head. Now the laws about garments [in the Old Testament] were legislated by man, even if God later ratified them. But the business of whether to cover one's head was legislated by nature (see 1 Cor 11:14-15). When I say "nature," I mean "God." For he is the one who created nature. Take note, therefore, what great harm comes from overturning these boundaries! And don't tell me that this is a small sin. In the first place it is serious in itself since it involves disobedience. But even if it were only a small sin, it becomes serious because it is a sign of important things. And here is the reason: it provides order to human life by assigning the ruler and the ruled their proper places. Thus the one who transgresses in this matter confuses everything and betrays the gifts of God and casts to the ground the **glory** (v. 7) given from above. This applies to the woman as well as to the man. For in fact it is the woman's greatest honor to maintain her own status, just as it is her greatest shame to rise in revolt.

(3) *Dialogue of a Montanist with an Orthodox Christian* on verse 5[2]

[But any woman who prays or prophesies with her head unveiled dishonors her head — it is the same as if her head were shaven.]

The Montanist: Why do you reject the holy women Maximilla and Priscilla and say that women are not allowed to prophesy? Did not Philip also have four daughters who prophesied (Acts 21:9)? And was Deborah not a prophetess (Judg 4:4)? And if it is not lawful for women to prophesy or pray, would the apostle say: **any woman who prays or prophesies with her head unveiled**? But if women pray, let them also prophesy.

The Orthodox: We do not reject the prophecies of women: the holy Mary also prophesied when she said: *henceforth all generations will call me blessed* (Luke 1:48). As you said

---

2. Gerhard Ficker published this work, found in the manuscript Escurial XII 11, in *Zeitschrift für Kirchengeschichte* 16 (1905) 447-58. Montanus was the leader of a second-century Christian movement called "the New Prophecy." He and his female followers, Maximilla and Priscilla, claimed to transcend the teaching of the apostles and to be bearers of the Paraclete or Holy Spirit (see John 14:16).

yourself, Philip had four daughters who prophesied, and Mary,[3] the sister of Aaron, prophesied (Exod 15:20). But we do not *allow them to speak in the churches* (1 Cor 14:34), nor *to have authority over* men (1 Tim 2:12), in that books are written in their names — for this is the meaning of their **praying and prophesying with unveiled head,**[4] and [the apostle did not allow a woman to do it because it][5] **dishonored** her **head**, that is, her **husband.** Mary, the holy Mother of God, was surely capable of writing books in her own name, was she not? But she did not do it, so as not to **dishonor her head**, by *having authority over* men (1 Tim 2:12).

The Montanist: So praying or prophesying with unveiled head means writing books?

The Orthodox: Exactly.

The Montanist: Then if the holy Mary says, *Henceforth all generations will call me blessed,* does she say this as one **unveiled**, that is, as one speaking freely, or not?

The Orthodox: She has the Gospel writer as a **veil**. She has not written the Gospel in her own name.

The Montanist: You should not take allegorical interpretations for authoritative teaching.

The Orthodox: But the holy Paul most certainly used allegory to confirm his teachings when he said, *Abraham had* two wives. *Now this is an allegory: these women are two covenants* (Gal 4:24). But for the sake of argument let us allow that **the veil** of the head is not meant as an allegory. If you want to dismiss all allegory, answer this for me: if a woman is poor and has nothing with which to veil herself, must she refrain from praying and prophesying?

The Montanist: Can she be so poor as to have nothing with which to cover herself?

The Orthodox: We have often seen women so poor as not to have anything with which to cover themselves. But since you refuse to admit that women can be so poor that they have nothing with which to cover themselves, what do you do in the case of those who are being baptized? Are those who are being baptized not required to pray?[6] And what do you say in the case of men, who often cover their heads because of illness. Do you forbid them from praying and prophesying?

The Montanist: During the time when such a man prays or prophesies he uncovers his head.

The Orthodox: Must he not *pray constantly* in order to obey the apostle who teaches him to *pray constantly* (1 Thess 5:17)? And are you also counseling the woman who is being baptized not to pray?[7]

---

3. The Greek equivalent for "Miriam" in the book of Exodus.

4. In this interpretation "unveiled head" is understood symbolically to refer to women writing books openly, under their own names.

5. The text appears to have a lacuna at this point; words in brackets are a conjecture of the translator.

6. The argument presupposes that people remove their headcovering for the baptismal immersion. Thus if women have to wear a headcovering in order to pray, they cannot pray during baptism, during which the covering would be removed.

7. The point of this whole argument seems to be that a literal interpretation of the text is insufficient because it is sometimes impossible for men and women to follow Paul's directives about headcoverings (e.g., when they are being immersed for baptism). Thus the allegorical interpretation — that women should not write in their own names — is correct after all.

The Montanist: So the reason you do not accept Priscilla and Maximilla is that they wrote books?

The Orthodox: Not for this reason alone, but also because they were false prophetesses, as their leader Montanus was a false prophet.

The Montanist: And what leads you to conclude that they were false prophetesses?

The Orthodox: Did they not teach the same things as Montanus?

The Montanist: Yes.

The Orthodox: We have shown that Montanus taught things contrary to divine Scripture, and so these women must be rejected along with him.

(4) Severian of Gabala on verse 7

Thus it appears that a human being is the **image of God** neither because of the soul nor because of the body. For if the **image** lay in one or the other of these, then the woman would certainly be called the **image of God** since she has the same form of body as a man and a soul like his. But if the woman, although she has the same soul and flesh (Gen 2:23) as the man, is not called the **image of God**, clearly what makes a human being the **image of God** is his ability to rule. For when Scripture speaks of the irrational creatures, then the woman is also the **image of God** (Gen 1:26). But when one speaks of man in relation to woman, only the man is called the **image**. For *male and female* human beings (Gen 1:27) rule over the creatures on the earth and in the sea and in the air, but man rules over woman, and no one on earth rules over man. So then just as nothing that exists rules over God, so nothing on earth rules over man.

(5) Augustine on verse 7

The serpent said that God forbade them to eat from the fruit of the tree because he knew that they would become gods, knowing good and evil, if they did so. If Adam was spiritual in his mind, though not in body, how could he have believed the serpent's words? Would the Creator begrudge his creation such a great blessing [as knowing good and evil]? It is strange that a man endowed with a spiritual mind could have believed this. Should we perhaps think that this is the reason for the addition of the woman? Adam himself could not have believed the serpent, but a woman is of lesser understanding who perhaps still lived *according to the flesh.* This may be the reason the apostle does not assign to her **the image of God. For,** he says, **a man ought not to cover his head, since he is the image and glory of God; but woman is the glory of man.** This is not because the mind of a woman cannot take the same **image** — since Paul maintains that in grace there is *neither male nor female* (Gal 3:28) — but because she had perhaps not yet taken this image, which comes with the knowledge of God. Perhaps she would have received it under the rule and dispensation of the man, and there is a point to what the apostle says: *For Adam was formed first, then Eve; and Adam was not deceived, but the woman was deceived and became a transgressor* (1 Tim 2:13-14), that is, through her the man also became a transgressor. For he also calls the man a transgressor when he says, *like the transgression of Adam, who was a type of the one who was to come* (Rom 5:14). But Paul denies that he was deceived. For Adam, when questioned, does not say, "The woman thou gavest to be with me deceived me and I ate," but *The woman whom thou gavest to be with me, she gave me fruit of the tree, and I ate* (Gen 3:12). But the woman says, *The serpent beguiled me* (Gen 3:13).

1 Corinthians 11:10-16

10That is why a woman ought to have authority[8] on her head, because of the angels. 11(Nevertheless, in the Lord woman is not independent of man nor man of woman; 12for as woman was made from man, so man is now born of woman. And all things are from God.) 13Judge for yourselves; is it proper for a woman to pray to God with her head uncovered? 14Does not nature itself teach you that for a man to wear long hair is degrading to him, 15but if a woman has long hair, it is her pride? For her hair is given to her for a covering. 16If any one is disposed to be contentious, we recognize no other practice, nor do the churches of God.

(1) Theodoret on verse 10

That is why a woman ought to have authority on her head, because of the angels. Paul calls the veil **authority**. This means: let her show her subjection, making herself humble, not least on account of the angels, who are set over human beings and are entrusted with their care. Thus in Acts someone says that it is not Peter [who appears] but *his angel* (Acts 12:15). And the Lord warns: *See that you do not despise one of these little ones; for I tell you that in heaven their angels always behold the face of my Father who is in heaven* (Matt 18:10).

(2) John Chrysostom

Paul had attributed great superiority to the man when he said that *woman is from man* (v. 8), *for man* (v. 9), and under him (v. 3). Notice, however, that in order to avoid exalting men or humbling women more than he needs to, he adds this correction: **Nevertheless, in the Lord woman is not independent of man nor man of woman.** This is what he means: "I want you not only to pay attention to the beginning and that first creation. If you look into the things that come after, you will see that each sex has its origin in the other, or, rather, each has its origin not in the other, but in the God of all." . . .

[*Later in the homily Chrysostom speaks again of the interdependence of man and*

8. RSV: "a veil." Others translate "a sign of authority."

woman. The context here is an exhortation to men not to beat their wives.] For this reason you were appointed as ruler [over the woman], and you were given the place of the *head* (1 Cor 11:3) so that you might bear the weakness of the woman whom you rule. Therefore, make your rule glorious — as it will be if you do not dishonor what you rule. . . . And think back to that evening when her father called you and entrusted his daughter to you, as a sacred trust, and after he had separated her from all others — from her mother and himself and his household — he gave the overseeing of her entirely into your hands. Bear in mind that, after God, she is the source of your children and the way you became a father, and for this reason be gentle to her.

Notice how farmers tend the earth once it has received seed, using various methods of cultivation — even if the ground has countless defects, if, for example, it has poor soil or produces weeds or is plagued by excessive rains because of its location. You should do the same, for thus you will be the first to enjoy both the fruit and the tranquility. For your wife is a safe haven and a medicine of contentment. If, then, you free your harbor from winds and waves, you will enjoy great security when you return from the marketplace. But if you fill this harbor with tumult and upheavals, you will make sailing more difficult for yourself. To avoid this, do as I say: when something unpleasant happens in the household, and it is her fault, console her and do not make the trouble worse. For even if you should lose everything, nothing is more troublesome than to have a wife who lacks goodwill sharing your house. And whatever offense you might mention, you can name nothing as painful as being at war with her. Thus, for these and other reasons, prize her love more than anything else. For if we must *bear one another's burdens* (Gal 6:2), how much more should you bear with your wife?

1 Corinthians 11:17-22

17But in the following instructions I do not commend you, because when you come together it is not for the better but for the worse. 18For, in the first place, when you assemble as a church, I hear that there are divisions[9] among you; and I partly believe it, 19for there must be heresies[10] among you in order that those who are genuine among you may be recognized. 20When you meet together, it is not the Lord's supper that you eat. 21For in eating, each one goes ahead with his own meal, and one is hungry and another is drunk. 22What! Do you not have houses to eat and drink in? Or do you despise the church of God and humiliate those who have nothing? What shall I say to you? Shall I commend you in this? No, I will not.

9. Or "schisms"; Greek *schismata.*
10. RSV: "factions." The Greek word is *haireseis,* from which the English word "heresies" is derived. Paul means simply "factions," but the church fathers often understood the term to mean "heresies" or "sects." See the commentaries of John Chrysostom and Clement of Alexandria.

(1) John Chrysostom

We must first explain the reason for this rebuke; then the argument will be easier to follow. What is it then? Just as in the days of the three thousand who first believed, all Christians feasted together and possessed everything in common (Acts 2:41-45), so it was when the apostle wrote these words, though not in every detail. Some echo of that early fellowship remained and was passed down to those who came after. And since some were poor and others rich, even though they did not contribute everything they had for common use, apparently it was their custom to prepare common meals on certain days. Once the worship service was over, after sharing the mysteries, they would all go to the common feast, with the wealthy bringing the food, and the poor and penniless as their guests, and all would feast together. But later even this custom was abandoned. A problem arose because the people were divided and championed different leaders, saying, "*I belong* to this one," and "*I belong* to that one," the very thing Paul had tried to address at the beginning of the letter (1 Cor 1:12). . . .

And do not marvel if Paul calls these groups **schisms**. As I said, he wants to get through to them with this term. But if the **schisms** were about doctrine, he would not have spoken with them as gently as he does. Indeed, take note how vehement he is, how firm and censorious, when he addresses doctrinal division. He is firm when he says, *But if an angel from heaven should preach to you a gospel contrary to that which you received, let him be accursed* (Gal 1:8). He is censorious when he says, *You who would be justified by the law, you have fallen away from grace* (Gal 5:4). And he also calls certain corrupters dogs, saying, *Look out for the dogs* (Phil 3:2). In another place he speaks of those *whose consciences are seared* (1 Tim 4:2), and again of *the devil's angels* (2 Cor 11:14-15). Yet in this text he does not say any such thing but speaks in a subdued and gentle way.

(2) Augustine on verse 19

[**For there must be heresies among you in order that those who are genuine among you may be recognized.**] You should note, holy people of God, the usefulness of heretics, usefulness in the plan of God, who uses even evil for good purpose. . . . For instance, how great was the good God derived from Judas! By the suffering of our Lord the nations were saved. But so that he might suffer, Judas betrayed him. . . . So in the case under discussion[11] no one would investigate the spiritual meanings that lie hidden in the text if he were content with a simpler faith. And so no one would discover these meanings since no one would investigate unless the slanderers were beating on the door. For when the heretics utter their calumnies, the little ones are troubled. When they are troubled, they ask questions. Their questions are like little children butting their heads against their mothers' breasts so that they will get enough milk to satisfy their hunger. These little ones are troubled and ask questions. But those who know and have learned — because they

11. Augustine is talking about people who raise doubts because of the differences between the genealogies of Christ in Matthew and Luke.

have investigated the matter and God has opened to their knocking — open in turn to those who are troubled. And thus it happens that heretics are useful for the discovery of truth even while they utter calumnies that lead people into error. If there were no deceitful adversaries, few would delve deeply into the truth. **For,** Paul says, **there must be heresies among you.** And as if we were asking the reason, he adds at once, **so that those who are genuine among you may be recognized.**

(3) Clement of Alexandria on verse 19

[**For there must be sects**[12] **among you in order that those who are genuine among you may be recognized.**] Our next task is to reply to the charges made against us by Greeks and Jews. But since, as we saw earlier, the existence of **sects** associated with the true teaching plays a role in some of their objections, it will be good first to clear away this obstacle and then proceed in the next book of the *Miscellanies,* after this preparation, to solve the other difficulties that have been raised.

The first criticism adduced against us is that one should not be a believer because Christian sects disagree among themselves. For where does the truth lie, if different sects teach different doctrines? Our answer is this: there have also been sects among you Jews, as well as among the most esteemed of the Greek philosophers, but you do not say that one must refrain from being a philosopher or a Jew merely because of your sects' disagreements with each other. In addition, the Lord, speaking prophetically, said that sects would be sown along with the truth, like *tares* with the wheat (Matt 13:25). And what was foretold must necessarily come to pass. Now the explanation for why the sects exist is that fine accomplishment attracts fault-finding. . . .[13]

Paul says that the **sects** exist for the sake of those who are **genuine.** Now by **genuine** he may be referring to those who are just coming to faith, who will approach the Lord's teaching in a more discriminating way,[14] like **genuine** money changers who distinguish the genuine coin of the Lord from the false one. Or perhaps he means those who have already become **genuine** in the faith, proven in both their conduct and their understanding.

For this reason, then, we must give greater care and consideration to investigating how we should live disciplined lives, and what true piety is. Clearly it is because truth is difficult to attain that questions have arisen. And because of these questions egotistical and vainglorious **sects** have emerged, when people have no learning and have not received genuine instruction but merely imagine that they have knowledge. We must then give more careful consideration to finding the real truth, the only truth about the true God. After such toil come the discovery and remembrance of the truth, which are sweet. Thus the **sects** make us get down to the toil of discovering, and we should by no means shrink from this task.

---

12. Or heresies. In this passage Clement is speaking primarily of Christian Gnostic groups.
13. See Bacchylides 13.202.
14. That is, because they are forced to make comparisons with the teaching of the heretics.

1 Corinthians 11:23-26

23For I received from the Lord what I also delivered to you, that the Lord Jesus on the night when he was betrayed took bread, 24and when he had given thanks, he broke it, and said, "This is my body which is for you. Do this in remembrance of me." 25In the same way also the cup, after supper, saying, "This cup is the new covenant in my blood. Do this, as often as you drink it, in remembrance of me." 26For as often as you eat this bread and drink the cup, you proclaim the Lord's death until he comes.

(1) John Chrysostom

For I received from the Lord, he says, **what I also delivered to you, that the Lord Jesus on the night when he was betrayed took bread, and when he had given thanks, he broke it, and said,** *Take, eat* [Matt 26:26]. **This is my body which is broken for you. Do this in remembrance of me.** Why does Paul mention the mysteries at this point in the letter? Because this subject was very necessary for his present argument. "Your Lord," he says, "considered all worthy of the same table, even though this table was far more precious and awe-inspiring than any other. But you consider your fellow Christians unworthy of your own table, which is paltry and insignificant, and though they do not take advantage of you in spiritual matters, you rob them in physical things. And these physical things are not even yours."

But Paul does not say this, lest his message become too harsh. He speaks more gently, saying, **That the Lord Jesus on the night when he was betrayed took bread.** And why does he remind us of that time, mentioning both that evening and the betrayal? It was not done foolishly or without reason, but in order that he might use that time to pierce them to the heart. Even if a person is made of stone, once he considers that night — how Christ in the presence of his disciples was deeply troubled, how he was betrayed, how he was bound, how he was led away, how he was condemned, how he suffered all that followed — he becomes softer than wax and is freed from the earth and all earthly imaginings. For this reason Paul reminds us of all these events, shaming us by mentioning the time and the table and the betrayal, and asking in effect: "Your Lord gave his very self for you; and will you not, for your own sake, share food with your brother?"

But why does Paul say that he **received** it **from the Lord**? For he was not even there at the time but was one of the persecutors. He says this so that you may realize that the table on that night has no advantage over the table that comes after it. For in fact today, too, the Lord himself is the one who does everything and delivers it to us, just as he did then. But this is not the only reason Paul recalls that night, but also to pierce our hearts in yet another way. We remember especially the last words of those who are departing this life, and if any of their heirs dare to transgress such commands, we shame them by saying: "Consider that your father left behind this parting word to you, and he kept enjoining these things right up to the night he was about to pass away." That is what Paul does here: wishing to strike awe in his hearers, he says, "Remember that the Lord gave you this initiation into the mysteries as his last gift, and **on the** very **night** in which he was about to be sacrificed for you, he gave these orders, delivering this supper to you, and after that he said nothing more."

(2) Prayers from *The Liturgy of Saint James*[15]

The priest stands, makes the sign of the cross over the gifts of bread and wine, and says quietly: You are holy, O King of the ages, Lord and Giver of all holiness. And holy is your Only Son, our Lord Jesus Christ, through whom you made all things (John 1:3). And holy is your Holy Spirit, *who searches everything, even the depths* of you, God and Father (1 Cor 2:10).

And bowing he says: Holy are you, Almighty One, all powerful, worthy of reverence, good, merciful, supremely compassionate to your creatures. You made man from the earth, in your *image and likeness* (Gen 1:26-27), and gave him the enjoyment of paradise. And when he had transgressed your commandment and was banished, you, O good One, did not neglect him or desert him, but like a merciful father you taught him. You called him through the Law and instructed him through the Prophets.

And later you sent your Only Son, our Lord Jesus Christ, into the world, so that by his coming he might renew and reawaken your image. He came down from heaven (John 3:13) and became incarnate from the Holy Spirit and the holy Mary, the perpetual virgin and mother of God, and dwelling among men, he arranged everything for the salvation of our race.

And when he who was without sin was about to undertake a voluntary and life-giving death on the cross for our sins (1 Cor 15:3), **on the night when he was betrayed**, or, rather, when he handed himself over for the sake of the life and salvation of the world —

Then the priest stands up and, taking hold of the bread and making the sign of the cross, says: — Taking the bread in his holy, undefiled, spotless, and immortal hands, and looking up to heaven, and showing it to you, O God our Father, **when he had given thanks**, he blessed it, and sanctified it, **broke it,** and shared it with his holy and blessed disciples (Matt 26:26) and apostles, saying,

And the priest puts down the bread and says aloud: Take, eat (Matt 26:26), **this is my body** which is broken and distributed **for you**, for the forgiveness of sins.

And the people say: Amen.

Then, taking the cup and making the sign of the cross, the priest says quietly: **In the same way after supper,** taking **the cup** and mixing wine and water, he looked up into heaven and showed it to you, O God our Father. And when he had given thanks (Matt 26:27), blessed it, sanctified it, and filled it with the Holy Spirit, he shared it with his holy and blessed disciples and apostles, saying,

And putting the cup down, the priest says aloud: Drink of it, all of you; this is the blood

---

15. These prayers, taken from an early Christian liturgy for the celebration of the Eucharist in the church in Jerusalem, are an example of how the words of institution found in 1 Cor 11:23-26 (with its parallels in Matt 26:26-29, Mark 14:22-25, and Luke 22:17-20) were expanded for use in early Christian worship. The prayers quoted here, which belong to the central part of the liturgy, the *anaphora,* or "lifting up," are punctuated by rubrics (printed here in italics) that explain the actions that accompany them.

of **the new covenant,** *which is poured out* for you and *for many for the forgiveness of sins* (Matt 26:27).

And the people say: Amen.

Then the priest stands and says quietly: **Do this in remembrance of me. For as often as you eat this bread and drink this cup, you proclaim the death** of the Son of Man and you confess his resurrection **until he comes.**

And the attending deacons answer: We believe and we confess.

And the people say: We **proclaim** your **death,** Lord, and we confess your resurrection.

Then the priest makes the sign of the cross, bows, and says: Therefore, we too who are sinners remember his life-giving sufferings and salvific cross and his **death** and burial and the resurrection from the dead on the third day (1 Cor 15:4) and his ascent to heaven and his sitting at the right hand of God the Father (Rom 8:34) and his second glorious and awesome coming (1 Cor 15:23), when he comes with glory to judge the living and the dead (1 Pet 4:5) and will render to every man according to his works (Rom 2:6).

He says three times: Spare us, Lord our God.

[*The priest continues*]: Nay, rather, it is by his mercy that we offer to you, O Master, this awesome and bloodless sacrifice, beseeching you not to deal with us according to our sins nor requite us according to our transgressions (Ps 103:10), but having in your gentleness and unutterable kindness passed over and canceled the bond that stood against your suppliants (Col 2:14), may you grant us your heavenly, eternal gifts *which no eye has seen, nor ear heard, nor the heart of man conceived, what you, O God, have prepared for those who love you* (1 Cor 2:9).

And he says three times: And do not reject your people because of me and because of my sins, O benevolent Lord.

And he says aloud: Your people and your church make supplication to you.

And the people say: Have mercy on us, O Lord, our God, Father Almighty.

And the priest stands and says quietly: Have mercy on us, O Lord our God, Father Almighty; have mercy on us, O God, our Savior; have mercy on us, O God, according to your great mercy, and send your Holy Spirit upon us and upon these holy gifts that are before us.

And bowing he says: Send down the sovereign and life-giving Spirit, who sits upon the throne with you, O God the Father, and with your Only Son, who rules with you and is consubstantial and co-eternal, who spoke in the Law and the Prophets and in your **new covenant,** who at the Jordan River descended on our Lord Jesus Christ in the form of a dove and rested upon him (Matt 3:16), who in the upper room of holy and glorious Zion descended on your holy apostles in the form of tongues of fire on the day of holy Pentecost (Acts 2:1-4).

And the priest stands and says quietly: Send, O Master, this same Holy Spirit upon us and upon these holy gifts that are before us.

And he says aloud: So that by coming with his holy, good, and glorious presence, he might sanctify and make this bread the holy **body** of Christ.

And the people say: Amen.

And the priest says: And make this cup the precious **blood** of Christ.

And the people say: Amen.

The priest stands and says quietly: That they [the bread and wine] might serve for all who partake of them for the forgiveness of sins and for eternal life, for the sanctification of souls and bodies, for bearing fruit in good works, and for the strengthening of your holy, catholic Church, which you founded on the *rock* of faith, so that *the powers of death shall not prevail against it* (Matt 16:18), saving it from all division and from the offenses of evildoers and from the enemies who have risen against it and continue to rise up until the end of the ages.

And the clergy alone say: Amen.

(3) Gregory of Nyssa

Since human nature is twofold, compounded of soul and body, those who are being saved must take hold of the Pioneer of life in both soul and body. Therefore, when the soul is united with him through faith, from this union it derives its impulse toward salvation, for being united with Life involves having a share in it. But the body comes to participate in and be united with the Savior in a different way. If a person is tricked into drinking poison, the poison's destructive effect can be neutralized by means of another drug, and the curative drug, like the destructive one, must enter the person's system so that the effect of the antidote may spread through the whole body. In the same way, given that we have tasted something that breaks apart our nature (Gen 3:6),[16] it necessarily follows that we also needed something to reunite what has been broken apart, a remedy that by entering us could serve as antidote to the harm the poison caused the body.

And what is this remedy? It is nothing other than that **body** that proved to be greater than death and became the source of life for us. For just as *a little leaven* makes the *whole lump of dough* like itself, as Paul says (1 Cor 5:6), so also the **body** that was made immortal by God,[17] when it enters us, refashions and transforms our whole body into its nature. When a destructive drug mingles with a healthy body, the whole mixture is corrupted. So also when the immortal **body** enters into the person who receives it, it changes his whole body to its own nature.

But there is no other way something can enter into our body than by being mingled with our internal organs by eating or drinking. Therefore, our bodies have to receive the life-giving power in a way that suits the capacity of our nature. But only the **body** that had held God[18] received this grace, and, as we have already demonstrated, our bodies can attain immortality only by sharing in what is immortal through participation in what is incorruptible. . . .

Now the substance of every body comes from nourishment, that is, from food and drink. (Food consists of bread and drink of water sweetened by wine.) And as we ex-

16. That is, evil — "tasted" along with the apple (Gen 3:6) — which separates us from God and results in the dissolution of the body. See Gregory's discussion of human sin earlier in this work (*Great Catechesis*, sections 7-8).

17. That is, the body of Christ, now present in the Eucharist.

18. That is, the body of Christ.

plained at the beginning of this work, the Word of God, who is both God and Word, was united with human nature. When he entered a human body, he did not invent some new constitution for our nature but sustained his body in the usual and appropriate way, maintaining its substance by means of food and drink. . . . A characteristic of all human beings we also acknowledge to be true of his flesh, that his body was kept alive by bread. But because the Word of God dwelt in it, his body was transformed so as to be worthy of God. We are right, then, to believe that now as well the **bread** that is sanctified by the Word of God is changed into the **body** of the Word of God. . . . Just as in his case the grace of the Word sanctified his body, a body that took its substance from bread and in a way was itself bread, so in the Eucharist the **bread**, as the apostle says, is sanctified by the Word of God and by prayer. In this case the bread does not become the Word's body by being eaten, but it is changed immediately into the **body** by the Word, as the Word says: **This is my body. . . .**

When God revealed himself, he joined himself with our mortal nature for this reason, so that humanity might be made divine through fellowship with the godhead. For this reason in the gracious plan of salvation he plants seeds of himself in all those who believe, by means of that flesh whose substance comes from wine and from **bread.** He mingles himself with the bodies of believers so that by union with what is immortal man might also have a share in incorruptibility. And this he grants, transforming the nature of the visible elements by the power of the blessing.[19]

(4) Ambrose

[This excerpt from Ambrose is included as an example of reflection on the meaning of the Eucharist in the patristic period. Although it does not contain a phrase-by-phrase exegesis of verses from 1 Corinthians, it is an interpretation of the words of institution, of which 1 Cor 11:23-26 is the earliest example (compare also Mark 14:22-25 and parallels).]
It has been shown that the Church's sacraments are older [than those of the synagogue]; now learn that they are more important. It is truly wonderful that God rained manna on the fathers and that they were fed every day by food from heaven (Exod 16:1-36). That is why it is said, *Man ate the bread of the angels* (Ps 78:25). All those who ate that bread, however, died in the wilderness (John 6:49), but this food which you are receiving, that *living bread which came down from heaven* (John 6:50), supplies the reality of eternal life, and whosoever eats this bread *will live for ever* (John 6:51), for it is the body of Christ.

Consider now which is more excellent, "the bread of the angels" or the flesh of Christ, which is the body of life. Manna came down from heaven, but this bread is above the heavens. The former bread belongs to the heavens, the latter to the heavens' lord; the former was subject to decay if kept until the next day, the latter is free from all corruption since anyone who tastes it faithfully will never be subject to corruption. To the people of Israel water flowed from the rock; to you flows Christ's blood; the water quenched

---

19. That is, the prayer of consecration spoken over the eucharistic elements. See prayers from *The Liturgy of Saint James*, translated above.

their thirst for the hour, but the blood irrigates you forever. The Jew drinks and is thirsty, but when you have drunk, you cannot longer be thirsty. That event was a shadow, this is reality. . . .

Perhaps you will ask, "How can you tell me that I will receive the body of Christ? For this is not what I see." This, too, remains for us to prove. Great are the precedents we can use to show that this [eucharistic] bread is not something nature has formed but something that a blessing has consecrated, and further that a blessing has greater power than nature because nature itself is changed by the blessing.

Moses held a rod, threw it down, and it became a serpent. Then when he took hold of the serpent's tail, it reverted to the nature of a rod (Exod 7:8-15). So you see that by the prophetic gift the nature of serpent and rod was twice altered. The rivers of Egypt were flowing with pure water; suddenly from their sources blood began to burst forth, and the rivers could not be drunk. Then when the prophet prayed, the blood in the river ceased and its watery nature returned (Exod 7:14-25). The Hebrew people were surrounded, fenced off by the Egyptians on one side and cut off by the sea on the other. Moses raised his rod, the waters parted and froze to form walls, and a pathway was made in the midst of the waves (Exod 14:15-25). The Jordan turned around and, contrary to its nature, flowed back to its source (Josh 3:7-17). Is it not clear that nature, whether that of waves of the sea or the flowing of rivers, was changed? Our fathers' people were thirsty: Moses touched a rock, and water flowed from the rock. Did grace not operate in contravention of nature, so that a rock gushed forth water that it did not naturally possess (Exod 17:1-7)? The river Marah was very bitter, so that the thirsty people could not drink from it. Moses threw a piece of wood into the water, and the water lost its bitterness, tempered by a sudden infusion of grace (Exod 15:22-25). In the days of Elisha the prophet, the axe head of one of the sons of the prophets came off and sank at once in water. The man who lost it asked Elisha, and he threw a piece of wood into the water and the iron head floated (2 Kings 6:1-7). Surely we recognize that this happened contrary to nature, for iron is heavier than water.

We see, therefore, that grace possesses greater efficacy than nature. Yet up to this point we have been adducing the grace of the prophets' blessing. Now if human blessing had enough power to change nature, what shall we say about consecration by God himself, where the very words of our Lord and Savior are at work? For the sacrament you are receiving is performed by the word of Christ. If the word of Elijah had so much power that it brought fire down from heaven (1 Kings 18:20-39), will the word of Christ not have enough power to change the nature of the elements? You have read about the creation of the world, *For he spoke, and they came to be; he commanded, and they were created* (Ps 33:9). Therefore, cannot the word of Christ, which could create from nothing, change things that are into what they are not? For it is no less a thing to give things their nature to begin with than to change that nature. . . .

The Lord Jesus himself cries out, **This is my body**. Before the blessing by heavenly words it was called something else; after the consecration it is designated as **body**. He himself speaks of his blood. Before consecration it was called something else; after consecration it is called **blood**. And you say "Amen," or "That is true." Let the mind within us confess what the mouth speaks, and let our hearts feel what our words utter.

With these sacraments, therefore, Christ nourishes his Church. By means of them he strengthens our souls.

1 Corinthians 11:27-34

27 **Whoever, therefore, eats the bread or drinks the cup of the Lord in an unworthy manner will be guilty of profaning the body and blood of the Lord.** 28 **Let a man examine himself, and so eat of the bread and drink of the cup.** 29 **For any one who eats and drinks without discerning the body eats and drinks judgment upon himself.** 30 **That is why many of you are weak and ill, and some have died.** 31 **But if we judged ourselves truly, we should not be judged.** 32 **But when we are judged by the Lord, we are chastened so that we may not be condemned along with the world.** 33 **So then, my brethren, when you come together to eat, wait for one another —** 34 **if any one is hungry, let him eat at home — lest you come together to be condemned. About the other things I will give directions when I come.**

(1) Theodore of Mopsuestia

Some people who do not pay close attention to the meaning of the text think that they carry out the apostle's intention if they partake of the mysteries[20] as seldom as possible. They must understand that if Paul expected us to be entirely free from sin in order to communicate, then he would be expecting us never to communicate. But in the first place, no one can be entirely free from sin. Secondly, even if this were possible, it would not be right for us to judge ourselves sinless and then take communion. And, further, what about Paul's words *as often as you eat* (1 Cor 11:26)? This shows that communion should be continual; and the rule of the Church, in agreement with Paul's words, enjoins us to celebrate the mysteries at all times. Therefore, it is proper for a person who has committed the gravest of sins to abstain — I mean those acts which the apostle explicitly says would keep a person from obtaining the kingdom (1 Cor 6:9-10). For he should partake of the mysteries only after fear of God's law has caused him to stop sinning.

As for lesser sins, however, which are an unavoidable part of human life — many of them occasioned by the chances of daily life but most caused by the weakness of our nature — we should of course strive to refrain from them as far as we can. For the pursuit of virtue and the daily practice of discipline can certainly make such sins less frequent. But if we should fall into these lesser sins, it is not good to deprive ourselves of the mysteries. Instead we should approach them with greater reverence, recognizing their magnitude but still participating in them in a spirit of hopefulness. For they bring us forgiveness, if while refraining from sin as much as we can we are clearly not neglectful of other things, in particular of the spiritual effort necessary to lead a more perfect life. It is appropriate that all the benefits that have come to us from the death of Christ are made effective

---

20. That is, the sacrament of the Lord's Supper.

through the visible tokens of that death. Therefore, I dare to say that even someone who has sinned gravely, if he resolves to refrain henceforth from all wrongdoing, seek virtue, and live according to the laws of Christ, and if he participates in the mysteries in the firm belief that he will receive pardon for all his sins, will obtain the object of his hopes.

(2) John Chrysostom

We too should pay attention to Paul's words of warning, we who approach this holy table together with the poor but when we go outside pretend not to see them. Instead we get drunk and walk past the hungry — the very charges that were made in those days against the Corinthians. Someone may ask, "When does this happen?" The answer is that it happens constantly, but especially at the feasts, when it least ought to happen. For at those times drunkenness and contempt for the poor follow immediately upon the communion. After having had a share in the blood, when you should observe a time of fasting and sobriety, you are drunk and disorderly. . . .

Therefore, I beg you: in order that we not engage in these acts to our **judgment**, let us feed Christ, let us give him drink, let us clothe him (Matt 25:35-36). That is conduct worthy of this table. Did you hear the sacred hymns? Did you see the spiritual wedding feast? Did you feast at the royal table? Were you filled with the Holy Spirit? Did you join the chorus of the seraphim? Did you become a partaker in the powers above? Do not cast such great joy to the ground. Do not pour out the treasure. Do not make room for drunkenness, that mother of discouragement and delight of Satan, which gives birth to countless miseries. . . .

Do you long for luxury? Then cease from drunkenness for this very reason. For I want you to enjoy luxury, the true luxury that never wastes away. What, then, is this true and ever fresh luxury? Summon Christ to your meal, give him a share of your goods, or rather of his. This will bring infinite and ever flourishing pleasure. But perceptible things are not like this; they appear and vanish in an instant. The one who has enjoyed them will be no better off than the one who has not, but rather worse. The one who has not enjoyed them is anchored as in a safe haven, but the other is flooded and besieged with plagues and cannot endure the high waves. To keep this from happening to us, let us pursue moderation. For in this way we will be physically sound, make our souls secure, and be freed from present and future evils.

1 Corinthians 12

This chapter continues the theme of worship in Corinth through a consideration of the gifts of the Spirit, especially prophecy and a gift that was especially prized by the Corinthians, speaking in tongues. Paul begins by referring to the pagan background of the Corinthian Christians (vv. 1-3). John Chrysostom explains this section by contrasting the practice of divination among the Greeks with Christian prophecy. The focus of Basil of Caesarea's comments on these verses is quite different: interpreting them in the context of fourth-century trinitarian debates, he finds here an argument for the divinity of the Holy Spirit. Much of the patristic commentary on this chapter emphasizes what Paul says about the Spirit. Thus Athanasius's comments on verses 4-7, where Paul speaks of the variety of spiritual gifts, argue for the divinity of the Spirit and the unity of the Trinity (see also his discussion of vv. 11 and 13). Paul's enumeration of specific spiritual gifts in verses 8-11 occasioned reflection on the relation of faith and knowledge (Augustine) and on divine grace (Chrysostom, who stresses Paul's choice of the word "gifts").

The chapter concludes with an extended comparison of the church with a body that is made up of diverse parts (vv. 12-31). In verse 13 Paul speaks of the Spirit as something given us "to drink." While Cyril of Alexandria explains this by comparing other biblical texts that use water imagery, John Chrysostom takes it as a reference to the Eucharist. The image of the Church as the body of Christ proved to be a fruitful one, as the excerpts from three of Augustine's sermons illustrate. In the first selection (on vv. 20-26) he uses this image to remind celibates not to scorn married Christians; in the last one (on vv. 27-31) it serves to correct the Donatists, who wanted to exclude from the body of Christ Christians who were not faithful in times of persecution. Both these interpretations focus on the need to honor the "weaker" parts of the body. The third excerpt (on vv. 20-26), from a sermon preached on the birthday of the martyrs Perpetua and Felicity, considers the "more presentable" members: Augustine reminds his congregation of the benefits these martyrs bring to the whole of the body.

1 Corinthians 12:1-3

1Now concerning spiritual gifts, brethren, I do not want you to be uninformed. 2You know that when you were heathen, you were led astray to dumb idols, however you may have been moved. 3Therefore I want you to understand that no one speaking in the Spirit[1] of God ever says "Jesus be cursed!" and no one can say "Jesus is Lord" except in the Holy Spirit.[2]

(1) John Chrysostom

This whole passage is hard to understand because we do not know the situation in those times and how this differs from our own experience. . . . What was it? When people were baptized, right away they would speak in tongues. Not only this, but in addition many would prophesy, and some displayed other powers as well. Because they were not raised on the ancient Scriptures but had worshiped idols, their understanding was insufficient. When they were baptized they immediately received the Spirit, yet they could not see the Spirit, who is invisible. So by divine grace they were given obvious evidence of the Spirit's activity. One would suddenly speak in Persian, another in Latin, another in the language of the Indians or of some other people (see Acts 2:1-13). And this made it clear to outsiders that the Spirit was present in the speaker. That is why Paul says, *To each is given the manifestation of the Spirit for the common good* (1 Cor. 12:7) and why he calls the gifts *the manifestation of the Spirit.* Once the apostles had received this first sign, other believers received the spiritual gift of tongues, and not only this gift but several others as well. Indeed, many of them raised the dead, cast out demons, and performed other miracles of this nature. They had spiritual gifts, some lesser, some greater. But the spiritual gift of tongues was preeminent.

These gifts, however, led to division, not because of the nature of the gifts themselves but because of the folly of those who received them. Those who received the greater gifts exalted themselves above those with lesser ones. The latter, for their part, were upset and envious of those with the greater gifts. Paul explains this later in the Letter. Since this situation caused serious injury, namely, the dissolution of their love, Paul takes great pains to correct it. . . .

But this was not the only thing that threw them into confusion. There were also many diviners in Corinth since it was a Greek city. This caused further upset and confusion. Thus at the beginning of his discussion Paul distinguishes prophecy from divination. This is why they also received *the ability to distinguish between spirits* (1 Cor 12:10), so that they could make distinctions and know who was speaking under the influence of a pure spirit and who of an impure one. . . .

Among those who worshiped idols, Paul says, whenever anyone was possessed by an unclean spirit to utter an oracle, as if **carried away**, he would be so constrained and driven by the spirit that he would not know what he was saying. Diviners are by nature out of their minds, under constraint, pushed, pulled, and swept away like madmen. That is not true of a prophet; everything the prophet says is spoken from a sober mind, with self-control, and full knowledge of what he is saying. Thus you should recognize

---

1. RSV: "by the Spirit."

2. RSV "*by* the Holy Spirit"; see Basil's commentary on this verse for one interpretation of the significance of the preposition.

diviners or prophets on the basis of their behavior, even before they are proved right or wrong.

Notice how Paul makes his argument plausible: he calls as witnesses those with firsthand experience. "As proof," he says, "that I am not just mocking pagan practices with lies born of enmity, you yourselves may bear witness for my case. **You know that when you were** Greeks, you were carried away and **led astray**." But if someone should object that the witness of believers is suspect, let me demonstrate Paul's point from the witness of outsiders. Here at any rate is what Plato says: "Just as the soothsayers and diviners say many beautiful things but know nothing of what they are saying."[3] Listen further to what another writer says on this subject. By means of rites and spells someone had bound a demon to a man. As the man was uttering an oracle, he was thrown about and suffered convulsions and could not endure the demon's attack. When he was so broken down that he was about to die, he said to those who had worked magic on him: "Let me go; I am mortal and can no longer contain the god who possesses me!" And again, "Tear the garland from my head, sprinkle my feet with clear water, erase the letters of the spell: let me go!"[4]

These quotations and others like them — for there are many more one could cite — prove two things to us: that demons serve by compulsion, and that those who abandon themselves to them and lose their natural sense suffer violence. Take the Pythia,[5] for example. I must now display to you another piece of pagan indecency. Although it would be good if I could avoid mentioning such indelicate things, I must speak so that you may see more clearly the indecency of the pagans. From this you can learn what a ridiculously stupid thing it is to consult diviners. We are told that this Pythia, who is a woman, sits on the tripod of Apollo with her legs spread. Then a wicked spirit, sent up from below, slips through her genitals and fills her with madness. Loosening her hair, she goes into bacchic frenzy and foams at the mouth. Thus intoxicated, she utters frenzied words. I realize that hearing these things has caused you to blush with embarrassment, but the pagans pride themselves on this indecency and madness. These things, and things like them, are what Paul calls to mind when he says, **You know that when you were heathen, you were led astray to dumb idols, however you may have been moved**.

(2) Origen on verse 3

There are many types of spirits, which no one will understand fully without the spiritual gift of discrimination of spirits (1 Cor 12:10). To keep us from hastily rejecting or approving those who speak under the influence of spirits, John says in his letter: *Beloved, do not believe every spirit, but test the spirits to see whether they are of God. . . . Every spirit which*

3. Apology 22c.
4. Chrysostom's source is Eusebius (*Preparation for the Gospel* 5.9), who quotes Porphyry, *On Deriving Philosophy from the Oracles*.
5. The priestess who spoke at the oracle of Delphi.

confesses that Jesus Christ has come in the flesh is of God, and every spirit which does not confess Jesus is not of God (1 John 4:1-3). He teaches us that we should neither give easy assent to what anyone says nor reject it hastily as not from the divine **Spirit**. Instead, each listener, knowing that he puts himself at risk by his approval or rejection of spirits, should take care not to believe falsehood or disbelieve the truth.

On this matter the apostle adds later on: *If any one among you is a prophet, or a spiritual person, he should acknowledge that what I am writing is of God. But if anyone does not recognize this, he is not recognized* (1 Cor 14:37-38). Not only is a person who does not recognize the words of the apostle *not recognized* by God; but also a person who speaks in the Spirit of God but denies speaking in the Spirit of God is *not recognized*. . . .

Let us now examine how we who are listening to the word of God must understand **no one speaking in the Spirit of God ever says "Jesus be cursed!"** Those who lack clear knowledge might be in doubt whether certain people are speaking **in the Spirit** when they curse Christ. If you ever see a Jew giving an impressive public exposition of the Holy Scriptures and the words of the prophets, it might not be clear whether the **Spirit of God** is in him. Therefore, to save you from vexatious doubt whether the Holy **Spirit** is in him or not, Paul teaches the following: Every Jew **says Jesus is accursed**. Given this, and since **no one can say "Jesus is Lord" except in the Holy Spirit**, the person who claims to know the Law and the Prophets but curses Jesus does not have the **Spirit of God**. In fact, there is a certain sect that will not accept as a member anyone who will not curse Jesus. And that sect is worthy of the name they delight in being called — "Ophites" — who say unholy things in praise of the snake, who is *cursed* by God (Gen 3:14).[6]

(3) Basil of Caesarea on verse 3

How could angels say *Glory to God in the highest* (Luke 2:14) if they were not empowered by the Spirit? For **no one can say "Jesus is Lord" except in the Holy Spirit**, and **no one speaking in the Spirit of God ever says "Jesus be cursed!"** — this is what our enemies, the wicked spirits, would say. And their fall proves my point, that the invisible powers have free will and are poised between virtue and vice, and for this reason they need the help of the Spirit. . . . It is the Spirit who reveals mysteries, according to the Scripture, for *God has revealed to us through the Spirit* (1 Cor 2:10).

How would *thrones or dominions* and *authorities* (Col 1:16) be leading a blessed life if they did not *always see the face of the Father who is in heaven* (Matt 18:10)? But this seeing does not happen without the Spirit. If at night you remove the light from your house, your eyes will be blind, your faculties will be useless, and even the different worth of things will not be recognizable. For example, in your ignorance you will trample on gold and iron alike. Without the Spirit there can be no genuinely spiritual life in accord with divine law, even as an army cannot maintain its ranks when the commander is absent or a choir stay in tune unless the director brings the voices into harmony. How could the sera-

---

6. A Gnostic group whose name is based on the Greek word for "snake."

phim say *Holy, holy, holy* (Isa 6:3) if they were not taught by the Spirit how often to express their devotion through this doxology? If all of God's angels praise him and all of his powers extol him, they do so because the Spirit works together with them. . . .

I attest to anyone who confesses Christ but denies God [the Father] that Christ will bring him no benefit. And if anyone calls upon God but denies the Son, his *faith is futile* (1 Cor 15:17). If anyone rejects the Spirit, his faith in the Father and the Son will turn out to be *in vain* (1 Cor 15:14): without the Spirit there can be no faith. For whoever does not believe in the Spirit does not believe in the Son, and whoever has not believed in the Son does not believe in the Father. For **no one can say "Jesus is Lord" except in the Holy Spirit.** And *no one has ever seen God*, but *the Only Son, who is in the bosom of the Father, he has made him known* (John 1:18). Anyone who makes such false claims has no part in true worship (John 4:24), for it is impossible to worship the Son without the Holy Spirit or to call upon the Father except in the *Spirit of adoption* (Rom 8:15).

When, through the illuminating power [of the Spirit], we fix our eyes on the beauty of the invisible image of God [the Son] and through this image are led up to the supremely beautiful sight of the archetype [the Father], there, surely, the Spirit of knowledge[7] is present, inseparable from the others. To those eager to see the truth he gives, in himself, the power to behold the image: he does not show it to them from any exterior source but leads them to knowledge in himself. Just as *no one knows the Father except the Son* (Matt 11:27), so **no one can say "Jesus is Lord" except in the Holy Spirit.** Paul does not say "through the Spirit," but **"in the Spirit."**[8] Furthermore, *God is spirit, and those who worship him must worship in spirit and truth* (John 4:24); the Scripture says, *In thy light we shall see light* (Ps 36:9), that is, in the illumination of the Spirit we will see *the true light that enlightens every man coming into the world* (John 1:9). Thus the Spirit exhibits in himself the *glory* of the *Only Son* (John 1:14), and in himself he provides the knowledge of God [the Father] to the *true worshipers* (John 4:24). Therefore the way to knowledge of God proceeds from the one Spirit, through the one Son, to the one Father.

1 Corinthians 12:4-7

4**Now there are varieties of gifts,**[9] **but the same Spirit;** 5**and there are varieties of service, but the same Lord;** 6**and there are varieties of working, but it is the same God who inspires them all in every one.** 7**To each is given the manifestation of the Spirit for the common good.**

---

7. Compare 1 Cor 12:8: "to another [is given] the utterance of knowledge according to the same Spirit."

8. RSV: "through the Spirit." The Greek preposition used in 1 Cor 12:3 can be rendered either way, but Basil's interpretation hinges on understanding it to mean "in."

9. RSV: "gifts."

(1) Athanasius

Such are the absurdities we encounter when it is claimed that God is a dyad.[10] But if God is a Trinity, which is in fact the case, and if it has been shown that there is no division or dissimilarity within the Trinity, then God is necessarily one in holiness and eternity and unchangeability. . . .

If the Holy Spirit is a created being, how can there be communion between the creature and the Creator? Or what unity between a lower creature and the Word that created him? The blessed Paul, knowing this, does not divide the Trinity, as you do; rather, he teaches its unity when he writes to the Corinthians about **spiritual gifts**. He presents God the Father as the source of them all, saying: **Now there are varieties of gifts, but the same Spirit; and there are varieties of service, but the same Lord; and there are varieties of working, but it is the same God who inspires them all in every one.** What the Spirit gives to each individual is furnished by the Father through the Word. For everything that belongs to the Father belongs also to the Son. Thus the **spiritual gifts** given by the Son in the Spirit are gifts of the Father. And when the Spirit is in us, the Word who gives the Spirit is also in us, and the Father is in the Word. And thus we find in Scripture, *We will come to him and make our home with him* (John 14:23). For where the light is, there too is its *radiance* (Heb 1:3). And where the *radiance* is, there is also its **working** and its luminous grace. Paul teaches this same thing when he writes a second time to the Corinthians, saying: *The grace of the Lord Jesus Christ and the love of God and the fellowship of the Holy Spirit be with you all* (2 Cor 13:14).

When Christ spoke in Paul — and Paul himself says, *since you desire proof that Christ is speaking in me* (2 Cor 13:3) — it was nonetheless the Spirit working in Paul who gave him the power of speech. For Paul himself writes of *the help of the Spirit of Jesus Christ given to [him]* (Phil 1:19). Again, when Christ was speaking in him, Paul said: *except that the Holy Spirit testifies to me in every city that imprisonment and afflictions await me* (Acts 20:23). For the Spirit is not separate from the Word, but since it is in the Word, it is in God the Father. Thus the spiritual **gifts** are given by the Trinity. For in the **variety** of these, as Paul writes to the Corinthians, is **the same Spirit** and **the same Lord** and **the same God who inspires them all in every one.** The Father himself works through the Word and in the Spirit in giving all these gifts.

Indeed, when Paul prayed for the Corinthians, it was in the name of the Trinity that he did so, saying: *The grace of the Lord Jesus Christ and the love of God and the fellowship of the Holy Spirit be with you all* (2 Cor 13:14). For when we participate in the Spirit, we have the grace of the Word, and in him we have the love of the Father. And since the grace of the Trinity is one, so the Trinity is indivisible. One can see this also in the account of the holy Mary. For when the angel Gabriel was sent to tell her that the Word was about to descend upon her, he says, *The Holy Spirit will come upon you* because he knows that the Spirit is in the Word. At any rate, he immediately adds, *and the power of the Most High*

---

10. In this letter Athanasius disputes a claim that the Holy Spirit was not divine, but was a creature. Compare his comments on 1 Cor 3:16-17, excerpted above.

will overshadow you (Luke 1:35). For *Christ is the power of God and the wisdom of God* (1 Cor 1:24). And since the Spirit was in the Word, it is clear that through the Word the Spirit was also in God. So also when the Spirit has come to be in us, the Son *will come*, and also the Father, and they will *make their home* in us (John 14:23).

(2) Theodoret on verses 4-6

Paul shows that while the spiritual gifts that are given are many and various, they have one source. For he describes the same things as being supplied by the All-holy Spirit, and by the Lord, and by God the Father. He calls the same things spiritual **gifts** and **ministries** and **workings**. They are called spiritual **gifts** because they are given by God's munificence, and **ministries** since they were given through men ordained for this service. Thus Paul writes in the Letter to the Romans: *Inasmuch then as I am an apostle to the Gentiles, I magnify my ministry* (Rom 11:13). And writing to Timothy in one place, he says, *Fulfill your ministry* (2 Tim 4:5), and in another, *I remind you to rekindle the spiritual gift of God* (2 Tim 1:6). Paul also calls spiritual gifts **workings** since they are effected by the divine nature.

Paul does not say, as certain of the foolish heretics have thought, that the Spirit **inspires** some gifts and the God of All inspires others. Instead, he shows that it is the Holy Trinity who is the giver of these same gifts. He teaches this more clearly in what follows: having said here [in v. 6] that it is God who **inspires** them, a little later he says: *All these are inspired by one and the same Spirit, who apportions* them *to each one individually as he wills* (1 Cor 12:11). In the present instance, moreover, the divine apostle sets down these things in opposition to the opinions of the Greeks, pointing out their discord, and he also gives encouragement to those who think they have received the lesser spiritual gifts and teaches them that both greater and lesser gifts have been given by the same Spirit.

This is also intimated in what follows: **To each person is given the manifestation of the Spirit for the common good.** Paul does not say "the grace" but **the manifestation.** For even now grace is given to those considered worthy of holy baptism, but not in a visible way. But at that time, immediately after baptism they proceeded to speak in different tongues and work wonders, and they were *confirmed* by these things (1 Cor 1:6) and learned that what they had been taught was true. It was necessary for Paul to say that **the manifestation of the Spirit** is given **for the common good,** so as to encourage those who were disheartened and teach them that everything is under the wise direction of the One with sure knowledge of everything, who knows what is beneficial to each person.

(3) John Chrysostom on verse 4

Now there are various types of spiritual gifts, but the same Spirit (1 Cor 12:4). He first soothes the feelings of the one who has the inferior gift and is troubled by this. "Why," he asks, "are you disheartened? Because you did not receive as much as the other? But if you understand that it is a gift and not a reward, your distress will be relieved." That is why he immediately says, **Now there are various types of spiritual gifts, but the same Spirit.** He does not say, "various types of signs" or "miracles," but "gifts," in order to persuade them by the designation "gift" not only not to be troubled but also to be thankful. "Consider another point as well," he says, "that even if you came in second in what was given, you have equal honor, since you have been deemed worthy to receive from him who also gave the other person the greater gift. It is not as if you could complain that he was shown favor by the Spirit but you were favored merely by an angel. The Spirit showed favor to both you and him." That is why Paul adds, **but the same Spirit.** So even if there is a difference in the gift, there is none in the Giver. Both you and he draw water from the same font.

1 Corinthians 12:8-11

8To one is given through the Spirit the utterance of wisdom, and to another the utterance of knowledge according to the same Spirit, 9to another faith by the same Spirit, to another gifts of healing by the one Spirit, 10to another the working of miracles, to another prophecy, to another the ability to distinguish between spirits, to another various kinds of tongues, to another the interpretation of tongues. 11All these are inspired by one and the same Spirit, who apportions to each one individually as he wills.

(1) Augustine on verse 8

The Greeks defined wisdom as follows: "Wisdom is the knowledge of things human and divine." That is why in the previous book[11] I made no secret of the fact that the knowledge of things human and divine could be called both wisdom and knowledge. But since the apostle says, **To one is given ... the utterance of wisdom and to another the utterance of knowledge,** the definitions of these words must be made distinct so that the knowledge of divine matters is called **wisdom,** while that of human matters is properly called **knowledge.** About this knowledge I wrote in Book 13, not of course attributing to it everything that can be known by a man about human affairs, since there is a great deal of superfluous vanity and harmful curiosity, but only that knowledge by which the saving faith that leads to true happiness is begotten, nourished, defended, and strengthened. Many of the faithful are lacking in this, even though they are mighty in faith. For it is one thing to know only those things a man must know in order to attain to that life which is eternal, another to know how one can help the faithful and mount a defense against the ungodly. It is knowledge of this kind that the apostle seems to call **knowledge.**

11. The reference is to *On the Trinity* 13.1.

(2) John Chrysostom

The universal medicine of consolation is that all receive from the same root, the same treasures, the same streams. Therefore, by continually pouring this remedy over them and using this word, Paul evens out and lessens the effects of their apparent inequality. Previously he showed that Spirit and Son and Father supply the gifts. Here he feels that it is enough to mention the Spirit, in order to show that his dignity is the same as theirs. But what is the **utterance of wisdom**? The very thing that Paul had, that John the son of thunder had. What, then, is the **utterance of knowledge**? It is what many of the faithful had, who possessed knowledge but were not able to the same degree to teach or easily convey their knowledge to another. **To another [he gives] faith**. He does not mean faith in the doctrines but the faith that produces miracles, concerning which Christ spoke, *If you have faith as a grain of mustard seed, you will say to this mountain, "Be moved," and it will move* (Matt 17:20). The apostles also requested this faith, saying, *Increase our faith!* (Luke 17:5). For, indeed, faith is the mother of miracles. Having the ability to work **miracles** is not the same thing as having the **gifts of healing**. Someone with the gift of healing healed, but someone with the ability to work **miracles** punished as well. It is the ability not only to heal but also to chastise: Paul maimed a man (Acts 13:11), and Peter put others to death (Acts 5:5, 10).

To another [he gave] prophecy, to another the ability to distinguish between spirits. What is the ability to **distinguish between spirits**? To know who is spiritual and who is not, who is a true prophet and who is a false one. He says the same thing to the Thessalonians, *Do not despise prophesying, but test everything; hold fast what is good* (1 Thess 5:20-22). There was a great plague of false prophets at that time since the devil maliciously delights in placing lies in the midst of truth (Rom 1:25).

To another various kinds of tongues, to another the interpretation of tongues. The one knew what he himself was saying, but he could not interpret for another. The interpreter had both of these abilities, or at least the second one. Now the former was thought to be a great gift since it was the first that the apostles received, and the majority of the Corinthians possessed it. But the word of instruction was deemed less important. That is why Paul puts tongues first and the word of instruction after it. And, in fact, the former gift is for the sake of the latter, and so are all the rest, prophesies and miracle working and various kinds of tongues and interpretation of tongues. Nothing is equal to it. That is why he says, *Let the elders who rule well be considered worthy of double honor, especially those who labor in preaching and teaching* (1 Tim 5:17). And he charges Timothy, saying, *Attend to the public reading of Scripture, to exhortation, to teaching. Do not neglect the gift you have* (1 Tim 4:13-14). . . .

Paul says, "Let us not be perplexed then or distraught, saying, 'Why did I receive this and not that?' Let us not demand a reckoning from the Holy Spirit. If you know that it was with careful consideration that he gave you his gift, realize that it was with the same care that he assigned you the proper measure, and be content and glad for what you have received. Do not be annoyed at what you have not received but show gratitude that you have not received more than you can handle.

Now if it is wrong to be overly inquisitive in regard to spiritual things, it is still more so in fleshly things: we should hold our peace and not meddle in the affairs of others, seeking to know why this man is rich and that one poor. To be sure, not all become rich by a gift from God: many do so by wrongdoing and robbery and greed, and how could the one who forbade this kind of wealth have given what he forbids them to receive? But in order to refute those who speak against us on this subject, let us apply our principle to those cases where wealth was given by God. Tell me: why was Abraham rich but Jacob went wanting for bread? Wasn't the latter righteous as well as the former? Does God not speak equally about all three, *I am the God of Abraham, the God of Isaac, and the God of Jacob* (Matt 22:32; Exod 3:6)? Why, then, was one rich and the other a hireling? What's more, why was Esau rich even though he was unrighteous and a fratricide, while his brother was in servitude for such a long time? Again, why did Isaac always live in prosperity while Jacob lived in trouble and toil, so that he said, *Few and evil have been the days of the years of my life* (Gen 47:9)? Why did David, who was prophet and king, live in distress all his life, while Solomon his son lived forty years rich beyond all other men, enjoying peace and security and receiving every form of glory, honor, and luxury? And among the prophets why did one suffer more and another less? The answer is that each received what was most beneficial. Therefore, in each case we say: *Thy judgments are like the great deep* (Ps 36:6). For if God did not train all these great and admirable men in the same way, but trained one through poverty and another through riches, one through relaxation and another through affliction, it is all the more necessary for us in the present time to bear these things in mind.

(3) Athanasius on verse 11

[**All these are inspired by one and the same Spirit, who apportions to each one individually as he wills.**] Again it is worthwhile to examine this question[12] in light of the following consideration: if the Son of God is the Word, he is one, as the Father is one — For *there is one God, the Father, from whom are all things . . . and one Lord, Jesus Christ* (1 Cor 8:6). For this reason we call him the *Only Son* (John 1:18), and so do the Scriptures. But as for creatures, they are many and various: angels, archangels, cherubim, rulers, authorities, and others, as we have said. But if the Son, because he does not belong to the many but is one as the Father is one (John 17:22), is not a creature, then certainly the Spirit could not be a creature since we must derive our knowledge of the Spirit from what we know about the Son. For the Spirit does not belong to the many but is himself one. And Paul understands this when he says: **All these are inspired by one and the same Spirit, who apportions to each one individually as he wills.** And a little further on he says: *For by one Spirit we were all baptized into one body . . . and all were made to drink of one Spirit* (1 Cor 12:13).

12. Whether the Spirit is divine, or merely a creature.

1 Corinthians 12:12-14

12For just as the body is one and has many members, and all the members of the body, though many, are one body, so it is with Christ. 13For by one Spirit we were all baptized into one body — Jews or Greeks, slaves or free — and all were made to drink of one Spirit.[13] 14For the body does not consist of one member but of many.

(1) Athanasius

[**All were made to drink of one Spirit.**] Since the Father is *light* (1 John 1:5) and the Son is his *radiance* (Heb 1:3), . . . in the Son we can also see the Spirit, in whom we are enlightened. For Paul prays *that God may give you a spirit of wisdom and of revelation in the knowledge of him, having the eyes of your hearts enlightened* (Eph 1:17-18). And when we are enlightened in the Spirit, it is Christ who enlightens us in him. *He was*, Scripture says, *the true light that enlightens every man who comes into the world* (John 1:9).[14] And again, since the Father is called a *fountain* (Jer 2:13; Bar 3:10-12) and the Son a *river* (Ps 65:9), we are said to **drink** the **Spirit**. For it is written: **we all were made to drink of one Spirit**. And being **made to drink** the **Spirit**, we drink Christ. *For they drank from the supernatural Rock which followed them, and the Rock was Christ* (1 Cor 10:4).

(2) Basil of Caesarea

[**For in one Spirit we were all baptized into one body.**] Let no one be misled because the apostle often omits the names of the Father and the Holy Spirit when he speaks of baptism or conclude from this that all three names were not invoked. Paul says, *As many of you as were baptized into Christ have put on Christ* (Gal 3:27); and, again, all of you *who have been baptized into Christ Jesus were baptized into his death* (Rom 6:3). For naming Christ involves a confession of the fullness of God. It reveals God who anoints and the Son who is anointed and the Spirit who is the chrism, as we learn from Peter in Acts: *Jesus of Nazareth, whom God anointed with the Holy Spirit* (Acts 10:38). And in Isaiah we read: *The Spirit of the Lord GOD is upon me, because the LORD has anointed me* (Isa 61:1). And the psalmist says: *Therefore God has anointed you with the oil of gladness* (Ps 45:7).

    Yet sometimes when Paul speaks of baptism, he mentions only the Spirit: **For in one Spirit we were all baptized into one body.** And in the same vein it is written: *You shall be baptized with the Holy Spirit* (Acts 1:5), and also: *He will baptize with the Holy Spirit* (Luke 3:16). Nonetheless, no one would call a baptism complete at which only the name of the Spirit was invoked.

---

13. The text as quoted by John Chrysostom reads, "And we were all given into one Spirit to drink."

14. RSV: "The true light that enlightens every man was coming into the world." In the Gospel text the Greek participle translated as "coming" can be taken to modify either "the true light" (so RSV) or "every man" (so Athanasius).

(3) Cyril of Alexandria on verse 13

We are united with each other and have become members of the same body in Christ (Eph 3:6) since he has raised us and bound us together through the one Holy Spirit who is the same in all of us and whom we have also been **given to drink** like a life-giving cup. At any rate, Christ, in his discussion with the woman at the well of Jacob, says: *Every one who drinks of this water will thirst again, but whoever drinks of the water that I shall give him . . . it will become in him a spring of water welling up to eternal life* (John 4:13-14). In another passage he says to the Jews: *He who believes in me, as the Scripture has said, "Out of his heart shall flow rivers of living water."* The Evangelist continues: *Now this he said about the Spirit, which those who believed in him were to receive* (John 7:38-39). This is not surprising; according to the psalmist's word, Christ is himself *the river of God* (Ps 65:9), which is full of waters, the richly flowing winter torrent, which God the Father is said to **give** to those who love him **to drink**; why, then, should his Spirit not be thought of as a life-giving cup of water? Therefore, since we have been called into unity through the Spirit and become members of the same body in Christ, let us keep the bonds of love unbroken.

(4) John Chrysostom

And we were all given one Spirit to drink. [15] For the body does not consist of one member but of many. That is, we have all been initiated into the same mysteries and take part in the same table. But why does he not say that we are nourished by the same body and drink the same blood? Because by saying Spirit he indicates both the flesh and the blood: through both of these we are **given one Spirit to drink**. But to me it now seems that Paul is speaking about the visitation of the Spirit which we experience after baptism and before receiving the Eucharist. He says that **we were given to drink** since this turn of phrase fits the matter at hand: it is as if he were saying that all the trees in a park are watered from the same source and by the same water. Here he says that we have all drunk the same Spirit, we have all enjoyed the same grace. If, then, one Spirit has formed us and has brought us all together into one body — that is, **we were baptized into one body** — and has given us a single table, he also gave the same watering to all, that is, **we were all given one Spirit to drink**. He has united those who were so divided, and the many become a body whenever they become one. Why then make so much of difference?

1 Corinthians 12:15-19

15If the foot should say, "Because I am not a hand, I do not belong to the body," that would not make it any less a part of the body. 16And if the ear should say, "Because I am not an eye, I do not belong to the body," that would not make it any less a part of

---

15. RSV: "and all were made to drink of one Spirit."

the body. 17If the whole body were an eye, where would be the hearing? If the whole body were an ear, where would be the sense of smell? 18But as it is, God arranged the organs in the body, each one of them, as he chose. 19If all were a single organ, where would the body be?

(1) John Chrysostom

The Corinthians were still being thrown into this kind of confusion, and so he does what he did before. Previously after an exhortation based on what was in their best interests he sternly rebuked them by saying, *One and the same Spirit works all these things, distributing them to each individually as he wills* (1 Cor 12:11). Here too he shows by reasoning that it is for their good that everything be thus, and again he appeals to the will of God, saying, **But as it is, God arranged the organs in the body, each one of them, as he chose.** Just as he used the phrase *as he wills* about the Spirit, so here he says, **as he chose.** So ask no more the question why it is thus and not some other way. Indeed, even if we could give ten thousand explanations, we could not as effectively demonstrate its goodness as by saying that this is the way the chief craftsman wanted it, and so it has come to pass. For what is best for us is what he wills.

1 Corinthians 12:20-26

20As it is, there are many parts, yet one body. 21The eye cannot say to the hand, "I have no need of you," nor again the head to the feet, "I have no need of you." 22On the contrary, the parts of the body which seem to be weaker are indispensable, 23and those parts of the body which we think less honorable we invest with the greater honor, and our unpresentable parts are treated with greater modesty, 24which our more presentable parts do not require. But God has so composed the body, giving the greater honor to the inferior part, 25that there may be no discord in the body, but that the members may have the same care for one another. 26If one member suffers, all suffer together; if one member is honored, all rejoice together.

(1) John Chrysostom

As it is, there are many parts, yet one body. We too, therefore, must keep this in mind and banish all jealousy. Let us not envy those who have the *higher gifts* (1 Cor 12:31) or look down on those who have the lesser ones, for this is the will of God. Let us not fight against him. And if you are still upset, understand that it is often the case that another cannot do what you can. Therefore, even if you are not as great, you are superior in this; and even if someone is greater in certain things, he is not as great as you are in what you can do. Thus there is equality. For in a body, too, the small parts make no small contribution, and their removal often harms the greater parts. What part of the body could be less

207

important than hair? But remove this small thing from the eyebrows and the eyelids, and you destroy the beauty of the entire face, and the eyes no longer appear lovely. Though the loss affects only a little thing, nevertheless it destroys all the beauty. And not only the beauty, but the eyes even lose much of their function. . . .

In the Church, too, there are many and diverse members, some **more honorable** and some less. For example, there are the choirs of virgins, the assemblies of widows, the company of those whose glory is in chaste marriage. These exhibit many degrees of virtue. The same is true of works of mercy. One person gives away everything, others desire only to be self-sufficient and to have the bare necessities, while still others give alms from their abundance. Nevertheless, all adorn each other, and if the greater reckons the lesser as nothing, he does great harm to himself. If the virgin treats the married woman with contempt, she loses no small part of her reward. If someone who gives everything away reproaches someone who does not, he has forfeited much of the fruit of his efforts.

But why do I speak of virgins and widows and the poor? What is of less account than beggars? Yet these, too, have a major role in the Church: they stand as fixtures and splendid adornment at the doors of the sanctuary. Indeed, without them the Church would not attain its full stature. . . .

No surgeon, extending his hand and applying his knife, removes the festering parts of the wounds as well as a poor man who, by extending his right hand and receiving alms, relieves you of the scars left by your wounds. And the amazing thing is that the poor perform this salutary operation without causing pain or discomfort. And while we preachers sit before you and recommend what will do you good, the one who sits before the doors of the church addresses you no less than we do, by his mere appearance, without saying a word. We drill our lessons into you day by day, saying, "My friend, do not be proud. Man's life is a shifting and precarious thing. Youth hastens to old age, beauty to deformity, strength to weakness, eminence to disgrace. Health passes to sickness, glory to insignificance, wealth to poverty. Our condition is like a swift river that never wants to stand still but always rushes downhill."

This advice and more like it the poor give us by their looks and by what has happened to them, which is an even clearer warning. How many of those now sitting outside flourished in their youth? How many of those who are ugly to look at were preeminent in bodily strength and beauty? Don't be a skeptic and mock what I am saying. Life is full of examples of this. If many who were lowly and insignificant have become kings, why is it a wonder that many who were great and honored have become lowly and insignificant? And in fact the former change is much more surprising, while the latter is an everyday occurrence. So we should not doubt that some of these beggars excelled as artisans or soldiers or had an abundance of possessions. Instead, we should have great pity on them and be afraid that we ourselves will suffer the same reverses. For we too are human beings who are subject to swift change.

Paul is right to say: **parts which seem to be weaker** and **which we think less honorable**. This shows that this description is not based on actual fact but on the opinion of the majority. There is nothing dishonorable in the body: it is God's workmanship. What is thought to be **less honorable** than our organs of generation? And yet they receive **greater honor**. Even the destitute, though the other parts of their bodies may be naked, will not allow those parts to be uncovered. . . .

That is why, when Paul calls these parts **weak** and **less honorable**, he adds **which seem to be**. But when he says that something is **necessary**, he does not add **which seem to be** but gives his own judgment that they are in fact necessary. And he is quite right. The **less honorable parts** are useful for procreation and the propagation of our race. Consequently, even Roman legislators punish those who mutilate these organs and make men eunuchs; such people harm the whole race and insult nature itself. But a curse be on all dissolute people who slander the handiwork of God! Just as many curse wine because there are drunkards or women's nature because of adulteresses, so they regard these organs as shameful because of those who make improper use of them. Yet that is not as it should be. Sin is not indissolubly bound up with these organs; it is born from the free choice of those who dare to transgress.

Some think that when Paul speaks of the **weaker, less honorable**, and **necessary** members that enjoy **greater honor** he means the eyes and the feet, and that he calls the eyes both **weaker** and **necessary** because they have less strength but are very useful. The **less honorable** members are the feet, and in fact these are given special care. . . .

God requires that we care for each other, and he established unity amid such great diversity so that all might share completely in everything that happens. For by caring for our neighbors we promote the salvation of all; thus all share in both glory and sorrow. So in this passage Paul is requesting three things: that they not be divided but perfectly united; that they care for each other one and all; and that they regard whatever happens as the common concern of all. . . .

But **members** are bound to each other not only in this way but also by experiences, both pleasant and painful. Often when a thorn has pierced the heel, the whole body feels it and becomes concerned. The back bends over, the abdomen and the legs join in, the hands, running forward like bodyguards and servants, remove the thorn, the head bows down, and the eyes look on with great concern. As a result, even if the foot is at a disadvantage because it cannot raise itself up, it is made equal by the lowering of the head and enjoys equal honor. . . .

Again, if something happens to the eyes, all the **members** feel pain, all are made idle. The feet do not walk or the hands work, and the stomach does not enjoy its usual foods. Yet the ailment belongs to the eye. Why does your stomach waste away? Why are your feet constrained? Why are your hands fettered? Because they are bound up with the eyes, and the whole body suffers more than it can say. If it did not suffer as a whole, it would not trouble itself with all this care for one part. Therefore, after saying **that the members may have the same care for one another**, Paul adds, **If one member suffers, all suffer together; if one member is honored, all rejoice together.** But how do they rejoice together? you may ask. The head is crowned and the whole person is honored. The mouth speaks and the eyes laugh with happiness, even though the credit does not belong to the beauty of the eyes but to the tongue. . . .

Let all of us keep these things in mind and imitate the love these **members** have for each other. And let us not do the opposite by exulting in the misfortunes of our neighbor or envying his good fortune. This would be to act like a madman. For to gouge out one's own eye or devour one's own hand is undeniable evidence of insanity. . . .

Nothing divides and tears us apart as much as malicious envy, that grievous and inexcusable disease, which is worse in a way than love of money, *the root of all evils* (1 Tim 6:10). At least the lover of money is happy if he gets some for himself. But the envious person is happy when the other gets nothing, not when he himself gets something. He thinks his own blessing lies in the misfortune of others, not in his own welfare. He storms about like an enemy of human nature and attacks the very **members** of Christ. What could be more deranged than this? . . . Tell me, why are you envious? Because your brother received some spiritual gift? And from whom did he receive it, pray tell? Was it not from God? Therefore, in envying you make yourself an enemy of the one who gave the gift. . . .

Let us flee this passion, then, beloved, and not be envious. Rather, let us pray for those who are and do everything that they may extinguish their passion. Fools who want to punish them do everything to fan this flame. Let it not be so for us. Rather, let us weep and mourn for their condition.

(2) Augustine

[*From a sermon preached to celibates*]
You have a higher purpose, you hold a higher place in the body of Christ because you practice celibacy. This is by his gift, not by your merits: it is the gift of God. This gift is suspected by the wicked who envy us. But it is attacked in order that it may be tested. For if in our profession of continence we seek the praises of men, the censures of men will cause us to fail. . . .

You must be aware of this first, dearly beloved, that in the body of Christ the more excellent members are not the only ones. The married life is worthy of praise and has its place in the body of Christ. So too in our bodies the things that are in the noblest place are not alone. The senses, for example, have a superior location in the head, but if the feet did not carry them, the parts with the most exalted place in the body would be lying on the ground. Hence the apostle's saying, **The parts of the body which seem to be weaker are indispensable. . . . God has so composed the body . . . that there may be no discord in the body.**

Members of Christ who live the married life — if they are members of Christ, if they are believers, if they hope for the life to come, if they know why they bear the sign of Christ — honor you, regarding you as superior to themselves. But as much as they honor you, you ought to honor them. If there is a special holiness in you, be careful you don't lose it. How? Through pride. The holiness of the celibate is lost one way if he commits adultery, another if he becomes proud. I make bold to say that those who live a married life, if they hold fast to humility, are better than the celibate. Consider, dear friends, what I mean. Take the devil: is he to be accused at God's tribunal of adultery and fornication? He is innocent of these since he doesn't have a body. It is pride and envy alone that send him into eternal fire.

As soon as pride steals into the servant of God, so too does envy. The proud man cannot help being envious. Envy is the daughter of pride, and the mother necessarily gives birth to the daughter; wherever she is, immediately she gives birth. But to keep pride and envy from residing in you, consider this: in the time of persecution it was not only Agnes the virgin who was crowned but also Crispina the wife. And it may be (it is not to be doubted) that some of the celibate fell away while many of the married fought and were victorious. And so it is to some purpose that the apostle says to all the members of Christ, *Count others better than yourselves; outdo one another in showing honor* (Phil 2:3; Rom 12:10). If you think these thoughts, you will not be great in your own estimation. You ought to think more about what you still lack than about what you possess. Take care that you do not lose what you possess. And pray that you may possess what you do not have.

[*From a sermon preached on the feast day of the martyrs Perpetua and Felicity*]
This day's annual return serves to remind us, and in a certain way make present again to us, the day on which the holy servants of God Perpetua and Felicity, made glorious with the crowns of martyrdom, came to flower in perpetual felicity. They held fast to the name of Christ in the battle, and at the same time found the meaning of their own names in the reward they were given. We have heard someone read how they were encouraged by a divine revelation they received and how they triumphed over suffering. All these things, set forth in glowing words, we have heard with our ears, seen in our mind's eye, honored by our piety, and praised with our love. . . .

Therefore, let us celebrate their feast, as we are doing, with great devotion, sober cheerfulness, chaste assembly, faithful contemplation, and confident preaching. It is no small part of imitation to rejoice in the virtues of those better than ourselves. They are great, and we are small. But God has blessed *both small and great* (Ps 115:13). They have gone before us; they towered over us. If we cannot follow them in deed, let us follow in affection; if not in glory, at least in gladness; if not in merit, at least in aspiration; if not in their passion, at least in compassion; if not in their preeminence, at least in our tie with them.

Let us not think it a slight thing that we are members of the same body with those whom we cannot equal. For **if one member suffers, all suffer together; if one member is honored, all rejoice together**. Glory be to the head, who looks out for the interests of the hands above and the feet below. Just as he laid down his life for us, so the martyrs imitated him and laid down their lives for the brethren. In order that this great harvest of peoples should spring up like seed sown, they watered the earth with their blood. So we too are the fruit of their labor. We admire them, they have pity on us. We praise their blessedness, they pray for us. They have spread out their bodies like those garments spread when Christ was carried by a foal into Jerusalem. Let us at least cut branches, as it were, from trees, plucking hymns and praises from the Holy Scriptures and offering them as our common joy (Matt 21:7-9). We all obey the same Lord, follow the same teacher, accompany the same leader, are joined to the same head, strive toward the same Jerusalem, pursue the same charity, and embrace the same unity.

1 Corinthians 12:27-31

27Now you are the body of Christ and individually members of it. 28And God has appointed in the church first apostles, second prophets, third teachers, then workers of miracles, then healers, helpers, administrators, speakers in various kinds of tongues. 29Are all apostles? Are all prophets? Are all teachers? Do all work miracles? 30Do all possess spiritual gifts[16] of healing? Do all speak with tongues? Do all interpret? 31But earnestly desire the higher gifts. And I will show you a still more excellent way.

(1) Augustine

If anyone possesses a gift in the Church and thereby enjoys preeminence, let him not boast of it, but let him see whether he has love. For when the apostle Paul enumerated the many gifts given to the body of Christ, which is the Church, he said that appropriate gifts have been given to each of the members and that it is impossible that all should have the same gift. Yet no one will be left without a gift: **apostles**, he says, **prophets, teachers, interpreters, speakers in various kinds of tongues, those who have the power to help, to administer, to speak languages**. That is what he said, and in fact we find different gifts in different people. No one, therefore, should grieve that he has not been given what someone else has been given. If he has love and is not envious of the gift's possessor, he possesses this gift jointly with him. Whatever my brother has, if I don't envy him but have love, is mine. I do not have it in myself but in him. It would not be mine if we were not in one body and under one head.

Take an example from your body: your left hand has a ring on it, let us suppose, and your right hand has none. Does the right remain without adornment? If you look at the hands individually, you will see that one has adornment and the other doesn't. But if you look at the whole body, to which the two hands are attached, you will see that the hand that lacks adornment possesses it in the hand that has it. The eyes can see where to walk and the feet walk where the eyes see. The feet cannot see, the eyes cannot walk. But the feet reply to you: "I too have light, not in me but in the eye. The eye does not see for its own sake without seeing for mine." The eyes also say: "We too walk, not in ourselves but in the feet. The feet do not carry themselves without carrying us." The individual members, assigned to their several functions, carry out the orders of the soul. All, however, are constituted in a single body and possess unity. They do not claim for themselves what other members have but they themselves lack. And they consider to be their very own what they hold in joint possession.

Therefore, brethren, if anything unpleasant happens to any member of the body, will any member refuse to come to its aid? What is as remote from the center as the foot? And in the foot what is as remote as the sole? And in the sole, what is as remote as the skin by which we touch the earth? But this remote member belongs to the body as a whole in such a way that if the sole treads on a thorn, the other members rush together to help re-

---

16. RSV: "gifts," as in vv. 4 and 9.

move it: immediately the knees bend, the spine curves over,[17] and you sit down to pull out the thorn. The sitting to do this belongs to the whole body. What a small spot is in trouble! The place that a thorn can puncture is tiny. And yet the pain felt in the tiny place is not left alone by the whole body: the other members feel no pain themselves yet all feel pain in that place. . . .

There is nothing higher and more honored in the body than the eyes. And nothing more remote than the little toe. Though that is so, it is better to be a toe in the body and enjoy health than to be an eye and to be inflamed and bleary. Health, which is common to all the members, is more valuable than the functions of them individually. Thus you see in the church a man with some small gift but possessing love; and another eminent in the church because of some greater gift but lacking love. Let us call the one the little toe, the other the eye. The former belongs more to the whole body since it has been able to share in its health. Whatever is diseased causes pain to the rest of the body. All the members make an effort to heal what is sick, and usually it is healed. But if it is not healed and catches gangrene that cannot be healed, it is in the interest of the rest of the body that it be amputated.

Let us grant that a certain Donatus was like an eye in the body. We don't know what he was like, but let us assume that he was as he is described. What benefit did he derive from his preeminence in honor and glory? He could not keep his health because he lacked love. And finally his followers became gangrenous and had to be amputated. . . . A member can admit health into itself only so long as it is not cut off from the body. Health flows from the other parts, which are sound, to the wounded place. But when the wounded part is cut off, there is no way for health to reach it. That is why they are compared to branches that are cut off, and the Gospel reading joins up with the reading of the apostle. There too the Lord recommends only love to us, that we may remain in him. *I am the vine,* he says, *you are the branches, and my Father is the vinedresser. Every branch of mine that bears no fruit he takes away, and every branch that does bear fruit he prunes, that it may bear more fruit* (John 15:1-2, 5). The fruit comes from charity, the only root from which fruit springs. And the apostle says, *being rooted and grounded in love* (Eph 3:17).

17. Augustine alludes to the double meaning of the Latin word *spina* ("spine" or "thorn"). In the Latin there is an explanation, omitted here, that he means the body's *spina*, not the *spina* or thorn to be removed.

1 Corinthians 13

It is no surprise that Paul's encomium of love, which is placed between two chapters on spiritual gifts, should have had great appeal for the fathers. Paul begins by describing love's superiority to all the spiritual gifts (vv. 1-3). Both John Chrysostom and Augustine interpret these verses in the context of other Scriptures. Augustine cites Old Testament examples (surprisingly) to illustrate how it is possible to prophesy or have faith without love. But he adds that prophecy brings no "gain" to such a person and that the life of one who believes and does not love is no different from that of demons. In verses 4-7 Paul then enumerates the many virtues of love. Origen and John Chrysostom provide examples of these from the Scriptures. Chrysostom also relates Paul's words to his own experience as a preacher. According to Augustine, love that is "not puffed up" (v. 4) is the antidote to the primary sins of pride and envy.

As Chrysostom points out, Paul returns in verses 8-10 to the subject of spiritual gifts that he had discussed in the previous chapter. Augustine refers to Paul's promise of perfect knowledge and perfect prophecy (v. 10) in the context of a discussion of the resurrection body. He uses a story about the prophet Elisha's clairvoyance as an analogy for the way God will be seen in the resurrection life. Verses 11-13 contrast the imperfect knowledge of the present time with future knowledge "face to face." John Chrysostom cites verse 12 ("now I know in part") to refute the claim of Eunomius and his circle to have complete knowledge of God, while Gregory of Nyssa understands the words "now we see in a mirror" to mean that the divine image in the human being can provide a glimpse of God.

Many patristic texts describe the beatific vision of God as the ultimate goal of the Christian life, and in discussions of this 1 Cor 13:12 is one of the most prominent biblical references, along with Matt 5:8 ("Blessed are the pure in heart, for they shall see God"). The comments included here give an example of the fathers' reflection on what seeing "face to face" can mean (Augustine) and illustrate how the verse inspired visions of the perfect, unending joy of divine contemplation (Gregory of Nyssa, Augustine). In a comment on verse 13 Augustine links Paul's praise of love that "never ends" to the contemplation of God: if the soul has already learned to love what it has not seen, love's flame can only grow brighter when the soul finally beholds God.

1 Corinthians 13:1-3

1If I speak in the tongues of men and of angels, but have not love, I am a noisy gong or a clanging cymbal. 2And if I have prophetic powers, and understand all mysteries and all knowledge, and if I have all faith, so as to remove mountains, but have not love, I am nothing. 3If I give away all I have, and if I deliver my body to be burned,[1] but have not love, I gain nothing.

(1) John Chrysostom

To make his argument more palatable, Paul does not confine himself to the gift of speaking in tongues but proceeds to other spiritual gifts. First he denigrates everything that is not accompanied by love and then sketches out what love is like. Since he had decided to demonstrate his point by amplification, he begins with the lesser things and moves on to the greater. For the gift of tongues, which he put last when he was ranking gifts (12:7-11), he now puts first, since he wants to advance by degrees from lesser to greater things. After he mentions speaking in tongues, he moves on at once to prophecy, saying, **if I have prophetic powers**. Here too he uses exaggeration. In the earlier sentence, after saying not just "tongues," but **the tongues** of all **men** and then adding those **of angels**, he then showed that this gift is nothing without love. In the same way, he now mentions not only prophecy but the most exalted form of prophecy. For after saying, **if I have prophetic powers**, he adds, **and I understand all mysteries and all knowledge**. This gift too he describes in heightened form.

After this, Paul goes on to the rest of the spiritual gifts. But to avoid being tiresome by reciting them all again one by one, he names the mother and source of them all, and this again in an exaggerated way, saying, **and if I have all faith**. And not satisfied with this, he adds something said by Christ to be a very great thing (see Matt 21:21): [faith] **so as to remove mountains, but do not have love, I am nothing**. See how here again he takes away the prestige associated with speaking in tongues. For in the case of prophecy he points to a great benefit, namely, understanding mysteries and possessing all knowledge, and in the case of faith he names removing mountains, no small accomplishment. About tongues, however, he says only that it is a gift and then moves on. Notice this as well, how in these few words he includes all the gifts when he mentions prophecy and faith. For miracles come about either through words or deeds. And so Christ says that the smallest portion of faith has the ability to remove mountains (Matt 21:21; Mark 11:23)....

If I divide up and give away[2] **all I have, and if I deliver my body to be burned, but have not love, I gain nothing.** What hyperbole! Here again Paul mentions the gifts and then adds a further description of them. He does not say, "If I give half of all my substance to the poor, or two-thirds or three-fourths," but **If I divide up and give away all I**

---

1. Some ancient manuscripts read "that I may glory."

2. Chrysostom calls attention to a nuance of the Greek verb Paul uses here: it can denote breaking food into small pieces to feed an infant.

have. Nor does he say, "if I give," but **if I divide up and give away**, with the result that to the expenditure is added the task of careful administration. **If I deliver my body to be burned**. He does not say, "If I am killed," but he speaks again in the strongest terms. He singles out the hardest death of all, being burned alive, and says that this is no great thing without love. Then he adds, **I gain nothing.** But the full extent of Paul's hyperbole becomes clear only when we compare Christ's testimonies about almsgiving and death. What, then, are these? Christ says to the rich man, *If you would be perfect, go, sell what you possess and give to the poor; and come, follow me* (Matt 19:21). Discussing love for one's neighbor, he says, *Greater love has no man than this, that a man lay down his life for his friends* (John 15:13). Thus it is clear that this is greatest in God's sight. "But I tell you" (says Paul), "if we give our life for God, and not only give it but in such a way that we are burned up (i.e., **if I deliver my body to be burned**), we will have little profit if we do not love our neighbor." To say that spiritual gifts bring no great gain when love is absent is not surprising since these gifts are less important than how we conduct our lives. . . .

But the question we are considering is this: if Christ associates these two things [i.e., selling possessions and giving up one's life] with perfection, why does Paul call them imperfect without love? He is not contradicting Christ (God forbid!) but is in perfect harmony with him. For Christ did not merely say to the rich man, *sell what you possess and give to the poor;* he added, *and come, follow me* (Matt 19:21). No form of following him is more characteristic of disciples of Christ than loving one another. *By this all men will know that you are my disciples,* he says, *if you have love for one another* (John 13:35). . . .

This is what one who has love is like. But anyone who performs miracles or has complete knowledge but has not love, even if he raises thousands from the dead, will do little good since he is separated from others and unwilling to associate with his fellow servants. That is why Christ says that the mark of perfect love is to love our neighbors. To Peter he says, if you *love me more than these, tend my sheep* (John 21:15-16). Do you see how even here he implies that this love is greater than martyrdom? Suppose a father had a beloved son for whom he would even give his life. Suppose too that someone loved the father but paid no attention whatever to the son. This would anger the father, and he would take no notice of the man's love for him because he neglected his son. If this is true for a human father and a son, it is much more so for God and human beings. For God loves us more than any father.

Thus, after saying, *This is the first and greatest commandment: You shall love the Lord your God,* Christ adds, making this explicit, *And a second is like it, You shall love your neighbor as yourself* (Matt 22:37-39; Deut 6:5; Lev 19:18). See how he requires love of the neighbor in nearly the same hyperbolic terms. In the case of God, he says, *with all your heart,* and in the case of your neighbor, *as yourself,* which is the same as *with all your heart.* If this commandment had been kept perfectly, we would have known no slave or free, no ruler or ruled, no rich or poor, no small or great, no devil. I don't mean merely *the* devil — even if there were another like him, or even ten thousand, where love is present they will have no power. For hay withstands fire better than the devil survives the flame of love. Love is stronger than a city wall; it is harder than steel. And even if you should think of some material stronger than these, love's strength exceeds them all. Neither wealth nor poverty overcomes it. No, there would be neither poverty nor immoderate wealth if there were love, but only the advantages associated with each: from the former we would enjoy freedom from being envied, and from the latter freedom from worry. We would suffer neither wealth's worries nor poverty's fear. But why am I talking about the advantages that derive from love? Think how extraordinarily great love is all by itself, how great is the joy it brings, how great the joy in which it sets the soul, a joy that it is the fairest flower!

(2) Augustine

It is good to speak about love to those who are guided by it, that love which, whatever is the object of your love, makes that love good. According to the apostle, it is in love that we find *a still more excellent way* (12:31). The passage was read just now, you have heard it: *And I will show you*, he says, *a still more excellent way* (12:31). Then he tells of many gifts, extraordinary gifts that are not to be made light of. But he says that these bring no benefit to those who **have not love**. Among these gifts he mentions **speaking in the tongues of men and angels, having prophetic powers, all knowledge, all faith, so as to remove mountains, giving away all one has to the poor, delivering one's body to be burned**. All these things are magnificent and from God, but only if they are set upon the foundation of love and rise from the root of love.

We would not dare to claim that people could actually possess these gifts without having love unless we were taught by examples from Holy Scripture itself. . . . Among the excellent gifts Paul names, the really important one seems to be either prophecy or faith. What about the others? If someone who has prophecy gains nothing without love, and if someone who has faith cannot come to the kingdom of God without love, do we need to speak about the other gifts? What is speaking in tongues in comparison with prophecy and faith? . . . These two are preeminent, and it is quite surprising to find that someone can have prophecy or faith without love.

The book of Kings gives us an example that concerns prophecy. Saul persecuted the holy David. When he had sent servants to haul him off for punishment, they found David among the prophets who were with Samuel, the son of the barren woman Hannah. . . . While they were prophesying, the men sent by Saul arrived, as I said, to haul David away to be killed. And upon them — the men who had come to take a holy and just man to be killed and to pluck him from the midst of the prophets — the Spirit of God descended, and they began to prophesy (1 Sam 19:18-20). Immediately they were filled with the Spirit of God and became prophets. It could be that this happened because of their innocence; perhaps they had not come of their own accord to arrest David but were only following the king's orders. Perhaps they came to where David was having no intention of carrying out Saul's order but intending to remain there themselves. Similar things happen today: sometimes a bailiff is sent by an authority to drag someone out of a church. He does not dare to act against God, and to avoid being executed himself he stays with his intended victim instead of dragging him off. So let us say that Saul's servants suddenly became prophets because they were innocent. . . . Let us believe this of them. Others were sent, and upon them the Spirit of God also descended, and they too began to prophesy. Let's count them with the first group as innocent. A third group was sent. The same happened to them. Presumably they too were innocent. Because of the delay in carrying out Saul's orders, Saul himself came. Was he too innocent? Was he sent under duress rather than in willful wickedness? On him too the Spirit of God descended, and he began to prophesy. Note, Saul is prophesying, but he has no love. He has become a vessel touched by the Spirit but not purified by him. . . .

And so the Spirit of God did not purify Saul the persecutor but touched him so that he prophesied. Another example: Caiaphas, the chief priest, persecuted Christ. And yet he spoke prophetically when he said, *It is expedient for you that one man should die for the people, and that the whole nation should not perish* (John 11:50). The Evangelist thereupon reveals that this was a prophecy and says, *He did not say this of his own accord, but being high priest that year he prophesied* (John 11:51). . . .

So we have proved that someone can have prophecy without love. But then prophecy has no benefit for him, according to the apostle: **if I have not love**, he says, **I am nothing**. He does not say, "prophecy is nothing" or "faith is nothing," but **I am nothing** if I do not have love. Although he has great things, he is nothing. For even the possession of the great things he has serves not to help him but to bring him into judgment. It is not a great thing merely to have great things: one must also use them well. But no one without love can use them well. Unless our will is good, we cannot use anything well. And when love is absent, the will cannot be good.

What about faith? Does anyone have faith but lack love? Indeed, many believe and do not love, too many to mention. We know that demons believe what we believe but do not love what we love. The apostle James upbraided those who thought it enough to believe but did not wish to live good lives, which one can do only by means of love — for a good life belongs to love, and one who loves cannot live badly since living well is nothing other than being filled with love. Since some boasted that they believed in God and yet did not live good lives in accordance with the faith they had received, James compared them to demons, saying: *You believe that God is one; you do well. Even the demons believe — and shudder* (Jas 2:19). So if you merely believe and do not love, your life is no different from that of demons.

1 Corinthians 13:4-7

4Love is patient and kind; love is not jealous or boastful; 5it is not arrogant or rude. Love does not insist on its own way; it is not irritable or resentful; 6it does not rejoice at wrong, but rejoices in the right. 7Love bears all things, believes all things, hopes all things, endures all things.

(1) Origen

In his praises of love, which is *more excellent* (1 Cor 12:31), Paul goes through the spiritual gifts one after another. For he had to teach both what love is and how the one who has love behaves. **Love is patient.** If you have patience, which is the *fruit of the Spirit* (Gal 5:22), you have it because of love. It is **kind**. What is the opposite of kindness? Wickedness. If you behave wickedly toward someone, you do not have love. If you are kind and pleasant to everyone, you have love. **Love is not jealous.** If you have envy like the envy Cain felt toward Abel or Joseph's brothers toward him, you do not have love. Loving and being jealous are at odds with each other. It is not **boastful**. When someone foolishly professes to understand either an art or a science or any form of knowledge, he is boastful because of not having love. It is **not rude**. No one who has love does anything shameful. Now if our brothers, claiming that it is according to God's plan that they love each other, *male and female* (Gen 1:27), should ever stumble because of their weakness masquerading as love, let us say to them that they do not have love.

Love does not insist on its own way. No one who has love insists on his own way. For example, mothers or fathers who love their sons **do not insist on** their own advantage but on that of their sons. For having love is not something selfish. If the Savior, who is *in the form of God* and *equal to God* (Phil 2:6), had insisted on his own way, he would have remained in that form. But because he wished to save a perishing world, *he emptied himself, taking the form of a servant, . . . and being found in human form he humbled himself and became obedient unto death, even death on a cross* (Phil 2:7-8). Consider the saints as well. Consider the love of Moses, who said, *If thou wilt forgive their sin, forgive it, and if not, blot me out of thy book, which thou hast written* (Exod 32:32). The apostle also says, *even as I myself seek to please everyone in every way, not seeking my own advantage, but that of the many, that they may be saved* (1 Cor 10:33), and *I could wish that I myself were accursed and cut off from Christ for the sake of my brethren, my kinsmen by race* (Rom 9:3). He prays to be *accursed and cut off from Christ* for the sake of the salvation of others.

(2) Augustine

Would that everyone would think of love, and love alone! That is the only thing that conquers all, the thing without which all else is worthless. Wherever it is, it draws everything to itself (John 12:32). This is the thing that **is not jealous**. Do you want to know why? Listen to what follows: **it is not arrogant.** As I started to say, first among the vices comes pride, then envy. Envy does not beget pride; it is the other way round. We do not envy unless we wish to be superior. Love of superiority is called pride. Since, therefore, pride is first in order, followed by envy, the apostle in his praise of charity does not first say **is not arrogant** and then **is not jealous**, but he first says **is not jealous** and thereafter **is not arrogant**. Why? Because when he had said **is not jealous**, as if you were about to ask the reason for this, he adds **is not arrogant**. . . . Let this grow up in you, and let your souls be strengthened because they are not arrogant.

What a great thing is love! It is the soul of Scripture, the force behind prophecy, the salvation inherent in the sacraments, the power that makes knowledge solid, the fruit of faith, the riches of the poor, the life of the dying. What is as generous as dying on behalf of those who are ungodly (Rom 5:8)? What is as kind as loving one's enemies (Matt 5:44)? Love alone is not oppressed by other men's good fortune since it is **not jealous**. Love alone is not elated by its own good fortune because it is **not arrogant**. Love alone is not stung by a bad conscience since it never acts wrongfully. Amid reproaches it is free from worry, amid hatreds it acts to do good, amid wrath it is calm, amid plots it is innocent, amid iniquities it maintains its innocence; it draws its breath from truth. What could be mightier than love, mightier not in paying back injuries but in ignoring them? . . .

The reason it **endures all things** in the present life is that it **believes all things** about the life to come. And it **endures all things** sent against it here because it **hopes all things** that are promised there. It is only right that it *never ends* (1 Cor 13:8). Therefore, pursue love, and by meditating on it in holiness bring forth the fruits of righteousness.

(3) John Chrysostom

Love is patient and kind; love is not jealous or boastful. Since Paul has already shown that if love is lacking there is no great benefit in faith, knowledge, prophecy, tongues, spiritual gifts, healings, self-sacrifice, or martyrdom, he must now sketch out the surpassing beauty of love. . . . See, then, where he begins and what he sets down first as the cause of all blessings. What is it? Patience. This is the basis for a disciplined life. That is why a wise man says, *He who is slow to anger has great understanding, but he who has a hasty temper exalts folly* (Prov 14:29). Comparing it to a city, and a strong one at that, Paul says that patience is even more secure. It is an invincible shield and an impregnable tower that easily repels all trouble. Just as a spark falling into a deep pit does no harm to the pit but is quickly extinguished, so whenever anything unexpected assails the **patient** soul, it quickly vanishes without causing any distress. Patience is indeed stronger than anything. If you mention armies or wealth or horses or fortresses or weapons or anything else, nothing will equal patience. For a man who relies on these other defenses is often himself overpowered by anger, like a frivolous young man, and he is upset and spreads confusion and troubles all around him. But the patient man enjoys complete peace, like a boat in a safe haven. If you grieve him with loss, you will not budge this rock. If you heap abuse on him, you will not jolt this tower. And if you rain blows on him, you will not shake this man of steel. . . .

This is love, when the lover and the beloved are no longer two distinct entities, but one person. This can never come about except through love. So to find your own good, do not seek it. The one who **insists on his own way** does not find it. That is why Paul also says, *Let no one seek his own good, but the good of his neighbor* (1 Cor 10:24). For your own advantage lies in your neighbor's advantage, as his does in yours. . . .

And if you would like an example, consider my situation as your preacher: my benefit lies in you, and your profit lies in me. It is to your advantage to learn what pleases God, but I have been entrusted with this so that you might learn it from me and hence be compelled to come to me. On the other hand, it is to my profit that you become better. I will receive a great reward for this. But again my profit lies in you, and so I am compelled to pursue you, so that you might be better and I might receive my gain from you. That is why Paul asks, *For what is our hope? Is it not you?* and again, my *hope,* my *joy,* and my *crown of boasting* (1 Thess 2:19). Thus Paul's disciples were his joy, and his joy depended on them. That is why he also wept if he ever saw them being corrupted. On the other hand, their profit was in Paul. So he could say, *It is because of the hope of Israel that I am bound with this chain* (Acts 28:20). And again, *I endure* these things *for the sake of the elect, that they may obtain* eternal life (2 Tim 2:10). . . .

Paul says, love **bears all things**. It bears them by its patience and its goodness even if things are burdensome and distasteful, even if love should suffer insults, blows, death, or anything at all. Once more, we can see this in the case of the blessed David. What could be more grievous than to see your son inciting rebellion, lusting for power, and thirsting for his father's blood (2 Samuel 15–18)? But that blessed man endured these things, and in spite of them would not utter a bitter word against the parricide. Leaving everything else to his generals' discretion, he gave strict instruction for his son's safety (2 Sam 18:5). Truly, love's foundation was strong. . . .

If you want to learn love's power, consider the case of a coward, who starts at every noise and trembles at shadows, or a violent man, who is more a savage beast than a human being, or a lustful and licentious man, who is given to every kind of vice. Turn the coward over to the care of love, enroll him in its school, and you will soon see that timid coward becoming brave, stout-hearted, and ready for any bold deed. What is truly marvelous is that these things do not take place by a transformation of his nature; rather, love demonstrates its own power within the timid soul itself. It is as if someone were to make a sword out of lead instead of iron, but while it remained lead by nature, it was ready to do what an iron sword can do. Here is an example. Jacob was *a plain man, dwelling in a house* (Gen 25:27), unpracticed in hardships and perils, enjoying a life of luxury and freedom like a virgin in her chamber. Remaining inside, he was mostly confined to tending the house. He was aloof from the market and its crowds and all such things, and enjoyed unbroken tranquility and peace. What happened then? When love's flame ignited him, see how it turned this same *plain man dwelling in a house* into a man of endurance capable of hard labor. Don't take my word for it, but listen to the patriarch himself. Accusing his father-in-law, he says, *These twenty years I have been with you* (Gen 31:38). And how did you behave during these twenty years, Jacob? He adds this: *By day the heat consumed me, and the cold by night, and my sleep fled from my eyes* (Gen 31:40). . . . It is plain that he was once a coward since, when he was expecting to see Esau, he was deathly afraid (Gen 32:7). But see again how love made the coward braver than a lion. He stationed himself in front of all the rest of his family as a kind of shield and was prepared to be the first to meet his brother, a man he believed was a savage breathing out murder (Gen 33:1-3). He protected the women with his own body. On the front line, he wanted to be the first to see the one he feared and dreaded. His love for his wives was stronger than his fear of his brother. Do you see how, even though he was fearful, he became wholly daring, not by changing his character but by being overpowered by love? . . .

What about Moses? Did he not run away in fear of one Egyptian and leave the country (Exod 2:14-16)? But nevertheless this same man, who fled and was unable to endure a single man's threats, once he had tasted the sweetness of love, gallantly hastened to perish with those he loved even though no one compelled him. *But now, if thou wilt for-give their sin — and if not, blot me, I pray thee, out of thy book which thou hast written* (Exod 32:32).

1 Corinthians 13:8-10

8**Love never ends; as for prophecies, they will pass away; as for tongues, they will cease; as for knowledge, it will pass away.** 9**For our knowledge is imperfect and our prophecy is imperfect;** 10**but when the perfect comes, the imperfect will pass away.**

(1) John Chrysostom

As for prophecies, they will pass away; as for tongues, they will cease; as for knowledge, it will pass away. Paul has shown the preeminence of love: he has demonstrated that spiritual gifts and right actions require love, he has enumerated all love's excellences and declared love to be the foundation of the truly virtuous life. Now again he shows love's value by means of a third argument. He does this because he wants to persuade those who were considered less favored that they too could possess the greatest of all wonders — that if they possessed love, their portion would be no smaller than that of those endowed with spiritual gifts. On the contrary, theirs will be far greater. At the same time, Paul is eager to humble those who have the greater gifts and are conceited because of this. He wants to show that they have nothing if they don't have love. His aim is that they would love each other and put malice and other such madness away, and the greater their love, the further away they would banish these passions. *Love is not jealous . . . it is not arrogant* (1 Cor 13:4-5). He surrounds them with an impregnable wall of concord and banishes every malady, so that they become even stronger. Therefore, he marshals a multitude of arguments to encourage their faint hearts. . . .

    For our knowledge is imperfect and our prophecy is imperfect; but when the perfect comes, the imperfect will pass away. It is not knowledge but partial knowledge that will be nullified. We will know not only as much as we know now, but much more besides. Let me make my point clearer by an example: we know that God is everywhere, but we do not know how. We know that he created the world from nothing, but we do not know how he did so. We know that [Christ] was born of a virgin, but we do not know how. In the future we will know about these things more completely and with more certainty.

(2) Augustine

Once we have been made partakers, as far as we are able, of God's peace, we experience the most perfect peace within ourselves and with each other and with him, whatever our "most perfect" may be; in similar fashion the holy angels experience it in accordance with

222

their capacities. But men are far below them, no matter how far they have advanced in knowledge. Consider how great a man it was who said, **Our knowledge is imperfect and our prophecy is imperfect** and *Now we see in a mirror dimly, but then face to face* (1 Cor 13:12). . . .

Therefore, when someone asks me what the saints will do in their spiritual bodies, I don't say what I can see at present but what I believe, just as it says in the psalm, *I have believed, and therefore I have also spoken* (Ps 116:10 Latin). So I say that they will see God while in their very bodies. But it is no easy question to say whether they will see him by means of them, just as we now see sun, moon, stars, sea, and earth and everything in it by means of our bodies. For it is hard to say that the bodies of the saints will be such that they cannot open and close their eyes when they wish. Yet it is even harder to maintain that in that future life someone who closes his eyes will not see God. Consider the prophet Elisha, who, though absent in body, saw his servant Gehazi accepting gifts from Naaman the Syrian, whom the prophet had cleansed from disfiguring leprosy (2 Kings 5:19-26). The wicked servant thought that his act had escaped notice since his master was not looking on. In view of this example, how much more clearly will saints be able to see in their spiritual bodies, not only if they close their eyes but also when they are physically absent! That will be the fulfillment of the apostle's words: **Our knowledge is imperfect and our prophecy is imperfect, but when the perfect comes, the imperfect will pass away.** Then, to demonstrate as well as he could how far the life to come outstrips our present life — the present life not merely of ordinary persons but of those endowed with special holiness — Paul says, *When I was a child, I spoke like a child, I thought like a child, I reasoned like a child; when I became a man, I gave up childish ways. For now we see in a mirror dimly, but then face to face. Now I know in part; then I shall understand fully, even as I have been fully understood* (1 Cor 13:11-12).

As a child compares to a man in his prime, so do the prophetic powers of those who are distinguished in this life compare to the powers of those in the life to come. So if in this life Elisha saw his servant accepting gifts when he was not present, can it be that when **the perfect** comes and our corruptible bodies no longer weigh down our souls and our incorruptible bodies offer no impediment — can it be that those saints, in order to see what they must, will need these bodily eyes when Elisha did not need them in order to see his servant? According to the seventy interpreters[3] here is what the prophet said to Gehazi: *Did not my heart go with you when the man turned from his chariot to meet you and you received money?* (2 Kings 5:26) and what follows. But the presbyter Jerome translates from the Hebrew as follows: "Was not my heart present when the man turned from his chariot to meet you?" So the prophet said that he had seen this with his heart, a heart, we may be sure, miraculously assisted by God. But how much more abundantly will all enjoy this gift when **the perfect** comes and *God shall be all in all* (1 Cor 15:28)? . . .

Just as it is certain that bodies are perceived by our spirit,[4] what if the power of the spiritual body were so great that spirit could also be seen by the body? For *God is spirit* (John 4:24). Moreover, it is by an inner sense, not by the bodily eye, that a man knows his

---

3. That is, the Septuagint.
4. Augustine has just argued that God, though bodiless, knows the physical world.

own life, that by which he now lives in the body and which quickens these mortal members and makes them living. But the life of others, which is invisible, he sees by means of the body. For how do we distinguish living bodies from dead except by seeing the body and its life at the same time, a life that we can see only through the body? But an incorporeal life cannot be seen with our bodily eyes.

Therefore, it is possible and even very probable that we will see physical bodies in the *new heaven and new earth* (Rev 21:1) in such a way that whichever way we turn our eyes we will behold with perfect clarity God present everywhere and governing all physical bodies, we will behold him, that is, by means of our bodies, the ones we will then be wearing. It will not be as it is now when God's *invisible nature has been clearly perceived in the things that have been made* (Rom 1:20), *in a mirror dimly* (1 Cor 13:12), and in an **imperfect** manner, where the faith by which we believe is more efficacious in us than the appearance of bodily things seen with bodily eyes. . . .

Perhaps, therefore, we will see God with those eyes in such a way that in their complete perfection they will be similar to that faculty of mind by which incorporeal nature is discerned — but this is difficult or impossible to show by any examples or scriptural testimonies. Or, as is easier to comprehend, God will be so known and manifest to us that each of us will see him by the spirit in each of us, each will see him in his neighbor and in himself, each will see him in the *new heaven* and the *new earth* and in the new creation of that time, will see him by means of the body in all bodies, wherever the eyes of the spiritual body are directed.

1 Corinthians 13:11-13

11**When I was a child, I spoke like a child, I thought like a child, I reasoned like a child; when I became a man, I gave up childish ways.** 12**For now we see in a mirror, in an enigma,**[5] **but then face to face. Now I know in part; then I shall understand fully, even as I have been fully understood.** 13**So faith, hope, love abide, these three; but the greatest of these is love.**

(1) John Chrysostom

For now we see through a mirror, in an enigma, but then face to face. Now I know in part; then I shall understand fully, even as I have been fully understood. But what do those impudent people say?[6] That **now I know in part** is in reference to God's plans for salvation since Paul himself possessed a perfect knowledge of God. But how is it, then, that the apostle calls himself a **child**? How is it that he sees **through a mirror**? How is it **in an enigma** if he possesses the fullness of knowledge? Why would Paul attribute full-

---

5. RSV: "dimly."

6. That is, the Eunomians, or Neo-Arians, followers of Eunomius, bishop of Cyzicus (d. 394), who claimed to have complete knowledge of God.

ness of knowledge to the Spirit as a function peculiar to him rather than to any created power? For he says, *For what person knows a man's thoughts except the spirit of the man which is in him? So also no one comprehends the thoughts of God except the Spirit of God* (1 Cor 2:11). Even Christ says that this knowledge is his alone, saying, *Not that any one has seen the Father except him who is from God; he has seen the Father* (John 6:46). When he speaks of seeing, he means the most certain and complete knowledge. . . .

Let no one think that this transgression [i.e., making arrogant claims] is small or simple: it is double and triple and many times multiple. It is strange that these braggarts claim to know things whose knowledge belongs to the Spirit and the Only Son of God alone. Strange, too, that while Paul was not able to gain even partial knowledge without a revelation from above, they say that they have grasped its entirety from their own reasoning. And in fact they cannot show us any Bible passage to convince us of their position.

(2) Gregory of Nyssa on verse 12

The divine nature transcends all knowledge and comprehension. The notion of God that springs up in us is a mere semblance of what we seek. For it does not represent God's true form, which no one *has seen* (1 Tim 6:16) or can see (1 Cor 2:9). Instead, **in a mirror and in an enigma** it is a sort of sketch or hint of what we seek arising in our souls as a kind of conjecture. . . .

Imagine a person who becomes perfect by collecting every sweet-smelling flower or spice from the variegated meadows of virtue and thus makes his whole life fragrant by the sweet odor of each of his actions.[7] Even though he is no more able to gaze directly on the divine Word itself than on the orb of the sun, still he beholds the sun in himself, as **in a mirror**. For the rays of that truly divine virtue shine on the life purified by the impassibility that emanates from them, and they make visible in us what is invisible and comprehensible what is incomprehensible, by picturing the "sun" **in** our **mirror**. . . .

Christ the bridegroom is the *true light* (John 1:9), the true *life* (John 1:3; 1 John 1:2), *true righteousness,* as Wisdom says (Prov 1:3, LXX), and everything else of like nature. So when someone by virtue of his works becomes what the bridegroom is and beholds the cluster of grapes[8] in his own conscience, he sees in it the bridegroom himself, since he sees as in a mirror the *light* of truth in his own luminous and spotless life. . . .

In the coming age, when everything visible has passed away, according to the word of the Lord, who says: *Heaven and earth will pass away* (Matt 24:34), and when we come into that life which is beyond *eye* and *ear* and understanding (1 Cor 2:9), we will perhaps no longer **know** the nature of the good **in part** through its works, as we do now, nor will the transcendent be known by its activity in the visible realm. Instead, we will grasp the

---

7. This excerpt is taken from Gregory's commentary on the Song of Songs; here he reflects on the image of perfume in Cant 3:6 and 4:6-16.

8. Gregory identifies the bridegroom of Song of Songs with Christ and the bride with the human soul. The image of a cluster of grapes is found in Cant 7:8, which Gregory associates with Christ's words "I am the true vine" from John 15:1.

beauty of inexpressible beatitude in an entirely different way and with a kind of joy that in the present *the heart of man* cannot conceive (1 Cor 2:9).

(3) Augustine on verses 11-12

He who is day by day renewed (see 2 Cor 4:16) by advancing in the knowledge of God and who, in the righteousness and holiness of truth, transfers his love from temporal things to eternal, from things seen with the eye to things understood with the mind, from carnal things to spiritual. Such a one perseveres diligently in reining in and diminishing his affection for the former things and binds himself in love to the latter things. He accomplishes this, however, only to the extent that he is helped by God. For God himself said, *Without me you can do nothing* (John 15:5). When the last day of this life finds anyone progressing toward God in this way and holding the faith of the Mediator, he will be received by the holy angels to be led to the God he has worshiped, and there he will be perfected by him and will, at the end of the age, receive an incorruptible body, not as a punishment but for glory. For it is in this image [i.e., the spiritual body] that the likeness of God[9] will be made perfect, when our vision of God is perfect. About this vision the apostle Paul says, **Now we see in a mirror dimly; but then face to face.** He also says, *And we all, with unveiled face, beholding the glory of the Lord, are being changed into his likeness from one degree of glory to another; for this comes from the Lord who is the Spirit* (2 Cor 3:18).

Now we see in a mirror dimly; but then face to face. Do not think here of a bodily face. If, fired by the desire to see God, you prepare your bodily face to see him, you will also desire such a face in God. But if you have a sufficiently spiritual idea of God that you do not think God is corporeal . . . if in your hearts, as in the temple of God, I have broken the image of human form, if there comes into your mind and possesses your inward parts that passage where the apostle denounces those who, *claiming to be wise, became fools, and exchanged the glory of the incorruptible God for images resembling mortal man* (Rom 1:22-23) — if you now denounce such an evil, if you turn away from it, if you cleanse the temple for the Creator, if you desire that he should come and make his dwelling with you, then *Think of the Lord with uprightness, and seek him with sincerity of heart* (Wis 1:1). See who it is to whom you say — if you do say and say truly: *To thee my heart said, "I will seek thy face."* Let your heart say this and add, *"Thy face, Lord, will I seek"* (Ps 27:8 Latin).

You are seeking well since you seek with the heart. We speak of God's face, God's arm, God's hand, God's feet, the footstool for God's feet. But do not think of human body parts. If you wish to be a temple of truth, smash the idol of falsehood. The hand of God is God's power; the face of God is knowledge of him; the feet of God are God's presence; God's seat, if you so desire, is yourself. You won't deny, by any chance, that Christ is God? "No," you say. Do you also admit that Christ is *the power of God and the wisdom of God* (1 Cor 1:24)? "I admit it," you say. Listen then: "The soul of the just is the seat of wis-

---

9. See Gen 1:26-27; 5:1; Jas 3:9.

dom."[10] Where does God have his seat if not in the place where he lives? And where does he live but in his temple? *For God's temple is holy, and that temple you are* (1 Cor 3:17). . . .

Now, then, extend yourself, if you can, to the recognition of Christ's love, a recognition that towers above other knowledge. When you have reached it, you will be filled with God in all his fullness. Then there will be that **face to face**. You will be filled with God's fullness, not in such a way that God will be filled with you but that you will be filled with God. There, if you can, look for a bodily face! Let all trivial things be removed from the vision of our minds! Let the **child** throw away his toys, let him learn to deal with greater things! In many things we are still children.

When we see **face to face** what we now see **in a mirror dimly**, then we shall say, with emotion far different, inexpressibly different, "It is true." And when we say this, we will also be saying "Amen," but with a satisfaction that never satiates. For it will be satisfaction since nothing will be lacking. But it will be satisfaction that never satiates since what is always present will always give pleasure. So just as truth will satisfy you without satiety, so with truth that never satiates you will say "Amen."

But who can tell the nature of *what no eye has seen, nor ear heard, nor the heart of man conceived* (1 Cor 2:9)? For since we will see the truth without its wearying us but with eternal delight, and since we will behold it plainly and surely, we will be set afire with the love of truth itself, cling to it with an embrace pleasurable, pure, and incorporeal, and with a voice to match this embrace we will praise him and say "Alleluia." All the citizens of that city,[11] exhorting each other to like praise in a spirit of burning love toward one another and toward God, will say "Alleluia" because they will say "Amen."

(4) Augustine on verse 13

If someone burns with a desire for eternal life, then wherever he lives . . . he must live patiently, longing for the day when his exile will end and he reaches his longed-for native land. The love that longs for what is absent is one thing; the love of what one sees is another. He who longs for something absent loves, and so does he who sees. He who longs has a desire that he may arrive, and he who sees has a desire that he may stay. But if the longing of the saints burns so hot in faith, what will it be in sight? If we love like this when we believe what we do not see, how will we love when we see?

So the apostle mentions three things that he especially recommends us to build in the inner man, faith, hope, and love, and when he has praised all three, he says at the end, **But the greatest of these is love.** *Make love your aim* (1 Cor 14:1). What then is faith? What is hope? What is love? And why is love **greatest**? *Faith,* as one passage in Scripture defines it, *is the substance of those who hope, the conviction of things not seen* (Heb 11:1 Latin). He who hopes does not have the thing he hopes for, but by believing it he resembles one who has it. For faith, he says, is the substance of those who hope; it is not yet the

---

10. The source of this quotation is unknown.

11. The heavenly city, which Augustine, in *The City of God*, contrasts with the earthly city of Rome.

thing we will possess, but faith itself takes the place of the thing itself. Someone who has faith does not have hold of nothing, and one who is full of faith is not empty. And so the reward for faith is great because it does not see and yet believes. If it saw, what reward would there be for believing? . . .

Faith does not fail since it has hope to support it. Take away hope, and faith fails. How does someone who does not hope to arrive even move his feet in walking? But if from the two, faith and hope, you take away love, what good does it do to believe, what good does it do to hope? It is not possible to hope for what one does not love. It is love that kindles hope; hope glows with love. But when we have arrived at what we hoped for in faith without seeing it, what faith will be left to praise since *faith is the conviction of things not seen?* When we see, it will no longer be called faith. You will see then; you won't believe. The same is true of hope itself. When the reality is present, you do not hope. For *hope that is seen is not hope* (Rom 8:24). There it is: when we have arrived, faith is ended, hope is ended. What happens to love? Faith turns to sight and hope to its reality. Now it is sight and reality, not faith and hope. What happens to love? Can it come to an end? No, for if the soul was already aflame with love for what it had not seen, certainly when it sees this it will burn all the brighter. So it was truly said that **the greatest of these is love**, since faith is succeeded by sight, hope by reality, but love has no successor. It grows, it increases, it is perfected in contemplation.

(5) Gregory of Nyssa on verse 13

If love is taken away from us, how will we be united to God? . . .

Love is the deep interior attachment to that which is desirable. When the soul has become pure and single-minded and perfectly godlike and finds that perfectly pure and spiritual good which is truly loveable and desirable, it attaches itself to this good and unites with it through the movement and energy of love, fashioning itself according to it and continually holding to it and discovering it anew. Because of its likeness to the good, the soul becomes that whose nature it shares.

We have instruction on this point from the holy apostle, who proclaims that all our strivings, even those directed toward the good, will cease and come to rest. Only love will have no end. *For prophecies will pass away, and knowledge will cease, but love never ends* (1 Cor 13:8). That is to say, it always remains the same. Although **faith** and **hope** accompany **love**, Paul says that it is proper to rank **love** higher than the others. For **hope** is active as long as we cannot enjoy that for which we hope, and **faith** lends support because of our uncertainty about that for which we hope. In fact, the apostle defines faith in that way: *Faith is the substance of things hoped for* (Heb 11:11). When, however, that for which one has hoped arrives, the other two pass away, and only love remains active.

1 Corinthians 14

In chapter 14 Paul continues the discussion of worship begun in chapter 11, with special attention to the spiritual gifts of prophecy and speaking in tongues. In first-century Corinth, worship was lively and sometimes disorderly, and the dramatic gift of speaking in tongues was especially prized. Paul's concern is that everyone in the church benefit from the spiritual gifts and that outsiders not be repelled. To this end he counsels the Corinthians to limit their own freedom to exercise the special gifts of prophecy (inspired speech) and speaking in tongues (speaking in unintelligible words, regarded as the speech of the angels),[1] and he orders women to be silent in public assemblies of the church.

Patristic authors (e.g., Theodoret and Severian on vv. 20-25) interpret the chapter by comparing two stories in Acts: the descent of "tongues of fire" at Pentecost (Acts 2) and Acts 5, a specific example of the use of prophetic powers. They also explore the implications of Paul's words for a new context, when the church is more established and the charismatic gift of ecstatic speech less prominent. John Chrysostom, commenting on verses 26-31, contrasts the church of Paul's day to that of his own day — here taking the Corinthian church as a pattern of order, a rather surprising point given his emphasis elsewhere in his homilies on the disorder in Corinth. Origen uses Paul's directives to women (vv. 34-35) to discredit the sectarian Montanist movement, in which prophecy was emphasized and female prophets took a leading role.[2] Both Cyril and Origen find lessons in this chapter for their own interpretation of Scripture. Cyril takes "prophecy" to mean the interpretation of prophetic Scripture, not ecstatic speech, and Origen understands the images of the flute, harp, and bugle in verses 7-8 as symbols of different types of exegesis. Basil of Caesarea and Theodoret consider the chapter's relevance to contemporary trinitarian debates, finding here a proof of the divinity of the Holy Spirit. As he does elsewhere in his Homilies on 1 Corinthians, John Chrysostom draws attention to Paul's rhetorical skill and explains how the chapter relates to other parts of the letter.

1. The story of Pentecost in Acts 2 describes a similar phenomenon, but here those upon whom the "tongues of fire" are poured out speak in different human languages, not in the "tongues of angels." Patristic authors, like many later interpreters, tend to understand 1 Corinthians 12–14 and Acts 2 to refer to the same phenomenon.

2. Montanus, a Christian prophet who lived in Asia Minor in the second century, was the head of a movement called the "New Prophecy," in which the female prophets Priscilla and Maximilla were also leaders. See the extract from *The Dialogue of a Montanist with an Orthodox Christian* in the section on 1 Cor 11:3-9 above.

1 Corinthians 14:1-5

₁Make love your aim, and earnestly desire the spiritual gifts, especially that you may prophesy. ₂For one who speaks in a tongue speaks not to men but to God; for no one understands him, but he utters mysteries in the Spirit. ₃On the other hand, he who prophesies speaks to men for their upbuilding and encouragement and consolation. ₄He who speaks in a tongue edifies himself, but he who prophesies edifies the church. ₅Now I want you all to speak in tongues, but even more to prophesy. He who prophesies is greater than he who speaks in tongues, unless some one interprets, so that the church may be edified.

(1) Cyril of Alexandria

Here Paul frees the Corinthians from the notion that speaking in tongues is a greater credit to them than interpreting the words of the prophets. For when we first possess and value faith and hope and also love (1 Cor 13:13) — love, that is, of God and our brothers, which fulfills the whole law (Rom 10:4) — then the other gifts can be added. Then, and only then, is the time right for us to be filled with God's spiritual gifts, and we will enjoy the richness of the Spirit's blessings. I mean the gift of prophecy, that is, the ability to interpret the words of the prophets. For once the Only Son had become man and suffered and been raised and the plan for our salvation had been accomplished, what sort of prophecy was required or what things still needed to be foretold? In these verses, therefore, prophesying must mean simply this: the ability to interpret the prophecies. And if we make them as clear as possible for our hearers and then confirm the truth of our own teaching from them, we will be faithful and unerring interpreters of what is most noble.

(2) Theodoret

Paul does two things at once: he condemns their ambitious rivalry and teaches them how to use the spiritual gift. Because of the diversity of human languages, preachers received the ability to speak in tongues so that when they came to the inhabitants of India, they could use their own language to bring them God's message. Again, by using the language of each people, they could proclaim the gospel to Persians or Scythians or Romans or Egyptians. But for anyone speaking in Corinth it was pointless to use the languages of the Scythians or Persians or Egyptians, since the Corinthians could not understand them. That is why the apostle says that **one who speaks in tongues speaks not to men but to God.** For he adds this: **for no one understands him.** But to show that the spiritual gift was not useless, he adds: **but he utters mysteries in the Spirit. . . .**

Now I want you all to speak in tongues, but even more to prophesy. He who prophesies is greater than he who speaks in tongues, unless some one interprets, so that the church may be edified. Paul explains clearly why he adds the words **even more.** "I do not make light of the gift," he says, "but I am eager that it be useful." When there is no interpreter for what is uttered in tongues, prophecy is better because it is more beneficial.

1 Corinthians 14:6-12

6Now, brethren, if I come to you speaking in tongues, how shall I benefit you unless I bring you some revelation or knowledge or prophecy or teaching? 7If even lifeless instruments, such as the flute or the harp, do not give distinct notes, how will any one know what is played? 8And if the bugle gives an indistinct sound, who will get ready for battle? 9So with yourselves; if you in a tongue utter speech that is not intelligible, how will any one know what is said? For you will be speaking into the air. 10There are doubtless many different languages in the world, and none is without meaning; 11but if I do not know the meaning of the language, I shall be a foreigner to the speaker and the speaker a foreigner to me. 12So with yourselves; since you are eager for manifestations of the Spirit, strive to excel in building up the church.

(1) Origen

Prophecy is knowledge that expresses invisible things through speech, for example, how the world is structured or how the elements and the seasons operate. **Teaching** is the instructive word that conveys knowledge to the many. **Revelation** occurs when the power of God frees the mind from earthly things and enables it to put off every fleshly activity. The one who achieves this experiences **revelation**. Perhaps the knowledge of coming things can also be called **revelation**. Those who understand the proper meaning of each of these words can use them in an extended sense. . . .

Those who speak in a tongue and do not interpret ought not to speak since their words are undifferentiated and unintelligible. Paul refers to teachings of a more theoretical or contemplative nature as a **flute and harp** since they do not treat the moral life, while he calls the exhortation to virtue a **bugle**. For this reason one could maintain that the obscure parts of Scripture, for example, the discussions of sacrifices in Leviticus and of the tabernacle in Exodus, should not be read unless someone interprets and makes their meaning clear.

(2) John Chrysostom

Now, brethren, if I come to you speaking in tongues, how shall I benefit you unless I bring you some revelation or knowledge or prophecy or teaching? "Why," Paul asks, "do I mention others? Let's assume that it is Paul who is speaking in tongues. Even in that case the hearers gain no benefit." Paul writes this to show that he wants what is best for them. He holds no grudge against those who have this gift and does not hesitate to use himself as an example of how unprofitable it can be. Paul always uses himself as an example when he discusses matters likely to cause offense. Thus he writes at the beginning of the letter, *What is Paul? What is Apollos? What is Cephas?* (1 Cor 3:5; compare 1:12). He does the same thing here, when he says, "Not even **I shall benefit you unless I bring you some revelation or knowledge or prophecy or teaching.**" What he means is this: "Unless I tell you something easy to understand, something that can be made clear, my speaking in tongues will demonstrate only that I have the gift. You will hear but gain no benefit." . . .

I shall be a foreigner to the speaker and the speaker a foreigner to me. Do you see how little by little Paul leads them to the point? This is his custom: he first brings in examples from far afield and then ends with something more germane to his point. After speaking about the flute and the harp, which have no practical use or meaning, he then comes to the bugle, which is more useful. Finally, he comes to language itself. He did the same thing earlier: when he argued that nothing prevented the apostles from receiving support (1 Cor 9:3-7, 13-14), he began with farmers and shepherds and soldiers and then introduced an example much closer to his present topic, namely, the priests of the Old Testament.

1 Corinthians 14:13-19

13Therefore, he who speaks in a tongue should pray for the power to interpret. 14For if I pray in a tongue, my spirit prays but my mind is unfruitful. 15What am I to do? I will pray with the spirit and I will pray with the mind also; I will sing with the spirit and I will sing with the mind also. 16Otherwise, if you bless with the spirit, how can any one in the position of an outsider say the "Amen" to your thanksgiving when he does not know what you are saying? 17For you may give thanks well enough, but the other man is not edified. 18I thank God that I speak in tongues more than you all; 19nevertheless, in church I would rather speak five words with my mind, in order to instruct others, than ten thousand words in a tongue.

(1) John Chrysostom

I thank God that I speak in tongues more than you all. He uses this same tactic elsewhere. When he wants to deny the advantages of Judaism and to show that henceforth they amount to nothing, he first shows that he himself possessed these advantages to the fullest. Then he calls them a loss. Here is what he says: *If any other man thinks he has reason for confidence in the flesh, I have more; circumcised on the eighth day, of the people of Israel, of the tribe of Benjamin, a Hebrew born of Hebrews; as to the law a Pharisee, as to zeal a persecutor of the church, as to righteousness under the law blameless* (Phil 3:4-6). Then, when he has indicated that he had more of such things than anyone else, he says, *But whatever gain I had, I counted as loss for the sake of Christ* (Phil 3:7). In this passage he does the same thing when he says, **I speak in tongues more than you all.** This means, "Do not be arrogant, then, as if you alone had this gift. Indeed, I possess it myself, even more than you do."

1 Corinthians 14:20-25

20Brethren, do not be children in your thinking; be babes in evil, but in thinking be mature. 21In the law it is written, "By men of strange tongues and by the lips of foreigners will I speak to this people, and even then they will not listen to me, says the Lord" [Isa 28:11-12]. 22Thus, tongues are a sign not for believers but for unbelievers, while prophecy is not for unbelievers but for believers. 23If, therefore, the whole church assembles and all speak in tongues, and outsiders[3] or unbelievers enter, will they not say that you are mad? 24But if all prophesy, and an unbeliever or outsider enters, he is convicted by all, he is called to account by all, 25the secrets of his heart are disclosed; and so, falling on his face, he will worship God and declare that God is really among you.

(1) Theodoret

The saying Paul quotes is really from a prophet, but Paul refers to the whole Old Testament as **the law**. After setting down this testimony, he adds the interpretation: **Thus, tongues are a sign not for believers but for unbelievers, while prophecy is not for unbelievers but for believers.** The unbeliever is amazed at the variety of tongues. This is what those gathered in Jerusalem at Pentecost experienced. They responded at once: *Are not all these who are speaking Galileans? And how is it that we hear, each of us in his own native language, Parthians and Medes?* — along with all the other peoples listed (Acts 2:7-9). **While prophecy is not for unbelievers, but for believers.** The apostle has only one goal: to benefit as many as possible. This is why he exhorts the Corinthians to prefer prophecy, since it brings benefit to the whole community. . . .

    And so, falling on his face, he will worship God. Thus everyone experienced fear when Ananias and Sapphira were rebuked (Acts 5:1-11). We should also note that in our text Paul clearly refers to the all-holy Spirit as God. For prophecy was the work of the Spirit of God: *All these are inspired by one and the same Spirit, who apportions to each one individually as he wills* (1 Cor 12:11). But in our text he says: **falling on his face, he will worship God and declare that God is really among you** — thus calling the all-holy Spirit *God*. The blessed Peter also charged: *Why has Satan filled your heart to lie to the Holy Spirit? . . . You have not lied to men but to God* (Acts 5:3-4).

(2) Severian of Gabala

It should be noted that the Jews are not able to explain the text Paul quotes (Isa 28:11-12). They cannot say when it was that God spoke to them through many tongues and they disobeyed him. But we can show that when the Holy Spirit came and distributed tongues, the Jews did not believe but said: *They are filled with new wine* (Acts 2:13).

3. Or "neophytes."

Thus, tongues are a sign not for believers but for unbelievers, while prophecy is not for unbelievers but for believers. . . . Clearly tongues are beneficial when the listener realizes that the one who speaks in tongues is using a language he does not know, one that has no human source. But the content of what is said does not help the hearer because he does not understand it. **Prophecy,** however, is given **for believers.** It tells of a future awaited by believers, not by all and sundry. The **sign** is given **to unbelievers,** so that they might believe what they see, but **prophecy** is given so they may accept what is said and bless the Lord. By **unbeliever** Paul means the Greek, and by **neophyte** he means the catechumen.[4] But in some passages the person whose faith is weak is called an **unbeliever.**

(3) Basil of Caesarea on verses 24-25

Let us return to our original point, that the Holy Spirit is completely indivisible and inseparable from the Father and the Son.[5] In the passage about the spiritual gift of tongues, Paul writes to the Corinthians: **But if all prophesy, and an unbeliever or outsider enters, he is convicted by all, he is called to account by all, the secrets of his heart are disclosed; and so, falling on his face, he will worship God and declare that God is really among you.** Prophecy, then, which operates by the gifts the Spirit distributes (1 Cor 14:1), makes it known that God is present in the prophets. Therefore, let those who contend against the Spirit decide what position they will assign to the Holy Spirit, whether it is more correct to rank him with God or to banish him to the created realm. Peter said to Sapphira, *How is it that you have agreed together to tempt the Holy Spirit? . . . You have not lied to men but to God* (Acts 5:9, 4).[6] This shows that sins against the Holy Spirit are the same as sins against God. From this one can learn that in every action the Holy Spirit is joined to, and inseparable from, the Father and the Son.

When God inspires *varieties of working* and the Lord *varieties of service* (1 Cor 12:4-6), the Holy Spirit is present along with them, distributing the gifts as he thinks best, according to the each person's merits (1 Cor 12:7-11). *Now there are varieties of gifts,* Paul says, *but the same Spirit; and there are varieties of service, but the same Lord; and there are varieties of working, but it is the same God who inspires them all in every one* (1 Cor 12:4-6). *All these are inspired by one and the same Spirit, who apportions to each one individually as he wills* (1 Cor 12:11). Now in this passage the apostle mentions the Spirit first, the Son second, and God the Father third, but it does not follow from this that in general their order should be reversed. Rather, Paul takes his point of departure from our experience. For when we receive the gifts, we encounter him who distributes them [the Spirit]. Then we

4. That is, a person undergoing instruction in preparation for baptism.
5. This discussion is taken from Basil's treatise *On the Holy Spirit,* in which he argues against a group called the Pneumatomachians ("fighters against the Spirit"), who had disputed that the Holy Spirit is fully divine. The debate about the Spirit is an extension of the controversy over the divinity of the Son. Compare Basil's comments on 1 Cor 2:10-12, cited above.
6. Basil has conflated Peter's rebuke of Sapphira in Acts 5:9 with the earlier rebuke of her husband Ananias in 5:4.

think of the one who sent him [the Son], after which our thoughts return to the source and cause of our blessings [the Father].

(4) John Chrysostom

Brethren, do not be children in your thinking; be babes in evil, but in thinking be mature. As is appropriate after his lengthy preparation and argument, Paul now speaks more strongly and gives harsh criticism. He uses an apt example, for little children show open-mouthed amazement at little things but are unfazed by very great things. So, since these men, because they had the gift of tongues, the ultimate gift, thought they had everything, Paul says, **do not be children.** That is, do not be foolish in matters where you ought to be wise, but be foolish and simple only when it comes to injustice, vanity, and arrogance. One who is a babe in evil is necessarily wise. For just as wisdom joined with wrongdoing would not be wisdom, so also simplicity joined with folly would not be simplicity. And as a simple person must flee folly, so a wise person must flee wickedness. Just as medicines that are unnecessarily bitter or sweet are ineffective, neither is simplicity or wisdom by itself a good thing. Therefore, Christ bids us to mix both together when he says, *Be wise as serpents and innocent as doves* (Matt 10:16). What does it mean to be a child in evil? Not even to know what evil is. This is how Paul wants them to be. That is why he said, *It is actually reported that there is immorality among you* (1 Cor 5:1). He did not say, "that immorality is practiced among you," but, *it is reported.* "You know the affair all too well," he says, "having heard about it." In fact he wanted them to be both men and children, the latter with respect to evil, the former with respect to wisdom. In this way, a man can still be a man even if he is also a little child. But if he does not become a child in regard to wickedness, he is not really a man. The person who does evil is not an adult, but a fool. . . .

Once again, someone might think that the gift of tongues is greater than prophecy. For if **tongues are a sign for unbelievers and prophecy for believers**, one might argue that what attracts strangers and makes them friends is greater than that which trains those who are already in the fold. What does Paul mean by this? There is nothing here that is difficult or unclear or contrary to what he said before. If we pay close attention, it is perfectly consistent. While prophecy is useful for both groups of people, speaking in tongues is not. . . . The believer does not need to see a sign; he requires only instruction and catechesis. You ask me: "How can you claim that Paul says prophecy is useful for both groups when he says that **prophecy is not for unbelievers but for believers**?" If you examine the text carefully, you will understand Paul's meaning. He does not say that prophecy is useless for unbelievers, but that it is not a **sign**, as tongues are, because it is obviously wasted on them. But neither are tongues of any use for unbelievers. Their only effect is to astound and disturb. A sign can be either good or bad. So the psalmist says, *Show me a sign,* and then adds, *of thy favor* (Ps 86:17); on the other hand, another psalm says, *I have been as a portent to many* (Ps 71:7),[7] that is, as a sign. . . .

---

7. In the context of Ps 71:7, "portent" indicates a sign of the wrath of God.

Therefore, what Paul means is this: prophecy is effective among both believers and unbelievers, but when unbelievers and fools hear a strange tongue, they receive no benefit and even mock the speakers as if they were madmen (Acts 2:13). It is only a **sign** for them, namely, something that perplexes them. But the sign was given so that those with understanding might profit from it. . . .

Prophecy is not merely a sign: it has value in leading unbelievers to faith and also benefits believers. If Paul does not say this right away, he explains it more clearly in what follows when he says: **he is convicted by all.** The whole verse reads: **But if all prophesy, and an unbeliever or an outsider enters, he is convicted by all, he is called to account by all, the secrets of his heart are disclosed; and so, falling on his face, he will worship God and declare that God is really among you.** It follows that prophecy is greater because it is effective among both groups and because it draws in those unbelievers who have no shame. Unbelievers experienced one kind of amazement when Peter rebuked Sapphira in a prophecy, and another when he spoke in tongues (Acts 5:9-11; 2:4-13). In the first case, they were all humbled, but when Paul was speaking in tongues, they regarded him as a madman. . . .

Paul says, **If, therefore, unbelievers or outsiders enter, they will say that you are mad**, just as the apostles themselves were suspected of being drunk. The people said, *They are filled with new wine* (Acts 2:13). But the fault does not lie with the sign so much as with the people's lack of understanding. That is why Paul specifies **outsiders and unbelievers**, to show that their judgment is due to ignorance of the faith and unbelief. As I have already said, he wanted to show that the gift of tongues was not to be criticized but rather regarded as not particularly beneficial. And he says this in order to restrain their eagerness and get them to seek an interpreter. Most of them were not concerned about this but instead were using the gift to show off and win admiration. So Paul draws them away from this by showing that their reputation was suffering because they were suspected of insanity.

Paul usually does this when he wants to deter people from a course of action: he shows that it is an impediment to the very thing they desire. You should do likewise. If you want to discourage some pleasure, show that it is painful. If you want to turn a person away from vanity, show that it involves dishonor. This is what Paul did. To wean the wealthy from their love of money, he says not only that wealth is harmful but also that it brings hardships. *Those who desire to be rich*, he says, *fall into temptation* (1 Tim 6:9). Since wealth is thought to bring release from trials and temptations, Paul demonstrates that the opposite of what the wealthy imagine is true.

Again, when others embraced the wisdom of nonbelievers (1 Cor 1:17-25), thinking that they could establish their teaching by using it, Paul shows that this gives no help to the cross but even nullifies it. The Corinthians were constantly bringing their lawsuits before outsiders (6:1-4) and thought it poor form to appear before their own members, since they believed that the pagans were more intelligent. Paul shows that using the courts of outsiders is actually disgraceful. They constantly ate meat offered to idols so as to demonstrate their perfected knowledge (8:1-13). Paul shows that not knowing how to accommodate to one's neighbors is a sign of imperfect knowledge. So also in this passage, when they were all excited about the gift of tongues and infatuated with the distinction it gave them, he shows that this is the very thing that brings them shame, for it not only deprives them of honor but also brings them under the suspicion of insanity.

Of course, Paul does not say this right out. Only after saying many other things to make it easier to accept does he introduce a quite unexpected point. This is another of his rhetorical principles. A person who wants to shake an established opinion and secure its opposite cannot set forth his position at once since he would be a laughingstock to those who hold the contrary view. Few would accept it at the outset. Instead, he must first use other arguments to thoroughly undermine the position of his opponents, and only after this try to persuade his hearers to accept the opposite of what they formerly believed.

At any rate, Paul does this when he is discussing marriage (1 Cor 7:1-40). Since many were turning to marriage as offering the easy course, he wanted to show that it was easier not to marry. Yet had he said this at the beginning, he would not have made it easy to accept. By making his point only after much argument and at the proper time, he achieves his intended effect on his audience. He also uses this strategy when discussing virginity. Only after discussing the topic at length does he say, *I would spare you* (1 Cor 7:28) and *I want you to be free from anxieties* (1 Cor 7:32).

1 Corinthians 14:26-33a

26What then, brethren? When you come together, each one has a hymn, a lesson, a revelation, a tongue, or an interpretation. Let all things be done for edification. 27If any speak in a tongue, let there be only two or at most three, and each in turn; and let one interpret. 28But if there is no one to interpret, let each of them keep silence in church and speak to himself and to God. 29Let two or three prophets speak, and let the others weigh what is said. 30If a revelation is made to another sitting by, let the first be silent. 31For you can all prophesy one by one, so that all may learn and all be encouraged; 32and the spirits of prophets are subject to prophets. 33a For God is not a God of confusion but of peace.

(1) Severian of Gabala

When Paul says **let him keep silent**, he teaches that a person who is speaking in the Holy Spirit speaks when he wishes and is silent when he wishes. This is the practice of the prophets, but not of those possessed by an unclean spirit. The latter speak when they do not wish and utter things they do not understand.

(2) Origen

I have often asked myself why it was that when there were prophets of God and also false prophets, the false prophets enjoyed greater favor with the kings than the prophets did, and yet the books of the false prophets were not written down and preserved among the people, while the books of the prophets, who were condemned and hated and endured well-known sufferings, were published and are held in honor. What was the reason for this? Taking my lead from the apostle, I would suggest that just as the spiritual gift of prophesying was present among the people, so also was the gift of distinguishing true prophets from false.

(3) John Chrysostom

For you can all prophesy one by one, so that all may learn and all be encouraged; and the spirits of prophets are subject to prophets. For God is not a God of confusion but of peace. You see, in its first days the Church was like heaven: the Spirit led the people in everything, moving and inspiring each of those who presided. But now we possess only tokens of these gifts. Even now, two or three of us speak by turns, and when one begins another remains quiet. Yet these are only signs and reminders of those earlier gifts. This is why, whenever we begin to speak, the people reply, "And with your Spirit," to indicate the way preachers used to speak of old, inspired not by their own wisdom but by the Spirit. . . .

Shall I tell you of another treasured inheritance the Church has lost? In former times, all would gather and sing psalms together. We still do this. But at that time there was *one heart and soul* among them all (Acts 4:32). Now such harmony cannot be found even in an individual soul; instead fierce war reigns everywhere. Today the one who presides over the church says a prayer for the peace of all, as if he were entering his father's house. But while there is much talk of this peace, the thing itself is nowhere to be found. Formerly, private houses were churches, but now the church is like a private house, or, rather, it is worse than any house. At least in other houses one can find things all in order. . . . But in the church there is great commotion and confusion, no different from a tavern. There is such laughing and uproar, people shout as if they were in a bathhouse or a marketplace, and everyone makes a racket. . . . The church is not a barbershop, or a perfume store, or a workshop in the marketplace. It is a place of angels and archangels, a kingdom of God, heaven itself. . . . If you don't believe me, just look at this table[8] and remember for whose sake it is standing there and for what reason. Consider who comes forth to this place, and feel a thrill of anticipation. Indeed, when someone sees the throne of a king, his spirits are raised as he awaits the king's coming. The same applies to you: don't wait until that awesome day to tremble; rise up. Even before you see the veil lifted and the chorus of angels advancing, ascend to heaven itself. . . .

The church is not a place for conversation but for teaching. But at present it is no different from the market; if it is not too audacious to say so, it is no different from the theater. The women assembling here adorn themselves more seductively than prostitutes who come to the theater. Hence they attract many licentious men, just as they do there. And if anyone wants to seduce a woman, no place, I suppose, appears to him more suitable than the church. And if anyone needs to buy something, the church seems better for

8. That is, the altar.

this than the marketplace. There are more conversations about such matters here than in the workshops. As for the trading of gossip, you can obverse this here more than in the market. . . .

There must always be one voice in the church since it is *one body* (1 Cor 12:12). For this reason only the reader speaks, and while he does so, even the bishop sits in silence. Only the chanter chants. If all join in, the voices come as if from a single mouth. And only the preacher is to preach. But when everyone is conversing about things many and sundry, why should we preachers vex you to no purpose? You all must assume that we are troubling you needlessly; otherwise you would not be talking about such irrelevant matters while we are discussing things of such magnitude.

1 Corinthians 14:33b-36

33bAs in all the churches of the saints, 34the women should keep silence in the churches. For they are not permitted to speak, but should be subordinate, as even the law says. 35If there is anything they desire to know, let them ask their husbands[9] at home. For it is shameful for a woman to speak in church. 36What! Did the word of God originate with you, or are you the only ones it has reached?

(1) Theodoret

Not only men but also women enjoyed the spiritual gift, as God announced beforehand through the prophet Joel: *I will pour out my spirit on all flesh; your sons and your daughters shall prophesy* (2:28). Thus Paul had to give rules about them as well.

(2) Origen

Realizing that all were speaking and had permission to speak if a revelation came to them (1 Cor 14:30), Paul says, **The women should keep silence in the churches.** Now the disciples of the women, who had become pupils of Priscilla and Maximilla,[10] not of Christ the bridegroom (see Eph 5:31-32), did not heed this commandment. Let us consider what they say fairly as we reply to their specious arguments. Indeed, let us consider their arguments fairly. They say that there were four daughters of Philip the evangelist, and that they prophesied (Acts 21:9). "And," they assert, "if these women prophesied, why is not appropriate for our prophetesses to prophesy?" Our response is as follows: First, if you say "our women prophesied," show us the signs of prophecy in them. Second, even if the daughters of Philip prophesied, they did not speak in the churches — we do not find this

---

9. Or "men." Origen construes the word in this more general sense; see the commentary below.

10. Female prophets who were associated with the second-century movement called Montanism. See also comments on 1 Cor 11:4-5 above.

reported in the Acts of the Apostles. Nor is this found in the Old Testament. Yes, it is attested that Deborah was a prophetess, and *Miriam the sister of Aaron, taking a drum, led off the women*[11] (Exod 15:20). But you will not find it written that Deborah publicly addressed the people, as Jeremiah and Isaiah did. Nor will you find that Huldah, who was a prophetess, spoke to the people, but only to a one person who came to her (2 Kings 22:14-20). "But," they will say, "the Gospel also mentions *Anna a prophetess, the daughter of Phanuel, of the tribe of Asher*" (Luke 2:36). Yes, but she did not speak in the church. Therefore, even if we should concede, on the basis of a prophetic sign, that a woman is a prophetess, still she is **not permitted to speak** in church. When Miriam the prophetess spoke, it was to certain women whom she was leading. **For it is shameful for a woman to speak in church.** And *I permit no woman to teach or to have authority over men* (1 Tim 2:12).

I will demonstrate this same point from another text. . . . *The older women should be reverent in behavior. . . . They are to be teachers of what is good, and so train the young women* (Tit 2:3). They are not to have general license to teach. Women are to be *teachers of what is good* but not so that men sit and listen to them, as if there were a lack of men capable of presenting the word of God.

If there is anything they desire to know, let them ask their men[12] **at home.** It seems to me that **their men** does not refer only to their husbands. For otherwise virgins will either speak in church or will have no one to teach them, and the same would be true of widows. But might **their men** perhaps indicate also their brothers, for example, and their kinsmen and sons? To put this simply: let a woman ask questions of **her own man**, understanding "man" as a generic noun, in contrast to "woman." **For it is shameful for a woman to speak in church**, whatever she might say, even if she should speak marvelous and holy words.

(3) John Chrysostom on verse 36

Did the word of God originate with you, or are you the only ones it has reached? At this point Paul introduces into the discussion the other churches that were keeping this rule, both in order to stop the confusion arising from the Corinthians' novel practices and to make his message more acceptable. For the same reason he says earlier, *I sent to you Timothy, my beloved child, to remind you of my ways in Christ, as I teach them everywhere in every church* (1 Cor 4:17). Again he says, *For God is not a God of confusion but of peace, as in all the churches of the saints* (1 Cor 14:33). . . . So he says here again, **Did the word of God originate with you, or are you the only ones it has reached?** That is, you are neither the first nor the only believers; instead the whole world believes. Writing to the Colossians about the gospel, he says, *as indeed in the whole world it is bearing fruit and growing* (Col 1:6). And he expresses the same idea in a different way when he wants to give his hearers encouragement, as when he says that their faith was first and manifest to all. In his Letter

11. Origen quotes and abridges the Septuagint, which differs from the Hebrew text. He does not mention that the verse calls Miriam a "prophetess."
12. RSV: "husbands."

to the Thessalonians he says, *The word of the Lord sounded forth from you in Macedonia and Achaia, [and] your faith in God has gone forth everywhere* (1 Thess 1:8). Again, he says to the Romans, *Your faith is proclaimed in all the world* (Rom 1:8). Both points serve to encourage and motivate Paul's hearers: that they are praised by others and that others share their belief. . . . Do you see how Paul uses weighty arguments to make them contrite? He introduces the law, he shows how disgraceful their whole situation is, and he sets before them the example of the rest of the churches.

1 Corinthians 14:37-40

37If any one thinks that he is a prophet, or spiritual, he should acknowledge that what I am writing to you is a command of the Lord. 38If any one does not recognize this, he is not recognized. 39So, my brethren, earnestly desire to prophesy, and do not forbid speaking in tongues; 40but all things should be done decently and in order.

(1) Ambrosiaster

If any one thinks that he is a prophet, or spiritual, he should acknowledge that what I am writing to you is a command of the Lord. In saying this Paul assails the false apostles already mentioned[13] by whom the Corinthians had been corrupted. Motivated by a desire to please men, they taught not divine but earthly things. Therefore, Paul says here that he is transmitting nothing of his own but rather the Lord's teaching, so that those he is trying to persuade should be won over for God, not for men. It is in this confidence that he constantly preaches, having a clear conscience because he wants to please God, not men. Thus he does not flatter sinners so that they sin all the more but warns them to cease.

If any one does not recognize this, he is not recognized. Properly so, since he who does not recognize that what the apostle says is of the Lord will not be recognized by the Lord on the day of judgment, when the Lord says, *Truly, I say to you, I do not know you* (Matt 25:12).

So, my brethren, earnestly desire to prophesy. Although he accuses and rebukes and chastises them about many things because they had departed from his teaching, nevertheless he calls them "brothers." . . . In order to console them after his criticisms, he calls them "brothers" and urges them to desire prophecy earnestly, so that they might become stronger through constant discussion and explanation of the law of God and learn that the preaching of the false prophets is wrong. . . . **But all things should be done decently and in order,** that is, according to the order mentioned earlier. A thing is done **decently** when it is done in peace and with discipline.

---

13. See 1 Cor 3:12-15 and compare 2 Cor 11:13.

1 Corinthians 15

This chapter, a concise summary of Paul's gospel (vv. 1-11) followed by the most detailed treatment in the New Testament of the general resurrection at the end of time, was of great interest to the fathers. It figured in debates about Christology and the nature of the afterlife, among other subjects. One early commentary is Tertullian's treatise defending the resurrection of the flesh against those who, like the Corinthians addressed by Paul, found it impossible to believe. Tertullian is especially concerned to explain verse 50, "Flesh and blood cannot inherit the kingdom of God." He gives several arguments to demonstrate that the flesh is included in the afterlife. His first argument, according to which "flesh" means sinful impulses, not the physical flesh, was facilitated by the Latin version of verse 49, which reads an imperative "let us bear the image of the heavenly man," instead of the indicative "we will bear" in the Greek text. In the fifth book of his refutation of Gnostic teachings, Irenaeus also gives much attention to verse 50. He sets it in the context of other passages from Paul's letters to show that the "flesh" that cannot inherit the kingdom of God is only that flesh which has not been animated by the Spirit. Origen argues a different point: he cites the verse to counter an attack on Christians for believing naively that the flesh will be raised without undergoing any change (see the comment on vv. 35-41). Augustine gives several possible interpretations of what the verse means.

Also much discussed was verse 28, which says that after Christ has defeated all the opposing powers, he will subject himself to God the Father, so that "God may be all in all." This verse was a favorite of Origen, who saw here a promise that ultimately all evil will be eradicated and all rational beings be restored to the contemplation of God. Gregory of Nyssa devoted a whole treatise to this one verse, in which he follows Origen in seeing here a promise that all will be saved. He also explores the verse's christological implications, arguing against those who held that Christ is subordinate to God the Father and not truly divine. John Chrysostom takes up this christological issue in his comments on verses 23-27, arguing that the "subjection" referred to here does not imply the Son's inferiority. Augustine did not agree with the universalism of Origen and Gregory of Nyssa, as his comments on the Adam/Christ typology of verses 21-22 indicate.

"That God may be all in all" (v. 28) was an inspired formulation that called forth some of the most profound commentary of any on 1 Corinthians. Augustine's description of God as the source of everything good and the ultimate satisfaction of all our desires is a particularly powerful example, as is Gregory of Nyssa's picture of God as the giver of all that is necessary for life. Another formulation that stimulated much reflection was Paul's paradoxical description of the resurrection

body as "a spiritual body" (v. 44). Origen describes the glory of this radically transformed body, arguing against those who denied that the body would figure in the future life and also against those who identified the "spiritual body" too closely with the present body. Paul uses the image of a seed that becomes a plant and the variety of heavenly and earthly bodies (vv. 35-41) to explain both the continuity and the discontinuity between the present body and the resurrection body. The fathers play on these images. John Chrysostom, for example, takes the various bodies Paul mentions to refer to different rewards and punishments, which gives him a starting point for moral exhortation. Augustine reflects on the image of the seed in an argument for the Christian hope.

Other themes taken up in patristic commentary on 1 Corinthians 15 include divine grace and the means of salvation. Augustine found verses 9-10 especially congenial because there Paul, the model Christian, attributes everything to divine grace. Augustine makes the text vivid by imagining a dialogue in which he poses questions to Paul and uses the words of the text as answers (on grace, see also Augustine's comments on vv. 54-58). John Chrysostom uses these same verses as the springboard for a sermon on humility. A common thread in the three excerpts from Gregory of Nyssa is his understanding of salvation as becoming incorporated into Christ, which is accomplished through imitation of his life, death, burial, and resurrection.

1 Corinthians 15:1-2

1Now I would remind you, brethren, in what terms I preached to you the gospel, which you received, in which you stand, 2by which you are saved, if you hold it fast — unless you believed in vain.

(1) John Chrysostom

Once he has finished teaching about spiritual gifts, Paul moves on to the most important subject of all, the matter of the resurrection. For the Corinthians had quite unsound views on this subject. . . . They were quarreling about the resurrection. Because this is the basis of all our hopes, the devil took a strong stand against it. At one moment he denied it altogether (see 15:12, 29, 31-32); in another he said that it had already taken place. Writing to Timothy, Paul calls such wicked teaching *gangrene* and singles out those who had introduced it: *Among them are Hymenaeus and Philetus, who have swerved from the truth by holding that the resurrection is past already. They are upsetting the faith of some* (2 Tim 2:17-18). These people said this some of the time, but at other times they denied that the body rises and claimed that resurrection means the purification of the soul. They were persuaded to say these things by that evil spirit who desires not only to overturn the resurrection but also to prove that all the things accomplished for our sakes are myths. For whenever people are persuaded that there is no resurrection of bodies, then the devil tries to persuade them little by little that Christ has not been raised. After this, proceeding methodically, Satan then tries to show that Christ did not come and did not do the things he did. Such is the devil's wicked work. This is why Paul also calls it *craftiness* (Eph 4:14), because Satan avoids showing his intention right away in order to escape detection; he wears a mask that disguises the nature

243

of his mischief. Like a shrewd enemy attacking a city's walls, he secretly undermines them from below so that their defenses may be breached and he can accomplish what he desires. For this reason the brilliant and distinguished Paul, who was always uncovering the devil's snares and hunting down his wicked traps, says, *We are not ignorant of his designs* (2 Cor 2:11). In the present text he also exposes the devil's plot and reveals his whole plan. He brings everything the devil wants to accomplish to light, and attacks each scheme in detail. . . .

By calling them **brothers** Paul is already laying an important foundation for his argument. We are **brothers** solely on account of the divine plan accomplished in the flesh of Christ. Thus Paul addresses them in this way to soothe and compliment them and at the same time remind them of their innumerable blessings. . . .

Do you see how he calls them as witnesses for what he is saying? He does not say, "which you heard," but **which you received**, as if asking them to return something entrusted to them. He indicates that they received it not in words alone but in deeds and signs and wonders, and that they must keep it safe. . . .

How can Paul say that those who are tottering **stand**? He conveniently feigns ignorance. He does something similar with the Galatians, but not in quite the same way. In their case it was not possible to feign ignorance, so he varies his strategy and says, *I have confidence in the Lord that you will take no other view than mine* (Gal 5:10). He does not say, "that you took no other view" since their error was open and acknowledged, but he expresses assurance about the future. This, however, was anything but certain. Paul does this in order to win them over more effectively. In our text, on the other hand, he feigns ignorance when he says, **in which you stand**. Next he mentions the benefit, **by which you are saved . . . in the terms I preached to you the gospel**. It follows that the instruction he is giving now is for clarification and explanation. He is saying, "You do not need to learn this doctrine, but to be reminded of it and corrected." . . .

Then, because he has stated, **in which you stand**, Paul wants to ensure that this formulation does not encourage laziness. So once again he frightens them by saying, **if you hold it fast — unless you believed in vain**. This indicates that their error strikes at the heart of things and that what is at stake is not matters of little consequence but the entire faith. In this verse he says this in a restrained way, but as he proceeds he warms to the task, bares his head, and shouts, *If Christ has not been raised, then our preaching is in vain and your faith is in vain . . . and you are still in your sins* (1 Cor 15:14, 17). But this is not how he expresses himself in these introductory remarks. Here it suited his purpose better to proceed gently and one step at a time.

1 Corinthians 15:3-7

3**For I delivered to you as of first importance what I also received, that Christ died for our sins in accordance with the Scriptures,** 4**that he was buried, that he was raised on the third day in accordance with the Scriptures,** 5**and that he appeared to Cephas, then to the twelve.** 6**Then he appeared to more than five hundred brethren at one time, most of whom are still alive, though some have fallen asleep.** 7**Then he appeared to James, then to all the apostles.**

(1) Cyril of Alexandria

Paul says that he **delivered** to them not simply whatever came into his mind without thought or examination, but the **gospel** that he **received**. For knowledge of it had been given to him by the one who became a man for our sake. The same Paul, speaking in another place about the gospel, says: *For I did not receive it from man, nor was I taught it, but it came through a revelation of Jesus Christ* (Gal 1:12). If, then, the one who delivers it has been taught by God, how can what he proclaims not be true, namely, that **Christ died for our sins in accordance with the Scriptures** (i.e., the Old and New Testaments)? For the witnesses to the death and resurrection of Christ are very numerous, removing any doubt that, on the one hand, Christ Jesus died in the flesh on our behalf, to *take away the sin of the world* (John 1:29), and, on the other, that **he was raised**, and that he trampled death, in order that we too might benefit. Further, in the present context Paul realizes that he has to say not only that **Christ died** but also that **he was buried**. For the death of Immanuel was truly confirmed and he was really placed in a tomb. But he came back to life, as I just said.

Now even though Christ is *the Word of God* (John 1:1), he completes his incarnation by dying in the flesh. By trampling on death he demonstrates clearly that he has a divine nature. But the Word who comes from God the Father brings back to life not the *temple* (cf. 1 Cor 6:19) of someone else, or the body of just anyone, but his very own body. It was in this body, we are told, that he died for our sake, to demonstrate further that the blessing of the resurrection happened for our sake. In him human nature as a whole tramples down death, and thus we are said to have been *buried with him* and to have been *raised with him* (Col 2:12) and to sit *in the heavenly places* (Eph 2:6). Therefore, Paul says that **he was raised in accordance with the Scriptures**, and **that he appeared** to the holy apostles, to some individually, as ones specially chosen, and then to a large group. *He appeared also to me, as to one untimely born* among the apostles (1 Cor 15:8). Paul shows great humility here in acknowledging that he *persecuted the church* and was called to be an apostle when Christ had mercy on him. He declares the great mystery of the resurrection (1 Cor 15:9-10), which was known both to the saints of old (for it had been foretold) and to those who had been chosen to be apostles and became *eyewitnesses and ministers of the word* (Luke 1:2).

(2) Gregory of Nyssa on verse 4

Now our descent into the water and triple immersion involve another mystery.[1] Our salvation is effected not so much by teaching and explanation as by the actions of the One who consented to share our human nature. By his actions he brought about life, so that

---

1. The context of this passage is a discussion of Christian baptism. Alluding to the phrase "on the third day" in 1 Cor 15:4, Gregory sees an analogy between the three days Christ spent under the earth and the three-fold formula used in baptism. Gregory's view that the believer must imitate the events of Christ's death, burial, and resurrection is also evident in his comments on 1 Cor 15:20-22, translated below.

through the flesh he assumed and deified everything akin to it might also be saved. Thus it was necessary that some way be devised so that there be a kinship and similarity between what the leader does and what his followers do. . . . Those being trained to handle weapons become acquainted with the soldier's art by watching the movements of trained soldiers, but if a man does not practice what he sees demonstrated, he will not learn this skill. In the same way all who are eager for the good must follow and imitate the One who led us to salvation by putting into practice the pattern he set forth. For it is impossible to arrive at the same end without traveling similar paths.

People who are lost in a bewildering labyrinth can escape its varied and deceptive turnings if they meet someone who knows the way and follow him. But without following a guide they could not escape. In a similar way, think of this life as a labyrinth from which human nature cannot extricate itself — unless we stick to the path taken by the One who entered it but escaped its confines. I use the labyrinth as a metaphor for the prison of death that confines the human race and from which there is no escape.

Now what have we observed in the case of the *pioneer of salvation* (Heb 2:10)? A death of **three days** and then a return to life. Therefore, something similar had to be devised for us. What, then, is this plan by which we too manage to imitate what Christ has done? Everything that has died finds its proper and fitting place in the earth, where it lies concealed. And earth and water are akin to each other as the only elements that are heavy, gravitate downward, and penetrate and mix with one another. Since, then, the initiator of our life died and was put in the ground in accordance with our common lot, our imitation of his death is represented through the element that is nearest to earth. Now after the *man from above* (1 Cor 15:47; John 3:31) took on death and was laid in the earth, he sprang back to life **on the third day**. In the same way everyone who is united to him in bodily nature fixes his gaze on the same deed — I mean his death — and has water poured over him instead of earth. He goes down into the water three times in imitation of the grace of the resurrection, which happened **on the third day**.

1 Corinthians 15:8-11

8**Last of all, as to one untimely born, he appeared also to me.** 9**For I am the least of the apostles, unfit to be called an apostle, because I persecuted the church of God.** 10**But by the grace of God I am what I am, and his grace toward me was not in vain. On the contrary, I worked harder than any of them, though it was not I, but the grace of God which is with me.** 11**Whether then it was I or they, so we preach and so you believed.**

(1) John Chrysostom

See how Paul is bursting with words of humility. For he says, **Last of all . . . he appeared also to me.** For this reason he does not put himself on a par with the others. And he adds, **as to one untimely born,** and that he is **the least of the apostles** and did not deserve the title "apostle." Not content with this, he gives reasons and proofs in order to make his humility not seem a matter of words alone: he was **as one untimely born** because he was the last to see Jesus; he was unworthy to be called an apostle because he persecuted the Church. Someone who has ordinary humility does not do this. A person who provides reasons why he should be humble speaks entirely from a contrite heart. This is why Paul mentions these same things in another text, saying, *I thank him who has given me strength for this, Christ . . . because he judged me faithful by appointing me to his service, though I formerly blasphemed and persecuted and insulted him* (1 Tim 1:12-13). But why does Paul also speak highly of himself, when he says, **I worked harder than any of them**? He saw that the situation required it. If he had not said this, but had only disparaged himself, how could he have the confidence to name himself as witness and count himself with the rest, saying, **Whether then it was I or they, so we preach** (1 Cor 15:11)? A witness must be trustworthy and a person of consequence. . . .

As we hear these words, let us parade our weaknesses and keep silent about our successes. And if we are forced to mention our successes, let us do so with humility and attribute everything to the **grace of God**. This is what Paul does: he condemns everything about his previous way of life and attributes everything subsequent to **grace** so as to use every means to demonstrate God's compassion: God saved someone like Paul and, once he had saved him, made him what he was. So, let no one living a wicked life despair; let no one living virtuously be overconfident. Let the former be fearful and the latter zealous. The careless and lethargic will not be able to maintain a virtuous life, and the zealous will not lack the means to escape evil. The blessed patriarch David is an example of both of these points. When he grew a little lethargic, he fell into great sin (2 Sam 11:2, 4). But when his conscience pricked him, he returned to his former greatness. You see, both despair and false security are equally bad. For despair quickly pulls a person down from the heights of heaven, and false security prevents the fallen from rising.

(2) Augustine

Now many people are kept from becoming strong because they believe that they are already strong. Only a person who realizes that he is weak in himself can derive strength from God. . . . Paul was weak enough to say, **I am unfit to be called an apostle, because I persecuted the church of God.** Then why, Paul, are you an apostle? **By the grace of God I am what I am.** I am not worthy, but **by the grace of God I am what I am.** Paul was weak; you, Lord, made him perfect. And now since he is what he is **by the grace of God**, see what follows: **and his grace toward me was not in vain, but I worked harder than any of them.** Take care, dear Paul, that you do not lose by arrogance what you earned by weakness. **I am unfit to be called an apostle**: well said, well said. **By his grace I am what I am, and his grace toward me was not in vain**: all very good. But **I worked harder than any of them** — this sounds as if you have begun to attribute to yourself what just now you ascribed to God. But see what follows: **though it was not I, but the grace of God which is with me.** Well done, weak man. You will be most highly exalted because you are not ungrateful. You are the same Paul, small in yourself[2] but great in the Lord. You are the one who asked the Lord three times that the *thorn in the flesh*, the *messenger of Satan* (2 Cor 12:7), by whom you were being buffeted, should be removed from you. What did God say to you? What did you hear when you asked this? *My grace is sufficient for you. For my power is made perfect in weakness* (2 Cor 12:9). Paul was indeed weakened, but you, Lord, strengthened him.[3]

1 Corinthians 15:12-19

12Now if Christ is preached as raised from the dead, how can some of you say that there is no resurrection of the dead? 13But if there is no resurrection of the dead, then Christ has not been raised; 14if Christ has not been raised, then our preaching is in vain and your faith is in vain. 15We are even found to be misrepresenting God, because we testified of God that he raised Christ, whom he did not raise if it is true that the dead are not raised. 16For if the dead are not raised, then Christ has not been raised. 17If Christ has not been raised, your faith is futile and you are still in your sins. 18Then those also who have fallen asleep in Christ have perished. 19If for this life only we have hoped in Christ, we are of all men most to be pitied.

(1) Tertullian

What is Paul trying to demonstrate by these words? You will answer: "the resurrection of the dead," which was being denied. Is it clear that he wishes us to be convinced by the example of the Lord's resurrection? "That is clear," you will reply. Is an example founded upon likeness or unlikeness? "Assuredly upon likeness," you will say. But how did Christ rise, in the flesh or not? If you read that he *died and was buried in accordance with the Scriptures* (1 Cor 15:3-4), certainly it was in the flesh, and you will grant that he was brought to life again in the flesh. The very thing that sank down in death, which lay in the grave, also arose, not so much Christ in the flesh as the flesh in Christ. Therefore, if we are to rise according to the example of Christ, who rose in the flesh, we will not be doing so if we do not also rise in the flesh.

(2) John Chrysostom

If Christ has not been raised, your faith is futile. Paul always presents the resurrection of Christ as a clear and accepted fact, and by means of this stronger point he makes assertions that seem weaker and more dubious convincing and certain. **You are still in your sins.** Paul's argument is this. If Christ was not raised, then he did not die. And if he did

---

2. *Paulus* (Latin) means "little."

3. Augustine's sermons contain many similar discussions of this text, often cast in the form of a dialogue with Paul; see, for example, *Sermons* 293B, 293C, 299B.5, 299C.4, 306B.2, and 333.5-6.

not die, then he did not take away sin, for his death brings the removal of sin. *Behold,* it says, *the Lamb of God, who takes away the sin of the world* (John 1:29). How does he take it away? By death. For this reason he was called the Lamb, as one who was sacrificed. But if he did not rise, then he was not sacrificed. And if he was not sacrificed, then sin has not been removed. And if it has not been removed, you are in sin. And if you are in sin, we have preached in vain. And if we have preached in vain, you have believed in vain. Furthermore, death continues to be immortal if Christ has not risen. For if he is held captive by death and did not *loose its pangs* (Acts 2:24), how did he free everyone else when he himself is still bound?

1 Corinthians 15:20-22

20But in fact Christ has been raised from the dead, the first fruits of those who have fallen asleep. 21For as by a man came death, by a man has come also the resurrection of the dead. 22For as in Adam all die, so also in Christ shall all be made alive.

(1) Origen

When the heretics claim to have the faith of the Church and yet ridicule it as "the faith of fools," they deny it in practice if not in word when they say that there is no resurrection, as the Church believes. Here is how we must answer them, using this passage from the apostle as well as countless others. Did Christ rise from the dead, or not? On this point even the heretics agree: Christ rose from the dead, and he is the *first-born from the dead* (Col 1:18). Now a firstborn child does not have a different nature from other children; it follows that Christ's resurrection must be like the resurrection of the others. For example, Reuben, the son of Jacob, is the firstborn (Gen 49:3-27), and his brothers have the same nature he does. It is not the case that Reuben has one nature and Simon and Levi and the rest have another. The same is true for others called *first-born.* So if Jesus is the *first-born from the dead,* he must be raised in the same way as the other dead who are raised. If Christ had a body (1 Cor 15:49), then his resurrection also was bodily; hence he partook of food, as we are told in the Gospel of John (John 21:9-13). Now the heretics suppose that the resurrection of those who believe in Christ is different from that of Christ himself, but they cannot explain in what sense Jesus is the *first-born from the dead* (Col 1:18). For *if we have been united with him in the death of Christ, we shall certainly be united with him in his resurrection* (Rom 6:5). And if their view is correct, how can Paul use the words: *who will change our lowly body to be like his glorious body* (Phil 3:21)? . . .

Now if **Christ has been raised,** the resurrection of the dead is demonstrated through him — unless we refuse to believe because we think the very idea of resurrection to be impossible, forgetting who it is that makes the promise. Among impossible things, which is (so to speak) more impossible: for the body to be brought to life or for heaven, the sun, and the rest of creation to be made from what does not exist? Consider also the origin of man, how he comes into existence. A human seed is shown to you, and someone says: "This seed will be a man, it will be transformed, it will become bones, flesh, sinews, and veins. It will walk. From this small and paltry seed, a man will be raised up on the earth and make use of his faculties." Would we not call someone a fool for making such claims if we had no experience of them? I make this comparison to commend the idea of resurrection, so that you will believe it more fervently because you have faith in God's perfection. Just as the seed stands in relation to the existing body — I mean the present body that we all share, which begets children and is the means for saying and doing just things — just so is this present body in relation to that future body. *Unless a grain of wheat falls into the earth and dies, it remains alone; but if it falls into the earth and dies* (John 12:24) and decays, from the decay of that grain of wheat comes a crop a hundred times greater (Matt 13:8). For Paul says that your body is a seed of the body that will rise. Hear his words: *What is sown is perishable, what is raised is imperishable. It is sown in dishonor, it is raised in glory. It is sown in weakness, it is raised in power. It is sown a physical body, it is raised a spiritual body* (1 Cor 15:42-44).

(2) Augustine

The scribe asks Jesus, *Who is my neighbor?* (Luke 10:29). Everyone is your neighbor. Aren't we all descended from two parents? Animals of every kind are neighbors to each other, dove to dove, leopard to leopard, asp to asp. And is man not neighbor to man? Recall how the creation was formed. God spoke, the waters brought forth. They brought forth swimming creatures, great whales, fish, birds, and things of that kind. Did all birds come from one bird? All vultures from one vulture? All doves from one dove? . . . Not at all: the earth produced whole species together. But when it came to the making of mankind, the earth did not bring it forth. A single progenitor — not two, father and mother — was made for us. . . . Instead, from the single father came the single mother. The one parent had no source but God, and the second was created from the first.

Consider our race: we have all issued from one font. And because that font has changed to bitterness, we have all become wild olive trees instead of domesticated olive trees (Rom 11:17). Grace also came. One man brought forth progeny destined to sin and death, but they are a single race, all neighbors to one another, not only similar but also related by birth. But in answer to that one man came another. In answer to him who scattered came the One who gathers together. In answer to the one who kills comes One who makes alive. For **as in Adam all die, so also in Christ shall all be made alive.** And just as everyone born from Adam dies, so in Christ everyone who believes is made alive.

By one man we are all saved, from the oldest to the youngest; by one man we are saved. *For there is one God, and there is one mediator between God and men, the man Christ Jesus* (1 Tim 2:5). **By one man came death, and by one man came the resurrection of the dead. As in Adam all die, so also in Christ shall all be made alive.** All are in Adam and all are in Christ. At this point someone might come along and say to me, "How can it be **all**? Does it include those destined to be sent to Gehenna, who will be damned with the devil, who will be tormented by eternal flames? How can Paul say **all** twice?" Because no one comes to death except through Adam, and no one comes to life except through Christ. If there were someone else through whom we came to death, not everyone would die in Adam. If there were someone else through whom we come to life, not all would be made alive in Christ.

(3) Gregory of Nyssa

We claim that God[4] became involved in both of the changes to which our nature is subject, both the uniting of the soul with the body and its separation from the body. And because God has become mingled with each of them (I mean with the sensible and intellectual parts of the human mixture), through this ineffable and indescribable commingling he brought it about that what was once united (I mean soul and body) would remain forever unified. For even in his case, human nature came in due course to the separation of body and soul, and then he joined together again what had been separated with a kind of glue (I mean divine power), and he made what had been divided into an inseparable unity.

And this is what **resurrection** means: that the parts that were joined together and then separated are restored to an indissoluble union in which they are fused together. Thus the first grace given to humanity is recalled, and we return to eternal life,[5] after the evil that has become mixed into our human nature has flowed away in the dissolution of death. Just so does a liquid flow out and disappear when its container is shattered, since there is nothing to contain it. And just as **death** originated **through one man** and was then distributed to the whole human race, so the **resurrection** originated **through one man** and extended to the whole of humanity. Christ reunited with his own body the soul he had assumed, reunited it by virtue of his own power, a power that was mixed with each of these elements when they were first formed. In a similar way but on a more general level: by this act he combined the intellectual nature with the sensible, and from this beginning resurrection proceeds by orderly progression to its conclusion.[6] For since in the case of the **man** assumed by Christ[7] the soul returned again to the body after the two had been separated, so, in the same way, from a certain beginning the reuniting of what was divided extends by this power to the whole human race.

This is the mystery of God's plan concerning death and the mystery of the resurrection from the dead. God does not prevent the inevitable natural course by which death releases the soul from the body, but he brings them back together by the resurrection so that he himself becomes the meeting point of both of them, of death and of life.

4. Gregory is speaking of Christ, the divine Logos. The context of this excerpt is an explanation of the incarnation — how and why God could enter the human realm whose weakness is contrary to the divine nature.

5. Gregory refers to life in the Garden of Eden before the fall. See Genesis 2–3, especially 3:22.

6. That is, until all of humanity follows Christ into the resurrection life.

7. That is, the human nature of Christ.

1 Corinthians 15:23-27

₂₃But each in his own order: Christ the first fruits, then at his coming those who belong to Christ. ₂₄Then comes the end, when he delivers the kingdom to God the Father after destroying every rule and every authority and power. ₂₅For he must reign until he has put all his enemies under his feet. ₂₆The last enemy to be destroyed is death. ₂₇"For God has put all things in subjection under his feet" [Ps 8:6]. But when it says, "All things are put in subjection under him," it is plain that he is excepted who put all things under him.

(1) John Chrysostom

"For God has put all things in subjection under his feet" (Ps 8:6). . . . Up to this point Paul has not said that it was the Father who **put in subjection**. He said that it was Christ who destroys. For Paul says that he, that is, Christ, will **destroy every rule and every authority** (v. 24). And again, **For he must reign until he has put all his enemies under his feet** (v. 25). Why does Paul now speak of the Father? And this is not the only thing that seems difficult in this text. Another is Paul's very odd worry — indicated by his adding the corrective **he is excepted who put all things under him** — that someone might suspect that even the Father could perhaps be subjected to the Son! What could be more ridiculous than this? . . .

What, then, is Paul's intent, and how does he carry it out? He expresses himself one way when he is talking about Christ's divine nature in itself and another way when he comes to God's sojourn on earth. For whenever he touches on the incarnation, he speaks boldly about all of Christ's humiliations, in the confidence that Christ's flesh is able to withstand all the humiliations he mentions. Let us see, then, whether in this text Paul's topic is the divine being in itself or whether his words about Christ refer to his sojourn on earth. But first, let me cite a passage where Paul does as I have indicated. . . . Writing to the Philippians, he says, *Though he was in the form of God, he did not count equality with God a thing to be grasped, but emptied himself, taking the form of a servant, being born in the likeness of men. And being found in human form he humbled himself and became obedient unto death, even death on a cross. Therefore God has highly exalted him* (Phil 2:6-9). Do you see how, when Paul discusses Christ's divine nature in itself, he says marvelous things — being in the form of God, being equal to the one who begot him — and assigns all these expressions to Christ; but when he tells you about the incarnate Christ, he speaks on a lower level? If you fail to distinguish these cases, you will think that what he says is clearly inconsistent. For if Christ was *equal to God,* how did God *exalt* his equal? And if he was *in the form of God,* how did God *bestow a name* on him (Phil 2:9)? He who bestows a gift gives it to one who lacks it, and he who exalts lifts up one who was lowly before. On this interpretation, the Son would be incomplete and deficient before he received the exaltation and the name, and countless other bizarre conclusions would follow. But if you attribute such things to God's sojourn on earth, you will not go wrong. . . .

At this point it is also necessary to point out that Paul's topic was the general resurrection, something that seemed impossible and utterly incredible. He was writing to people in Corinth, where there were many philosophers who were always mocking such assertions. For though the philosophers were at odds on everything else, on this point they all agreed: that there is no resurrection. Since Paul was arguing for an idea they considered incredible and absurd, both because of their innate prejudice and because of the difficulty of the subject, Paul first wants to argue the possibility, and he does this on the basis of the resurrection of Christ. Once he has demonstrated Christ's resurrection from the prophets, the eyewitnesses, and fellow believers (1 Cor 15:3-11) and has made them agree that to deny it would be a *reductio ad absurdum* (1 Cor 15:12-18), he next establishes the resurrection of humanity: *For if the dead are not raised, then Christ has not been raised* (1 Cor 15:16). Since he has already thoroughly refuted such a supposition, he now turns to another argument, calling Christ *the first fruits* (1 Cor 15:20) and showing that he destroys **every rule and every authority and power** and also **death** as the last enemy (vv. 24, 26). "How, then, will death be destroyed," Paul asks, "if it does not first yield up the bodies it possesses?"

Paul makes powerful claims about the only-begotten Son — that he **hands over the kingdom** (v. 24), that is, that he himself accomplishes the things described here; that it is he who wins the war and **puts everything under his feet**. After this, to correct the skepticism of many of his hearers, he adds: **For he must reign until he has put all his enemies under his feet** (v. 25). Paul does not use the word **until** in order to indicate that the kingdom will end but rather to make his message more credible and give them greater confidence. What he means is this: "When you hear that Christ will destroy **every rule and every authority and power**, and all the devil's legions, and the multitude of unbelievers, and the tyranny of **death**, and all other evils, do not fear that his power will become exhausted. He must reign **until** he does all this." Paul does not mean that after doing all this Christ will no longer reign; his point is that even if this has not yet been accomplished, it certainly will be. Indeed, Christ's kingdom is not cut off, for his rule and power remain **until** he sets everything right. . . .

It is the height of impiety to suspect the Son of weakness, and Paul corrects any such notion when he says that **he will put all his enemies under his feet**. It is even more irreverent to suppose that the Father is inferior to the Son. And so, in similar fashion, Paul completely refutes such an idea. Notice how he does this. He is not content to say, **he is excepted who put all things under him**, but adds, **it is plain that**. "For even if this point is granted," he says, "still I want to establish it beyond all doubt." And to show you that this is why Paul says these things, let me ask you this question: "Is the Son to undergo another subjection at that future time?" Would this not be very odd and unworthy of God? For the greatest subjection and obedience was this, that the Son, who was God, took the form of a servant (Phil 2:7). How, then, could he be subjected in the future? Don't you see that Paul added these words in order to eliminate such a ridiculous idea and did so in an appropriately indirect way? The Son obeys in a way befitting one who is both Son and God, not like a human being, but acting freely and with full authority. Otherwise how could he be enthroned with the Father (Rev 22:1, 3)? How could he raise those whom he wishes to raise up just as the Father does (John 5:21)? How could all that belongs to the Father be his and all that belongs to him be the Father's (John

16:15)? These passages show us that Christ has an authority perfectly matched to that of his Father.

(2) Augustine on verse 26

To what extent does anyone become good in the present life? I will tell you. However much progress someone makes, he will still be battling against desires, battling against lusts.[8] However much progress he makes — even someone who is at peace with those in his household and those outside of it — he will have war within himself, he will be waging a contest within himself and will do so constantly under the eye of him who is ready to help him in his struggles and to crown him when he is victorious. But one day all the dissension and discord within us will pass away; for our weakness and quarreling is not some alien nature but the weakness that has become habitual to us. We were not that way in paradise. Nothing in us fought against us. But we sent away the One with whom we were at peace and began to be at war with ourselves, which is the source of our misery (Genesis 3). It is a marvelous thing in this life if we are not overcome in this war — and it is not possible for us to be without a foe in this life. But there will be another life, our final life, when we have no enemy without or within. For **the last enemy to be destroyed is death.** Then we shall live in blessedness in the house of God and praise him forever and ever. Amen.

1 Corinthians 15:28

28**When all things are subjected to him, then the Son himself will also be subjected to him who put all things under him, that God may be all in all.**

(1) Origen

We must examine more carefully what it will be like when blessedness is perfect and when the world will end, when God is said not only to be **in all** but to be **all**. Let us ask what this **all** is that God will be **in all** things.

For my part I think God is said to be **all in all** because even in individual beings he is everything. He will be **all** in individual beings in the sense that when the rational mind is freed from the dregs of vice and has the clouds of wickedness swept away, whatever it can feel or understand or think will be God; henceforth, besides God it will feel nothing, think nothing, see nothing, possess nothing, all its movements will be God, and thus to it **God** will be **all**. There will no longer be discernment of good and evil, for evil will be no-

---

8. Augustine here applies the battle imagery of 1 Cor 15:24-27 to the Christian life, viewed as an inescapable battle against evil that will end only in the future life, with the destruction of death. Compare the commentary of Gregory of Nyssa on v. 28, translated below.

where to be found (for **God** is **all** to the creature, and there is no evil in him). And one who lives always in the good and for whom **God** is **all** will no longer desire to eat from the tree of the knowledge of good and evil (Gen 3:1-7). The restoration of the end to the beginning and the bringing of the final state back to its origins will restore that state which rational nature possessed when it felt no need to eat from the tree of the knowledge of good and evil. When all sense of evil is removed and swept away to produce wholeness and purity, only the **God** who is *one* and *good* (Matt 19:17) will be **all** to the creature. It is not in a number of creatures, whether many or few, that God will be **all**, but **in all**, since there will be no death, no sting of death, and no evil at all. Thus truly **God** will be **all in all**.

(2) John Chrysostom

What does it mean, **that God may be all in all**? That everything may depend on him, that no one will suppose that there are two principles, neither one of which rules the other, or that there is another sovereignty separate from God's sovereignty. When the Son's enemies lie under his feet, since there is no disagreement but rather perfect harmony between the Son who has subjected them and his Father, then the Father himself will be **all in all**. Some argue that Paul says this to indicate [only] that all evil will be removed, that everything will yield to God and nothing will resist or sin. When sin no longer exists, it is clear that **God** is **all in all**. But if our bodies are not raised, how can this be true? **Death**, the worst **enemy** of all, is still there, and he has had his way. Someone might reply, "Not so, since they will no longer sin at that time." Yet what does that amount to? Paul is not talking in this text about the death of the soul but of the body. How, then, is Death annulled? Victory entails taking back what Death has seized and now holds. If bodies are always going to be held in the earth, then Death's tyranny endures because he holds those bodies and there is no other body in which his defeat may be accomplished. But if what Paul describes takes place, as indeed it will, this will make clear the glorious victory of the God who is able to raise bodies that are under Death's control.

(3) Augustine on verse 28

Can anything be so completely **all** as the one who made **all**? But all things would not have been made by him unless he had known them. Who would dare to say, "God made this but did not know it"? He made what he knew. Before he made his creatures he held them. But he held them in wondrous fashion, far beyond the way he made them: he made them temporal and transitory, but held them in the manner of a craftsman, who holds inwardly what he makes outwardly. In God, therefore, all things are excellent, immortal, unfailing, and permanent, and **God** himself is **all in all**. But to his saints he will be **all in all**. So he himself is sufficient, he suffices all alone. About him is said, "Show us the Father, and we shall be satisfied." But Christ said, *Have I been with you so long, and yet you do not know me? He who has seen me has seen the Father* (John 14:8-9). God — Father,

Son, and Holy Spirit — is **all**, and so it is quite proper that he alone is sufficient for us. If we are avaricious, let us love him. If we desire wealth, he alone can satisfy us, he of whom it is said, *Who satisfies your desire with good things* (Ps 103:5).

That God may be all in all. What is the meaning of **all**? He will be for you whatever you looked for here on earth, whatever you considered important. What did you want here, what did you love? To eat and drink? He himself will be food for you; he himself will be drink. What did you want here? A fragile and transient bodily health? He himself will be immortality for you. What did you look for here? Wealth? Greedy man, what will satisfy you if God himself does not? Well, what did you love? Glory, honors? God will be your glory. To him we now say, *My glory, and the lifter of my head* (Ps 3:3). He has already lifted up my head. Our *head* is Christ (Eph 5:23). But why feel surprise? For the other members of the body will be exalted, along with the head; then **God** will be **all in all**. This is our belief, our hope. But when we arrive, we will have it as a possession. Then it will be a matter of sight, not faith. When we arrive, we will have it as a possession. Then it will be fact, not hope. What of love? Can it be that it exists now but will not exist then? If we love now when we believe but do not see, what will our love be when we see and possess? So there will be love, but perfected. As the apostle says, *Faith, hope, and love, these three; but the greatest of these is love* (1 Cor 13:13). If we have love and foster it in ourselves, let us persevere confidently in him with his help and say: *Who shall separate us from the love of Christ?* — until he himself in his mercy brings our love to perfection. *Shall tribulation, or distress, or famine, or nakedness, or sword? For thy sake we are being killed all the day long; we are regarded as sheep to be slaughtered.* Who can endure, who can tolerate all of this? *But in all this we are conquerors.* How? *Through him who loved us* (Rom 8:35-37). Therefore, *If God is for us, who is against us?* (Rom 8:31).

(4) Gregory of Nyssa

When all things are subjected to him, then the Son himself will also be subjected to him who put all things under him, that God may be all in all. I first will set forth in my own words the general sense of what Paul has written; then I will quote the words of the apostle in which the ideas I have presented are stated. What, then, is the point the divine apostle is making in this text? That at some time evil will recede into nonbeing and be completely eradicated and that God's perfect goodness will enfold in itself every rational being, and nothing God has made will be cast out of his kingdom. This will come to be when all the evil mixed in with what exists has been consumed, like dross, by the purifying fire, and everything God has made will be as it was at the beginning, before evil entered the world.

Paul says that this happens in the following way: the pure, perfect divinity of the Only Son entered into human nature, which is subject to death. The human Christ came to be from the mingling of the divine with human nature as a whole, a kind of *first fruits* (1 Cor 15:20) from the one *lump of dough* (Rom 11:15; 1 Cor 5:7), and by this all humanity was attached to the godhead. In him all evil was completely obliterated since he did not

256

commit sin — as the prophet says, *nor was there any deceit in his mouth* (Isa 53:9) — and in him death, which follows sin, was also totally wiped out since there is no other cause of death except sin (Rom 5:12). Thus both the obliteration of evil and the dissolution of death had their beginning in him.

Then an *order* (1 Cor 15:23) and sequence were imposed on what was to happen. As they turned away from the good, inevitably some departed further from what was at first and some not so far. And so each one, according to his own merit and ability, will follow after the one who goes before him. Therefore, we follow the man Christ, who became the *first fruits* of our nature (1 Cor 15:23) when he received divinity in himself; he is also *the first fruits of those who have fallen asleep* (1 Cor 15:20) and *the first-born from the dead* (Col 1:18), because he dissolved the bonds of death. So first comes this man, who was wholly free from sin and had abolished the power of death in himself and destroyed *all its rule and authority and power* (1 Cor 15:24). Then at the time of his coming there will follow closely behind this *first fruits* anyone who is like Paul, who imitated Christ as closely as possible (1 Cor 11:1) in his rejection of evil.

Next, I suppose, might come Timothy, who imitated his teacher as closely as possible (1 Cor 4:17), or someone else like him, and then would come all those who follow their predecessors, each in order — even as they have fallen away little by little from the good — until we reach those in whom there is more evil than good. In this way the sequence of those moving toward the good starts with those who are less evil and moves to those who are more so, until the procession of goodness reaches the extreme of evil and obliterates it. This is the final stage of our hope, when nothing contrary to the good will remain and the divine life will permeate all, first by destroying sin, which as I said before is the source of death's rule over humanity (Rom 5:12-14, 17), and then wholly obliterating death.

When every evil *authority and power* (1 Cor 15:24) in us is destroyed and no passion has any power over our nature, then it necessarily follows — since there is no other ruler — that everything will be **subject** to the ruler of all. Subjection to God means the complete removal of evil. Therefore, when by imitation of Christ the *first fruits* we all become separated from evil, then the whole of our nature's *lump of dough* (1 Cor 5:6), mixed with the *first fruits* and having become *one body* (1 Cor 12:12-20) in its closeness to Christ, will accept the rulership of the one who alone is good (Matt 19:17). Thus, when the whole *body* of our nature has been folded into the pure divine nature, what Paul calls the subjection of the Son will take place through us. This subjection, which is accomplished in his *body*, is attributed to Christ because he works in us the grace of subjection.

This, then, is the general sense of what the great Paul teaches in this passage, as we understand it. It is now time to set down the apostle's words: **For as in Adam all die, so also in Christ shall all be made alive. But each in his own order: Christ the first fruits, then at his coming those who belong to Christ. Then comes the end, when he delivers the kingdom to God the Father after destroying every rule and every authority and power. For he must reign until he has put all his enemies under his feet. The last enemy to be destroyed is death. "For God has put all things in subjection under his feet" [Ps 8:6]. But when it says, "All things are put in subjection under him," it is plain that he is excepted who put all things under him. When all things are subjected to him, then the Son himself will also be subjected to him who put all things under him, that God may be all in all** (1 Cor 15:22-28).

At the end of the passage Paul clearly teaches that evil will have no existence when he says that **God** is **in all**, becoming **all** to each one. It is clear that when no evil is to be found in anything that exists, then it will be true that **God** is **in all**. For it would be impossible for God to be present in evil. Thus either God will not be **in all** — if any evil remains in what exists — or, if we are correct in believing that he will be truly **in all**, then it follows from this that evil will have no existence. For there is no place for God in evil.

That **God** becomes **all** for everything that exists shows the simple and uniform character of the life for which we hope. For by teaching that **God** will be for us **all** those things that are necessary in the present life, Paul shows that when this comes to be, our life will no longer be sustained by many and various things, as it is now. Rather, by analogy with the things considered necessary in the present life, each of us will receive **all** these things, but understood in a more divine sense. Thus God will be food for us since it is fitting that God be eaten (John 6:53); he will be drink, and likewise clothing and shelter, air, space, wealth, enjoyment, beauty, health, strength, wisdom, glory, happiness, and everything else considered good and which our nature needs. We understand all these words in a higher sense that befits God. From this we learn that the person who is in God has all things in having him (1 Cor 3:21). For having God is the same as being united with God.

But no one can be united with him without becoming *one body* with him, as Paul puts it (Eph 3:6). All of us, joined together through participation in the one body of Christ, become his *one body* (1 Cor 12:12). Therefore, when the good pervades everything, then the whole of Christ's *body* will be subject to the power that gives life. Thus the subjection of this body of his is called the **subjection** of the **Son**, who has become united with his own body, which is the Church. So the apostle says to the Colossians, in these exact words: *Now I rejoice in my sufferings . . . and in my flesh I complete what is lacking in Christ's afflictions for the sake of his body, that is, the church, of which I became a minister according to the divine office* (Col 1:24; see also Eph 5:23). And to the church in Corinth he says: *Now you are the body of Christ and individually members of it* (1 Cor 12:27). And Paul entrusts this teaching to the Ephesians in an even clearer way, when he says: *Rather, speaking the truth in love, we are to grow up in every way into him who is the head, into Christ, from whom the whole body, joined and knit together by every joint with which it is supplied, when each part is working properly, makes bodily growth and upbuilds itself in love* (Eph 4:15-16). So Christ builds himself up through those who are constantly being *added* to the faith.[9] And Christ will stop building himself up when the growth and perfection of his body reaches its proper *measure* (Eph 4:13), and the body is no longer in need of this building up. This will happen when all are built *upon the foundation of the prophets and the apostles* (Eph 2:20) and all have been *added* to the faith, when, as the apostle says, *we all attain to the unity of the faith and of the knowledge of the Son of God, to mature manhood, to the measure of the stature of the fullness of Christ* (Eph 4:13).

Christ then, as head, is gradually building up his body through those who are constantly being added, and he *joins* and *knits* them all together (Eph 4:16) so that they fulfill the functions for which the *measure* (Eph 4:13) of each one's activity naturally suits him.

9. See Acts 2:47: "And the Lord added to their number day by day those who were being saved." See also Acts 5:14.

In this way a person becomes, in proportion to his faith, a hand, a foot, an eye, an ear, or any other of the things that complete the body. By doing these things, Christ builds up his body, as Scripture says (Eph 4:12-13). From this it should be clear that by being **in all** Christ receives into himself all those who are united to him through *fellowship in the body* (1 Cor 10:16), and he makes them all members of his own body, so that there are *many members* but *one body* (1 Cor 12:12). Christ, then, who has united us to himself and become one with us — becoming one with us **in all** things — makes **all** that we possess his own. And the primary good we can possess is subjection to God, when all creation becomes harmonious and *every knee bows, in heaven and on earth and under the earth, and every tongue confesses that Jesus Christ is Lord* (Phil 2:10-11). When all creation has become *one body* and all are united with each other in him through obedience, then Christ speaks of the subjection of his *body* to the Father as the subjection of himself. . . .

And since everything that comes to be in him (John 1:4) is saved, and since subjection means salvation, just as the psalm leads us to suppose,[10] what the apostle teaches us to believe in the present passage is consistent with this, namely, that outside the company of those who are being saved, nothing at all will remain. This is shown in the present passage by the destruction of death and the subjection of the Son, because the two things, the nonexistence of death and the entrance of all into life, are simultaneous. The Lord is life (John 1:4), and through him, as the apostle teaches, his whole body receives access to his Father (Eph 2:18), *when he delivers the rule* over us *to God the Father* (1 Cor 15:24). His body, as I have said many times, is humanity as a whole, with which he has been united. And this is why Paul called the Lord the *mediator between God and men* (1 Tim 2:5). For the one who is in the Father (John 1:1) and came to be in men (John 1:14) performs his mediation by uniting all men with himself and, through himself, with the Father. That is what the Lord says in the Gospel, addressing himself to the Father: *even as thou, Father, art in me, and I in thee, that they also may be in us* (John 17:21).

*   *   *

In the case of those who are called enemies (1 Cor 15:24-28) salvation is clearly designated by the word "subjection." This is proved by how Paul in this part of the letter distinguishes two different senses of the word "enemy." For he says that some of the enemies will become subject, while others will be destroyed. Now the one who is by nature an enemy, that is, *death*, will be *destroyed* (1 Cor 15:26), as will the *rule and authority and power* (1 Cor 15:24) of sin that accompanies death. But those called "enemies" of God in another sense, who have deserted the kingdom of God for that of sin, will be **made subject**. Paul mentions this second group in the verse from Romans: *if while we were enemies we were reconciled to God by the death of his Son* (Rom 5:10). Here he calls "reconciliation" what he called "subjection" in the text from Corinthians, expressing with both words the same idea, namely, salvation. For just as subjection leads to salvation, so Paul says in the other passage, *now that we are reconciled, we shall be saved by his life* (Rom 5:10).

10. Ps 61:2 (LXX), which Gregory discusses at beginning of this treatise. It reads: "Will not my soul be subjected to God?"

Now *enemies* like this, Paul says, will become **subject** to God the Father, but *death* and its *rule* will no longer exist. This is shown by the phrase *will be destroyed* (1 Cor 15:25-26). From this it is clear that the rule of evil will be entirely done away with, but that those called "enemies of God" because of their disobedience (see Rom 5:10; Eph 2:1-13) will become "friends of the Lord" through obedience, when they obey the one who says: *So we are ambassadors for Christ, God making his appeal through us. We beseech you on behalf of Christ, be reconciled to God* (2 Cor 5:20). And according to the promise given in the Gospel, when they have been reconciled they are no longer counted by the Lord as his *servants* but as his *friends* (John 15:14-15).

But as to the verse *For he must reign until he has put all his enemies under his feet* (1 Cor 15:25), we must, it seems to me, take it in a way befitting God[11] and understand "reigning" to mean excelling in battle. For the one who is mighty in battle (Ps 24:8) stops excelling in warfare when everything opposed to the good is destroyed and he gathers up his entire *kingdom* and brings it to *God the Father* (15:26), after he has united **all** (15:28) to himself. Now Christ's *delivering the kingdom to the Father* (15:24) means the same as that he, *through whom we have access* to the Father (Eph 2:18), brings **all** to the Father. Therefore, when all those who were once enemies have become a *footstool under the feet* of God (Ps 110:1) — in that we receive a footprint of the divine in ourselves — and when death has been destroyed (for when no one dies, death will have no existence), and when all of us have been subjected, then, as Paul tells us, the Son who lives in us **will be subjected**. This subjection is not to be understood as the humiliation of a slave, but rather as receiving kingship and immortality and blessedness. It is Christ who in himself brings what is good in us to perfection and works in us what is pleasing to him.

This is our understanding of Paul's great wisdom, as it is contained in this passage, insofar as we are able to comprehend it, to the limit of our capacities. We have aimed to show that the proponents of heretical teachings have not paid attention to the apostle's purpose, which I have been concerned to examine in this discussion. If what I have achieved is sufficient for you, may the credit be rendered to God. But if you think that something is lacking, I shall be glad to receive what is missing, if you show it to me from the Scriptures, and if the Holy Spirit, through our prayers, reveals what is hidden.

1 Corinthians 15:29-34

29Otherwise, what do people mean by being baptized on behalf of the dead? If the dead are not raised at all, why are people baptized on their behalf? 30Why am I in peril every hour? 31I protest, brethren, by my pride in you which I have in Christ Jesus our Lord, I die every day! 32What do I gain if, humanly speaking, I fought with beasts at Ephesus? If the dead are not raised, "Let us eat and drink, for tomorrow we die." 33Do not be deceived: "Bad company ruins good morals." 34Come to your right mind, and sin no more. For some have no knowledge of God. I say this to your shame.

11. Not in the sense in which Arius and his followers took this verse, as a proof that Christ was subordinate to the Father and that his kingdom was not eternal.

(1) Tertullian on verse 29

Moreover, if some people are **baptized on behalf of the dead**, we must see whether this practice is reasonable. Plainly Paul shows that they had instituted it because they assumed that baptism leads to the hope of the flesh's resurrection, even if done vicariously. Yet if resurrection is not resurrection of the body, it would have no connection with bodily baptism. Why, Paul asks, are they baptized if the dead do not rise, that is, if bodies that are baptized do not rise? For the soul is sanctified not by washing but by its confession of faith.

(2) John Chrysostom

Whenever we are about to baptize, we proclaim the sacred and awe-inspiring words of the Creed, its teachings revealed from heaven, and at the end we bid each one say, "I believe in the resurrection of the dead," and on the basis of this faith we are baptized. After making this profession along with the others, we then descend into the font of those holy waters. Paul, reminding the Corinthians of this, says, **If the dead are not raised at all, why are you baptized on their behalf?** — that is, for their bodies. This was the basis for your baptism, that you believe in the resurrection of the dead body, that it does not remain dead. . . . Indeed, to be baptized by sinking down and rising again is a symbol of the descent into hell and the ascent from there. That is why Paul calls baptism a burial, saying: *We were buried therefore with him by baptism into death* (Rom 6:4). In this way he makes the future event (I mean the resurrection of bodies) more believable. The removal of sins is a much greater thing than the resurrection of the body. . . .

I protest, brethren, by my pride in you which I have in Christ Jesus our Lord, I die every day! By this **pride** he means their advancement. He has showed that the perils he endured were many, but not wishing to appear to be complaining about them, he says, "Not only do I not lament my condition, I even boast in suffering these things on your behalf." He says he is doubly proud, both in being endangered for their sakes and in seeing their progress. Then he does what is customary for him: since he has uttered great boasts, he ascribes both works to Christ.

But how can he **die every day**? By being eager and prepared for death. And why does he say this? Again, with this too he is proving what he says about the resurrection of the dead. For who, he says, would choose to endure so many deaths if there is no resurrection or life after this? . . .

What do I gain if, humanly speaking, I fought with beasts at Ephesus? He says all this, not because he had no benefit from his suffering, but because of the weakness of the majority. He wished to fix firmly in them the truth about the resurrection. It was not because he himself was running for a reward: doing what seemed good to God was return enough for him. So also when he says, *If for this life only we have hoped in Christ, we are of all men most to be pitied* (1 Cor 15:19), he has a similar motivation. He is condescending to their weakness in order to shake their doubts about the resurrection when he appeals to their fear of such a miserable life. But the great reward is this, to please Christ in every way. Apart from any other return, the greatest recompense is to place oneself at risk for his sake.

(3) Augustine

Those who love food and drink, who pursue them, who think this life is the only one and do not hope for another, who either do not pray to God or pray to him only for these things, who find talk of diligence tiresome — such persons must feel great sadness when they hear us saying these things. They want to eat and drink, for tomorrow they die. How I wish they truly thought that they were going to die tomorrow! For who is so crazy and wrongheaded, who is so hostile to his own soul, as not to reflect, when he is going to die the next day, that everything for which he has worked is over? For Scripture says, *On that very day his plans perish* (Ps 146:4). If men take care, with their death day approaching, to make a will for the sake of those they leave behind, how much more should they have a care for their own souls? A man thinks of those he leaves behind: Does he have no thought for the one who is leaving all this behind? Consider this: your children will have what you lay aside, and you will have nothing! All your thought is expended on how travelers coming after you shall pass through life, not on the destination to which their traveling will take them.

How I wish, therefore, that they truly thought about death! Now when funerals are being conducted, people think of death and say, "Poor fellow! He was walking around yesterday well enough," or "I saw him a week ago, and he said thus and so to me; man amounts to nothing." They mutter these sentiments. Perhaps when the deceased is being mourned, when the funeral is being prepared, when the procession is being arranged, when the body is brought out of the house, is on its way, is being lowered into the ground, this kind of talk is rife. But once the deceased is buried, thoughts like these are buried with him. The preoccupations that kill us return. A man forgets whom he has buried, and though he is himself bound to depart, he thinks about success, though he is doomed to die. He returns to fraud, robbery, perjury, drunkenness, the countless pleasures of the body, pleasures of which it is not enough to say that they will perish when they have been used up — rather, they are perishing in the very act of being enjoyed. Worst of all, from the burial of a dead man he makes a case for burying his heart and says, **Let us eat and drink, for tomorrow we die.** . . .

As I started to say, let us take a look at this question because of those who mutter in the ears of the weak, **Let us eat and drink, for tomorrow we die.** They say, "No one has risen from there: from the time when my grandfather was laid to rest, or my great-grandfather, or my father, I have heard no one's voice; no one's voice have I heard." Answer him, Christians, if you really are Christians — unless perhaps you wish to get drunk with the multitude and are therefore ashamed to answer your corrupters. You have a reply to make. But you are tossed about by desire for pleasures and you want to be sucked down and buried alive by them. The desire for drunkenness rises up and like a wave washes over the soul, a wave pushed on by the breath of the tempter. . . .

All my words, brethren, are intended to equip you in case people say that the dead do not rise (1 Cor 15:12). You remember that I said all the necessary things that God had deigned to show me and that I made my testimony on the basis of the natural world and everyday examples; I spoke about the omnipotence of God, for whom nothing is difficult: just as he was able to create something that once did not exist, so he is able to restore what once existed; I spoke about our Lord and Savior Jesus Christ, who we agree rose from the dead. . . . Therefore let the tongues of those who say, **Let us eat and drink, for tomorrow we die** fall silent. Reply at once, "Let us fast and pray, for tomorrow we die."

1 Corinthians 15:35-41

35But some one will ask, "How are the dead raised? With what kind of body do they come?" 36You foolish man! What you sow does not come to life unless it dies. 37And what you sow is not the body which is to be, but a bare kernel, perhaps of wheat or of some other grain. 38But God gives it a body as he has chosen, and to each kind of seed its own body. 39For not all flesh is alike, but there is one kind for men, another for animals, another for birds, and another for fish. 40There are celestial bodies and there are terrestrial bodies; but the glory of the celestial is one, and the glory of the terrestrial is another. 41There is one glory of the sun, and another glory of the moon, and another glory of the stars; for star differs from star in glory.

(1) Origen

Let us examine Celsus's next statements addressed to us:[12] "Furthermore, are your teachings not absurd? On the one hand you yearn for the body and hope that this very body will rise again as if you possessed nothing better or more valuable than this, but on the other hand you consign it to punishments as if it had no value. But it is not worth our time to discuss this point with those who believe as you do, people who are so entwined in the body. These are the same people who in other respects are uncultured, unclean, and infected with mindless sedition. But I am ready to discuss this matter with those who hope with God's help to possess the soul or the mind for all time, whether they prefer to call it 'spiritual,' or 'a holy and blessed intellectual spirit,' or a 'living soul,' or 'an incorruptible offspring of the divine and bodiless nature that comes from beyond the heavens,' or whatever other name they like to give it."

Neither we nor the holy Scriptures say that those who died long ago will rise up and live, flesh and all, without this flesh undergoing any change for the better. Celsus maligns us when he claims that we do. Many Scriptures speak about resurrection in a way that is

---

12. Origen is responding to an anti-Christian work called *The True Doctrine*, written by the Platonic philosopher Celsus around the year 248. This work is lost and known only through Origen's quotations from it.

worthy of God, but for the present it is enough to cite the words of Paul from his First Letter to the Corinthians, where he says: **But some one will ask, "How are the dead raised? With what kind of body do they come?" You foolish man! What you sow does not come to life unless it dies. And what you sow is not the body which is to be, but a bare kernel, perhaps of wheat or of some other grain. But God gives it a body as he has chosen, and to each kind of seed its own body.** Notice how Paul says here that it is **not the body which is to be** that is sown; he says instead that from what is sown and put naked in the ground a kind of resurrection happens when **God gives to each kind of seed its own body.**

From seed put in the ground in some cases an ear of corn is raised up, in others a tree, as in the case of the mustard plant (Matt 13:31-32), or an even larger tree, as in the case of the olive pit or another fruit. **God** then **gives to each a body as he has chosen.** Just as in the case of seeds that are sown, so also for those who are "sown" in dying and at the proper time take up from what has been sown a **body** — the body with which God clothes each one in accordance with his worth. Scripture teaches us in many passages the difference between what is "sown" and what is "raised" from it. It says: *What is sown is perishable, what is raised is imperishable. It is sown in dishonor, it is raised in glory. It is sown in weakness, it is raised in power. It is sown a physical body, it is raised a spiritual body* (1 Cor 15:42-44).

Let anyone who is able understand also what Paul means when he says: *As was the man of dust, so are those who are of the dust; and as is the man of heaven, so are those who are of heaven. Just as we have borne the image of the man of dust, let us also bear*[13] *the image of the man of heaven* (15:48-49). Now the apostle wants to conceal the things that cannot be uttered here (2 Cor 12:4) and that are not suited for simpler believers or for a general audience of those being brought through faith to higher things. Nonetheless, in what follows, out of a concern that we not misunderstand his words, after he says *let us also bear the image of the man of heaven,* he is compelled to add: *I tell you this, brethren: flesh and blood cannot inherit the kingdom of God, nor does the perishable inherit the imperishable* (15:50). And then, knowing well that there was a secret and mysterious sense to this teaching, he adds the following, as befits one who leaves for his followers a written record of what he has thought and said: *Lo! I tell you a mystery* (15:51), a term he customarily uses to indicate the deeper and more mysterious teachings that are appropriately hidden from the many. . . .

Therefore [contrary to what Celsus says],[14] our hope is not a hope "of worms," nor does the soul long for "the body that has rotted." To be sure, the soul needs a body for the sake of moving from place to place. But a soul that has cultivated wisdom — following the text *The mouth of the righteous will practice wisdom* (Ps 37:30) — this soul understands the difference between the earthly *dwelling,* doomed to destruction, where our *tent* is, and the tent in which those who are righteous *sigh, being weighed down* (2 Cor

---

13. Origen's text reads the hortatory subjunctive of this verb (which stands for the imperative), not the future indicative.

14. Here Origen uses two phrases from allegations of Celsus that he quotes at greater length in 5.14. Celsus, making fun of the Christian hope for resurrection of the body, had said that only worms would want to be raised in the same body after it has rotted.

5:4). It is not that they wish to put off the tent *but to be further clothed,* so that from this putting on *what is mortal may be swallowed up by life* (2 Cor 5:4-5).

(2) John Chrysostom

And what you sow is not the body which is to be, but a bare kernel, perhaps of wheat or of some other grain. Yet the heretics, understanding none of this, pounce on us and say, "One body falls and another rises. How, then, is that a resurrection? For the resurrection is of what has fallen. Where is the astounding and unexpected victory over death if one thing falls and another rises? On that showing it will be plain that death has not given back what he took captive." But on this interpretation how would Paul's illustration fit the context? It is not that one essence is sown and another rises, but the same one rises in a better condition. Otherwise, Christ, as the *first fruits* of those who rise (1 Cor 15:20), would not have been revived in the same body. But on your view, he would have cast one body aside, although there was nothing sinful about it, and taken up another. Where did this other come from? If the first body is from the virgin, where is the second one from? Don't you see what absurdity this line of reasoning entails? Why did Christ show the imprints of the nails (John 20:19-28)? Was it not to show that this same body was nailed to a stake and rose again? And what is the sign of Jonah supposed to mean to him? Surely it is not that one Jonah was swallowed up and another came forth on the land. And why did Christ say, *Destroy this temple, and in three days I will raise it up* (John 2:19)? The body that was destroyed is clearly the one he raised. That is why the Evangelist adds, *But he spoke of the temple of his body* (John 2:21). Why, then, does Paul say, **What you sow is not the body which is to be** — that is, not an ear of corn? Well, in one sense they are the same and in another not. They are the same in that the essence is the same. They are different in that the mature corn is better. Although the essence remains the same, its glory is greater and the same thing rises in newness. . . .

There is one glory of the sun, and another glory of the moon, and another glory of the stars; for star differs from star in glory.** Since Paul has established the doctrine of the resurrection, he goes on to show that even though the resurrection is singular, there will be a great difference in glory. For the present he divides everything into two groups, heavenly things and earthly things. That bodies rise he showed by speaking of the kernel of wheat (v. 37); in the present verse he is showing that all will not have the same glory. Just as disbelief in the resurrection makes people lazy, so they become indifferent if they think everyone will get the same reward. Hence Paul sets both groups straight: he has already corrected the first in the preceding verses, and now he begins to address the second. Having made a twofold classification, the righteous and sinners, he then divides these two into several subcategories, showing that neither the righteous and sinners will get the same things nor will all the righteous or all the sinners receive the same rewards. He makes the first and primary distinction between the righteous and sinners when he says, **There are celestial bodies and there are terrestrial bodies** (v. 40). The earthly bodies, he implies, are sinners; the celestial bodies the righteous. Then he adds a further distinction, between one sinner and another, when he says: **For not all flesh is alike, but there is one** kind for . . . animals, another for birds, and another for fish (v. 39). All will have bodies, but some are more worthy and others less, and similarly in their manner of life and their very constitution. . . . [**There is one glory of the sun, and another glory of the moon, and another glory of the stars.**] Now what do we learn from this? That even if all the righteous will be in the kingdom, not all will enjoy the same benefits; and if all sinners will be in hell, all will not endure the same things. That is why Paul adds, *So is it with the resurrection of the dead* (1 Cor 15:42).

(3) Augustine

But some one will ask, "How are the dead raised? With what kind of body do they come?" (v. 35). You are made sad by the burial of your loved one because you do not immediately hear his voice. He used to live but is dead. He used to eat but eats no more. He used to have sensation but now does not: he has no part in the joys and delights of the living. Would you mourn for the seed while you were plowing? Suppose there were someone so ignorant of the world that when the seed was being carried out to the fields and put in the earth and buried in the furrow, he had so little knowledge of what was shortly to come that he mourned for the wheat because he remembered the summer. He thinks to himself, "This grain, which has just been buried — how much work did it cost us to harvest, transport, thresh, clean, and store it in the barn! We saw its beauty, and we congratulated ourselves. Now it is taken away from our sight. I see the land plowed up, but neither in the barn nor here before me do I see the grain." . . . What would those who know the truth say to him if ignorance of the facts caused him to mourn? "Do not be sad. What we have buried is certainly not in the barn and not in our hands. We will come to this field, and you will be delighted to see the beauty of the crop where you now weep for the bare furrowed land." The one who knew what was going to come forth from the grain would rejoice in the act of plowing, and the foolish and incredulous one — or (to speak more accurately) the one had no experience of this — would perhaps grieve at first but would go away consoled, trusting the man of experience and sharing his hope for the harvest to come.

Now harvests are regularly seen every year, but the one final harvest of the human race will spring up at the end of the age. It cannot now be shown to our eyes; but we have been given an experience of it in one principal "grain." The Lord himself says, *If a grain remains thus and is not put to death, it remains alone* (John 12:24). He speaks of his own death and makes plain that there is to be a resurrection of those multitudes who believe in him. The precedent has to do with a single grain, but this precedent is such as to call forth the faith of all who wish to be grains. Yet the whole creation also speaks of resurrection — if we are not too deaf to hear. From this we ought to guess what God is going to do once at the end of time since we see so many similar things every day. The resurrection of Christians will occur once, but the sleep and waking of living things is a daily occurrence. Sleep is like death, waking is like resurrection. So, on the basis of a thing that happens every day, believe in that which will happen once. In the course of every month the moon is born, waxes, is full, wanes, is spent, and is renewed. What happens to the moon every month happens once for all time at the resurrection, even as what happens to sleepers every day happens to the moon every month. Why do the leaves depart, why do they return? . . . The year comes back in due season: shall men, made in the image of God, perish utterly once they die? . . .

I don't want you to raise your usual objection: "The body of a person dead and buried does not remain whole; if it did, I would believe it could rise." So would you say that only the Egyptians believe in the resurrection since they diligently care for the bodies of the dead? It is their custom to dry out corpses and make them the color of bronze. So would people who hold your views — being ignorant of the hidden recesses of nature where everything is securely preserved for the Creator even when it is withdrawn from our mortal senses — maintain that only the Egyptians do well to believe in the resurrection, while the hopes of Christians are in doubt?

Often when tombs are opened or laid bare — they may have gotten too old or there may have been some pious reason to open them — it is found that the bodies have decayed, and men whose pleasure is in bodily appearance sigh and groan and say in their hearts, "Can this dust ever become beautiful, will it be restored to life and to the daylight? When will this be? When can I hope to see anything that is alive rise from this dust?" You who say this can at least see the dust in the tomb. Consider your own lifetime — let's say you are thirty or fifty years old or even more. In the grave there is at least the dust. But fifty years ago, what were you? Where were you? The bodies of all of us, speaker and listeners alike, will be dust within a few years. But a few years ago they were not even dust. Shall he who could make what once was not be unable to restore what already is?

Now then, brethren, let no one ask with wrongheaded cleverness what sort of shape bodies will have in the resurrection of the dead, how tall they will stand, what kind of motion or gait they will have. It is enough for you to know that your flesh will rise in the same form as that in which our Lord appeared, the form of a human being. . . .

If you ask what kind of life the resurrected will have, what human being could give an account? It will be the life of the angels. . . . But if the life of the angels is kept secret, we should ask no further questions. Otherwise we may wander around and never reach what we are looking for but only something we have imagined for ourselves. . . . Keep walking on the way: you will arrive at your home country if you don't leave the way. So hold fast to Christ, brethren, hold fast to the faith, hold fast to the way. It will lead you to what you cannot now see. . . .

You will ask, "How do the angels live?" It is enough for you to know that they live a life not subject to decay. It is easier to tell you what that life lacks than what it has. . . . There will be no marrying wives in order to have children since there is no death there. There will be no growing up because there is no growing old either. There will be no replenishing of the body because there is no lack to replenish. There will be no occupation we do not choose because we will lack nothing. . . .

It will be a perpetual sabbath. In the temporal sphere the sabbath is celebrated by the Jews, but we understand it as eternity. There will be inexpressible peace, peace impossible to describe. . . . Toward this peace we travel, for it we are spiritually reborn. For just as we are born in the flesh for toil, so we are spiritually reborn for rest, and Christ calls out: *Come to me, all who labor and are heavy laden, and I will give you rest* (Matt 11:28).

Here he feeds us, there he perfects us; here he promises, there he makes good; here he gives us hints, there the full expression. . . .

What, then, will be going on there? Have I not already said that I could more easily tell you what that life will lack than what it will have? This much I know, brethren, that we will not be asleep and inert. Sleep itself is given to the soul to supply what is lacking. It would be too much for our frail bodies if our mortal senses were continually awake: our frailness must be repaired by the slumbering of our senses so that it can endure this activity. Our waking from sleep is now what our renewal from death will one day be. Therefore, there will be no sleep there: where there is no death, there is also no image of death.

1 Corinthians 15:42-49

42So is it with the resurrection of the dead. What is sown is perishable, what is raised is imperishable. 43It is sown in dishonor, it is raised in glory. It is sown in weakness, it is raised in power. 44It is sown a natural body,[15] it is raised a spiritual body. If there is a natural body, there is also a spiritual body. 45Thus it is written, "The first man Adam became a living being" [Gen 2:7]; the last Adam became a life-giving spirit. 46But it is not the spiritual [body] which is first but the natural [body], and then the spiritual. 47The first man was from the earth, a man of dust; the second man is from heaven. 48As was the man of dust, so are those who are of the dust; and as is the man of heaven, so are those who are of heaven. 49Just as we have borne the image of the man of dust, we shall also bear[16] the image of the man of heaven.

(1) Tertullian

But certain persons argue that the **natural body** is the soul; they hope to show that its coming back to life has nothing to do with the flesh. . . . But it is the flesh about which the apostle is writing and speaking. It is sown as a **natural body** and raised as one that is **spiritual**. To help you understand the matter thus, Paul again lends you a hand by showing, on the authority of the same Scripture, that the first man Adam **became a living soul** (Gen 2:7).[17] Now if Adam was the first man, and the man was flesh before he was soul, it is beyond doubt that flesh **became a living soul**. And then having become **a living soul**, since he was already a body, he of course became a **natural body**. What would they[18] prefer the flesh to be called other than what it became through the soul, what it was not before the soul entered it, and what it will not be after the soul's departure except when it

15. The Greek phrase, a combination of the adjective "of the soul" *(psychikos)* and the word "body," is difficult to render in English. Other possible translations are "ensouled body," "physical body" (RSV), "body animated by soul." In translating 1 Cor 2:14 (see above) I have rendered the adjective *psychikos* as "unspiritual."

16. Variant reading: "let us bear"; this reading is presupposed in the comments on vv. 35-41 by Origen and John Chrysostom, translated above, and Tertullian's comments on v. 50, translated below.

17. RSV: "living being."

18. Tertullian refers here to those who denied the resurrection of the body.

rises again? For when it gets the soul back, it again becomes a **natural body**, so that it may become a **spiritual body**. Only something that existed before rises again. Therefore, the reason why it is fitting for the flesh to be called a **spiritual body** does not apply to the soul. For flesh was body before it was a **natural body**; it was only afterward, when it was animated, that it became a **natural body**. . . .

Therefore, just as previously the flesh became a **natural** [or **ensouled**] **body** when it received the soul, so afterward it becomes a **spiritual body** when it puts on the spirit. When the apostle sets out this ordering, he rightly makes this distinction also in the case of **Adam** and **Christ**, since they are the heads from which the distinction comes. And when he calls Christ the **last Adam**, you must recognize that he uses all his authority as a teacher to establish the resurrection of the flesh, not of the soul. For if the **first man Adam** was flesh, not soul, and then **became a living soul**, and the **last Adam**, Christ, is Adam because he is man and man because he is flesh, not because he is soul — and thus he adds, **it is not the spiritual which is first, but the soul-informed and then the spiritual** in regard to the two Adams — does he not seem to be distinguishing **natural body** and **spiritual body** in the same flesh since he previously built up this distinction in the two Adams, that is, two men? On the basis of the substance Christ and Adam share (i.e., their flesh, though also their soul; but it is in virtue of flesh that each is a man, for man was first flesh) on the basis of that substance they can be set in an order so that the one is called the first, the other the last man, that is, Adam.

(2) Origen on verses 42-44

But to approach this subject [the last judgment] in its proper order, it seems that I must first speak about the resurrection, so that we may know what it is that will come either to punishment or to rest and blessedness. I have discussed this subject at length in other books I have written about the resurrection, making plain what my views on it are.[19] But because of the subject of this present work it does not seem out of place to repeat a few things from those works, especially since some people, principally sectarians, take offense at the faith of the church and maintain that our beliefs about the resurrection are stupid and utterly without sense.[20]

To these sectarians I think we must reply as follows. If they admit that there is a resurrection of the dead, let them answer us: What is it that is dead? Is it not the body? Therefore, there will be a resurrection of the body. Then let them tell us this: Do they think we shall have the use of bodies or not? Since the apostle Paul says, **It is sown a natural body, it will be raised a spiritual body**, I do not think they can deny that the body rises or that we will have the use of bodies in the resurrection. What follows? If it is clear that we shall have the use of bodies, and if it is foretold that those bodies that have fallen

19. Only small fragments of the work to which Origen alludes survive.
20. Origen probably refers to Gnostics such as the followers of Valentinus, who had a spiritual view of the resurrection. In the next excerpt he argues against a very different front: Christians who think the resurrection body will be identical to the present body.

will rise again (for nothing that has not previously fallen can properly be said to rise again), no one can doubt that these bodies rise again so that we may put them on again (2 Cor 5:2-4) in the resurrection. The two statements cohere closely. For if bodies rise, clearly they will rise to clothe us, and if it is necessary for us to be in bodies (as it clearly is), we must be in no other bodies than our own. If it is true that these rise, and rise as **spiritual bodies**, it cannot be doubted that they are said to rise from the dead, their corruption discarded and their mortality laid aside. Otherwise it will seem pointless and redundant for someone to rise from the dead only to die once more. . . .

Our understanding is that the apostle, when he wanted to indicate how great was the difference among those who will rise in glory, that is, the saints, drew his comparison from celestial bodies, saying: *There is one glory of the sun, and another glory of the moon, and another glory of the stars* (1 Cor 15:41). And again when he wanted to show the difference among those who come to the resurrection without being purified in this life, that is, as sinners, he draws the comparison from earthly creatures, saying: *There is one flesh for birds and another for fish* (1 Cor 15:39). It is proper to compare saints to heavenly things and sinners to earthly things. Let this suffice as a reply to those who deny the resurrection of the dead, that is, the resurrection of bodies.

I now turn the discussion toward some of our own people who put forward a trivial and contemptible view of the resurrection of the body, because of their limited intelligence or because they are not skilled in explaining things. I ask them, how do they understand that the **natural body** will be changed thanks to the resurrection and become **spiritual**, and how do they think that **what is sown in weakness** is **raised in power**. How can it be that **what is sown in dishonor** is **raised in glory**, and how can **what is perishable** be brought to imperishability? If they believe the apostle that the body that rises in glory, power, and imperishability is already **spiritual**, it is absurd and contrary to the apostle's meaning to say that it will be embroiled in the passions of flesh and blood since the apostle says plainly, *Flesh and blood cannot inherit the kingdom of God, nor does the perishable inherit the imperishable* (1 Cor 15:50). And how do they interpret the passage where the apostle says, *We shall all be changed* (1 Cor 15:51)? We must expect that change will occur according to the example described above, and we clearly must look for a result worthy of divine grace. We believe that it will happen according to the apostle's model of a bare grain of wheat or some other plant sowed in the ground: to it God gives the body he wishes when the grain itself has died (1 Cor 15:37-38).

Now since we find mention in the apostle Paul of a **spiritual body**, let us consider as best we can what we should think about this. As far as our intellects can grasp it, the **spiritual body** ought to be of such a kind as to be the fit dwelling not only for all holy and sanctified souls but also for that whole creation which *will be set free from its bondage to decay* (Rom 8:21). About this body the apostle also says, *We have . . . a house not made with hands* (2 Cor 5:1), that is, in the dwelling places of the blessed. We may guess what great purity, what extreme fineness, and what glory this body will possess if we compare it with those bodies that, while being heavenly and splendid, are nevertheless *made with hands* and visible. Of the former it is said that it is *a house not made with hands, eternal in the heavens*. Since *the things that are seen are transient, but the things that are unseen are* *eternal* (2 Cor 4:18), all those bodies that we see in the heavens, which can be seen, are *made with hands* and are not eternal — all these are far surpassed by that body which cannot be seen and is not made with hands, but is eternal. From this comparison one may guess what beauty, what splendor, what brightness the **spiritual body** will have, and how true is the saying that *no eye has seen, nor ear heard, nor the heart of man conceived, what God has prepared for those who love him* (1 Cor 2:9). We must not doubt that these bodies of ours, by the will of God who made them thus, can be brought to such a state of fineness, purity, and splendor by the Creator as the nature of things and the merits of their rational nature demand. A last point: when the world required variety and diversity, matter offered itself, in all obedience, to the Creator, its lord and maker, through various forms and species, so that he might draw from it all the different forms of earthly and heavenly things. But now that all things have begun to hasten toward the goal that all may be one, just as the Father is one with the Son (John 17:21), we must understand, consistent with this, that there will no longer be diversity.

(3) Didymus of Alexandria on verses 42-44

At the resurrection we will not receive something other than the *perishable*, but precisely the perishable now changed into something *imperishable* (1 Cor 15:53-54) and the *natural*[21] now become *spiritual* (1 Cor 15:44). Consider what this means: what is other than the body is incorporeal. And if someone should say that what we will receive is other than the body, he does not know what he is talking about. For Paul has used the word "body" for both things: "It is sown a perishable body, it is raised an imperishable body. **It is sown a weak and dishonored body, it is raised a strong and glorious body, It is sown a natural body, it is raised a spiritual body.**"[22] Somehow, then, what is raised is both other than and the same as the body that perishes. When Paul says: **If there is a natural body, there is also a spiritual body,** he is referring to a difference in aspect. He says, **But it is not the spiritual which is first but the natural [body], and then the spiritual.** When Paul says **first** and **then**, this seems to refer to two different entities, but I understand this by way of an analogy: if I should say that a person is first an infant and then a child — not first a child but first an infant — I am of course not speaking of two subjects or two persons, but only one, in two different stages. The existence of two stages of life does not mean that as a person ages he takes on a different nature; rather, his behavior and thinking are transformed and changed. So the child becomes a man, and this man is not someone different from the child, but the same person.

Therefore, at that time a person will truly live in heaven, in bodily form, and enjoy the sabbath rest. He will no longer walk on the earth while having his *citizenship in heaven* (Phil 3:20), but he will now be seated in the heavenly places (Eph 2:6) and live under the authority of the *great high priest who has passed through the heavens* (Heb 4:14).

21. The Greek word is *psychikos,* an adjective derived from the word "soul" *(psychē).* It refers to what belongs to the natural world, apart from the Spirit of God. See p. 268 n. 15.

22. Didymus, probably quoting from memory, cites 1 Cor 15:42-44 in a variant form.

(4) John Chrysostom on verse 44

It is sown a natural body, it is raised a spiritual body. If there is a natural body, there is also a spiritual body. What do you think? Is the present body not **spiritual**? Yes, it is spiritual, but that one will be much more so. For now the abundant grace of the Holy Spirit often flies away when people commit grave sins, and even while the Spirit is present, the life of the fleshly soul can depart. Such a body is destitute without the Spirit, but then it will not be so. Then the Spirit will continually remain in the flesh of the righteous and will be in control, with the soul also being present. Either Paul implies some such thing when he says **spiritual** [body], or he means that the body will be lighter and more refined, so that it will even be able to float on air. Very likely he means both.

1 Corinthians 15:50-53

50I tell you this, brethren: flesh and blood cannot inherit the kingdom of God, nor does the perishable inherit the imperishable. 51Lo! I tell you a mystery. We shall not all sleep, but we shall all be changed, 52in a moment, in the twinkling of an eye, at the last trumpet. For the trumpet will sound, and the dead will be raised imperishable, and we shall be changed. 53For this perishable nature must put on the imperishable, and this mortal nature must put on immortality.

(1) Tertullian

We have now come to **flesh and blood**, in truth the hinge of the whole question.[23] Here, no less than before, we can learn from Paul's earlier statements under what conditions the apostle denies that these substances inherit the kingdom of God. *The first man,* he says, *was from the earth, a man of dust,* that is, a man of mud, who was Adam; *the second man is from heaven* (1 Cor 15:47), that is, the word of God, who is Christ. But though he was *from heaven,* Christ was a man because he himself was flesh and spirit, which is what man is and Adam was. He was described in an earlier verse as *the last Adam* (1 Cor 15:45), and he derives this shared name from shared substance: Adam was flesh not derived from human seed, and so was Christ. Therefore, *as was the man of dust, such are those who are of the dust; and as is the man of heaven, such are those who are of heaven* (1 Cor 15:48). Does Paul mean that they are *such* in present substance? Or does he mean that at first they are being trained to be *such* and later they will receive the dignity at which this teaching aims? It is the latter. Men of heaven and men of dust are in no way different in substance since the apostle calls them both men. For if Christ, . . . who is man in being flesh and

23. The difficulty is that when Paul says that "flesh and blood" cannot inherit the kingdom of God, he seems to deny the resurrection of the flesh. Tertullian gives several arguments against this understanding of Paul's words. Two points made earlier were that "flesh" means sinful impulses, not the physical flesh, and that the flesh cannot inherit the kingdom by itself, without the gift of the Spirit. Tertullian's argument in the present text is based on Christology; he emphasizes the reality of Christ's flesh in both incarnation and resurrection.

soul, is in substance indistinguishable from the *man of dust,* it follows that those who like him are *heavenly* are so regarded not because of their present substance but because of their future glory. . . .

Finally, once Paul has established that within the one substance [i.e., the flesh] there is a difference of dignity — the dignity that is now to be pursued and that will then be attained — he also exhorts us, first by means of discipline in the present life to seek to be clothed in Christ, and then in the life to come to attain in our glorified state his exalted rank: *Just as we have borne the image of the man of dust, let us also bear the image of the man of heaven* (1 Cor 15:49). We have worn the image of the *man of dust* (1 Cor 15:48) by sharing in transgression, by partaking in death, by being exiled from paradise. For though it is in the flesh that we wear the image of Adam, still it is not the flesh that we are bidden to *put off* (Eph 4:22). If not the flesh, then it must be our way of life that is to be put off, so that we might likewise *bear in us the image of the heavenly man,* being not yet gods and not yet established in heaven but walking according to the pattern of Christ in holiness and righteousness and truth. In all this Paul is so much concerned for our instruction that he says we must bear the image of Christ in the flesh and in this time of training. For in saying *let us bear,* a prescriptive form of the verb, he speaks to the present time in which man is no other substance than flesh and soul, so that even if our faith looks forward to another, heavenly substance, this has been promised to one who has been commanded to work toward it. Paul describes the image of the *man of dust* and the *man of heaven* in terms of different ways of life, the former to be avoided, the latter to be pursued. Afterward he adds, **For I tell you this** (i.e., "because of what I have said above" — **for** being a conjunction that a completes the thought to what precedes), **that flesh and blood cannot inherit the kingdom of God**. Thus he requires that we understand by **flesh and blood** nothing other than the previously mentioned *image of the man of dust:* if this image consists in our former manner of life, and the former manner of life **cannot inherit the kingdom of God**, similarly **flesh and blood** in their inability to **inherit the kingdom of God** are restricted to our old manner of life. . . .

Even if the apostle had burst out suddenly and without any preparation with this banning of **flesh and blood** from **the kingdom of God**, would we not immediately interpret those two substances as the old man, given over to flesh and blood, that is, eating and drinking, the kind of man who would say, against the resurrection faith, *Let us eat and drink, for tomorrow we will die* (1 Cor 15:32)? . . .

Flesh and blood cannot inherit the kingdom of God alone and by themselves: Paul says this quite rightly to show that the Spirit must be present in them. For it is the Spirit that *makes alive* for **the kingdom of God**; *the flesh helps not at all* (John 6:63). But it may be helped by something else, that is, the Spirit and the works of the Spirit, which are accomplished by the Spirit's agency. So all **flesh and blood** rises to an equal degree, each in its proper quality. But those who can gain the kingdom of God must put on, before they can gain it, the power of incorruptibility and **immortality**, without which they cannot gain **the kingdom of God**. So, as I said, it is quite right that **flesh and blood** by themselves are incapable of **inheriting the kingdom of God**. But since that **perishable nature,** that is, flesh, is destined to be **swallowed up** by **the imperishable**, and that **mortal nature,** that is, blood, by **immortality** after the resurrection and as a result of the change it brings, it is right that **flesh and blood**, changed and swallowed up, can **inherit the kingdom of God**, but only if they are raised again. . . .

But what I have reserved for last will stand as a defense of all the rest and also of the apostle himself. We really must accuse him of thoughtlessness if he really acted as abruptly as some claim — with eyes closed, as the saying is — and thrust **all flesh and blood**, without distinction or condition, from **the kingdom of God**, from the very palace of heaven, even though Jesus still sits there at the right hand of the Father. Jesus is man though God, he is *the last Adam* (1 Cor 15:45) though the first Word, he is **flesh and blood** though in him these are purer than in us, and he is the same man in substance and form as when he ascended. He will come down in like fashion, the angels tell us (Acts 1:11; compare John 1:51), and will be recognized by those who wounded him (John 19:37; Rev 1:7). He is called the *mediator* between God and men (1 Tim 2:5), having received a deposit from both sides, and he keeps a deposit of flesh in himself as an earnest of the whole sum. For just as he left us the *earnest of the Spirit* (2 Cor 5:5), so he received from us the earnest of the flesh and took it up to heaven, a pledge of the complete sum that is to be brought there. Do not worry, **flesh and blood**: you have already taken possession of heaven and **the kingdom of God** in the person of Christ. Otherwise, unless our opponents deny that you (i.e., these elements) are in Christ, let them deny that Christ is in heaven, even as they deny that flesh and blood are there.

(2) Irenaeus

The apostle expresses this thought [that unregenerate persons are properly called *carnal* and *unspiritual*][24] in another context: **flesh and blood cannot inherit the kingdom of God**. This is the passage cited by all the heretics in their perverse attempt to show that what God has created [i.e., the flesh] is not saved. They do not see that, as I have shown, the perfect man consists of three elements, flesh, soul, and spirit. One of these, namely, spirit, saves and forms; another, namely, flesh, is saved and formed; and the third, soul, stands between the two, sometimes following the spirit and being raised up by it, sometimes consenting to the flesh and falling into earthly lusts. Therefore, all those who lack the element that saves and forms are properly called **flesh and blood** since they do not have the spirit in them. That is why our Lord calls such persons "dead": *Leave the dead to bury their own dead* (Luke 9:60), he says, since they do not have the life-giving spirit.

But all those who fear God, believing in the coming of his Son and by faith allowing the Spirit to dwell in their hearts, will properly be called *pure* (Matt 5:8) and *spiritual* (1 Cor 2:15) and *alive to God* (Rom 6:11) since they have the Spirit of the Father, who purifies them and raises them up to the life of God. For just as our Lord testifies that *the flesh is weak*, so he says that *the spirit is willing* (Matt 26:41), which means capable of doing whatever it wills. If, therefore, one adds the willingness of the spirit, as if it were a goad, to the weakness of the flesh, what is strong must necessarily overcome what is weak, and the

---

24. See 1 Cor 2:14–3:1.

weakness of the flesh must be swallowed up by the strength of the spirit. Such a person will no longer be fleshly but spiritual because of his communion with the Spirit. . . .

Since, therefore, we cannot be saved without the Spirit of God, the apostle exhorts us to preserve this Spirit by faith and a chaste way of life. He is afraid that we may fail to participate in the Holy Spirit and so lose the kingdom of heaven, and so he cries aloud that **flesh and blood** by themselves cannot possess **the kingdom of God**. . . .

To keep us from losing the Spirit who possesses us and thereby losing life, the apostle correctly exhorts us to share in the Spirit and says the words I have cited, **flesh and blood cannot inherit the kingdom of God**. This is as if to say, "Be not deceived: if the Word of God and the Spirit of the Father do not dwell in you and if you live a planless and random life as if you were only flesh and blood, you will not be able to possess the kingdom of God." . . .

So the apostle was right to say that **flesh and blood cannot inherit the kingdom of God** and that *those who are in the flesh cannot please God* (Rom 8:8). He does not reject the substance of the flesh but calls for an infusion of the Spirit. That is why he says, **This perishable nature must put on the imperishable, and this mortal nature must put on immortality.** Again he says, *But you are not in the flesh, you are in the Spirit, if in fact the Spirit of God dwells in you* (Rom 8:9). He expresses the point still more clearly when he says, *Although your bodies are dead because of sin, your spirits are alive because of righteousness. If the Spirit of him who raised Jesus from the dead dwells in you, he who raised Christ Jesus from the dead will give life to your mortal bodies also through his Spirit which dwells in you* (Rom 8:10-11). In the same Epistle to the Romans he also says, *If you live according to the flesh, you will die.* He does not mean to reject life in the flesh, since he was living in the flesh when he wrote. Rather, he is trying to prune away their fleshly lusts, which condemn a person to death. And that is why he adds, *But if by the Spirit you put to death the deeds of the body, you will live. For all who are led by the Spirit of God are sons of God* (Rom 8:13-14). . . .

[*In a section omitted here Irenaeus quotes Paul's contrasting description of the "works of the flesh" and the "fruits of the Spirit" in Gal 5:19-23.*] Therefore, just as he who makes progress and produces the fruits of the Spirit will be completely saved because of his participation in the Spirit, so he who remains in the works of the flesh named above and is called "carnal" because he has not received the Spirit of God will not be able to inherit the kingdom of heaven.

The apostle bears witness to this again when he says to the Corinthians, *Do you not know that the unrighteous will not inherit the kingdom of God? Do not be deceived; neither the immoral, nor idolaters, nor adulterers, nor sexual perverts, nor thieves, nor the greedy, nor drunkards, nor revilers, nor robbers will inherit the kingdom of God. And such were some of you. But you were washed, you were sanctified, you were justified in the name of the Lord Jesus Christ and in the Spirit of our God* (1 Cor 6:9-11). Paul shows plainly the things by which a man is destroyed if he persists in living according to the flesh, and also the things by which he is saved. The things that save him, he says, are *the name of our Lord Jesus Christ* and *the Spirit of our God*. Since, therefore, he has here enumerated the works of the flesh, which lack the Spirit and produce death, it is consistent with what has gone before when he exclaims at the end of the epistle, as a summation, *Just as we have borne the image of the man of dust, we shall also bear the image of the man of heaven.* **I tell you this,**

brethren: flesh and blood cannot inherit the kingdom of God (1 Cor 15:49-50). The sense of the clause *Just as we have borne the image of the man of dust* is similar to that of *And such were some of you. But you were washed, you were sanctified, you were justified in the name of the Lord Jesus Christ and in the Spirit of our God* (1 Cor 6:11). When did we bear the image of the man of dust? It was when the works of the flesh Paul has mentioned were being done in us. And when did we bear the image of the man of heaven? It was when *you were washed* and believed in the name of the Lord and received his Spirit. What we have been cleansed of is not the substance of our bodies or the image we bear as creatures but our former vain way of life. So in the very members in which we were perishing when we performed the works of corruption we are now being made alive when we perform the works of the Spirit. For just as the flesh admits of corruption, so it admits of imperishability, and just as it admits of death, so it admits of life.

*   *   *

Those who refuse to see what is so plain and clear and flee from the light of truth are foolish and truly miserable. Like poor Oedipus, they blind themselves. An inexperienced wrestler seizes some part of the opponent's body with all his might, and as a result he is thrown by the very part he has taken hold of. As he falls, he imagines that because he has a firm grasp of the limb he seized at the start he is winning the match, but he not only suffers a fall but is made a laughingstock. The heretics resemble such a wrestler. In Paul's clause **flesh and blood cannot inherit the kingdom of God,** they take two words, **flesh** and **blood,** and consider neither the apostle's meaning nor the force of the words. They grab on to these words without further addition, and with them in their grasp they die, having overturned, as far as they are able, God's whole plan of salvation.

For if they claim that Paul's words refer to flesh in its primary sense rather than the works of the flesh, they will prove, as I have demonstrated, that the apostle contradicts himself, since a little later in the same epistle he says plainly, **For this perishable nature must put on the imperishable, and this mortal nature must put on immortality.** *When the perishable puts on the imperishable, and the mortal puts on immortality, then shall come to pass the saying that is written: "Death is swallowed up in victory"* (Isa 25:8). *"O death, where is thy victory? O death, where is thy sting?"* (Hos 13:14; 1 Cor 15:54-55). But it will be proper to say this only when this mortal and corruptible flesh, which is under death's influence and suffers its dominion, arises to life and puts on **imperishability** and **immortality.** For death will be truly conquered only when the flesh that is in its power has passed from its dominion.

(3) Augustine

I tell you this, brethren: flesh and blood will not possess[25] **the kingdom of God, nor does the perishable possess the imperishable** (v. 50). Some people raise a problem for us based on the apostle's words: see what objection they raise against what we are argu-

---

25. The Latin text followed by Augustine differs from the Greek text, which RSV renders: "cannot inherit."

ing. "Flesh," they say, "will not rise. For if it rises, it will possess **the kingdom of God**. But the apostle says plainly, **Flesh and blood cannot possess the kingdom of God**." . . . So are we preaching something contrary to the apostle, or is he preaching something contrary to the gospel? . . .

We could solve the problem in the following way and thereby resist the foolish faultfinders: . . . The apostle says, **Flesh and blood will not** gain possession of **the kingdom of God** by inheritance. He speaks the truth. For it is not the role of flesh to possess but to be possessed. For your flesh does not possess anything: it is your soul that possesses by means of your body, it is your soul that possesses your body itself. So if the flesh is raised in such a way that it is possessed but does not possess, what is so strange if **flesh and blood will not possess the kingdom of God** since they will themselves be possessed? The flesh possesses those who are not of the kingdom of God but of the devil: that is why they are subject to the pleasures of the flesh. That is why the famous paralytic was carried on his bed. But when the Lord had healed him, he said, *Take up your bed and walk* (Mark 2:11). Thus when his paralysis is healed, he possesses his flesh and takes it where he likes. He is not dragged by the flesh where he does not wish to go. . . . So when we have risen, flesh will not carry us but we it. If we carry it, we will be its possessors, and if we are its possessors, we will not be possessed by it because, being freed from the devil, we will be **the kingdom of God**. And thus **flesh shall not gain possession of the kingdom of God**. . . .

The problem could also be solved in another way. The sort of people who are called **flesh and blood** — and it is of such that the apostle says, *We are not contending against flesh and blood* (Eph 6:12) — **will not be able to possess the kingdom of God** unless they turn to a spiritual kind of life and *by the Spirit put to death the deeds of the body* (Rom 8:13).

"But," someone might say, "what does the apostle mean?" The truer sense is the one that takes account of the context. . . . The theme Paul had set himself was this: *But some one will ask, "How are the dead raised? With what kind of body do they come?"* (1 Cor 15:35). And the reason he says, *The first man was from earth, a man of dust, the second man is from heaven. As was the man of dust, so are those who are of the dust; and as is the man of heaven, so are those who are of heaven* (1 Cor 15:47-48), is that we may hope for the occurrence in our bodies of what happened in Christ's body; and that, though we do not perceive this as a fact, we might hold fast to it by faith. And so he adds, *Just as we have borne the image of the man of dust, let us also bear the image of the man of heaven* (1 Cor 15:49). And that we might not suppose that we will rise to the sort of corrupt actions that we did according to the first man, he adds at once, **I tell you this, brethren: flesh and blood will not be able to possess the kingdom of God by inheritance**.

And he wants to show what he means by **flesh and blood**, namely, that he uses the phrase **flesh and blood** to signify not merely being a body but rather the fact of decay, a decay that will not exist at that future time. For the body, without reference to its decay, is not properly called **flesh and blood** but a body. For if it is flesh, it is subject to decay and death. But if it *dies no more* (Rom 6:9), it is no longer subject to decay. And so if its appearance remains the same but without decay, it is no longer properly called flesh but body. And if it is called flesh, it is not properly so called but only by a certain analogy of appearance. For example, we could speak of the "flesh" of angels when they appear to men as men, even though what they have are actually "bodies," not flesh, because there is nothing in them that brings on corruption. So therefore, using an analogy, we can refer to a body that is not subject to corruption as "flesh." But the apostle was concerned to show what he meant by **flesh and blood**: that these words signify decay, not merely anything that looks like a body. So he immediately adds, **nor will corruption possess by inheritance what is incorruptible**, as if to say, "What I meant by **Flesh and blood will not possess the kingdom of God** is the same as when I said, **corruption will not possess by inheritance what is incorruptible**."

[. . . **in the twinkling of an eye**] The twinkling of an eye is not the opening and closing of the eyelid. For that happens more slowly than the act of seeing. It takes more time to lift your eyelid than to direct its ray.[26] It takes less time for the ray to go to heaven than to raise your eyelid to your eyebrow. You see what is meant by **the twinkling of an eye**; you see how easy the apostle makes the resurrection of bodies. How slowly were these formed and created! Let us remember how long it takes to conceive and for the seeds of children to coalesce in their mothers' wombs. After an interval their limbs are formed, over a fixed number of days and many months, until what was created and formed within is brought forth into the light. Then what time the child takes to grow, how long until adolescence succeeds childhood, young manhood adolescence, old age young manhood, and death everything! Then there is another interval. The newly dead body seems whole, but it is dissolved into putrescence. And for that dissolution time is needed until the body flows away into decay and dries up into dust. From the first beginnings in the womb until the last dust of the grave, what is the interval? How many days, what length of time? But when it comes to the resurrection, the body is all reconstituted **in the twinkling of an eye**.

But who could find the words to express what will be the glory of this flesh in the resurrection? None of us has yet had any experience of it. Now we carry our flesh around as a burden since it is needy, weak, mortal, and corruptible. For *the body which is perishing weighs down the soul* (Wis 9:15). But have no fear of this in the resurrection. **This perishable nature must put on the imperishable, and this mortal nature must put on immortality** (v. 53). What now is onerous will then be honorific; what was once a load to be borne will be a relief. For it will not have weight so that you feel you have a body.

Look, dearest friends, at our body, even this fragile and mortal body, when it is healthy, when it is ruled by the just tempering of its parts, when no part of it is at strife with some other part, when heat does not beset and fight against cold, when excessive cold does not put out its heat . . . but all of its parts are balanced in a relation of mutual harmony which is called health. Health, in a word, is the harmony of the body's constituent parts. This health is the harmony of parts and humors in a perishable object, an object needy and weak, that can still feel hunger and thirst, grow weary from standing, be restored by sitting, be wearied once more by sitting, grow faint from being hungry, be restored by eating. It cannot help its earlier deficiencies except by beginning new ones. For

26. The ancients thought that in the act of seeing the eye emits a ray.

whatever you in your weariness take for refreshment is the beginning of a new weariness since, if you persist in the thing you took to help you, it also will be a source of weariness. In this weak and perishable body what does any sort of health amount to? For this health, which we say our mortal and corruptible flesh possesses, is in no way comparable to the health of the angels, with whom we are promised equality in the resurrection (Luke 20:36). . . .

The body which is perishing (Wis 9:15), that is, perishable, *weighs down the soul* even when it is healthy. It weighs down the soul, that is, it does not obey the soul's every wish. In many things it obeys: the soul moves the hands to do work, the feet to walk, the tongue to speak, the eyes to see, the sense of hearing to hear voices. In all these things the body obeys. But when we desire to move from one place to another we feel a burden, a weight. The body does not move so easily to arrive at its destination. Someone, in the body, desires to see his friend, in the body. He knows that he lives far away, with a many days' journey in between. In his spirit he has already gone ahead, and when he arrives in body, then he feels what a burden he carries. The weight of the flesh is not able to obey the will as speedily as anticipated. . . . But when it is a *spiritual body,* about which it has been said, *It is sown a natural body and rises a spiritual body* (15:44), what ease, what swiftness, what obedience to desire it will show! It will have no weight, no neediness, no weariness, nor will one part fight against or resist another.

1 Corinthians 15:54-58

54When the perishable puts on the imperishable, and the mortal puts on immortality, then shall come to pass the saying that is written: "Death is swallowed up in victory" [Isa 25:8]. 55"O death, where is thy struggle?"[27] O death, where is thy sting?" [Hos 13:14] 56The sting of death is sin, and the power of sin is the law. 57But thanks be to God, who gives us the victory through our Lord Jesus Christ. 58Therefore, my beloved brethren, be steadfast, immovable, always abounding in the work of the Lord, knowing that in the Lord your labor is not in vain.

(1) Augustine

Without doubt, my brethren, there will be a **victory**. Let us believe, let us hope, let us love: there will be a victory someday at the dedication of the house now being built after the captivity.[28] For the last enemy, Death, will be destroyed when **this perishable nature puts on the imperishable, and this mortal nature puts on immortality**. Let us practice beforehand the words of the victors, **"death, where is thy struggle?"** . . .

27. According to Augustine's Latin text. The Greek, followed by RSV, reads "victory."

28. This seems to be an allusion to the superscript of Psalm 30, which Augustine quotes earlier in this sermon in the form: "When the house was being rebuilt after the captivity." Citing 1 Cor 3:16, in which Paul calls the Christian community the "temple of God," Augustine applies this to Christians who are freed from captivity to sin.

[*In the omitted section Augustine returns to the present time, in which Christians are still struggling, and recommends humility as the means to victory.*] You proudly rely on the law (Rom 2:17), since the law and its command have been given to you. It is good that the Spirit should make you alive so that the letter may not kill you (2 Cor 3:6). I want you to wish this, but it is not enough to wish it. You need help in order that you may wholeheartedly wish it, and fulfill what you wish. Do you want to see what power the letter that commands has without the help of the Spirit? Paul has said it here. Having said **O death, where is thy sting? The sting of death is sin**, he immediately adds, **and the power of sin is the law**. What does it mean, **the power of sin is the law**? It is not by enjoining evil things or forbidding good things. Quite the reverse: it is by enjoining good things and forbidding evil things. **The power of sin is the law** because, as Paul says, *the law came in to increase the trespass* (Rom 5:20). What does it mean "to increase the trespass"? That where there was no grace, the prohibition increased desire. And when men became presumptuous about their own virtue, it became a great vice.

But what has grace done? *Where sin increased, grace abounded all the more* (Rom 5:20). The Lord came. All that you drew from Adam, all that you added by your own wicked character, he forgave it, erased it all. He taught us to pray, he promised grace; he announced the contest, came to the struggler's aid, and crowned him as victor. . . .

Therefore, since **the sting of death is sin, and the power of sin is the law**, this happened by God's good providence, so that all men might be consigned to sin (Gal 3:21) and seek for a helper, seek for grace, seek for God, instead of trusting presumptuously in their own virtue. Therefore, after saying **But the sting of death is sin, and the power of sin is the law** — why are you afraid, why anxious, why in such a sweat? Listen to what comes next: **But thanks be to God, who gives us the victory through our Lord Jesus Christ.** Do you really give yourself the victory? **Thanks be to God, who gives us the victory through our Lord Jesus Christ.**

So when you begin to struggle in your fight against the lusts of the flesh, walk by the Spirit, call upon the Spirit, seek the gift of God. And if *the law in* your *members* fights from below (i.e., from the flesh) against *the law of* your *mind* and holds you *captive to the law of sin* (Rom 7:23), even this will be set right, even this will pass over into the victor's power. Just call out, just call upon God. We *ought always to pray and not lose heart* (Luke 18:1). Call on him always, ask for his help. *While you are still speaking, he will say, "Look, here I am"* (Isa 58:9 Latin). Then understand, and you will hear him saying to your soul: *I am your deliverance* (Ps 35:3).

In baptism iniquity is blotted out, but weakness remains. But in the resurrection there will be no iniquity and weakness will be destroyed. **When the perishable puts on the imperishable, and the mortal puts on immortality, then shall come to pass the saying that is written: "Death is swallowed up in victory"** [Isa 25:8]. **"O death, where is thy struggle?"** (Hos 13:14). And if the struggle with death is our contest, *it is no longer I that do it but sin which dwells within me* (Rom 7:17). The concupiscence of the flesh is what Paul calls sin. I desire, but I do not consent in my mind, and yet concupiscence does not cease to goad me on to evil. This is the struggle with death. But one day the external enemy, the devil, will be beneath our feet and the internal enemy, concupiscence, will be healed, and we will live in peace. What sort of peace? A peace *which no eye has seen, nor ear heard* (1 Cor 2:9). What sort of peace? A peace no heart imagines and which is followed by no discord. What sort of peace? The peace of which the apostle said, *And the peace of God, which passes all understanding, keep your hearts* (Phil 4:7). About this peace the prophet Isaiah says, *O Lord, thou wilt ordain peace for us, thou hast made good all things for us* (Isa 26:12). Lord, you promised us Christ: you made good the promise. You promised his ascension and the sending of the Holy Spirit from heaven: you made good the promise. You promised the Church spread abroad in all the world: you made good the promise. You promised that there would be heretics to try us and test us and that the Church would triumph over their errors: you made good the promise. You promised that the idols of the Gentiles would be abolished: you made good the promise. *O Lord, thou wilt ordain peace for us, thou hast made good all things for us.*

1 Corinthians 16

The last chapter of 1 Corinthians, which focuses on Paul's situation, his travel plans, and final greetings, did not occasion as much patristic commentary as did other, more theologically sugges-tive chapters. The most extensive commentary comes from John Chrysostom, who considers in detail how the chapter relates to other parts of the letter and its place in Paul's rhetorical strategy. In his comments on verses 1-4 he notes that the letter's conclusion differs from that of Paul's other letters in that it contains little ethical advice. Nonetheless, he finds in Paul's directives to make a collection for the saints in Jerusalem a theme dear to his own heart, the value of giving alms. Origen, Didymus, and Augustine derive other generally applicable lessons from the concrete ma-terial of this chapter as well as from the brief exhortations in verses 13-14, which conclude with "Let everything be done in love." The image of the "open door" was particularly suggestive of wider applications. To Augustine it shows that the beginning of faith is itself is a gift from God.

1 Corinthians 16:1-4

1Now concerning the contribution for the saints: as I directed the churches of Galatia, so you also are to do. 2On the first day of every week, each of you is to put something aside and store it up, as he may prosper, so that contributions need not be made when I come. 3And when I arrive, I will send those whom you accredit by letter to carry your gift to Jerusalem. 4If it seems advisable that I should go also, they will accompany me.

(1) John Chrysostom

Having finished his discourse on Christian doctrine and ready to engage a topic more re-lated to Christian ethics, he leaves everything else aside and goes to the chief good, the topic of almsgiving. After that he brings the letter to a close. Nowhere else does he do this. In the other epistles he concludes with discussions of mercy, moderation, gentleness, pa-tience, and all the other virtues. Why, then, does he instruct them here only in this one as-pect of ethics, almsgiving? Because most of what he said before was already concerned with Christian behavior: chastising the fornicator, correcting those going to pagan courts, frightening drunkards and gluttons, condemning the factious, the contentious, and the power-hungry, passing a crushing verdict upon those who approached the holy mysteries unworthily, and discoursing about love. Because the saints in Jerusalem were in great need, he mentions only almsgiving here.

Consider his good sense: once he had convinced them about the resurrection and awakened their yearning, he then goes on to talk about this topic. Of course he had also talked about this with them before, when he asked, *If we have sown spiritual good among you, is it too much if we reap your material benefits?* (1 Cor 9:11) and *Who plants a vineyard without eating any of its fruit* (1 Cor 9:7)? But because he knows the importance of this endeavor, he does not shrink from adding it again to the end of the letter.

He calls the collecting of funds a **contribution**, and thereby immediately lightens the topic by the way he introduces it. Whenever a financial burden is borne by all, the demand on each individual becomes light. In speaking about the fund-raising, he does not immediately say, **Each of you is to put something aside and store it up** (v. 2). That came later. Only after saying, **As I directed the churches of Galatia** (v. 1), does he introduce this idea, causing them to emulate others by talking about their good works and setting his command in a narrative context. He does the same thing in writing to the Romans. While his apparent point is the reason for his trip to Jerusalem, he inserts a discussion of the offering, saying, *At present, however, I am going to Jerusalem with aid for the saints. For Macedonia and Achaia have been pleased to make some contribution for the poor among the saints* (Rom 15:25-26). Just as he urges the Romans on by the example of the Macedonians and the Corinthians, so he urges the Corinthians on by the example of the Galatians. . . .

On the first day of every week, that is, on the Lord's Day, **each of you is to put something aside and store it up, as he may prosper**. See how he uses the particular time to incite them. The day itself was enough to move them to compassion. "Be mindful," he says, "of what you gained on this day. Unutterable good, the root and source of our life, happened on that day." But this is not the only reason why the day can stir up the desire for charity; it also involves a slackening or cessation of labor. When a soul is freed from hard work, it becomes more cheerful and more suited to works of mercy. . . .

[*Chrysostom applies Paul's message to his own audience.*] With all boldness I will tell you, "Give to the needy." I will not stop saying this, and I will be a harsh critic of those who do not give. If I were a general and had soldiers under me, I would feel no shame in asking rations for my men. I long earnestly for your salvation. To make my message even more emphatic and effective, I will take Paul as my ally and say along with him, **Each of you is to put something aside and store it up**. Notice his gentleness even here. He does not say "such and such an amount" but **as he may prosper**, whether much or little. And he does not say, "whatever profit he has made," but **as he may prosper**, showing that the resources are from God. Furthermore, by not ordering them to collect it all at one time, he makes the contribution easy. Since it is collected little by little, the offering and the expenditure are imperceptible. . . .

Let each of us make a little chest for the poor and let it sit there next to the place where you stand to pray. And as often as you enter to pray, first put in your alms and then send up your prayer. Just as you would not pray with unwashed hands, do not pray without alms. To lay alms next to your bed is just as good as hanging a Gospel next to it. If you just hang up a Gospel without doing anything, you are not benefited in the least. But if you have such a little chest, you possess a defense against the devil, you give your prayer wings, and you make your home holy since you will have stored food for the King inside it (see Matt 25:35, 40). Put your bed next to this little chest and your night will be free of bad dreams.

1 Corinthians 16:5-9

₅I will visit you after passing through Macedonia, for I intend to pass through Macedonia, ₆and perhaps I will stay with you or even spend the winter, so that you may speed me on my journey, wherever I go. ₇For I do not want to see you now just in passing; I hope to spend some time with you, if the Lord permits. ₈But I will stay in Ephesus until Pentecost, ₉for a wide door for effective work has opened to me, and there are many adversaries.

(1) Pelagius

I will visit you after passing through Macedonia. That is, the Macedonians' conduct is such that I need not stay any longer with them; but with you I must tarry, even spending the winter — there are many things to correct in you — just as a doctor tarries where many people are sick.

(2) Didymus of Alexandria

Paul wrote this letter to the Corinthians in Ephesus. He says that he will spend the winter there for a good reason. **A door,** large and very productive for his hearers, **has opened** to him. Because of this he had many opponents — wandering demons and those who were magicians and deceivers. For the wicked mount a strong opposition when they see the word of faith working mightily in those who hear it. Boldness in the preaching of godliness Paul is accustomed to call a **door** (see 2 Cor 2:12; Col 4:3).

(3) John Chrysostom

I will visit you, he says, **after passing through Macedonia.** He had said this before, but in anger, for he added, *I will find out not the talk of these arrogant people but their power* (1 Cor 4:19). But here he speaks more gently, so that they might even look forward to his coming.... **And perhaps I will stay with you or even spend the winter.** I do not intend, he says, for you to be incidental to my journey, but I want to stay with you for a long time. When he wrote this, he was in Ephesus and it was winter, since he says, **But I will stay in**

Ephesus until Pentecost. Thereafter, he says, I will depart for Macedonia and, passing through it, I will come to you in the summer. Perhaps I will spend the winter with you.

Why does he say **perhaps** rather than speak with certainty? Because Paul did not know the future, and it was good that he did not. He does not speak with certainty so that, if what he said should not happen, he might have an excuse — namely, that he had spoken indefinitely, and the power of the Spirit was leading him wherever it wished and not where he himself wanted. He also says this in the Second Letter when he is defending his delay, *Do I make my plans like a worldly man, ready to say Yes and No at once?* (2 Cor 1:17). . . .

For a wide door for effective work has opened to me, and there are many adversaries. If there are many conspiring against him, this, too, is an indication that the gospel is going forward. The devil never gets angry except when he sees many of his instruments snatched away (see Matt 12:29; Mark 3:27). Whenever we desire to perform some great and noble deed, let us not consider the great labor it involves but let us look at the gain. See, then, how Paul does not hesitate or hold back because there are **many adversaries**, but because the **door** was opened **wide** he pressed his attack and stayed the course. As I have said, this was a clear indication that the devil was being plundered. It is not small and trivial accomplishments that provoke that wicked monster. Thus, whenever you see a just man accomplishing great things and yet suffering from countless misfortunes, don't be surprised. On the contrary, it would be surprising if the devil should keep quiet and meekly bear his wounds while receiving many blows. There is no need to wonder if a snake gets angry when repeatedly poked and strikes the one who was poking at it. Indeed, the devil slithers about more ill-tempered than any snake, striking at everyone, and like a scorpion he rises up with his sting raised. But don't let this trouble you. The man who returns from battle, victory, and slaughter is necessarily spattered with blood and often is wounded. . . .

When someone who does good suffers terrible things and gives thanks through it all, the devil is beaten down. It is impressive to show mercy and to cling to virtue when the winds of heaven are blowing your way, but it is far greater for those who suffer terribly to persevere in doing good. That is true most of all for someone who does this for God's sake. Accordingly, beloved, whatever risk we endure, whatever we suffer, let us hold fast with greater zeal to the works of virtue. For, you see, the season of our reward is not this age.

(4) Augustine

The Apostle makes clear to us that it is by the gift of God that we begin to believe when he says in the Epistle to the Colossians, *Continue steadfastly in prayer, being watchful in it with thanksgiving; and pray for us also, that God may open to us a door for the word, to declare the mystery of Christ, on account of which I am in prison, that I may make it clear, as I ought to speak* (Col 4:2-4). How is *a door for the word* opened? Is it not when the hearer's understanding is opened so that he may believe . . . and not close his heart in disbelief and reject what is being said? Hence Paul says to the Corinthians, **I will stay in**

Ephesus until Pentecost, for a wide door for effective work has been opened to me, and there are many adversaries. What should we understand in this passage? Is it not that when he preached the gospel to begin with, many believed, and that many adversaries of the faith arose in accordance with the Lord's saying, *No one can come to me unless it is granted him by the Father* (John 6:65) and *To you it has been given to know the secrets of the kingdom of heaven, but to them it has not been given* (Matt 13:11)? So a **door** was **opened** in those to whom it was given, but the **many adversaries** were those to whom it was not given.

And likewise the same apostle says to the same people in his Second Letter: *When I came to Troas to preach the gospel of Christ, a door was opened for me in the Lord; but my mind could not rest because I did not find my brother Titus there. So I took leave of them and went on to Macedonia* (2 Cor 2:12-13). Of whom did he take leave except those who had believed, those, that is, in whose hearts Paul's preaching had found a **door open**? But hear what he adds: *But thanks be to God, who in Christ always leads us in triumph, and through us spreads the fragrance of the knowledge of him everywhere. For we are the aroma of Christ to God among those who are being saved and among those who are perishing, to one a fragrance from death to death, to the other a fragrance from life to life* (2 Cor 2:14-16). See why the keen warrior and unvanquished defender of grace gives thanks. See why he gives thanks that the apostles are *the aroma of Christ*, both in those who are being saved by his grace and in those who are perishing by his judgment. But he advises them not to feel anger at those who do not understand these things when he adds, *Who is sufficient for these things?* (2 Cor 2:16). But let us return to the opening of the **door**, by which the apostle meant the beginning of faith in his hearers. What does it mean, *pray for us also, that God may open to us a door for the word* (Col 4:3)? Is it not an utterly plain demonstration that even our beginning to believe is the gift of God? For God would not have been asked for it in prayer unless he was thought to grant it. This gift of heavenly grace had descended also to that *seller of purple goods,* whose heart, as the Scripture says in the Acts of the Apostles, *the Lord opened to give heed to what was said by Paul* (Acts 16:14). For she was called to be a believer. God does what he wants in the hearts of men, either by helping or by judging, so that what his hand and his counsel predestined should be fulfilled through them.

1 Corinthians 16:10-12

10When Timothy comes, see that he be without fear[1] among you, for he is doing the work of the Lord, as I am. 11So let no one despise him. Speed him on his way in peace, that he may return to me; for I am expecting him with the brethren. 12As for our brother Apollos, I strongly urged him to visit you with the other brethren, but it was not at all his will to come now. He will come when he has opportunity.

---

1. RSV: "you put him at ease."

(1) Didymus of Alexandria

When their pupils are firm and steadfast in their piety, teachers can live among them **without fear**, without the worry that there be any laxity among their hearers. Therefore, Paul says this: "Pay attention to yourselves, so that Timothy will be encouraged to come to you, without having to fear that you will have a change of heart." Here Paul expresses this by the word **fear**. And in the next letter he says: *But I am afraid that as the serpent deceived Eve by his cunning, your thoughts will be led astray* (2 Cor 11:3).

"Now this Timothy," Paul goes on to say, "about whom I write these things, is one of the genuine servants of God, who carries out the works of his master just as I do. Therefore, let him not be slighted by you, but see that he is received with genuine love and given help for his journey. For I am waiting in Asia until he returns to me with the brothers."

(2) Origen

At the beginning of the letter, Paul says, *I hear that there are divisions among you*, for *each one of you says, "I belong to Paul," or "I belong to Apollos"* (1 Cor 1:11-12). It was around Apollos, he says, that there were division and unrest in the Corinthian church. This remarkable Apollos, who was a bishop at that time, resorted to Paul to judge the matter. Paul was engaged in his apostolic work. He was residing at the time in Asia, and it was not possible for him to leave his pressing work there and come to Corinth. But he chose Timothy as his substitute and sent him to straighten out matters in Corinth. . . . When the holy ones made visits and sought to help their hearers, they did not come *in weakness* or in *fear and trembling* (1 Cor 2:3). But when they came to those who were weaker, they did visit *in weakness and in much fear and trembling*. Because the Corinthians were weak, it was not the great Paul but the weak Paul who resided with them, as he says: *To the weak I became weak, that I might win the weak* (1 Cor 9:22). And for this reason he says: *And I was with you in weakness.* This is also why he was *in much fear and trembling* (1 Cor 2:3), so that he might outdo his hearers in this. Since, then, it is for the sake of his hearers that their benefactor visits them *in fear and trembling*, it is Paul's wish that Timothy may come to them **without fear, for he is doing the work of the Lord, as I am**. "What I would have done if I were visiting you," says Paul, "this Timothy will do."

So let no one despise him. If you despise him, you also despise me. **Speed him on his way in peace, that he may return to me.** He comes to you now in order to make peace, for he finds dissension in your church. But once you have come to agreement and been set right by his words and the peace is restored, **speed him on his way** through your concord and **in peace, that he may return to me; for I am expecting him with the brethren.** Which brethren? Those about whom Paul said, *I will send those whom you accredit by letter* (1 Cor 16:3). **For I am expecting him** since I hear that he is about to return to bring me news about your affairs.

(3) John Chrysostom

When Timothy comes, see that he be without fear among you, for he is doing the work of the Lord, as I am. Perhaps someone might think that this advice insults Timothy's courage. But it is not said for Timothy's sake but for the sake of Paul's audience, that they might not bring themselves harm by plotting against him. For Timothy was always exposed to perils. Paul says, *As a son with a father he has served with me in the gospel* (Phil 2:22). But he fears that boldness toward the disciple will lead them to attack the teacher and to become even worse, so he restrains them beforehand by saying, **See that he be without fear among you.** That is, see that none of those desperate ones rises up against him. For Timothy was probably going to censure them for what Paul had written. Paul had already said that this is why he sent him. He says, *Therefore I sent to you Timothy, my beloved and faithful child in the Lord, to remind you of my ways in Christ, as I teach them everywhere in every church* (1 Cor 4:17).

1 Corinthians 16:13-14

13Be watchful, stand firm in your faith, be courageous, be strong. 14Let all that you do be done in love.

(1) Theodoret

Paul writes **be watchful** on account of the deceivers, and **stand firm** and **be courageous** because of his hearers' open adversaries. For the pious were being persecuted by the impious. And he says, **Let everything be done in love**, to those who were dividing the body of the church by their passionate desire to rule, and those who partook of food offered to idols and despised those who were offended by this.

(2) John Chrysostom

To show that their hopes of salvation depend not only on who their teachers are but also on themselves, he commands, **Be watchful, stand firm in your faith.** Salvation is not a matter of pagan wisdom (1 Cor 1:20), for one cannot "stand" in pagan wisdom: one can only be swept along. In faith, however, one can stand. **Be courageous, be strong. Let all that you do be done in love.** In saying these things, Paul appears to give a warning, but actually he is accusing them of laxity. Thus, he says, **be watchful** because they are sleeping, **stand firm** because they are tottering, **be courageous, be strong** because they have grown soft, **let all that you do be done in love** because they are factious. The phrase **be watchful, stand firm** is directed at the deceitful; the phrase **be courageous** is directed at the schemers; and to those warring factions that try to tear everything in pieces he addresses the clause **Let all that you do be done in love**, *which is the bond of perfection* (Col 3:14), the fount and root of everything good.

What does this mean, **Let all that you do be done in love**? It means that whether a person rebukes or rules or is ruled, or learns or teaches, everything should be done in love because everything Paul writes about arose from neglect of this very thing. If they had not neglected love, they would not have been puffed up and would not have said, *"I belong to Paul,"* or *"I belong to Apollos"* (1 Cor 1:12). If there had been love, they would not have gone to court outside the church; indeed, they would not have gone to court at all (1 Cor 6:1). If there had been love, that man would not have taken his father's wife (1 Cor 5:1), they would not have looked down on their weak brothers (1 Cor 8:11), they would not have had divisions (1 Cor 1:10), they would not have been arrogant about spiritual gifts (1 Cor 13:4). That is why Paul says, **Let everything be done in love.**

(3) Origen

Be watchful. There is a sleep of the soul, and an awakening. Thus the Word speaking through Solomon forbids the soul to sleep: *Give your eyes no sleep and your eyelids no slumber; save yourself like a gazelle from the hunter, like a bird from the hand of the fowler* (Prov 6:4-5). And the Savior says, *Watch* at all times, *and pray* that you may be able to flee the *temptations* that are about to come (Matt 26:41).

　　Stand firm. Do not be shaken but be steadfast. The one who is double-minded does not stand in faith, nor does the one who is doubtful about matters of faith. **Be courageous.** Paul says this as if speaking to soldiers. For he charges, *Put on the whole armor of God, that you may be able to stand against the wiles of the devil* (Eph 6:11). **Be strong.** That is, assume strength in order that with it you can say, *I can do all things in Christ Jesus who strengthens me* (Phil 4:13). **Let all that you do be done in love.** It is characteristic of beginners to act out of fear, but the mature act out of love.

(4) Augustine

[**Let all that you do be done in love.**] "And so," our opponents say,[2] "let those in authority over us merely instruct us in what we ought to do and pray that we may do it. But let them not rebuke us if we fail to do it." On the contrary, let all these things be done. The teachers of the Church, the apostles, did all these things: they said what was to be done, they offered rebuke if it was not done, and they prayed that it might be done. The apostle gave instruction when he said, **Let all that you do be done in love.** He rebuked when he said: *To have lawsuits at all with one another is sin for you. Why not rather suffer wrong? Why not rather be defrauded? But you yourselves wrong and defraud, and that even your own brethren. Do you not know that the unrighteous will not inherit the kingdom of God?* (1 Cor 6:7-9). Let us also hear him praying: *May the Lord make you increase and abound in love to one another and to all men* (1 Thess 3:12). He instructs them that they should have

---

2. Some of the monks at Hadrumetum had drawn the false conclusion from Augustine's work "On Grace and Free Will" that, since grace is necessary, fraternal correction was useless.

love; he rebukes them for not having it; and he prays that love may abound. Friend, in Paul's instruction learn what you ought to have; in his rebuke learn that you are at fault in not having it; in his prayer learn from what source you may receive what you desire to have.

1 Corinthians 16:15-18

15Now, brethren, you know that the household of Stephanas was the firstfruits[3] in Achaia, and they have devoted themselves to the service of the saints; 16I urge you to be subject to such men and to every fellow worker and laborer. 17I rejoice at the coming of Stephanas and Fortunatus and Achaicus, because they have made up for your absence;[4] 18for they refreshed my spirit as well as yours. Give recognition to such men.

(1) John Chrysostom

Now, brethren, you know that the household of Stephanas was the firstfruits in Achaia, and they have devoted themselves to the service of the saints.... Paul also mentions this man at the beginning of the Letter when he says, *I did baptize also the household of Stephanas* (1 Cor 1:16). Now he says that he is the **firstfruits** not only of Corinth but of all of Greece. This is no small compliment, to be the first to come to Christ. For the same reason Paul compliments certain people in the Epistle to the Romans by saying, *And they were in Christ before me* (Rom 16:7). He does not say that they were the first to believe but that they were the **firstfruits**, which shows that in addition to their faith they displayed an exemplary life, since by their fruits they showed themselves worthy in every way. Indeed, the **firstfruits** are necessarily better than the rest since they are the first offerings to God. Paul's comments about them make this clear. Not only did they genuinely believe, as I said, but they also demonstrated deep piety, mature virtue, and an eagerness to help the poor....

I rejoice at the coming of Stephanas and Fortunatus and Achaicus, because they have made up for your absence; for they refreshed my spirit as well as yours. The Corinthians would naturally be angry with these men since they are the ones who came to Paul and informed him about the discord, for it was through them that the congregation had presented their written questions about virgins and married couples (1 Cor 7:1). Accordingly, see how Paul soothes their anger. At the beginning of the letter he says, *For it has been reported to me about you by Chloe's people* (1 Cor 1:11), thereby concealing the other group and bringing Chloe's people to the fore, who had probably made their disclosure through Stephanas and the others. And so he writes here, **They have made up for your absence; for they refreshed my spirit as well as yours,** pointing out that they came representing all the Corinthians and chose for their sake to be sent on such a long journey.

---

3. RSV: "were the first converts."
4. Or "they made up for what you lacked."

(2) Didymus of Alexandria

They are called **firstfruits** either because they were believers before the others, or because they excel in piety, or because they are the best of their kind. These men, because of their natural humility, were elected to no office. Instead, on their own impulse they made themselves Paul's servants. Therefore, **be subject to such men**, since you have them as images and patterns, so that you might appoint yourselves as servants of the saints.

Fortunatus and Achaicus, along with Stephanas, **made up for what you lacked** since they made the same choice as he did, and **they refreshed your spirit as well as mine.**[5] The one who thinks and acts in accord with piety refreshes the spirit of the saint, for one's spirit desires what is good as much as it desires to exist.

1 Corinthians 16:19-24

19The churches of Asia send greetings. Aquila and Prisca, together with the church in their house, send you hearty greetings in the Lord. 20All the brethren send greetings. Greet one another with a holy kiss. 21I, Paul, write this greeting with my own hand. 22If any one has no love for the Lord, let him be accursed. Our Lord has come [Maranatha]![6] 23The grace of the Lord Jesus be with you. 24My love be with you all in Christ Jesus. Amen.

(1) Didymus of Alexandria

He gives them sufficient incitement to love by writing that **the churches of Asia send greetings,** including all the saints and pious ones who were in them. . . . To keep them from being deceived if someone else should write in the name of the apostle, Paul distinguishes letters written by him from those that are not by marking the former with his own hand. What is written here is from his holy right hand. **If any one has no love for the Lord, let him be accursed. Our Lord has come!** One who does not keep his commandments does not love the Lord. Therefore, this person is **accursed,** since he knows that the Lord, who judges human works, has come, saying: "I love those who love me." But if he loves those who love him, consider what will befall those who do not love.

(2) John Chrysostom

The churches of Asia send greetings. Paul always uses his greetings to bring the members of the church together. **Aquila and Prisca, together with the church in their house,**

---

5. RSV: "my spirit as well as yours."

6. RSV: "Our Lord, come!" Paul here uses an Aramaic word, "maranatha." Didymus and John Chrysostom take this as a reference to Christ's incarnation. The RSV and other modern translations take it to refer to Christ's second coming and translate, "Our Lord, come."

send you hearty greetings in the Lord. For Paul stayed with them, since he was a tent maker. And it was no small virtue that they made their house into a church. **All the brethren send greetings. Greet one another with a holy kiss.** Only in this letter does Paul add this command. Why does he do this? They were very divided among themselves in that they said, *"I belong to Paul,"* or *"I belong to Apollos,"* or *"I belong to Cephas,"* or *"I belong to Christ"* (1 Cor 1:12). They were divided when one went hungry and another was getting drunk (1 Cor 11:21), and when they had fights, rivalries, and lawsuits (1 Cor 6:1). In addition, there was much jealousy and pride over spiritual gifts (1 Cor 12:1-31; 13:4). Since his exhortation has served to bring them together, it is fitting that he tells them to be united through a **holy kiss**, which brings to birth *one body* (1 Cor 12:12-14). This kiss is holy, without guile or hypocrisy. **I, Paul, write this greeting with my own hand.** This indicates the earnestness with which Paul has written the letter.

For the same reason, he adds, **If any one has no love for the Lord, let him be accursed.** With this one word **accursed** he makes them all afraid — those who were making their members the members of a prostitute (1 Cor 6:15), those who offended their brothers by eating food offered to idols (1 Cor 8:13), those who named themselves after human beings (1 Cor 1:12), and those who did not believe in the resurrection (1 Cor 15:12). He not only frightens them, but he also shows them the way of virtue and the source of vice. When our love for the Lord is strong, it blots out and repels all forms of sin. Likewise, when love grows weak, it makes these same sins sprout up.

Our Lord has come [Maranatha]! Why does he say this? Moreover, why does he say it in Hebrew? It is because vanity was the cause of all their troubles, and vanity came from pagan wisdom, which was the main thing that divided Corinth (1 Cor 1:20). So to check their vanity, Paul does not use Greek but Hebrew. This shows that he is not ashamed of his lack of sophistication but happy to acknowledge it. But what does **"Maranatha"** mean? **Our Lord has come.** Why does Paul say this? To confirm what he has said about God's plan for salvation, which is particularly evident in his discussion of the *seeds* of resurrection (1 Cor 15:1-58). Not only this, but he makes them feel ashamed, as if he were saying, "The one universal Lord has deigned to come down, and yet you continue in the same state of sin? Are you not overcome by awe at the abundance of his love, the chief of blessings?" . . .

My love be with you all, as if he were saying, "I am with you all." By this Paul shows that what he has written does not come from anger or wrath but from concern. After chastising them so strongly, he has not turned away from them but loves and embraces them though they are absent, throwing his arms about them through these epistles. Anyone who corrects others has to do this. One who acts only in anger gives vent to his own strong feelings. One who corrects someone who has gone astray and then demonstrates the way of love makes clear that even what he said by way of rebuke was said out of love. Let us admonish each other in this way.

Authors of Works Excerpted

Ambrose (ca. 339-97), a powerful bishop of Milan, the capital of the western Roman Empire, exerted much influence on the emperors of his time. He was a defender of Nicene orthodoxy against Arianism and was also partly responsible for the conversion of Augustine. He is one of the four "doctors" (i.e., teachers) of the Latin church. Fluent in Greek, he was acquainted with the biblical commentaries of Origen and other Greek fathers. His comments on 1 Corinthians are taken from *On the Mysteries,* a collection of homilies that discuss Baptism and the Eucharist and explain their symbolism.

Ambrosiaster (probably fourth century) is the name by which scholars refer to the unknown author of commentaries in Latin on the thirteen letters of Paul, who may have lived in Rome at the time of Pope Damasus (366-84). Our manuscripts attribute these commentaries to St. Ambrose (ca. 339-97). A work called *Questions on the Old and New Testaments* is probably also by the same person. His commentary on 1 Corinthians, the first in the Latin-speaking West, uses an Old Latin form of the biblical text that precedes Jerome's *Vulgate* (begun in 382). His succinct comments on 1 Corinthians focus on the historical sense of the text and on theological and moral themes, avoiding allegorical interpretation. Ambrosiaster is especially interested in Jewish institutions.

Augustine (354-430), the preeminent Western theologian of the patristic period, was trained in rhetoric in North Africa and Rome and taught it in Milan. He was a follower of Platonic philosophy and then of Manicheanism before his conversion to Christianity and his baptism by Ambrose in 387. Forcibly ordained priest of Hippo (in modern Algiers) and shortly thereafter bishop, he spent much of his time defending the catholic faith in opposition to Manicheans, Donatists, and Pelagians. (On these groups see Appendix 3.) His vast surviving output embraces exegesis (sermons, commentaries), theology and dogma (e.g., *On the Trinity*), apologetics *(City of God),* and autobiography *(Confessions).* Among the central themes of his work are God as the supreme object of human desire, evil as a purely negative privation of the good, the radical dependence of man upon the grace of God, and the doctrine of original sin. Although he did not write a commentary or a series of sermons on 1 Corinthians, his sermons and theological works are full of comments on passages in this letter.

Athanasius (ca. 296-373), bishop of Alexandria, was a strong supporter of the creed adopted at Nicea (325). Against the Arians (see Appendix 3), he championed the view that the Son is fully divine. His works include *On the Incarnation* and a life of the hermit Anthony. His comments on 1 Corinthians are excerpted from his first letter to the monk Serapion, in which he argues for the divinity of the Holy Spirit, and from his treatise *On Virginity.*

Basil of Caesarea, or Basil "the Great" (ca. 330-79), was bishop of Caesarea in Cappadocia (in modern Turkey) and founder of a monastery and charitable institutions. One of the three Cappadocian fathers, he was the brother of Gregory of Nyssa and close friend of Gregory of Nazianzus. His rules for monks, published in several different forms, are still influential in Eastern churches. Basil defended the Christology of Nicea against the Neo-Arians, who denied the full divinity of Christ. His treatise *On the Holy Spirit* is concerned to defend the divinity of the Spirit.

Cassiodorus (485/90–ca. 580) was a Roman statesman who served the Ostrogothic rulers in Ravenna and the founded a monastic community near Naples. There he arranged for the copying of manuscripts and collected many theological writings, including biblical commentaries. His works include the *Institutes of Divine and Secular Literature,* a church history, and a commentary on the Psalms. His commentary on thirteen letters of Paul (excluding Hebrews) is a revision of the commentary of Pelagius.

Clement of Alexandria (ca. 150–ca. 215), a Christian apologist, philosopher, and polymath, was the first Christian to attempt a thoroughgoing synthesis of the Bible and Greek philosophy. He is known primarily for a trilogy that consists of the *Exhortation,* an invitation to the Christian faith directed at educated Greeks, the *Pedagogue,* a moral treatise that focuses on the elementary stages of the Christian life, and the *Stromateis* or *Miscellanies,* an enigmatic, diffuse work in seven books that discusses various theological and moral topics. Book 3 of this work, which is devoted to the subject of marriage and takes issue with the views of Gnostic groups, contains much discussion of 1 Corinthians 7.

Cyril of Alexandria (d. 444), patriarch of Alexandria and an influential theologian, played an important role in the formulation of the classic doctrines of the person of Christ. He is known especially for his opposition to the teaching of the Antiochene Nestorius, bishop of Constantinople, who had opposed applying the term "mother of God" to the Virgin Mary. Cyril's writings include theological treatises, letters, and commentaries. One noteworthy feature of his *Commentary on 1 Corinthians,* of which fragments were preserved in medieval chain-commentaries, is his exploration of how Paul's words relate to various parts of the Old Testament.

Dialogue of a Montanist with an Orthodox Christian (probably third century) is the work of an anonymous Christian whose views are probably represented by "the orthodox" speaker in the dialogue. The work purports to give the teachings of a representative of the sectarian Montanist movement on subjects such as female prophets, which views are then refuted by the orthodox speaker. Montanus was the leader of a second-century Christian movement called "the new prophecy." He and his followers, Maximilla and Priscilla, claimed to go beyond the teaching of the apostles, under the influence of the Holy Spirit.

Didymus the Blind (ca. 313-98) was an influential biblical scholar and teacher in Alexandria, whose students included Jerome, Rufinus, and Palladius. Much influenced by Origen, he was condemned posthumously, along with Origen, by the fifth ecumenical council in 553. His writings include a treatise on the Holy Spirit and many commentaries on Scripture, most of which are lost. In 1941 his commentaries on Genesis, Job, Psalms 20–44, Ecclesiastes, and Zechariah were rediscovered in a collection of papyri at Toura in Egypt. Didymus interprets biblical narratives as describing a quest for union with the divine life. Of his *Commentary on 1 Corinthians* only a few comments on chapters 15 and 16 survive.

Gregory of Nazianzus (329-89), known as "the Theologian," was bishop of Sasima in Cappadocia (in modern Turkey) and a prominent preacher in Constantinople. Along with the other two Cappadocian fathers (Basil of Caesarea and Gregory of Nyssa), he was a strong supporter of the creed formulated at Nicea in 325 and a contributor to the resolution of the Arian controversies at the Council of Constantinople in 381. Well educated in Greek culture and rhetoric, he was known for his eloquence, evident, for example, in his *Five Theological Orations* and his many poems.

Gregory of Nyssa (ca. 330–ca. 395), bishop of Nyssa and an important theologian, was the brother of Basil of Caesarea and one of the three Cappadocian fathers. He championed the creed of Nicea (325) against followers of Arius who denied the full divinity of Christ (see the excerpts from his treatise on 1 Cor 15:28 and his polemical work *Against Eunomius*). Among his many works are the *Great Catechesis,* an introduction to the Christian faith and sacraments; *On Virginity,* which recommends the ascetic life; the *Life of Moses;* and homilies on the Beatitudes, the Lord's Prayer, and the Song of Songs. His exegesis, influenced by Origen, emphasizes the mystical sense of Scripture.

Irenaeus (ca. 130–ca. 200), bishop of Lugdunum in Gaul (modern Lyon), wrote *Against the Heresies* to oppose Gnostic teachers such the followers of Valentinus. He defends the Christian use of the Old Testament and argues for its unity with the New Testament, of which he is an important early interpreter. His theology emphasizes God's providential direction of history and the central biblical themes of creation, redemption through the incarnation, and eschatological fulfillment. Irenaeus uses 1 Corinthians 15 as an argument against the Gnostic dualism of flesh and spirit and for the resurrection of the body.

Jerome (ca. 345-420), an influential biblical scholar and ascetic, was educated in Rome and then devoted himself to the ascetic life, spending several years as a hermit in the Syrian desert and serving as head of a monastery in Bethlehem. He is best known for the Vulgate, his translation of the Bible from Hebrew and Greek into Latin, and for his many biblical commentaries (including works on the Prophets, Matthew, Galatians, Ephesians, and Philemon). He was much influenced by Origen, some of whose works he translated into Latin, but later in life he denounced some of Origen's ideas. His *On Illustrious Men*, a catalogue of Christian writers, contains a brief biography of the apostle Paul and a description of his letters. Jerome's extreme asceticism is evident in his *Against Jovinian*, where he opposes a monk who had used 1 Corinthians 7, along with other texts, to argue that marriage and celibacy had equal merit.

John Chrysostom (ca. 347-407) studied rhetoric under the pagan orator Libanius and theology under Diodore of Tarsus, head of the Christian school in Antioch. As a priest in Antioch and later bishop at Constantinople he was known especially for his uncompromising morality, his courage in difficult political circumstances, and his eloquence. His honorific title "Chrysostom" means "golden-tongued" and reflects his great reputation as a preacher. He preached extended series of sermons on many biblical books. His extensive *Homilies on 1 Corinthians* resemble a commentary in that they go through the book chapter by chapter and deal with historical and theological questions. Their setting in preaching is evident especially in the moral exhortation that takes up the last half of each sermon; frequent subjects are the danger of wealth and the need to care for the poor. Anticipating modern critics, Chrysostom is interested in reconstructing the historical situation presupposed in Paul's letter, and he emphasizes Paul's rhetorical skill.

John of Damascus (ca. 655–ca. 750), an official in the court of the Arab caliph, resigned his position to become a monk and priest in Jerusalem. He defended the use of images during the Iconoclasic Controversy (726-73). His major work, *The Fount of Wisdom*, is a synthesis of the teaching of the Greek fathers on central points of Christian doctrine. His lengthy commentary on the letters of Paul is a compilation based on the commentaries of John Chrysostom, Theodoret, and Cyril of Alexandria.

Leo the Great (Leo I, d. 461) became pope in 440. During an unstable time he greatly enhanced the authority of the see of Rome over all the Western provinces. His many letters and sermons are forcefully written.

The Liturgy of Saint James is an early Christian order for eucharistic worship associated with the church in Jerusalem and used in Syria, Egypt, Ethiopia, Armenia, and Georgia. It dates from the fifth century, if not earlier. Its *anaphora*, or prayer for offering up the elements of the Eucharist, includes an elaboration of Paul's words in 1 Corinthians 11.

Maximus the Confessor (ca. 580-662), synthesized, extended, and deepened the insights of Greek theologians such as Origen, Gregory of Nazianzus, Basil of Caesarea, and Gregory of Nyssa. He was imperial secretary in Constantinople under the emperor Heraclius before becoming a monk. He is called "Confessor" because of his heroic sufferings for his faith: as a result of his involvement in doctrinal controversy his tongue and hand were cut off and he was exiled. His many writings on theological, exegetical and ascetical topics include *The Four Hundred Chapters on Love; Questions to Thalassius*, which explains difficult texts from Scripture; *The Church's Mystagogy*, a mystical interpretation of the liturgy; and the *Ambigua*, which explains passsages from Gregory of Nazianzus and Dionysius the Areopagite. Maximus taught that the purpose of the incarnation of the Son of God was the deification of man, the restoration of the divine "image and likeness."

Oecumenius, author of brief glosses on the letters of Paul preserved in medieval chain-commentaries, is a shadowy figure. He was probably a sixth-century writer who copied John Chrysostom's homilies on the letters of Paul and added brief comments. A long chain-commentary on the letters of Paul published by Migne in PG 118, probably composed at the end of the eighth century, was once attributed to Oecumenius, but this attribution is now rejected and the work's unknown author referred to as "Pseudo-Oecumenius."

Origen of Alexandria (ca. 185–ca. 254) was a leading third-century theologian and exegete who lived in Alexandria and later in Caesarea in Palestine. He wrote many commentaries and homilies on Old and New Testament books (e.g., on Genesis, Exodus, Leviticus, Jeremiah, Luke, and John) and apparently commented on all the Pauline epistles (of these only the commentary on Romans survives in substantial quantity). His other works include *Against Celsus*, a defense of Christianity against the attack of the Platonic philosopher Celsus, and *On First Principles*, a compendium of Christian theology. Origen's works show particular interest in 1 Corinthians. Excerpts from these works are cited here, along with the substantial fragments of his *Homilies on 1 Corinthians*.

Pelagius (born ca. 354), a British monk and leader of an ascetic movement, was active in Rome from 384 to 410. He taught that human beings were blessed with a free will and could choose the good with the help of the commandments and the example of Christ. His views were strongly opposed by Augustine and condemned by several church councils. The *Commentary on the Thirteen Letters of Paul*, his main surviving work, makes use of earlier commentaries including those of Ambrosiaster, Origen, and Theodore of Mopsuestia. It consists mostly of brief notes and displays a particular interest in moral progress and in the power of imitating exemplary lives, such as that of St. Paul.

Photius (ca 810–ca. 895), patriarch of Constantinople and statesman, was involved in conflicts between the Greek and Latin churches. He was a scholar of wide interests, and his *Bibliotheca* preserves extracts of hundreds of works, many otherwise lost. Fragments of his *Commentary on the Letters of Paul* survive in medieval chain-commentaries.

Severian of Gabala (fl. ca. 400), an exegete of the Antiochene school, was a well-known preacher in Constantinople, where he was popular with the imperial court. Appointed by John Chrysostom as his vicar, he later turned against John and was one of his accusers at the Synod of the Oak (403). Fragments of his *Homilies on 1 Corinthians* were preserved in medieval chain-commentaries.

Tertullian (ca. 160–ca. 225), from Carthage in North Africa, the first to write theological treatises in Latin, also wrote apologetic, antiheretical, and moral works, all of which display great rhetorical skill. In his *On the Resurrection of the Dead,* which is directed against Gnostics, he makes use of 1 Corinthians 15 to mount a vigorous argument for the physical reality of the resurrection body. For a time Tertullian was a Montanist (see Appendix 3), attracted in part by the rigorous moralism of this movement. His ascetic views are reflected in his comments on 1 Corinthians 7 in *On Monogamy* and in his *Letter to His Wife.*

Theodore of Mopsuestia (ca. 350-428), a friend of John Chrysostom and bishop of Mopsuestia in Cilicia, was a representative of Antiochene exegesis and theology. In his biblical commentaries, surviving only in fragments, Theodore emphasizes philological and historical questions and avoids Alexandrian allegorical interpretation.

Theodoret (ca. 393–ca. 460), bishop of Cyrus (near Antioch), was educated in monastic schools in Antioch and defended Nestorius and Antiochene Christology against the criticisms of Cyril of Alexandria. His works include an apology that compares Christian and pagan teaching, a church history, biographies of monks, a refutation of heresies, and commentaries on many Old Testament books and on all the letters of Paul. His *Commentary on 1 Corinthians* gives terse comments on every section. It frequently opposes the teachings of groups such as Montanists and Manichees (on which see Appendix 3).

Sources of Texts Translated

See Bibliography for editions used.
Note the following short titles used in the references below:
    Commentary = Commentary on 1 Corinthians
    Homilies = Homilies on 1 Corinthians

Abbreviations

CCSL   Corpus Christianorum: Series latina. Turnhout (Belgium): Brepols, 1953ff.
CSEL   Corpus scriptorum ecclesiasticorum latinorum. Vienna, 1866ff.
Denis   M. Denis, ed. *Sancti Aurelii Augustini Hipponensis episcopi sermones inediti admixtis quibusdam dubiis.* Vienna, 1792.
FC   Fontes Christiani. Freiburg and New York: Herder, 1990ff.
GCS   Die griechischen christlichen Schriftsteller der ersten drei Jahrhunderte. Berlin: Akademie Verlag, 1901ff.
GNO   W. Jaeger et al., eds. Gregorii Nysseni opera. Leiden: Brill, 1960-72.
JTS   *Journal of Theological Studies.* London: Oxford University Press, 1899ff.
LCL   Loeb Classical Library. Cambridge, Mass.: Harvard University Press, 1912ff.
MA   *Miscellanea Agostiniana,* 2 vols. Rome, 1930-31. Vol. 1: *Sermones post Maurinos reperti,* ed. G. Morin.
PA   Papyrologische Texte und Abhandlungen. Bonn: Habelt, 1958ff.
PG   J.-P. Migne, ed. Patrologiae cursus completus: Series graeca. 161 vols. Paris, 1857-66.
PL   J.-P. Migne, ed. Patrologiae cursus completus: Series latina. 221 vols. Paris, 1878-90.
PLS   A. Hamann, ed. Patrologiae latinae supplementum. Paris, 1957ff.
PO   Patrologia orientalis. Paris, 1907ff.
RB   *Revue bénédictine.* Abbaye de Maredsous, Belgium, 1890ff.
SC   Sources chrétiennes. Paris: du Cerf, 1948ff.
Staab   K. Staab, ed. *Pauluskommentar aus der griechischen Kirche aus Katenhandschriften gesammelt.* Münster: Aschendorff, 1933.

On the Author: St. Paul

(1) Jerome, *On Illustrious Men* 5, A. Ceresa-Gastaldo, 80-86.
(2) Origen, *Homilies on Leviticus* 4.6, SC 286:182-84.
(3) Augustine, *Sermon* 333.2-4, PL 38:1464-46; *Sermon* 168.3-4, PL 38:913.
(4) John Chrysostom, *In Praise of Paul, Homily* 1: 1.1-11, 2.1-7, 3.1-8, 4.1-15, 6.1-12, 8.1-12, 13.1-10, SC 300:112-32; *Homily* 2: 8.1-14, SC 300:156; *Homily* 4: 10.11-31, SC 300:202-6; *Homily* 5: 4.1-18, SC 300:236-38; *Homily* 7: 1.1-11, SC 300:292-94; *Homily* 4: 21.1-9, SC 300:228.

General Comments on the Letter

(1) Ambrosiaster, *Commentary*, CSEL 81/2:3-4.
(2) John Chrysostom, *Homilies on 1 Corinthians*, Introductory Summary, PG 61:9-12.
(3) Theodoret, *Commentary*, Introductory Summary, PG 82:225-28.

1 Corinthians 1:1-3

(1) Severian of Gabala, *Commentary*, Staab 225-26.
(2) Ambrosiaster, *Commentary*, CSEL 81/2:4-6.
(3) Origen, *Homilies, JTS* 9 (1908) 232.

1 Corinthians 1:4-9

(1) Ambrosiaster, *Commentary*, CSEL 81/2:6-8.
(2) Origen, *Homilies, JTS* 9 (1908) 232-34.
(3) Theodoret, *Commentary*, PG 82:229-32.

1 Corinthians 1:10-17

(1) John Chrysostom, *Homily* 3, PG 61:21-28.
(2) Ambrosiaster, *Commentary*, CSEL 81/2:10-13.

1 Corinthians 1:18-25

(1) Origen, *Homilies, JTS* 9 (1908) 235; *Homilies on Luke*, SC 87:150-52.
(2) Ambrosiaster, *Commentary*, CSEL 81/2:15.
(3) John Chrysostom, *Homily* 4, PG 61:31-32.
(4) Cyril of Alexandria, *Commentary*, Pusey 253-55.
(5) Theodoret, *Commentary*, PG 82:236-37.

1 Corinthians 1:26-31

(1) Origen, *Homilies, JTS* 9 (1908) 237.

(2) John of Damascus, *Commentary*, PG 95:580-81.

(3) Severian of Gabala, *Commentary*, Staab 230-31.

(4) Ambrosiaster, *Commentary*, CSEL 81/2:20-21.

(5) Gregory of Nazianzus, *Oration* 30.16-20, SC 250:260, 266-70.

(6) Gregory of Nyssa, *Commentary on the Song of Songs* 11, GNO 6:331-32; *On the Beatitudes* 5, GNO 7.2:119-22.

(7) Maximus the Confessor, *Ambiguum* 7, PG 91:1081-84.

(8) Basil of Caesarea, *Homily* 20, PG 31:528-32.

(9) Augustine, *Sermon* 160.1-5, PL 38:873-76.

1 Corinthians 2:1-5

(1) John Chrysostom, *Homily* 6, PG 61:49-51.

1 Corinthians 2:6-8

(1) Origen, *Homilies*, JTS 9 (1908) 238-39; *On First Principles* 4.2.1-4 (Greek), SC 268:292-312.

(2) Cyril of Alexandria, *Commentary*, Pusey 256-57.

(3) Oecumenius, *Notes on 1 Corinthians*, Staab 432.

1 Corinthians 2:9-12

(1) Leo the Great, *Treatise* 95.8, CCSL 38A:588-89.

(2) Augustine, *Sermon* 331.4-5, PL 38:1460-61.

(3) Athanasius, *Letter to Serapion* 1.22, PG 26:581.

(4) Basil of Caesarea, *On the Holy Spirit* 24.55-57, 6.40, SC 17:450-54, 390.

(5) Augustine, *Confessions* 13.28-31, O'Donnell 1:201-3.

1 Corinthians 2:13-16

(1) John of Damascus, *Commentary*, PG 95:588.

(2) Cyril of Alexandria, *Commentary*, Pusey 257.

(3) Origen, *Homilies*, JTS 9 (1908) 240.

1 Corinthians 3:1-3

(1) Ambrosiaster, *Commentary*, CSEL 81/2:31-33.

(2) Origen, *Homilies*, JTS 9 (1908) 241-42.

(3) Severian of Gabala, *Commentary*, Staab 235-36.

(4) Augustine, *Commentary on John* 98, CCSL 36:576-81; *Sermon* 71, 30-31, PL 38:461-62.

(5) John Chrysostom, *Homily* 8, PG 61:69-70.

1 Corinthians 3:4-8

(1) John Chrysostom, *Homily* 8, PG 61:70-71.
(2) Ambrosiaster, *Commentary*, CSEL 81/2:33-34.
(3) Origen, *Homilies*, JTS 9 (1908) 243.
(4) Augustine, *Sermon* 340.1, PL 38:1483-84.
(5) Theodoret, *Commentary*, PG 82:248.

1 Corinthians 3:9-11

(1) Origen, *Homilies*, JTS 9 (1908) 244.
(2) John Chrysostom, *Homily* 8, PG 61:72-73.
(3) Cyril of Alexandria, *Commentary*, Pusey 259-60.
(4) Augustine, *Sermon* 337.1-2, PL 38:1475-77.

1 Corinthians 3:12-15

(1) Cassiodorus, *Commentary*, PL 68:513-14.
(2) John Chrysostom, *Homily* 9, PG 61:75-80.
(3) Origen, *Homilies*, JTS 9 (1908) 244-45; *Homily on Jeremiah* 16.5, SC 238:144-46.
(4) Ambrosiaster, *Commentary*, CSEL 81/2:37-38.

1 Corinthians 3:16-17

(1) Origen, *Homilies*, JTS 9 (1908) 245-46.
(2) Athanasius, *Letter to Serapion* 1.24, PG 26:585-88.
(3) Augustine, *Sermon* 82.13, PL 38:512.
(4) Theodore of Mopsuestia, *Commentary*, Staab 176.
(5) Ambrosiaster, *Commentary*, CSEL 81/2:38-39.

1 Corinthians 3:18-23

(1) Ambrosiaster, *Commentary*, CSEL 81/2:39.
(2) Pelagius, *Commentary*, Souter 2:144-45.
(3) Origen, *Homilies*, JTS 9 (1908) 247, 353.
(4) Theodore of Mopsuestia, *Commentary*, Staab 176.
(5) Severian of Gabala, *Commentary*, Staab 238.

1 Corinthians 4:1-2

(1) Origen, *Homilies*, JTS 9 (1908) 354.
(2) John Chrysostom, *Homily* 10, PG 61:84-85.

1 Corinthians 4:3-5

(1) John Chrysostom, *Homily* 11, PG 61:87-92.
(2) Origen, *Homilies,* JTS 9 (1908) 355-56.
(3) Augustine, *Sermon* 71.21, PL 38:456.

1 Corinthians 4:6-8

(1) John Chrysostom, *Homily* 12, PG 61:95-98.
(2) Photius, *Commentary,* Staab 551.
(3) Ambrosiaster, *Commentary,* CSEL 81/2:45-46.
(4) Augustine, *Sermon* 333.6; PL 38:1466-67.

1 Corinthians 4:9-13

(1) Origen, *Homilies,* JTS 9 (1908) 360.
(2) Augustine, *Sermon* 51.2, PL 38:333.
(3) John Chrysostom, *Homily* 12, PG 61:100-101.
(4) Ambrosiaster, *Commentary,* CSEL 81/2:48.

1 Corinthians 4:14-16

(1) Augustine, *Sermon* 16A.10, CCSL 41:227.
(2) John Chrysostom, *Homily* 13, PG 61:110-12.

1 Corinthians 4:17-21

(1) Theodoret, *Commentary,* PG 82:260.
(2) Severian of Gabala, *Commentary,* Staab 242.
(3) John Chrysostom, *Homily* 14, PG 61:117.

1 Corinthians 5:1-5

(1) Cyril of Alexandria, *Commentary,* Pusey 261.
(2) Origen, *Homilies,* JTS 9 (1908) 364.

1 Corinthians 5:6-8

(1) John Chrysostom, *Homily* 15, PG 61:124-26.
(2) Origen, *Homilies,* JTS 9 (1908) 365.

1 Corinthians 5:9-11

(1) Origen, *Homilies,* JTS 9 (1908), 366-67.

(2) Photius, *Commentary*, Staab 553.
(3) Augustine, *Letter* 29, LCL 239:70, 74-76, 86-90.

1 Corinthians 5:12-13

(1) Origen, *Homilies, JTS* 9 (1908) 367.
(2) John Chrysostom, *Homily* 16, PG 61:131.

1 Corinthians 6:1-6

(1) John Chrysostom, *Homily* 16, PG 61:132-33.
(2) Severian of Gabala, *Commentary*, Staab 245-46.
(3) Theodoret, *Commentary*, PG 82:265.

1 Corinthians 6:7-8

(1) John Chrysostom, *Homily,* 16, PG 61:136-38.

1 Corinthians 6:9-11

(1) Origen, *Homilies, JTS* 9 (1908) 368-69.

1 Corinthians 6:12-14

(1) Theodoret, *Commentary*, PG 82:268.
(2) Severian of Gabala, *Commentary,* Staab 246-47.

1 Corinthians 6:15-18

(1) Augustine, *Sermon* 161.1-4, 7-9, PL 38:877-83; *Sermon* 162.1-4, PL 38:885-89.
(2) Oecumenius, *Notes on 1 Corinthians,* Staab 434-35.

1 Corinthians 6:19-20

(1) Theodoret, *Commentary,* PG 82:269-72.
(2) John Chrysostom, *Homily* 18, PG 61:148-49.

1 Corinthians 7:1-7

(1) Clement of Alexandria, *Miscellanies* 3.6.51-53; 3.7.57-59, GCS 2:219.25–220.6; 220.14-27; 222.14-19; 222.27–223.10.
(2) Origen, *Homilies on 1 Corinthians, JTS* 9 (1908) 500-503.
(3) John Chrysostom, *Homily* 19, PG 61:151-53.
(4) Jerome, *Against Jovinian* 1, PL 23:211-21.
(5) Augustine, *On the Good of Marriage* 1, 3-4, Walsh 2, 6-8; *Sermon* 332.4, PL 38:1463.

1 Corinthians 7:8-11

(1) Cyril of Alexandria, *Commentary*, Pusey 267-70.
(2) Clement of Alexandria, *Miscellanies* 3.1.4; 3.18.108, GCS 2:197.3-15; 246:10-20.
(3) John Chrysostom, *Homily* 19, PG 61:153-54.
(4) Augustine, *Sermon* 354A, *RB* 84 (1974) 267; *On the Good of Marriage* 6-7, Walsh 14-16.

1 Corinthians 7:12-16

(1) Tertullian, *To His Wife* 2.1-2, SC 273:122-26.
(2) John Chrysostom, *Homily* 19, PG 61:155.
(3) Augustine, *Sermon* 294.18, PL 38:1346-47.

1 Corinthians 7:17-24

(1) John Chrysostom, *Homily* 19, PG 61:156-57.
(2) Basil of Caesarea, *Shorter Rules* 136, 141, 147, PG 31:1172, 1177, 1180.

1 Corinthians 7:25-31

(1) Jerome, *Against Jovinian* 1.12, PL 23:227-28.
(2) Augustine, *Sermon* 161.11, PL 38:884; *On the Good of Marriage* 12-13, Walsh 26; *Sermon* 125.7-8, 11, PL 38:694-97; *Sermon* 301A.4, *MA* 1:84-85.

1 Corinthians 7:32-35

(1) Clement of Alexandria, *Miscellanies* 3.12.88, GCS 2:236.28–237.4.
(2) John Chrysostom, *Homily* 19, PG 61:159-60.
(3) Basil of Caesarea, *Longer Rules* 5, PG 31:920-21.
(4) Athanasius, *On Virginity* 2-3, Von der Goltz 36-37.
(5) Augustine, *Sermon* 161.12, PL 38:884.
(6) Gregory of Nyssa, *On Virginity*, Introduction and section 9, GNO 8/1: 247.1–248.16; 287.17–288.9.

1 Corinthians 7:36-40

(1) Theodoret, *Commentary*, PG 82:284-85.
(2) Augustine, *On the Good of Marriage* 8, Walsh 18; *Sermon* 354.9, PL 39:1567-68.

1 Corinthians 8:1-3

(1) Ambrosiaster, *Commentary*, CSEL 81/2:91-92.
(2) John Chrysostom, *Homily* 20, PG 61:159-62.
(3) Augustine, *Sermon* 354.6-7, PL 39:1566.

(4) Gregory of Nyssa, *Commentary on the Song of Songs* 12, GNO 6:352.

1 Corinthians 8:4-6

(1) John Chrysostom, *Homily 20*, PG 61:162-65.
(2) Theodore of Mopsuestia, *Commentary*, Staab 183-84.
(3) Gregory of Nyssa, *Against Eunomius* 3.8 (= book 10, PG 45:844-45), GNO 2:254-56.
(4) Theodoret, *Commentary*, PG 82:289.
(5) Ambrosiaster, *Commentary*, CSEL 81/2:93-94.

1 Corinthians 8:7-9

(1) Ambrosiaster, *Commentary*, CSEL 81/2:94.
(2) John Chrysostom, *Homily 20*, PG 61:165-66.

1 Corinthians 8:10-13

(1) John Chrysostom, *Homily 20*, PG 61:167-68.
(2) Cyril of Alexandria, *Commentary*, Pusey 277.
(3) Augustine, *Sermon* 62.7-11, PL 38.417-20.
(4) Gregory of Nyssa, *Against Eunomius* 1.37 (= book 1, PG 45:417-20), GNO 1:183-84.

1 Corinthians 9:1-2

(1) John Chrysostom, *Homily* 21, PG 61:169-71.

1 Corinthians 9:3-7

(1) Augustine, *The Work of Monks* 5-6, CSEL 41:538-40.
(2) Severian of Gabala, *Commentary*, Staab 256.
(3) Origen, *Homilies*, JTS 9 (1908) 510-11.
(4) John Chrysostom, *Homily* 21, PG 61:172-73.

1 Corinthians 9:8-12a

(1) Augustine, *Sermon*, Dolbeau 29,9, *Revue des Études Augustiniennes* 41 (1995) 286.
(2) John Chrysostom, *Homily* 21, PG 61:173-74.
(3) Origen, *Homilies*, JTS 9 (1908) 511-12.

1 Corinthians 9:12b-18

(1) John Chrysostom, *Homily* 21, PG 61:175-76.
(2) Oecumenius, *Notes on 1 Corinthians*, Staab 439.
(3) Augustine, *The Work of Monks* 10, CSEL 41:546-47.

(4) Origen, *Homilies, JTS* 9 (1908) 512.

1 Corinthians 9:19-23

(1) Origen, *Homilies, JTS* 9 (1908) 512-14.
(2) Augustine, *The Work of Monks* 12, CSEL 41:550-51.

1 Corinthians 9:24-27

(1) Severian of Gabala, *Commentary,* Staab 257.
(2) Origen, *Homilies, JTS* 9 (1908) 514.
(3) Augustine, *The Usefulness of Fasting* 5, PL 40:710-11.

1 Corinthians 10:1-5

(1) Origen, *Homilies on Exodus* 5, SC 321:148-50.
(2) John Chrysostom, *Homily* 23, PG 61:191.
(3) Augustine, *A Reply to Faustus* 12.29, PL 42:269-70; *Sermon* 4.9-10, CCSL 41.25-27.

1 Corinthians 10:6-11

(1) Cyril of Alexandria, *Commentary,* Pusey 278-80.
(2) Augustine, *The Literal Meaning of Genesis* 1.1.1, CSEL 28/1:3-4.

1 Corinthians 10:12-13

(1) John Chrysostom, *Homily* 23, PL 61:194.
(2) Origen, *On First Principles* 3.2.1-3, SC 268:152, 156-66.

1 Corinthians 10:14-17

(1) John Chrysostom, *Homily* 24, PG 61:199-202.

1 Corinthians 10:18-22

(1) John Chrysostom, *Homily* 24, PG 61:202.
(2) Clement of Alexandria, *Instructor* 2.1.8.3–9.4, GCS 1:159.12-60.11.

1 Corinthians 10:23-26

(1) Clement of Alexandria, *Instructor* 2.1.14.3-6, GCS 1:163.30-64.17.
(2) John Chrysostom, *Homily* 24, PG 61:202-3.

1 Corinthians 10:27-33

(1) Clement of Alexandria, *Instructor* 2.1.10.1-4; 13.2, GCS 1:160.16-161.6; 163.14-17.
(2) Theodoret, *Commentary*, PG 82:308-9.
(3) John Chrysostom, *Homily* 25, PG 61:208-12.

1 Corinthians 11:1-2

(1) Ambrosiaster, *Commentary*, CSEL 81:119-20.
(2) John Chrysostom, *Homily* 26, PG 61:213.

1 Corinthians 11:3-9

(1) Theodore of Mopsuestia, *Commentary*, Staab 187.
(2) John Chrysostom, *Homily* 26, PG 61:214, 216.
(3) *Dialogue of a Montanist with an Orthodox Christian*, Gerhard Ficker, *Zeitschrift für Kirchengeschichte* 26 (1905), 456-58.
(4) Severian of Gabala, *Commentary*, Staab 261.
(5) Augustine, *The Literal Meaning of Genesis*, 1.42, CSEL 28/1:376-77.

1 Corinthians 11:10-16

(1) Theodoret, *Commentary*, PG 82:312-13.
(2) John Chrysostom, *Homily* 26, PG 61:218-19, 222-23.

1 Corinthians 11:17-22

(1) John Chrysostom, *Homily* 27, PG 61:223, 226.
(2) Augustine, *Sermon* 51.11, PL 38:339.
(3) Clement of Alexandria, *Miscellanies* 7.15.89.1–91.3, GCS 3:63.19-34; 64.15-30.

1 Corinthians 11:23-26

(1) John Chrysostom, *Homily* 27, PG 61:228-29.
(2) Prayers from *The Liturgy of St. James*, PO 26:200-206.
(3) Gregory of Nyssa, *Great Catechesis* 37, GNO 3/4:93-94, 96-98.
(4) Ambrose, *On the Mysteries* 47-48, 50-52, 54-55, FC 3.240-48.

1 Corinthians 11:27-34

(1) Theodore of Mopsuestia, *Commentary*, Staab 189.
(2) John Chrysostom, *Homily* 27, PG 61:230-32.

1 Corinthians 12:1-3

(1) John Chrysostom, *Homily* 29, PG 61:239-42.
(2) Origen, *Homilies, JTS* 10 (1909) 29-30.
(3) Basil of Caesarea, *On the Holy Spirit* 16.38, SC 17:382-84; 11.27, SC 17:342; 18.47, SC 17:412.

1 Corinthians 12:4-7

(1) Athanasius, *Letter to Serapion* 1.30, PG 26:597-600; 3.5-6, PG 26:633.
(2) Theodoret, *Commentary,* PG 82:321-24.
(3) John Chrysostom, *Homily* 29, PG 61:243.

1 Corinthians 12:8-11

(1) Augustine, *On the Trinity* 14.1.3, CCSL 50A:423-24.
(2) John Chrysostom, *Homily* 29, PG 61:244-47.
(3) Athanasius, *Letter to Serapion* 3.3-4, PG 26:629.

1 Corinthians 12:12-14

(1) Athanasius, *Letter to Serapion* 1.19, PG 26:573-76.
(2) Basil of Caesarea, *On the Holy Spirit* 12.28, SC 17:344-46.
(3) Cyril of Alexandria, *Commentary,* Pusey 290-91.
(4) John Chrysostom, *Homily* 30, PG 61:251.

1 Corinthians 12:15-19

(1) John Chrysostom, *Homily* 30, PG 61:252.

1 Corinthians 12:20-26

(1) John Chrysostom, *Homily* 30, PG 61:253-55; *Homily* 31, PG 61:258-59, 261-64.
(2) Augustine, *Sermon* 354.3-5, PL 39:1564-65; *Sermon* 280.1, 6, PL 38:1281-84.

1 Corinthians 12:27-31

(1) Augustine, *Sermon* 162A.4-5, 6-7, Denis 19, *MA* 1:101-4.

1 Corinthians 13:1-3

(1) John Chrysostom, *Homily* 32, PG 61:268-72.
(2) Augustine, *Sermon* 162A.1-4, Denis 19, *MA* 1:98-101.

1 Corinthians 13:4-7

(1) Origen, *Homilies, JTS* 10 (1909) 34-35.
(2) Augustine, *Sermon* 354.6, PL 39:1565-66; *Sermon* 350, PL 39:1535.
(3) John Chrysostom, *Homily* 33, PG 61:275-85.

1 Corinthians 13:8-10

(1) John Chrysostom, *Homily* 34, PG 61:285-87.
(2) Augustine, *City of God* 22.29, LCL 7:356-62, 368-70.

1 Corinthians 13:11-13

(1) John Chrysostom, *Homily* 34, PG 61:288-89.
(2) Gregory of Nyssa, *Commentary on the Song of Songs*, GNO 6:86, 90, 98, 336.
(3) Augustine, *On the Trinity* 14.17, CCSL 50A:454-55; *Sermon* 53.6-7, 16, PL 38:366-67, 371-72; *Sermon* 362.29, Lambot 4, PL 39:1632-33.
(4) Augustine, *Sermon* 359A, PLS 2:759-61.
(5) Gregory of Nyssa, *On the Soul and the Resurrection* 6, PG 46:65, 93-96.

1 Corinthians 14:1-5

(1) Cyril of Alexandria, *Commentary*, Pusey 291-92.
(2) Theodoret, *Commentary*, PG 82:337-40.

1 Corinthians 14:6-12

(1) Origen, *Homilies, JTS* 10 (1909) 36.
(2) John Chrysostom, *Homily* 35, PG 61:297-99.

1 Corinthians 14:13-19

(1) John Chrysostom, *Homily* 35, PG 61:300-301.

1 Corinthians 14:20-25

(1) Theodoret, *Commentary*, PG 82:344.
(2) Severian of Gabala, *Commentary*, Staab 269.
(3) Basil of Caesarea, *On the Holy Spirit* 16.37, SC 17:374-76.
(4) John Chrysostom, *Homily* 36, PG 61:305-9.

1 Corinthians 14:26-33a

(1) Severian of Gabala, *Commentary*, Staab 270.
(2) Origen, *Homilies, JTS* 10 (1909) 41.

(3) John Chrysostom, *Homily* 36, PG 61:312-15.

1 Corinthians 14:33b-36

(1) Theodoret, *Commentary,* PG 82:345-48.
(2) Origen, *Homilies, JTS* 10 (1909) 41-42.
(3) John Chrysostom, *Homily* 37, PG 61:317.

1 Corinthians 14:37-40

(1) Ambrosiaster, *Commentary,* CSEL 81:160-63.

1 Corinthians 15:1-2

(1) John Chrysostom, *Homily* 38, PG 61:321-23.

1 Corinthians 15:3-7

(1) Cyril of Alexandria, *Commentary,* Pusey 297-99.
(2) Gregory of Nyssa, *Great Catechesis* 35, GNO 3/4:86-88.

1 Corinthians 15:8-11

(1) John Chrysostom, *Homily* 38, PG 61:328-29.
(2) Augustine, *Sermon* 76.6-7, PL 38:481-82.

1 Corinthians 15:12-19

(1) Tertullian, *On the Resurrection* 48.6-8, Evans 138.
(2) John Chrysostom, *Homily* 39, PG 61:335.

1 Corinthians 15:20-22

(1) Origen, *Homilies, JTS* 10 (1909) 45-47.
(2) Augustine, *Sermon* 90.7, PL 38:563-64; *Sermon* 293.8-9, PL 38:1333.
(3) Gregory of Nyssa, *Great Catechesis* 16, GNO 3/4:48-49.

1 Corinthians 15:23-27

(1) John Chrysostom, *Homily* 39, PG 61:338-41.
(2) Augustine, *Sermon* 61A.7, *RB* 79 (1969) 184.

1 Corinthians 15:28

(1) Origen, *On First Principles* 3.6.2-3, SC 268:238-40.
(2) John Chrysostom, *Homily* 39, PG 61:341-42.
(3) Augustine, *Sermon* 177.9, PL 38:958; *Sermon* 158.9, PL 38:867.
(4) Gregory of Nyssa, *Treatise on 1 Cor 15.28*, GNO 3/2:13-21, 26-28.

1 Corinthians 15:29-34

(1) Tertullian, *On the Resurrection* 48.11, Evans 138-40.
(2) John Chrysostom, *Homily* 40, PG 61:348-51.
(3) Augustine, *Sermon* 361.5, 7, 18, PL 39:1601-2, 1609-10.

1 Corinthians 15:35-41

(1) Origen, *Against Celsus* 8.49, SC 150:280-82, *Against Celsus* 5.18-19, SC 147:58-62.
(2) John Chrysostom, *Homily* 41, PG 61:356-58.
(3) Augustine, *Sermon* 361.9-12, PL 39:1603-5; *Sermon* 362.27-29, PL 39:1630-32.

1 Corinthians 15:42-49

(1) Tertullian, *On the Resurrection* 53.1, 4-8, 10-14, Evans 156, 158-60.
(2) Origen, *On First Principles* 2.10.1, SC 252:374-76; 2.10.3, SC 252:378-80; 3.6.4, SC 268:242-44.
(3) Didymus of Alexandria, *Commentary on the Psalms* 259, PA 6:130-32.
(4) John Chrysostom, *Homily* 41, PG 61:359.

1 Corinthians 15:50-53

(1) Tertullian, *On the Resurrection* 49.1-5, 6-10, 13; 50.4-6; 51.1-3, Evans 140-48.
(2) Irenaeus, *Against the Heresies* 1.5.9.1-4, 10.2, 11.1–12.1, 13.2-3, SC 153:106-11, 114-16, 120-22, 130-32, 134-40, 166-70.
(3) Augustine, *Sermon* 362.13-17, PL 39:1619-22; *Sermon* 277.11, PL 38:1263; *Sermon* 277.4, 6-7, PL 38:1259-61.

1 Corinthians 15:54-58

(1) Augustine, *Sermon* 163.7, 10-12, PL 38:892-95; *Sermon* 77A.2, PLS 2:650-51.

1 Corinthians 16:1-4

(1) John Chrysostom, *Homily* 43, PG 61:367-69, 373.

1 Corinthians 16:5-9

(1) Pelagius, *Commentary,* Souter 227.
(2) Didymus of Alexandria, *Commentary,* Staab 12.
(3) John Chrysostom, *Homily* 43, PG 61:370-72.
(4) Augustine, *On the Predestination of the Saints* 40-41, PL 44:989-90.

1 Corinthians 16:10-12

(1) Didymus of Alexandria, *Commentary,* Staab 12.
(2) Origen, *Homilies, JTS* 10 (1909) 50.
(3) John Chrysostom, *Homily* 44, PG 61:373.

1 Corinthians 16:13-14

(1) Theodoret, *Commentary,* PG 82:372.
(2) John Chrysostom, *Homily* 44, PG 61:374-75.
(3) Origen, *Homilies, JTS* 10 (1909) 51.
(4) Augustine, *On Rebuke and Grace* 5, PL 44:918-19.

1 Corinthians 16:15-18

(1) John Chrysostom, *Homily* 44, PG 61:375-76.
(2) Didymus of Alexandria, *Commentary,* Staab 13.

1 Corinthians 16:19-24

(1) Didymus of Alexandria, *Commentary,* Staab 13-14.
(2) John Chrysostom, *Homily* 44, PG 61:376-77.

APPENDIX 3

Glossary of Proper Names

Arius, Arians. Arius (d. 336) was a priest in Alexandria who was excommunicated from the church for teaching that Christ the Son was neither fully divine nor eternal, but rather a "creature," the first creation of the Father before the ages. The views of Arius were strongly opposed by Athanasius, deacon and then bishop of Alexandria, and condemned at the ecumenical council at Nicea in 325, but they continued to spark theological controversy for centuries. Later followers of the teachings of Arius included the "Neo-Arians" Aetius (d. ca. 366) and Eunomius (d. 394), who developed his teaching in a more radical form. Arian views had wide influence, especially in the eastern parts of the Roman Empire, and they found favor with Constantine (for a time) and with the eastern emperors Constantius and Valens. Among those who disputed Arian teachings were the three Cappadocian fathers (Basil of Caesarea, Gregory of Nyssa, and Gregory of Nazianzius), whose views prevailed at the Council of Constantinople in 381. (See also "Eunomius, Eunomians.")

Celsus. A Platonic philosopher who around the year 248 composed an attack on Christianity called *The True Doctrine*. This work is lost, but portions are quoted by Origen in *Against Celsus,* in which he defends the Christian faith against the criticisms of Celsus.

Donatus, Donatists. Donatus (fl. 315-355), a teacher in North Africa, was a leader of a rigorist schismatic group that came to be known by his name. He was appointed bishop by a group that opposed the catholic bishop of Carthage, Caecilian, on the grounds that he had been consecrated by a bishop who had compromised with pagan authorities. The Donatists broke off from the catholic church in North Africa in the early fourth century because they thought the catholics were too lenient with Christians who were not entirely faithful during the persecution of Diocletian (303-12). The Donatists claimed that theirs was the only "holy" church and held that sacraments administered by unworthy priests were invalid, insisting that catholic converts to their church be rebaptized. Augustine led theological opposition to the Donatists. In a comment on 1 Cor 12:27-31, for example, he concedes that Donatus may be "holy" but accuses him of lack of love for the "body of Christ." The group was condemned at an imperial council in 411 but survived in Africa until the eighth century.

314

Eunomius, Eunomians. Eunomius (d. 394), bishop of Cyzicus in Mysia (in modern Turkey), is called a Neo-Arian because he followed and developed in a more radical direction the teaching of Arius (d. 336). He studied in Alexandria with the Arian teacher Aetius (d. ca. 366). Like Arius, Eunomius taught that the Son was a "creature," subordinate to the Father. In addition, he claimed that the supreme being, whom he called "the Ungenerated," was totally intelligible. He wrote a commentary on Romans (now lost). His *First Apology* and *Second Apology,* both lost, called forth refutations by Basil of Caesarea and Gregory of Nyssa. The Eunomians, his followers, are also called Neo-Arians, extreme Arians, and Anomeans. The last epithet derives from the Greek word meaning "dissimilar" and reflects this group's emphasis on the difference between the Father and the Son. (See also "Arius, Arians.")

Gnostics. "Gnostic" (literally, "possessing knowledge") is a general name used to designate various groups in the ancient world, both within and outside of Christianity, who claimed to have special secret knowledge and who had a dualistic view of the world. Church fathers such as Irenaeus, Tertullian, Clement of Alexandria, and Origen argued against their views, especially their assertion that there are two different gods, the inferior Creator God of Old Testament and the perfectly good Father of Jesus Christ.

Marcion-Marcionites. Marcion (d. ca. 160) was excommunicated from the church at Rome in 144 because of his teaching that the Creator God of the Old Testament was entirely different from the God of love proclaimed by Jesus. In his work *Antitheses* (now lost except for sections quoted by Tertullian and other opponents), Maricon sharply contrasted law and gospel and held that the Old Testament had no place in the Christian religion. The communities he established around the Roman Empire were a significant threat to the orthodox church in the second and third centuries.

Mani, Manicheans. Mani or Manicheus (216-76), a teacher born in the Persian Empire, where he belonged to a Jewish Christian sect, and later exiled to India, developed a strongly dualistic version of Gnostic teaching (see "Gnostics"), which emphasized the primeval conflict of light and darkness. His teaching spread widely. His followers, the Manicheans or Manichees, were active in Egypt in the third century, in Rome by the fourth century, and in North Africa by the later fourth century; they survived in Chinese Turkestan through the tenth century. Their religion was concerned with the release of particles of Light imprisoned by Satan, a drama in which the whole cosmos was involved. The sect was strongly ascetic. Augustine was a Manichean for nine years but then rejected their teachings and argued against them.

Montanus, Montanism. Montanus (second century) was the leader of a Christian movement called "the New Prophecy" that centered in Phrygia in Asia Minor (modern Turkey). He and his followers, including the female prophets Maximilla and Priscilla, claimed to transcend the teaching of the apostles and to be bearers of the Paraclete or Holy Spirit. Montanus expected that the heavenly Jerusalem (see Revelation 21–22) would soon descend in Phrygia. The Montanist movement emphasized ecstatic experience and vivid eschatological expectation. A form of Montanism that emphasized asceticism and denounced second marriage spread to North Africa, where it was embraced for a time by Tertullian (ca. 160–ca. 225).

Novatianists. A rigorist schismatic group that arose under the leadership of a Roman presbyter, Novatian, after the persecution by the emperor Decius (249-50). Novatian and his followers said that those who had renounced their faith under threat of persecution could not be received back into the church. The movement lasted through the early fifth century.

Tropici. A group that denied the divinity of the Holy Spirit, whom they called a "creature." Athanasius (ca. 296-373) argues against their views in a letter to Bishop Serapion.

Pneumatomachians. A fourth-century group who denied the full divinity of the Spirit. Their teaching was attacked by Basil of Caesarea (in *On the Holy Spirit*), and by the other two Cappadocian theologians, Gregory of Nyssa and Gregory of Nazianzus. The debate they sparked was an extension of the Arian controversies, in which the divinity of the Son was at issue.

Bibliography: Editions of Patristic Texts

Note: *English titles for patristic works are those used in the list of sources in Appendix 2; these are followed by the full bibliography of the editions from which the translations have been made. For abbreviations, see Appendix 2.*

Ambrose, *On the Mysteries: De sacramentis; De mysteriis.* O. Faller, ed.; Josef Schmitz, tr. FC 3:206-55. Freiburg: Herder, 1990.

Ambrosiaster, *Commentary on 1 Corinthians: Commentarius in Epistulas Paulinas.* Heinrich Josef Vogels, ed. CSEL 81/2:3-194. Vienna: Hoelder-Pichler-Tempsky, 1966-1969.

Athanasius, *Letter to Serapion: Epistola I ad Serapionem.* PG 26:529-608.

Athanasius, *On Virginity: De virginitate.* Eduard Freiherr von der Goltz, ed. TU 14, 2a. Leipzig: J. C. Hinrichs, 1905.

Augustine, *City of God.* W. M. Green, ed. and tr. Vol. 7. LCL 417. Cambridge, Mass.: Harvard University Press, 1972.

Augustine, *Commentary on John: In Iohannis Evangelium tractatus CXXIV.* Radbodus Willems, ed. CCSL 36. Turnhout: Brepols, 1954.

Augustine, *Confessions.* James J. O'Donnell, ed. 3 vols. Oxford: Clarendon, 1992.

Augustine, *The Literal Meaning of Genesis: De Genesi ad litteram libri duodecim.* Joseph Zycha, ed. CSEL 28/1. Vienna: F. Tempsky, 1894.

Augustine, *On the Good of Marriage: De bono coniugali; De sancta virginitate.* P. G. Walsh, ed. Oxford: Clarendon, 2001.

Augustine, *On the Predestination of the Saints: De praedestinatione sanctorum.* PL 44:959-92.

Augustine, *On Rebuke and Grace: De peccatorum meritis et remissione.* PL 44:109-52.

Augustine, *On the Trinity: De trinitate libri XV.* W. J. Mountain, ed. 2 vols. CCSL 50-50A. Turnhout: Brepols, 1968.

Augustine, *On the Usefulness of Fasting: De utilitate jejunii tractatus unus.* PL 40:707-16.

Augustine, *On the Work of Monks: De opere monachorum.* Joseph Zycha, ed. CSEL 41. Vienna: F. Tempsky, 1900.

Augustine, *A Reply to Faustus: Contra Faustum Manichaeum libri XXXIII.* PL 42:207-518.

Augustine, *Select Letters.* J. H. Baxter, ed. and tr. LCL 239. Cambridge: Harvard University Press, 1965.

Augustine, *Sermons.* PL 38-39; PLS 2.

Augustine, *Sermons. Sancti Augustini Opera XI/1: Sermones de vetere testamento.* Cyril Lambot, ed. CCSL 41. Turnhout: Brepols, 1961.

Augustine, *Sermons. Miscellanea Agostiniana.* G. Morin, ed. Vol. 1: *Sermones post Maurinos reperti.*

Augustine, *Sermons. Revue biblique* 79 (1969) 180-84; 84 (1974) 267.

Augustine, *Sermons:* "Sermon inédit de saint Augustin sur la providence divine." F. Dolbeau, ed. *Revue des Études Augustiniennes* 41.2 (1995) 267-89.

Basil of Caesarea, *Homily* 20. PG 31:527-40.

Basil of Caesarea, *On the Holy Spirit: Sur le Saint-Esprit.* Benoit Pruche, ed. 2d ed. SC 17. Paris: Cerf, 1968.

Basil of Caesarea, *Longer Rules.* PG 31:889-1052.

Basil of Caesarea, *Shorter Rules.* PG 31:1080-1305.

Cassiodorus, *Commentary on 1 Corinthians: In Epistolam I ad Corinthios.* PL 68:505-54.

Clement of Alexandria, *Instructor: Protrepticus und Paedagogus.* Otto Stählin, Ludwig Früchtel, and U. Treu, eds. GCS 1. Berlin: Akademie, 1972.

Clement of Alexandria, *Miscellanies,* Book 3: *Stromata Buch I-VI.* Otto Stählin, Ludwig Früchtel, and Ursula Treu, eds. GCS 2. Berlin: Akademie, 1985.

Clement of Alexandria, *Miscellanies,* Book 7: *Stromata Buch VII und VIII. Excerpta ex Theodoto. Eclogae Propheticae. Quis Dives Salvetur. Fragmente.* Otto Stählin, Ludwig Früchtel, and Ursula Treu, eds. GCS 3. Berlin: Akademie, 1970.

Cyril of Alexandria, *Commentary on 1 Corinthians: Sancti patris nostri Cyrilli Archiepiscopi Alexandrini in D. Joannis Evangelium: accedunt fragmenta varia necnon tractatus ad Tiberium diaconum duo.* Philip Edward Pusey, ed. Vol. 3:249-318. Brussels: Culture et Civilisation, 1965.

Dialogue of a Montanist with an Orthodox Christian. Gerhard Ficker, ed. *Zeitschrift für Kirchengeschichte* 26 (1905) 447-63.

Didymus of Alexandria, *Commentary on 1 Corinthians. Pauluskommentar aus der griechischen Kirche aus Katenenhandschriften gesammelt.* Karl Staab, ed. Münster: Aschendorff, 1933. 6-14.

Didymus of Alexandria, *Commentary on the Psalms: Psalmenkommentar.* 5 vols. Louis Doutreleau, Adolphe Gesché, and Michael Gronewald, eds. Papyrologische Texte und Abhandlungen 4, 6-8, 12. Bonn: Habelt, 1968-70.

Gregory of Nazianzus. *Oration* 30: *Discours 27-31.* Paul Gallay, ed. SC 250. Paris: Cerf, 1978.

Gregory of Nyssa, *Against Eunomius: Contra Eunomium Libri.* Werner Jaeger, ed. GNO 1:3-409 and 2:3-311. Leiden: Brill, 1960.

Gregory of Nyssa, *Commentary on the Song of Songs: In Canticum canticorum homiliae 15.* Hermann Langerbeck, ed. GNO 6:3-469. Leiden: Brill, 1960.

Gregory of Nyssa, *Great Catechesis: Oratio catechetica.* Ekkehard Mühlenberg, ed. GNO 3/4. Leiden: Brill, 1996.

Gregory of Nyssa, *On the Beatitudes: De Oratione Dominica; De Beatitudinibus.* Johannes F. Callahan, ed. GNO 7/2:75-170. Leiden: Brill, 1992.

Gregory of Nyssa, *On the Soul and the Resurrection: Dialogus de anima et resurrectione qui inscribitur Macrinia.* PG 46:11-160.

Gregory of Nyssa, *On Virginity: Opera Ascetica.* W. Jaeger, J. P. Canarvos, and V. W. Callahan, eds. GNO 8/1:215-343. Leiden: Brill, 1952.

Gregory of Nyssa, *Treatise on 1 Corinthians 15:28: Opera Dogmatica Minora.* J. Kenneth Downing, ed. GNO 3/2:3-28. Leiden: Brill, 1987.

Irenaeus, *Against the Heresies: Contre les Hérésies,* Book 5. A. Rousseau, B. Hemmerdinger, L. Doutreleau, and C. Mercier, eds. SC 153. Paris: Cerf, 1969.

Jerome, *On Illustrious Men: Gli uomini illustri.* Aldo Ceresa-Gastaldo, ed. Florence: Nardini, Centro internazionale del libro, 1988.

Jerome, *Against Jovinian.* PL 23:211-338.

John Chrysostom, *Homilies on 1 Corinthians.* PG 61:7-382.

John Chrysostom, *In Praise of Paul: Panégyriques de saint Paul.* Auguste Piédagnel, ed. SC 300:112-320. Paris: Cerf, 1982.

John of Damascus, *Commentary on 1 Corinthians.* PG 95:569-705.

Leo the Great, *Tractates: Tractatus Septem et Nonaginta.* Antonius Charasse, ed. 2 vols. CCSL 138-138A. Turnhout: Brepols, 1973.

The Liturgy of Saint James: La liturgie de saint Jacques. B.-Ch. Mercier, ed. PO 26:160-249, Turnhout: Brepols, 1974.

Oecumenius of Tricca. *Notes on 1 Corinthians.* In *Pauluskommentar aus der griechischen Kirche aus Katenenhandschriften gesammelt.* Karl Staab, ed. Münster: Aschendorff, 1933. 432-43.

Origen, *Against Celsus: Contre Celse.* Marcel Borret, ed. 5 vols. SC 132, 136, 147, 150, 227. Paris: Cerf, 1967-76.

Origen, *First Principles: Traité des Principes.* 5 vols. Henri Crouzel and Manlio Simonetti, eds. SC 252-53, 268-69, 312. Paris: Cerf, 1978-84.

Origen, *Homilies on Exodus: Homélies sur l'Exode.* Marcel Borrett, ed. SC 321. Paris: Cerf, 1985.

Origen, *Homilies on 1 Corinthians:* "Documents: Origen on I Corinthians" [fragments from catenae]. Claude Jenkins, ed. *Journal of Theological Studies* 9 (1908) 232-47, 353-72, 500-514; 10 (1909) 29-51.

Origen, *Homilies on Jeremiah: Homélies sur Jérémie.* Pierre Nautin, ed. Pierre Husson, tr. 2 vols. SC 232, 238. Paris: Cerf, 1977.

Origen, *Homilies on Leviticus: Homélies sur le Lévitique.* Marcel Borret, ed. SC 286-87. Paris: Cerf, 1981.

Origen, *Homilies on Luke: Homélies sur saint Luc.* Henri Crouzel, F. Fournier, and P. Périchon, eds. SC 87. Paris: Cerf, 1962.

Pelagius, *Commentary on 1 Corinthians: Expositions of Thirteen Epistles of St. Paul.* Alexander Souter, ed. 3 vols. Cambridge: Cambridge University Press, 1922-31.

Photius, *Commentary on 1 Corinthians.* In *Pauluskommentar aus der griechischen Kirche aus Katenenhandschriften gesammelt.* Karl Staab, ed. Münster: Aschendorff, 1933. 544-83.

Severian of Gabala, *Commentary on 1 Corinthians.* In *Pauluskommentar aus der griechischen Kirche aus Katenenhandschriften gesammelt.* Karl Staab, ed. Münster: Aschendorff, 1933. 225-77.

Tertullian, *On the Resurrection: De resurrectione carnis liber.* Ernest Evans, ed. London: S.P.C.K., 1960.

Tertullian, *To His Wife: À son Épouse.* Charles Munier, ed. SC 273. Paris: Cerf, 1980.

Theodore of Mopsuestia, *Commentary on 1 Corinthians.* In *Pauluskommentar aus der griechischen Kirche aus Katenenhandschriften gesammelt.* Karl Staab, ed. Münster: Aschendorff, 1933. 172-96.

Theodoret, *Commentary on 1 Corinthians: Interpretatio Epistolae I ad Corinthios.* PG 82:225-376.

Index of Names

Alpius (bishop of Thagaste), 89n.7

Ambrose, xvii, xviii, xxiii, xxiv, xxv, 104, 177, 191-93, 293

Ambrosiaster, xvii, xx, xxiv, xxv, 8-9, 12-13, 14, 16, 21-22, 23-24, 28-29, 48-49, 54, 62, 65-66, 75, 78-79, 131, 132, 138, 178, 241, 303

Antony (Egyptian monk), xvi

Aquila, xxvi

Aristophanes, 171n.12

Arius, xiii, xxvi, xxix, 18n.4, 26, 137, 142, 177, 260n.11, 314

Athanasius, xiii, xxiii, xxvi, 36, 42, 63-64, 101, 104-5, 126, 195, 200, 204-5, 294

Augustine, xvi-xviii, xxiii-xxvi, xxvii, xxviii, 1, 3-5, 13, 33-35, 36, 41-42, 43-44, 50-53, 55, 57-58, 64-65, 69, 73, 75-77, 79, 83, 89-90, 92, 98-101, 104-5, 111-13, 115-18, 121-24, 127, 129-31, 133-34, 141-42, 144-47, 149, 152-53, 156-59, 162-63, 165, 178, 182-83, 185-86, 195, 202-3, 210-14, 217-20, 222-24, 226-28, 242-43, 247-48, 250-51, 254-56, 262-63, 266, 268, 276-82, 285-86, 289-90, 293, 314

Bacchylides, 186n.13

Basil of Caesarea (Basil "the Great"), xxiii, xxiv, 13, 32-33, 36, 42-43, 105, 119-20, 125-26, 131, 142-43, 195, 198-99, 205, 229, 234-35, 294

Cassiodorus, xxiv, 58-59, 294

Celsus, xxiv, 263-65, 314

Clement of Alexandria, xiii, xxiii, 104-5, 106-7, 114-15, 124, 160, 170-72, 178, 184n.10, 186, 294

Cyril of Alexandria, xvi-xviii, xx, xxiii-xxviii, 13, 25-26, 36, 40, 45, 47, 57, 83-84, 113-14, 140, 159, 165-65, 177, 195, 206, 229, 245, 294

Didymus of Alexandria ("The Blind"), xxiii, 271, 282, 284, 287, 291

Diodore of Tarsus, xxiv

Donatus, xxvi, xxix, 314

Euhemerus, 135n.3

Eunomius, xxv-xxvi, 136-37, 142, 214, 224n.6, 315

Euripides, 84n.3

Eusebius, 197n.4

Fee, Gordon, 83n.1

Felicity (martyr), 211

Ficker, Gerhard, 180n.2

Gallio, 9

Gregory the Great, xviii

Gregory of Nazianzus, 13, 29-30, 295

Gregory of Nyssa, viii, xiii, xv, xviii, xxiii-xxvii, 13, 30-31, 104-5, 127-28, 131, 134, 136-37, 142-43, 177, 190-91, 214, 225-26, 242, 245-46, 251, 256-60, 295

Homer, 9n.1

Ignatius, xi

Irenaeus, vii, xii, xiii, 174-76, 242, 295

James, Saint, 177, 188-90,

Jerome, xv, xvii, xviii, xxiv, xxvi, 1-2, 104, 110-11, 121, 223, 295

John Chrysostom, xvii, xviii, xx, xxiii-xxvi, 1, 4-7, 8, 9-11, 12, 13, 19-20, 24-25, 36, 37-38, 47-48, 53, 54, 56-57, 59-61, 69-70, 71-72, 74-75, 77-78, 79-81, 82, 83-84, 85-87, 90-91, 92-93, 95-96, 101, 102-3, 104-5, 109-10, 115, 117-19, 125, 131, 132-33, 135-36, 138-40, 144-46, 148-50, 151-52, 159-60,

161-62, 165-66, 168-69, 170, 172, 173-76, 177, 178, 179-80, 183-85, 187-88, 194, 195-97, 203-4, 206, 207-10, 214-17, 220-22, 224-25, 229, 231-32, 235-37, 238-39, 240-41, 242-44, 246-47, 248-49, 252-54, 255, 261-62, 265-66, 272, 282-84, 284-85, 288-89, 291-92, 296

John of Damascus, xxiv, 13, 27-28, 37, 45, 296
Jovinian, 104, 110, 121

Leo the Great (Leo I), 36, 41, 296
Leontius (bishop of Hippo), 89-90
Libanius, xxiv

Manicheus (Mani), xxvi, 315
Marcion, xxvi, 15, 109, 315
Maximilla (Montanist), 180-82, 229n.4, 239
Maximus the Confessor, 31-32, 296
Mitchell, Margaret, xxvi n.11
Montanus, 180n.2, 182, 229n.2, 315

Nautin, Pierre, xx n.4

Oecumenius, 36, 40, 92, 101-2, 152, 296
Origen of Alexandria, vii, viii, xiii, xv, xvi-xviii, xx, xxiii, xxiv, xxvi-xxviii, 1-3, 13, 15, 16-17, 22-23, 27, 36, 38-39, 45-46, 47-48, 49-50, 54-55, 56, 61-62, 63, 66-67, 70, 72-73, 76-77, 83-85, 87-88, 90, 92, 96-97, 104-5, 107-9, 144-45, 147-48, 150-51, 153-55, 157, 159-61, 166-68, 197-98, 214, 218-

19, 229, 231, 237-38, 239-40, 242-43, 249-50, 254-55, 263-65, 269-71, 282, 287, 289, 296

Pelagius, xxiv, 48, 66, 284, 296
Perpetua (martyr), 211
Photius, 69, 75, 88, 296
Plato, 20, 197
Plutarch, 9n.2
Porphyry, 197n.4
Priscilla (Montanist), 180-82, 229n.4, 239

Severian of Gabala, xxiii, 12, 14, 28, 50, 67-68, 70, 81, 94, 98, 101, 144, 147, 156-57, 182, 229, 233-34, 237, 296
Staab, Karl, xxiii n.8, 101 n.6

Tertullian, xiii, xx n.2, 2, 105, 116-17, 242, 248, 261, 268-69, 272-74, 297
Theodore of Mopsuestia, xvii, xxiii, 65, 67, 136, 177, 179, 193, 297
Theodoret, xviii, xx, xxiv-xxvi, 8, 11, 12, 18, 26, 55, 69, 81, 92, 94, 97-98, 102, 104, 128-29, 131, 137, 173, 183, 201, 229, 233, 239, 288, 297
Theseus, 84

Valentinus, 269n.20
Victorinus, xviii

Wilken, Robert, xxix n.15

Index of Subjects

Abraham, 5, 112, 174-75, 181, 204

Abstinence, 108, 112, 114, 125

Adam, 30, 110, 157, 177, 179, 182-83, 242, 249-51, 257, 268-69, 272-74, 277, 280; sin of, 60, 157, 188

Age: end of, 58, 163, 190, 226, 266; this, 17, 38, 58, 162, 166, 285

Allegory. *See* Scriptural exegesis

Angels, xi, 7, 51-52, 76-77, 78, 92, 93-94, 140, 175, 183, 185, 191, 198-99, 202, 215, 217, 222, 226, 229, 238, 267, 274, 277, 279

Anxiety, 124-28

Apollos, 11, 19, 21, 47, 51-54, 65, 70, 73-75, 148, 232, 286-87, 289, 292

Apostles, xii, 21, 27, 67, 74, 76-77, 78, 104, 106, 110, 123, 144, 146-51, 153, 177, 188, 196, 203, 212, 232, 236, 244-46, 258, 286, 289; false, 15, 49, 63, 66, 75, 241; twelve, 94, 147

Arians, xxv, 21, 131, 142, 179n.1, 224n.6, 260n.11, 314

Arrogance, xxi, 10, 20, 69, 72, 73-76, 81, 155, 218-20, 222, 235, 247, 284, 289; prohibition of, 13, 14, 21, 26. *See also* Boasting, Pride

Ascent, 261; of Christ, 124, 189, 274, 281; to God, 32, 41. *See also* Vision of God

Asceticism, xxiii, xxv, 104, 106, 110, 144-45; sexual, 144-45

Baptism, xi, xii, 19-21, 48, 64-65, 83, 89, 92, 117-18, 159, 160-65, 181, 196, 201, 204-6, 260-61, 280, 290; as rebirth, 48, 53, 234n.4, 245-46

Battle, Spiritual, 159, 166-68

Beauty, 122, 127, 208-9, 220, 226, 258, 266; of God, 123, 199; of heaven, 96, 103; of Paul, 80

Believer, 93-94, 118, 135, 138, 167, 186, 191, 197, 202, 210, 233-34, 240, 253, 286, 291; simple, 35, 264

Bible. *See* Scriptures

Bishop, vii, xxiv, xxv, 56, 83-84, 90, 112, 115, 239, 287

Blood of Christ, 40, 100, 102, 118, 162, 164, 168, 189, 192-94, 206. *See also* Cross of Christ, Death of Christ

Boasting, 74-76, 133, 151, 153, 155, 165, 218-21, 224-25; in the Lord, 29, 32, 33-35; prohibition of, 13-14, 21, 26-28, 32-33, 65-67, 85. *See also* Arrogance, Pride

Body, 58, 64, 73, 77, 80, 83, 84, 92, 95, 97-103, 105, 112, 114, 117, 120, 122, 126, 156-58, 160, 177, 179, 182, 190-91, 206-8, 210, 212-13, 224, 226, 245, 251, 255, 262-65, 267-72, 275-79, 292; for God, 102-3; heavenly, 270; incorruptible, 223, 226; natural (ensouled), 268-72; spiritual, xxii, 223, 226, 268; as temple, 64-65, 122. *See also* Resurrection

Body of Christ, xi, 20, 56-57, 92, 98-101, 140, 157, 162, 168-69, 187, 190-93, 195, 205-13, 239, 256-58; believer as, 56-57, 98-101, 243; church as, xxii, 20, 57, 98-101, 168, 205-13, 239

Brother (fellow Christian), 87, 93-94, 99, 116, 138-41, 146, 149, 152, 157, 160, 162, 169, 173-75, 187, 193, 210, 212, 230-31, 233, 235, 237, 241, 244, 268, 279, 286-87, 289-90, 292

Carnal. *See* Fleshly

Celibacy, xxviii, 104-6, 109, 111, 113-14, 116, 121, 126, 129-30, 195, 210-11. *See also* Asceticism, Virginity

Cephas. *See* Peter

Charity. *See* Love

322

Chastity, 55, 88, 108, 110, 112, 121-22, 125, 130, 147, 275.

Choice, free, 31, 32, 38, 66-67, 70, 81, 99, 117, 151, 153-54, 209

Christ: divinity of, xiii, xxv, xxiv, 136-37, 141, 179, 204, 219, 226, 242, 245, 252, 254, 256-57; God and man, 21, 51, 98, 274; image of, 242, 268, 273, 275, 277; as Lord, 134-38; as mediator, 51-52, 226, 259, 274; titles of, 13, 21, 30. *See also* Christology, Incarnation, Son of God, Word

Christology, xiv, 136-38, 177, 134, 242, 253-54, 256-60, 272n.23; debates about, xxiii, xxv, 12, 21, 131, 135-38, 142-43, 177-80, 199, 204, 242, 253-54, 256-60. *See also* Christ, Incarnation, Son of God, Word

Church, xxi, 47, 73, 85-86, 88, 89, 141, 147, 157, 159, 160-61, 166, 171, 184, 189, 193, 208, 213, 229, 230-33, 237-41, 246, 249, 258, 281, 291-92; as Christ's body, 57, 98-101, 205-13, 239; dedication of a, 57; early, vii-viii, xviii, 238; of God, 172-73; Holy Catholic, 190; rule of the, 193

Commandments, 50, 88, 89, 94, 101, 105, 107, 109, 118, 120-21, 125, 144, 150, 180, 188; of Christ, 120-22, 126, 128, 152, 173, 216, 241, 291; of the Lord, 147; of Paul, 172, 239

Concealment, 2-4, 6, 36, 47, 49-51, 70, 74, 264, 267-68. *See also* Teaching, different levels

Conscience, 138-42, 170, 172, 241

Contemplation, of God, 41, 126, 160, 171, 211, 214, 228, 231, 242. *See also* Vision of God

Continence. *See* Moderation

Corinthians, 8, 9, 10, 11, 13, 14-15, 132, 140, 151-52, 159, 168, 170, 229-30, 233-34, 236, 240-41

Covenant, 181; new, xi, 150, 187-89

Creation, xii, 13, 24, 66, 135, 183, 192, 224, 249-50, 259, 266, 270, 274; new, 224. *See also* Creator

Creator, xiii, 60, 64, 71, 72, 78, 101-3, 104, 109, 121-22, 127, 135-38, 182, 188, 200, 222, 250, 255, 263, 267, 271; Christ as, xvi, 51, 58, 64, 135-38, 188, 192, 200

Creed, 261; Nicene, xxv. *See also* Faith, confession of

Cross of Christ, xii, xvii, xxi, 4, 7, 13, 17, 19, 34, 36, 38, 50-51, 126, 166, 188-89, 219, 236, 252, 265; debate about 13, 24; delight in, 34; denial of, 15; and the Devil, 12, 22, 40; effects of, 12, 22-24; as hidden treasure, 34-35; and pagan wisdom, 20, 24; as paradox, xxi, 12; as power of God, 20, 22-26; signs of, 188-90. *See also* Blood of Christ, Death of Christ

David, xiv, 30, 31, 91, 108, 174, 204, 214, 217, 221, 247

Deacons, 106, 189

Death, 65-67, 77, 171, 175, 216, 246, 249, 250-53, 261, 262, 265-67, 273-81, 286; victory over, 245, 252-55, 257-60, 276, 279-81; to the world, 23

Death of Christ, xi, xii, xxi, xxii, 13, 17, 36, 74, 124, 139, 188-89, 193, 205, 211, 219, 230, 243-46, 248-49, 252, 259-60, 266. *See also* Blood of Christ, Cross of Christ

Deeds, xii, 61-63, 72-73, 75-76, 81, 88, 92, 93, 102, 106, 189, 211, 244, 285; of the body, 275, 77; evil, 86, 98-99; good, 173, 175, 190, 194, 222, 225. *See also* Works

Delight, 247, 266

Demons. *See* Powers, demonic

Desire, xv, 83, 100, 106-7, 114, 119, 123, 127-28, 163, 167, 175, 227, 256, 280, 288; for Christ, xiv; sexual, 100-101, 104, 109, 112, 114-15; true, 82, 127. *See also* Lust

Devil, 6, 83, 96, 106, 124, 129-30, 134, 140, 148, 162-63, 166-67, 203, 210, 216, 233, 243-44, 248, 250, 253, 277, 284-85, 289; in Corinth, 9; and the cross, 36, 40; victory over, 13, 29, 95, 102, 280

Devotion, 104-5, 122, 124-28; to prayer, 105, 110-11

Discipline, 80, 84, 95, 103, 108, 125, 145, 147, 186, 193, 220, 241, 273; lack of, xxi; monastic, 105, 120; spiritual, 5, 6

Divinization, 32, 64, 191, 227, 246, 260

Divisions, xi, 18, 72, 133, 169, 177-78, 183-86, 190, 196, 210, 230, 283, 287-90, 292; in the church, 10, 109, 184-86, 178; in Corinth, xxi, 8, 9, 10, 11, 12, 14, 18, 19-20, 21, 47, 52-53, 107; doctrinal, 185

Divorce, 113-17, 120

Donatists, 21, 195, 314

Drunkenness, 83, 87-90, 96, 99, 166, 184, 194, 209, 262, 275, 283

Earthly, 127, 231, 264, 270; appetites, 157; creatures, 171; things, 6, 82, 126, 150, 241, 265; realm, 40

Economy of redemption. *See* Plan, divine; Incarnation

Elijah, 192

Elisha, 85, 192, 214, 223

Eloquence, xxiv, 8, 11, 20, 22, 81. *See also* Rhetoric

Emotions. *See* Passions

End, ultimate, xxvii, 242, 252, 254; Christ as, 13; God as, 31-32, 214, 257-60, 254

Envy. *See* Jealousy, Passions

Epicureans, 48, 66n.11

Error, 22, 73, 79, 137, 168, 186, 244

Eternal: life, 190-91, 202, 221, 227, 251, 267; things, 226-27

Ethics. *See* Morality

Eucharist, xi, xiii, xxi, xxii, 83, 89, 109n.5, 159-62, 168-69, 177, 179, 184, 187-94, 205

Eunomians, 137, 142-43, 224n.6, 315

Eve, 182-83

Evil, 4, 52, 61-62, 84, 86-87, 95, 126, 129, 143, 163, 185, 190n.16, 204, 233-35, 247, 251, 253-56, 280; obliteration of, 257-60; victory over, xxi, xxii, 242

Excommunication, 73, 83-85, 90-91

Exegesis. *See* Scriptural exegesis

Exodus, the, xxiii, 83, 159, 161-65, 175

Faith, x, xii, xxii, xxv, 2, 16, 24, 37, 38, 51, 75-78, 110, 117, 124, 131, 135, 138, 140, 144, 145, 149, 160, 162, 168, 173, 185-86, 190, 195, 199, 202-3, 214-15, 217-20, 223-24, 226-28, 230, 234, 236, 240-41, 243, 248-49, 256, 258, 264, 266-67, 273, 275, 277, 284-86, 288, 290; of the church, 249, 269; confession of, xi-xiii, xvi, xxi-xxii, 114, 189, 261

Fasting, 55, 144-45, 151, 157, 174, 194, 263

Father. *See* God, as Father

Fellowship, 83, 136; in Christ, 15, 17, 47; with Christ, 259; with demons, 174; with God, xxvii, xxviii, 63, 191; human, 111, 116. *See also* Participation

Festival, xxi, 83, 85-87, 90, 194, 211; pagan, 89-90

Flesh, 57, 64-65, 83, 84, 98, 101-2, 112-13, 134, 137, 153, 157-58, 160, 166-67, 169, 182, 232, 242, 250, 258, 263, 265, 267-70, 272-80; of Christ, 169, 191, 206, 244-46, 252, 274; of the Word, 49, 50. *See also* Resurrection, of the flesh

Fleshly, 65, 77, 125, 162, 169, 226, 231, 274-75; lust, 100-101; soul, 272; things, 204

Folly, 65-66, 133, 136, 140, 164, 235; cross as, x, xxi, 13, 22, 47, 48; human, 11, 27, 196

Forgiveness, 16, 60, 88, 96, 115, 124, 174, 188-90, 193-94, 280

Freedom, xxi, 79, 97, 102, 105, 108, 117-19, 125, 131, 138-39, 145-46, 152, 154, 160, 170, 172, 221, 229. *See also* Choice, free; Free will

Free will, 75-76, 97, 106, 123, 151, 153-54, 198, 274. *See also* Choice, free

Gentiles, 14, 15, 121, 156, 160, 201, 281

Glossolalia. *See* Tongues, speaking in

Gnostics, vii, xii, xxiii, 104, 157n.13, 186, 198n.6, 242, 269n.20, 315

God: all in all, 223, 254-60; as Father, xxvi, 5, 13, 63, 102, 123, 126, 135-37, 142-43, 183, 188-89, 199, 201, 204-6, 225, 242, 245, 252, 255, 257, 271; impassibility, 225; incomprehensibility, 225; incorruptibility, 226; infinity, 134; nature of, 78, 200, 225; omnipotence, 263; omnipresence, 224; omniscience, 72, 78, 142, 201; as one, 109, 134-38. *See also* Christ, Creator, Holy Spirit, Son of God, Trinity

Good, the, 220; God as, 31; in man, 31-32; supreme, 66

Gospel, xi, xii, xv, xviii, 11, 12, 13, 73, 79, 109-10, 113, 125, 136, 139, 141, 145, 147-48, 151-56, 160, 181, 230, 240, 242-43, 260, 277, 284-86, 288

Grace, xx, xxv, 32, 102, 134, 136, 162, 168, 182, 190-92, 195-96, 201, 206, 226, 243, 246-48, 250-51, 257, 270, 272-74, 280, 286, 291; in Christ, 16, 21, 176; of God, 1, 4-5, 11, 13, 15, 20, 21, 22, 71, 75-76, 80, 106, 114, 117; and law, 100, 185; of the Spirit, 179. *See also* Mercy

Greeks, 103, 108, 135, 155, 57, 172-74, 197, 201, 205, 234; debates with, 20-21, 186; teachings, 22, 25, 38. *See also* Philosophy

Heaven, 6, 24, 35, 60, 72, 80, 82, 95, 99, 102-3, 124, 130, 135-36, 159, 161-62, 164, 166, 173, 175, 183, 188-89, 191, 224-25, 245, 247, 259, 261, 263, 265, 268, 271-72, 274, 277-78, 285; ruled by Christ, 13, 23

Hell, 100, 250, 261, 266; fire, 59-61

Heretics, 8, 9, 14, 17-18, 21, 64, 69, 73, 90, 104, 109-10, 128, 143, 157, 179, 184-86, 198, 201, 249, 260, 265, 269, 274, 276, 281

Holiness, 116-18, 122, 124, 126-27, 130, 188, 200, 210, 220, 223, 226-27, 273. *See also* Sanctification

Holy Spirit, xiii, xxviii, 5, 30, 31, 32, 36, 37, 62-65, 73, 77, 89, 96, 100, 102, 106, 124-25, 128, 131, 135-36, 161, 164, 167, 188-89, 194, 195-207, 219, 225, 229-31, 233-35, 237-38, 272, 274-75, 280-81, 285; in the believer, 48, 52-53, 64-65, 99, 121, 201, 273; debates about, xxv, 36, 42-43, 63-65, 195, 198-200, 229, 234; divinity of, xxiii, 64-65, 131, 229, 233-35; as revealer, xxvii, 33, 36, 40-41, 44-45, 260. *See also* Trinity

Homilies, vii-viii, xiii-xx, xxii-xxiv, xxvi-xxvii, 229

Hope, xv, xxi, 73, 75, 108, 117, 123, 128, 149-51, 153,

162, 168, 193-94, 210, 218-19, 221, 224, 227-28, 230, 243, 248, 256-58, 261, 263, 266, 277

Humility, xxi, 12, 32-33, 34-35, 76, 79, 126, 128-30, 183, 210, 132, 219, 222, 243, 245-47, 280; of Christ, 179; of the cross, 13; of Paul, 19

Hymns, 126, 194, 211

Idolatry, 83, 87-88, 96-97, 99, 131-32, 134-35, 138-42, 159, 163-65, 168-70, 174, 281; food of, xxii, 131-43, 144-45, 148, 151, 159, 160, 165, 169-70, 173-74, 236, 275, 288, 292

Ignorance, 22, 137-38, 198, 266

Image of God, 123, 188; Christ as, xv, 30, 199, 264; in man, 123, 177, 179, 182, 188, 214, 226, 267

Imitation, xxviii, 211; of Christ, xxi, 7, 36, 69, 79-81, 96, 111, 143, 173-74, 178, 243, 246, 257, 273; of Old Testament figures, 174-75; of Paul, 7, 69, 79, 111, 143, 144, 160, 166, 174-75, 178, 231-32

Immorality, 69-70, 83, 84, 87-89, 96-101, 105, 107-9, 155, 159, 163, 235, 275

Immortality, xv, 58, 98, 169, 179, 190-91, 256, 260, 270, 272-73, 275-76, 278-81

Imperishability, 156-57, 250, 263, 268, 270-71, 273, 275-76, 278-81

Incarnation, xii, xiii, xvi, 13, 33, 43, 48, 66, 77, 83, 86, 92, 179, 188, 190, 198, 230, 243-46, 251-53, 269, 274, 280. *See also* Plan, divine

Incorporeality, 224, 227; of God, 226

Incorruptibility, 190-91, 223, 263-64, 267, 270, 277-78; of God, 226

Irony, 69, 74-75

Interpretation of Scripture. *See* Scriptural exegesis

Jealousy, 53, 207, 210, 218-20, 292; God's, 170

Jerusalem, 61, 80, 124, 188n.15, 211, 233, 282-83

Jews, xxv, 13-14 24, 22, 25-26, 40, 73, 87, 93, 124, 137, 145, 150, 154-57, 161-63, 166, 169-70, 172-74, 186, 192, 198, 205-6, 219, 233, 267

Judgment, 65, 69, 71-73, 81, 90-91, 92-97, 109, 120-21, 123, 133, 152, 183, 193-94, 209, 236, 287; by Christ, 291; final, 12, 15, 16, 47, 58, 61-62, 69, 78, 84, 96, 189, 193, 241, 269; by God, 13, 24, 61, 72-73, 78, 142, 157, 167, 204, 210, 286; human, 78; by pagans, 92-94; in the present, 193

Justice, xiii-xiv, 67, 171. *See also* Righteousness

Justification, 96

Kingdom of God, xii, xxii, 62, 70, 81, 88, 89, 92, 96-97, 99, 106, 113, 118, 121, 129-30, 147, 160,

165, 193, 217, 238, 242, 252-53, 256-57, 259, 264, 266, 270, 272-73, 286, 289

Knowledge, xiv, xv, xxiii, 15, 17, 32, 33, 70, 80, 107, 131, 132-34, 138-42, 148, 164, 186, 195, 198, 201-4, 214-17, 219-20, 222-27, 231-32, 236, 245, 255, 258, 286; of God, xvii, xxvii, 125, 131, 171, 182, 199, 205, 223-27, 260; known by God, 131-33

Lamb, 249; Christ as, 85

Law, 145, 148-49, 154-55, 157, 159, 161, 171-72, 185, 188-89, 193, 198, 230, 232-33, 241, 279-80; of Christ, 113, 154-55, 194; of Moses, 15, 49, 87, 91, 100, 109, 121, 149-50; Old Testament, 113-14; and the prophets, 198

Letters of Paul, xx, 2, 8, 87-88, 160, 282, 292; Ephesians, xviii, 63; First Corinthians, 8, xx-xix, 284, 286; list of, xx; lost letter, xxi n.6, 83, 87-88, 107; Romans, xviii, 14, 133, 283; Second Corinthians, 85, 285-86; Titus, 64

Life, 65-67, 83, 85, 169, 219, 224, 251, 268, 275, 286; Christ as, 190, 225, 259; to come, 223, 225; eternal, 190-91, 221, 227, 251, 267; present, 165-67, 175, 223, 226, 254, 258, 273; true, 73; way of, 80, 155, 273, 276

Light, 173; Christ as, 30, 57, 225; God as, 205; true, 199, 205

Likeness to God. *See* Image of God

Liturgy, vii, xvi, xxvii, 83, 188-90

Logos. *See* Word

Lord's Supper. *See* Eucharist

Love, xv, xvii, xxi, xxii, 81, 89, 100, 107, 109, 127, 131-33, 169, 171, 175, 184, 196, 209, 211-13, 214-28, 230, 256, 258, 279, 282-83, 287-92 ; of Christ, 79, 126, 169, 256; for God, xxvii, 105-6, 122-23, 125, 128, 256, 271; God's, 79, 126, 200; virtues of, 218-22; works of, 57; of the world, 122-23

Lust, 118-19, 167, 170-71, 221, 274-75, 280. *See also* Desire

Manicheans, xxix, 21, 43-44, 52n.3, 104, 110, 315

Marcionites, 104, 109, 315

Marriage, xxi-xxiii, xxv, xxviii, 9, 10, 86, 97, 101, 104-30, 155, 208, 210-11, 237, 267, 290; second, 105, 111, 113-17, 128-29

Martyrdom, 3, 23, 49, 69, 77, 175, 195, 211, 216, 220

Mary the Virgin, xv, 111, 180-81, 188, 200, 222, 265

Mercy, 89, 96, 120-21, 156, 173, 179, 188-89, 208, 247, 256, 283, 285. See also Grace

Miracles, 36, 38, 50, 103, 126, 140, 174, 201-3, 212, 215-16, 223, 243

Moderation, 80, 89, 98, 104-9, 112-15, 126, 156-57, 160, 171-72, 194, 210, 282. *See also* Self-control

Money. *See* Wealth

Monks, xxv, 144, 153; rules for, 105, 119. *See also* Asceticism

Montanists, xxix, xxvi, 180-82, 229, 239, 315

Morality, xxi, xxvi, 12, 53, 104, 141, 157, 231, 265, 273, 276, 282; levels of, xxiv, 47, 49, 122, 128, 130, 144, 152, 154-55, 210

Moses, 80, 108, 160-62, 164, 170, 174, 214, 219, 221; law of, 15, 49, 87, 91, 100, 109, 121, 149-50; as mediator, 164; as prophet, 192

Mystery, x, xvi, xxviii, 22, 38, 66, 70, 126, 138, 160, 168, 185, 187, 193-94, 198, 206, 215, 230, 245, 251, 264, 272, 283, 285

Name: of Christ, 18, 84, 89, 96, 211, 252, 275-76

Nature, xiv, 183, 192, 209, 267; divine, 225, 251n.4, 252, 256-57, 263; of Christ, 190-91, 225; of God, 224, 227; of the Good, 225; human, 32, 78, 190-91, 210, 245-46, 251, 256-57; rational, 271

New Testament, vii, x-xix, 86, 91, 110, 114, 162, 165-66, 169, 245

Nicea: Council of, xiii, Creed of, xxv

Novatianists, 21, 129, 316

Old Testament, vii, xi, xiii, xxiii, xxv, xxviii, 52, 83, 84, 86, 109-10, 114, 137, 150, 159-60, 162, 165-66, 169, 177, 180, 214, 232-33, 240, 245; and New Testament, 90-91

Omniscience: of God, 142, 201

Pagans, 73, 84, 88, 92, 95, 116, 131, 139, 141-42, 156, 164, 186, 229, 232, 236; courts of, 92-94, 282, 289; eating with, 131-32, 135, 141-42, 164, 168, 170, 172; laws of, 209; marriage to, 116-17; practices, 197; religion, xxii, 131, 134-42, 144, 159, 166, 168-70; wisdom of, 288, 292; writings, 83

Paradise, 188, 254, 273

Participation: in Christ, 56-57, 64, 160, 168-69, 190-91, 258; in God, 32, 65, 194, 222, 256; in the Spirit, 65, 275. *See also* Fellowship

Passion, of Christ. *See* Blood of Christ, Cross of Christ, Death of Christ

Passions, 96, 98, 101, 103, 112, 115, 167, 179, 210, 222, 227, 257, 270; anger, 220; envy, 102, 210-12; of the flesh, 128; jealousy, 53, 207, 210; purification from, 53; worldly, xvi, 65

Passover, xxi, 87

Patience, 132, 139, 219-21, 227

Paul: activity, 7, 16; adaptability, xxii, 1, 7, 109, 121, 143, 145, 154-56, 160, 172-74, 219; defense of, 144, 146; letters of, xx, 2, 10, 56, 87-88, 160, 282, 292; life, xxviii, 1-5, 8-9, 11, 80, 81, 154, 282, 284, 292; perfection, 154; as persecutor, 1, 3-5, 187, 232, 246-47; as prophet, 85; rhetorical skill, 2, 12, 229; soul of, xx, 80, 175, 182; sufferings, 6-7, 9, 33, 37, 69, 79-81, 96, 145, 151-52, 156, 175, 200, 221, 258, 260-62; teaching, 2-3, 11, 16, 81, 161; virtues of, 5-7, 80-81

Peace, 13, 73, 106, 109, 116, 204, 220-22, 237-41, 254, 267, 281, 286-87

Pelagians, 117n.11, 117

Pentecost, 86, 124, 189, 196, 229, 233, 236, 284-86

Perfect, 74, 133, 139, 144, 152, 154-55, 164, 175, 216, 222-23, 225-26, 236, 247-48, 274; the, 10, 36, 38, 39, 214, 256; love, 216; more, 77, 107; teaching, 49, 113

Perfection, 3, 48, 122, 139, 167, 216, 224, 226, 254, 260, 268, 288; degrees of, 114; of God, 250; of love, 256; pursuit of, xxiv, 12, 113, 154-55, 193. *See also* Progress, spiritual

Persecution, 76, 79, 123-24, 211, 218, 223, 245-47, 288

Peter (Cephas), x, xi, 19, 21, 50, 58, 65, 69-70, 71, 108, 110, 123, 140, 146-47, 150, 183, 205, 232-34, 236, 244, 292

Philosophy, xiv, 15, 253; pagan, xxv, 8, 10, 66, 106, 136, 154, 157, 186; worldly, 8, 34

Piety, 80, 142, 186, 287, 290-91; true, 186

Plan, divine: for redemption, xii, 6, 13, 26, 47, 50, 179, 185, 191, 219, 224, 244, 246, 251-52, 276, 292. *See also* Incarnation

Pleasure, 31, 77, 89, 98, 112, 170-72, 236, 262, 267, 277; in God, 227; slaves of, 48; true, 194

Poor, the, 10, 124, 140, 144, 171, 185, 194, 208, 219; alms for, 154, 194, 208, 215-17, 282-84, 290; care of, xxiv, 144-45, 152

Poverty, 69, 77-78, 81, 86, 123, 175, 204, 208, 216

Power, 81, 82, 84, 156, 158, 168, 176, 192, 219, 223, 250-51, 258, 264, 270; Christ as, 13, 22-23, 25, 29, 190, 201, 226; of death, 190; of God, xxi, 13, 28, 97-98, 103, 134, 200, 226; of the gospel, 37; of love, 221; of the Spirit, 81

Powers: demonic, 6, 36, 38, 40, 83, 106, 135, 139, 141, 145, 148-49, 160, 166-70, 174, 218, 223, 242, 252-53; heavenly, xi, 6, 38; spiritual, 199, 204; victory over demonic powers, 252-53, 257. *See also* Angels

Prayer, vii, xiii, xv, xviii, 55, 63, 67, 89, 105-6, 108,

110-11, 115, 118, 120-21, 174, 180, 183, 188-91, 210-
11, 232, 238, 260, 262-63, 280, 283-86, 289-90

Preaching, vii, 18, 36, 59, 106, 145, 151, 153, 156-57,
203, 208, 211, 214, 220, 230, 238-39, 241, 243,
246-49, 284, 286. *See also* Homilies

Pride, 13, 27-28, 32-33, 75, 77, 101, 130, 131-34, 139,
150, 165, 170, 183, 197, 208, 210-11, 214, 219,
260-61, 292. *See also* Arrogance, Boasting

Priest, xxiv, 94, 109, 144, 152, 218, 232; Christ as,
271; duties of, 55; office of, 55, 63

Progress, spiritual, 15, 49, 51-52, 69-70, 107, 114,
134, 144, 160, 179, 223-25, 228, 251, 254, 257-58,
261, 275. *See also* Perfection, pursuit of

Promises, 75, 102, 123, 162-63, 175-76, 242, 249,
260, 268, 273, 281; of Christ, 75

Prophecy, 77, 80, 85, 97, 177, 180, 186, 195-98,
202-4, 212, 214-15, 217-20, 222-23, 229-31, 233-
41; compared to love, 222-24

Prophets, xii, xxvii, 39, 63, 83, 94, 109, 148, 154,
177, 188-89, 192, 204, 212, 217, 230, 233-34, 237-
41, 253, 258; false, 182, 237-38, 203; true, 203;
women, xxvi, 177, 179-82

Providence, 39, 89, 114, 149, 167, 201, 207, 280;
denial of, 13, 23, 25, 48, 66

Psalms, vii, 31, 90, 119, 238

Punishment, 58-65, 71, 84-86, 91, 100-101, 116,
120-21, 124, 127, 137, 145, 148, 154, 203, 217, 226,
243, 263, 265, 269; eternal, 48, 59-61, 99, 115,
210, 250; purifying, 48, 83

Purgatory, 48

Purification, 48, 62, 70, 83, 85-86, 108, 113, 243,
256, 276

Purity, 93, 97, 105, 107-9, 112, 117, 255, 270-71

Pythia, the, 197

Reason, 45, 225-26

Reconciliation, 259

Redemption, xii, 83, 86, 102, 118, 155, 188, 219,
244-45, 249; Christ as, 13, 24-27, 29, 30, 32, 40,
79. *See also* Plan, divine; Salvation

Repentance, 69, 73, 81, 83, 84, 85, 88, 91

Reserve, pedagogical. *See* Concealment

Resurrection, 242-81, 283, 292; of believers, 97;
Christ as, 57; of Christ, x-xii, xvii, xxii, 97-98,
140, 160, 189, 230, 243-46, 248-53, 257, 263,
265-67, 275, 277; of the body, x, xxiii, 10, 11,
98, 214, 243, 249-51, 255, 261, 263-70, 275, 277-
78; of the flesh, 13, 48, 66, 242, 248, 261-62,
268-60, 272-78; denial of, 243, 248-49, 253,
261-63, 265, 267-70, 272-74, 276-77, 292; general, xxi, xxii, 10, 11, 179, 243, 248-53, 257, 260-

61, 266, 268-69, 272; in the present, 30, 206,
245, 275-76

Reward, xxvii, 70, 96-97, 121, 123, 144-45, 148, 151,
153-54, 156-57, 173-74, 176, 189, 211, 220, 228,
243, 261, 273, 285; ultimate, 36, 42, 99; variety
in, 129-30, 265

Rhetoric, xxiv n.8; xxviii, 93, 229; Paul's strategy,
xxvi, 14, 16, 19-20, 54, 56, 74-75, 109, 131, 132-
33, 135-36, 146, 148-49, 170, 172, 174, 177, 187,
197, 201-2, 207, 215, 222, 232, 235, 236-37, 241,
244, 248-49, 252-53, 282-83, 285, 290-92

Rhetorical figures: amplification, 215; climax 33;
exaggeration, 215; hyperbole, 19, 215. *See also*
Irony

Righteous, 77, 92, 95, 99, 107, 125, 204, 226, 264-
66, 272

Righteousness, xiii, xxvii, 13, 29, 33, 103, 106, 150,
220, 226, 232, 273, 275; Christ as, 13, 26, 92, 96,
225; through faith, 32. *See also* Justice

Sabbath, 267, 271

Sacrament, 104, 115-16, 160, 190-93, 219

Sacrifice, 102, 231; of Christ, 14, 22, 29, 80, 83, 85,
140, 169, 188, 249; Eucharist as, 189; in Old
Testament, 113, 151-52, 169; pagan, 13, 23, 139,
141, 168, 172; spiritual, 63. *See also* Blood of
Christ, Cross of Christ, Death of Christ.

Saints, 93-94, 219, 227, 245, 255, 270, 283, 290-91

Salvation, xv, xvi, 39-40, 58-62, 66, 73, 76-77, 81,
84, 114, 116, 118, 124, 126, 139-40, 142-43, 152,
155, 157, 172-73, 175, 177, 185, 188-90, 209, 219,
242-43, 245-47, 250, 259, 274, 276, 283, 286,
288, 292. *See also* Plan, divine; Redemption

Sanctification, 14, 15, 89, 92, 96, 117-18, 177, 190,
261, 275; Christ as, 13, 26, 30, 31; of Eucharist,
188-89, 191-92

Satan. *See* Devil

Savior, 98, 114, 189, 219, 289

Scriptural exegesis, vii-viii, x-xix, xx-xxix, 12, 13,
16-17, 36, 38-39, 49, 83, 144, 150, 155n.10, 159,
160-65, 159-65, 229, 230-34; allegorical, xxiii-
xxv, 181; attention to textual variants, xxiv,
xxvi; christological, 159, 160-64; figurative
sense, xxiii, 159, 162-65; foreshadowing, 86,
192; historical, xv, xxiv-xxvi, 159, 161, 177, 196;
intrabiblical, xxvii-xxviii, 105, 195, 206; by
Jews, 198; literal, 159, 161-62; multiple senses,
xxiii, 47-48, 63, 66, 69, 83, 101; paradigm of,
159, 160-63, 165; philological, xxiv, xxvi, 145;
plain sense, 39, 61; spiritual sense, xxv, 36, 39,
144, 150, 155n.4, 159, 162-64, 185; typology, 159,
177, 191-92, 242, 249-51, 257-58, 268-69

Scriptures, xx, 13, 45. 67, 84, 111, 113, 137, 159, 163-66, 182, 185, 203-4, 211, 217, 219, 231, 244, 260, 263-64; inspiration of, 31, 39, 136. *See also* Scriptural exegesis

Second coming, of Christ, xxi, xxii, 38, 58, 71, 72-73, 187, 189, 238, 257, 274, 291

Self-control, 144-47, 156-57, 160, 170. *See also* Moderation

Septuagint (LXX), xiv, xxvi, xxviii-xxix

Sermons. *See* Homilies

Sexual relations, xxi, xxii, 100, 104-16. *See also* Marriage; Sin, sexual; Virginity

Sin, 8, 10, 15, 23, 40, 61-65, 71-72, 80, 83, 85, 87, 89, 97, 100-101, 103, 106, 113, 115, 120, 122, 127, 137, 139-43, 155, 159, 162-63, 166-69, 174, 180, 182-83, 189, 190n.16, 193, 222, 234, 241-43, 247-48, 250, 255, 257, 259-61, 270, 272-73, 275, 279-80, 289, 292; of Adam, 157, 188, 117n.11; sexual, xxi-xxii, 8, 10-11, 63-65, 81, 83-86, 88, 89, 91, 92, 96-102, 109, 111-13, 115, 121-22, 129, 153, 165-66, 209-10, 265-66, 275, 282, 289, 292

Slavery, 97, 105, 117-18, 122, 154, 175

Solomon, 61, 204, 289

Son of God, xiii, 253; divinity of, xxiii, 135, 204, 234n.5, 256; equality with Father, 18, 135-38, 142-43; as Lord, 134-38; names of, 29-30; only, 189, 199, 204, 225, 230. *See also* Christ, Christology, Incarnation, Word

Sosthenes, 13, 14

Soul, 7, 30, 80, 84-85, 99-103, 112, 114, 120, 122, 134, 150-51, 162, 166, 169, 173, 190, 221, 223, 225, 228, 238, 251, 255, 261-64, 268-69, 272-74, 277-80, 283, 289; of Christ, 98, 251; longing of, xxvii, 13, 123; nature of, 53; of Paul, xx, 80, 175, 182

Spirit, 98, 126, 242, 268, 277; evil, 243; God as, 223; of God, 217-18; of man, 41, 84-85, 102, 122, 124, 157, 223-25, 232, 274, 291; of Paul, 290; of this world, 75. *See also* Holy Spirit

Spirit, Holy. *See* Holy Spirit

Spiritual, vii-viii, xiii-xv, xviii, 49, 65, 77, 80, 86, 90, 150, 153, 159-61, 163, 166, 182, 193-94, 198, 203, 226, 241, 263, 267, 274-75, 277, 283; body, 223-24, 243, 268-72; contrast fleshly, 47, 84; gifts, xxvi, 8, 10-12, 15-16, 17, 124, 136, 177, 195-97, 199-204, 207-13, 214-18, 220, 222, 225, 229-34, 238, 243, 289, 292; good, 149-51; life, vii, 13, 48, 153; person, xxviii, 48, 48-53, 156, 241; things, 48-50, 150, 187, 213

Stoics, 48, 67

Suffering, 34, 75, 76, 78, 92, 95, 103, 139, 207, 209-11, 215, 221, 256; of the apostles, 76-78; of

Christ, xi, 96, 185, 187, 189, 230, 258; of the Hebrews, 175; of the just, 285; of martyrs, 211; of Moses, 175; of Paul, 6-7, 9, 33, 37, 69, 79-81, 96, 145, 151-52, 156, 175, 200, 221, 258, 260-62; of the prophets, 204, 238

Teachers, 212, 287; in Corinth, 9, 12; task of, 61-62, 150-51

Teaching, 10, 36, 136, 143, 153, 173, 203, 231-32, 238, 240, 245; catechetical, xi; of Christ, 241; different levels of, xxiv, xxviii, 2-4, 47, 48-50, 69-70, 107, 109, 121, 144, 150, 164; false, 8, 14, 62, 66; pagan, xxv, 67; of Paul, 10, 148, 161, 241, 288; rival, 10-12; of the Spirit, 46; true, 142, 157; of women, 240

Temple, 88, 89, 97, 245, 265; believer as, 63-64, 89, 92, 99-102, 112, 121, 226; the body as, 64-65, 122; church as, 47-48, 56-57, 61, 62-65, 279n.28; pagan, 139; service of, 151-52

Temptation, 107, 128, 134, 155, 159-60, 162-63, 165-68, 236, 289

Textual variants, xxviii, 108n.4

Thanksgiving, 33, 90, 124, 160, 168, 172, 187-88, 202, 232, 247, 279, 285-86

Timothy, 10, 46, 81, 240, 243, 257, 286

Tongues: interpretation of, 230, 232, 236-38; speaking in, 11, 177, 195, 201, 215, 217, 220, 222, 229-37, 241

Tradition, x-xiii, 187, 244

Transformation, 41, 191-92, 221, 226, 250, 270-74; spiritual, xxviii

Trinity, xiii, xxv, 28, 63-64, 70, 102, 109, 131, 135-36, 176, 195, 199, 201, 204-5, 234, 256; debates about, xxiii, xxvi, 63-64, 229, 234-35; unity of, 36, 43, 53, 189, 199-201, 203-4, 229, 234. *See also* God, Christ, Son of God, Holy Spirit

Truth, xi, 73, 80, 85, 137, 142, 160, 165, 171, 186, 198-99, 203, 225-27, 230, 243, 273, 276-77; Christ as, 30, 137

Unity, 12, 63, 209, 211-12, 239, 292; appeal for, 18, 206; of body and soul, 251; in Christ, 57, 169; with Christ, 68, 126, 190-91, 246, 249, 258-60; of church, 58; with God, 258-59, 271

Universalism, 242, 259-60

Virginity, xxiii, xxv, 10, 49, 104, 107, 109-10, 121, 125, 126-28, 130, 152-53, 237; of Christ, 111. *See also* Asceticism, Celibacy

Virgins, 9, 11, 110, 120-29, 208, 211, 221, 240, 265, 290

Virtue, xx, 31, 79, 81, 100, 103, 106, 119, 127, 166-

67, 173, 198, 208, 211, 214, 222, 225, 231, 247, 280, 282, 285, 290, 292; of Paul, 5-7; pursuit of, 193-94; true, 31

Vision of God, xiii, xiv, xv, 41, 134, 214, 223-28; by angels, 140. *See also* Contemplation

Wealth, xv, xxiv, 67, 78, 95-96, 101, 106, 119, 123-24, 126, 128, 152, 171, 173-75, 185, 204, 208, 216, 220, 236, 256, 258; love of, 96

Widow, 113-14, 126, 128, 208

Will of God, 123, 126, 207, 271

Wisdom, xxviii, 12, 13, 28, 32, 65-67, 76, 78, 81, 94, 143, 148, 155, 164, 202-3, 205, 225, 235, 258, 264; Christ as, xv, 13, 17, 22, 25, 26, 28-29, 32, 51, 201, 226; definition of, 202; false, 11, 136, 166; and folly, 65-67; of God, xxi, 22, 47; hidden 36, 38; human, 9, 12, 22, 24, 44, 65-67; pagan, 20, 22, 45, 66-67, 236, 288, 292; of Paul, 137, 260; perfect, xxviii

Women, 144, 146-47, 177, 179-84, 209, 221; deacons, 106; and divine image, 182; and men, 179-84; Midianite, 165; and mission, 144, 146-47; prophets, xxii, 177, 179-84, 229, 239-40; status of, 177, 179-80; teachers, 106; in worship, xxii, 179-84, 229, 239-40

Word, 200, 204, 225, 241, 251n.4, 289; Christ as, 17, 29, 31, 63, 64, 272, 275; of Christ, 192; of God, xv, 156, 191, 240, 245; incarnate, xvi, 25. *See also* Christ, Christology, Incarnation, Son of God

Works, 144, 146-49, 153, 286-88, 291; of the flesh, 274-75; good, 283; of virtue, 285. *See also* Deeds

Worldly. *See* Earthly, Fleshly

Worship, vii, xi-xii, xv-xvi, xxi-xxii, xxvii, 38, 90, 185, 226, 229, 233-35, 236-40; Eucharistic, 177, 179-94; pagan, 142; true, 199; women in, xxii, 179-84, 229, 239-40

Index of Scripture References

OLD TESTAMENT

Genesis

1:1	42
1:11-12	45
1:26	32, 182
1:26-27	177, 188, 226n.9
1:27	179, 182, 219
1:28	171
1:31	43
2–3	177, 251n.5
2:7	30, 268
2:9-23	45
2:10-14	5
2:17	30
2:18-23	111
2:18-24	179
2:21-23	101
2:23	182
2:24	98, 101
3	254
3:1-7	166, 255
3:6	190
3:12	183
3:13	183
3:14	198
3:16	109
3:22	251n.5
3:24	105, 126
4:4	5
4:25	30
5:1	226n.9
6:1-4	94n.2
12:1	5
13:9	174
18:22-33	174

19:24-29	174
25:27	221
29:15-30	6
30:29-30	174
31:38	221
31:40	221
32:7	221
33:1-3	221
37:13	174
39	119
47:9	204
49:3-27	249
49:27	3-4

Exodus

1–15	159
2:11-15	175
2:14-16	221
3:6	204
3:10-12	54
3:14	44
7:8-15	192
7:14-25	192
12	86
12:21	87
12:37	161
13:20	161
13:21	160-61, 163n.5
14–15	159
14:15-25	192
14:22	160-61
15:20	181, 240
15:22-25	192
16–Numbers 21	159
16	159, 191
16:1	161

16:4-35	160
17:1-7	160, 192
17:6	160n.2
17:8-13	163n.4
19:10	59
19:15	108
19:21	59
20:2	137
20:12	50
20:14	50
30:29	3
32	84
32:4	163
32:6	163, 165n.8
32:31-32	6
32:32	174, 219, 222
32:33	141

Leviticus

6:8-13	2
19:18	216
26:12	42

Numbers

11:24	3
14:29-30	160
16:14	163
16:49	163
20:2-13	160
20:7-11	160n.2
21:4-9	49
21:5-6	163
25	163
25:1-3	159, 164
25:6-9	165n.8
31	163n.4

Deuteronomy

6:4	137
6:5	105, 216
17	84
17:7	90
18:3	152
22:5	180
25:4	148-50
29:29	73
32:21	170

Joshua

3:7-17	192

Judges

4:4	180

1 Samuel

2:1-10	32n.13
2:3	32n.13
2:30	63
9:24	106
19:18-20	217
21:1-6	108n.4
21:4	108
21:6	108
22:20-23	108n.4

2 Samuel

8:17	108n.4
11:2	247
11:4	247
12	91
15–18	221
18:5	221
24:17	174

1 Kings

6:20-22	61
8:11	63
17:6	106
18:20-39	192

2 Kings

5:19-26	223
5:23-26	85
5:26	xxvi, 223
6:1-7	192
22:14-20	240

Job

1–2	95

1:21	123
5:13	65-66
11:16	166
42	95

Psalms

3:3	256
8:6	252, 257
8:6-8	171
12:6	78
14:1	42
17:15	31
19:1-4	103
19:4	23
22:16	73
22:16-17	77
24:1	171
24:8	260
27:8 Latin	226
30	279n.28
32:1	88
33:9	192
34:8	31, 90, 163
34:16	99
35:3	280
36:6	204
36:9	199
37:30	264
39:1	79
40:2	30
42:2	31
45	105
45:2	127
45:7	205
61:2 LXX	259n.10
65:9	xxviii, 205-6
71:7	235
73:27	56, 100
73:28	101
78:25	191
86:17	235
94:11	65
97:7	29
102:25	24
103:5	256
103:10	3, 189
103:12	3
103:29-30 LXX	64
104:1	137
110:1	260
115:13	211
116:10 Latin	223

118:22	58
119:130-31	30
139:12	72
141:5	79
146:4	262

Proverbs

1:3 LXX	225
1:6	39
6:4-5	289
8:22	26n.10
13:20 LXX	164
14:29	220
18:4	164
20:10	107
22:20-21 LXX	39
27:1	17

Ecclesiastes

1:2	78
1:14	4

Canticles

3:6	225n.7
4:6-16	225n.7
5:3	30
5:5	31
5:5-6	134
7:8	225n.8

Isaiah

1:19	82
5:4	55
5:5	55
6:3	199
25:8	276, 279-80
26:12	281
26:19	15
28:11-12	233
28:16	57-58
29:13	142
29:14	22
40:6	64, 99
40:13 LXX	45
40:23	24
52:7	80
52:15	40n.5
53:9	257
54:11-12	61
55:1	148n.3
56:4-5	114
58:9 Latin	280

61:1	205	**Zechariah**		12:42	93-94
64:4	40n.5	10:3	148n.3	13:3	150
				13:4	150
Jeremiah		**Malachi**		13:8	250
2:13	205	2:7	94	13:11	286
3:16	40n.5			13:23	150
4:3	150			13:25	186
6:10 LXX	166	**NEW TESTAMENT**		13:31-32	264
6:16	56			13:33	173
8:4	166	**Matthew**		13:52	165
9:23	32	3:16	189	14:19	173
9:23-24	29, 51	4:1-11	166	15:4	50
9:24	26, 32	4:3	40	15:8	142
16:18	62n.7	4:23	27	15:11	170
17:5	29	5:5	13	15:13	54
23:4	148n.3	5:6	xxvii, 31	15:17-18	132
25:34	148n.3	5:8	41, 214, 274	16:6	86
33:12	148n.3	5:13	173	16:18	134, 190
		5:14	173	16:23	52
Ezekiel		5:16	63, 102-3, 173	17:1-9	49
3:18-19	59	5:27	50	17:20	203
18:4	67	5:29-30	142	18:10	140, 183, 198
18:23	73	5:32	111, 115	18:19	63
34:2	148n.3	5:39	66	19:3	113
		5:40	95	19:8	114
Daniel		5:44	88, 220	19:9	111, 113
3:19-26	24	6:9	102	19:10	113
3:28 LXX	103	6:12	115	19:10-12	114, 121
		6:18	142	19:12	113, 115, 152
Hosea		6:25-26	171	19:17	255, 257
4:14	164	6:25-32	149	19:21	50, 152, 216
13:14	276, 279-80	7:1	71, 73	19:25	123
		7:3	71	19:27	71
Joel		7:6	84, 89	19:28	94
2:14	84	7:7	17	20:16	76
2:28	239	7:19	55	21:7-9	211
		7:22-23	60	21:21	215
Amos		7:24-25	58	21:23	25
2:7	84	7:24-27	57	21:38	40, 57
		8:28-34	166n.10	22:2	86
Jonah		10:10	153	22:11-14	86
1:1–3:3	54	10:16	235	22:30	97
		10:19-20	43	22:32	204
Habakkuk		10:33	23	22:37-39	216
3:3	31	11:4	25	23:8-9	136
		11:27	29, 199	23:8-10	46
Zephaniah		11:28	267	24:14	18
2:6	148n.3	12:25	9	24:34	225
		12:29	285	25:1-7	56
Haggai		12:31	73	25:1-13	60
2:8	67	12:38	25	25:12	241
		12:41	93-94	25:24-30	174

25:34	58	17:5	203	7:39	164
25:35	284	18:1	280	8:12	30, 57
25:35-36	194	20:36	279	9:5	57
25:40	284	22:17-20	188n.15	10:11	56, 147
25:41-46	154			10:27-28	43
25:46	60	**John**		11:25	30, 57
26:26	187-88	1	13	11:50	218
26:26-29	188n.15	1:1	17, 29, 245, 259	11:51	218
26:27	188-89	1:3	18n.4, 58, 171, 188, 225	12:24	250, 266
26:39	34	1:4	30-31, 259	12:32	219
26:41	274, 289	1:4-5	30	12:35	30
26:67-68	96	1:9	57, 199, 205, 225	12:46	30
27:41-42	24	1:12	27	13:2	166
		1:13	28, 107	13:13	136-37
Mark		1:14	51, 59, 199, 259	13:27	40, 166
2:11	277	1:18	29, 142n.8, 199, 204	13:35	216
3:27	285	1:29	245, 249	14:6	30-31, 56-57, 137
4:10-12	49	1:51	274	14:8	42, 123
8:33	52	2:1-11	111	14:8-9	255
9:48	59	2:6	25	14:9	29
10:37	34	2:18	25	14:15	126
10:38	34	2:19	265	14:16	180n.2
11:23	215	2:21	265	14:17	125
14:22-25	188n.15, 191	3:5	161	14:19	57
		3:13	188	14:21	56
Luke		3:14	49	14:23	31, 200-201
1:2	245	3:27	76	15:1	54, 225n.8
1:32	23	3:31	246	15:1-2	213
1:35	201	4:10	31, 164	15:4-5	76
1:48	180	4:13-14	xxviii, 206	15:5	56, 76, 213, 226
1:51-52	129	4:22	15	15:10	56, 126
2:14	198	4:24	199, 223	15:13	216
2:36	240	4:35	150	15:14-15	260
3:16	205	5:21	253	15:16	33
6:28	103	6:27	30	15:19	105, 125
6:36	126	6:32-35	171	15:22	137
6:48	56	6:42	162	16:12	50
8:1-3	147	6:42-49	159	16:15	253-54
9:60	274	6:46	225	17:18	178
9:61	67	6:48-51	171	17:19	178
10:7	153	6:49	191	17:21	259, 271
10:27	105, 128	6:49-51	161	17:22	204
10:29	250	6:50	31, 191	17:25	125
11:52	39	6:51	191	18:14	22
12:42	70	6:53	258	19:34	165
12:44	70	6:55	49	19:34-35	168
13:6-7	54	6:63	43, 273	19:37	274
14:11	129	6:65	286	20:19-28	265
14:27	126	7:37	121	20:29	38
14:28	124	7:37-38	33	21:3	140
14:33	105, 126	7:38	5, 164	21:7	140
15:11-13	171	7:38-39	xxviii, 206	21:9	173

21:9-13	249	17:28	30, 32, 155	7:17	280
21:15-16	216	18	8	7:23	128, 280
		18:1-17	xxi n.6	7:24	61
Acts		18:3	6	8:2	43
1:5	205	18:9-10	11	8:6-7	83, 85
1:8	43	18:10	9	8:8	275
1:11	274	18:11	8	8:8-17	27
2	124, 229	18:17	9	8:9	275
2:1-4	189	19:13-17	9	8:10	43
2:1-13	196	19:19	9	8:10-11	275
2:4-13	236	20:23	200	8:11	43, 56
2:7-9	233	20:30	56	8:13	27, 277
2:13	233, 236	20:34	140	8:13-14	275
2:24	249	21:8-9	106	8:15	199
2:41-45	185	21:9	180, 239	8:17	17, 57, 114, 168
2:43-45	124	22:3	1	8:20-21	43
2:47	258n.9	22:21	14	8:21	270
3:12	71	22:24	6	8:24	228
4:12	57	28:20	221	8:26	142
4:13	20			8:29	57
4:32	63, 169, 238	**Romans**		8:31	256
5	229	1:8	241	8:32	43
5:1-11	91, 233	1:14	155	8:34	189
5:3-4	233	1:20	24, 224	8:35	79
5:4	234	1:22-23	226	8:35-37	256
5:5	203	1:25	203	8:38-39	5, 17
5:9	234	2:6	30, 189	9:3	175, 219
5:9-11	236	2:11	24	9:3-4	6
5:10	203	2:17	280	9:5	137
5:14	258n.9	2:28-29	155	9:22	4
7:54–8:2	4	2:29	156n.11	10:2	80
8:3	20n.7	5:5	44	10:4	230
9:1	4	5:8	220	11:1	3
9:3-6	81	5:10	259-60	11:13	201
9:4	5	5:12	257	11:15	256
9:10-16	54	5:12-14	257	11:17	250
9:15	1, 4-5, 112	5:14	183	12:1	102
10:26	71n.1	5:17	257	12:2	46
10:38	205	5:20	280	12:10	211
12:15	183	5:21	61	12:11	16
13:8-11	81	6:2	67	13	92
13:11	203	6:3	205	13:1-2	94
14:15	71n.1	6:4	57, 261	13:3	59
14:19	6	6:5	249	13:13	107
15:19-29	156n.11	6:9	277	13:14	107
16:14	286	6:11	274	14:1-2	133n.1
17:17	6	6:14	30	14:2	3, 49
17:17-18	67	7:1-4	114	14:3	172
17:18	26	7:2-3	111	14:6	172
17:21	10	7:4	150	14:10	133
17:23	155	7:13	140	14:13	140
17:26	111	7:14	39	14:15	107

334

14:17	106	1:31	13, 33	3:12-15	48, 58-62, 241n.13
14:21	133n.1	2	36-37	3:13-15	xxiii
15:1	133n.1	2:1	16, 34, 50	3:15	48, 62
15:3	172	2:1-2	13	3:16	53, 56, 61, 65, 112,
15:19	80	2:1-5	36-38		279n.28
15:19-20	56	2:2	xxvii, 3, 34, 47, 50, 74	3:16-17	36n.1, 47-48, 62-65,
15:20	77	2:3	36, 287		200n.10
15:24	80	2:5	36, 38	3:17	58, 65, 88, 97, 227
15:25-26	283	2:6	4, 45, 49, 155, 166	3:18	48, 65-66
16:7	290	2:6-7	50	3:18-23	47, 65-68
		2:6-8	3, 36, 38-40	3:19	67
1 Corinthians		2:6-11	xxviii	3:19-20	48
1	12-13	2:7	33	3:20	53
1:1-3	12-15	2:8	32, 36, 166	3:21	67, 258
1:1-9	xxi, 12	2:9	xxvii, 34, 36, 41, 134,	3:21-22	48
1:2	12, 16-17		189, 225-27, 271, 281	3:22	67
1:4-9	15-18	2:9-10	43	4	69-70
1:6	201	2:9-12	36, 40-44	4:1	107
1:6-7	12	2:10	43, 188, 198	4:1-2	70-71
1:7	12, 20	2:10-11	36	4:1-5	69
1:7-8	12	2:10-12	36, 42	4:2	69
1:9	12	2:10-16	xxiii	4:3	10
1:10	16, 63, 289	2:11	xxvii, 225	4:3-5	69, 71-73
1:10-12	8, 47-48, 52	2:11-12	42-43	4:3-6	11n.5
1:10-16	109	2:12	36, 43, 76	4:5	72
1:10-17	12, 18-22	2:12-13	39	4:6	11, 19, 52, 69
1:10–4:21	xxi	2:12-16	36	4:6-8	73-76
1:11	290	2:13	36-37	4:6-13	69
1:11-12	287	2:13-16	36, 44-46	4:7	33, 71
1:12	51, 185, 232, 289, 292	2:14	25, 27, 37, 45, 51-52,	4:8	10, 69, 75
1:16	290		268n.15	4:9	69, 77, 80
1:17	8, 12, 38	2:15	274	4:9-13	69, 76-79
1:17-25	xxi, 236	2:16	39, 110, 113, 137	4:11	6, 69, 96, 151
1:17–2:16	xxi	3	47-48	4:11-12	78
1:18	12, 22, 143	3:1	9, 45, 51n.2, 65, 74, 77	4:12	88, 103
1:18-21	13, 24	3:1-2	10, 34	4:14-16	79-81
1:18-25	12, 22-26, 47	3:1-3	xxviii, 47-53	4:14-21	69
1:18-31	12	3:1-5	47	4:16	69
1:20	13, 15, 23, 136, 288, 292	3:1–4:13	xxi	4:17	240, 257, 288
1:22	13	3:2	3-4, 115	4:17-21	69, 81-82
1:22-25	13, 25-26	3:3	47, 53	4:18	8
1:23	13, 15	3:4-5	52	4:19	284
1:23-24	51	3:4-8	53-55	4:21	70, 81-82
1:24	xxvii, 13, 17, 22, 23n.9,	3:5	54, 232	5-7	xxi
	30, 67, 201, 226	3:6	54-55, 148	5	83-84
1:26	13	3:6-9	47	5:1	8, 11, 65, 70, 81, 235,
1:26-27	27	3:8	47, 55, 60		289
1:26-31	13, 26-35	3:9	55, 60-61, 147	5:1-5	83-85
1:27	27	3:9-11	47, 56-58	5:1-8	109
1:29-30	28	3:10	51, 61, 77	5:2	10, 72, 88
1:30	13, 29-31, 92, 96, 135	3:10-15	47	5:4	23
1:30-31	28, 32, 51	3:11	56	5:5	73, 83

5:6	88, 190, 257	7:10-11	104	9:1-2	145-46
5:6-8	83, 85-87	7:12	114	9:1-3	4, 144
5:7	83, 88, 256	7:12-14	105	9:1-26	xxii
5:7-8	xxi, 83	7:12-16	116-18	9:2	10
5:9	xxi n.6, 8, 83	7:14	114, 117	9:3	144
5:9-11	83, 87-90	7:17	9	9:3-7	144, 146-49, 232
5:9–6:11	109	7:17-24	118-20	9:4	153, 170
5:11	83	7:18	119n.13	9:4-12	9
5:12	69, 73	7:21-23	105	9:5	106, 108, 144, 147
5:12-13	84, 90-91, 94	7:24	105, 119	9:7	144, 147-48, 283
6	48, 92	7:25	4-5, 9	9:8	148
6:1	9-10, 92, 289, 292	7:25-26	121	9:8-12	149-51
6:1-4	236	7:25-31	120-24	9:9	144
6:1-6	92-94	7:27	106-7	9:9-10	xxiii
6:1-11	xxii	7:28	237	9:9-11	144
6:2	92	7:29-31	59	9:11	283
6:3	92	7:29-32	105	9:12	108, 144, 148, 151, 172
6:7	94	7:32	237	9:12-18	144, 151-54
6:7-8	92, 95-96	7:32-35	104-5, 124-28	9:13	152
6:7-9	289	7:33	125n.15	9:13-14	232
6:9-10	59, 99, 193	7:33-34	128	9:14	145
6:9-11	84, 89, 92, 96-97, 100,	7:34	122, 127	9:16-17	144, 153
	275	7:34-35	125	9:18	148
6:10	88	7:35	106	9:18-19	172
6:11	276	7:36	122	9:19-23	1, 144-45, 154-56
6:12	92, 102	7:36-40	104-5, 128-30	9:20	172
6:12-14	97-98	7:37-38	128n.16	9:21	172
6:12-20	92	7:38	104, 129	9:22	7, 79, 121, 287
6:13	80	7:39	104, 110, 116	9:23-24	144
6:15	88, 97, 100-101, 292	8	131, 159, 164, 236	9:24	144, 156
6:15-18	98-102	8:1	xxii, 129, 136, 145, 148	9:24-25	37
6:16	126	8:1-2	10	9:24-27	145, 156-58
6:17	126	8:1-3	131-34	10	131, 159-60
6:18	92	8:2	134	10:1-5	160-63
6:19	56, 63-65, 92, 99, 101,	8:4	132, 137	10:1-11	xxiii, 159
	122, 245	8:4-5	131	10:2	159, 161, 164-65
6:19-20	65, 100, 102-3	8:4-6	134-38	10:3	165
6:20	92, 99	8:5	137	10:4	31, 57-58, 134, 164, 205
7	xxi, xxiii, xxviii, 104-5,	8:6	xxiii, xxvi, 36n.1, 57,	10:6	xxiii, 159, 162-63
	237		131, 136-38, 204	10:6-10	159
7:1	xxi, 9-10, 104, 290	8:7-8	133n.1, 170	10:6-11	163-65
7:1-5	105	8:7-9	131, 138-39	10:6-14	159
7:1-7	104-13	8:8	170	10:9-10	49
7:2	155	8:9	170	10:11	xxiii, 150
7:3	122	8:9-11	141	10:11-12	159
7:3-4	112	8:10	xxii, 143	10:12	114
7:4	105, 109, 126	8:10-13	131, 139-43	10:12-13	165-68
7:5	105, 108, 112, 121	8:11	289	10:13	159-60, 166
7:6	49, 104, 111, 122	8:11–10:33	xxii	10:14-17	168-69
7:7	104	8:13	80, 131, 142, 145, 292	10:14-22	160
7:8-11	113-16	9	144-45	10:15-22	159
7:9	105, 114-15, 155	9:1	146, 172	10:16	160, 259

10:17	157	12:4-6	201, 234	14:26-31	229
10:18-22	160, 169-71	12:4-7	36n.1, 63n.8, 195, 199-	14:26-33	53, 237-39
10:20	142, 174		202	14:30	239
10:21	145, 171	12:4-13	xxiii	14:33	109, 240
10:23	xxii	12:6	201	14:33-36	xxii, 239-41
10:23-26	160, 171-72	12:7	196	14:34	181
10:24	220	12:7-11	215, 234	14:34-35	229
10:25	172	12:8	18, 199n.7, 202	14:36	240
10:27	xxii	12:8-11	195, 202-4	14:37-38	198
10:27-33	160, 172-76	12:9	212n.16	14:37-40	241
10:28-29	170	12:10	196-97	15	xxi, xxiii, 242-43, 292
10:32-33	173	12:11	36n.1, 63n.8, 195, 201,	15:1-2	243-44
10:33	160, 172, 219		204, 207, 233-34	15:1-7	xxii
11–14	xxii, 177	12:11–14:40	xxii	15:1-11	242
11	xxvi, 177-78, 229	12:12	101, 157, 239, 258-59	15:3	188
11:1	79n.2, 111, 143, 174, 257	12:12-14	205-6, 292	15:3-4	248
11:1-2	178	12:12-20	56, 120, 140, 257	15:3-7	244-46
11:1-16	177	12:12-30	xxii	15:3-11	253
11:2-16	xxii-xxiii	12:12-31	195	15:4	189, 245
11:3	112, 177, 179, 183-84	12:13	xxviii, 36n.1, 63n.8,	15:8	245
11:3-5	179		195, 204, 206	15:8-11	246-48
11:3-9	179-83, 229n.2	12:15-19	206-7	15:9-10	243, 245
11:5	180	12:20-26	195, 207-11	15:10	33, 71, 146
11:7	177, 180, 182	12:25	169	15:11	247
11:8	183	12:27	157, 169, 258	15:12	10-11, 243, 263, 292
11:9	183	12:27-31	195, 212-13	15:12-18	253
11:10	183	12:31	85, 207, 217-18	15:12-19	248-49
11:10-16	183-84	13	xxi-xxii, 133, 214	15:14	199, 244
11:14	10	13:1-3	214-18	15:16	253
11:14-15	180	13:3	175	15:17	199, 244
11:16	178	13:4	214, 289, 292	15:19	261
11:17	16	13:4-5	222	15:20	253, 256-57, 265
11:17-20	10	13:4-7	214, 218-22	15:20-22	245n.1, 249-51
11:17-22	177, 184-86	13:5	107	15:21-22	242
11:17-34	xxii, 177	13:8-10	214, 222-24	15:22	157
11:19	178, 185-86	13:9-10	74	15:22-28	257
11:20	16	13:10	67, 214	15:23	189, 257
11:20-22	89	13:10-12	xxvi	15:23-27	242, 252-54
11:21	292	13:11-12	223, 226	15:24	252-53, 257, 259-60
11:23-25	xxi	13:11-13	214, 224-28	15:24-27	254n.8
11:23-26	177, 187-93	13:12	214, 223-25	15:24-28	259
11:26	193	13:12-13	xxiii	15:25	252-53, 260
11:27-34	177, 193-94	13:13	58, 214, 227, 230, 256	15:25-26	260
11:34	109	14	229	15:25-28	38
12–14	17-18, 177, 229n.1	14:1	85, 227, 234	15:26	253-54, 259-60
12	xxvi, 195, 292	14:1-5	230-31	15:28	xxii-xxiii, xxv, 58, 223,
12:1	10	14:6-12	231-32		242, 254-60
12:1-3	195-99	14:7-8	229	15:29	243, 261
12:1–14:33	11	14:13-19	232	15:29-34	260-63
12:2	132	14:20-25	229, 233-37	15:31	5, 77
12:3	36n.1, 197-99	14:21	xxvi	15:31-32	243
12:4	136, 201, 212n.16	14:24-25	36n.1, 42n.10, 179, 234	15:32	273

15:33	141	2:16	286	1:10	128
15:35	266, 277	2:17	113	1:12	245
15:35-41	242-43, 263-68	3:6	280	2:20	67
15:37	265	3:12-18	163n.5	3:13	49, 155
15:37-38	270	3:17	43	3:21	280
15:39	266, 270	3:18	226	3:24	100
15:40	265	4:10	5, 77	3:27	205
15:41	270	4:16	226	3:28	157, 182
15:42	266	4:18	271	3:29	57
15:42-44	250, 264, 269, 271	5:1	270	4:4	37
15:42-49	268-72	5:2-4	270	4:7	57
15:44	xxii, 243, 271-72, 279	5:4	7, 264-65	4:9	33
15:45	272, 274	5:4-5	265	4:13	37
15:45-46	177	5:5	274	4:21-31	xxiii
15:47	246, 272	5:7	38	4:24	181
15:47-48	277	5:10	97	5:4	185
15:48	272-73	5:15	22	5:10	244
15:48-49	264	5:20	260	5:16-23	27
15:49	242, 249, 273, 277	6:1	55	5:17	157, 167
15:49-50	276	6:14	136	5:19-23	275
15:50	242, 264, 268n.16, 270, 276	6:16	42, 56, 63	5:22	219
		9:15	168	5:24	128
15:50-53	272-79	10:3-5	67	6:2	114, 184
15:51	264, 270	10:5	61	6:14	22-23, 34-35
15:53	58, 278	11:2	6		
15:53-54	271	11:3	287	**Ephesians**	
15:53-57	31	11:6	6	1:17-18	205
15:54-55	276	11:8-9	151	1:18	57
15:54-58	243, 279-81	11:13	241n.13	1:22	98, 101
16	282	11:14-15	185	1:22-23	80
16:1	283	11:20	150	2:1	169
16:1-4	282-84	11:23-24	81	2:1-13	260
16:1-12	xxi	11:25	6	2:3	157
16:2	283	11:25-26	6	2:6	245, 271
16:3	287	11:27	6	2:8-9	76
16:5-9	284-86	11:27-29	79	2:12	168
16:10	10	11:30	37	2:13	168
16:10-12	286-88	11:32	37	2:15	135
16:13-14	282, 288-90	12:2-4	6	2:18	259-60
16:15-18	290-91	12:4	264	2:19-22	63
16:17	10	12:7	134, 248	2:20	258
16:19-24	291-92	12:7-9	134	2:21	63
		12:9	155, 248	3:6	168, 206, 258
2 Corinthians		12:10	37, 75	3:8	76
1:9-10	33	12:19	113	3:17	213
1:17	285	13:3	200	4:10	23
1:22	32	13:4	27	4:12-13	259
2:7	85	13:14	136, 200	4:13	157, 258
2:11	244	15:32	6	4:14	243
2:12	284			4:15	98
2:12-13	286	**Galatians**		4:15-16	258
2:14-16	286	1:8	185	4:16	258

4:22	48, 273	**Colossians**		4:5	118
4:27	166	1	13	4:13-14	203
5:5	137	1:6	240	5:9-10	106
5:6	96	1:15	30	5:14	110
5:12	129	1:16	30, 198	5:17	203
5:19	120	1:17	29-30	6:9	236
5:23	6, 56, 98, 256, 258	1:18	57, 98, 101, 249, 257	6:10	210
5:23-24	126	1:24	258	6:13	18
5:24	105, 126	2:3	34	6:16	41, 225
5:25	109	2:8	34		
5:31-32	239	2:12	245	**2 Timothy**	
5:32	22, 105, 126	2:13	169	1:6	201
5:33	109	2:14	40, 189	2:4	148
6:6	119	2:14-18	22	2:10	221
6:11	166, 289	2:18	106	2:11	67
6:12	166-67, 277	2:23	106	2:17-18	243
		3:9	48, 87	4:5	201
Philippians		3:14	288	4:6	2
1:6	76	3:22	119	4:7-8	3
1:11	150	4:2-4	285	4:16-17	2
1:19	200	4:3	284, 286	4:18	2
1:23	7				
1:24	7	**1 Thessalonians**		**Titus**	
1:29	76	1:8	241	1:6	115
2:3	211	2:19	221	1:14	161
2:4	107	3:12	289	2:3	240
2:6	219	5:17	110, 181	2:13	137
2:6-8	179	5:20-22	203	3:5	65
2:6-9	252	5:23	39	3:5-6	64
2:7	253				
2:7-8	219	**2 Thessalonians**		**Hebrews**	
2:9	252	1:9	59	1:2	57
2:9-11	179	3:6-12	153n.6	1:3	30, 200, 205
2:10	23	3:11	148	1:14	57
2:10-11	259			2:4	17
2:13	32	**1 Timothy**		2:10	246
2:15	173	1:3	70	2:11	57, 168
2:17-18	5	1:12-13	247	2:17	57
2:22	288	1:13	3-4	4:12	72
3:2	185	2:5	250, 259, 274	4:14	23, 271
3:4-6	232	2:6	164	5:12	49
3:7	95, 232	2:7	160	5:12-14	50
3:9-11	32	2:12	181, 240	5:14	3, 39, 49
3:10	77	2:13-14	182	9:5	96
3:12	33	2:14-15	110	9:25	96
3:13	79, 134	3:2	56, 115	10:1	39
3:20	105, 125, 271	3:4	115	10:32	57
3:21	58, 249	3:16	23, 38	11	175n.14
4:3	104, 106	4:1	106	11:1	38
4:4	86	4:2	110, 185	11:1 Latin	227
4:7	281	4:3	106	11:10	175n.14
4:13	289	4:4	143	11:26	175

12:14	60	**1 John**		22:1		253
12:23	57	1:2	225	22:3		253
13:4	101, 104, 110, 129	1:5	205			
		2:6	111			
James		3:7	96	**APOCRYPHA**		
1:17	76	4:1-3	198			
2:19	218	4:13	64	**Wisdom of Solomon**		
3:9	226n.9	4:18	100	1:1		226
				7:17		17
1 Peter		**Jude**		9:15		278-79
2:2	50	19	52			
2:4	58			**Sirach**		
2:5	57, 63	**Revelation**		1:10		40n.5
2:11	71	1:7	274	1:26		39
3:3-4	105, 127	3:5	141	10:12		101
3:6	112	14:4	97	15:16		82
3:15	17	21:1	99, 224			
4:5	189	21:2	56	**Baruch**		
4:10	107	21:6	31	3:10-12		205
4:11	23	21:9	6, 56			
		21:11	63	**1 Enoch**		
2 Peter		21:16	63	6–16		94n.2
3:15-16	xx n.3	21:19-21	61